The Routledge Handbook of Transatlantic Security

This new Handbook provides readers with the tools to understand the evolution of transatlantic security from the Cold War era to the early twenty-first century.

After the Second World War, the United States retained a strong presence as the dominant member of NATO throughout the Cold War. Former enemies, such as Germany, became close allies, while even countries that often criticized the United States made no serious attempt to break with Washington. This pattern of security cooperation continued after the end of the Cold War, with NATO expansion eastwards extending US influence. Despite the Iraq war prompting a seemingly irreparable transatlantic confrontation, the last years of the Bush administration witnessed a warming of US–European relations, expected to continue with the Obama administration.

The contributors address the following key questions arising from the history of transatlantic security relations:

- What lies behind the growing and continuing European dependency on security policy on the United States and what are the political consequences of this?
- Is this dependency likely to continue or will an independent European Common Foreign and Security Policy eventually emerge?
- What has been the impact of 'out-of-area' issues on transatlantic security cooperation?

The essays in this Handbook cover a broad range of historical and contemporary themes, including the founding of NATO; the impact of the Korean War; the role of nuclear (non-)proliferation; perspectives of individual countries (especially France and Germany); the impact of culture, identity and representation in shaping post-Cold War transatlantic relations; institutional issues, particularly EU–NATO relations; the Middle East; and the legacy of the Cold War, notably tensions with Russia.

This Handbook will be of much interest to students of transatlantic security, NATO, Cold War Studies, foreign policy and International Relations in general.

Basil Germond is Research Associate at the Centre for Sustainable Development, University of Central Lancashire.

Jussi M. Hanhimäki is Professor of International History and Politics at the Graduate Institute of International and Development Studies in Geneva.

Georges-Henri Soutou is Professor Emeritus at Paris-Sorbonne (Paris IV) University.

The Routledge Handbook of Transatlantic Security

Edited by
Basil Germond, Jussi M. Hanhimäki and
Georges-Henri Soutou

LONDON AND NEW YORK

First published 2010
by Routledge
2 Park Square, Milton Park, Abingdon, Oxon, OX14 4RN

Simultaneously published in the USA and Canada
by Routledge
270 Madison Avenue, New York, NY 10016

Routledge is an imprint of the Taylor & Francis Group, an informa business

© 2010 Basil Germond, Jussi M. Hanhimäki and
Georges-Henri Soutou for selection and editorial matter, individual contributors; their contributions

Typeset in Bembo and Helvetica by
Taylor & Francis Books

All rights reserved. No part of this book may be reprinted or reproduced or utilised in any form or by any electronic, mechanical, or other means, now known or hereafter invented, including photocopying and recording, or in any information storage or retrieval system, without permission in writing from the publishers.

British Library Cataloguing in Publication Data
A catalogue record for this book is available from the British Library

Library of Congress Cataloging in Publication Data
　The Routledge handbook of transatlantic security / edited by Basil Germond, Jussi M. Hanhimäki, and Georges-Henri Soutou.
　　p. cm.
　1. Security, International–North Atlantic Region. 2. North Atlantic Treaty Organization. 3. National security–Europe. 4. National security–United States. 5. United States–Military relations–European Union countries. 6. European Union countries–Military relations–United States. I. Germond, Basil. II. Hanhimäki, Jussi M., 1965- III. Soutou, Georges-Henri.
　JZ5930.R38 2010
　355'.03301821–dc22
　　　　　　　　2010004241

ISBN 978-0-415-57283-5 (hbk)
ISBN 978-0-203-84669-8 (ebk)

Contents

List of contributors viii
Preface xii
Introduction xiv

Part I
Transatlantic security in the Cold War era 1

1 Three ministers and the world they made: Acheson, Bevin and Schuman, and the making of the North Atlantic Treaty, March–April 1949   3
   Anne Deighton

2 The Korean War: miscalculation and Alliance transformation   17
   Samuel F. Wells, Jr.

3 The doctrine of massive retaliation and the impossible nuclear defense of the Atlantic Alliance: From directive MC 48 to MC 70 (1953–59)   32
   François David

4 The Fourth Republic and NATO: loyalty to the Alliance versus national demands?   45
   Jenny Raflik

5 The Fifth Republic and NATO: odd-man out or the only country in step?   58
   Georges-Henri Soutou

6 NATO forever? Willy Brandt's heretical thoughts on an alternative future   74
   Benedikt Schoenborn

CONTENTS

7 Negotiating with the enemy and having problems with the allies: the impact of the Non-Proliferation Treaty on transatlantic relations   89
Leopoldo Nuti

8 Power shifts and new security needs: NATO, European identity, and the reorganization of the West, 1967–75   103
Andreas Wenger and Daniel Möckli

9 West Germany and the United States during the Middle East Crisis of 1973: 'nothing but a semi-colony'?   123
Bernhard Blumenau

10 The United States and the 'loss' of Iran: repercussions on transatlantic security   138
Barbara Zanchetta

Part II
Transatlantic security beyond the Cold War   153

11 The Warsaw Pact, NATO and the end of the Cold War   155
Jérôme Elie

12 The road to Saint-Malo: Germany and EU–NATO relations after the Cold War   169
Wolfgang Krieger

13 EU–NATO relations after the Cold War   180
Hanna Ojanen

14 Security of the EU borders in the post-Cold War era   194
Axel Marion

15 Venus has learned geopolitics: the European Union's frontier and transatlantic relations   206
Basil Germond

16 The rise and fall of criticism towards the United States in transatlantic relations: from anti-Americanism to Obamania   218
Tuomas Forsberg

17 Strategic culture and security: American antiterrorist policy and the use of soft power after 9/11   231
Jérôme Gygax

18 European security identity since the end of the Cold War   250
Guillaume de Rougé

19 A realistic reset with Russia: practical expectations for US–Russian relations 263
James M. Goldgeier

20 The Obama administration and transatlantic security: problems and prospects 273
Jussi M. Hanhimäki

21 Is the present future of transatlantic security already history? 287
Jean-Jacques de Dardel

Index 301

Contributors

Bernhard Blumenau is a PhD student at the Graduate Institute in Geneva, working on West Germany's strategies against international terrorism in the 1970s. His research interests include German foreign policy since World War II, European integration, the history of terrorism and the Cold War. He is also a Research Associate at the Fondation Pierre du Bois pour l'histoire du temps présent.

François David is Lecturer at the Jean Moulin University, Lyon III, and the Centre Lyonnais d'Etudes de Sécurité et de Défense (CLESID). He is a former student of the Ecole Normale Supérieure (Ulm) and former pensionnaire of the Fondation Thiers (Institut de France–CNRS), 'agrégé d'histoire'.

Jean-Jacques de Dardel is Head of the Swiss Mission to NATO and Ambassador to Belgium. Former Head of the Political Affairs Division of the Swiss DFA in charge of Europe, Central Asia, Council of Europe and OSCE. In 2001, he founded the Centre for International Security Policy of the DFA, which he directed until 2004.

Guillaume de Rougé holds a PhD in Contemporary History (2010) from the University of Paris III–Sorbonne Nouvelle. The topic, 'Ariadne's thread, France and European defence, 1991–2001', consists of a historical and strategic analysis of French policy with regard to European defence in the post-Cold War era. He has also gained valuable policy-oriented experiences at the French Ministry of Defence.

Anne Deighton is a Professor of European International Poitics at the University of Oxford, United Kingdom. She has published extensively on British foreign policy both during and after the Cold War, as well as on issues relating to European integration and contemporary European security. She is currently working on a study of British foreign secretary, Ernest Bevin. In the University of Oxford's 'Changing Character of War' project, she is writing on contemporary European multilateral security institutions and the use of force.

CONTRIBUTORS

Jérôme Elie recently completed a PhD in History at the Graduate Institute, Geneva, on the end of the Cold War as a period of 'Systemic Transition'. He is currently the Coordinator of Activities of the Programme for the Study of Global Migration and the lead researcher on a UNHCR history project.

Tuomas Forsberg is Professor of International Politics at the University of Tampere. Previously he has worked at the University of Helsinki, at the George C. Marshall European Center for Security Studies, Garmisch-Partenkirchen, Germany, and at the Finnish Institute of International Affairs. His most recent (co-authored) book is *Divided West. European Security and the Transatlantic Relationship* (2006).

Basil Germond is Research Associate at the Centre for Sustainable Development, University of Central Lancashire. He was previously Research Fellow at the University of St Andrews and Visiting Research Fellow with the Changing Character of War Programme (University of Oxford). He has also taught at the Geneva School of Diplomacy, as well as at the Graduate Institute of International Studies, Geneva. Trained in International Relations, Basil is specialized in European security in general and in the maritime and naval dimensions of security in particular, on which he has widely published in French and English.

James Goldgeier is Professor of Political Science at George Washington University and a senior fellow at the Council on Foreign Relations. His most recent book (co-authored with Derek Chollet) is *America Between the Wars: From 11/9 to 9/11*, named 'A Best Book of 2008' by *Slate*.

Jérôme A. Gygax is Associate Researcher at the Pierre du Bois Foundation. He obtained his MA from Lausanne University (Switzerland) and a PhD in International Relations from the Graduate Institute, Geneva. He is a lecturer for the Master programme in Sport Administration and Technology (at AISTS), and has been guest lecturer at the University of Queensland (Brisbane, Australia). He is co-author of *Le pouvoir des anneaux: les jeux olympiques à la lumière de la politique 1896–2004* (Paris, Vuibert ed, 2004).

Jussi M. Hanhimäki is Professor of International History and Politics at the Graduate Institute of International and Development Studies in Geneva, Switzerland. His most recent publications include *The United Nations: A Very Short Introduction* (2008) and *The Flawed Architect: Henry Kissinger and American Foreign Policy* (2004). Professor Hanhimäki is one of the founding editors of the journal *Cold War History* and a member of the editorial boards of *Relations Internationales*, *Refugee Survey Quarterly*, and *Ulkopolitiikka*.

Wolfgang Krieger is University Professor of Modern History and History of International Relations at Universität Marburg, Germany. He held fellowships at St Antony's College Oxford and at Harvard University and has taught at Universität München, Johns Hopkins University (Bologna), Princeton University, University of Toronto and Institut d'Études Politiques ('Sciences Po'), Paris. He has published widely on the history of the Cold War, on European–American relations after 1945, on German and British foreign policy, on military history as well as on the history and politics of secret intelligence services. His most recent book is a history of intelligence from Ancient Egypt to the present.

Axel Marion is a PhD student at the Graduate Institute of International and Development Studies. His research interests centre on the history of the European construction, particularly through political geography and transnational identity aspects. His interests extend to the polar regions.

Daniel Möckli is a Senior Researcher at the Center for Security Studies at ETH Zurich. Recent publications include *European Foreign Policy during the Cold War* (I.B. Tauris 2009) and *European–American Relations and the Middle East: From Suez to Iraq* (Routledge 2010, with Victor Mauer).

Leopoldo Nuti is Professor of History of International Relations at the University of Roma Tre. His latest publications are *La sfida nucleare. La politica estera italiana e le armi nucleari, 1945–1991* (2007) and, as an editor, *The Crisis of détente in Europe. From Helsinki to Gorbachev, 1875–1985* (2008).

Hanna Ojanen works as Research Director at the Swedish Institute of International Affairs. Previously, she was Programme Director at the Finnish Institute of International Affairs. Doctor of the European University Institute (Florence), her research interests include the EU's relations to other international organisations and security and defence policy in Europe.

Jenny Raflik is Lecturer in contemporary history at the Cergy-Pontoise University, member of the CICC (Civilisations et Identités Culturelles Comparées des Sociétés européennes et occidentales) and Associate Researcher at the UMR IRICE. Her research is focused on transatlantic relations and the relations between France and NATO.

Benedikt Schoenborn is a Fellow at the University of Tampere (Finland), in a research project on transatlantic relations. Doctor of the Universities of Geneva and Paris-Sorbonne, he is the author of the prize winning book *La mésentente apprivoisée: de Gaulle et les Allemands, 1963–1969* (Paris 2007), and of various articles on German and French foreign policies.

Georges-Henri Soutou is Professor Emeritus at Paris-Sorbonne (Paris IV) University. He works particularly about the First World War, Franco-German relations and the Cold War. Major publications in the context of this book: *L'Alliance incertaine. Les rapports politico-stratégiques franco-allemands, 1954–1996*, Paris, 1996; *La Guerre de Cinquante Ans. Les relations Est-Ouest 1943–1990*, Paris, 2001.

Samuel. F. Wells, Jr. is a Senior Scholar at the Woodrow Wilson Center in Washington, DC. A specialist on international security affairs, he has published widely on US strategy and transatlantic relations. He was a contributor to *The Strategic Triangle: France, Germany, and the Shaping of the New Europe* (2006).

Andreas Wenger is Professor of International and Swiss Security Policy and Director of the Center for Security Studies at ETH Zurich. He recently co-edited *Transforming*

NATO in the Cold War: Challenges Beyond Deterrence in the 1960s (Routledge 2006) and *Origins of the European Security System: The Helsinki Process Revisited, 1965–75* (Routledge 2008).

Barbara Zanchetta is a Researcher at the Finnish Institute of International Affairs in Helsinki currently focusing on US policy towards Iran and Afghanistan. She has worked on US–Soviet détente and is completing the book *From Dominance to Leadership: The Transformation of American Power in the 1970s* (tentative title). She is also the co-author of the textbook *Transatlantic Relations since 1945: An Introduction* (Routledge, forthcoming).

Preface

On behalf of the Fondation Pierre du Bois pour l'histoire du temps présent it is a great privilege and pleasure for me to introduce this Routledge Handbook on Transatlantic Security. It represents the outcome of the first scientific conference organized by the Foundation in conjunction with the Graduate Institute of International and Development Studies in Geneva, Switzerland.

But it is also with deep emotion that I am writing these words. The Foundation carries the name of Pierre du Bois, my husband, who, for 15 years, was Professor of International History and Politics at the Graduate Institute of International Studies in Geneva. He was an expert in European integration, in security issues and contemporary international relations. Pierre du Bois left us prematurely, suddenly and extremely sadly in June 2007 at the age of 64.

In keeping with his wishes, the Foundation was established, which aims at promoting and supporting research in the area of current history. It awards scholarships, research and publication grants, as well as the Pierre du Bois Prize. The Foundation organizes public conferences and symposia and thus encourages interaction among researchers and the creation of networks. The research and interest focus of the Foundation are, to start with, Europe and the challenges of European construction, security-related issues and Latin America.

The symposium, which represented the basis of this Handbook, fits perfectly within the framework of security-related issues, in an interdisciplinary manner and within the broadest sense of this word. It was organized by Professor Jussi Hanhimäki, Graduate Institute of International and Development Studies in Geneva, together with Professor Georges-Henri Soutou, University of Paris-Sorbonne (Paris IV) and Dr Basil Germond, PhD, University of Central Lancashire – and took place on the occasion of the 60th anniversary of NATO in April 2008. Beyond this anniversary, the organizers intended to create a forum for a frank exchange of views on the past, present and future of transatlantic security relations. We wished to place specific emphasis on the changing nature of security over the past six decades and analyse the challenges that lie ahead of us.

This Handbook brings together well-known historians with many young and brilliant researchers. Several among them worked with Pierre du Bois and he would have been the happiest man on earth to see them grow, develop and take flight. An extraordinary network of young researchers has begun to evolve within the Foundation. They are united by common interests and projects. This network aims to widen and establish contact with other researchers in Switzerland, Europe, North and Latin America, and across the world. I express the wish – and I will work to this effect – that the Foundation in the future offers a platform where skilled researchers can meet, share their learnings and 'cross swords' with each other to help us better understand and develop the world in which we live today.

My deep thanks go to the brilliant thinker, organizer, animator of the Symposium and editor of this Handbook, Professor Jussi Hanhimäki, one of the foremost specialists in transatlantic relationships after 1945, in the history of the Cold War and in American foreign policy. Also, many thanks to the other two co-editors: Professor Georges-Henri Soutou, renowned scholar and historian of international relationships and an old friend of Pierre du Bois', and Dr Basil Germond, expert in European security and in naval forces and maritime issues. Basil Germond was the last student to obtain his PhD with Professor Pierre du Bois in May 2007. I would also like to express my profound gratitude to Philippe Burrin, Director of the Graduate Institute of International and Development Studies in Geneva for his extraordinary support. Last but not least my thanks go to Bernhard Blumenau, who is preparing his PhD with Professor Jussi Hanhimäki and who has been the 'good fairy' behind the Symposium and is editing assistant for this Handbook.

I hope this first volume will be followed by many more, as the Foundation grows and develops its association with scholars across disciplines and continents, all sharing a common interest in current history.

Irina du Bois
Fondation Pierre du Bois pour l'histoire du temps présent
March 2010

Introduction

Jussi Hanhimäki, Georges-Henri Soutou and Basil Germond

'NATO was created to keep the Russians out, the Americans in, and the Germans down.' The famous dictum from Lord Ismay, the first Secretary General of NATO (1952–57), has been repeated so many times in conferences and textbooks as to appear quite banal. For a book dealing with transatlantic security since the end of the Second World War and written amid the 60-year anniversary of history's longest-lasting military alliance, however, there appears no better starting point. For not only does the citation neatly sum up the multiple rationales behind the founding of NATO but it also helps to put some of the Alliance's present-day concerns into their proper perspective.

In April 1949 NATO was, first and foremost, a collective defence organization addressing joint transatlantic concerns and fears. The Soviet Union controlled one half of Europe and maintained a formidable military force capable, in theory, of rolling into Western Europe. The weakness of the West Europeans necessitated – in the minds of British, American and even French leaders – the continued presence of Washington's military guarantee. Whether the Americans were 'invited' to establish an imperial-like hold over Western Europe or not, post-war transatlantic security cooperation was initially established with this reality in mind. For the next four decades it remained a central rationale behind the endurance of a transatlantic security community with NATO as its institutional and organizational backbone. And, to the surprise of a number of observers, the Alliance created to contain a common threat has not only endured, despite the disappearance of the Soviet Union, it has continued to expand to include a number of former Warsaw Pact – the Soviet-led institutional counterweight to NATO – countries. The story of transatlantic security since the Second World War cannot be understood without acknowledging the remarkable endurance and growth of this multinational defence organization.

Even a brief review of the literature on NATO, however, reveals a simple fact: historians, political scientists and other scholars prefer analysing situations of crisis to discussing periods of harmony. As the Norwegian historian Geir Lundestad has noted, a 'crisis perspective' dominates the literature on European–American relations in general and NATO in particular.[1]

And yet, the American role in Europe during the second half of the twentieth century seems, in security terms, to have experienced a virtually linear course. Since the end of the Second World War, Americans retained a strong presence as the dominant member of NATO throughout the Cold War. Former enemies, such as Germany, became close allies, whereas countries that often criticize(d) the USA have made no serious attempt to break completely with Washington. Even France's dramatic exit from NATO's integrated military structure in 1966 did not amount to a full 'withdrawal'. Nor has this pattern of security cooperation changed dramatically since the end of the Cold War. NATO expansion has, in fact, extended US influence while the American role in the conflicts following the break up of former Yugoslavia illustrated the relative incapacity of Europeans when faced with the need to take decisive military action. More recently, the Iraq war may have prompted a seemingly irreparable transatlantic confrontation. Yet, already the last years of the Bush administration witnessed a gradual warming of American–European relations that most expect will continue with the new Obama administration. Talk of renewal has replaced alarmist reports about transatlantic drift.[2]

The 60-year anniversary of NATO in April 2009 was in itself a reminder of the continuing strength of transatlantic cooperation. The occasion turned into a festival of renewal and unity of purpose, highlighted by the addition of two new members (Albania and Croatia) from Europe's most troubled region and by France's full return to NATO's integrated military structure. As President Barack Obama put it on 3 April 2009: 'Today I'm confident that we took a substantial step forward to renewing our alliance to meet the challenges of our time.'[3]

What explains these developments? What lies behind the growing and continuing European dependency – in security policy – on the USA? What have been the political consequences of this European dependency? Is it likely to continue to the foreseeable future or – given recent disagreements and the lack of a unified external threat – will an independent European Common Foreign and Security Policy eventually become an alternative to NATO? These are some of the key questions that will be addressed in the chapters of this book.

Yet, the story of NATO is only part of the past, present and future of transatlantic security. The bilateral context was central, but already during the Cold War a number of other developments shaped and transformed transatlantic security. Although Americans stayed 'in', they also gradually became to view Europe as less central in their overall security policy. The impact of the Korean War in the early 1950s – explored in this volume by Samuel Wells – was an early indication of the difference between America's increasingly global concerns. Over the years Americans became accustomed to using military force on a global scale while Europeans – having withdrawn from their empires by the 1970s – became increasingly critical of such military interventions (whether in Vietnam, the Middle East or elsewhere). Simultaneously, Europeans were engaged in the gradual process of integration that, by the close of the Cold War, prompted the creation of the European Union (EU).

These factors – extra-European conflicts and integration – have influenced transatlantic relations much more since the end of the Cold War and the demise of extreme bipolarity. But whereas the world of the 1990s may have seemed rather 'unipolar' given the USA's global pre-eminence, the relationship between the USA and Russia is still crucial in influencing transatlantic relations in the twenty-first century. As James Goldgeier's chapter in this volume makes clear, Russia's willingness to cooperate with the West remains a crucial question today. At the same time, however, the role of the EU has also become very important: the EU's dynamics are crucial to understanding the nature of transatlantic relations in the twenty-first century. The EU is a new political and military actor; it offers a new framework for political and military cooperation to the EU and NATO Member States, which, since 2007, are almost the same (the principal exception being Turkey and some small neutral states such as Austria, Finland and Sweden). In her chapter, Hanna Ojanen argues that the EU now offers an alternative to NATO; according to Basil Germond it has even developed some geopolitical ambitions and started to exercise its power beyond its external boundaries. However, whereas the EU seems preponderant regarding civilian aspects of crises management and post-conflict reconstruction, NATO remains the main actor when it comes to high-intensity warfare. And, unlike in the 1960s when French President Charles de Gaulle removed his country from NATO's integrated military structure, the defence alliance is today as popular as ever, symbolized by de Gaulle's successor Nicolas Sarkozy's decision to fully reintegrate France into the Alliance.

The future of transatlantic security depends on a number of factors. Internal politics of the states in question, geopolitics (such as the growing EU's ambitions, Russia's aspirations, America's role in the Middle East, etc.); American and European views of each other; the perception of risks and threats (common or not) rank among the top – but not only – issues that will continue shaping transatlantic relations in the future. While 'hardcore' territorial defence missions are not likely to induce operations in the forthcoming future, stabilization missions in Europe (Balkans) are about to be completed and/or transferred to the EU. So, what is left? Clearly, NATO is going to be an instrument to project security (power, forces, but also stability and good governance), far away from Europe. Afghanistan is an obvious example of this ongoing trend that may, though, create political difficulties in the countries that choose to cooperate with what remains an American-led operation. Such missions may even create crises between, as well as within, the major nations (and other actors) that are part of twenty-first century transatlantic security structures. It seems clear, however, that with the number of institutional structures and common interests at stake, no sudden and cataclysmic collapse of transatlantic security cooperation is in sight.

The present volume tackles a multitude of issues related to the evolution of post-Second World War transatlantic security. Instead of a thematic division, we chose to divide the book chronologically. The first part deals with the various challenges during the Cold War, which we consider as being a historically distinct period, with its specific international – ideological, military and political – structures. The second part of the book is focused on the challenges that have shaped the structure of transatlantic security since the collapse of the USSR. Perhaps because the editors are all historians we felt that such a chronological division was eminently justified.

A note of caution is in order here. Although the book is entitled *Handbook on Transatlantic Security*, we do not claim that this book is a 'handbook' in the sense of covering every conceivable angle of transatlantic security issues. Nevertheless, we believe that the wide variety of topics discussed – as well as the fact that the selection of authors range from PhD students to senior scholars and are roughly equally divided between historians and International Relations specialists – offers the reader a good sense of the multiple issues that shape and inform scholarship on transatlantic security today.

The chapters in Part I of the book offer a series of analyses of the key questions that shaped transatlantic security during the Cold War. Anne Deighton's opening chapter focuses on the initial negotiations of the North Atlantic Treaty (NAT) and emphasizes the military–defensive nature of the organization created in 1949. Samuel Wells calls the readers' attention to the sometimes forgotten impact that the outbreak of the Korean

War in 1950 had on the 'militarization' of NATO and transatlantic security. In two subsequent chapters François David and Jenny Raflik look at the role of France during the first decade of NATO's existence; David from the perspective of nuclear defence plans, Raflik within the context of French overall foreign policy during the Fourth Republic.

Several chapters deal with the challenges of the 1960s and 1970s. Georges-Henri Soutou analyses de Gaulle's policies and the impact of 'gaullism' on France's often turbulent relationship with its NATO partners. Benedikt Schoenborn looks at Willy Brandt's *détente* policies and the foundations of the Federal Republic of Germany's (FRG's) *Ostpolitik*. In his chapter Leopoldo Nuti examines the negotiations leading to the signing of the Nuclear Non-Proliferation Treaty (NPT) from the perspective of two non-nuclear powers, Italy and West Germany. Daniel Möckli and Andreas Wenger turn their attention to the broader context in which *détente* emerged and its impact on transatlantic relations. Finally, Bernhard Blumenau and Barbara Zanchetta address different aspects of the increasingly important role that the Middle East played in transatlantic security relations; Blumenau from the perspective of German–American relations during the 1973 October War and Zanchetta within the context of the Iranian revolution.

The end of the Cold War in 1989–91 fundamentally changed the rationale of transatlantic security. This is a key issue addressed in the first chapter of Part II of the book, in which Jérôme Elie places the dissolution of the Warsaw Pact within the context of ongoing Soviet–American negotiations that began at least as early as 1987. Wolfgang Krieger then takes the story into the late 1990s by introducing the EU–NATO dichotomy in his chapter on the background and relevance of the Franco-British St-Malo declaration of 1998. Hanna Ojanen's chapter on the current state of EU–NATO relations further examines this post-Cold War institutional dichotomy, a mixture of cooperation and competition. The next two chapters, by Axel Marion and Basil Germond, revolve around the question of boundaries; in particular, on the evolving frontiers of the new EU and the impact that the extension of the European project has had on transatlantic relations.

From different angles, the chapters of Tuomas Forsberg, Jérôme Gygax and Guillaume de Rougé address the much talked about question of soft power. By looking at anti-Americanism in Europe (Forsberg), strategic culture (Gygax) and European identity (de Rougé), these chapters further underline the complexity of present-day transatlantic relations. James Goldgeier's chapter, however, serves as a good reminder about the continued significance of Russian–American relations for transatlantic security, whereas Jussi Hanhimäki's chapter cautions against the inflated expectations placed upon the new American president.

In the concluding chapter Ambassador Jacques de Dardel – the keynote speaker of the conference in which most of the chapters were initially discussed – provides an overview of the difficulties that NATO faces in trying to adapt to the evermore quickly changing times. The title of his chapter, 'Is the present future of NATO already history?' is a provocative reminder of the rapidity and unpredictability of our current era in general and transatlantic relations in particular.

Most of the chapters in this volume were originally presented in late April 2009 at an international conference on 'Transatlantic Security Issues from the Cold War to the 21st Century'. The conference was hosted at the Graduate Institute of International and Development Studies, Geneva, and mainly funded by the Fondation Pierre du Bois pour l'histoire du temps présent. The editors would like to express their heartfelt thanks to the

Graduate Institute and to the Fondation Pierre du Bois for their generous support. We are particularly grateful to the efforts of Mme Irina du Bois, whose commitment made the conference not only possible but into a truly memorable occasion.

We would also like to express our gratitude to those who were instrumental in bringing this book into fruition. At the Graduate Institute Bernhard Blumenau worked tirelessly to put the lengthy manuscript together, while Lisa Komar and Jaci Eisenberg provided valuable assistance with translation and editing. At Routledge, we owe a heartfelt thanks to Andrew Humphrys and Rebecca Brennan.

Notes

1 Geir Lundestad (ed.), *No End to Alliance: The United States and Western Europe: Past, Present and Future,* (London: Macmillan, 1998), p. 4. See also Lundestad (ed.), *Just Another Major Crisis: The United States and Europe Since 2000,* (Oxford: Oxford University Press, 2008).
2 Literature on NATO is massive. One recent book that includes a wide array of perspectives and issues is Vojtech Mastny, Sven G. Holtsmark and Andreas Wenger (eds), *War Plans and Alliances in the Cold War: Threat Perceptions in the East and West,* (London: Routledge, 2006). The most up-to-date overall account is Lawrence Kaplan, *NATO Divided, NATO United: The Evolution of an Alliance,* (New York: Praeger, 2004). See also the Parallel History Project www.isn.ethz.ch/ (accessed 10 March 2010).
3 The full text of the speech can be found on numerous websites, for example www.cbsnews.com/stories/2009/04/03/politics/100days/worldaffairs/main4918137.shtml (accessed 10 January 2010).

Part I
Transatlantic security in the Cold War era

Three ministers and the world they made

Acheson, Bevin and Schuman, and the North Atlantic Treaty, March–April 1949

Anne Deighton

Introduction

The North Atlantic Treaty (NAT) defined and then cemented the institutional shape of the bipolar system and the ideological contours of the Cold War world. The alliance became the key vehicle for both East–West and West–West communication during the Cold War, and it also shaped the politics of West European states. It has continued to survive and to expand its membership and its functions for over 20 years since the end of the Cold War.

This would have surprised the three leading foreign ministers, Dean Acheson (USA), Ernest Bevin (UK) and Robert Schuman (France), who signed the NAT with nine other foreign ministers on 4 April 1949. It would have amazed them that they had devised such enduring institutional and military structures, and that, over the next 60 years, NATO would both survive and continue to enlarge. For in 1949, all three were far more conscious of the history of the previous 50 years. Etched on their minds – but in different ways – were the disasters of European and global wars; the consequences of the USA's refusal to sign the Versailles Treaty; the failure of appeasement in the 1930s to deal with nazism and fascism; and the frailty of the wartime alliance that had been forged to fight the war after 1939. All three were more concerned with how Germany's future might look in the short term; with the nature and strength of the Soviet threat in Europe and the kind of political deal that was now required to meet it; and with resource and reconstruction issues.

This chapter will examine what Acheson, Bevin and Schuman thought they were creating in April 1949, and the high-level personal diplomacy that took place in Washington from 31 March to 7 April 1949. It will show that there were substantive areas of disagreement, and that compromises had to be made to secure a general treaty, as there was no agreed view about the form it should take or of its membership. Yet, it was clear by the end of 1949 that the NAT had triggered a profound strategic and psychological revolution among the Western allies, despite the fact that the militarization of the NAT took several years more. By the mid-1950s, the NAT had facilitated a more activist US policy over West Germany which involved empowering France as the lead nation on the European continent, but which also left the UK as a global strategic partner to the USA, yet also outside the integrative efforts on the continent.

The chapter will conclude by reflecting on the footprint of the 1949 settlement that remains today, at least in two important respects. The first is that the idea of an existential external threat remains the necessary driver for the institutional success of NATO. That is to say, NATO remains at heart primarily a defence alliance, driven primarily by Article 5 of the NAT. This helps us to understanding the continuing perceptions of both Russia and now also of terrorism as existential 'others', as this serves to legitimize the continuing presence of NATO. The dominance of the USA over European politics from 1949 has also shaped the direction and depth of subsequent European integrative efforts, and has contributed to a European-wide cultural and political internalization of Atlanticism that has become a part of the politics of European security and integration over and beyond the end of the Cold War. This reveals the 'stickiness' of NATO's institutional presence in the Euro-Atlantic sphere to this day, although the extent to which this continues to depend upon the 'defence' dimension of the Alliance remains unknown.

Secret and public diplomacy: 1948

The year of 'la grande peur' was 1948. Between 1945 and 1947 diplomacy had failed to secure a post-war settlement, and the risks of an ideological and power political conflict seemed high. Germany, Austria and Japan were still under military occupation. In February, the Soviets masterminded a coup in Prague. In June they blockaded Berlin. Economic crisis loomed in Western Europe and the sterling area, despite the promise of dollars through Marshall Aid. Intelligence reports about the attraction of communist propaganda were mounting. Politicians and planners on both sides of the Atlantic were divided on how to assess the future: they were mindful of the baleful memory of appeasement, yet aware that popular pressures were for domestic reconstruction and peace. The nature of Soviet policy was hard to assess beyond observation of policy on the ground, and analysis of the ideological and geostrategic tenets of the Soviet Union/Russia.

It was against this background of real fear and insecurity that the Brussels Treaty (BT) was drawn up by the UK, France and the Benelux countries. It was Bevin who made the early running for the treaty, particularly with his famous House of Commons 'Western Union' speech of 22 January 1948.[1] The BT, which was then agreed less than two months later, was multilateral, secured within the UN Article 51, with defence automaticity in Article IV. It received public endorsement from Truman, as well as his private promise of support.[2] Before the ink was barely dry the signatories began talks on how to bind the USA to a European project to deliver military security to the western part of Europe.

The welter of negotiations that took place over the rest of the year has been covered in a number of accounts.[3] There were private trilateral talks between the USA, UK and Canada from March (about which the other BT powers were not informed); sessions of the BT Consultative Council; and many sets of bilateral negotiations. At the public level, the Vandenberg resolution of June 1948 was a significant indication that public opinion in the USA might now move to a new defence policy, and the BT powers, the USA and Canada then opened negotiations. Negotiators on both sides of the Atlantic moved from the hope that the USA would give military support to the BT or an expanded model of the BT, to exploration of the USA joining the BT, or even creating a new treaty. Military discussion also got under way.[4] By September 1948, the planners had come up with the skeleton of what was to become the NAT: while not naming the Soviets or the Germans as the future threat, the draft mentioned mutual defence against an armed attack. It also touched upon economic and social cooperation, self-help and mutual aid. The form, membership, duration and geographical scope of the treaty were not mentioned.[5] Hard negotiating then lapsed because of the American presidential elections in which Truman was wrongly but widely expected to lose.[6]

January–April 1949

As the new year opened, ministers once again began their negotiations. What were the expectations of the ministers as the preparatory talks reached their climax, and preparations were made for the three foreign ministers to meet in Washington at the end of March 1949?

Dean Acheson, appointed as Secretary of State by Truman after his own successful election campaign, was to be the host of this three-way meeting. It was to be the first time he had met his fellow foreign ministers.[7] Acheson was a lawyer–politician and had already served under Truman, taking a leading role in the Marshall Plan before leaving office to make money as a lawyer. Acheson's views hardened over time, but he was still by temperament a classic east-coast American liberal with a natural sympathy for the UK. Urbane, quick-witted, yet with a sharp tongue, he sought to activate a 'preponderance' of power in the furtherance of American interests in Europe.[8] Acheson saw the treaty instrumentally, as part of a wider European project to deal with the major strategic question of Germany's future in the face of the Soviet menace. He was irritated by the complexity of the two-, three- and four-power negotiations about Germany, reconstruction and defence, thought that the path towards the creation of West Germany was irreversible, and that the USA had to use the NAT as a 'carrot to elicit France's cooperation' to bring a West Germany into a West European community.[9] Truman later reflected that there would have been no NATO without Acheson, who drove through both the decisions on Germany and the treaty's own institutional arrangements.[10]

Robert Schuman's career and approach to life were totally different. A borderland man from Lorraine, Schuman was unmarried, gaunt, aesthetic and almost clerical in demeanour. Yet he was a tough political survivor. He came to the post of foreign minister in 1948 from being prime minister, and was an emblem of stability in the tumultuous politics of the Fourth Republic. He knew both the depth of insecurity about German power that existed in France, and also the importance to the national psyche of the idea of France as a major continental and imperial power. He knew that French leadership in Europe would never be easy, not least because of France's large communist party, and he was also not a natural Atlanticist. Yet it was clear to him that the USA had now to be an ally of France in peace as it had been in war: how this was to be operationalized in a way that enhanced France's role in the international system drove Schuman's strategy.[11] So Schuman went to Washington with the intention of seeking progress on Germany, but also with a clear agenda about the ways in which the treaty could benefit France's own European, geostrategic and economic interests.[12] He would have to be flexible on currency reform, a possible new constitution for western Germany and the Ruhr, while playing a hard, two-level game between French domestic opinion and international ambitions and pressures.

Ernest Bevin was one of the most senior trade unionists in Britain, and had held senior government office longer than his other two colleagues. Minister of Labour between

1940 and 1945 in Winston Churchill's coalition wartime government, he then took office in the 1945 Labour Government of Clement Attlee at the age of 64. He was already tired and in poor health. Bevin's view of Britain's role in the world was largely formulated before 1945. In his union career he had seen the malign influence of communist doctrine upon the working man and upon social democratic trade unionism. Yet he appreciated that communism was a force that could be neither ignored nor easily stamped out, and that the Soviet Union – like the interwar employer bosses – was a power with which Britain would have to live. He favoured an intergovernmental, Commonwealth-like approach to the management of Britain's role as a world power. He also favoured a close collaboration with France, but there is little evidence of a natural affinity with the USA. He had opposed the 1946 US loan, and was on the secret cabinet committee for Britain's own independent nuclear bomb project. However, Bevin, always a subtle observer of the workings of power, was well aware of the unbalanced power distribution among the USA, Europe and the Soviet Union that the Second World War had exacerbated.

In 1948, Bevin's sights were set high. He sought actively to promote the role of the UK as a third world force; to lead continental Europe, and to re-animate imperial–commonwealth connections through development, strategic bases, and financial links. Such a scenario would have brought strategic strength, and greater independence, as well as access to the raw materials and labour that Britain and continental Europe needed for reconstruction. So he wanted the NAT to be a short-term military alliance, to have the BT powers hold a privileged place in the arrangement and thus to privilege it as the premier European organization. He preferred the phrase 'collective defence arrangements of the Brussels treaty powers in association with the United States' to the wording of the NAT. For the Five Powers

> had their own identity and common purpose and were what he called at the time of the signature of the Brussels Treaty the "hard core" to undertake the leadership of Western Europe. He would be reluctant to hand the whole business over to the United States ... If Western Europe developed on the right lines and again got on her feet, the difference in power between her and America would not be so great and it was important to keep Western Europe's position of leadership even during the present time of temporary difficulties.[13]

Bevin was the key player among the BT foreign ministers, to whom the others, especially the Benelux countries, deferred. But both he and Schuman needed to achieve military security and funding to enable them to restore confidence at home; they both wanted to be leaders, although it would be fairer to say that theirs was rather a competitive dependence upon the USA.

The issues

What issues were most contentious for the NAT negotiators? The most important issue was the wording of Article 5, as this was the 'key article of the treaty' and underpinned the whole military alliance. The Europeans watched anxiously as the 'deplorable' debate on Article 5 flowed through the US decision-making system and the American press in early 1949. The article became a painstaking compromise for Americans between the continuing lure of isolationism and the responsibility of guarantees.[14] Bevin knew that, while he wanted Article 5 to include the word 'military' and to follow the model of automaticity in the BT, a weaker clause could not be a reason for not signing the NAT, for the psychological importance of even a weak NAT would better than no treaty at all, as 'we should still secure consultative machinery, and above all, the establishment of a military committee'.[15]

If Article 5 provoked widespread debate, membership and thus the structure of the NAT did not cause so much consternation, although the issues were strategically just as important, and were unclear until the last moment. The BT powers were late to move to serious consideration of adhering individually to an Atlantic Pact rather than negotiating as a block. However, the Americans expressed concern about the Scandinavian region; Spain (whose admission was out of the question for the Europeans); Greece; Turkey (Bevin also sought but failed to secure a public commitment to Iran as well); and Portugal. Here, US officials said the need for the Azores as a base trumped concerns about the Portuguese dictatorship.[16] Sweden was also of concern, for it sought a Nordic bloc which would draw in its immediate neighbours and be less provocative to the Soviet Union than a transatlantic pact – and Bevin was always very attracted to interlocking regional security blocs. But the Americans were opposed to this idea – and the Norwegians were not so keen either. The Scandinavian debate was taken right up the wire, and not resolved until mid-March when the Americans got their way, and Norway and Denmark, but not Sweden, were invited to accede.[17]

The case of Italy caused endless diplomatic trouble, and was also not resolved until late in the negotiations.[18] The French, who had originally been happy to leave the Italians out, then saw that admitting Italy could be a prelude to also admitting Algeria – both Mediterranean countries. This change of heart infuriated both the Americans and Bevin. However, the French would then only support the admission of Norway, which the Americans insisted upon, if Italy could be considered too. Ambassador Bonnet even threatened withdrawal from the process if this were not done.[19] As with Article 5, Bevin relented again. As he said to his BT colleagues, the British were not now 'masters of the situation, and if the United States were keen on the admission of Italy, then the United Kingdom would not object'. He just hoped that something might be done for Greece and Turkey, 'or the Soviet Union might assume that we had decided upon a certain line of defence which did not cover Greece and Turkey, which would thereby be endangered'.[20] The significance of all this is that key leaders were very unclear of exactly what they were trying to do beyond pen in communism: it is startling to see how uncertain the institutional shape of the NAT looked, even in March 1949.

Other issues that had to be considered in the last hectic weeks were those of aid for the Europeans; the relationship between the proposed treaty and the UN; the wording of Article 2; and the duration of the alliance (20 years was as long as the Europeans thought they could get the USA to agree to). European requests for aid were rejected as being underprepared and underscrutinized, although the BT countries had actually stated their request for aid that was based on considerations of solidarity and that, 'the attainment of [their] economic viability should accordingly have priority': the USA should provide the hard military cover for European economic revival, an issue that starkly revealed the real uncertainty about exactly the type of threat from the Soviets that they were all facing.[21]

The relationship between NATO and the UN was also of importance, not least because the UN was the most public aspect of inclusive international diplomacy to date: if the NAT was not to be seen as a deliberate attempt to undermine the UN (which was the Soviet claim), then the treaty had to be constructed in such a way that at least the appearance of universalism had been retained. It was not until 16 March that Acheson the lawyer stepped in to resolve the difficulties of dovetailing UN Articles 51, 53 and 54 to the proposed NAT text.[22] Of course, Soviet diplomats were quick to complain that Article 5 was detached from the UNSC and could alone trigger war without any reference to the UN.

There was another debate that centred on Article 2 – the Western community-building clause.[23] The Canadians, who sponsored this article, were in part concerned to open a firmer trilateral trade space between the USA, the UK and themselves in the context of the negotiations about freeing up trade within Western Europe, while giving themselves an explanation at home for adherence to the treaty.[24] It is significant that neither Bevin not Acheson favoured Article 2, largely because they thought it would complicate and slow down the implementation of the military treaty. However, the Canadians also reserved their position on adherence at all until Article 2 was included.[25] Given the subsequent debates and difficulties relating to this dimension of the treaty, and the imaging of NATO as a collective security institution, this is highly significant and underdiscussed.

To the end of the negotiation process

The text of the Pact was published 18 March.[26] Bevin had had to make many compromises, while Schuman had his way on Italy. Acheson was not happy about the successes the French and Canadians had scored. One might have expected that spirits would be high, but this was not the case, not least because the Americans had outmanoeuvred their BT colleagues and invited the Canadians and all the other future European members of the NAT to the signing ceremony, although the BT powers had hoped only to allow the others to accede to the treaty later, thus reinforcing the role of the BT at the European heart of the treaty.[27] At the end of March the foreign ministers then met face-to face to discuss not only the NAT but future strategy more generally, a pattern much favoured in the growing phenomenon of multilateral institutional negotiations.

Bilaterals and multilaterals

The first meeting between Bevin and Acheson was on 31 March – the first time that the two had met. After the pleasantries, they discussed the fact that the Soviets seemed interested in finding a way out of the Berlin blockade and reopening negotiations on Germany. Bevin sought to hold back for, 'I saw no objection to continuing sounding the Russians, but I thought it was essential that we should consolidate the situation in Western Europe before we went any further with them … We did not want to rush ahead too fast'.

However, Acheson disagreed with Bevin's view that the Soviets were trying to block the NAT by making some concessions on Berlin, and argued that, by contrast, ending the blockade immediately might encourage the US Senate towards the NAT. Bevin now reported that he sensed a 'very dangerous situation arising' with this form of issue linkage to US domestic politics. It was, instead, important to build upon the growing confidence and participation of France, and not 'put the clock back' by either making too early an agreement with the Soviets over Berlin or allowing the Germans greater freedom of action, both of which would make France fearful and obstinate. While seeking also to ensure a privileged position for Britain in American eyes vis-à-vis France, he knew that keeping Americans on board was the top priority: a repetition of the events of 1919 when the Americans failed to secure agreement to the Versailles Treaty would be disastrous.[28]

Schuman's meeting with Acheson covered much of the same ground. Schuman wondered how the NAT would really stop French fears of a Soviet invasion of France, which could not be countered by use of the bomb in Western Europe. Yet, Acheson admitted that Congress might find the delivery of large quantities of military aid difficult to agree to. On Germany, Schuman finally agreed to a trizonal solution. Like Bevin, he was more cautious about the next steps towards the Soviets, but broadly agreed with Acheson that the initiative here should not be lost.[29]

The three men met together in the afternoon of 1 April.[30] They discussed the possibility of a simplified Occupation Statute for the Western zones. Acheson suggested retaining reserved powers, while allowing the Germans greater freedoms, and also completing the Ruhr agreement.[31] He later recalled that they all agreed that none of them actually fully understood the existing complexities of the situation. However, the record of the meeting reveals a good deal of residual tension: Bevin in particular was truculent, as immediate four-power talks could 'split the western front' for neither the Pact, nor a European Council, nor even the decisions on West Germany had yet been finalized or ratified. His idea of negotiation from strength essentially stemmed from his trade union experience of collecting negotiation chips to improve bargaining power, while Acheson's tactics displayed a confidence that Western unity would oblige the Soviets to be more accommodating. Schuman was more pliable than Bevin, indicating that the Western powers should not fall into a trap of rejecting the possibility that the Soviets wished to negotiate again.[32]

On 2 April, Acheson met all the other Pact foreign ministers who had now arrived in Washington. The final wording of the Pact was now nodded through, and talks opened on the Soviet responses and follow-up machinery for the Council.[33] However, there was disagreement with the Dutch about Indonesia (Dutch Foreign Minister Dirk Stikker even threatened not to sign the Pact – the third foreign minister to do so).[34]

The Americans lecture the Europeans

That evening, a Sunday, the Pact foreign ministers met with Truman, accompanied only by Acheson and Forrestal. The meeting was, as Spaak said, 'blunt', and was dominated by Acheson and Truman, and not even included in the UK record of these days.[35] It is here that we can see the longer strategic vision of the Americans – this was real, hard, no holds barred 'grand strategy', in which their view of communism as an 'egalitarian, dynamic social force' was developed, and in which the particularities of the Europeans and their own national preoccupations were thought of as being of secondary importance. Truman asserted that 'none of us are under illusion that the Atlantic Pact itself is more than a symbol of our common determination'. He then set out how the future would involve 'sacrifices of traditional security and economic objectives which they may be most unwilling to make', but which were necessary if they were to ensure their survival, and then 'the eventual triumph of the West'. Truman said that vast military expenditure was out of the question: US public opinion would not stand for it. The Europeans, and especially the French and Dutch, were told that they had to give up their colonial fantasies – their 'hopeless colonial warfare' (Forrestal) – and stop the risk of communism spreading to support nationalism. However, USA estimates were that there was a breathing space of 'several years' for the West, during which time Truman proposed 'to carry the ideological war to the Soviet sphere itself'.

Germany and Japan were both major power centres: they had to be rehabilitated. In the case of Germany, this had to be done through a 'reasonably centralised West German government ... And the integration of the Reich as a full-fledged partner in an increasingly unified Western Europe', politically, economically and militarily, to capture the imagination of Germans in a way that would protect them against Soviet influence.

However, although the Europeans had to start being more effective collectively, it would be impossible to defend Europe at the Rhine in the near future, and they now required a combined command led by the USA, UK and France 'with liaison missions from the other members'.[36] Under this would be the Western Union organization, perhaps joined by Italy, in a scenario in which only the USA and the UK would have naval missions, while the others built up their forces, all of which would require integrated equipment, training and operational techniques, supplied by an integrated armaments production division. The UK and the USA, 'the farthest removed from the Soviet threat', would become the arsenals of this Atlantic combine. The president added that a dynamic political and psychological warfare programme was needed to seize the initiative, as well as a strengthening of the UN 'as a focal point for rallying and tying together the entire non-Soviet world', and to reinforce the core effort of turning the Pact from 'a paper plan to a solid reality'. To support this, the European Reconstruction Programme (ERP) must be revitalized through a 'whole new approach' of closer economic and political cooperation (although Eastern Europe was 'gone semi-permanently from the Western orbit'). Revitalization would be an antidote to the appeal of international communism, though a United States of Europe was not immediately favoured. However, '[i]n this connection, Mr Bevin', Acheson said, 'we are somewhat concerned over the evident UK hesitation about proceeding too far along these lines ... for the continent is Britain's shield against attack'. Britain must sacrifice some of her traditional aloofness.

The meeting must have particularly humiliating to Bevin and Schuman, as it became clear that far from being able to use the Americans for British or French interests, the new arrangements implied a grand strategic re-evaluation led by the USA. Bevin's fear of European federalism came to the fore, for 'we do not consider ourselves as a continental nation: we have a worldwide commonwealth to look after and our attitude toward the continent is somewhat like that of the US ... we do not wish to rush headlong into entangling commitments'. To which Schuman replied tartly that perhaps 'Mr Bevin would prefer to wait until the Communists had "stabilised" Western Europe?' Acheson had to calm both down after this exchange, and the meeting seems to have ended rather abruptly.

The USA had now fully turned the corner and would now be leading its Western European allies forward, listening and empowering Bevin and Schuman in different ways. The two strongest features of the treaty were already the dominant role of the USA, which was prepared to tell the Europeans how they develop their region, and the hopefully distant but fairly solid commitment to military defence through Article 5. This difficult evening meeting made it all too clear that negotiating from weakness with the USA in the context of the NAT would be the way forward from now on.

Short-term outcomes

The next day – no doubt with a return of good diplomatic manners – the treaty was signed. The treaty's institutional framework was set after September 1949, when the first meeting of the Council was held, which also established the Defence Committee. It was not until October that the Mutual Defence Act finally went through Congress, freeing up aid for the European militaries. In January 1950, the first strategic plan was agreed by the North Atlantic powers: by now the BT was clearly not going to retain its independent military dimension.

The NAT was a military, psychological and diplomatic gateway to the subsequent dominance by the USA of German and, to a certain extent, also West European politics. Outstanding issues over policy were taken forward by the three foreign ministers in five intensive meetings over three days after the signature of the NAT, and they agreed a four-power conference and laid out the lines of a new civilian government for the three Western zones, with high commissioners, a new funding mechanism and with the empowerment of German civilian rule with allied control only exercised over specific security arenas. Although this was not widely discussed at the time, all three also knew full well that the three German zones were now indeed militarily defended by the NATO treaty.[37] These decisions were unequivocally driven by Acheson.[38]

In late May, the abortive four-power Palais Rose Council of Foreign Ministers was held in Paris, following on from the Soviets agreement to end the blockade of Berlin on 12 May. This was the meeting about which Bevin had had such reservations when he was in Washington. While Acheson came increasingly to admire Bevin's dogged approach to dealing with the Soviets over Germany, he suggested that they should nevertheless have constructive proposals to hand to the Soviets, even if only for propaganda purposes.[39] It was not until July 1949 that the NAT was ratified in the UK, USA and France, and it did not come into operation until August 1949, so Bevin and Schuman had to be content with the publicity surrounding the treaty to give them the psychological boost needed to have the confidence to take forward these solutions for Western Germany. As a result of Acheson's German policy both Bevin and Schuman came to realize and appreciate that Acheson did have a strategic vision that they had to accept. Acheson's personal relations with Bevin were stronger than those with Schuman, and Bevin's growing compliancy in NATO matters was part of that package. Yet, retrospectively, it cannot be forgotten that Acheson 'almost thought of Bevin and Schuman as one. They had both emerged from Europe's "tragic" century and agreed on the "menace of communism"'. They had both realized that for Acheson, 'power talks'.[40]

Bevin was feted for the treaty, yet it can be argued that both the detail and the strategic thrust of the NAT were a setback for his most ambitious personal aims.[41] Bevin had opposed Article 2, but favoured a stronger Article 5; opposed a wider treaty, and particularly the membership of Italy; had vigorously sought to empower the BT powers to a far greater extent than materialized; and had unsuccessfully sought a speedy resolution to both the military aid and the planning issues. In short, he wanted US support and money in the short term, to allow the UK to recover its own autonomy in the world.

At the same time, Acheson was seeking to empower Schuman, who was 'one of the greatest strokes of luck that has come along for a long time'.[42] The moment when the USA turned unequivocally to France was 15 September 1949. In their tripartite meeting in Washington, and in the midst of a long and painful discussion about dismantling and reparations, Acheson turned to Schuman and said, '[p]erhaps the situation is hopeless. Maybe Germany can't be a useful quiet member of the European community. The best chance and hope for us seems to be under French leadership. It doesn't work for us to take the lead. We are too far away and to a lesser extent this is also true of the British. In the long run if there is to be an answer, there must be a solution of Franco-German troubles under French leadership'.[43]

This was the decisive moment, made possible through the psychological advantage of NATO as a gateway to a stronger German policy, and in part in view of the help that

11

the Americans had given to the UK during their terrible currency crisis of the previous month. Acheson thought that Britain would be kept on board through the military context, financial and global conversations, while France could ensure its security vis-à-vis Germany through West European institutional structures.

So from the autumn of 1949, Bevin's world power plans were in tatters, and the increasingly ill foreign secretary was to see the Foreign Office (FO) – always sceptical about European cooperative schemes – now make the running over the treaty at home, and argue that the fist aim of British policy should be to further empower the treaty, drop his world power proposals, use Article 2 to build an Atlantic rather than European community (i.e. against the Council of Europe), and to encourage further positive gestures from the USA, which they did in a very vigorous series of papers between the autumn of 1949 and April of 1950.[44] However, it was actually France that was the *sine qua non* of the strategic impulses of the NAT. For in June 1950, France could pick up the gauntlet thrown by Acheson six months earlier and lead the way towards a reconceptualization of the Franco-German dilemma through Jean Monnet's 'Schuman' Plan, confident of US backing. No wonder the FO was dejected and Bevin infuriated by events on the continent. Indeed, by the autumn of 1950, the Americans had begun a tortuous four-year period of negotiations over the full return of Germany to the centre of the European balance of power with the Pleven Plan/European Defence Community proposals, which left the UK as pliant supporters of an American policy that accommodated itself to the time needed by France to allow West German admission to NATO.

Conclusion

A strategic revolution took place as a result of the NAT, which, as we have seen, was not fully anticipated at the time: it shaped Western defence, the rehabilitation of West Germany and the nature of transatlantic relations. It set a pattern of US support of West Germany through French leadership on the continent, and UK compliance to US demands and to NATO (in the name of the 'special relationship'). There are many characteristics of the foundation days that were to dominate the 1950s and beyond which still resonate today.

First, it seems that the idea of an existential external threat remains a driving – and perhaps necessary – force for the continuation of NATO.[45] In 1948–49, the fear of the Soviet Union and its communist ideology seemed real enough. While planners and politicians did not expect an immediate invasion or war, the territorial gains of the Soviet Union, the nature of an ideology which argued that the forces of history were on its side, were cause for alarm. Yet a residual fear of German power had not disappeared, through its military potential as an aggressive power, as an economic competitor or as a possible future ally of the Soviet Union, although Germany was recognized to be the necessary driver for economic recovery in Europe. The NAT initially gave military protection to the western zones of Germany until a new Germany that was embedded in Western Europe could be created. The treaty took the western part of the defeated Germany inside the new system, even as the structure, thinking and planning of NATO was predicated upon the external, Soviet threat.

Nothing like this happened after the end of the Cold War. Intuitively, one might have expected the institutional structure of NATO to change after the relatively peaceful collapse of the Soviet Union. Debates and initiatives in the 1990s to explore the possibility of weaving Russia into the NATO fabric however were tepid and feeble, and excluded the possibility of Russian membership. Yet at the same time the USA developed a policy of NATO enlargement to parts of the former Soviet empire, which has continued to divide Europe and upset the Russians. This focus on the Russian 'other' shifted after 9/11, as NATO planners saw the possibility of 'reinventing' NATO to fight terrorism in Afghanistan, a new enemy. The consequences of this have been on the one hand to transform the alliance into a fighting force in a region beyond Europe, yet at the same time without having managed to reinvent Russia as a long-term partner of NATO. Now, there is a rising public and private concern, once again, about Russian policy. If one leaves aside the politics of this shift, it is not hard to see, in pure strategic terms, the continued value of the enemy, the 'other', for a 'sticky' institution as large and as dependent upon public messages, rhetoric and psychology as is NATO.

Second, the two institutional features of NATO in the Cold War were US hegemony and the assumption that there would be an increasingly united Europe under a benign American supervision. This was clear in Truman's important dressing down to the foreign ministers. This assumption has changed perhaps less than might have been expected. Institutional theory suggests that institutions continue to behave in similar ways, unless and until affected by a major 'shock' or paradigm shift. This was and is still true in the case of NATO. During the Cold War, the West European powers were firmly 'nested' within the Atlantic structure, even if there were disagreements within the organization. No country defected from NATO – even France, despite its histrionics about the military command structure. Indeed, France, the UK and West Germany all performed an elaborate and competitive dance for the attentions of the USA throughout the Cold War.

In 1949 there was also a widely held assumption that West Europe should cooperate or integrate further – if only to stop Europeans fighting each other again. The Americans had been disappointed by the lack of integrative impulses in the ERP. Although they privileged the UK, France and the Federal Republic, this was in different ways for each country, and there always remained an element of 'managing' the West Europeans. Within NATO, the institutional and particularly the military structure were US-dominated, affecting planning, purchasing and grand strategy. Historians have not yet satisfactorily assessed the extent to which NATO has shaped the way in which European integration developed in the Cold War, and the extent not only to which the USA worked against European defence/military integration, but also, for example, the participation of the neutrals in the European Community during the Cold War.

In the post-Cold War world, the negative response of the USA to the St Malo initiative in 1998 indicated very starkly that the hegemonic structure remained appealing to the USA, which feared both a threat to the military role of NATO and the weakening of the institutional loyalty of its European Union (EU) partners. Institutional competition between NATO and the EU is a powerful reason for the relative lack of subsequent success – or at least the very slow progress – of the ESDP since 1998. Indeed, Europeans remain culturally Atlanticist (even through the Iraq War), despite the new dimensions NATO. Thus, in these two illustrative areas, the overlay of the NAT remains extraordinarily powerful, showing that this international organization gave a shape to the current transatlantic system that was not understood at the moment of its creation.

Notes

1 The signatories were the UK, France, The Netherlands, Belgium, Luxembourg, *Treaty of Economic, Social and Cultural Collaboration and Collective Self-Defence*, Cmd. 7599, (London: HMSO, 1948); Anne Deighton, 'Entente neo-coloniale: Ernest Bevin and the proposals for an Anglo-French Third

World Power, 1945–49', *Diplomacy and Statecraft*, no. 17, 2006, pp. 835–52; Gladwyn Jebb, *The Memoirs of Lord Gladwyn*, (London: Weidenfeld and Nicolson, 1972), chapter 13. I am grateful to Georges-Henri Soutou, Nadia Hilliard, Robert Ayson and Christian Huber for perceptive and positive comments.

2 Harry S. Truman, *Years of Trial and Hope*, Vol II, (London: Hodder and Stoughton, 1956), pp. 256–57.

3 *Events Leading up to the Signature of the North Atlantic Treaty*, Cmd. 7692, (London: HMSO, 1949); Lawrence S. Kaplan, *NATO 1948: the Birth of the Transatlantic Alliance*, (Plymouth: Rowman and Littlefield, 2007), the most recent of Kaplan's distinguished publications on this theme; Nicholas Henderson, *The Birth of NATO*, (London: Weidenfeld and Nicolson, 1982); Escott Reid, *Time of Fear and Hope; the Making of the North Atlantic Treaty, 1947–1949*, (Ontario: McClelland and Stewart, 1977); Francis H. Heller and John R Gillingham, *NATO: The Founding of the Atlantic Alliance and the Integration of Europe*, (New York: St Martin's Press, 1992); Timothy P. Ireland, *Creating the Entangling Alliance: the Origins of the North Atlantic Treaty Organization*, (London: Aldwych Press, 1981); John Baylis, *The Diplomacy of Pragmatism: Britain and the Formation of NATO*, (Kent, OH: Kent State University Press, 1993); Maurice Vaisse et al, *La France et l'OTAN, 1949–1996*, (Paris: Complexe, 1996); Olav Riste (ed.), *Western Security: the Formative Years, European and Atlantic Defence, 1947–1953* (Oslo: Norwegian University Press, 1985). The US/UK/Canadian Pentagon talks were a well-kept secret for many decades. All these negotiations were more complex because the names of these organizations had not yet been fully agreed, and there was also much uncertainty about their relative positions in the emerging European system.

4 This was through the Western Union Defence Organisation (WUDO). The British Plan was called Doublequick, the US one, Halfmoon, Kaplan, *NATO 1948*, pp. 87, 161. On plans to expand the BT, NSC1/9, April 1948, *Foreign Relations of the United States (FRUS), 1948: III* (Washington: US Government Printing Office, 1974), p. 86. The Ambassadors' talks lasted for six weeks from July 1948, before being turned over to a working group that was able to move ahead with concrete proposals.

5 It is this draft that leads Kaplan to use the title *NATO 1948*, pp. 129, 132. NSC 9/3 and NSC 14/1 formed the planning basis of the talks from July 1948, *FRUS, 1948: III*, pp. 140–41, 587f.

6 *FRUS, 1948: III*, p. 324; Kaplan, *NATO 1948*, pp. 186–88. Germany was under four-power military occupation, and there were many sets of talks under way about what to do with Germany, see generally, Anne Deighton, *The Impossible Peace* (Oxford: Oxford University, Clarendon Press, 1993). The German Anglo-American bizone agreement was due to end in March 1949, while reparations, the level of industry agreements and coal production were all under discussion. After May 1948, discussions about a Council of Europe also started.

7 See generally, Robert L. Beisner, *Dean Acheson: a Life in the Cold War*, (New York: Oxford UP, 2006).

8 Melvyn P. Leffler, *A Preponderance of Power: National Security, the Truman Administration, and the Cold War*, (Stanford: Stanford UP, 1992), chapter 7.

9 US Department of State, Memoranda of conversations (henceforth USDSmem), 1949, 9 March, 1949, reel no. 860; John Lewis Gaddis, *The Long Peace: Inquiries into the History of the Cold War*, (New York: Oxford UP, 1987), chapter 3 is a lucid overview of competing American perspectives. Leffler, *Preponderance*, pp. 280, 281; *FRUS, 1949: IV*, p. 109, 14 February 1949.

10 Harry S. Truman, *Memoirs of Harry S Truman, Vol II: Years of Trial and Hope, 1946–1953*, (London: Hodder and Stoughton, 1956), p. 267.

11 Raymond Poidevin, *Robert Schuman, 1886–1963*, (Paris: Imprimerie Nationale, 1986); Georges-Henri Soutou, 'France', in David Reynolds (ed), *The Origins of the Cold War in Europe: International Perspectives*, (New Haven: Yale UP, 1994), p. 105, and 'La sécurité de la France dans l'après-guerre', in, Vaïsse et al (eds), *La France et l'OTAN 1949–1996*; John Young, *France, The Cold War and the Western Alliance, 1944–49*, (Leicester: Leicester UP, 1990). The Americans gave France considerable sums of interim aid from the end of 1947.

12 Kaplan, *NATO 1948*, p. 19.

13 United Kingdom National Archives, (henceforth, UKNA), FO800/448, Five Power Consultative Committee, London, 14–15 March 1949, pp. 6–7. Bevin called this 'an historical occasion', as all the details, including aid required, were agreed before the foreign ministers left for the US.

14 *Events*, p. 5. There is a general assumption about automaticity, which of course does not exist in Article 5 itself. Under the American Constitution, treaties were under the purview of the Senate, not the House of Representatives. The use of the word 'military' was removed from Article 5, and 'such action as it deems necessary, including the use of armed force' was substituted. Bevin used the word 'deplorable', UKNA, CAB129/ 32, CP(49)34, 18 February 1949, 'North Atlantic Pact'.

15 UKNA, CAB129/32, CP(49)34, 18 February 1949, 'North Atlantic Pact', and telegram 965, Franks to FO, 16 February 1949. Bevin was not sure that France would accept such a treaty, however.
16 UKNA, FO371/79239, Woton to FO, no. 1644, 22 March 1949; FO to Lisbon, no. 75, 19 March 1949. Britain had to invoke the long-standing Anglo-Portuguese alliance to help the Americans achieve this. Spain was working against such an outcome.
17 Bevin thought as late as 10 March 1949 that Sweden might yet accede to the Treaty, UKNA CM (49) 19th Conclusions, 10 March 1949; Juhana Aunesluoma, *Britain, Sweden and the Cold War: Understanding Neutrality, 1945–1954*, (Basingstoke: Palgrave Macmillan, 2003). Bevin was also interested in Ireland joining, which however, refused to join, given the status of Northern Ireland: however, this issue was not of concern to the Americans, and so was left.
18 UKNA, CAB129/32, CP (49) 37, 21 February 1949.
19 UKNA, FO800/448, 27–29 January 1949, meeting of Consultative Committee of Five-Power Brussels Treaty for the BT ministers' discussion, inter al, of Italy, p. 15.
20 UKNA, FO800/448, 27–29 January 1949, meeting of Consultative Committee of Five-Power Brussels Treaty, p. 14; CAB129/32, CP(49)37, 21 February 1949: Bevin originally included Iran alongside Greece and Turkey, but was overruled by Acheson.
21 UKNA, FO800/448, Meeting of Consultative Committee of Five-Power Brussels Treaty, London 14–15 March, Annex E, p. 21. They hoped for 600 million dollars over two years.
22 The difficulty was whether the treaty was a regional organization; when the UNSC could have been called into play; and the difference between enforcement and collective actions. The UNSC was essentially relegated to Article 7, while the UN Charter in general was referred to in nearly every paragraph. The legal relationship between UN Article 51 and the proposed Atlantic Pact exercised lawyers and politicians on both sides of the Atlantic, see UKNA, FO371/79235, Z2314, 10 March 1949.
23 'The Parties will contribute toward the further development of peaceful and friendly international relations by strengthening their free institutions, by bringing about a better understanding of the principles upon which these institutions are founded, and by promoting conditions of stability and well-being. They will seek to eliminate conflict in their international economic policies and will encourage economic collaboration between any or all of them', Article 2, North Atlantic Treaty.
24 Canada's 'object is to secure provision whereby it may be possible to handle US-UK-Canadian trade on a three cornered basis', UKNA, FO371/ 79232, Shuckburgh minute.
25 Indeed, it has been argued that eliding anti-communism with free institutions and democracy became one of the less fortunate features not only of the idea of the cold war security community, but more generally of the management of US foreign policy throughout the cold war.
26 It was presented to the UK Cabinet on 10 March, 1949, UKNA, CM (49) 19, 10 March 1949.
27 UNKA, FO371/79238, Brief for the Secretary of State.
28 UKNA, FO800/448, pp. 3, 4, 29; USDSmem, Box 418 Lot 53D444, no 890, 31 March 1949, microfilm; *FRUS 1949:III*, pp. 156–58. The two accounts are different in emphasis, recording of the order of the conversation, and in the tone of the meeting. Bevin also agreed to the creation of the Trizone.
29 USDSmem, 000474, US microfilm, 1949, 891; Acheson and Schuman, 1 April 1949, *FRUS, 1949: III*, pp. 158–59. The role of the British Ambassador to the US, Sir Oliver Franks was central during the final days, Alex Danchev, *Oliver Franks: Founding Father*, (Oxford: Oxford University Clarendon Press, 1993).
30 Bevin had earlier given a talk at the National Press Club over lunch, with an up-beat speech, explaining that Britain had decided it must become European, 'Mr Bevin at the National Press Club', UKNA, FO371/74184, British Information Services, T59, 1 April 1949.
31 UKNA, FO800/448, 12; Dean Acheson, *Sketches from Life: Of Men I Have Known*, (London: Hamish Hamilton, 1961), p. 16. Kirkpatrick sent a cable to Bevin on his way to the States with a short brief on what the administrative situation in Germany actually was, UKNA, FO 800/516, no. 3517, 30 March 1949.
32 USDSmem, 1949, microfilm, 894, 896, Acheson, Bevin, Schuman meeting, 1 April 1949.
33 UKNA, FO371/79239, Brief on Soviet accession to the North Atlantic Pact.
34 UKNA, FO800/448, pp. 29–31, 33–35.
35 In FO800/448. I could not find a UK account of the meeting in other relevant FO files. This could be because the foreign ministers were specifically not permitted to have advisors present, and Bevin, at least, would not have been capable of keeping a note of the meeting. It is recorded in USDSmem,

1949, Lot 53 D444, Box 418, microfilm, 987ff. The long report, which is barely legible in parts, is not in *FRUS*.
36 It is worth noting that the USA both allocated jobs and divided up European responsibilities in a way that reinforced their own military dominance.
37 Beisner, *Acheson*, pp. 136–40; UKNA, CAB128/15, CM (49) 26th Conclusions, 7 April 1949; North Atlantic Treaty, Article 6.
38 *FRUS, 1949: III*, 178ff; UKNA, CAB, CAB128/15, CM (49) 26th Conclusions, 7 April 1949: Attlee explained that the new proposals overturned the earlier drafts which had become very complicated, by proceeding on the principle of turning over power to the Germans subject only to a limited number of specific reservations. Truman said the German agreement was 'the best thing that had been done in his administration', *FRUS, 1949: III*, p. 174.
39 UKNA, FO 800/516, Franks to Bevin, no. 2467, 2 May 1949. This would also please German opinion.
40 Beisner, *Acheson*, pp. 145, 150.
41 UKNA, CAB128/15, CM(49) 32nd Conclusions, 5 May 1949.
42 Quoted in Leffler, *Preponderance*, p. 285.
43 USDS, MemCon 1019, 14 September 1949, Acheson–Bevin meeting, microfilm.
44 R. Bullen and M.E. Pelly (eds), *Documents on British Policy Overseas, 1950: II, II*, (London: HMSO, 1987), nos. 46, 60, 100.
45 The troubled relationship between NATO and the UN in 1949; the under-researched impact of domestic politics – double-edged diplomacy – in all three countries; the problems related to the public characterization of NATO's non-military functions – the Article 2 issue; and the rationale of NATO enlargement particularly after the end of the cold war are among some of the other important issues that still resonate powerfully.

2

The Korean War
Miscalculation and alliance transformation

Samuel F. Wells, Jr.

As the events of the early days of the Cold War developed after 1946, the US administration of Harry S Truman demonstrated its continued commitment to the strategic priorities of World War II. In the increasingly heated competition with the Soviet Union, Europe remained Washington's primary concern. To the challenges of Communist subversion in Greece and Turkey and to economic collapse and security anxiety across Western Europe, the United States responded with the Truman Doctrine, the Marshall Plan, the Brussels Pact, and eventually in April 1949 the North Atlantic Treaty. At the same time, the Truman administration reduced its obligations in East Asia by withdrawing its military forces from South Korea (June 1949) and limiting its commitment to the Chinese Nationalist government in Taiwan. The National Security Council (NSC) formalized these policies in December 1949 when it adopted NSC-48 which outlined future strategy for Asia and excluded the Asian mainland from the US defensive perimeter. Secretary of State Dean Acheson presented this new Asia strategy to the public in a speech at the National Press Club on 12 January 1950. This statement clearly excluded South Korea from American defense commitments.[1]

Yet when North Korea invaded the south on 25 June 1950, the United States intervened by sending its available military forces from Japan. This was largely because the political climate in Washington had changed and because new forceful personalities had taken over critical positions in the administration. Dean Acheson replaced General George C. Marshall as Secretary of State in January 1949, and Paul Nitze took over from George Kennan at the Policy Planning Staff of the State Department a year later. In September 1949, President Truman surprised the world with the announcement that the Air Force had detected fallout from a successful Soviet atomic test. Shortly afterward, on 7 October, the Soviet Union established the German Democratic Republic in its zone of occupation, thereby creating a divided Germany for the post-war period. That same week, on the other side of the world, the Chinese Communists celebrated their victory in the civil war by establishing the People's Republic of China. The two giants of international Communism consolidated their forces by signing on 14 February 1950 a Treaty of Mutual Friendship, Alliance and Mutual Assistance. Adding further cause for concern, British police arrested scientist Klaus Fuchs for atomic espionage early in February. Capitalizing

17

on this series of unwelcome events, Senator Joseph R. McCarthy launched his first attacks on the Truman administration for harboring Communists in its ranks in a speech in Wheeling, West Virginia, on 9 February.[2]

A debate on defense expansion

Following the detection of the Soviet atomic test, President Truman established a committee to examine the question of whether to develop a fusion (hydrogen) bomb. Aggressive Russian actions in Eastern Europe, especially the blockade of Western occupation zones in Berlin, persuaded the president that leaders in Moscow would pursue a fusion capability in any event. This conviction led Truman to approve a report recommending an accelerated research program on the fusion bomb on 31 January 1950. To put the weapons decision in a wider strategic context, at the same time he ordered a broad evaluation of US national security policy in the light of the new Soviet nuclear capability.[3]

Paul H. Nitze chaired the policy review group which worked through the late winter and reported to the NSC in April 1950. Nitze and the members of his *ad hoc* group contended in their report, called NSC-68, that US defenses needed significant strengthening in order to be able to confront a time of "maximum danger" from the Soviet Union in 1954. They declared that the goal of the Soviet leadership was "to impose its absolute authority over the rest of the world" and called for a serious political mobilization of the West, a major build-up of conventional and nuclear military power, and an expansion of covert operations in economic, political, and psychological warfare. The report concluded by declaring: "The whole success of the proposed program hangs ultimately on recognition by this Government, the American people, and all free peoples, that the cold war is in fact a real war in which the survival of the free world is at stake."[4]

Truman received this alarming report with considerable skepticism. He realized that the Soviet Union would be a growing problem, but he firmly believed that the United States needed to limit its defense budget to 15 billion US dollars a year in order to maintain a strong economy and continue the conversion to a peacetime nation. As recently as October 1949 he had confronted a defense appropriation bill containing an unwanted requirement to spend 800 million US dollars for long-range bombers and an additional 10 groups for the Air Force with a declaration that he would not spend the extra funds and would restrict the Air Force, to his requested strength of 48 groups. The president asked a special committee of budget specialists to analyze the recommendations of NSC-68 and report how much it would cost to implement them.[5]

The authors of NSC-68 had omitted cost estimates because they were well aware of the president's views on a 15 billion US dollars spending ceiling for defense. Some important members of the review group admitted to colleagues that they believed the full implementation of the report would cost 45 billion US dollars a year for a number of years. The new committee studying the possible cost of NSC-68 had met eight times before war broke out in Korea, but they had reached no conclusion. The records of their deliberations indicate that their likely direction was to implement only part of the recommendations and hold the spending increases to no more than 3 billion US dollars per year. NSC-68 had forced a reconsideration of how to meet a growing Soviet threat, but it took war in Korea to reverse Truman's budgetary constraints.[6]

A military build-up

In responding to the North Korean invasion, US officials assumed the attack was directed by the Soviet Union in an effort to establish Communist control over all of Korea while testing American will to act in East Asia. The administration's response transformed military policy. On 19 July the president requested supplemental appropriations for defense, indicating that most of the funds would be used, not for Korea, but for a general military build-up. The NSC on 30 September approved NSC-68 as US policy, and the president directed all agencies to implement its recommendations. By early December Congress had passed two appropriations bills totaling 35.3 billion US dollars in addition to the previous administration budgeted bill for fiscal year 1951 of 13.3 billion US dollars. After the massive intervention of "volunteer" Chinese troops in late November, Truman declared a state of national emergency on 16 December, asserting that the Communists "are now willing to push the world to the brink of general war to get what they want." The administration increased the armed forces by 1 million men to a size of 3.5 million, and within the first year of the war expanded the orders for aircraft by 500 percent and for combat vehicles by 450 percent. The build-up prepared to send significant additional forces to Europe and began a series of steps that transformed NATO from a treaty for political reassurance to a full-fledged military alliance.[7]

The Korean build-up greatly expanded US military capabilities. Shortly before the war began, the Joint Chiefs of Staff set its force goals for fiscal year 1952 at 10 divisions for the Army, 281 major combat vessels for the Navy, and 58 wings for the Air Force. Given pre-war political and economic attitudes, it was unlikely that these force increases would be funded. But by the end of December 1950, the administration had approved all the recommendations of NSC-68 and accepted force goals for fiscal year 1952 of 18 divisions for the Army, 397 major combat vessels for the Navy, and 95 wings for the Air Force.[8]

The focus on Europe

Although US forces in Korea were driven back into a narrow redoubt around the port of Pusan, officials in Washington concentrated on expanding defenses in Europe. On 14 July, Secretary of State Dean Acheson reported to the Cabinet that anxiety was sweeping across Europe. Declaring that the situation was "one of gravest danger," he said the war in Korea indicated to the world that US forces were not adequate to counter the threat. "The feeling in Europe is changing," he said, "from one of elation that the United States has come into the Korean crisis to petrified fright. People are questioning whether NATO means anything […]."[9]

Europe's defenses were clearly inadequate for any serious challenge from Soviet forces. NATO was a new organization without any central staff or a single commander, and its "strategic concept" allowed each member's military to specialize in the missions for which it was best suited. Although allied planners agreed that 54 divisions would be needed to hold a line of defense at the River Rhine, NATO had only 10 understrength divisions in West Germany. Within this force, the United States had one infantry division, three armored cavalry regiments, and two fighter-bomber groups. The allied war plan assumed that NATO could not withstand a major Soviet attack and planned for its forces to withdraw to Spain, North Africa, and Great Britain to wait for massive reinforcements.[10]

After extensive discussions among military, diplomatic, and political leaders, the Truman administration agreed on a plan for greatly improved European defense. Secretary Acheson presented this package to the British and French foreign ministers on 12 September at the Waldorf-Astoria in New York before a meeting of the North Atlantic Council. The proposal consisted of three elements: sending four additional US combat divisions to Europe with added air and naval support, creating a unified command for the alliance with an American Supreme Allied Commander, Europe (SACEUR), and establishing an integrated NATO defense force including German units of up to a division in strength. The French government strongly objected to rearming Germany so soon after the devastating war. It took General George C. Marshall, now returned to government as Secretary of Defense, to negotiate a compromise that included delaying German rearmament. At the same time as the terms of the European build-up were being resolved, the United States approved a massive increase in defense assistance for European rearmament. In addition to a planned appropriation of 1.2 billion US dollars in July, Congress approved the president's request for an additional 4 billion US dollars in late September. Of the new amount, 3.5 billion US dollars was designated for Western Europe.[11]

NATO restructured

Despite continued economic dislocation in Europe and the reluctance of national leaders to devote more funds to defense, NATO made significant progress in reforming its organization and in expanding its military capabilities. At a joint meeting of the North Atlantic Council and the Defense Committee in Brussels on 18–19 December 1950, the allies agreed to create an integrated defense force, approved the Medium Term Defense Plan, and created the office of SACEUR. They called on President Truman to appoint General Dwight D. Eisenhower to this position, and he took that step the following day. Over the next year the expanded alliance staff under Eisenhower's leadership organized the command structure, planned for various possible military contingencies, and worked to gain the resources to implement the Medium Term Defense Plan. According to one of his staff assistants, who later served as SACEUR, Eisenhower spoke often of the main task of NATO during his first year in command being to create "spirals of strength and confidence."[12]

While the alliance advanced its organization and planning capacity, the United States worked to prepare and send to Europe additional forces and equipment. To accomplish this task the administration had to overcome serious political opposition led by Senator Robert A. Taft, who with his Republican allies in Congress strongly opposed sending additional ground forces to Europe and wanted the US contribution to continue being mainly limited to air and naval forces. The argument that proved decisive came from Dwight Eisenhower, who made a tour of allied capitals and returned to testify in February 1951 before the Senate Armed Forces and Foreign Relations Committees. The incoming allied commander asserted that a defense of Western Europe could be constructed but only with a significant US ground force. Such an American contribution would be both the backbone of the NATO defense and the all-important US moral commitment to the protection of Europe. On 4 April 1951 the Senate voted 69–21 to approve the transfer of four additional divisions to Europe and endorsed the appointment of Eisenhower as SACEUR. By the end of 1952 the US force presence in Western Europe had grown to five divisions and seven air wings.[13]

The role of Germany within the alliance remained in dispute for some years. Washington firmly believed that German rearmament was a central part of creating an adequate European defense, but the French and a substantial number of German leaders found a wide range of proposals all unacceptable. After extensive negotiations the allies signed a treaty in May 1952 creating the European Defense Community (EDC). Opposition to the treaty continued, however, until it was defeated by the French National Assembly in 1954. The treaty also failed to win the needed two-thirds vote in the German Bundestag and was withdrawn by the government. Some other parts of the American defense build-up, not subject to the foibles of European politics, fared much better.[14]

The expansion of Strategic Air Command and the atomic strategy

The most important outcome of the Korean War build-up for national security policy was the development of the strategy of nuclear deterrence of the Soviet Union. Sparked by the new Soviet atomic capability, guided by the recommendations of NSC-68, and fuelled by the build-up for Korea, the US Air Force launched a successful campaign to become the primary element of national defense. Within the Air Force the spearhead of this expansion was the Strategic Air Command (SAC), which by the end of 1955 had doubled its assigned mission and tripled the number of its operational bomber fleet. With a strength of 87 wings in June 1951, the Air Force advanced an ambitious request for an increase to 140 wings by the end of fiscal year 1954. This proposal included a striking growth of SAC from 34 to 70 wings. After months of debate over missions and resources among the services and some changes demanded by Congress, the administration settled at the end of 1951 on a program of 137 wings for the Air Force.[15]

The SAC soon became the dominant component within the Air Force. General Curtis E. LeMay, Commanding General of SAC from October 1948 through June 1957, became the face of the Air Force for the public and Congress. With LeMay providing dynamic leadership, organization, and the rationale, the air staff in Washington won the resources for rapid expansion. As it phased out the World War II workhorse B-29 fleet, SAC introduced the B-36 and the all-jet B-47, and in mid-1955 received its first B-52. From the end of 1950, SAC grew from a total force of 962 operational bombers to a total of 1,830 by the end of 1953 and 3,068 by the end of 1955.[16]

General LeMay developed a broader mission to justify SAC's growing force structure. Before the Korean War, SAC had focused its limited resources on a strategic air campaign against "war-supporting targets in the Soviet Union." But when the Soviets demonstrated an atomic capability and supported aggression in Korea, the Air Force had to plan for the time when its likely opponent would have a long-range atomic strike force of its own. Contending that the mission of SAC had essentially doubled, Air Force planners laid out a new mission containing three elements: to destroy any bases that could be used for an atomic attack on the United States, to eliminate Russian industrial capacity, and to attack massed conventional forces and retard their advance against NATO defenses. During the early 1950s, the campaign of selling SAC and its deterrent mission was extremely successful and led to the creation of a strategic nuclear capability which has been aptly termed "overkill".[17]

To accomplish its expanded mission SAC needed access to numerous overseas bases ringing Russia and Eastern Europe. Medium bombers such as the B-29, B-47, and B-50 could only reach targets in the Soviet Union from overseas bases. Only the B-36 and B-52 had intercontinental range, and the B-52 only became available in usable numbers after 1955. SAC had constructed 14 overseas bases for its primary operations by the end of 1955, and it had also gained landing rights at bases in Newfoundland, Labrador, Iceland, the Azores, Morocco, Libya, Turkey, and Saudi Arabia. This ring of bases was clearly directed against the Soviet Union, and their bombers could be used to deter a Soviet first strike by an assured response, to impede a conventional attack, or to make a pre-emptive strike against the Soviet homeland.[18]

The final component of the atomic strategy was the rapid increase in the types and numbers of nuclear weapons available for US forces. The Korean build-up generated three important advances in nuclear policy. The Atomic Energy Commission budget for fissionable materials and weapons production increased sharply with supplemental appropriations of 260 million US dollars in 1950, an additional 1 billion US dollars in 1951, and a further 5 billion US dollars in 1952 for new production facilities. The vast increase in available nuclear weapons was matched by an equivalent growth in the target list for SAC. Unclassified estimates indicate that the US nuclear weapons stockpile grew from about 1,000 warheads in 1953 to almost 18,000 by 1960. Second, expanded funding supported accelerated development of the hydrogen bomb and led to the detonation of the first "true" thermonuclear device in October 1952. Finally, scientific breakthroughs and the promise of almost unlimited supplies of fissionable material led to a rapid development of tactical nuclear weapons. Based on studies showing the value of tactical nuclear weapons in the defense of Western Europe, the Army and the Navy developed doctrine and delivery systems for their use. The first low-yield tactical nuclear bombs were deployed for Air Force use in Europe in 1953, while large numbers of rockets and artillery shells with nuclear warheads arrived for battlefield use by the Army in 1954–55. By the latter date Washington's reliance on conventional deterrence of the Soviet threat in Europe had been replaced by nuclear deterrence at both the strategic and tactical levels.[19]

The rapid growth of intelligence operations

The Korean War caused a major expansion of the size and nature of intelligence operations sponsored by the United States. Although very little can be said about the activities of the military intelligence agencies or those divisions of the intelligence community dealing with cryptography and covert and electronic surveillance, it is safe to assume that their size and scope also increased dramatically in this period. We know much more about the activities of the Central Intelligence Agency (CIA) as a result of the lengthy investigations of the Senate Select Committee on Intelligence Activities (the Church Committee). Created by the National Security Act of 1947, the CIA was originally set up as a coordinating staff for information collected by other agencies, but by 1950 it had developed its own collection capability and added the missions of intelligence analysis and covert operations. These activities were conducted in separate organizations and initially had little supervision or coordination.[20]

With the approval of NSC-10/2 in June 1948, the CIA was authorized to begin covert operations. The agency's mandate was to create a unit to conduct political and psychological warfare and economic and paramilitary operations against the Soviet Union. This unit of the CIA was to be directed in its operations by the State Department, and it was misleadingly named the Office of Policy Coordination (OPC). After a slow beginning in its first two years, OPC experienced a massive expansion during the

Korean build-up. In 1949 OPC operated with 302 employees, while in 1952 its personnel numbered 2,812 plus 3,142 overseas contract employees. In 1949 OPC had seven overseas stations, whereas three years later it operated 47. The unit's budget of 4.7 million US dollars in 1949 exploded to 82 million US dollars in 1952. When the Truman administration left office, clandestine collection and covert action consumed 74 percent of the CIA's total budget and employed 60 percent of its personnel.[21]

In its first five years, the OPC developed a wide range of activities in Western Europe. Officials in Washington viewed Europe as the region most vulnerable to Communist penetration as well as the area of greatest value to the United States. Europe also benefited in OPC's allocation of assets because until the start of war in Korea General Douglas MacArthur refused to allow the CIA and OPC to operate in the Pacific theatre under his command. In Europe, OPC activities focused on projects dealing with labor organization, refugee assistance, media development, and political action. With the outbreak of war in Korea, paramilitary operations expanded greatly in North Korea and later in China, and they remained the principal activity of the CIA in Asia.[22]

Prior to October 1950, when General Walter Bedell Smith became Director of Central Intelligence, OPC had operated with almost complete independence. Step by step Smith assumed administrative control of OPC and coordinated it with other parts of the CIA. In April 1951, at Smith's urging, the NSC created the Psychological Strategy Board as a subcommittee of the NSC to provide general direction to psychological warfare and to approve all covert operations. General Smith is credited with improving the professional quality of covert operations and with coordinating them effectively with expanded analytical activities, especially with the work of the new Office of National Estimates.[23]

The creation of the National Security Agency (NSA) in 1952 is the other major Korean era development in the intelligence community. Organized as part of the Department of Defense, the NSA has the mission of collecting and decoding foreign communications and electronic signals. Although it does not produce intelligence analysis, it does collect massive amounts of data and is the largest of US intelligence agencies.[24]

The Korean build-up stimulated a massive expansion of the CIA. Between 1947 and 1953 the agency grew by six times, most growth coming after war began in Korea. The CIA's missions expanded even more dramatically. By the end of the war the CIA had developed the organization, missions, and patterns of influence that would function over the next two decades.

The impact of the Korean War

When the fighting in Korea came to a stalemate at roughly the 38th parallel where it had begun and truce negotiations started in July 1951, the Truman administration began to slow its military build-up. Except for the Army the force structure goals remained the same, but the time span for their achievement was lengthened. Congress and the public were no longer willing to support the high level of expenditure necessary to maintain the building program needed for the major weapons systems for the Air Force and the Navy as well as the rapid expansion of the nuclear stockpile. Reinforcing this general resistance to high defense spending was the fact that the Soviet Union had made no new aggressive steps in Europe and the prospects of a major crisis in the near future seemed sharply reduced.[25]

As public support for a deadlocked conventional war in Northeast Asia declined, Robert A. Lovett, who became Secretary of Defense in September 1951, realized that he had to reduce the annual cost of defense. During 1951–52, Lovett directed the design of a military force that would reduce the size of its ground component and rely much more heavily on SAC's strategic nuclear deterrent. This reduced force structure and the military doctrine for its use would be passed on to the new Republican administration of Dwight D. Eisenhower early in 1953. The new president would continue these general trends and baptize the approach as the New Look and its strategy massive retaliation.[26]

The Korean War had an immense impact on US strategic programs and doctrine as it launched the military build-up which NSC-68 had been unable to initiate. The major enemy was assumed to be the Soviet Union; its most likely objective, the domination of Western Europe. In meeting this challenge and demonstrating the will to defend its vital interests, the Truman administration vastly increased its expenditures for the defense of Europe. In the process it transformed NATO from a loose organization with minimal military capability to an integrated military force with a unified command and significant military potential. Expanded intelligence and covert operational activities were also a critical dimension of the American build-up. The most important long-term result of the war was the US commitment to a nuclear deterrent strategy. This new approach would rely on nuclear weapons delivered by bombers and later by land and sea-based intercontinental missiles as well as shorter range tactical nuclear weapons based in Europe and in Asia.

Western Europe continued to be the principal strategic interest of the United States. The Korean War initiated the implementation of containment by military means, and the North Korean attack was the principal cause of the first Cold War defense build-up and a major escalation of the military competition between the United States and the Soviet Union.

An evaluation of US policy and strategy

The foregoing description and analysis of the military build-up launched by the Korean War was based entirely on US records and sources. It reflects the thinking and actions of officials in the Truman administration and the subsequent analysis of scholars and policy specialists. Recently available archival materials now allow scholars to examine the plans and choices made by Soviet, Chinese, and North Korean leaders. These records come from Moscow and Beijing and also from fraternal Communist states such as the German Democratic Republic and Albania. We can benefit, in addition, from studies by scholars in Russia and China who have access to archives not open to foreigners. Although the new sources for the Korean War period are tantalizing and important, they are presently limited in scope and fragmentary. They can raise questions about US assumptions and decisions, but they are seldom conclusive. In light of this opportunity and with this limitation in mind, we will explore several key questions regarding US policy and strategy for this period.

What was the role of Joseph Stalin and the Soviet leadership in the North Korean invasion? What were their goals and assumptions?

Stalin wanted to reunify Korea under Kim Il Sung's leadership, but he needed to find the time when the costs were low and the task relatively easy. For the Soviet leader, a cautious approach was necessary because his nation's resources were devoted to a massive reconstruction program at home and to solidifying control over Eastern Europe.

Also, the North Korean military was poorly equipped and trained and, by all accounts, not ready for war. US forces only withdrew from South Korea at the end of June 1949, and before approving a North Korean attack Stalin wanted to be sure that the United States would not intervene. On the other hand, the Soviet Union could not afford to wait too long because Japanese economic recovery was well-advanced due to US assistance, and leaders in Moscow feared revived Japanese involvement in Korea. They wanted to avoid the threat posed by the development of Korea under Japanese influence within an American sphere of interest. Finally, the Soviet leadership was concerned about rivalry with China. Mao Zedong's Communists were close to complete victory in the civil war, and they would be certain to show a strong interest in unifying Korea under Communist rule. Stalin wanted to establish that he, not Mao, was the undisputed leader of Communism in Asia as well as in Europe.[27]

After repeated requests from Kim Il Sung for approval to attack the south, Stalin agreed in a telegram of 30 January 1950 that the Soviet Union would provide assistance and invited the North Korean leader to visit Moscow to discuss preparations. Arriving in Moscow in late March, Kim held extensive discussions with the Soviet leadership in the first half of April. Records of Kim's exchanges show that several factors persuaded Stalin that late June was the right time for the North Korean attack. American troops withdrew from Korea at the end of June 1949, and the Soviet Union gained an immense boost in prestige when its successful atomic test in August became known to the world the following month. Soon thereafter the Communist forces declared victory in China, and the defeated Nationalists evacuated the mainland for Taiwan in December. As a result, 14,000 Korean troops returned to North Korea from fighting in the Chinese civil war, providing a substantial battle-hardened addition to Kim's forces. Meanwhile in a speech at the National Press Club in Washington on 12 January 1950, Secretary of State Dean Acheson set forth the administration's policy for Asia in the aftermath of the Communist victory in China. In a passage of his speech that was not intended to be a major statement of policy, Acheson described the US defense perimeter in Asia in the case of general war in terms that clearly excluded Korea. Although a minor point in Washington, this exclusion was carefully noted by Stalin and in the April discussions in Moscow was emphasized by Kim as a reason for an early attack. Also influential in Stalin's decision to approve an invasion was the fact that negotiations were well-advanced for a treaty of alliance with China, and the Soviet leader was convinced that this alliance (formally signed on 14 February 1950) would alter the global constellation of forces in favor of Communism under his leadership.[28]

The April negotiations about the essential preparations for the invasion provide interesting insights into Stalin's thinking about the Soviet role in coming years. Eager to have a short and successful campaign against South Korea in order to eliminate the possibility of US reinforcements from the occupation army in Japan, Stalin insisted on the development of a fully detailed plan of attack and sent Soviet advisers to North Korea to help draft it and to train the Korean forces, especially their inexperienced commanding officers. The Soviet military transferred massive amounts of equipment, supplies, and ammunition to the North Korean army, but Stalin firmly declared that Soviet forces would not participate directly in the fighting. The Soviet leader wanted to win Mao's endorsement of the attack, but wished to do so without allowing the Chinese Communists' victory in the civil war to provide a basis for Mao to challenge Stalin as the leader of the Communist movement. Thus, after working out the detailed plans for the attack under Soviet guidance, Kim was required by Stalin to get Mao's approval for the attack which he accomplished during a trip to Beijing in May.[29]

Soviet actions after the outbreak of war strongly indicate that Stalin and his colleagues were thoroughly surprised by the American intervention, and they took a series of steps to avoid any direct conflict with US forces. The Truman administration responded immediately to the North Korean invasion by sending supplies to South Korea, and on 26 June authorized the use of US air and naval bombardment to slow the North Korean advance. The next day the United States won a second resolution in the United Nations (UN) Security Council authorizing member states to assist South Korea in repelling the invasion and restoring peace and security, and on 29 June Truman approved the use of air power against North Korean targets above the 38th parallel. Despite these strong US responses, the Soviet Foreign Ministry took until 4 July to issue its first statement of concern over American involvement in the conflict. Immediately after fighting began, Moscow ordered all Soviet naval vessels to leave North Korean ports and waters and to avoid contact with US forces. The Central Committee refused the pleas of Soviet citizens of Korean origin to join the fighting, and when it belatedly sent Air Force units to assist the Chinese volunteers in November 1950, the Soviet airmen took extensive measures to maintain secrecy using North Korean aircraft markings, Chinese uniforms, and made halting attempts to communicate over the radio in Korean.[30]

Available evidence clearly establishes that Kim Il Sung initiated the war and that Stalin agreed to support it only when convinced that the United States would not intervene. The Soviet leader also wanted to assert his leadership over the international Communist movement and insisted that Kim get Mao's endorsement after Moscow had pledged its support and basically completed developing the plan of attack. Soviet approval and support of the invasion was essentially a defensive strategy to secure the Korean peninsula for a friendly government under Moscow's tutelage and to deny it to the United States and a revived Japanese government at a later date. Soviet actions were not a probe of US will to defend its larger interests overseas, and Stalin was highly upset when the United States intervened and began a major military build-up. He castigated Kim for a serious misjudgment of the international situation and worked hard to avoid any direct Soviet confrontation with the United States during the war.

Why did US leaders approve General MacArthur's proposals to cross the 38th parallel and advance to the Yalu River?

The outbreak of war found US occupation forces in Japan and Okinawa completely unprepared for combat and officials in Washington uneasy about the personality and prospects of their regional commander to lead a multinational force under a UN Security Council mandate. General Douglas MacArthur had frequently shown disregard for instructions from the president and the Joint Chiefs of Staff, and his thinly disguised ambition to run as the Republican candidate for president was widely known. In late July MacArthur made an unauthorized trip to Taiwan to provide support for the exiled Chinese Nationalists who were eager to revive their war with Mao Zedong's Communist government. This highly publicized trip angered the new government in Beijing while winning enthusiastic support from the Republican Party's leading advocates for the Chinese Nationalists. When Mao in late August was evaluating the military situation in

Korea with key advisers, he asked a senior military official who had studied the US forces about MacArthur's personality. The official replied that MacArthur as a commander was noted for his arrogance and stubbornness. Showing great interest in this assessment, Mao declared: "Fine! Fine! The more arrogant and more stubborn he is, the better. An arrogant enemy is easy to defeat."[31]

With US and South Korean troops driven into a narrow perimeter around Pusan, MacArthur wanted to use his additional forces to achieve a quick, dramatic breakthrough. Based on his experience in a victorious series of amphibious assaults against Japanese-held islands in World War II, the general planned a daring amphibious landing at Inchon, a port on the western coast of Korea 25 miles from Seoul. When confronted by military planners with the immense difficulties of an assault at Inchon, MacArthur firmly replied: "I realize that Inchon is a 5,000 to 1 gamble, but I am used to taking such odds. We shall land at Inchon and I shall crush them!" MacArthur beat down all attempts to delay or modify his plans, and on 15 September the first wave of US troops landed at Inchon. The enveloping assault was more successful than anyone expected. By 26 September UN forces had captured Seoul and linked up with troops who had broken through the Pusan perimeter and pushed rapidly northward.[32]

Prior to the Inchon landing, officials in Washington had carefully analyzed the question of whether to cross the 38th parallel if the assault proved successful and Seoul were recaptured. On 11 September, President Truman approved the recommendations of NSC-81/1 and ordered them implemented. This report stated that it expected the UN commander would be authorized to pursue military operations to achieve "a roll-back in Korea north of the 38th parallel [...] provided that at the time of such operations there has been no entry into North Korea by major Soviet or Chinese Communist forces, no announcement of intended entry, nor a threat to counter our operations militarily in North Korea." In order to minimize the risk of general war with the Soviet Union, the UN commander should get the approval of the president before executing this plan and should use only South Korean troops in operations bordering the Soviet Union or Manchuria. But the great success of the Inchon landing and the rapid retreat of North Korean troops across the border removed these limitations and constraints. US officials were united in supporting operations above the 38th parallel, and MacArthur declared that he intended to vanquish the North Korean forces and unify the country.[33]

Even if MacArthur's goal was set, administration officials still had to determine how far to advance into North Korea and what to do if the Chinese intervened. On 27 September, Truman authorized MacArthur to cross the 38th parallel. On 3 October, Chinese leaders sent messages through the Indian ambassador in Beijing and through the UN that Chinese forces would intervene if UN troops crossed the border. US intelligence sources reported that at least 300,000 Chinese troops had been moved into Manchuria near the border with North Korea. MacArthur insisted that the Chinese were not serious and would not intervene. The vast majority of US intelligence analysts, diplomats, and political leaders agreed that the Chinese were bluffing. They all assumed that Beijing was merely a pawn of Moscow, and they were convinced that Stalin was cautious and wanted to avoid a wider war. Even the few military officials in the Pentagon who had apprehensions about Chinese intervention did not want to countermand the UN commander who had crafted the stunning victory at Inchon. In the background for the policymakers loomed the offyear Congressional elections and public opinion polls showing strong majorities favoring completing the defeat of the North Koreans and unifying the country.[34]

With South Korean forces operating across the border starting on 1 October, MacArthur launched his major advance with US troops on 9 October. The UN forces moved steadily northward, and as they approached the Manchurian border MacArthur sent US units into areas that were forbidden by orders from the Joint Chiefs. At the end of October the first contingent of Chinese volunteers entered North Korea, and they were soon sufficiently strong to stop the UN offensive. When the Chinese forces appeared to withdraw, MacArthur planned a final drive to seize control of all North Korea. Key officials in Washington had misgivings, but again they were unwilling to overrule MacArthur. With the president's approval, the final offensive began on 24 November. The following night 300,000 Chinese troops entered the battle and drove UN forces back toward the 38th parallel. In Washington officials raged at MacArthur for his willful misreading of the situation, while the general responded with charges that his hands had been tied when he was several times refused approval to bomb the bridges carrying troops and supplies over the Yalu. By early December 1950 the Korean War had entered a new and much more dangerous phase.[35]

Why did the Chinese intervene in Korea in October 1950? What were their goals?

The decision by the Truman administration to defend South Korea sharply increased the likelihood that Chinese Communist troops would intervene in the conflict. Mao Zedong understood immediately that North Korea would be unable to win against the combined forces of South Korea and the United States. He began to assess the significance for China of a North Korean defeat. As Chen Jian argues persuasively in his *China's Road to the Korean War*, Mao's analysis involved three dimensions of threat. There was a direct threat to China's security posed by the presence of a hostile Korea under US protection on the border of Manchuria with its wealth of natural resources, as well as the challenge posed by the US decision to station the 7th Fleet in the Taiwan Straits to protect the Nationalists. Mao saw an additional threat to the consolidation of the Communist revolution in China, where the new regime still faced significant opposition from merchants and large landowners. Finally, there was a threat to China's ability to establish itself as the leader of Asian Communism independent of Soviet tutelage.[36]

Mao was persuaded of the necessity of Chinese intervention by mid-August, well before the UN breakthrough victory at Inchon. At the chairman's urging, the People's Liberation Army had established the China Northeast Border Defense Force in early July and issued orders to move 120,000 soldiers there within the next month. But many of Mao's colleagues in the Politburo disagreed on the question of intervention feeling that China was not prepared for the financial and human costs of a war against the United States and its allies from the industrial world. Even after South Korean forces had crossed the 38th parallel and US units were expected to follow in a short time, a majority of the enlarged Politburo in a long meeting on 4–5 October still had significant reservations about intervention.[37]

Mao also had difficulty winning the support of Kim Il Sung and Stalin for Chinese intervention. Kim wanted to avoid asking for assistance from China until it was absolutely necessary, and he needed to gain Stalin's approval. With his forces near collapse, Kim urgently requested assistance on 30 September, and early the next morning Stalin endorsed this request in a telegram to Mao. The Chinese gave an ambiguous reply saying they wanted to help but could not do so immediately. The reasons for delay were to win a consensus in the Chinese Politburo, and the necessary precondition was to gain a pledge of Soviet support with military equipment and supplies and the commitment to provide combat air support. After dramatic negotiations between Zhou Enlai and Stalin, the Soviet leader pledged his support on 14 October and the Chinese decision to intervene was confirmed to Kim.[38]

While Mao's goal of intervention in Korea was achieved, it almost came too late. Mutual suspicion and mistrust among the three main leaders—Stalin, Mao, and Kim—and the resistance of key members of the Chinese Politburo delayed intervention to the point where Mao's strategic objective of driving UN forces out of Korea proved to be beyond reach. The first engagement between Chinese volunteers and South Korean forces came on 25 October. But when Stalin delayed in providing substantial air support, the Chinese units pulled back into defensive positions. By the time MacArthur launched his planned final offensive on 24 November, Chinese forces were reinforced, had the needed air support, and were able to drive the UN coalition back below the 38th parallel.

Lessons drawn and an alternative history

The actual lessons drawn from the Korean War by the political classes in the United States and the Soviet Union were self-serving and unproductive. American political and military leaders concluded from the Korean experience that the Soviet Union and its Chinese junior partner would exploit every opening in western defenses so that the United States should never be unprepared and weak in response to Communist challenges. Russian leaders drew from their experience that the United States would use every opportunity and mobilize its allies, including Germany and Japan, to defeat the Soviet Union and overthrow Communism, so that their response should be to match Western military power in Europe and create opportunities for expanding their influence in developing countries.

While it is good that the Korean conflict did not expand into general war with nuclear exchanges, the course of events could have been even more limited and less destructive if several alternative outcomes could have been attained.

- If the United States had understood that the initiative for the war came from Kim Il Sung and that Stalin had relatively limited goals and wanted to avoid confrontation with Washington, the fighting could have been limited to Korea with a much smaller build-up of NATO and SAC.
- If Stalin had controlled North Korean forces more effectively and acted on warnings of an envelopment at Inchon, the conflict might have been limited to South Korean territory.
- If the United States had not attempted to cross the 38th parallel and unify the country under South Korean leadership, the Chinese might not have intervened. Or, if the UN forces had stopped at the narrow neck of North Korea (a line roughly between Pyongyang and Wonsan), a negotiated settlement might have been easier to reach with many lives saved.

Notes

1 Harry S. Truman, *Memoirs*, vol. 2, *Years of Trial and Hope,* (Garden City, NY: Doubleday & Company, 1956), pp. 328–30; Gaddis Smith, *Dean Acheson,* (New York: Cooper Square Publishers, 1972),

pp. 173–76; Kathryn Weathersby, '"Should We Fear This?": Stalin and the Danger of War with America', *Cold War International History Project (CWIHP) Working Paper* No. 39 (Woodrow Wilson Center, July 2002), pp. 5–11.
2. Dean Acheson, *Present At The Creation: My Years in the State Department*, (New York: W. W. Norton, 1969), pp. 321, 355, 362; Richard G. Hewlett and Francis Duncan, *Atomic Shield, 1947–1952*, (Washington: US Atomic Energy Commission, 1972), pp. 362–69; Paul H. Nitze, 'Recent Soviet Moves', February 8, 1950, *Foreign Relations of the United States, 1950*, I, p. 145.
3. Hewlett and Duncan, *Atomic Shield*, pp. 373–405; National Archives, Washington, DC, Records of the Policy Planning Staff, R. G. 59, Paul Nitze, memorandum of December 19, 1949; Report by the Special Committee of the NSC to the President, January 31, 1950, President to the Secretary of State, January 31, 1950, *Foreign Relations, 1950*, I, pp. 513–17, 141–42.
4. NSC-68, April 7, 1950, *Foreign Relations, 1950*, I, 235–92 (quotations on pp. 237, 285, and 292).
5. Louis Fisher, *Presidential Spending Power*, (Princeton: Princeton University Press, 1975), pp. 162–63; Congressional Quarterly, *Congress and the Nation, 1945–1964*, (Washington: Congressional Quarterly, 1965), pp. 253–54; Samuel F. Wells, Jr., 'Sounding the Tocsin: NSC 68 and the Soviet Threat', *International Security*, no. 4 (Fall 1979), pp. 116–58.
6. Wells, 'Sounding the Tocsin.', pp. 137–39.
7. Truman, *Memoirs*, II, pp. 331–48; Report to the National Security Council by the Executive Secretary, September 30, 1950, *Foreign Relations, 1950*, I, p. 400; Congressional Quarterly, *Congress and the Nation*, pp. 259–60; Harry S. Truman, *Public Papers of the Presidents, 1950*, (Washington: Government Printing Office, 1965), pp. 741–46.
8. Walter S. Poole, *The History of the Joint Chiefs of Staff: The Joint Chiefs of Staff and National Policy*, Volume IV, 1950–52 (Washington: Joint Chiefs of Staff, 1979), p. 71.
9. Memorandum by Charles E. Bohlen, July 13, 1950, Memorandum of conversation by Dean Acheson, July 14, 1950, *Foreign Relations, 1950*, I, pp. 342–45.
10. Poole, *Joint Chiefs of Staff*, IV, pp. 180–85; Lawrence S. Kaplan, *A Community of Interests: NATO and the Military Assistance Program, 1948–1951*, (Washington: GPO, 1980), pp. 73–79, 85–90.
11. Secretaries of State and Defense to the President, September 8, 1950, Secretary of State to the President, September 14 and 20, 1950, *Foreign Relations, 1950*, III, pp. 273–78, 301–2, 335–37; Acheson, *Present At The Creation*, pp. 436–45; Poole, *Joint Chiefs of Staff*, IV, pp. 191–213, 47; Kaplan, *Community of Interests*, pp. 104–7.
12. Report of the North Atlantic Military Committee to the North Atlantic Defense Committee, December 12, 1950, US Delegation Minutes of the First and Second Meetings of the Sixth North Atlantic Treaty Council With the Defense Ministers, December 18 and 19, 1950, President to General Dwight Eisenhower, December 19, 1950, *Foreign Relations, 1950*, III, pp. 548–64, 585–605; Lord Ismay, *NATO: The First Five Years, 1949–1954*, (Paris: NATO, 1955), pp. 34–35; Poole, *Joint Chiefs of Staff*, IV, pp. 226–46, 276–84, 287–96; author's interview with General Andrew J. Goodpaster, USA (Ret.), June 14, 1983.
13. David S. McLellan, *Dean Acheson: The State Department Years*, (New York: Dodd, Mead & Co., 1976), pp. 337–46; James T. Patterson, *Mr. Republican: A Biography of Robert A. Taft*, (Boston: Houghton Mifflin Co., 1972), pp. 477–82; Poole, *Joint Chiefs of Staff*, IV, pp. 135, 185, 221–24; Congressional Quarterly, *Congress and the Nation*, pp. 264–66.
14. Interim Report of the Delegations to the Conference for the Organization of a European Defense Community to the Participating Governments, July 24, 1951, Memorandum from the Secretary of State and the Acting Secretary of Defense to the President, July 30, 1951, *Foreign Relations, 1951*, III, Part 1, pp. 843–46, 849–52; Lawrence S. Kaplan, 'The Korean War and US Foreign Relations: The Case of NATO,' in Francis H. Heller (ed.), *The Korean War: A 25-Year Perspective*, (Lawrence, Kansas: Regents Press of Kansas, 1977), pp. 58–60; Poole, *Joint Chiefs of Staff*, IV, pp. 247–64, 289–96, 323–28.
15. Samuel P. Huntington, *The Common Defense: Strategic Programs in National Politics*, (New York: Columbia University Press, 1966), pp. 60–62, 306–12; Poole, *Joint Chiefs of Staff*, IV, pp. 88, 96–101; Samuel F. Wells, Jr., 'The Origins of Massive Retaliation,' *Political Science Quarterly*, no. 96, Spring 1981, pp. 31–52.
16. J.C. Hopkins, *The Development of the Strategic Air Command, 1946–1981* (Omaha, NB: Strategic Air Command, 1982), pp. 20, 40, 51.
17. Robert Frank Futrell, *Ideas, Concepts, Doctrine: A History of Basic Thinking in the United States Air Force, 1907–1964*, (Maxwell Air Force Base, AL: Air University, 1971), pp. 149–67, 216–22; David Alan Rosenberg, 'The Origins of Overkill: Nuclear Weapons and American Strategy, 1945–60,' *International Security*, no. 7 (Spring 1983), pp. 3–71.

18 Poole, *Joint Chiefs of Staff*, IV, pp. 168–70; Rosenberg, 'The Origins of Overkill,' pp. 18–21.
19 Richard G. Hewlett and Francis Duncan, *A History of the United States Atomic Energy Commission: Atomic Shield*, II, *1947–1952*, (Washington, DC: US Atomic Energy Commission, 1972), pp. 528–33, 580–81, 592; Rosenberg, 'The Origins of Overkill', pp. 21–25; Futrell, *Ideas, Concepts, Doctrine*, pp. 167–69; Stockholm International Peace Research Institute (SIPRI), *Tactical Nuclear Weapons: European Perspectives*, (New York: Crane, Russak & Co., 1978), pp. 10–14; Samuel R. Williamson, Jr. and Steven L. Rearden, *The Origins of US Nuclear Strategy, 1945–1953*, (New York: St Martin's Press, 1993), pp. 149–54, 168–74.
20 The best single source for the history of the CIA is a staff study compiled by Ann Karalekas for the Church Committee. Her study is properly titled: US Senate, Select Committee to Study Government Operations with Respect to Intelligence Activities, *Final Report*, Book IV, April 1976, Report Nr. 904-755 (94th Cong., 2nd Sess.). Hereafter cited as Karalekas, *History of the CIA*.
21 Ibid., pp. 29–41.
22 Ibid., pp. 35–36.
23 Ibid., pp. 11–12, 31–41. For a more personal view of these same events, see Ray S. Cline, *Secrets, Spies, and Scholars: Blueprint of the Essential CIA*, (Washington: Acropolis Books, 1976), pp. 104–18.
24 Karalekas, *History of the CIA*, p. 3. For a critical, but generally accurate assessment of the operations and influence of NSA, see James Bamford, *The Puzzle Palace: A Report on America's Most Secret Agency*, (Boston: Houghton Mifflin Co., 1982).
25 Poole, *Joint Chiefs of Staff*, IV, pp. 109–26; Futrell, *Ideas, Concepts, Doctrine*, pp. 172–73.
26 Wells, 'Origins of Massive Retaliation,' pp. 31–52.
27 Kathryn Weathersby, 'To Attack, or Not to Attack? Stalin, Kim Il Sung, and the Prelude to War', CWIHP, *Bulletin*, no. 5, Woodrow Wilson Center, Spring 1995, pp. 1–8; Kathryn Weathersby, 'Soviet Aims in Korea and the Origins of the Korean War, 1945–50: New Evidence from Russian Archives,' *CWIHP Working Paper* no. 8, Woodrow Wilson Center, November 1993, pp. 9–28.
28 By one count, Kim made forty-eight requests for authorization to attack the south before he won approval. Kathryn Weathersby, 'New Findings on the Korean War,' CWIHP, *Bulletin*, no. 3, Woodrow Wilson Center, Fall 1993, pp. 14–16; Weathersby, 'Should We Fear This?', pp. 4–13; Weathersby, 'To Attack, or Not to Attack?', pp. 1–9; Melvyn P. Leffler, *A Preponderance of Power: National Security, the Truman Administration, and the Cold War*, (Stanford: Stanford University Press, 1992), pp. 337–38.
29 Weathersby, 'Should We Fear This?', pp. 9–15; Weathersby, 'Soviet Aims in Korea', pp. 29–31; Weathersby, 'New Findings on the Korean War', pp. 14–18.
30 Leffler, *Preponderance of Power*, pp. 365–67; Weathersby, 'Soviet Aims in Korea', pp. 31–33; Weathersby, 'New Findings on the Korean War', pp. 15–16.
31 William Stueck, *The Korean War: An International History*, (Princeton: Princeton University Press, 1995), pp. 65–70; James F. Schnabel and Robert J. Watson, *The History of the Joint Chiefs of Staff: The Joint Chiefs of Staff and National Policy*, Volume III, The Korean War, Part I (Washington: Joint Chiefs of Staff, 1978), pp. 43–45; Chen Jian, *China's Road to the Korean War: The Making of the Sino-American Confrontation*, (New York: Columbia University Press, 1994), pp. 142–43, 147–48.
32 Schnabel and Watson, *Joint Chiefs of Staff*, III, pp. 201–18; Stueck, *Korean War*, pp. 85–87.
33 Report by the National Security Council to the President, 'United States Courses of Action With Respect to Korea (NSC-81/1),' September 9, 1950, *Foreign Relations, 1950*, VII, pp. 712–16; Leffler, *Preponderance of Power*, pp. 377–78; Schnabel and Watson, *Joint Chiefs of Staff*, III, pp. 220–28.
34 Chen, *China's Road to the Korean War*, pp. 164–71; Schnabel and Watson, *Joint Chiefs of Staff*, III, pp. 230–49; Stueck, *Korean War*, pp. 88–106.
35 When under the pressure of massive Chinese intervention Truman on 30 November mentioned at a press conference the possible use of atomic weapons, the British Prime Minister Clement Attlee flew to Washington with Foreign Secretary Ernest Bevin to argue strongly, with the support of Robert Schuman, against the use of nuclear weapons. Leffler, *Preponderance of Power*, pp. 378–80, 398–99; Stueck, *Korean War*, pp. 106–19; Schnabel and Watson, *Joint Chiefs of Staff*, III, pp. 249–84.
36 Chen, *China's Road to the Korean War*, passim.
37 Shen Zhihua, 'China and the Soviet Union Dispatch Troops to Aid Korea: the Establishment of the Chinese-Soviet-Korean Alliance in the Early Stages of the Korean War,' *CWIHP draft Working Paper*, pp. 1–14; Alexandre Y. Mansourov, 'Stalin, Mao, Kim, and China's Decision to Enter the Korean War, September 16 – October 15, 1950: New Evidence from the Russian Archives', CWIHP, *Bulletin*, no. 6–7, Woodrow Wilson Center, Winter 1995/1996, pp. 94–101.
38 Mansourov, 'Stalin, Mao, Kim, and China's Decision', pp. 101–5.

3

The doctrine of massive retaliation and the impossible nuclear defense of the Atlantic Alliance

From directive MC 48 to MC 70 (1953–59)

François David

> The eternal night begins and it will be terrible.
> What will happen when men realize that there will be no more sun?
>
> Gérard de Nerval, *Aurélia*

Nuclear deterrence is seemingly very simple: if the enemy attacks me, he knows that I will wipe him off the map. In reality, the doctrine of "massive retaliation", expounded for the first time in 1954 by Secretary of State John Foster Dulles,[1] quickly raised questions about its military effectiveness and whether it compromised the quality of Western relations. Originally, the nuclear New Look launched by the Eisenhower administration was meant to provide the means of finally defending Europe against the Red Army, while being fiscally sound. Indeed, it is (wrongly) assumed that atomic weapons are less expensive than conventional weapons (the Lisbon Conference of February 1952 initially planned for about 100 American and European divisions, instead of 30, at an astronomical cost). Nevertheless, one fact is certain: firepower increased tenfold. In reality, the New Look profoundly modified the nature of the Atlantic Alliance while cruelly emphasizing the attrition of the allied armies. The following is a non-exhaustive list of vital questions raised by this doctrine.

From the point of view of inter-allied relations: how was the protection of the North American continent and the defense of Europe articulated in the New Look?

From a specifically European point of view: did the European governments not risk sheltering themselves behind the American nuclear umbrella instead of improving their own defenses?

From a tactical and operational point of view: what mission did the New Look assign to American divisions in Europe? Are they still useful? What was forecasted for the future of European ground forces and tactical aviation? Who supports what? Would the nuclear fire cover the ground divisions, or would they only serve to flank the atomic artillery? In these conditions, what was the place of French and German units in the reformed Atlantic battle group? What of the Anglo-Saxon naval aviation and the advanced line that would absorb the first shock of a Soviet invasion?

In terms of strategy: can the nuclear all or nothing be avoided? At what point can the assumption of a "local and limited war" still be reconciled with the principle of general deterrence?

On the general plan of the Cold War: did Eisenhower and Dulles really strengthen the vitality of the Alliance? Would not they have devised a Maginot Line strategy, behind their row of nuclear rockets?

These issues boil down to one central question: could Europe really be defended with nuclear arms without buttressing it? The attempts at formulating politicomilitary responses during the 1950s will be discussed through the two major Atlantic nuclear guidelines of the 1950s: directive MC 48 adopted by the North Atlantic Council in December 1954, and directive MC 70, started in 1956, long classified as "Cosmic Secret" and applicable from 1960 to 1965.

The origins of Western nuclear defense: American Executive Directive NSC 162

Upon taking office, the Eisenhower administration spent its first eight months developing a secret internal directive: NSC (National Security Council) 162. NSC 162 was a complicated document, because it attempted to reduce the contradictions resulting from the Cold War. In particular, the Pentagon and the State Department disagreed over the most important clause, paragraph 39(b): would nuclear retaliation be automatic in the case of Soviet aggression, even if it was limited or indirect? What could atomic weapons do if the USSR seized a country by internal subversion, like the Prague coup in 1948? What if a satellite state crossed the iron curtain to achieve its own territorial objectives: for example, an incursion by East German forces into the Federal Republic of Germany (FRG), with Berlin and Hamburg making an agreement, a hypothesis considered plausible at the time by the military staffs? Or Romania fighting against Yugoslavia to rectify a boundary line? Or even Yugoslavia reconciled with the USSR, confronting Italy about Trieste?

Most importantly, when would Soviet aggression justify a nuclear response? At the first mushroom cloud of enemy origin, or from an aerial violation of NATO's borders? Similarly, how should a high concentration of troops at the iron curtain be considered? Should it be interpreted as an act of war, on the same basis as a general mobilization (cf. July 1914), and thus trigger "pre-emptive" nuclear fire before being caught by surprise?

Paragraph 39(b) of NSC 162 did not provide an answer and merely states that "in the event of hostilities, the United States will consider nuclear weapons to be as available for use as other munitions." The Pentagon saw this as a green light to freely develop its war plans, privileging the use of special weapons over conventional means. According to its scheme, US commanders would only consider the use of atomic weapons according to the evolution of operations and based on tactical objectives. To increase its responsiveness, the Pentagon sought and obtained from President Eisenhower the possession of bombs in peacetime.[2] Hitherto, nuclear warheads had been kept by the Atomic Energy Commission (AEC), a civilian agency created by Truman in order to circumscribe the military staff.

Vis-à-vis the Pentagon, Dulles and the State Department approved the "militarization" of the nuclear arsenal, but strongly contested the systematic use of nuclear fire. This decision should come exclusively from the president of the United States at the appropriate time, and not from the generals. According to American diplomacy, one must always wonder whether tactical nuclear weapons would widen a conflict, or upset allied cohesion, for fear of an even more deadly Soviet nuclear retaliation. The State Department accepted only one case justifying an automatic response: a nuclear Pearl Harbor against American territory.[3] Regarding the rest, John Foster Dulles secretly doubted the pertinence of the New Look.

Secretary of State Foster Dulles painfully enunciated the formal presentation of the New Look at the Atlantic Council of April

In fact, the allies had to wait for Dulles' speech at the next Atlantic Council in April 1954 to hear the first coherent description of the New Look. The Secretary of State linked the five aspects of the problem: (1) the Sino-Soviet threat; (2) the strategic concept of massive retaliation on a global scale; (3) the inclusion of tactical nuclear weapons in the conventional arsenal of NATO; (4) planning in times of peace and the procedure for inter-allied consultation in case of war; and (5) the right of the United States to use the atomic bomb first, in the event of war being started by the USSR, on behalf of overall Western interests.[4]

However, in the autumn of 1954, the most difficult task remained to be done: turning American directive NSC 162/2 into an Atlantic doctrine. This was the issue at stake in the MC 48 document, and which resulted, in the Atlantic case, in deliberations similar to those of the American National Security Council.

MC 48: A directive to Atlanticize nuclear war: to deter before defending?

Analysis

Formally, MC 48 initially resulted from the policy decisions of the North Atlantic Council in December 1953, and from the studies of the Military Committee at the request of the United States, to adapt the Atlantic strategy to the New Look.[5] But in reality, the basis of MC 48 was the "Capabilities Studies" of the three main commanders of the Alliance, in particular General Gruenther, commander-in-chief of NATO (SACEUR). Unsurprisingly, it contained the plans adopted by the American National Security Council. In particular, it took into account Western economic resources.[6] In the second place, the Standing Group of Washington (the United States, Great Britain, and France) synthesized the multiple sources and wrote the first draft of MC 48, drawn especially from the SACEUR (September–October 1954). The Standing Group concluded that the "immediate" outbreak of nuclear fire, tactical and strategic, would be the only way to deter or defeat the USSR, if it initiated a war, even a purely conventional one. Then, the MC 48 draft obtained the *nihil obstat* of the other military delegations that were convened in the NATO Military Committee (MC) and was adopted without any real debate at the end of November 1954. The Military Committee transmitted its "report" to the Atlantic Council on 22 November 1954. Outside the Standing Group, the allies of the Big Three thus only became aware of the text 15 days before the official Atlantic Council. This procedure proved to be a bit cavalier for a document that involved the survival of the entire Western world, and in this context discord was inevitable.[7]

MC 48 was entitled: "The most effective pattern of NATO military strength for the next few years." It was subdivided into seven parts: "The defensive aims of NATO"; "Probable nature and duration of future war involving NATO"; "Factors affecting the outcome of the initial phase"; "Factors affecting the outcome of subsequent operations"; "Examination of Soviet capabilities and probably strategy"; "The task of NATO forces in Europe"; and "Control of sea communications."[8]

MC 48 thus sought a large counterattack during the first days of the conflict, so as to prevent the enemy from retaking the nuclear initiative and make it capitulate. This assumed three essential conditions: first, the existence of an instantaneous air alarm system; next, the ability of SACEUR to react instantly, while launching tactical nuclear fire in response without waiting for orders from political bodies; and, finally, that the industrial capacity of the West could mass-produce the maximum number of bombs possible, to "provide us with a residual for use in the subsequent phase of operations."[9]

Comment

In spite of European fears about an excessive and dangerous doctrine, MC 48 contained a bold and innovative subtlety. Hitherto, and in spite of official discourse, the USSR could succeed in a conventional invasion of Europe. Much later, the United States would attempt to recover the lost continent. It was also known that America possessed, thanks to its atomic bombs, the means of cruelly wounding the Soviet bear, but undoubtedly not of killing it, given its insufficient stockpiles. Basically, everything rested on the question of whether the Kremlin leadership would sacrifice Moscow and Leningrad to install itself in Western Europe. The precedent of 1812–14 makes one wonder. Furthermore, the American–Atlantic "new approach" was no longer content with simply deterring the Soviet threat. From then on, in the event of war, not only was defeat no longer certain against the USSR, but victory became possible on the condition of replying within the hour after the first violation of the original Soviet boundary, and possessing an atomic arsenal superior in numbers. The productivist and quantitative logic of the two previous world wars accelerated. The new dogma of European defense rested as much on the moral determination of the allies to combat the USSR as on the industrial productivity of the United States. The America of Eisenhower launched itself on the race for nuclear armament. It went from 1000 nuclear warheads in 1953 to 18,000 in 1960 (against only 200 in the USSR[10]).

A fortiori, the possibility of victory strengthened deterrence. The Kremlin, in effect, could doubt Atlantic reprisals if they led to the automatic suicide of Western civilization. In this case, Western leaders might prefer subjugation to annihilation. However, from the moment when the immediate use of American weapons permitted a forward strategy and the possibility of a victory for the Alliance, the Soviets would worry and would hesitate a long time before taking the plunge. Perhaps the apocalypse would occur but the angel of destruction would not maintain an equal balance. Still American diplomacy needed to convince the allies of the relevance of the new doctrine.

The European authorities struggled to discern the boundary between conventional war and nuclear war

In 1954, the dogma cracked and gaps appeared. In France, for example, Raymond Aron criticized the modalities that accompanied the new doctrine, namely the announced withdrawal of two divisions from Korea and, implicitly, American divisions from the FRG. The French philosopher noted that Eisenhower and Dulles had paradoxically reverted to the strategy that Truman had used before 1950, in relying excessively on atomic weapons and the mobility of a strategic reserve, based in North America:

> To say that "the mobile reserve" and "strategic aviation" will prevent an attack is excellent, but if, after all, local aggression occurs, we may be torn as it almost was in 1950, by the choice between surrender or general war, two possibilities that we want to avoid. In other words, the concentration of military resources on a single weapon, contrary to the assertions of M.J.F. Dulles, would tend to reduce, and not expand the freedom of decision.[11]

How, in these conditions, could the Europeans rely on the New Look to protect their interests and their security? A new feeling of dependence towards the United States was created. The future of the continent rested in foreign hands, friends today but perhaps indifferent tomorrow. Consider the ambiguity of Atlantic integration that was increasingly unequal and discriminatory: only the American forces in Europe wielded atomic weapons and they remained under the orders of the White House. The president of the United States, the commander-in-chief of American forces in Europe, and all the military subordinates, would consider European security alone, relying exclusively on American nuclear weapons. As Dulles declared in April 1954 to G. Bidault "no power has ever given another power the option of determining its entry into war."[12] Eisenhower or his successors could decide either not to defend Europe or to plunge it into nuclear apocalypse. Understandably, the French and European governments had difficulty conceiving an intermediate situation between these two disasters.

Military Committee and the equipping of the allied forces with tactical nuclear weapons: a disguised return to the excessive figures of the Lisbon Conference (1952)?

When leaving behind theory to elaborate a practical doctrine, everything needs to be reinvented. A privileged witness of the American strategic evolution, General Valluy commented from his post as French representative to the Permanent Group in Washington:

> The American military chiefs who, not without pride, are conscious of shaping the military thought of the free world, today feel, as General Taylor [Chief of Staff of the Army], unable to declare a simple and revolutionary doctrine, speaking instead, without dogmatism, of slow evolution, of contradictory needs, of necessary compromises, of the durability of the heroic soldier.[13]

This approximation involuntarily weighed heavily on everyone, including the British heads of staff, who held the closest known point of view to that of the United States and believed in keeping with their own government.

Even the Committee of the British Joint Chiefs of Staff doubted the soundness of US plans to defend Europe and the United Kingdom

In contradiction to the American executive, the English generals criticized the optimism of MC 48 for its decrease in conventional forces in favor of an atomic build-up. From September 1954, even before the adoption of MC 48, they denounced the insufficiency of the "forces-in-being" intended for the forward defense.[14]

Like the French, the British Chiefs of Staff feared that they should have to pay the costs of the persistent myth of the "American fortress." Did they fear becoming victims of a "peripheral super-strategy" that haughtily ignored the security of the British Isles? In any case, they thought that, strategically, "as rapid and decisive as nuclear strikes are, aerial responses are not guarantees of an immediate cessation of enemy attacks, ground or naval." Tactically, it seemed inconceivable to them to ever regain the lost regions of Western Europe devastated by nuclear weapons: "The idea of liberating the lost ground, using nuclear weapons, is so serious that it becomes unthinkable." Finally, the British High Command returned to the inadequacy of the nuclear response to local crises: "If the Communists returned to an aggressive policy, "conventional forces" would be necessary to oppose their threats and their bluff." In short, the British command called for a serious re-evaluation of MC 48.[15]

However, despite the warnings of their military advisors, British political leaders wanted to return to New Look orthodoxy, and confirm the primacy of tactical and strategic nuclear technology over conventional units. From a chronological perspective, it was therefore up to the governments of Eden and Macmillan, in 1956–57, to launch the first studies that led to MC 70. To the great displeasure of the British Government, the drafting of MC 70 led to diametrically opposite results: the strengthening of conventional units and the augmentation of military budgets. Until this paradoxical result, the English concerns in 1956 attracted the sympathetic attention of SACEUR, General Gruenther, who decided to rethink the doctrine of the employment of forces.

From MC 48 to MC 70: the tactical will of General Gruenther (autumn 1956)[16]

General Gruenther was aware of the criticisms of the doctrine that he himself had inspired. Before handing over his post to General Norstad, he provided a more nuanced reading of MC 48, which paved the way for directive MC 70, adopted in 1958.

Let us be wary of the legend at the time attributed to US officials: no American officer, and no serious study by the Pentagon, ever believed that nuclear war would abolish land combat. The question was rather the degree of confidence given to tactical nuclear weapons to win the battle of Europe. In September 1956, General Gruenther weighed in on a report about the desirable ratio between nuclear forces and conventional elements. He proposed four series of adjustments to dispel allied concerns. The first change: he adjusted the automatic nature of the atomic response and considered it more and more as one option among others. The implacable resolve of the allies would achieve the real goal of never resorting to nuclear fire.

The second innovation: General Gruenther admitted the possibility of a purely local and conventional conflict. He proposed "to give Europeans an environment of military confidence and security," which implied that

> the maintenance of forces on the ground, adequate, properly arranged, and highly trained, which would constitute evidence that any local aggression – from a small

scale that could lead to general war – could be contained and would not give the advantage to the enemy.[17]

Consequently, a NATO rapid reaction force ("ready reserves") would be created, preferably multinational, under the direct command of SACEUR, which would immediately be assigned to the threatened region.

The third novelty: the "shield" must be reinvigorated, i.e. the army, navy, and air force in Europe. This term replaced the expression "forces in being", used in MC 48. The shield

> must possess sufficient power and a deployment on the ground such that there does not exist in the mind of the aggressor any hope of obtaining a partial gain nor of reaching a favourable compromise.[18]

In particular, it must commit the enemy to making massive and overt conventional preparations, which would leave no doubt about its intentions. Next, "the shield must raise the stakes so that the aggressor, who decides to attack, faces the devastating consequences of total nuclear war." If war broke out, then the first five days would be characterized by an intense tactical nuclear duel. SACEUR would no longer settle for

> launching an immediate nuclear retaliation campaign to neutralize the military capabilities of the enemy, beginning by destroying its nuclear delivery systems. It would also *defend* [emphasis added] the populations, territories, vital maritime regions and offensive capabilities of NATO.[19]

Note that this view already agreed with the conceptions of the French High Command, for whom real deterrence was both nuclear (sword) and conventional (shield).[20]

Fourth, the Gruenther report largely considered the second phase of the conflict. MC 48 did not exclude a conflict that exceeded 30 days, but deemed it impossible at the time to prepare, due to the lack of resources available.[21] SACEUR now emphasized the second month of war (M + 30) and the phase of reconditioning and restocking, essential to victory. Gruenther asked Eisenhower to maintain two divisions in the United States as reinforcements for the European theatre during the first month of the conflict. (It should be specified from the start that the president refused to provide these strategic reserves, initially due to budgetary considerations, and, besides, because he did not see how to send forces out of America in a nuclear context when the United States itself would be devastated and in need of all available support.)

The "policy directive" launching the preparatory studies for MC 70 (Atlantic Council, 14 December 1956)

The report of General Gruenther received the approval of the European Staffs, unlike the American Joint Chiefs of Staff, who accused him of "continuing to develop its recommendations according to the norms of Lisbon."[22] SACEUR's recommendations led to the "policy directive" of 14 December 1956, itself the direct cause of MC 70. Given the difficulty of moving MC 48 beyond theory, the Military Committee of NATO formally requested that the Council of Ministers initiate the studies in order to create a more coherent new text on "the minimum level of Atlantic forces" that took into account the gradual arrival of "new weapons"[23] and the possibility of "local" infiltrations, incursions, or actions, so as to repel them without drifting towards nuclear conflict.[24]

The stages of writing (December 1956—December 1957): the maximalism of the Pentagon overrode the flexibility recommended by the State Department

MC 70 experienced a paradoxical fate. Unlike MC 48, it was not a NATO version of an internal directive of the American National Security Council. The new regulation stems only from the cogitation of SHAPE (Supreme Headquarters Allied Powers Europe). The White House and the Pentagon considered it with suspicion at the outset because the Atlantic Staffs judged that it was necessary to temper the systematic use of atomic weapons and enhance the function of conventional forces. Note that Great Britain took a great interest in this doctrinal evolution, provided that the other states applied it in its place: to the Anglo-Saxons, nuclear fire—prestigious and reputedly inexpensive—to the continental allies, the traditional troops. In 1957, intervening in its turn, France, its Staff, and the *"services des pactes,"* attempted to persuade the United States to finance the upgrading of the conventional and nuclear shield in Europe, and especially the French army.

Finally, the Pentagon overrode these tendencies and imposed its radical views. For the first time since Hiroshima, American war plans coordinated the strategic war with the tactical battle. The American generals wanted to reinforce the *tactical* atomic component of European defense, because they realized that *strategic* bombing would require more than a month to bleed the USSR, its vast territory, and dispersed facilities. Meanwhile, it would have to hold. The Joint Chiefs of Staff drew directly from the lessons of World War II. Indeed, any current analysis, supported by the American Army, denounced the overconfidence that had hitherto been accorded to the *strategic* bombings on Germany. The American military also did not forget the classic victories in the battle of the Pacific that preceded the strategic destruction of Hiroshima and Nagasaki. The tactical war and the strategic war must thus support each other. The two, hand in hand, would lead to victory. Consequently, the Pentagon used MC 70 to reinforce the tactical nuclear weapons and to settle the unresolved problem of the conventional inferiority between East and West. The first consequence: in 1957, the war plans of SACEUR now rested on 1700 tactical bombs instead of 170, as in 1954.[25]

The final text and the essence of MC 70: in times of war, the European allies would handle tactical nuclear weapons on an equal footing with the American divisions, all under the command of SACEUR

MC 70 is entitled: "The Minimum Essential Force Requirements 1958–1963".[26] It introduced a massive program to modernize the weapons and infrastructure of NATO: 28 Atlantic divisions in the first day of mobilization (M) and 50 divisions at M + 3. France, for example, had to maintain four divisions on M and mobilize 12 divisions on M + 3. In absolute terms, the increase in manpower did not exceed MC 48. The volume of troops even decreased due to the adaptation of the size of the divisions to nuclear war: more lightness and responsiveness. This also applied to tactical aviation.[27]

The big innovation was the qualitative jump required of the allies, with the gradual introduction of atomic weapons in the units as the United States produced them:[28]

MC 70 anticipated that not only 270 American units be equipped but also European short-range tactical aircraft. However, the Western divisions had to be able to fight with conventional weapons at the same time, or to launch their atomic weapons in the first hour of war. Atomic bombs were no longer reserved for the delayed battle and stopped at the Oder or the Rhine, but were also for the defense of national territories, behind the lines. This required providing the allied armies with short range tactical nuclear missiles with limited power, since the concerned countries (and benevolent allies) would bomb their own national territory. This measure primarily concerned the FRG, but could eventually also concern France or the Po valley. This makes it easier to understand why MC 70 remained classified until 2000. The successive plans no doubt inherited this drastic measure and would not have pleased these countries' citizens.[29]

The procedure of the "double key" governed the use of atomic warheads: in times of peace, the American forces kept the nuclear warheads in 147 principle depots and 161 other secondary stocks or in transit (very expensive indeed).[30] During a conflict, American forces would immediately hand over the atomic warheads to the allied units, on the order of the president of the United States. The host nation would handle and maintain the vectors.[31] This was a belated and inevitable consequence of the New Look and MC 48: the exact role of the conventional European divisions beside the nuclearized American units on the same battle field was ill-conceived (unless imagining an American division integrated in each French, German or Italian army corps). The inclusion of tactical weapons in European arsenals (Honest John, Nike, Hawk, and Sergeant missiles, with a range of 50–150 km) would multiply Atlantic firepower. This would lead, for France and the FRG, to considerable positive consequences, for example giving their F100 airplanes tactical nuclear capabilities.[32] These two principal nations left behind the role of "foot soldiers" that MC 48 had assigned them—which should have pleased them, in theory.

The second objective of MC 70: to survive Soviet strikes and to win the second month of war, to reinforce the capacity to survive and to prepare for a considerable logistical effort, on land and on sea

Indisputably, MC 70 offered attractive prospects to the American allies. However, this new military regulation would also carry a heavy price for the Western economies, because of the intensification of the logistical and conventional aspects of MC 48. From then on, MC 70 planned the second month of war on the assumption that the tactical and strategic bombings against the Communist armies and territories would not in and of themselves bring victory. MC 70 renounced the old theory which postulated that a nuclear war would not last longer than a month (cf. the "concept of thirty days" of MC 48). After the first round of annihilation, NATO would reorganize the surviving units to reconquer lost territories. This is why MC 70 gave prominence to logistical questions and stressed the vital link between the protection of American industry and the rehabilitation of battered Europe.

MC 70 was thus logically interested in maritime communications.[33] To preserve the vital link between North America and Europe, the directive ordered the evacuation of the entire European and British merchant fleet at the start of the war (3,500 ships), to be dispersed offshore of the United States and in the South Atlantic, in order to conserve the possibility of later sending reinforcements and supplies to the old continent.[34] In this vein, MC 70 distributed considerable financial resources to the anti-submarine fight, at a comparable level to investments on land, as well as an expensive increase in the power of American and British fleets under the orders of SACLANT (Supreme Allied Commander Atlantic). In parallel, SACEUR recommended financing and stocking 90 days' worth of war reserves in Europe, a considerable immobilization of capital. All these accumulated factors made the cost of MC 70 skyrocket. For financial reasons, the European governments, led by France, initially supported the new directive in the hope of receiving subsidies from the United States, then rejected it when they understood that they had to pay their share.

The fantastic accounts of MC 70

From the start, the Eisenhower administration maintained MC 70 to impose a "Fair Share" on the Europeans and a rationalization of the costs of Western security.[35] In fact, the trap closed almost immediately on the American budget: not only did the European allies continue to hide behind the American military presence in Europe, but the United States had to continue to increase their Atlantic contribution, in absolute and relative value.

After an initial setback in December 1957, from 15 to 17 April 1958 the NATO Council of Defence Ministers tried, and failed again, to adopt MC 70:[36] one by one, the European ministers slipped away and hid their reluctance behind a veil of good intentions. For example, the Belgian government calculated that the execution of MC 70 would impose an increase of 35 percent of their military budget.[37] On behalf of the FRG, Franz Josef Strauss worried about financing nuclear missiles while the Bundeswehr had not achieved the first stage of its rise to power, and had not yet received all of its conventional material. And yet, the tactical weapons of high technology necessitated even more land, infrastructure, engineers, not to mention constant revisions and updates.[38]

The position of the United Kingdom was no more coherent than that of its neighbors. The British complained that MC 70 raised their defense budgets. For example, MC 70 required 100,000 additional troops be added to the 50,000 soldiers forced to remain in the FRG and to modernize them quickly.[39] Her Majesty's Government also quickly understood that a significant naval contribution was required in order to ensure that the sea routes between North America and Europe were secure. The new directive therefore directly contradicted the British Defence White Paper of 1957. Paradoxically, the United Kingdom, though originally in favor of MC 70, criticized the maximalist ambitions, including and especially the naval component. At the North Atlantic Council of December 1958, Duncan Sandys argued that MC 70 was not a minimum, but an ideal (whereas it is actually a "minimum" understood in "a spirit of strict economy").[40]

The logical outcome: at the Atlantic Council of December 1959, no one mentioned MC 70, which lasted in theory until 1963. Drawing lessons from the fiasco, the Secretary-General of the Organization, Paul-Henri Spaak, renounced the principal of the "long term Atlantic plan" and returned to the system of the "annual review."[41]

The technocratic and strategic bankruptcy of MC 70

On the whole, the nuclearization of the European armies is only now being understood (including the Luftwaffe), the price of the double key. On the whole, the nuclearization of the European Armies (with the double key system) has been the only concrete achievement of MC 70. In particular, the fracture between the military staffs and the political authorities should be mentioned. The Military Committee of NATO and the Standing Group, as the principal military leaders of the Atlantic Alliance wanted to impose a vital minimum, which quickly appeared to civilian authorities as a deadly maximum. The European governments, particularly France and Great Britain, but also President Eisenhower only wanted to consider budgetary savings.

By refusing to finance the conventional section of MC 70 and by giving budgetary priority to the welfare state, the European members of NATO refused the possibility of conducting conventional combat initially and thus resolved to have nuclear war in the case of a Soviet attack, even a limited one. The fact that World War III fortunately did not break out does not prove the suitability of their position. European leaders had *de facto* accepted the prospect of suicide: either the European continent was a lightning rod of East–West conflict, sparing North America and Soviet Russia; or the president of the United States would refuse to take any risks and would not authorize nuclear fire in Europe, strategic or tactical, letting the Red Army crush the European armies; or, alternatively, the member states of NATO would behave collectively as a large Denmark in 1940: Amsterdam, Brussels, Rome, Paris … open cities!

Between these two options, life or death, the United States resigned itself to the riskiest option. They maintained their divisions in the FRG on the frontline of a potential conflict, if only a local one. The large American units voluntarily served as hostages for European security. Yet the successive presidential administrations could have been much more restrictive and coercive towards their allies, including and especially France, by requiring them to actually finance the necessary defense.

Notes

1 'Evolution of Foreign Policy', address to the Council on Foreign Relations; New York 12/1/1954. Princeton, *Mudd Library, Dulles Papers*, box no. 322.
2 Talk on 6/8/1956 between Eisenhower and Lewis Strauss in Shaun R. Gregory, *Nuclear Command and Control in NATO. Nuclear weapons Operations and the Strategy of Flexible Response*, (Macmillan, 1996), pp. 168–70.
3 Memo from Walter Bedell Smith, to President Eisenhower; 3/12/1953. *Foreign Relations of the United States (FRUS), 1952–1954*, (Washington: United States Government Printing Office), vol. II, p. 607–8.
4 Statement by the Secretary of State to the North Atlantic Council Closed Ministerial Session; Paris, 23/4/1954. *FRUS 1952–1954*, vol. V, pp. 509–14.
5 For the stance of the French general staff: 'Possibilités d'obtenir un meilleur rendement militaire des ressources de l'alliance', note no. 4152/11-D.30; 27/11/1953. Ministère des Affaires étrangères français (hereafter, MAEF) série *Service des pactes 1947–1970* (hereafter, *Pactes*, box no. 38.
6 The American origin of this is confirmed by the memo of the *Service des pactes*; 13/12/1955. Quai d'Orsay, MAEF, *Service des pactes*, ibid.
7 'Etude par le Conseil des ministres du rapport du Comité militaire sur le nouveau plan d'organisation des forces de l'OTAN'. Tg. no. 50 424/pol. 256 from M. Couve de Murville present representative to the NAC; 29/11/1954, ibid; *'Dossier remis au ministre de la Défense nationale et des forces armées en vue de la réunion des ministres de la Défense des 10—11 & 12 octobre 1955'*. Working paper no. 1730/DN/AG/EX from the Secrétariat général permanent de la Défense nationale (35 pp.); 5/10/1955. Memo A.2: 'MC 48—Principes sur lesquels repose la stratégie OTAN'. Ibid.
8 'Système le plus efficace à adopter pour la force militaire de l'OTAN pendant les prochaines années—MC 48'. 22/11/1954. In G. Pedlow (ed.), *Documents sur la stratégie de l'OTAN 1949–1969*, (SHAPE: 1997), p. 273, §6.
9 Ibid., p. 275, §8.
10 Georges-Henry Soutou, *La Guerre de Cinquante Ans. Les relations Est-Ouest, 1943–1990,* (Paris: Fayard, 2001), p. 345.

11 'Une nouvelle stratégie américaine? L'arme atomique ne répond pas à toutes les formes d'agression'; 22/3/1954. Raymond Aron, *Les articles de politique internationale dans le Figaro de 1947 à 1977*, (Paris: éditions de Fallois, 1990), t. I, pp. 186–88.
12 Meeting Dulles-Bonnet; 16/6/1954. *FRUS, 1952–1954*, vol. XIII, t. 2, pp. 1710–13.
13 Note no. 97/DFGP/C of the general Valluy; February 1956. MAEF, Pactes no. 38.
14 For the following development: 'The Most Effective Pattern of NATO Military Strength for the Next Few Years. Report by the Joint Planning Staff (Chiefs of Staff Committee)'. No. J.P. (54) 77; 3/9/1954. Public Record Office, Kew Gardens, DEFE 6/26.
15 Ibid.
16 'Force Posture Allied Command 1960/62'. Memo of the SACEUR no. 56/230 and no. 56/231; September 1956. Collected, analyzed, and commented in 'SACEUR's Force Requirements 1960/62'. Report of the British Chiefs of Staff, no. J.P. (56) 162. Kew Gardens, DEFE 4/92. Actually General Gruenther voiced some criticism concerning the new doctrine in December 1953. Tg. no. 50 109–50 112 for Washington; 24/12/1953. MAEF, Pactes, b. no. 38.
17 Ibid.
18 Ibid.
19 Ibid.
20 'Préparation de la conférence des ministres de la Défense des nations OTAN (15 avril 1958)'. File no. 3603/11/B. 39 of the general staff to the French ministers of defence; 5/4/1958. MAEF, Pactes, b. no. 40.
21 'Système le plus efficace à adopter pour la force militaire de l'OTAN pendant les prochaines années—MC 48'. 22/11/1954, in Pedlow (ed.), *Documents sur la stratégie de l'OTAN*, p. 278, § 13.
22 2850 National Security Council; 17/5/1956. *FRUS 1955–1957*, vol. XIX, doc. no. 79, pp. 305–11. See also in the same tone the lengthy analysis by General Jean Piatte, head of the French delegation to the Standing Group: personal letter to General Ely; Washington, 4/4/1958. No. 141/DFGP/S. MAEF, b. No. 40.
23 'Directive du Conseil aux autorités militaires de l'Alliance', position paper of the 'Pactes' before the North Atlantic Council of December 1956; 10/12/1956. MAEF, Pactes, b. no. 38 bis.
24 Abstract of the 'political directive' of 1956 in: 'Forces de l'OTAN'. Memo of the 'Pactes' le secrétaire général du Quai; 13/3/1958. MAEF, Pactes, b. no. 40.
25 Georges-Henri Soutou, *L'alliance incertaine. Les rapports politico-stratégiques franco-allemands. 1954–1996*, (Paris: Fayard, 1996), p. 64.
26 '*The Minimum Essential Force Requirements 1958–1963*', President's Committee to Study the United States Military Assistance Program (Draper Committee) Records, 1958–59, box 17, Dwight D. Eisenhower Library, Abilene, Kansas.
27 Circular Tg. of the Pactes, summing up the North Atlantic Council of Defence ministries; 17/4/1958. MAEF, Pactes, b. no. 40.
28 'Besoins en forces', analysis of MC 70 by French General J. Piatte; 28/3/1958. Letter no. 136/DFGP/S is meant to go directly to General Ely. Ibid.—'MC 70', memo of the 'Pactes' to the Minister; 10/4/1958. Ibid.
29 '22° session du Comité militaire de l'OTAN', report by the SACEUR L. Norstad. Tg. REPAN Chaillot no. 50 174; 12/12/1958. MAEF, Pactes, b. no. 40.
30 Ibid.
31 'Preliminary United States Views and Proposals for the December NATO Meeting'. Department of State memo to the allied powers; 3/12/1957. MAEF, Pactes, b. no. 39.
32 Tg. no. 782–85, signed by Alphand; Washington, 8/2/1958. MAEF, Pactes, b. no. 82.
33 For the origins see 'Dossier remis au ministre de la Défense nationale et des forces armées en vue de la réunion des ministres de la Défense des 10—11 & 12 octobre 1955'; 'Exposé de SACLANT' at the Atlantic conférence of 1956. Included in document no 564 DN/AG/EX of the SGPDN; 15/3/1956, MAEF, Pactes, b. no. 38; principles repeated by Admiral Wright, SACLANT, en mars 1958: 'Réunion commune du Comité militaire et du Conseil permanent'. Tg. REPAN Paris, signed by Crouy; 17/3/1958—MAEF, Pactes, b. no. 40; North Atlantic Council of December 1958. *FRUS 1958–1960*, vol. VII, doc. no 172, p. 388.
34 'Chiefs of Staff Committee. NATO Minimum Forces Studies' (4 p.). Summary report of the meeting of the committee of the British chiefs of staff to serve as instructions for the British representative at the standing group in Washington, in order to finalize MC 70. C.O.S. (57) 244. Public Record Office, Kew Gardens (PRO), DEFE 5/79, § 16.

35 Report by the NATO general secretary (P. H. Spaak) about his trip to Washington, P. H. Spaak. Tg. REPAN Paris no. 50 460, signé Crouy; 12/11/1957. MAEF, Pactes, b. no. 39.
36 Report by the French permanent representative to the North Atlantic Council, Etienne de Crouy-Chanel; 15/4/1958. Tg. no. 50 120. MAEF, Pactes, b. no. 40.
37 Concerns expressed by the American delegation to the North Atlantic Council 18/12/1958. Tg. Polto no.1742, *FRUS 1958–1960*, vol. VII, doc. no 173, p. 393.
38 Ibid.
39 In May 1958, the Macmillan government asked Washington to pay for 10,000 to 55,000 troops of the British Army on the Rhine (BAOR). The following October, Eisenhower agreed to pay 26 million dollars within the framework of the Mutual Weapons Development Program (installation of the intermediate range ballistic missile Thor) for the budgetary year 1958–59. See conversation Dulles–Lloyd at the Atlantic Council in Copenhagen, 7/5/1958. *FRUS 1958–1960*, vol. VII, doc. no 147, p. 348 and note no. 1.
40 Address of the British Defence minister to the North Atlantic Council of December 1958. See the summary report of the plenary session, 17/12/1958. Analysis of the point no. 11 ('Military issues') in the circular Tg. signed by Courcel. MAE, Pactes, b. no. 40—Tg. Polto no. 1741 of the American delegation; 18/12/1958. *FRUS 1958–1960*, vol. VII, doc. no. 172, p. 389.
41 Verbatim of the North Atlantic Session of December 1959. NATO document transmitted to the allied governments, 12/19/1959. MAEF, Pactes, b. no. 40 bis.

4

The Fourth Republic and NATO

Loyalty to the Alliance versus national demands?

Jenny Raflik

The French Fourth Republic has too often been caricatured as a weak regime subjected to American influence in contrast to the strong and independent France of General Charles de Gaulle. However, the creation of the Atlantic Alliance coincided with the Fourth Republic. France played an original and decisive role during the first years of the Alliance, which is important for understanding the subsequent relationship between France and NATO.

In order to understand the transatlantic policies of the Fourth Republic, the circumstances in which they were formulated must be recalled:

- the continuous engagement of France in colonial conflicts, in Indochina and then Algeria
- a French Communist Party which obtained on average 25 per cent of the vote in the country
- a Gaullist opposition, aggressive in foreign policy which was echoed loudly in public opinion.

The definition of France's transatlantic policy also rested on contradictory political preferences among the French leadership. However, if these preferences had conflicting objectives, they sometimes, and even often, coincided on the means of policy implementation. Thus, alongside a preference that is often too quickly termed 'Atlanticist', expressing early attachment to the Atlantic Alliance as a nationalist objective,[1] there developed a more Europeanist preference[2] attached to the idea of a European Third Way. On the whole, the transatlantic view and the European view concealed the same nationalist interest based on the Cold War and the decline of the traditional European powers. This interest was the need to adapt French policy to the realities of the post-war world.

It is in this context that, under the Fourth Republic, the Atlantic Pact began to impose itself in multiple fields. It is thus reflected in questions of domestic policy (the role of the Communists, concessions on sovereignty, etc.), foreign policy (German rearmament, the European Defence Community, European construction, etc.) and defence policy

(European defence strategy, the Military Aid Program, Mediterranean Command, general rearmament, etc.).

Since it is impossible to outline the entire transatlantic policy of the Fourth Republic here, the focus will be the growing frustration of the Fourth Republic and its leadership with the transatlantic institutions, and some of the lasting tendencies of this policy will be highlighted in order to shed light on the subsequent relationship between France and NATO. Behind the constant loyalty of the Fourth Republic to the Atlantic alliance, there were national claims which preceded those of the Gaullist regime. In order to illustrate this, the initiatives that made the Fourth Republic an essential actor in the Alliance will first be considered, then the elements of tension surrounding French participation before finally highlighting some of the lasting tendencies of the transatlantic policy of the Fourth Republic.

The Fourth Republic: an essential actor in the genesis and original organization of the Alliance[3]

A brief initial desire to remain outside the power blocs

In the immediate post-war period, France began to redefine its security policy, taking into account the emerging new geopolitical situation of a bipolar world. At first tempted by a policy of neutrality between the two great powers, France was quickly forced to choose as the Soviet threat soon became military and no longer only political. The Fourth Republic had inherited the foreign policy of General de Gaulle's provisional government. France was a permanent member of the United Nations Security Council and an occupying power in Germany. However, this status was due more to the pugnacity of and, above all, Churchill's desire to avoid isolation in the face of the two great powers than to the actual military status of the country.

France's foreign policy in fact evolved in relation to the stages of the Cold War and the increasing realization of the Soviet threat.[4] What marks French particularism during the period of the genesis of the Alliance was the progressive change from the conception of a purely German threat to the perception of a combination of German and Soviet threats.[5] Thus, the 1947 Treaty of Dunkirk[6] and even more so the 1948 Treaty of Brussels explicitly mention the German threat, while the United States, with Truman's speech of 12 March 1947 on aid to Greece and Turkey, was already engaged in the Cold War.[7] Nevertheless, the first concrete work of the Military Staff of the Treaty of Brussels showed that the military envisioned Soviet aggression and not only German. The chronology of events that led France to perceive a German–Soviet threat rather than an exclusively German one was not agreed on by all French leaders. Thus, important divergences appeared between the principal leaders of the Fourth Republic. Some leaders envisioned an Atlantic alliance early on, even if its content remained uncertain. It was these men who took the early initiatives that can be interpreted as being at the origins of the Alliance. Thus, from February 1946, the Minister of the Armies, Edmond Michelet (from the Mouvement Républicain Populaire), with the agreement of Georges Bidault, the Foreign Minister, decided to send General Billotte on a secret mission to Washington to 'test' the Americans on a transatlantic military alliance. Once informed, however, the head of the government, the Socialist Félix Gouin, put a stop to the mission.[8] General Billotte, member of the United Nations General Staff Committee, nonetheless proceeded with these more or less official consultations, with Bidault's consent.

The governmental coalition was divided over this question. Whereas Bidault is seen as a very early champion of Atlanticism, the Socialists, in particular, continued to advocate the idea of a European third force. In 1947, Prime Minister Paul Ramadier decided to evict Communist ministers, without including transatlantic ideas in the area of national defence. President Auriol also illustrated this tendency. Convinced of the danger and the incapacity of France to resist international tensions alone, he did not want to provoke the USSR and remained partisan to a prudent, though firm, policy. There was no doubt as to his opposition to Communism when he felt it endangered domestic order, but it did not extend to foreign policy with the USSR. The evolution of the socialists can be observed in a number of stages; with the Soviet refusal of the Marshall Plan, the Szlarzka Poreba conference in October 1947, then the serious strikes in November–December and finally the Prague coup in 1948.

French initiatives at the origin of the Alliance

Although George Bidault demonstrated an early Atlanticism, his role in the genesis of the Alliance seems essential. But the events which led to the negotiation of the Washington Treaty have multiple historiographies, resulting from the ambiguities and hesitations of French leaders at the time. Thus, the Brussels Pact can be perceived in two ways, and it seemed so at the time as well. For some French diplomats, such as Jean de Hautecloque, France's ambassador to Belgium, the Brussels Pact really had a Europeanist end. Georges Bidault, in contrast, seemed to conceive it as an invitation to the Americans to invest in the defence of Europe. This was the tone of the correspondence he kept with US Secretary of State George Marshall during the European negotiations and is also the only logical explanation for the steps taken with General Billotte. On 4 March, at the same time as the negotiations between France, Great Britain and the three Benelux countries, he delivered a note to Caffery, the American ambassador, to be forwarded to Marshall, requesting direct American involvement in Europe.[9] Marshall's response was rather lukewarm.[10] The Americans encouraged the Europeans to take responsibility for their own collective defence. However, negotiations opened in Washington on 22 March 1948 between the Americans, Canadians and the English. The exclusion of France was justified by the fear of leaks coming from the numerous Communist sympathizers still present within the French administration. These first negotiations contributed to giving France the impression of an Anglo-American club, within which it would be difficult to find a place. Faced with this obvious diplomatic isolation, Bidault addressed a second personal letter to Marshall on 14 April 1948. At the moment of the signing of the Brussels Pact, President Truman's declaration seemed encouraging:

> At the very moment I am addressing you, five nations of the European community, in Brussels, are signing a 50-year agreement for economic cooperation and common defense against aggression. This action has great significance, for this agreement was not imposed by the decree of a more powerful neighbor.[11]

However, the major obstacle to American participation was a legal one: a two-thirds majority vote in the Senate was required or the Senate would continue to consider any permanent peacetime alliance unconstitutional, since it would threaten to bring the United States into a war without the required Congressional authorization. It was the Vandenburg resolution, voted on 11 June 1948, that finally cleared up the situation by allowing the

United States to participate as an observer during the meetings of the Brussels Treaty Staff Committee, starting on 20 July, and which signalled the beginning of official negotiations over the Atlantic Pact.[12] For Bidault, it was a success, although it took some time to happen.

Once again, it was a crisis, the Berlin blockade, that served as a catalyst for the negotiation of the Atlantic Pact and which provided the context for all of the discussions. Conversations began on 6 July 1948 in Washington at the request of the State Department between the representatives of the Western European Union, the United States and the Canadian embassy.[13] France's priority was for a simple association of the United States to the Brussels Pact. However, the United States firmly rejected this idea.

The French position during the Atlantic Pact negotiations largely explains subsequent relations between France and NATO. While agreement on the principle of common defence came easily, the consultations highlighted the existing gap between French and Anglo-Saxon proposals. French leaders made the efficiency of the Alliance an absolute priority during the negotiations. However, the United States refused to agree to an automatic response in case of attack. France had to retract this request. This represented the first failure of the French negotiators. Subsequently, this weighed heavily on the perception of the Atlantic Pact in France, since it appeared as a failure in the efficiency of the system put into place.[14]

Divergences also existed between the French and the Americans on the geographic area of the Alliance. The United States wished for a large area, anchored in Northern Europe with Scandinavia, whereas the French wanted their own country to be the centre of gravity for the future alliance, and included Italy within it to provide a Mediterranean orientation. Furthermore, for strategic as well as political reasons within the French Union, the government did not envision its defence without including its overseas territories, the Algerian *départements*, and the North African protectorates. The only concession finally accorded to the French was Algeria being included in the zone covered by the treaty, to counterbalance the Scandinavian participation demanded by the Americans.

Finally, always anxious about efficiency and to make the Alliance operational immediately, the French demanded the immediate delivery of arms whereas the Americans made signature of the treaty a condition. On this point as well, France was required to content itself with American promises.

From these first negotiations, contradictions appeared in French discourse. This discourse focused on obtaining treaty coverage of North Africa, but without allowing American interference in this zone. It aimed at integrating Western defence, but without renouncing national sovereignty. It wanted to fight in Germany, but without the Germans. All of these demands resurfaced during the following phase, the implementation of the Alliance's structures.

French initiatives at the origin of Atlantic integration

In effect, if France did not obtain total satisfaction during the negotiation phase, it at least retained the hope of seeing the organization further its own projects, via Article 9:

> The Parties hereby establish a Council, on which each of them shall be represented, to consider matters concerning the implementation of this Treaty [...]
> The Council shall set up such subsidiary bodies as may be necessary; in particular it shall establish immediately a defence committee [...].[15]

NATO's institutions progressively developed between 1949 and 1952. The implementation of transatlantic structures led to a number of disappointments for the French, who showed themselves to be the champions of integration within the Alliance. In fact, there were misunderstandings between the French and Americans very quickly, which stemmed from different interpretations of the concept of integration. As Frédéric Bozo remarks:

> despite its frequent use, the word [integration] never had an official existence within the structure of the Atlantic Alliance, and it did not appear within NATO's lexicon. It is difficult to give it a concrete, precise, and unique meaning as long as the realities it covers are multiple, diverse, and often ambiguous.[16]

In its politico-military interpretation, the word designates an organizational process and the implementation of a common defence policy in the transatlantic framework, thus it signifies the organization process flowing from the treaty. In its military interpretation, it designates the structures and procedures adopted within the Alliance, aiming towards a merger rather than simply the coordination of allied forces in times of war.

The politico-military aspect was the first to develop, beginning in 1949. During the construction of the political structures of the Alliance, the French position seemed guided by both power politics (aimed at making France, if not a Great Power, at least a great Western power) and the strategic interest of the country (ensuring a forward defence of Europe, and not a peripheral defence as the Anglo-Saxons preferred).

Without going into exhaustive detail, one can bring forth some of the lasting tendencies of French policy during the negotiations that took place from 1949 to 1952.[17] First, the French focused their attention on a three-power leadership of the Alliance. The existence of a small committee at the head of the Alliance was a means of weighing in on the transatlantic future. France wanted to create a permanent strategic planning organ which would have authority over all of the Alliance structures, particularly over the regional general staffs that could be created. For the French, this question was vital: they needed to influence the strategic decisions of the Alliance and defend, within an organ adapted to this purpose, their idea of forward defence. In actuality, the Permanent Group, put into place at the level of the chiefs of staff and charged with preparing the Council's decisions and supervising their execution, coordinated rather than led the policies of the Alliance. Its competences were far less than what the French had expected,[18] but they represented the most the Americans were willing to concede. For French leaders, the necessity of preventing an Anglo-American tête-à-tête from emerging justified this 1949 compromise. After 1950, with the creation of integrated commands, the French wanted to give the Permanent Group direct responsibility for Alliance strategy in all theatres, but the American and British allies refused. In practice, the Permanent Group was supplanted by the Supreme Headquarters Allied Powers Europe (SHAPE), despite the official endorsement of the French position by the Council in 1950. The government could at least avail itself of this endorsement in the face of public opinion, although it would not fool any connoisseur of the Alliance. The French never stopped defending the competences of the Permanent Group. There are traces of this in the proposal for a High Atlantic Council made by Georges Bidault in 1950. He declared:

> Feeling that the time has come to ensure that the unity of the free countries is simpler, more concrete, and more efficient, I believe that it would be wise and timely to

create a High Atlantic Council aimed at ordering and orienting the development of the community on two inseparable levels, that of defence and that of the economy, with the hope of being able to add, without too much delay, the political level as well.[19]

It was this same position that influenced a Gaullist memorandum from 17 September 1958 where de Gaulle demanded a bigger role for France alongside the United States and Great Britain and the creation of a tripartite leadership over the West. The discourse was the same, but the tone had changed and had become more threatening.

Another essential lasting tendency was the attention that France gave to European institutions within the framework of the Alliance. The desire to maintain the Brussels institutions despite the 1949 Atlantic Pact can be seen as the desire to create a European pillar within the Alliance, a point to which President Auriol, Robert Schuman and even General de Lattre de Tassigny attached a great deal of importance. This idea aimed at unifying the continental powers to make their positions better known to Washington and London, notably to defend the forward defence strategy over the peripheral defence option. Additionally, the Brussels Pact had a juridical advantage over the Atlantic Pact: the automatic response to aggression, which did not appear in the Washington Treaty. Finally, via a European body, French leaders felt there was the possibility of a European mediator emerging between the two blocs, and of defending French leadership on the continent. On this last aspect, the attachment of some French leaders to the Brussels Pact, as well as the European Defence Community (EDC), represented a resurgence of the neutralist tendencies present in the immediate post-war period.

The outbreak of the Korean War launched the purely military aspect of the integration of the Atlantic Alliance. It also constituted a test for the Atlantic nations and the first results were strongly negative. American reinforcements took time to deploy. Drawing lessons from the Korean War, the French addressed a memorandum to the allies on 5 August 1950[20] and complemented it with a second on 17 August.[21] These memoranda summarized the French position regarding the largest NATO questions: Western rearmament and its economic conditions (particularly American aid), the reorganization of the organization's general structures at the military and political levels, and finally the growing engagement of the Anglo-Saxons in Europe through a direct contribution of troops to the continent.

This memorandum shared a conviction, already widely held among much of the French leadership, with the allies of the necessity of enlarging the attributions of the Permanent Group by making it the leading organ at the strategic level of the Pact as the military equivalent of the North Atlantic Council. To a large extent, the French were satisfied with the acceleration of Atlantic integration. The Americans recognized the immediate danger threatening Europe. However, the conclusions drawn by the French and the Americans differed on one essential point: the French concluded that this threat required a massive engagement of American troops, whereas the Americans felt that this danger highlighted the indispensable contribution of German forces. The decision to create an integrated military structure in Europe by the attribution of national forces to a Supreme Allied Commander in Europe (SACEUR), understood to be American, constituted a guarantee of American engagement in the defence of Europe, which greatly satisfied the leaders of the Fourth Republic. The creation, at Rocquencourt, of SHAPE further made this engagement a reality. The installation of NATO infrastructure in France, after the 1952 Lisbon reform, also reinforced the strategic weight of France in the Alliance. By hosting NATO's General Secretariat and the Pact's permanent installations, France became, in a spectacular way, the centre of gravity and its defence in case of attack became everyone's concern. However, this presence also became the source of a new misunderstanding: to France, hosting the Atlantic forces was seen as constituting a considerable effort for the Alliance, which should have justified a political preponderance for France due to the large presence on its territory. To the allies, it was simply a geographical location, which should not act as a substitute for increased military and financial contributions. In fact, during this early phase of the creation of the Alliance and its structures, it is notable that each time France took the initiative, it found itself overtaken and confronted with pre-established scenarios. Demanding in terms of the integration and efficiency of the Alliance, the French government found itself confronted with dramatic choices that it could not handle and which encouraged growing doubts about the Alliance.

From initial doubts to the progressive divorce between France and NATO

German rearmament: initial French doubts towards the Alliance?

The German question was an early subject of French distrust of the Atlantic Pact and the debates surrounding its ratification. The famous quotation by Beuve-Méry in *Le Monde* 'German rearmament is contained in the Atlantic Pact like an embryo within an egg'[22], was echoed by French parliamentarians during the ratification vote: any new member of the Atlantic Pact would not be permitted without the president receiving prior authorization from parliament.[23]

French leaders thus found themselves in a paradoxical situation: they demanded that their British and transatlantic allies send troops to Europe and defend the continent along a line located as far east as possible (i.e. in Germany), but refused the use of German troops, whose forces were situated on the envisaged battlefield. Discordant voices within France highlighted this paradox. Some in the military attracted the attention of politicians to the fragility of the French position: in November 1948, Admiral Lemonnier had already asked the Comité des chefs d'État-major généraux to open the question of German rearmament, calling it 'a current issue with primordial importance'.[24] General Stehlin also evoked the possibility of German rearmament benefiting Western defence within the framework of the Brussels Treaty.[25] However, the government refused to accept this hypothesis. In September 1950, the time bomb exploded, through the mouth of Dean Acheson in the middle of the North Atlantic Council meeting: the Americans demanded a German contribution of ten divisions to the common defence. On 8 September, the 'package', an integrated transatlantic army including German troops, became the official policy of the United States.[26]

For four years, this issue weighed heavily on France's transatlantic policy, whose first objective was to minimize the effects of a German military renaissance. The Pleven Plan, proposed on 23 October 1950, took into account both American demands and French prejudices. It aimed at permitting a German military contribution while avoiding the creation of a German Army. It also gave new life to the initial idea of a 'European pillar' of the Alliance. The objective was to remain the European leader and to thus prevent Germany from holding this position. This would allow the complete integration of German forces into the EDC while France would escape from this total integration through its overseas forces. If here France was the champion of integration, it was due to national interest: it aimed at controlling German rearmament, ensuring French leadership in continental Europe and reaffirming its international status.

There are multiple explanations for the failure of the EDC: the changes in the majority within the French National Assembly following the 1951 elections, the declining perception of a Soviet threat after Stalin's death, awkward pressures from the United States (the 'agonizing reappraisal' of John Foster Dulles), from Germany itself (untimely statements from Adenauer) a poorly conceived military project and the hostility of the military hierarchy, and the weight of the war in Indochina, which burdened the French military effort within the EDC and provoked fears of German preponderance in the European zone. Whatever the explanation, by 1954 the EDC had lost the meaning it had at the beginning: Paris was required, under allied pressure, to abandon most of the discriminatory clauses with respect to Germany. Control over German rearmament was becoming less and less assured. The increasingly rapid recovery of the Federal Republic of Germany (FRG) endangered French leadership on the continent. American pressures gave the project a negative image, that of a foreign imposition. In short, by 1954, the EDC no longer had the interest it had initially held in 1950:

> Fundamentally, the failure of the EDC marked the realization by French leaders of their true margin of manoeuvre and of the reality of their country's power which they had overestimated for years.[27]

However, it is important to note that the resolution of the Franco-American conflict opened by the EDC debate took place within the Atlantic framework with German participation in NATO, according to the formula proposed by Anthony Eden at the London Conference (28–30 September 1954) and on which the French Foreign Ministry was already working. The entry of the FRG and Italy into the Western European Union gave a 'European' colour to this approach and allowed, via the Agency of the Western European Union for the Control of Armaments, to ensure relative control over German rearmament, safeguarding the appearance, at least, of French interests, but it placed German forces, in peacetime, under the authority of SACEUR. Thus, rather than just being a transatlantic crisis, the EDC quarrel was a Franco-American crisis resolved within the framework of NATO.

The difficult Franco-American relations regarding military aid

There was another source of transatlantic tension: the issue of American military aid. Here again French policy was paradoxical. It aimed at managing the contradiction between a lack of means, requiring France to look for allied aid, and lasting national and imperial ambitions. In short, France was trying to defend its political independence within a context of financial dependence. Here too, misunderstandings with the American government multiplied. The French gave the impression of a beggar who refused to say thank you and whose prideful reactions were not at all understood on the other side of the Atlantic.

The civilian and then military aid mechanisms began to take shape in 1948.[28] At the military level, the United States accorded a billion dollars to the Western European Union, aid that was extended and then inserted into the framework of the Atlantic Pact. This extension derived from the Mutual Defence Assistance Act (MDAA) of 6 October 1949, applied to France by the Franco-American agreement of 27 January 1950. The 10 October 1951 Mutual Security Act, modified on 20 June 1952, succeeded the MDAA, even if the 27 January agreement remained the basis for American aid to France. The geographical situation of Indochina did not allow for the application of these agreements, which only referred to the Atlantic Pact. An agreement was signed by the United States, Cambodia, Laos, Vietnam and France on 23 December 1950 to manage mutual defence aid in Asia. This military support took the following forms: the delivery of military material stocked in the United States and sent to Europe (this was only end-item materials grouped within annual Mutual Aid Plans) and supplementary financial aid, called Additional Military Production, which functioned similarly to the Marshall Plan. Under these, conventions and bilateral aid were put into place between each Western European country on one side, and the United States or Canada on the other.

However, the two Franco-American crises over *off-shore* purchases of 1951 and 1952 demonstrated the weaknesses of this system. These crises were once again rooted in misunderstandings: thus, in 1951, the difficulties resulted from an American promise, made on 18 December 1950, to pay 200 million dollars before 30 June 1951.[29] The French thought that this aid would be in addition to Marshall Plan aid, but the Americans counted it as part of the European Recovery Program. If the French took the 200 million *off-shore* dollars for granted, the Americans requested a users programme over which they demanded oversight. These continual misunderstandings led Jules Moch to propose a common budget on 29 June 1951:

> We must absolutely move from an integrated army to an integrated budget. The parliaments of the various countries must vote for a budget that would no longer be American, English, or French budgets, but an international budget.[30]

The North Atlantic Council meeting in Lisbon vindicated him by adding a multilateral mechanism to bilateral aid: that of a common infrastructure within the framework of NATO. This mechanism was a partial (and the only) success of the common budget proposal that had originated in the French memorandum of 5 August 1950.[31]

However, the definition of the 1952–53 budget was again the cause of a serious diplomatic crisis, more important than that of 1951. Aside from the exceptional cases of Schuman, who was anxious about the strained Franco-American relations, notably over Tunisia and Morocco, plus the issue of aid, and Monnet, who tried to calm things down, the leaders of the two countries sunk into deepening hostility. In France, anti-Americanism became a theme of electoral campaigns based on the serious crisis of transatlantic relations. How did the two allies reach such a degree of tension? The American tone was brutal and contemptuous. Disappointed, the French dug their heels in with attitude of excessive national pride in relation to the nature of the requests.

This situation led the French delegation to the Atlantic Alliance to submit a memorandum to the Permanent Group on 16 September, and then one to the Council of Deputies on 22 September 1952. It proposed that on the basis of a critical examination of the military effort of each country, the expenses of each member be defined in accordance with norms applicable to everyone.[32] The North Atlantic Council decided that an annual review would be completed by a ministerial meeting.[33] Once again, in order to resolve a Franco-American quarrel, French leaders turned to the Atlantic Alliance.

Colonial policy: factor of discord

Another theme of continual discord between France and its Atlantic allies, notably the United States: the colonial question. For the leaders of the Fourth Republic, the continued engagement of France in colonial conflicts, in Indochina and then Algeria, diverted some French forces away from the European theatre. However, at the same time, French engagement in Indochina represented participation in the struggle against international Communism, for which the French expected recognition from their allies. Here again, there were increasing misunderstandings. The French felt that the struggle in Indochina should have been counted within the general French effort within NATO, whereas the United States considered it a separate issue. From these distant engagements came a progressive marginalization of France's role in the defence of the Central European theatre.

The Algerian conflict could not be compared to Indochina in this respect. In the first case, American policy followed a precise chronology, which followed that of the Cold War. Indeed, it was not until 1950, after the start of the Korean War, that the American administration became interested in Indochina. From then on, their interests, hoped for to that point by French leaders, became more and more difficult to handle for the leaders of the Fourth Republic. While military operations in Southeast Asia were presented to international public opinion as a contribution to the general effort in the defence of the free world against Communism, French leaders implicitly opened the door to other powers expressing themselves on the question. Since national interests were no longer the only stakes in the conflict, France could no longer be the sole master of its decisions. Once again, to better manage American tutelage, French leaders decided to submit the Indochina issue to the North Atlantic Council: they aimed to go beyond the framework of bilateral negotiations with the United States and Great Britain on aid in Asia, by gaining recognition from France's NATO allies of the international character of the struggle in Indochina, and to demonstrate France's role as a Great Power through this engagement, while its place within the EDC seemed to endanger this status through Germany's potential role.[34]

The result was satisfactory: allied representatives recognized the importance of the French struggle for the general interest of the Western powers. However, as expected, apart from the United States, who highlighted their contribution, no one intended to support France with anything except words.[35]

The Suez Crisis offers another example of the consequences of the tensions between the allies. While the events in the Suez illustrated the gap existing between the American position on one hand, and the British and French on the other, and offers an image of a divided Alliance, it was yet again within the framework of NATO that solutions to the bilateral tensions were sought. The work of the 'Three Wise Men' (Halvord Lange, Gaetano Martino and Lester B. Pearson) had begun before the crisis, but the report that they submitted to the North Atlantic Council on the ways and means of improving NATO cooperation in non-military areas, particularly with the aim of developing greater unity within the Alliance, was strongly influenced by Suez.[36]

Finally, in all of these examples, which are not exhaustive, when Franco-American relations had deteriorated, NATO served as the ultimate recourse to resolve these bilateral difficulties.

Conclusion: lasting French demands?

During the Fourth Republic it is evident that some of the logic that guided subsequent Gaullist polices was expressed by French leaders within the Alliance, albeit discreetly: national independence, rejection of the blocs and, of course, the struggle against

American tutelage and its corollary, European construction. These were expressed through specific demands.

- A tripartite leadership group, which recurred regularly in French requests in order to insure direct French influence on Alliance strategy-making (as far east as possible), and to ensure its leadership role over the other continental members of NATO. It was important to France to see its particular status within the Alliance recognized, justified by its key strategic position in defence plans, the installation on its territory of much of the Alliance's infrastructure and by France's global role. In this respect, there was an undeniable continuity between French demands surrounding the creation of the Permanent Group, its demands on the competences of this group, Bidault's High Atlantic Council idea and finally de Gaulle's 1958 memorandum.
- The European pillar, incarnated by the Brussels Pact or the EDC, which would also ensure France's continental leadership and a European solidarity vis-à-vis the United States and Great Britain.

We must thus nuance the image of a continual and 'resigned' adherence to American dominance by the first governments of the Fourth Republic. Transatlantic engagement was permanent, but even those French who demanded this engagement defended their own national interests with no less rigour, whether it was in confrontation with the Soviets or with their Western allies. This was sometimes done in bad faith, but it was always done with force.

It is nonetheless fundamental to note the Fourth Republic's constant loyalty to the Alliance. Transatlantic tensions never truly threatened this loyalty, rather it seems that NATO played a stabilizing role in the bilateral relations between France and the United States. At the worst point of Franco-American tensions over the negotiations of the off-shore contracts, the government turned to the Alliance. To overcome problems after the failure of the EDC, it was again towards NATO that the Mendès government turned. The president of the Council moreover judged it useful, immediately after the vote on 30 August, to make a declaration of loyalty to the Alliance before the National Assembly. It is also important to note that the Paris Accords not only sanctioned the entry of the FRG into the Alliance, but also reinforced the structures of the Alliance through enlarging its competences and deepening the powers of the Atlantic Council, despite the fact that this was hidden somewhat by the reactivation of the Western European Union. The same was true for the Suez Crisis. The Fourth Republic perceived the Atlantic Alliance as a multilateral recourse to overcome bilateral difficulties with the United States. It is this last point, without doubt, where the rupture between this and the Gaullist period appeared.

Notes

1 Figures such as Georges Bidault or Marshal Juin fit into this category.
2 For example, Robert Schuman or Jean de Lattre de Tassigny.
3 Michael M. Harrisson, *The Reluctant Ally: France and Atlantic Security*, (Baltimore: John Hopkins University Press, 1981); Irwin M. Wall, *L'influence américaine sur la politique française, 1945–1954*, (Paris: Balland, 1989).
4 One finds this action–reaction phenomenon at every stage of the genesis of the Alliance (the Prague coup–Treaty of Brussels; Berlin blockade–Treaty of Washington; Korean War–German rearmament; Sputnik–tactical nuclear weapons).

5 Georges-Henri Soutou, 'La perception du problème soviétique par le Quai d'Orsay entre 1945 et 1949', *Revue d'Allemagne*, no. 3, 1998.
6 Preamble to the Treaty of Dunkirk: 'preventing Germany from becoming again a menace to peace'
7 'Soutien aux peuples libres', 'La politique étrangère: l'aide à la Grèce et à la Turquie', *Notes documentaires et études*, 17 March 1947, no. 573, p. 6.
8 'I had spoken of an Atlantic Pact for the first time with De Gaulle in the autumn of 1945, and seeing the influence that the communists were gaining every day thanks to Soviet control developing in Europe, I thought that something needed to be done. Michelet, who was minister of the Armed Forces gave me his agreement [...] Bonnet implored me to make no contact with the Americans. The Communist ministers would be filled with rage, which would be a catastrophe. And he wrote to Gouin on the subject, and Gouin told Thorez. There was no question of an Atlantic Pact occurring until 1947', CARAN, 561AP1, papers of Georgette Elgey, account of an interview accorded by General Billotte to Georgette Elgey, 3 October 1963. See also Georges-Henri Soutou, 'Les Dirigeants français et l'entrée en guerre froide', *Trimestre du Monde*, 3e trimestre 1993, pp. 135–47.
9 MAE, Archives privées et papiers d'agents (APPA), Henri Bonnet, volume 1, lettre de Bidault à Marshall, remise le 4 mars 1948.
10 MAE, APPA, Henri Bonnet, volume 1, communication de l'ambassade des États-Unis d'Amérique à Paris, 13 mars 1948.
11 Harry Truman, 'Special Message to the Congress on the Threat to the Freedom of Europe,' 17 March 1947.
12 SHAT, 1Q26–4, Institut des hautes études de Défense nationale, section politique, travail en comité, sur le Pacte Atlantique, conférence d'introduction de Noël Henry, ministre plénipotentiaire, chef de la section politique, 15 février 1949.
13 Pierre Nora, Jacques Ozouf, René Rémond (ed), Vincent Auriol, *Journal du septennat, 1948,* (Paris: Colin, 1974), p. 690.
14 From 1949 onwards, neutralist intellectuals attacked NATO on the failure of the lack of an automatic clause in the Atlantic Pact. The fear of the United States not engaging in case of a war and staying outside of a conflict that they would have provoked through their bellicose attitude was very strong and was the primary source of resentment against the Americans. If the United States really intended to engage in case of war, why not officially recognize this?
15 The North Atlantic Treaty, Article 9, 4 April 1949, http://www.nato.int/cps/en/natolive/official_texts_17120.htm
16 Frédéric Bozo, *La France et l'OTAN*, (Paris: Masson, 1991), p. 35.
17 Jenny Raflik, 'La France et la genèse institutionnelle de l'Alliance atlantique, 1948–52', *Relations Internationales*, no. 131, été 2008.
18 Archives départementales de l'Aveyron, papiers Ramadier, 52J86/4, télégramme de Bonnet, Washington, metric, 13 août 1949.
19 'M. Georges Bidault propose la création d'un haut Conseil atlantique pour la paix', *Le Monde*, 18 avril 1950.
20 OTAN, IS002, *memorandum* du gouvernement français au gouvernement des États-Unis, D-D-26, confidentiel, 5 août 1950.
21 OTAN, IS002, réponses adressées au gouvernement des États-Unis au sujet de l'accroissement des efforts de défense et de l'assistance supplémentaire nécessaire à la mise en œuvre du programme de défense (doc D-D/6), memorandum additionnel du gouvernement français, D-D/34, très secret, 17 août 1950.
22 FNSP, BM133, 'Un nouveau pilier de la paix?', *Le Monde*, 6 avril 1949.
23 *Journal officiel de la République française, Assemblée Nationale, compte rendu intégral des séances*, 26 juillet 1949.
24 SHAT, 6R2, lettre du vice-amiral Lemonnier, chef d'État-major général de la Marine, au général d'armée Lechères, président du CCEM, no. 425EMG, très secret, 16 novembre 1948.
25 AN, 561AP3, interview du général Stehlin par Georgette Elgey, 22 janvier 1966.
26 Pierre Mélandri, 'Les États-Unis et le plan Pleven, octobre 1950–juillet 1951', *Relations Internationales*, no. 11, 1977, p. 205; J. Martin, 'The American Decision to Rearm Germany', in Harold Stein (ed.), *American Civil Military Decisions. A Book of Case Studies,* (Birmingham, AB: University of Alabama Press, 1963), pp. 647–51.
27 Frédéric Bozo, *La France et l'OTAN*, (Paris: Masson, 1991), p. 41.
28 SHM, 136GG2/14, Historique de l'aide alliée depuis 1950, cours supérieur de logistique prononcé à l'Ecole de Guerre Navale par le contrôleur de 1ère classe Appert, 26 novembre 1954.

29 MAEF, Service des Pactes, 81, aide mémoire du gouvernement des États-Unis, Washington, 18 décembre 1950.
30 AN, 484 AP 24, bilan d'un an au ministère de la Défense nationale, 29 juin 1951.
31 OTAN, AC/29-D/3, Groupe de travail sur la définition de l'Infrastructure commune, rapport au Conseil, 20 janvier 1953.
32 OTAN, IS002, *memorandum* de la délégation française, CM(52)78, secret, 22 septembre 1952.
33 PRO, FO371, 105840, cabinet, Mutual Aid Committee, Briefs for Ministers for Talks with French Ministers, objectives in 1952 NATO Annual Review, note by the treasury, confidential, MAC(53) 48, 7 February 1953.
34 CARAN, papiers Auriol, 552AP46, PV du CDN du 11 décembre 1952. no. 706CDN du 16 janvier 1953, très secret, exemplaire 18/30.
35 OTAN, C-R (52)38, 16 décembre 1952.
36 Pitman, 'The consequences of the Suez Crisis for the Transatlantic System', intervention présentée lors du colloque organisé par le Service Historique de la défense en novembre 2006, à paraître.

5

The Fifth Republic and NATO

Odd-man out or the only country in step?

Georges-Henri Soutou

It is widely believed the French Fifth Republic has been cool towards NATO, if not actually opposed to it. French foreign policy under Charles de Gaulle took a specific position inside the North Atlantic Alliance (France would be allied, but not integrated), a position which was later repeated by Spain when it joined the Alliance, and was briefly suggested by Moscow in 1990 as an option for reunified Germany. 'The French solution' was often considered a special case, if not an outright oddity, explained by the idiosyncrasy of the 'Grande Nation'.

There is no dispute that many in France, even at the government level, felt the same way. They were quite happy with their special status, and did not wish to see it extended to other Alliance members, certainly not to the Federal Republic of Germany: France strongly believed, even under the Fourth Republic, the purpose of NATO was to control Germany, in turn deterring the Soviet Union. Although integration was, therefore, seen by many French officials as a hindrance to French independence, it was a useful means to restrict Germany, and yet simultaneously harness its power to contain the Soviet Union.

At the same time others believed (including de Gaulle himself, at times) that the French position was not merely accidental, politically convenient or even self-serving, but rather to have evolved from the idea the Alliance could be valid, in Kantian terms, for all its members. Many French sincerely believed they had the best concept for NATO, and it was other countries which did not want to fall in step. They stressed in the great crises of the Cold War (Berlin in 1958, Cuba in 1962, the Pershing crisis in Germany and the speech of François Mitterrand to the Bundestag in January 1983) France had been one of the staunchest supporters of the USA and the Alliance. As Valéry Giscard d'Estaing told US Vice President Walter Mondale in January 1977, traditionally the French nurtured good relations with America, but they did not like to be 'overcrowded or manipulated; [...] with some adaptation [they] are probably the most reliable allies of the US, because [they] are a serious people'.[1]

It could be argued there was a French concept for the Atlantic Alliance for which, at times, Paris tried to gain approval from the other NATO countries. The concept was such that the Alliance would remain an organization of sovereign States, without any loss of independence or freedom of decision for its members. Integration was acceptable at command level in times of war, yet it was always rescindable (the French expression for this concept is *mise à disposition opérationelle*, which could be translated as 'temporary subordination to an allied command for a defined operation or set of operations'). Moreover, the Alliance should not impair the development of a European foreign policy and defence entity. Generally speaking, if taken too far, instituted in peacetime, integration had the effect of depriving national governments of their democratic legitimacy (based on their independence at the international level), leading to a reduced commitment to national defence in each country, and thus diminishing the overall effectiveness of the Western defence system.

The need for national independence inside the Alliance was also rationalized at the nuclear level. Nuclear weapons could not be shared; their only possible use was deterrence ('graduated response' was too dangerous for the Europeans, as it left the possibility for war in Europe, and it gave the USA an opportunity to downgrade their commitment). The existence of several national nuclear decision centres created uncertainty for the adversary, thus enhancing deterrence.

The Alliance was certainly directed against the Soviet threat. Founded on common values, it was not established with the aim of producing a Western bloc under American leadership, which would harden the divide of the Cold War, possibly blocking any evolution towards a West European Union and thus a new security system for the whole continent which could overcome the Cold War. The Atlantic Alliance was acceptable, but atlanticism was not. 'Out-of-area' was not unthinkable, but only provided the European allies, particularly Great Britain and France, had their say, and that it remained in existence on an *ad hoc* basis (and did not become a substitute for the UN).

Moreover, prior to 1958, the French believed division of labour (each country doing what it could do best) to be better than integration, which was perceived as demotivating. The idea was the French, like the British, had a special role in world politics because of their global responsibilities and relatively important military establishment among Alliance members, save the USA.

These views held credence in Paris, notwithstanding variations, from 1958 to 2007. This essay explores this continuity, and also some occasions when Paris attempted to persuade its partners to agree to reform the Alliance along these lines. President Sarkozy announced in 2007 that France would rejoin the integrated NATO structures, provided a European decision centre be accepted inside the Alliance. It is argued in some quarters that if such a reform were actually achieved, it would not be a complete change in direction. Yet other observers see in President Sarkozy's move a momentous change in French policy. The jury is still out, but this work will clarify the argument.[2] A complete study, reaching beyond the parameters of a synthetic chapter, should stress the different approaches to the problem in France, emanating from many different strains of a political, yet social or ideological, nature. During the Cold War, and at least through the 1970s, atlanticist Socialists and, on the Right, conservatives or even Gaullists were unenthusiastic about NATO integration not because they were reticent about the Alliance, but because they feared the USA was far too willing to strike a deal with the Soviets – a very Gaullist theme, but which could be understood in some parts of the Gaullist rank and file in a far more anti-Soviet and thus 'Western' frame of mind, than the General himself intended.

The problem of NATO command integration and French independence

An issue at the forefront of the Fifth Republic, generally speaking and in particular, pertaining to NATO was the full independence of French foreign policy and defence.

This strongly held conviction derives from a long history: particularly from the Second World War, but dating also from some humiliating experiences under the Fourth Republic.

NATO was not what the French had first anticipated

In 1948–49, when the West discussed the Atlantic Alliance, the French imagined it would rest on close cooperation between the Big Three: the USA, Great Britain and France. Their belief was such that France would finally be able to join the US–British Combined Chiefs of Staff group, founded during the war, which the French erroneously believed had not been disbanded after 1945. They ascribed a paramount importance to the Standing Group in Washington, which was, as early as 1949, an American–British–French military staff entrusted with the provision of overall strategic advice for the various Alliance bodies. The French believed that they would be full participants in the overall definition of Western strategy. Although understanding perfectly that the USA would be the lead country, they expected equal status with the UK, the actual yardstick of international influence for the French well into the 1960s.

The French were quickly disappointed: for grand strategy and for more specific issues (such as sea power, closely linked to world strategy) there was an 'Anglosphere', in which the French were not really allowed to participate. This situation became more acute when, in 1954, NATO adopted a nuclear strategy for the defence of Europe. This came to a head at the Bermuda summit in December 1953, when Eisenhower and Churchill refused to grant France a seat at the head table of the Alliance.[3]

The issue came to a head during the Suez crisis (1956) when the French felt Washington had let them down: what was seen in Paris not only as a fight against Nasser to help the war in Algeria, was also an operation on behalf of the West to prevent the Soviets from setting foot in the Middle East.[4] The lack of support from the USA for the war in Algeria completed the picture: before de Gaulle came back to power in June 1958, there were few supporters of NATO in France, and the last governments of the Fourth Republic had, from 1957, begun to organize a common defence system with Germany and Italy that included nuclear weapons.

It could be argued that de Gaulle ensured French participation in NATO by, upon his return to power, shelving the most taxing part of the defence agreements concluded with Bonn and Rome since 1957 and by proclaiming French solidarity with the Western allies and the Germans when the Berlin crisis started (with the Khrushchev ultimatum of November 1958).[5] De Gaulle also kept France in NATO by instantly reducing the communist vote from 25 to 15 per cent and by swiftly silencing the extremely nationalist part of the military and political spectrum, where, contrary to what is generally believed, there was little love lost for the 'Anglo-Saxons'.

The September 1958 memorandum

Upon his return to power, de Gaulle convened the Defence Council, on 17 June 1958, stating the transformation he sought regarding NATO. He carved out a worldwide role for NATO, so as to include areas of particular interest to France, such as Africa and the Middle East. France was to be allowed to share planning for all theatres (including nuclear targeting) with London and Washington.[6] Finally, NATO must be revised in order to end the integration of French forces.[7] Those ideas, and the fresh experience of Anglo-American intervention in Lebanon in July without consulting Paris, led to de Gaulle's 17 September memorandum to Dwight D. Eisenhower and Harold Macmillan. De Gaulle asked for both the enlargement of the Atlantic field of action to what is known today as 'out-of-area' and French participation in global strategic planning on the same footing as the USA and UK, including for nuclear weapons.[8]

De Gaulle was serious at the time

The 1958 memorandum has been frequently described as a manoeuvre to force the Anglo-Americans to come out into the open and provide proof they did not really want to treat France as an equal. According to this view, de Gaulle anticipated the probable failure of his memorandum, and intended from the beginning to use the anticipated failure as justification to move to a more aggressive agenda.[9] Early on there were signs the new French president was about to reduce the scope of NATO integration: as early as March 1959 French ships in the Mediterranean were removed from integrated NATO command. However, at the same time, there is no doubt the French memorandum of September 1958 was serious: the papers of General Ely (then Chief of the General Staff) in the Military Archives at Vincennes prove that tripartite cooperation 'out-of-area', especially in Africa, was studied in earnest (Ely had been the first French representative at the Standing Group).[10] At a so-called Defence Council on 31 January 1959, a meeting attended by the military chiefs, Prime Minister Michel Debré, Foreign Minister Maurice Couve de Murville and Minister of Armed Forces Pierre Guillaumat, de Gaulle explained he wanted discussions with the USA and Great Britain to set guidelines in advance of concerted military action in different parts of the world, including guidelines for the eventual use of nuclear weapons, so that one 'would not sit helpless at the first crisis coming out of the blue'.[11]

As for NATO integration, during that meeting de Gaulle was initially opposed to it, accusing advocates of 'denationalizing the defence of a country'. General Ely had to explain that de Gaulle misunderstood the scope of NATO integration, which was more limited than he had imagined. For instance, the French Tactical Air Force Command, otherwise known as CATAC (NATO air units were just beginning the process of integration), could be withdrawn at any time. The real problem for France was the procurement of nuclear weapons, which would go a long way towards ameliorating the situation. Finally, de Gaulle accepted the existence of NATO commands, provided forces remained national and could be eventually withdrawn. Even if later in the same year Ely regretted Paris's rejection of NATO-integrated air defence, or the withdrawal of the French navy from the Mediterranean NATO command: the positions then advanced were still very far from 1966.[12]

An intriguing document from December 1961 details a conversation between a Quai d'Orsay diplomat and de Gaulle about NATO integration.[13] De Gaulle states he is not so much against integration *per se* as against what it had actually become inside the Alliance: 'there was actually no integration, but one or two superpowers which decided everything and the others were to obey without consideration of their national imperatives'. 'Integration died under its own excesses', underlined the General, because 'first-rate European officers and good national contingents were swamped inside an enormous and amorphous Anglo-Saxon coalition system, under an American general taking, for his most important decisions (about the use of nuclear and thermo-nuclear weapons), only the orders of the US President'.

De Gaulle then described the kind of 'so-called integration' he could accept:

> a participation of French generals in great commands, a participation of French officers in interallied staff, the putting at the disposal of the coalition of major national units, provided that the strategy and war plans of the said coalition or alliance have been settled and approved beforehand by the governments, which have to answer, for their national defence, in last resort to God, to their people and to History.

It must be understood though 'that the national forces components put at the disposal of the coalition could be taken back if a national imperative were to transcend the interests of the coalition'. It should be pointed out here that most clearly de Gaulle was convinced that that system would apply to *all member countries*: it was a matter of general principle, not just a strictly French agenda.

Clearly, it was not exactly the kind of integration which had evolved inside NATO, and the use of the word 'coalition' as a synonym for 'alliance' is very telling. But it was not so far from the actual NATO system: apart from German forces, which already stood under integrated NATO command in peacetime, other national forces (apart from the air defence of Europe) came under NATO command only in the case of war, after a decision by their national governments.

At the same time, de Gaulle's model was not far from the Brussels Pact military arrangements of 1948: its scope was more encompassing. It accepted the very important fact that units put at the disposal of the Alliance would then no longer be under national command, but under the different NATO commands, where, of course, French officers would participate. The French expression for this concept is *mise à disposition opérationnelle*, which goes beyond earmarking and cooperation. This model did not provide for the certainty of French participation, but nor did the NATO practice of integration, as such. The only feature of NATO defence which could provide reasonable confidence that all members would participate in the common defence was the interlocking of troops from various allies on the central front. NATO could have lived with such a concept. All the more because this concept included, as we have seen, a permanent and important participation of French officers in all NATO staff, also a point of major importance.

De Gaulle's opposition to integration was first and foremost politically motivated, because he felt it was an essential instrument of American hegemony over Europe. About practical aspects, however, he remained flexible for a time.

De Gaulle's conception of strategic division of labour among allies: a general concept

De Gaulle was convinced that defence tasks should not be integrated, but rather divided among major allies according to their geostrategic situation and military capabilities. As he explained to Konrad Adenauer on 29 July 1960, Germany constituted the vanguard (clearly in his view a rather expendable one); France the main line of resistance, but fully involved in the Battle of Germany; and Great Britain would be in charge of protecting the Northern Flank and keeping sea lanes open. As for the USA, they were 'the reserve, the arsenal'.[14]

Needless to say, that concept went directly against NATO as it had evolved since the Korean War. However, it was sincere (and never completely left Paris, although it was unclear which tasks 'smaller' but crucial allies, like the Dutch, were supposed to fulfil): de Gaulle was convinced each ally would contribute more effectively to nationally assigned tasks rather than to an anonymous integrated system, lacking clear national responsibilities.

De Gaulle's stance hardens

After several developments (the Multilateral Force saga, the evolution of East–West relations and the war in Vietnam), de Gaulle announced in March 1966 that France would leave the NATO integrated command structure, and thus all NATO staff and foreign troops would have to leave France inside the year.[15] Beyond that decision in itself, there was an indisputable hardening of de Gaulle's views about the very nature of NATO: at a press conference on 28 October 1966, he set the March decision to leave the integrated structure of NATO in the context of France's recovery of full independence, its world role against US hegemony, and finally against 'both hegemonies'. At the same time he stated he 'most sincerely believed that the US would find it in their own interest' to follow suit.[16] In his view, the French model for the Alliance was valid also for other partners.

However, de Gaulle quickly discovered a NATO reality: since the 1954 Paris Agreements, the presence of French forces in Germany was determined by the Atlantic Alliance, not the 1945 occupation rights. Bonn was quite clear: without an agreement between Paris and SACEUR (Supreme Allied Commander in Europe), French troops would have to leave;[17] de Gaulle had actually wished for such an agreement from the beginning. On 2 June 1966, he explained to the Defence Council what he wanted: a staffing agreement between the French chief of staff, General Ailleret, and SACEUR, General Lemnitzer.[18] Such an agreement was finally reached in September 1967.

For long kept secret, the Ailleret–Lemnitzer exchange of letters has now been published.[19] It was actually much more restrictive than what was previously believed: this discussion was very strictly limited to French forces in Germany. There would be no French participation in NATO staff, neither in peacetime nor in wartime, even if France decided to join the fight. The only staff would be liaison staff, in limited numbers during peacetime. NATO commands would get operational control (whereby one should remember that the French word *contrôle* has a less stringent meaning than the English control: the real meaning is more 'authority') upon French forces when decided by the French Commander in Chief in Germany, but only through the French national command and only in the scope of war plans agreed beforehand.

It was also stated the role of French forces would be limited to that of a 'regional reserve', meaning they would essentially be mobilized near their peacetime bases. Of course, it was impossible to go further, because the engagement of those forces remained a question mark until the end. This dovetailed with the French tactical nuclear 'last warning' concept, which French staff studied assiduously from 1968 onwards. The national role of French forces in Germany, beyond potentially a short phase of cooperation with NATO, would be to hold off the Soviet advance long enough to apply the 'last warning' tactical nuclear strike. Needless to say, no other parties to the Alliance, especially not the Germans or Americans, were enthusiastic about this strategy. However, the French were convinced the new 'graduated deterrence' strategy of NATO (discussed since 1963 but only adopted in 1967, once the French had left the command structure, and thus forgoing their veto power) was senseless and dangerous. It was a national nuclear stance, but in Paris's view it could be meaningful at the Alliance level.

Two major differences with the views pronounced by de Gaulle in December 1961 were the absence of the French from NATO staff, even in wartime, and the fact that NATO commands, if granted operational control over French forces in wartime, would lead French forces through French national commands.

A major problem was Paris wanted to retain its freedom of action until the last moment (and internal French documents show de Gaulle meant it, even intending to see how the first actions against the Warsaw Pact turned out before intervening).[20] Beyond that basic uncertainty, the French decision, and the way in which it was implemented, posed the allies two difficult problems. First, how could European airspace now be effectively controlled, given the independence of the French air defence, and, moreover, the independent (even if cooperating) alert and communications systems? (Although the French did remain in the NADGE (NATO Air Defence Ground Environment) radar system, so they could be alerted as early as possible in case of Soviet air attack). A second, and less well-known problem: NATO logistics (including pipelines which went from the Atlantic ports to Germany through French territory). The French consistently refused to give any assurance in advance about the Alliance's ability to use these facilities, which was crippling. Even when he tried to repair the relations with Washington, President Georges Pompidou remained adamant on that point: nothing should prejudice the French decision to apply Article V.[21] NATO had to reroute its logistics through German ports, much nearer to the eventual frontline.

The nuclear issue

It is well known, in de Gaulle's view, that France's acquisition of a nuclear deterrent was a major factor necessitating a key transformation of NATO. One frequent argument to justify the French move in 1966 was that decisions about the use of nuclear weapons could not be shared. Also, there was a reaffirmation of national sovereignty, difficult to reconcile with any kind of integrated alliance. Many interpreted, and still interpret today, this position as the epitome of French policy at the time: a sort of neutralism between the two blocs, supported by the national nuclear deterrent. Additionally, it is true in operational terms that the problem of nuclear weapons, and particularly so-called 'tactical' nuclear weapons, hampered any effort to coordinate Alliance plans with eventual French participation because of widely divergent nuclear doctrines.[22]

There is another explanation: the French sincerely believed, beyond their own national interest, that nuclear weapons (even so-called 'tactical' ones) had only one possible purpose: deterrence. In 1963–64 they rejected the so-called 'graduated deterrence' or 'flexible response' (it was a major accelerator contributing to the 1966 decision) because they feared two consequences: the reduction of the US commitment to couple their central strategic systems with the defence of Europe, which could in French eyes only lessen their deterrent effect and thus enhance the chances of war; and also the possibility the new doctrine could lead to destructive and inconclusive nuclear war in Europe.[23]

The French were consistently opposed to the notion of tactical nuclear war (apart, perhaps, from two short episodes at the beginning of Giscard d'Estaing's presidency, and in 1986–88 during the François Mitterrand–Jacques Chirac 'cohabitation'). They were opposed for two reasons: first, it ruined the very concept of nuclear deterrence and thus opened the possibility of a still devastating protracted conventional war in Europe. Second, it was not feasible: it is impossible to plan, command and control a series of nuclear exchanges beyond a compact tactical salvo in order to eventually restore deterrence (the so-called *ultime avertissement*) because of the disruptions caused by those weapons: the collateral damage and fall-out and the electromagnetic pulses which would block all radar and wireless transmissions; and the devastating psychological consequences to the soldiers themselves.

At the time of the discussions about the Soviet SS 20 leading to the NATO 'double decision' of December 1979, the French were adamant: one should not speak of 'Euro-strategic weapons' or imagine a sort of regional deterrence or exchange between US weapons based in Europe and the Soviet Union. The only serious issue in their view was the coupling of the European theatre with the US central strategic system.[24]

President François Mitterrand was much clearer regarding this issue than his predecessors, although his France possessed many more nuclear warheads than before. De Gaulle may have wavered,[25] Giscard also; there was a notion of using the tactical nuclear component both to provide the 'ultime avertissement' and to wipe out 'a whole segment of the Soviet manoeuvre', which was ambiguous; and there were recurring military temptations in that direction. Mitterrand restored a strictly deterrent nuclear stance for France itself: he rebranded tactical weapons as 'pre-strategic' weapons and reacted forcefully to the 1990 NATO decision to consider nuclear weapons as 'weapons of last resort', which in his view opened a broad avenue to actual war-fighting, conventional or even nuclear.[26] Once again, in his view it was not just a problem of divergent strategies between France and the Alliance: he felt that NATO nuclear strategy was misguided, ineffective and dangerous by itself, beyond the particular French nuclear agenda.

There emerges a very clear French model for the nuclear aspects of NATO, of course self-serving but in Paris's view applicable to all NATO members: only deterrence is admissible; it is provided by the central strategic systems; nuclear weapons cannot be shared; the existence of the French (and the British) national nuclear deterrent reinforced the security of the Alliance because it complicated, through the inherent uncertainty of the decisions of Paris (and London), any possible scheme in Moscow to wage war under the nuclear threshold. This was officially stated as Alliance policy in the Ottawa Declaration of June 1974, which became a mantra for the French (and the British).

Making the relationship with NATO bearable

Evidently the French decision in 1966 confronted NATO with serious problems. Apart from politics and strategy, it was mostly about nuts and bolts such as logistics. There was no progress in these fields under President Pompidou, who studiously avoided any such commitment, even regarding the possibility of NATO using pipelines traversing French territory, so as to avoid compromising France's pro-choice stance.[27]

Some movement first occurred after 1974, under President Giscard d'Estaing. In July, the Valentin–Ferber agreements extended the Ailleret–Lemnitzer agreements of 1967 to the whole First Army (five divisions, not just the two stationed in Germany). On 10 July 1975, Giscard d'Estaing explained to Henry Kissinger, without renouncing its freedom of choice, Paris could prepare for the eventual engagement of its forces with NATO, including the use of tactical nuclear weapons.[28]

Indeed, the new Chief of Staff, General de Méry, wrote in the June 1976 issue of *Défense nationale*, that, although retaining its freedom of decision, France could participate in the forward battle of the Alliance, thus moving from the strict position as second-line reserve it had maintained since 1964. Of course, this statement was much criticized. Despite the fact the mood towards NATO was generally improved in Giscard d'Estaing's France (one of his close advisers, Ambassador François de Rose, published *La France et la défense de l'Europe* in 1976, supporting closer cooperation with the Alliance and stating, which goes to the heart of the argument presented here, there was no real contradiction between French and NATO strategy), nothing very practical seems to have come out of that evolution, or of the discussions which took place between Méry and General Haig (SACEUR) about the vexing question of coordination of tactical nuclear weapons on both sides.[29]

There were discussions with Washington about logistic facilities on French territory in wartime; we do not know to what extent those discussions were fruitful.[30] We do, however, know that several agreements were reached with the USA, particularly with Navy staff.[31]

François Mitterrand, after 1981, and at least until the end of the Cold War, followed a more independent line towards NATO.[32] Whether under the more engaging attitude of Giscard or the more restrictive attitude of Mitterrand, the French were sincerely convinced, because of the different agreements signed since 1967, that their special position in the Alliance would not cause any serious problems to their partners.[33] It is a view which can be disputed, but it was undoubtedly sincere and contributed to the French conviction that their model for NATO was not just a national peculiarity, but could be valid for other countries as well (but not Germany: when President Mitterrand feared, at the beginning of 1983, that Bonn under the pressures of the Pershing question could be tempted by some kind of neutrality, he flew to Bonn for his famous Bundestag speech on 20 January, in which he stressed the importance of the Atlantic Alliance for both countries).[34]

Since 1990, creeping back inside NATO

At first, Mitterrand doubted NATO would survive the Cold War, and he decided in 1990 to evacuate the majority of French forces stationed in Germany. Additionally, he opposed two important NATO undertakings that year: the formation of a multinational corps and the adoption of an 'out-of-area' agenda. Mitterrand evidently followed a very Gaullist line against those who wanted to rejuvenate the Alliance. Soon the French realized two things: first, despite what they had believed in 1990, NATO was not going to wither; and, second, their special status in the Alliance was not aiding them in maximizing their dividends of the Cold War (a divided Germany, an automatic guarantee from the USA, generally speaking a bigger role than otherwise). As early as 1992, when the Franco-German Eurocorps (which was conceived as the nucleus of a future European defence force) was created, the French understood its command would be fraught with insuperable problems if France did not inch closer to NATO. Moreover, in 1993, in the wake of the Yugoslav crisis and the NATO engagement in Bosnia, Mitterrand decided France would once again take part in some sessions of the military committee of NATO.[35] In order to further the European defence identity, so dear to the French, and in order to convince the Germans and to calm the many NATO countries opposed to French views about European Security and Defence Policy (the so-called *Europe-puissance*), Paris realized it had to warm to NATO. The last move by President Sarkozy at the Strasbourg Atlantic Council of April 2009 can be seen as the completion of this long evolution.[36]

At the time, Paris only stood at the very beginning of that evolution. Of course, Mitterrand's views were disputed among French specialists, some of them believing after the end of the Cold War that France should move faster towards integration into NATO. A group of retired high-ranking military officers and diplomats, along with some academics and a few opposition (at the time, conservative) politicians, called *Renouveau Défense*, circulated a paper in chosen circles in December 1991 under the title *La France et l'Alliance atlantique: le faux problème de l'intégration*. The thrust of the paper was to dispel the bogey of integration: French forces were, in fact, already cooperating with the Alliance to a greater extent than most French people realized, and it was detrimental to French influence to abstain from all integrated structures. Yet, this was a minority view, even in conservative circles. When, in 1993, after the general elections, President Mitterrand was forced to accept a new period of 'cohabitation' with a conservative government led by Edouard Balladur, the Defence White Book of 1994 remained quite orthodox. France had not changed its position since 1966, and, regardless, with the end of the Cold War, NATO was bound to evolve towards a French conception of the entity, and a European defence identity was the most pressing issue. However, there was an opening: when French forces were involved, and on an *ad hoc* basis, French foreign and defence ministers and chiefs of staff could now participate in meetings of NATO councils.[37] Yet, it was still quite an aloof stance, with the general idea in Paris that NATO and European defence were competitors rather than partners, and with the delusion that, ultimately, with the end of the Cold War, Europeans would support the French and that Americans would be less adamant in defending an integrated NATO as it had existed since the Korean War.

The problem of a European pillar inside or beside the Alliance

The balance between France's European project and France's NATO commitment has been at the heart of the matter since the beginning. I have shown elsewhere that for de Gaulle, as early as 1958, NATO reform and the formation of a 'European personality in foreign policy and defence', to use his expression, were both sides of the same coin. De Gaulle envisioned a strong system of military cooperation among the Six, which would then, as a group, conclude agreements with Washington; it had been one of the objectives of the Fouchet Plan in 1961–62, and then of the Elysée Treaty in 1963. De Gaulle had to put the issue on the backburner, yet he never abandoned it.[38] An option for action was described in an officious article, written by a work group with near official status, in the October 1965 issue of *Politique étrangère*. It suggested the juxtaposition of a Western alliance without integration, dealing essentially with nuclear cooperation between the three nuclear powers of the Alliance, and a much closer European group, which would constitute a true European pillar inside the Alliance.[39]

It is worthwhile noting here how the idea of restructuring the Alliance around a cooperative system with the USA and a European pillar inside NATO emerges again and again: it did so at the time of the negotiations in view of the Maastricht Treaty (1992), and, again, when President Chirac suggested France could return to the integrated command if NATO agreed to recognize a European defence identity (1995–96). This idea is once again gaining momentum: apparently some (and not only the French) are currently suggesting that the USA and the European Union (EU) should sign a treaty of alliance.[40]

After the Cold War, the problem of restructuring NATO with a European pillar became pressing once again, in the context of the preparation of the Maastricht Treaty. It was so because Mitterrand wished to keep reunified Germany firmly inside the European framework. On 6 December 1990, Mitterrand and Helmut Kohl wrote a joint letter to their European partners, suggesting the main features of what was to become the EU with the entry into force of the Maastricht Treaty two years later. There would ultimately be a 'common foreign policy' and a 'common defence'. However, Paris and Bonn diverged on one capital issue: for the French, the European defence system should evolve from the WEU and thus be independent from NATO; for the Germans, it would have to evolve as a European pillar inside NATO. The issue was obfuscated in the joint letter, which retained both ideas, and still remained unresolved in the final Maastricht Treaty; it became even more complex with the proviso the WEU should establish strong links with NATO, all the more so that Great Britain would not accept any kind of European defence system outside NATO.

There is no doubt Mitterrand was engaging in political manoeuvres: he was convinced, despite his concessions to the German and British position, that an autonomous European defence was necessary and would bring a deep transformation of NATO (11 April 1991 speech at the Ecole militaire in Paris). The problem was, of course, to convince the partners to accept France's European scheme. The preceding ones, including the Fouchet Plan and the first French version of Maastricht, had failed because nobody wished to cross the USA and because Germany easily deciphered the French ulterior motives of leadership in Europe. It had been clear since 1961 a European defence pillar *inside* NATO was not inconceivable, even if difficult to achieve, but *outside* NATO was out of the question.

Mitterrand realized it and, deliberately, on 14 January 1991, told John Major the USA wanted to reinforce their influence in Europe, and that he believed an independent European defence was necessary, but that for the time being 'NATO was a declining reality' and 'European defence a growing virtuality'. For years it would be neither necessary nor advisable to make a choice.[41]

When Chirac became President in 1995, he tried to cut the Gordian knot. He decided to break the deadlock by having France first rejoin NATO, and then working within NATO to promote a European defence identity inside rather than outside the Atlantic Alliance. Chirac's proposal, put forth in 1995 and 1996, would have fully returned France to NATO's integrated command structure, which France had left in 1966. NATO, in turn, would recognize the existence of a European identity inside the Alliance and establish a special European chain of command within the different NATO staff, allowing the Europeans to use NATO assets in operations in which the Americans chose not to participate. That compromise was accepted and promulgated by the Atlantic Council in Berlin in June 1996,[42] but it ultimately failed because of a major disagreement between Paris and Washington about the commanding officer for NATO's Mediterranean forces (headquartered in Naples.) The Americans wanted to retain the position (the American admiral in Naples was also the commander of the Sixth Fleet) while the French felt it should go to a European admiral.

Beyond that surface difference the real reason for this new Franco-American clash lay in diverging ulterior motives on both sides. Almost certainly France wished to retain, through an agreement with NATO promoting a European defence set-up, a greater weight in Washington than reunified Germany, and to continue to distinguish itself from its Eastern neighbour by its prime world role at the highest level of the Alliance, on par with Washington and London.[43] Comparatively, Washington was convinced it should keep a tight grip on NATO as an instrument of regional and global security against the new threats arising after the end of the Cold War, consistent with the 'New Concept for NATO' adopted in Washington on 25 April 1999. It bears noting this New Concept explicitly opened the possibility of 'out-of-area' action for NATO forces acting without a UN mandate, a feature of the new strategy the French tried hard to tone down. In any event, the tentative Franco-American agreement of 1996 ultimately failed.[44] Of course that failure did not prevent close Franco-American cooperation in Bosnia in 1995 and in Kosovo in 1999 (in a NATO framework). But the lack of a real solution to deep-seated Franco-American differences, including coming to grips with the relationship between NATO and a European foreign policy and defence identity, greatly contributed to the transatlantic break over Iraq in 2002–3. The French attempted, once again, to explain that their proposal was in the best interest of all partners, yet they still retained ulterior motives, or at least had not been convincing enough.

In 2003, Chirac, in the wake of the Iraq crisis, reverted to a more Gaullist approach. This aim was relaunched on 22 November 2002, with a new Franco-German proposal to the EU suggesting the adoption of a clause of mutual assistance between members of the EU and the establishment of a core group of countries willing to collaborate more closely in matters of security and defence; the joint proposal also suggested an increase in cooperation regarding armaments.[45] This led to a summit meeting in Brussels between the leaders of France, Germany, Belgium and Luxembourg at the end of April 2003, endorsing those proposals and proposing the establishment of a European military staff independent of NATO.

Of course, it was widely noted the Brussels summit took place without the participation of Great Britain, despite the fact that its military contribution would be essential and that Prime Minister Tony Blair had been instrumental in relaunching the idea of a European defence with the Saint Malo Declaration of December 1998 (signed by Blair and Chirac).[46] Blair's absence from the Brussels summit was a result of the deep European rift induced by the Iraq crisis, and it is certain that a majority of European countries were not willing to follow the French lead if it meant setting up a European defence system outside NATO. Additionally, Washington did everything to torpedo the notion of an independent European command.

Finally, at the European summit of Brussels in December 2003, a compromise was reached. It did not go so far as to set up a true operational staff for the EU independent from NATO, as the French and Germans had envisioned in April, mainly due to Anglo-American opposition. Notwithstanding, it was decided to form an operational nucleus (but not a command) inside the pre-existing European staff, which would advise the European Council on strategic matters. That nucleus would provide operational plans for the national commands which would be in charge of eventual EU operations. The EU was making slow, yet deliberate, progress towards an independent command capability.[47]

President Nicolas Sarkozy's 2007 initiative, whereby France would join the integrated command structure, and, in exchange, a European defence identity inside NATO would be clearly recognized, could be seen not so much as a new departure than as the accomplishment of a long process, and as a final reconciliation of all Alliance members with the most palatable (and in some respect the most permanent) parts of the French agenda.

The overall Atlantic environment

Of course, the French position towards NATO was not determined only by considerations about integration, the chain of command and the European pillar. There was a wider agenda. The very crucial issue of 'out-of-area' extension elicited very different French reactions as time passed (but, on the other hand, also from on part of the USA): in 1958 de Gaulle wanted that extension, but after 1965 and the onset of the Vietnam War he most strongly opposed it. Pompidou was against, but Giscard d'Estaing was a champion of the issue, wishing that President Carter would engage more in Africa. Mitterrand was absolutely against, and would have preferred NATO to wither after the end of the Cold War. The nicest double-step was danced by Chirac, who in 1999 supported NATO intervention in Kosovo without a UN mandate and took the reverse position in 2003. Now, with the French Defence White Book of 2007 and President Sarkozy's position, 'out-of-area' is *in* again.

Yet, on other issues, the French have been remarkably consistent. If they have at times accepted a sober recognition of common Western values as one of the fundamentals of the Atlantic Alliance (but the current president was the first to go as far in that direction), there has been continuing strong opposition to a more ideological vision of atlanticism. The French (meaning the elites, as well as a majority of the population) have consistently preferred a more realistic view of NATO, resulting in strenuous opposition of 'bloc to bloc' negotiations, in order not to consolidate the Cold War divide which was one of their main reasons for not participating in the multilateral balanced forces reduction negotiations. Furthermore, after the end of the Cold War until the Sarkozy presidency, anything which would seemingly pit the 'West' against the rest of the world in a sort of 'culture clash' was vehemently avoided.

Another major issue has been the dollar. De Gaulle was convinced the world currency role of the dollar was another powerful means other than NATO to promote American hegemony, in particular because Washington did not have to finance the US world role, but could rather borrow the money without problem. This was the rationale for his public stance against the gold standard in 1965; however, his successors pursued that line in a more astute way (the world economy did have to be financed in some way), as Pompidou tried to do at the time of the 'Nixon shock' in 1971, Giscard with the EMS in 1979 and Mitterrand with the Euro. Along the way Paris was convinced opposition against the monetary 'benign neglect' of Washington was absolutely necessary for Europe at large, not just France. A new, more durable Atlantic balance would rest on a reformed NATO and a new monetary order.

Epilogue: France back into the fold or the triumph of French views?

On 17 June 2008, President Sarkozy, on the occasion of the presentation of the conclusions of the review undertaken by the Defence White Book Commission, expressed his views about French security and defence policy, particularly regarding NATO and the European pillar.[48] In terms of unmistakable Sarkozian flavour, he uncovered some realities for the French public: the previous policy of aloofness towards NATO had led to diminished French influence, not an increased one. In that speech, President Sarkozy explained the only way out of this situation was to return to the integrated NATO command structure; this, after all, was the only way to bring its partners to accept the necessary establishment of a European defence identity inside NATO, but that it would have to happen before France came back. Years later, exactly the same conditions stated by de Gaulle applied: full freedom of choice, exclusive national nuclear deterrent power, no French troops under permanent NATO command in peacetime. The wording employed by President Sarkozy is similar to the one invoked by de Gaulle, attributable to an unnamed French diplomat, in December 1961 (see above). Apparently, the French return to NATO does not extend to the Nuclear Planning Group, a limitation quite consistent with Paris' longstanding stance of permanent nuclear independence.

President Sarkozy's decision to return to the NATO integrated command structure was announced in his speech of 11 March 2009 and confirmed by a vote in the French Parliament.[49] To date, the counterpart Sarkozy insisted upon since 2007 (the recognition of a European defence identity inside NATO) has not been forthcoming. At the EU summit in December 2008, it was only decided to create an 'informal group' of NATO–EU representatives, to enhance 'pragmatic cooperation of both organizations in the field'. Of course, the blocking, as of now, of the Lisbon Treaty (which covers important defence developments) is a big question mark.

Many commentators believe that, after this return of France into the NATO fold, the programme of *Europe-puissance* (another expression which was quite à la mode at the turn of the millennium to describe a European identity) is out for good.[50] However, at least in strategic matters, the Germans are no longer obliged to navigate between Paris and Washington, which was, for them, a very uncomfortable situation. It may be true, then, that the only way out of the old dispute about the European defence identity, and the only option promoting true Franco-German strategic cooperation, is the full return of Paris to NATO.

The return of France to NATO happened inside the framework laid out by de Gaulle in 1961: the conditions of French re-entry into the NATO integrated common structure, with two commands for the French and 800 positions for French officers in the different NATO staff (but not in the Nuclear Planning Group, which deals with nuclear weapons) look quite similar to the ideas expressed by de Gaulle in December 1961.[51] In fact, France limits integration to staff, retains freedom of decision and full control over its forces as well as its nuclear deterrent. Sarkozy has accepted an 'out-of-area' role for NATO, but de Gaulle believed in 1958 it was a necessary component. One could say there is now a full reconciliation between France and its partners, and that French views about NATO are no longer just tolerated but accepted. Yet, if many politicians accuse Sarkozy of returning to NATO without gaining much, some experts believe he remains basically a Gaullist.[52] Considering present conditions, which are very much different from those in the 1960s, can de Gaulle count a posthumous victory?

At the same time, in a wider context, it is less evident: there is still no real effective European defence personality, save peacekeeping tasks. Indeed, the G20 summit in London in April 2009 has likely reaffirmed the supremacy of the dollar: it is a far cry from de Gaulle's stance in 1965.[53] Washington's new push towards nuclear disarmament assures pressure will likely be applied to France to encourage reduction of its nuclear forces: the French nuclear arsenal is no longer quantitatively negligible if Russian and American stockpiles fall in line with the 1,500 weapon benchmark.[54] If France ever had an idea to more effectively influence Washington through constructive engagement, this notion was put to rest on the very same day as France's re-entry into NATO by President Barack Obama's forceful endorsement of Turkey's application to the EU, a move which has clearly restated American leadership of the West. The new overall transatlantic balance de Gaulle had in mind is not yet in place. And Paris has not yet truly convinced its partners of the validity of France's world view. France's return is an inevitable move, but also a turning point, which may well be a nice funeral wreath for *Europe-puissance*. Many will think France quickly shuffled to once again be in step. Only the future will tell if this is the case, or if Paris has finally managed to advance decisively, under present-day conditions, its old agenda.[55]

Notes

1 Archives nationales, Paris (AN) 5AG3/AE92.
2 For an introduction to France and NATO see Maurice Vaïsse, Pierre Mélandri, Frédéric Bozo (eds), *La France et l'OTAN 1949–1996*, (Brussels: Complexe, 1996); Frédéric Bozo, *Deux stratégies pour l'Europe. De Gaulle les Etats-Unis et l'Alliance atlantique 1958–1969*, (Paris: Plon, 1996); Frédéric Bozo, *La France et l'OTAN. De la guerre froide au nouvel ordre européen*, (Paris: Masson, 1991).
3 Georges-Henri Soutou, 'Frankreich und das atlantische Bündnis 1949–56', in Norbert Wiggershaus, Winfried Heinemann (eds), *Nationale Aussen-und Bündnispolitik der NATO-Mitgliedstaaten*, (Munich: Oldenbourg, 2000).
4 See my paper 'Les objectifs politico-stratégiques des responsables français au lendemain du cessez-le-feu: Algérie française ou défense de l'Occident?' for the 2006 international conference in Paris about the Suez crisis (Paris: Presses de la Sorbonne, in press).
5 Georges-Henri Soutou, *L'Alliance incertaine. Les rapports politico-stratégiques franco-allemands, 1954–1996*, (Paris: Fayard, 1996), chapter V.
6 Protocol of the June 17 meeting and note of July 1st approved by de Gaulle, Ministère des Affaires étrangères (MAE), Pactes, box 34. About the relations between de Gaulle and the Atlantic Alliance see Frédéric Bozo, *Deux stratégies pour l'Europe*.
7 Conclusions of the Defense Council on 31 January, MAE, Pactes, carton 34.
8 Charles de Gaulle, *Lettres, Notes et Carnets 1958–1960*, (Paris: Plon, 1980), pp. 83–84.
9 I do not believe in that interpretation, even if at times de Gaulle himself mentioned it (Alain Peyrefitte, *C'était de Gaulle*, (Paris: Fayard, 1994), vol. 1, p. 352).
10 Service Historique de la Défense, Département Terre (SHD/DT), 233 K 60.
11 In March Ely's staff refined that concept: there should be permanent commands for the different parts of the world, also out-of-area; the French should receive a command covering the Western Mediterranean and French Africa down to Dakar and Chad, with an operative direction towards Libya, Egypt, Suez and the Red Sea. The British should get such a command for the Indian Ocean, owing to their bases in Aden and Singapore. A new organization, more powerful than the current Standing Group, should coordinate, under the instructions of the three governments, the different regional commands in the context of a worldwide strategy ('Projet d'instructions pour Washington', March 23 1959, SHD/DT, 233 K 60). But de Gaulle did not go as far: he wanted French national commands established in all theatres, which would eventually collaborate with NATO (letter to Michel Debré on April 21 1959).
12 Ely to Debré on June 6 and October 6 1959, SHD/DT, 233 K 60.
13 19 December 1961, MAE, Service des Pactes, carton 266.
14 MAE, Cabinet, Entretiens 1960.
15 Georges-Henri Soutou, *L'Alliance incertaine*, pp. 289–93.
16 Charles de Gaulle, *Discours et Messages*, (Paris: Plon, 1979), vol. V, pp. 98–106.
17 Georges-Henri Soutou, *L'Alliance incertaine*, pp. 293–96.
18 Note from the Service des Pactes of 27 May, alluding to the conclusions of the Defence Council of 7 May, MAE, Service des Pactes, box 263.
19 *Documents diplomatiques français*, 1967–2, (Brussels: Peter Lang, 2008), pp. 182–88.
20 Georges-Henri Soutou, *L'Alliance incertaine*, p. 298.
21 Georges-Henri Soutou, 'Le Président Pompidou et les relations entre les Etats-Unis et l'Europe', *Journal of European Integration History/Revue d'Histoire de l'intégration européenne*, 2000, vol. 6, no. 2.
22 Georges-Henri Soutou, *L'Alliance incertaine*, pp. 300–301.
23 Ibid., pp. 266–69. See also the recent and very comprehensive article, about a complex issue, by Dieter Krüger, 'Schlachtfeld Bundesrepublik? Europa, die deutsche Luftwaffe und der Strategiewechsel der NATO 1958 bis 1968', *Vierteljahreshefte für Zeitgeschichte*, no. 2, 2008.
24 My paper for the 'Double-track decision' conference in Berlin, March 2009, publication forthcoming.
25 Général François Valentin, *Une politique de défense pour la France*, (Paris: Calmann-Lévy, 1980), 91ff.

26 Amiral Jacques Lanxade, *Quand le monde a basculé*, (Paris: NiL éditions, 2001), pp. 208–17.
27 Georges-Henri Soutou, 'Le Président Pompidou et les relations entre les Etats-Unis et l'Europe'.
28 Archives Nationales-Paris (AN), 5AG3/AE91.
29 Georges-Henri Soutou, *L'Alliance incertaine*, pp. 360–64.
30 Note from Dutet after a conversation with Defence Minister Bourges to prepare the visit of the American Secretary of Defense Schlesinger, 24 September 1975, AN, AG3/AE91.
31 Note from the military staff at the Elysée, 12 May 1976, AN, 5AG3/AE96.
32 Georges-Henri Soutou, *L'Alliance incertaine*, pp. 373–77.
33 See Frédéric Bozo, *La France et l'OTAN*, for a general and well-grounded presentation of that thesis.
34 My paper for the 'Double-track decision' conference in Berlin, March 2009, publication forthcoming.
35 For a very good description of that creeping back and its causes, see Louis Gautier, *Mitterrand et son armée, 1990–1995*, (Paris: Grasset, 1999), 77ff.
36 For a more detailed description see Jeremy Ghez and F. Stephen Larrabee, 'France and NATO', *Survival*, April–May 2009.
37 *Livre Blanc sur la Défense*, Paris: 10/18, 1994, pp. 64–68.
38 Georges-Henri Soutou, 'La France et la défense européenne du traité de l'Elysée au retrait de l'OTAN (1963–66)', in Wilfried Loth (ed.), *Crises and Compromises: The European Project 1963–1969*, (Brussels: Bruylant, 2001.)
39 'Faut-il réformer l'Alliance atlantique?', *Politique étrangère*, no. 3, 1965 (republished in issue number 4, 1995, of the same journal, with an introduction explaining its origins).
40 Natalie Nougayrède, 'Le sommet de l'OTAN et le retour du lien transatlantique', *Le Monde*, 3 April 2009.
41 Louis Gautier, *Mitterrand et son armée, 1990–1995*, pp. 77–78.
42 Georges-Henri Soutou, *L'Alliance incertaine*, pp. 423–29.
43 Article by Lothar Rühl in the *Neue Zürcher Zeitung* of 30 November to 1 December 1996.
44 Gilles Delafon and Thomas Sancton, *Dear Jacques, Cher Bill*, (Paris: Plon), 1999.
45 See Henri de Bresson and Daniel Vernet in *Le Monde* of 26 November 2002.
46 Laurent Zecchini in *Le Monde*, 29 May 2003, and Isabelle Lasserre in *Le Figaro*, 14 July 2003.
47 See Jeremy Ghez and F. Stephen Larrabee, 'France and NATO'.
48 Elysée Website.
49 Speech on March 11 2009.
50 Hubert Védrine in *Le Monde*, 6 March 2009.
51 Apart from the speech of Sarkozy himself in 2008 quoted, the point has been made, for instance, by François d'Orcival in the weekly *Valeurs actuelles* of 2 April 2009.
52 Justin Vaïsse, 'A Gaullist By Any Other Name', *Survival*, vol. 50. no. 3, pp 5–10.
53 Pierre-Antoine Delhommais in *Le Monde* of 5–6 April 2009, and Yves de Kerdrel in *Le Figaro* of 7 April 2009.
54 As has been reportedly noted by the Elysée diplomatic staff, *Le Figaro*, 9 April 2009.
55 Evidently there is a debate in France about the consequences of France's return. Two interesting studies, stating the pros and cons: Benoît d'Aboville (former French ambassador to NATO), 'Les soixante ans de l'OTAN: un point de vue européen', *Politique étrangère*, no. 1, 2008 and Lionel Grange (alias for a high ranking civil servant), 'La France dans l'OTAN. Les vraies questions', *Commentaire*, no. 126, Summer 2009.

6

NATO forever?

Willy Brandt's heretical thoughts on an alternative future

Benedikt Schoenborn[1]

> Allegorically speaking, we can say that a new building will have to be constructed between the two blocs. This building will gradually outgrow the blocs and make them dispensable, one day.
>
> Willy Brandt to George Macovescu, 4 June 1969[2]

> The Germans are really insane. They have nothing to offer the Russians. The only thing they have left to offer the Russians is to wreck NATO. After that is done they will have nothing to offer them. The Russians will never permit a powerful block in Central Europe led by Germany. Only if Bonn becomes like Helsinki.
>
> Henry Kissinger to Joseph Luns, 13 April 1973[3]

Since the aftermath of the Second World War, NATO has been the main framework of transatlantic cooperation. The goal of integrating Germany, or 'to keep the Germans down' like Lord Ismay famously put it, was still part of the organization's *raison d'être* in the 1960s and 1970s.[4] A German chancellor exploring scenarios about the end of NATO and thus challenging the core idea of transatlantic cooperation was most disconcerting for the other allies. And yet, they saw evidence of this in an earlier planning document, which was leaked to the press in 1973.[5]

The present chapter intends to show that Willy Brandt had indeed wished to examine alternative concepts to NATO, although not with the intention of degrading German–American cooperation. I further propose to put Brandt's thoughts in the perspective of the time and of his political evolution.

The good German

Willy Brandt was born 1913 as Herbert Karl Frahm in Lübeck, Northern Germany. In his youth, he was already an active member of the Social Democrat Party (SPD), and later of the Socialist Workers Party (SAP). By the early 1930s, Frahm disapproved of both the SPD's passivity and of the Communist Party's submission to Moscow. He left for Norway in April 1933, to build up the SAP's office in Oslo and to avoid impending arrest by the

Nazis. As a journalist and political activist against the Nazi regime, he adopted the name Willy Brandt. He spent the years of the Second World War in Norway and Sweden, escaping imprisonment several times. He returned to Berlin in 1945 as a correspondent for Scandinavian newspapers. With his German citizenship reinstated, Brandt joined the SPD leadership in Berlin and was elected deputy of the *Bundestag*, the West German parliament, in 1949.

The major steps of his political rise are well known. Brandt became mayor of West Berlin in 1957, West German foreign minister and vice chancellor in 1966, then chancellor in 1969. In 1971, he received the Nobel Peace Prize. Upon the unveiling of an East German spy in his inner circle, Brandt stepped down from the chancellorship in 1974, but remained SPD party leader until 1987. For almost 30 years, he also headed Socialist International and launched various initiatives against poverty in the world. In 1990, Brandt prominently participated in the ceremonies for Germany's reunification. He died of cancer in 1992.[6]

Today, Willy Brandt is widely recognized as one of the most important European politicians of the twentieth century, mostly because of the *Ostpolitik* he implemented as chancellor. Unlike his predecessors, who had tried to use any leverage to put political pressure on the Soviets, Brandt instead opted for open dialogue with the East. Even if the communist system was fundamentally wrong, Brandt argued, the West Germans had a vital interest in steady contacts with Eastern leaders, to avoid a possible war and to improve daily life in a divided Germany.[7]

Upon his election as chancellor, Brandt complied with the Soviet demands that all previous West German governments had rejected. He acknowledged the de facto loss of German territories attributed to Poland in 1945, he accepted that the Federal Republic of Germany (FRG) would never possess nuclear weapons and he recognized the German Democratic Republic (GDR) as a state. The subsequent moves towards East–West détente and the signing of Germany's Eastern Treaties profoundly changed the face of Europe.[8]

To a large extent, historians have established a consensus on the concrete aspects of Brandt's foreign policy. In contrast, questions about the long-term effects of *Ostpolitik* and its impact on the end of the Cold War continue to trigger lively academic debates. Was Brandt's *Ostpolitik* a clever time bomb undermining the Soviet empire, or did it help prolong the life of a communist system already doomed to failure?[9]

While these debates have made their way into newspapers and public consciousness, another intriguing argument has recently been raised questioning Brandt's stance on NATO and European security. The orthodox historiography presents Brandt as an unconditional supporter of NATO. According to leading German professors such as Gottfried Niedhart and Helga Haftendorn, Chancellor Brandt's loyalty to the Atlantic Alliance lay at the core of his political thoughts. He was deeply aware, these scholars argue, that the naked survival of West Germany and West Berlin would be jeopardized without straightforward American protection. Unwavering membership in NATO was a crucial element of Brandt's *Ostpolitik*, the reasoning further goes. Contacts with the USSR and Eastern Europe could only be fruitful with the FRG solidly anchored in the Western framework.[10]

The evidence supporting this argumentation seems to be overwhelming. Chancellor Brandt emphasized the importance of NATO for his country time and again. Most spectacularly, in a televised address to the German people from Moscow on 12 August 1970, he insisted on West Germany's 'firm embedding in the Western Alliance' and the 'reliable partnership with America'.[11] Any idea of weakening NATO, Chancellor Brandt maintained repeatedly, would 'endanger the process' launched by *Ostpolitik*.[12]

And yet, a thorough analysis reveals some ground for speculation. For example, a detailed study established by the American State Department in 1970 suggested that

Brandt's emphasis on NATO served his interests in the short run, to strengthen his relations with the Western allies and to put him in a better position to reach a *modus vivendi* with the East. But in the middle run, a softening of Brandt's stance on the American presence in Europe could be a potential bargaining chip in his discussions with Moscow.[13] Moreover, this chapter will show that it was possible to imagine a persistent American protection for West Germany even outside of NATO structures. In other words, Brandt's sticking to his partnership with the United States did not necessarily exclude the option of modifying the security structures in the longer run.

In France, Sorbonne professor Georges-Henri Soutou stirred up a controversy when claiming that Brandt had been able to realize only half of his political goals by 1974, the creation of a new European security system remaining unachieved. Italian scholar Giovanni Bernardini drew a similar picture in his studies on German–American relations 1969–72.[14] In Britain and Germany, Christoph Bluth and Wilfried Loth have argued that chancellor Brandt's far-reaching ambitions for mutual and balanced force reductions (MBFR) had initially been driven by his attempt to fundamentally affect the structure of European security.[15] This gives further substance to the hypothesis that Brandt did in fact consider, at some point, the modification of the military structures.

In a widely noted PhD thesis, Andreas Vogtmeier laid out Egon Bahr's studies on the creation of a new European security system, without answering the essential question about their impact on Brandt's foreign policy however.[16] In my opinion, it would not be conclusive to attribute these plans solely to Bahr and dissociate them from Brandt, although this appears to be the widespread assumption. After all, Brandt had himself chosen Bahr for the planning task, which he considered highly important, and made sure that Bahr kept this responsibility over many years. Every time Bahr had concluded a study, he discussed it with Brandt. Hence, Bahr's conceptual framework was at least partly linked to Brandt's own assumptions, which Bahr continuously took into account in his planning.[17] And undeniably, the two men were politically very close throughout the period described here. For example, when preparing for the crucial meeting with Leonid Brezhnev in Oreanda in September 1971, Brandt insisted he wanted to be accompanied by Bahr instead of foreign minister Scheel.[18]

Although the mentioned publications have brought fresh perspectives, none of them has elucidated the evolution of Brandt's own thoughts over a longer time period. In order to better understand his long-term goals as chancellor it appears imperative to take into account the evolution of Brandt's thinking from his taking office as mayor of West Berlin in 1957, until his stepping down as chancellor in 1974.

Mayor Brandt calls for new concepts

Brandt's years as mayor of West Berlin from 1957 to 1966 were deeply marked by the Second Berlin crisis.[19] In November 1958, Soviet leader Khrushchev addressed an ultimatum to the Western Powers, accusing them of having violated the Berlin agreements. Unless the allied troops were evacuated from West Berlin, Khrushchev threatened to sign a 'Peace Treaty' with the GDR and to transfer all rights on Berlin to the East Germans. This ultimatum endangered not only the Western access rights to West Berlin, but jeopardized the city's very existence. For a few years, the spectre of a nuclear war over Berlin lurked on the horizon. In August 1961, Khrushchev opted for the construction of a wall through Berlin, in order to stop the steady flow of refugees from East to West.

Compared to his 1958 ultimatum Khrushchev had backed down, although the Wall was a very hard piece to swallow for the Germans. From Brandt's point of view, the crisis and the Soviet threat against West Berlin were finally over in June 1964, when Khrushchev signed a rather insubstantial 'Friendship Treaty' with the GDR.[20]

These years of crises had a double impact on Brandt. On the one hand, they made him an even stauncher defender of German–American friendship. He clearly perceived that only the United States was powerful enough to guarantee the freedom of the FRG and West Berlin against the very real Soviet menace. Brandt thus aspired to 'a maximum of Atlantic partnership'.[21] He saw a strong convergence of American and German interests during the Kennedy presidency and still in 1965, with Lyndon B. Johnson in the White House, he led his election campaign with the telling slogan 'What is good for the US is also good for us'.[22]

On the other hand, Washington's acquiescence in the Wall puzzled and upset mayor Brandt. He recognized in 1961 that the West Germans had to develop their own political concepts and contacts with the East even without US support, otherwise Germany would remain a divided country forever.[23] Yet, these concepts should be elaborated and discussed secretly, not publicly. When in June 1962 one of Brandt's party fellows shared his opinion on Berlin and the East–West conflict with an American journalist, Brandt was upset to see these views revealed to the press. The mayor insisted that any statement on these matters be prepared in strictest confidence because of Berlin's delicate situation. He even advocated that the undisciplined party official be excluded from the SPD.[24] Such secrecy generally applied to Brandt's long-term plans even in later years and provided a fertile ground for rumours and suspicion.

Although the events of 1961 strongly influenced Brandt's will to develop his own approach to the East–West conflict, the recent studies by Wolfgang Schmidt, Peter Speicher and Arne Hofmann have shown convincingly that Brandt had already started to do so.[25] Ever since 1955, he had promoted the idea of peaceful coexistence, based on the assumption that nuclear arms prevented any direct war between the superpowers. He thereby ranged the FRG clearly in the Western camp and favoured American leadership, in contrast to some of his fellow social democrats. Throughout the 1950s, Brandt repeatedly spoke out against the 'illusionists' dreaming of an alternative position for Germany or pleading for the misconception of Europe as a 'Third Force' between East and West. At the same time, he criticized chancellor Adenauer's unilateral Western policy and lack of serious discussions with the East. Brandt considered accepting an invitation to meet with Khrushchev in early March 1959 and again in January 1963, but Adenauer's CDU and the Americans intervened.[26]

Mayor Brandt was eager to explore and widen the perspectives of German foreign policy, while safeguarding the FRG's and West Berlin's security. In this context he didn't rule out structural changes involving NATO. This is not surprising, as US President Eisenhower repeatedly announced throughout his years in office (1953–61) that he wanted to 'bring the boys home'.[27] According to Brandt, at least a partial withdrawal of American troops from Europe would eventually happen and had to be dealt with. Brandt's own position on the issue was somewhat ambiguous. As mayor of the easily jeopardized city of West Berlin he valued highly the presence of American forces and later on opposed concrete plans by the US Congress to reduce the troops stationed in Germany. On the other hand, the idea of disarmament had been a permanent feature in his thinking from early on. 'More than anything else, progress in the field of controlled disarmament could bring us closer to our goal of international détente and thus to the solution of the German question', he declared in June 1960.[28]

In the SPD's *Deutschland-Plan* (plan for Germany) of March 1959, disarmament played a central role. It called for the creation of a denuclearized zone in Central Europe, including both parts of Germany, Poland, Czechoslovakia and Hungary. The United States and the Soviet Union would guarantee the security of the newly established *Entspannungszone* (zone of détente), but would withdraw all their troops from it. These ideas were much in line with the 1957 proposal by Polish foreign minister Rapacki, aiming at the denuclearization of East and West Germany, Poland and Czechoslovakia. But the SPD plan further suggested, in a second part, the election of a pan-German parliament to be entrusted with the task of organizing the cooperation and eventually the reunification of both parts of Germany.[29]

Willy Brandt – not yet SPD party leader at that time – criticized the forward-rushing spirit of the plan and the unlikely expectation of obtaining any serious Eastern support for German reunification. Instead, he suggested a more modest but perseverant attitude in order 'to get, one day, the Soviet Union's green light for the re-establishment of our national unity'.[30] His fundamental criticism was mostly about the second part of the plan dealing with reunification and less about the disarmament ideas expressed in its first part. As Brandt had anticipated, Moscow was not interested in the least and the SPD plan had to be shelved.

In Brandt's far-reaching lectures at Harvard University in October 1962, as well as in his and Egon Bahr's meanwhile famous Tutzing speeches in July 1963, concrete visions of German reunification were carefully avoided.[31] And yet, Brandt considered the long-term planning of the future a matter of highest importance. He acknowledged that the division of Germany and Berlin pushed him 'daily to reflect' on long-term political objectives.[32] For the task of elaborating such plans under his supervision, Brandt chose Egon Bahr, 'conceptually the most capable' and one of the most loyal of his advisers.[33]

Brandt and Bahr had known each other since the 1950s. Originally from Thuringia in the Eastern part of Germany, young Egon Bahr served as soldier in the German *Wehrmacht* until his dishonourable discharge in 1944, on the grounds of Jewish ancestry. Aged 23 after the war, Bahr started a career as a journalist in Berlin. By 1950 he was chief editor of the American–German radio channel RIAS. On Brandt's request, Bahr became the spokesman of the West Berlin Senate in 1960. One of his main duties was to write speeches for the mayor. He quickly evolved into Brandt's 'Brain-Truster' and for at least 15 years, Bahr put all his political activities to the benefit of his mentor.[34]

As Brandt's long-term planner, Bahr finished a 180-page manuscript in March 1966. It basically projected eight steps towards German reunification. Bahr assumed that reunification would inevitably happen if Soviet troops left the GDR, because the factitious East German regime, if left alone, would not be able to resist the will of the people.[35] This opinion was also shared by other Western politicians of the 1960s.[36]

Bahr further argued that Moscow might even consider West German suggestions, if the prospected development would not endanger Soviet interests. A permanently peaceful and unified Germany could possibly become a tempting perspective for the USSR, but only if the military balance would not be tipped in favour of the West. With a united Germany as a member of NATO, however, the balance would certainly be harmed. On the other hand, Germany's security as well as the Western allies would not allow any change in favour of the East. Hence a unified Germany could not join the Warsaw Pact. In order to keep the East–West balance untouched, a unified Germany could thus not be part of either military alliance, Bahr concluded.[37]

According to the concept he presented, the FRG and the GDR would first intensify their contacts, then negotiations of the Four Powers and the two German parts would start, a European security system and a peace treaty for Germany would be drafted, free elections organized in all Germany and finally a pan-German army established and foreign troops withdrawn. The Four Powers would guarantee both Germany's security and the security of the neighbouring countries from Germany. For Bahr, the military protection by the United States was indispensable, but 'NATO becomes replaceable' if the American security guarantee was maintained otherwise.[38]

Brandt's reaction to this draft was cautious. He commented that 'the best way to stay out of trouble is to stay out of sight', and ruled out the publication of the text in its existing form. Brandt also encouraged Bahr to continue working on the topic.[39] Overall, Bahr's manuscript was not designed as a plan to be put into practice at once, but as a 'positive political utopia' exploring a possible way towards German reunification. It was thus in line with Brandt's general ambitions 'to seek ways to surmount and to permeate the blocs of today' and 'to constantly reconsider the tasks and possibilities of German foreign policy'.[40]

Minister Brandt explores alternatives to NATO

When Brandt became foreign minister in Kurt Georg Kiesinger's Grand Coalition government in December 1966, the overall European situation was moving towards détente. US President Johnson endeavoured to 'thaw out' the Cold War and launched a series of discussions with the Soviets, notably on arms control. Johnson's bridge-building initiatives with Eastern Europe illustrated that Washington now favoured a more encompassing Eastern policy also by West Germany.[41]

At the same time, the United States grew increasingly preoccupied with South-East Asia and started to shift troops from Germany to Vietnam. French withdrawal from NATO command, announced in March 1966, shocked the other members and triggered further discussions on the future of the Atlantic Alliance. As the NATO treaty was about to expire in 1969, European uncertainties became tangible. In December 1966, the NATO members created a study group headed by Belgian foreign minister Pierre Harmel in order to elaborate the 'Future Tasks of the Alliance'. By adopting the Harmel Report on 14 December 1967, the Atlantic Council redefined the organization's goals in a context of East–West détente. It notably stated that 'the ultimate political purpose of the Alliance is to achieve a just and lasting peaceful order in Europe accompanied by appropriate security guarantees'.[42]

Much in line with the work of the Harmel Group, foreign minister Brandt often used the terms 'European security system' and 'European peace order' in his speeches.[43] While Brandt's Eastern policy was widely commented at that time, his queries about the future of the Atlantic Alliance attracted relatively little attention. To be sure, he reaffirmed the vital importance of NATO for his country and deplored French President de Gaulle's reluctance towards this organization. Brandt also specified that essentially, NATO meant protection by the United States: 'When we say Alliance, we say USA.'[44]

On the other hand, Brandt made clear that far-reaching changes for NATO and the organization of European security were to be expected in the following 20 years. At his very first appearance as foreign minister at the Western European Union (WEU), Brandt suggested that a possible replacement of NATO and of the Warsaw Pact by a European security system be examined.[45] He alluded to a possible end of the two military alliances publicly a few months later. In an interview with the German radio station Deutschlandfunk he explained that two different models of European security system were thinkable. Either the existing alliances would continue to exist and develop their relations, or 'NATO and the Warsaw Pact would be gradually dissolved in Europe and replaced by something new'.[46]

The American security guarantee would continue to exist in both models, he added, and once again emphasized the need for new forms of contact and collaboration between the Eastern and Western parts of Europe. In an article published one month later, he elaborated on the topic more carefully. Brandt wrote that he did not believe that NATO had already achieved its purpose and become superfluous. When it came to the choice between the two models of European security, many reasons would point to sticking to the existing alliances. Still, given the importance of the topic, especially for the Germans, Brandt encouraged his fellow countrymen to consider all options and to generate constructive proposals for a European peace order.[47]

In 1967, Brandt also initiated a Franco-German 'Study group on European security problems in the 1970s'. He wanted this group to push its thoughts beyond the limits of NATO, but chancellor Kiesinger as well as US ambassador McGhee successfully intervened to cut down the ambitions of the project.[48] In October 1967, McGhee informed Washington that Brandt's preoccupation with 'European security presents the most significant potential source of misunderstanding', but, overall, the Americans did not seem to worry too much about the German foreign minister's wish to explore this topic. His room for manoeuvre was considered too narrow.[49]

France, the second most important ally according to Brandt, complied with the German wish to create a study group on security issues, but kept the discussions on a rather conventional level.[50] Another French contact turned out to be more inspiring for Brandt and his team: the Centre d'études de politique étrangère in Paris, perceived by the Germans as a non-official think tank of the French foreign ministry. In November 1967, and a few weeks later in German translation, this institute published a rather detailed outlook on three possible security models for Europe. The notes taken by the *Planungsstab* (planning group) in Bonn make clear that the similarity of that study to Bahr's secret paper of June 1968 was no coincidence.[51]

Bahr had become chief of the *Planungsstab* in November 1967, supervised directly and only by Brandt. The purpose of this planning group in the foreign ministry was to provide thoughts and studies on long-term aspects of German foreign policy. Since its creation in January 1963, it had organized various colloquia with academics, researchers and journalists. Already before Bahr's arrival, the *Planungsstab* had manifested a special interest for the idea of a nuclear-free zone in Central Europe and the notion of a European security system.[52] According to Bahr's explanation in May 1968 at one of these colloquia, his own studies on European security issues were 'a mere speculative game, a glass bead game'.[53] And yet, several indications suggest that his June 1968 paper entitled 'European security' was more than just a hypothetical, intellectual exercise.[54]

Shorter and farther reaching than the manuscript of 1966, Bahr's 1968 study sketched three models of European security under the viewpoint of German reunification. Only one model (C) would provide a promising political basis in that respect, Bahr concluded. Model A foresaw a continuation of the existing alliances and an easing of tensions through partial disarmament. Bahr advised that the West German government follow this concept in the short run only. In model B, common organs cramped together the Warsaw Pact and NATO in a permanent institutional framework, topping both pacts. Bonn should avoid this concept, Bahr insisted, because it would freeze the status quo and offer no perspective for German reunification.[55]

Finally, model C proposed to replace NATO and the Warsaw Pact by a new European security system. The United States and the USSR – possibly also the UK and France – would guarantee the new system but not be part of it. Geographically, it would include East and West Germany, Belgium, Holland, Luxemburg, Poland and Czechoslovakia. These member states would have their own armies, but all nuclear weapons and foreign troops would be withdrawn from their territories. A new European security council would be established in Berlin, and the GDR formally recognized as a state. Bahr estimated, however, that the East German government would ultimately collapse, as no foreign power would be allowed to intervene without permission by the new council.[56]

Although Bahr's paper and the French study of November 1967 outlined different methods for setting up the new security organ in Berlin, they basically shared the same assumptions. (1) The gradual abolition of the two military alliances would represent major challenges in both East and West, but promised substantial benefits with regard to détente and the German question. It would also create a suitable framework, militarily and psychologically, for the likely withdrawal of American troops. In any case, major long-term challenges were to be expected even if the European status quo should be maintained. (2) The denuclearization of Central Europe would not undermine the 'balance of terror', since modern warfare did not depend on short-range nuclear missiles anymore. Quite the opposite, the region would become safer when cleared of its foremost military targets. (3) American protection would be maintained, as Washington would never want to allow the USSR to take possession of the new security area in Central Europe.[57]

Bahr's judgment about the practical impact of his June 1968 document was ambiguous. On the one hand, he saw little immediate effect and advised Brandt to keep only the conclusions in mind, since achieving model C would not happen any time soon. Well aware of the obstacles, Bahr also listed the expected counter-arguments by the American, French, British, Soviet and East German governments. On the other hand, he encouraged Brandt to move ahead and to sound out the Yugoslav government, in order to know if Yugoslavia would be interested in joining the project. Brandt indeed followed this advice during a visit to Belgrade in June 1968, but the Yugoslavs flatly rejected the idea of a new European security system.[58] Not discouraged in the least and clearly turning away now from a mere theoretical approach, Bahr informed Brandt on 19 August 1968 that the document on European security, with an updated section on the denuclearized zone, would become operational by September. After consultations with the allies and chancellor Kiesinger 'the federal government could apply the whole program by the end of the year', Bahr concluded with pronounced self-confidence.[59]

The very next day, however, the Warsaw Pact's invasion of Czechoslovakia brutally changed the international context. From an American point of view, this event shifted NATO's emphasis from Harmel's approach of 'peaceful engagement with the East' back to the more basic problem of defence. And, most importantly, the Czechoslovak crisis had the effect of 'stalling the process of NATO's disintegration' and brought all members 'to accept the necessity of preserving an effective alliance beyond its twentieth anniversary' in 1969.[60] German chancellor Kiesinger repeatedly commented that, if the Russians had not invaded Prague, the Atlantic Alliance might have ceased to exist within two years.[61] While the accuracy of this opinion may be contested, it nevertheless reveals some serious West German doubts about the future of NATO, rarely expressed in official statements of the time.

After the Czech tragedy, Brandt and Bahr exerted themselves to strengthen NATO beyond 1969. But Brandt's faith in the alliance was not unconditional, as a CIA agent reported in September 1968: 'It is impossible, Brandt said, to rid oneself of the feeling that one day American leaders will change their policy' and 'rid themselves of their military obligations' in Europe. The agent pointed out that 'the foreign minister sometimes has such moments of disenchantment with the Atlantic Alliance'.[62]

Anyhow, Brandt's basic interest in alternative perspectives did not seem to fade after August 1968. Bahr's *Planungsstab* continued to work on the three different models of European security and upheld, in March 1969, that only model C would offer a promising framework for the solution of the German question.[63] Much to his later regret, Bahr also disclosed his views to American professor Walter Hahn in early 1969. In Hahn's presence Bahr elaborated on force reductions in Germany and, compared to the June 1968 document, projected an even wider scope of a European security system: Romania, Bulgaria and Yugoslavia would also be potential members from the Eastern side, as well as Denmark, Norway and Sweden from the Western side. Hahn left the meeting with a sense of disbelief and the impression that Bahr single-mindedly followed a strategy leading to the dissolution of the Atlantic Alliance. The evidence suggests that professor Hahn already shared his impressions with American officials before he decided to publish the entire interview, in 1973.[64]

At least to some extent, Brandt adopted the conclusions of his planning staff. When meeting with adjunct Romanian foreign minister Macovescu in June 1969, Brandt manifested clear sympathies for Romanian appeals to abolish the two military blocs. In a first step, Brandt explained, the efforts to achieve a European security system should aim at modifying the relationship between NATO and the Warsaw Pact. Then, a new system could gradually come to overlie the two blocs. Non-aligned and neutral countries – Yugoslavia, Austria, Finland, even Ireland or Spain – should be included in that process. As quoted at the beginning of this chapter, Brandt prospected that this new system would 'gradually outgrow the blocs and make them dispensable, one day'.[65]

Chancellor Brandt maintains the NATO framework

When the two men met again in February 1972, Brandt took a distinctly different stance. He now emphasized that both Romania and West Germany should act as loyal members of their respective blocs. Macosvescu tried hard to continue their 1969 discussion on the abolition of NATO and the Warsaw Pact, but to no avail.[66]

The modification of Brandt's position may have had different reasons. An obvious explanation would be that he could not speak as frankly any more, due to his responsibilities as chancellor and his acquired international posture. The task of developing new ideas and concepts, of looking for alternative ways of German foreign policy, certainly corresponded better to the mayor of West Berlin or the junior partner of the Grand Coalition than to the chancellor. After Brandt took office in October 1969, he indeed advised his staff not to use the word 'reunification' anymore and to avoid talking about long-term visions for Europe. It would be foolish to create the impression, Brandt explained, that the Germans intended to tell the others how the continent should look like in the future.[67]

Chancellor Brandt also had a clear political interest not to mention any perspective of ending NATO. He was much aware that his policy of détente towards the East could only be successful with the FRG firmly anchored within the Atlantic Alliance.[68]

So far I have found no evidence of Brandt mentioning the dissolution of NATO during his almost five years as West German chancellor. His carefulness alone doesn't seem to entirely explain the situation. While Brandt had manifested sympathies for 'Model C' in the 1960s, several indications suggest that he quite significantly reassessed the international context once he had started to put his *Ostpolitik* into practice.

First of all, the Soviet Union turned out to have no interest in exploring new formulas for military structures. Despite the Warsaw Pact's previous calls for the abolition of the blocs or its support of the Rapacki proposals, the USSR in fact opposed any modification of the status quo. Brandt concluded in early 1972 that Moscow would not take the risk of losing control over Eastern Europe. Even the presence of American troops in Western Europe and the existence of NATO were beneficial to the Soviet Union, in the sense that the United States helped stabilize the European status quo.[69]

As to American foreign policy, a substantial troop withdrawal from Europe had become less likely by the early 1970s. According to Brandt's analysis, the Nixon government had resolved to keep the military alliance untouched, a strong US presence in Europe being in Washington's own interest. German *Ostpolitik* had given new political meaning to NATO and to the presence of American troops, since Washington wanted to ensure that the FRG remain a part of the West.[70] Henry Kissinger, a key figure in Nixon's European policy, clearly had no sympathies for German 'romantic ideas' of ending the military blocs in Europe. 'If the Germans go that route they will be crushed', he stated bluntly.[71]

In the mid-1960s, Egon Bahr had assumed that Kissinger and other American thinkers were considering the creation of new transatlantic structures, because NATO would not be a suitable instrument of détente.[72] In April 1965, Bahr had even visited Kissinger at Harvard University 'to explore some ideas he and Brandt were mulling over'. According to Kissinger's memo sent to the White House, Bahr had outlined a vision of foreign troop withdrawal, of a unified Germany leaving NATO and of the organization's eventual disintegration.[73] Right from the start, Kissinger had thus been informed first-hand of these ideas. In retrospect, Bahr's 1965 trip to Boston could be judged as naive, but at the same time it may show that he perceived American support for his plans as a viable option for the future. This impression turned out to be too optimistic.

As for France, experience showed that the 1967 study by the Centre d'études de politique étrangère had no positive impact on the planning of French foreign policy. And despite de Gaulle's rather enigmatic statements on the renewal of the Atlantic Alliance treaty, France remained a member beyond 1969. In the early 1970s, President Pompidou was horrified by the idea of troop reductions or a partial American withdrawal from the FRG, fearing Germany's neutralization. 'NATO is irreplaceable', French foreign minister Schumann declared in that context. The British government adopted a similar attitude.[74]

Hence, the officials of the *Auswärtiges Amt* in Bonn noted that all three major allies vigorously opposed the idea of a denuclearized and disarmed zone in Central Europe, or the dissolution of NATO. Partly for that reason, Bahr's successor as chief of the *Planungsstab* dismissed the study of June 1968 as utopian, naive and outdated.[75]

Finally, several clues can be interpreted in the sense that Brandt himself developed some reluctance towards the enormous changes Bahr's initial plans would have brought about. For example, the absence of the chancellor's comments on this issue, throughout the years 1969–74, could be a sign of this. Most officials of the Nixon government started to differentiate between Brandt's long-term objectives and those of Bahr, who reportedly was still fond of his 1960s concepts.[76] An American diplomat also recorded that Brandt, after the first months of active *Ostpolitik*, felt rather overwhelmed by the 'excessive activities' of his aids. 'As Brandt put it, he woke up one morning to find that, not only was Bahr in Moscow and Duckwitz in Warsaw, but Emmel was in Moscow, Wischnewski turned up in Budapest, and, as if this were not enough, Arndt also turned up in Budapest on yet another mission.'[77]

Although this quote does not deal directly with Bahr's concepts on European security, it nevertheless conveys the impression that Brandt was not eagerly looking for more transformation, at least not at that time. One of his discussions with Soviet leader Brezhnev, some three years later, points in a similar direction. After mentioning that many perceptions had changed over the past 20 years, Brandt said that 'maybe, at some point in the future, the two military blocs would cease to exist, but for the time being, they did exist' and suited the situation 'better than chaos'.[78]

This statement appears to be a genuine expression of Brandt's approach to the question. Whereas Bahr had reasoned in the 1960s that German reunification was more important than integration in NATO, Brandt had always stressed that peace was more important than Germany's unity. This fundamental attitude implied his intention to respect the will of the other international actors. When planning German foreign policy, Brandt once said he was not in a situation to choose the most beautiful among many beautiful things, but he had to do what was possible.[79] Plausibly, Brandt had accepted in the early 1970s that Bahr's initial plans were not within the range of the possible for the time being.

Still, in the years 1971–73, Brandt repeatedly voiced support for the idea of partial disarmament in the 'Rapacki zone', thereby contributing to the Western allies' suspicions that he might consider a long-term modification of the military structures.[80] Together with Brandt's sympathy for the notion of a permanent CSCE organ to be established in Berlin,[81] this may indicate that he still cherished some of the ideas Bahr had outlined in June 1968. Although tilting towards the longer term maintenance of NATO, it appears that chancellor Brandt wanted to keep all options open.

After the fall of the Wall, Brandt dismisses the alternative

In conclusion, strong evidence suggests that during the 1960s, Brandt considered the creation of a new European security system as a possible long-term policy goal. Upon his election as chancellor in 1969, he was more reluctant to this idea, although he never excluded that NATO and the Warsaw Pact might disappear some day. Well aware of Germany's unfortunate past, he also took care to avoid the impression that the Germans wanted to tell the other Europeans how the continent should look like in the future.

Later events support the assessment that the concepts described in this chapter were more than just intellectual exercises. A few days after the unexpected fall of the Berlin Wall in November 1989, Bahr publicly claimed that Germany's unity could only be achieved in the framework of a new European security system, and called for the dissolution of NATO and the Warsaw Pact. And in June 1990, when the events had already developed very differently from his expectations, Bahr advanced a specific outline for the creation of a new European security system, along the very lines of his 1968 concept. When Gorbachev acquiesced in Germany's unification within NATO a few weeks later, Bahr's theories all crumbled. He had never believed this possible.[82]

Willy Brandt's position was quite different at this point. He had built up good personal relations with Mikhail Gorbachev since 1985. Accompanied each time by Bahr, Brandt had visited the Soviet leader three times in Moscow. These visits, and even previous concepts on Common Security written by Bahr, influenced Gorbachev's plan to create a

Common European Home, beyond the existing security structures.[83] Nevertheless, unlike Bahr, Brandt changed his attitude after the fall of the Wall on 9 November 1989. He quickly grasped the new situation and the imminent changes. Going against the flow of his SPD, Brandt backed up christian-democrat chancellor Kohl, who sought to achieve Germany's quick reunification within NATO. As we all know, Kohl was successful by October 1990. This may illustrate that Brandt, although still sympathizing with the idea of new European security structures in the 1980s, finally dismissed these plans as inadequate at the decisive moment.[84]

Notes

1 I would like to express my gratitude to the Academy of Finland, who has been financing my research at the University of Tampere. I would also like to thank the Lyndon Baines Johnson Library for the Moody Research Grant, and Egon Bahr for the inspiring interview.
2 *Akten zur Auswärtigen Politik der Bundesrepublik Deutschland* (hereafter AAPD), edited by H.-P. Schwarz, vol. 1969/1 (Munich: Oldenbourg, 2000), pp. 672–79, Gespräch Brandt–Macovescu, 4 June 1969.
3 National Archives and Records Administration (hereafter NARA), College Park MD, Nixon Presidential Materials, NSC Files, HAK Memcons, Box 1027, Conversation Kissinger–Luns, 13 April 1973.
4 Quoted in Geir Lundestad, *The United States and Western Europe since 1945,* (Oxford: Oxford University Press, 2003), p. 8. Lord Ismay was the first Secretary General of NATO, 1952–57.
5 On 27 September 1973, the German pictorial *Quick* printed parts of Egon Bahr's planning study of 27 June 1968. In early 1973, the American journal *Orbis* published a related document. See the section on 'Minister Brandt'.
6 For more details, see Helga Grebing, *Willy Brandt. Der andere Deutsche,* (Paderborn: Wilhelm Fink, 2008). Peter Merseburger, *Willy Brandt, 1913–1992. Visionär und Realist,* (Stuttgart: DVA, 2002). Gregor Schöllgen, *Willy Brandt. Die Biographie,* (Berlin: Ullstein, 2003). Carola Stern, Willy Brandt (Berlin: Rowohlt, 2009).
7 Willy Brandt, *The Ordeal of Coexistence,* (Cambridge MA: Harvard University Press, 1963), pp. 1–11.
8 For good overviews, see Peter Graf Kielmansegg, *Nach der Katastrophe. Eine Geschichte des geteilten Deutschland,* (Berlin: Siedler, 2000). Helga Haftendorn, *Coming of Age: German Foreign Policy since 1945,* (Lanham: Rowman & Littlefield, 2006).
9 For an extensive discussion, see Timothy Garton Ash, *In Europe's Name. Germany and the Divided Continent,* (New York: Random House, 1993). For a critical view on Brandt, see Vladimir Boukovsky, *Jugement à Moscou. Un dissident dans les archives du Kremlin,* (Paris: Robert Laffont, 1995). For a recent overview, see Frédéric Bozo et al. (eds), *Europe and the End of the Cold War. A reappraisal,* (London: Routledge, 2008).
10 See the various contributions in Georges-Henri Soutou et al. (eds), *The Making of Détente. Eastern and Western Europe in the Cold War, 1965–1975,* (London: Routledge, 2008). Both Gottfried Niedhart and Helga Haftendorn have vastly published on this topic, e.g. Gottfried Niedhart, 'Ostpolitik: Phases, short-term Objectives and Grand Design', *GHI Bulletin Supplement,* no. 1, 2003, pp. 118–36. Helga Haftendorn, *German Ostpolitik in a Multilateral Setting,* in *The Strategic Triangle. France, Germany and the United States in the Shaping of the New Europe,* edited by H. Haftendorn et al. (Washington: Woodrow Wilson Center Press, 2007), pp. 209–27. For an overview of the historiography, see Oliver Bange, 'Ostpolitik – Etappen und Desiderate der Forschung. Zur internationalen Einordnung von Willy Brandt's Aussenpolitik', *Archiv für Sozialgeschichte,* no. 46, 2006, pp. 713–36.
11 *Bulletin des Presse-und Informationsamtes der Bundesregierung,* 14 August 1970, no. 108, pp. 1083–1984, Fernsehansprache des Bundeskanzlers aus Moskau, 12 August 1970.
12 *Der Spiegel,* 27 September 1971, no. 40, p. 28, Spiegel – Gespräch mit Bundeskanzler Willy Brandt.
13 Declassified Documents Reference System (hereafter DDRS), accessed from the Norwegian Nobel Institute on 12 June 2007, Report by the Department of State, A longer term perspective on key issues of European security, Washington 1970.
14 Georges-Henri Soutou, *La guerre de Cinquante Ans. Les relations Est-Ouest 1943–1990,* (Paris: Fayard, 2001), p. 501. Giovanni Bernardini, *'Le relazioni politiche hanno voltato l'angolo'. L'Amministrazione*

Nixon e il governo Brandt: Europa, Occidente, rapporti con l'Est, 1969–1971, (University of Florence, PhD Thesis, 2006). G. Bernardini, 'West German–American Relations and a New Order of Peace for Europe', *Journal of Transatlantic Studies,* vol. 8, no. 1, 2010, pp. 19–31.

15 Wilfried Loth, *The road to Vienna. West German and European security from 1969 to 1973,* in *The Making of Détente. Eastern and Western Europe in the Cold War, 1965–1975,* edited by W. Loth and G.-H. Soutou (London: Routledge, 2008), pp. 153–67. Christoph Bluth, 'The Origins of MBFR: West German Policy Priorities and Conventional Arms Control', *War in History,* vol. 7, no. 2, 2000, pp. 199–224.

16 Andreas Vogtmeier, *Egon Bahr und die deutsche Frage. Zur Entwicklung der sozialdemokratischen Ost- und Deutschlandpolitik vom Kriegsende bis zur Vereinigung,* (Bonn: Dietz, 1996). See also Alexander Gallus, *Die Neutralisten. Verfechter eines vereinten Deutschland zwischen Ost und West 1945–1990,* (Düsseldorf: Droste, 2001).

17 This was also the conclusion by the US State Department in 1970, in the mentioned document on Key issues of European security, p. 44.

18 Archiv des Liberalismus, Gummersbach, Bestand N82–87, Brandt an Scheel (handwritten letter, undated).

19 The Berlin Blockade of 1948–49 is generally referred to as the First Berlin crisis.

20 John Gearson and Kori Schake (eds), *The Berlin Wall Crisis. Perspectives on Cold War Alliances,* (Basingstoke: Palgrave, 2002). For Brandt's assessment of the Friendship Treaty, see Archives du Ministère des Affaires Etrangères (hereafter AMAE), Paris, RFA 1603, conversation Brandt–Winckler, 20 June 1964.

21 *Willy Brandt – Berliner Ausgabe* (hereafter WBBA), edited by H. Grebing et al., vol. 3 (Bonn: Dietz, 2004), p. 401, Brandt an Kennedy, 7 February 1963.

22 'Was für die USA gut ist, ist auch gut für uns', quoted in Reiner Marcowitz, *Option für Paris? Unionsparteien, SPD und Charles de Gaulle, 1958 bis 1969,* (Munich: Oldenbourg, 1996), p. 223. In the 1965 elections to the *Bundestag,* Brandt's SPD was defeated quite clearly by the christian-democrat CDU. As a consequence chancellor Erhard was re-elected.

23 Hope Harrison, 'The Berlin Wall, Ostpolitik, and Détente', *GHI Bulletin Supplement,* no. 1, 2003, pp. 5–18.

24 WBBA, vol. 3, pp. 41–42, 368–71, 601–2.

25 Wolfgang Schmidt, *Kalter Krieg, Koexistenz und kleine Schritte. Willy Brandt und die Deutschlandpolitik 1948–1963,* (Wiesbaden: Westdeutscher Verlag, 2001). Peter Speicher, *The Berlin origins of Brandt's Ostpolitik, 1957–1966,* (University of Cambridge: unpublished PhD thesis, 2001). Arne Hofmann, *The Emergence of Détente in Europe. Brandt, Kennedy and the formation of Ostpolitik,* (London: Routledge, 2007).

26 Willy Brandt, *Begegnungen und Einsichten: Die Jahre 1960–1975,* (Hamburg: Hoffmann und Campe, 1976), pp. 110–12. WBBA, vol. 3, pp. 48–49, 258–65, Aufzeichnungen Brandt, 8–19 March 1959.

27 Quoted in Lundestad, *The US and Western Europe,* pp. 87–88.

28 WBBA, vol. 3, p. 302, Bemerkungen zur Berlinfrage, 27 June 1960.

29 *Archiv der Gegenwart* (hereafter AdG), CD-Rom (Sankt Augustin: Siegler Verlag, 2000), pp. 13129–40, Deutschland-Plan der SPD, 18 March 1959.

30 WBBA, vol. 3, pp. 269–70, Schreiben Brandt an von Knoeringen, 27 August 1959.

31 For the Harvard lectures, see Brandt, *The Ordeal of Coexistence.* For the Tutzing speeches, see *Dokumente zur Deutschlandpolitik* (hereafter DzD), 1963, vol. IV, no. 9, edited by the Bundesministerium für Innerdeutsche Beziehungen (Frankfurt: Alfred Metzner Verlag, 1978), pp. 565–75.

32 Brandt, *Ordeal of Coexistence,* p. 11.

33 Brandt, *Erinnerungen,* (Frankfurt: Propyläen, 1989), p. 73.

34 Vogtmeier, *Egon Bahr,* pp. 20–61, p. 59 for the Brandt quote.

35 Archiv der sozialen Demokratie (hereafter AdsD), Bonn, Depositum Bahr, Box 465, Manuskript *Was nun?* 1966.

36 For example, French foreign minister Couve de Murville: 'Once the Soviet army leaves the GDR, Germany will be reunified in five minutes.' AMAE, EM 23, Entretien Couve de Murville–David, 26 November 1964.

37 AdsD, Bonn, Dep. Bahr, Box 465, Manuskript *Was nun?,* 1966, pp. 17–21, 89–92.

38 Ibid., pp. 93–119 (quote p. 95). For a critical analysis, see Vogtmeier, *Egon Bahr,* pp. 80–95. For Bahr's view in retrospect, see Egon Bahr, *Sicherheit für und vor Deutschland. Vom Wandel durch Annäherung zur Europäischen Sicherheitsgemeinschaft,* (Munich: Carl Hanser, 1991), pp. 18–35.

39 AdsD, Dep. Bahr, Box 466, Brandt an Bahr, 6 April 1966.
40 Quotes from Brandt's speeches in Harvard and Tutzing: Brandt, *Ordeal of Coexistence*, p. 77. WBBA, vol. 3, p. 445.
41 Thomas Alan Schwartz, *Lyndon Johnson and Europe. In the Shadow of Vietnam,* (Cambridge MA: Harvard UP, 2003), pp. 226–30.
42 North Atlantic Council, Brussels, 13–14 December 1967, Harmel report on the future tasks of the Alliance, available on the NATO website, www.nato.int/cps/en/natolive/official_texts_26700.htm (accessed 10 March 2010).
43 These were recurring themes in Brandt's speeches throughout the years of the Grand Coalition: WBBA, vol. 6.
44 WBBA, vol. 6, p. 199, Rede vor dem Bundestag, 26 September 1968.
45 Politisches Archiv des Auswärtigen Amts (PAAA), Berlin, B43, Box 797, Aufz. Strenziok, 20 December 1966.
46 AdG, p. 23305, Brandt im Deutschlandfunk, 2 July 1967.
47 WBBA, vol. 6, pp. 130–37, Artikel Brandts in *Aussenpolitik: Zeitschrift für internationale Fragen*, August 1967.
48 AAPD, 1968, pp. 1084–1985, Gespräch Kiesinger-McGhee, 17 July 1967. NARA, Record Group 59, State Department, Central Foreign Policy Files 1967–69, Box 2117, Intelligence Note by Thomas Hughes, 20 July 1967.
49 NARA, RG 59, CFPF 1967–69, Box 2136, McGhee (Bonn) to DepState, 12 October 1967 (quote). Ibid., Memo for the Secretary by Th. Hughes, 20 July 1967.
50 See the records of conversation in AMAE, RFA, Box 1457.
51 PAAA, B9, Box 178364 (various notes). The German translation of the complete French study was also published in DzD, 1966–67, vol. V/2, pp. 1923–35.
52 PAAA, B9, Box 179346, Aufz. Müller-Roschach, 10 December 1964. Ibid., Box 178344, Aufz. Diehl, 2 June 1967.
53 PAAA, B9, Box 178345, Kolloquium der Naturwissenschaftler, 27 May 1968.
54 On this point, see also my article 'Willy Brandt infidèle? Les incertitudes françaises durant le Printemps de Prague, 1968', *Relations Internationales* no. 134, printemps 2008, pp. 69–81.
55 AAPD, 1968, pp. 796–814, Aufz. Bahr, Europäische Sicherheit, 27 June 1968.
56 Ibid.
57 Ibid. DzD, 1966–67, pp. 1923–35.
58 AdsD, Dep. Bahr, Box 399, Memo Bahr for Brandt, 11 June 1968. AAPD, 1968, pp. 714–15, Telegram Ruete (Belgrade) to Bonn, 13 June 1968.
59 AAPD, 1968, pp. 1006–7, Letter Bahr to Brandt (Hamar), 19 August 1968.
60 Foreign Relations of the United States (hereafter FRUS), vol. XIII (Washington DC: US Government printing office, 1995), Document 334, Intelligence Memorandum, 4 November 1968. See also ibid., Doc. 337, Telegram Rusk (Brussels) to DepState, 16 November 1968.
61 Bundesarchiv, Koblenz, Nachlass Guttenberg (NL 397), Box 94, Gespräch Kiesinger-Clifford, 11 October 1968. Archiv für Christlich-Demokratische Politik (ACDP), Sankt Augustin, Nachlass Kiesinger (NL 226), Box 008–1, Informationsgespräch des Kanzlers im Watergate Hotel, 3 April 1969. Ibid., Box 310, Kiesinger in *Bild am Sonntag*, 26 September 1971.
62 Lyndon B. Johnson Library (LBJL), Austin, NSF, Country File 189/6, CIA report, 13 September 1968.
63 AAPD, 1969, vol. 1, pp. 428–33, Aufzeichnung des Planungsstabs, 24 March 1969.
64 Walter F. Hahn, 'West Germany's Ostpolitik: The Grand Design of Egon Bahr', *Orbis: a journal of world affairs*, vol. 16, no. 4, Winter 1973, pp. 859–80. NARA, RG 59, Subject Numeric Files 1970–73, Box 2301, Telegram Hillenbrand (Bonn) to DepState, Orbis Article on Bahr Plan, 17 April 1973.
65 AAPD, 1969, pp. 672–79, Gespräch Brandt–Macovescu, 4 June 1969.
66 AAPD, 1972, pp. 179–84, Gespräch Brandt–Macovescu, 22 February 1972.
67 AdsD, Depositum Ehmke, Box 217, Vermerk Ehmke, 30 January 1970. WBBA, vol. 6, p. 404, *Spiegel* – Interview mit dem Bundeskanzler, 27 September 1971.
68 Willy Brandt, *Über den Tag hinaus. Eine Zwischenbilanz,* (Hamburg: Hoffmann und Campe, 1974), pp. 499–504. Brandt, *Erinnerungen*, pp. 185–95.
69 AAPD, 1972, pp. 112–23, Gespräch Brandt-Pompidou, 10 February 1972. Brandt later repeated this argument on several occasions.

70 Brandt's office correctly understood that the launch of *Ostpolitik* had reinforced this American objective: AdsD, Dep. Bahr, Box 439, Vermerk Ehmke, 23 December 1970. AAPD, 1973, pp. 862–63, Gespräch Brandt–Heath.
71 NARA, Nixon Presidential Materials, NSC Files, HAK Memcons, Box 1027, Conversation Kissinger–Luns, 13 April 1973. For detailed accounts of German–American relations 1969–74, see the PhD theses by Petri Hakkarainen (University of Oxford, 2008), Giovanni Bernardini (University of Padova, 2005) and Werner Lippert (Vanderbilt University, 2005).
72 AdsD, Dep. Bahr, Vermerk Bahr, 26 January 1967.
73 LBJL, NSF, Bundy Files, Box 15, Conversation Kissinger–Bahr, 10 April 1965.
74 AAPD, 1972, pp. 1791–92, Krapf (Brüssel, NATO) ans Auswärtige Amt, 8 December 1972. On French and British attitudes in that context, see Gottfried Niedhart, *The British Reaction towards Ostpolitik*, in *Debating Foreign Affairs. The Public and British Foreign Policy since 1867*, edited by Ch. Haase (Berlin: Philo, 2003), pp. 130–52, as well as the contributions by Georges-Henri Soutou, Hans-Peter Schwarz and Wilfried Loth in *Willy Brandt und Frankreich*, edited by H. Möller and M. Vaïsse (Munich: Oldenbourg, 2005).
75 AAPD, 1971, pp. 1731–32, Aufz. von Staden, 16 November 1971. Ibid., pp. 49–63, Aufz. Oncken, 14 January 1971.
76 NARA, Nixon Presidential Materials, NSC Files, Box 688, Conversation Kissinger–Strauss, 18 October 1973.
77 NARA, Nixon Presidential Materials, NSC, Country Files, Box 683, Bonn Embassy to Secratary of State, 11 February 1970.
78 AAPD, 1973, pp. 763, Gespräch Brandt–Breschnew, 20 May 1973.
79 WBBA, vol. 6, p. 454, Regierungserklärung, 18 January 1973, and p. 495, Gespräch mit Rovan, 22 August 1973.
80 See e.g. Brandt's conversations with Pompidou: AAPD, 1971, pp. 1078–80, 6 July 1971. *Idem*, 1972, pp. 896–97, 3–4 July 1972. *Idem*, 1973, pp. 1018–19, 21 June 1973.
81 AAPD, 1973, pp. 801–4, Aufz. Roth, 24 May 1973. While Bahr clearly favoured this idea, Brandt showed his support more carefully. CSCE: Conference on Security and Cooperation in Europe, opened in Helsinki in July 1973.
82 Egon Bahr, 'Sicherheit durch Annäherung. Eine europäische Sicherheitsgemeinschaft in Zentraleuropa: Modell für den alten Kontinent', *Die Zeit*, 29 June 1990, p. 6. Bahr's statements of 14, 16 and 30 November 1989 are quoted by Vogtmeier, *Egon Bahr*, pp. 322–32. For a critical view on Bahr's position in 1989–90, see Daniel Friedrich Sturm, *Uneinig in die Einheit. Die Sozialdemokraten und die Vereinigung Deutschlands 1989–90*, (Bonn: Dietz, 2006).
83 Wilfried Loth, 'Mikhail Gorbachev, Willy Brandt, and European Security', *Journal of European Integration History*, vol. 11, no. 1, 2005, pp. 45–59. Loth convincingly illustrates Brandt's influence with quotes from different documents and with Gorbachev's own testimony.
84 Ibid. Schöllgen, *Willy Brandt*, pp. 270–80. Merseburger, *Willy Brandt*, pp. 836–49. Sturm, *Uneinig in die Einheit*, pp. 464–72. WBBA, vol. 10, pp. 87–101.

7

Negotiating with the enemy and having problems with the allies

The impact of the Non-Proliferation Treaty on transatlantic relations

Leopoldo Nuti

This chapter focuses on one of the tensest moments in the history of the Atlantic Alliance's nuclear dilemmas, namely the latest phase of the negotiations that led to the signature of the Non-Proliferation Treaty (NPT). As the USA, Great Britain and the USSR drew near the conclusion of a treaty, two of the key Western European allies, namely West Germany and Italy, displayed a growing resentment towards what they saw as an unprecedented turnaround, and forced the Johnson administration to adjust to at least some of their requests before they joined the NPT.

After a brief survey of the early phase of the NPT negotiations, the chapter focuses on the crucial period between late 1966 and early 1968, when the USA reached an agreement with the Soviet Union for a joint draft treaty. The chapter then explores the criticism levelled by West Germany and Italy against the Soviet–American draft. Particular attention is given to the Italian–German bilateral discussions, in which representatives of the two governments frankly expressed their disappointment at the evolution of the NPT talks. Finally, the chapter evaluates somewhat more in depth the motivations of this hostile attitude and also tries to interpret the significance of this episode for the evolution of the alliance. The major sources used for this chapter include US (Foreign Relations of the United States; National Archives, Johnson and Kennedy Libraries, Declassified Documents Reference Service), Italian (Ministry of Foreign Affairs, the private collections of Aldo Moro and Amintore Fanfani papers) and German ones (Politisches Archiv des Auswärtiges Amt, AAPD).

The early phase of the NPT negotiations

As is well known, the event that pushed the USA to step up its dialogue with the Soviet Union was the first nuclear test by the People's Republic of China in October 1964.[1] Shortly after the event, President Johnson appointed a Special Committee led by Roswell Gilpatric, which concluded that the diffusion of atomic weapons was fast becoming a key threat for the USA and urged the administration to sign a non-proliferation treaty as early as possible.[2]

The Gilpatric report became the basis of US policy at the eighth session of the so-called Eighteen Nations Disarmament Committee (ENDC), which was the main international body dealing with disarmament and arms control issues. Negotiations, however, moved slowly, as the USA had to balance its new interest on non-proliferation with the need to reassure the NATO allies about its nuclear guarantee to Western Europe. The debate about how best to implement that guarantee had been going on for several years without reaching a satisfactory conclusion, but most NATO members continued to display a strong interest in the principle of sharing control of the US nuclear arsenal – even if the latest scheme, the so-called Multilateral Force (MLF), was so convoluted that few seem to have seriously believed in its actual fulfilment. And yet the principle of nuclear sharing that the MLF proposal embodied was too important to be dismissed. NATO registered an intense exchange of opinions on the compatibility of the MLF with non-proliferation,[3] and the non-proliferation draft tabled by the USA on 17 August 1965 'was carefully phrased to keep open the possibility both of the MLF/ANF and of an eventual European force'.[4]

The Soviet Union, however, made it clear that it would not discuss – let alone sign – a non-proliferation treaty which would not explicitly ban the creation of any of NATO's nuclear sharing schemes. For almost two years the Soviets would systematically repeat at each session of the ENDC that these NATO projects had no other goal than to provide a revanchist West Germany with some form of control over the US atomic arsenal, thereby introducing an element of profound destabilization in the European status quo.

We are moving away from the realization of a non-proliferation treaty – said for example on June 23, 1966, the Head of the Soviet Delegation in Geneva, Alexei Roshchin – because the United States have put their NATO policies and their plans for strengthening their military alliance with the Federal Republic of Germany above the problem of non-dissemination, and above the exigencies of the UN General Assembly.[5]

A similar position was also held throughout the bilateral US–Soviet talks.[6] For a while the Johnson administration tried to persuade the Soviets that the NATO nuclear sharing schemes had actually been conceived to prevent, and not to encourage, nuclear proliferation.[7] The Kremlin, however, constantly refused this interpretation and inexorably pushed the USA towards a choice that Washington tried to avoid or, if possible, to delay. Both Johnson and his key collaborators shared the belief that the creation of a NATO MLF was unlikely if not entirely impossible. At the same time they were also aware of the possible repercussions on alliance cohesion if the project was dropped, particularly because NATO was going through a difficult adjustment to the new international challenges of the 1960s.[8]

Until the USA modified its approach, therefore, the Geneva negotiations were mostly an opportunity for the delegates of both blocs to hurl insults at each other and score propaganda points. The repeated hints to Vietnam, which were a main staple of the meetings, however, make clear that there was another dimension in the US–Soviet dialogue which must be taken into account to explain what went on in Geneva, namely the rapid escalation of the US war in South-East Asia. The US involvement in the Vietnam War was, in fact, predicated from the start on the assumption of a bipolar co-division of responsibilities in which one superpower understood and reacted to the gestures of the other. As Lloyd Gardner has argued, much of the carefully implemented escalation of the conflict was calculated and designed with Moscow in mind as much as Hanoi. The 'signals' that were to be sent by the gradual application of military pressure were supposed to be picked up in the Kremlin, according to the theories of 'crisis management' whose soundness was believed to have been proved in the Cuban missile crisis.[9] Even when the beginning of the bombing elicited a strongly negative Soviet response, there were hints on both sides about the need to cooperate. Soviet Ambassador Anatoly Dobrynin, for instance, told Vice President Humphrey that 'there were other ways' to discuss the issue beside formal negotiations, adding that 'during the Cuban confrontation, his house had been used for various things, not for negotiations, but for things that have been instrumental in getting a settlement'.[10] Linkage between Vietnam and arms control was also made quite explicit by the Soviet diplomat:

> it can be said that tensions that recently increased in connection with the United States' acts in Southeast Asia create the atmosphere which by no means facilitates negotiations on disarmament. One cannot ignore in this connection also the plans for creating the NATO nuclear forces in any of their variations – in the form of 'multilateral force' or 'Atlantic Force'.[11]

In the following years the USSR would continue to issue its warnings, either insisting that no agreement on non-proliferation could be reached until the 'Vietnam issue leaves the scene', or placing Vietnam and NATO nuclear sharing on the same level as the major obstacles to an improvement of the bilateral relations.[12]

Fully aware of the linkage established by the Soviets, the Johnson administration debated what issue should be given top priority. Some denied that there could ever be a 'grand global deal' with the Soviets, and those who held a strong Eurocentric view, à la George Ball or à la John McCloy, criticized any inversion which might place Vietnam and US–Soviet détente above US–European relations.[13] Initially it looked as if this view might gain the upper hand. Détente with Moscow was not worth the 'sacrifices' that the Soviets demanded, be they either the negotiation of 'a settlement in Vietnam on Hanoi's terms', or the abandonment of any 'plans for nuclear sharing in NATO'.[14] As the war dragged on, however, it became clear that a possible way to break the deadlock in US–Soviet relations would lay in a possible reversal: rather than yielding in Vietnam to achieve an agreement on non-proliferation, the USA might be willing to soften its position on nuclear sharing in order to get possible Soviet help in South-East Asia. Averell Harriman clearly spelled this option out in October 1966:

> I believe the only chance now to induce Hanoi to negotiate a settlement depends on the influence Moscow is willing and able to exert [...] If Moscow is to take on the task of persuading Hanoi to move towards a settlement, the USSR will probably have to assume certain risks and obligations. Thus I believe we must offer some compensating inducements.
>
> In my judgement, the overpowering desire of Moscow today is for greater stability in Europe. Regardless of how we assess developments in Germany in the years ahead, I am convinced that the Soviet leaders are deeply concerned over a possible re-emergence of a German threat to Russian security. The Kremlin desires a nuclear non-proliferation pact with Germany particularly in mind. I seriously doubt that the Soviet Union will be satisfied with a formula which would permit 'hardware participation' by the Germans. A possible quid pro quo for Moscow's action in Southeast Asia would be our abandoning the hardware option in our proposals for

the pact. Although few Germans really believe a NATO hardware deal is probable, its abandonment would mean to the Germans the giving up of a hope which has some political appeal.[15]

Harriman's ideas do not necessarily represent the position of the whole Johnson administration. Yet one should note that as the ENDC negotiations moved towards the drafting of a non-proliferation treaty which accepted the Soviet requests, the Soviet position on Vietnam underwent a sensible change. In his talk with Soviet Foreign Minister Gromyko on 10 October 1966, President Johnson felt he detected such a change, namely that 'Gromyko had indicated that the Soviets now have some influence in North Viet-Nam and that, if the bombing were to cease, there was reason to hope that this would be followed by positive action on the part of the North', a comment which according to Ambassador Thompson was because 'the Soviets probably consider that a posture of improved relations will help bring pressure on us for agreements they would like to achieve, such as a non-proliferation treaty'.[16] Shortly afterwards, in Moscow, the Politburo approved a report drafted from the Soviet Foreign Ministry which stated that 'putting an end to the Vietnam conflict would undoubtedly have a positive effect on Soviet–American relations and open up new possibilities for solving certain international problems'.[17] At about the same time, or shortly afterwards, two important secret diplomatic efforts (Marigold and Sunflower, the latter directly involving Soviet Premier Kosygin) tried to clear the path towards a negotiated settlement of the Vietnam War, until the dismal failure of Sunflower brought to a temporary halt all Soviet attempts to broker an end to the conflict.

A first sign of change in the US attitude towards the NPT could be detected during the twenty-first Session of the United Nations General Assembly, in the autumn of 1966, when the Johnson administration made a new, sustained effort to persuade the Soviet Union of its own will to reach a joint solution to the issue of non-proliferation. Rusk, in particular, told Gromyko that the real obstacle did not lie in the relations between the USA and the Soviet Union but in those which each one of them had with the non-nuclear powers:

> He said that if the US and the USSR could reach agreement on a treaty, while they would still be unable to force other countries to sign it, they would be in a much better position to influence them to do so. He pointed out that many of the arguments used by non-nuclear countries against non-proliferation were merely contrived pretexts, designed to hold their positions open for future negotiating purposes. He did not accept such arguments as genuine. The Secretary went on to say that he could not see why our two countries could not agree about the heart of the matter and then put their heads together to see what could be done to make other countries, which were presently merely 'flirting', sign the treaty.[18]

And Gromyko, in his reply, was hardly less clear:

> He wanted to ask the question very clearly, whether the US was ready to say so in the treaty. He defined what he meant by saying that the treaty must contain a prohibition against non-nuclear countries producing or receiving nuclear weapons directly or indirectly. Nuclear countries must be forbidden to transfer nuclear weapons into the national hands of any non-nuclear country, directly or indirectly.

He added that the Secretary knew what he meant by the word 'indirectly'. He meant by that transfer of nuclear weapons *through an alliance*. [my emphasis] If the treaty could contain such a prohibition, he would think that the major part of the difficulties was already behind us.

In spite of such blunt language, finding a mutually agreeable formula still required time, particularly because the US as Rusk told Gromyko later on, was not willing to simply say to their allies that 'that the nuclear problem is none of their business. Mr. Gromyko must understand that this would be an absolutely untenable position for us and one which would not be understood or supported by our allies since they, after all, are targeted by Soviet nuclear weapons'. This position was, incidentally, also shared by the US president himself.[19] And yet the inner logic of Rusk's first statement seems to go straight to the heart of the matter, insofar as it seemed to reverse the conceptual mindset of 20 years of Cold War when it hinted at the necessity to overcome the resistance that the allies might put up against any entente between the two superpowers. The final success of the non-proliferation negotiation, therefore, depended on the US capacity to persuade its non-nuclear European allies to drop any nuclear aspiration they might have nurtured and to abandon for good the perspective of a possible MLF. From the Soviet point of view, this was the first important – indeed crucial – step towards the consolidation of the status quo in East-central Europe and the definite dismissal of any revisionist trend in West German foreign policy.

Between September and October 1966 the delegates of the two superpowers saw a significant rapprochement between their positions. By early December, they had achieved a general agreement on the first two articles of the treaty, which prohibited nuclear states from transferring their weapons to non-nuclear ones and explicitly stated that the latter should not try to procure them. The key of the whole agreement was in the formulation of article I which, rather than explicitly declaring the prohibition to transfer nuclear weapons to states or 'groups of states', as the Soviets would have preferred, now stated that each nuclear power committed itself not to transfer nuclear weapons, or control over such weapons 'directly or indirectly' 'to any recipient whatsoever' – which was a formulation specifically conceived to make less brutal the prohibition to transfer them to any such alliance as NATO.[20]

Hostile reactions: West Germany and Italy

As the US–Soviet negotiations inched their way forward towards a conclusion which would sacrifice the MLF, a crucial role in making the cancellation of the project more palatable to the European allies was played by the establishment of the Alliance's Nuclear Planning Group (NPG). This was the invention of US Secretary of Defense Robert McNamara, conceived to replace the sharing of the 'nuclear hardware' (the weapons) with the 'nuclear software' (the plans for the actual use of the US weapons).[21] In spite of the implementation of the NPG, however, the reactions of the Western European allies to the new NPT draft were remarkably hostile.[22] Only Great Britain, which had been involved in the NPT negotiations and had played an important role in trying to bridge the gap between the different US and Soviet points of view, stood out in supporting it.

Reactions in West Germany and Italy, in particular, featured a remarkable degree of resentment. Chancellor Ludwig Erhard seemed to be willing to go along with the draft, but only as long as it allowed German participation to a future multilateral force in NATO, which was exactly what the Russians did not want. Only the SPD seemed to be willing to accept the treaty, provided it did not prevent at least a German participation in the alliance's nuclear planning. The so-called 'Gaullist' faction inside the CDU, however, would not settle for anything less than the theoretical perspective of a 'European option', advocating a treaty that should explicitly mention the possibility of setting up a fully nuclear European defence community of which Germany would be a core member. 'The emphasis and emotive quality of the arguments used to sustain' this European option, Helga Haftendorn has written, 'can only be understood in light of the shock produced by the USA and the Soviet Union reaching a common ground on the issue of non proliferation'.[23] The range of epithets that were hurled at the treaty by its German opponents is indeed an impressive one: Adenauer called it a 'Morgenthau plan squared' and Franz-Josef Strauss 'a Versailles of cosmic proportions'. More subtly, Erhard's successor, the new chancellor Kurt-Georg Kiesinger saw in the treaty 'a kind of atomic complicity' between the superpowers.[24]

The German hostility can be roughly divided in two phases: while Erhard was chancellor, criticism was much more outspoken, particularly as it became more and more unlikely that there would be an Atlantic Nuclear Force or MLF which might give Germany 'a finger on the nuclear trigger'. The second phase, during the grand coalition government with Kiesinger and Brandt, coincided with the emerging of the close US–Soviet cooperation and it elicited an even stronger criticism from the Gaullist factions of the CDU. Yet the government took a slightly different attitude towards the treaty: as Brandt hastened to point out in his first visit to Washington in February 1967, it was acceptable, provided that a large number of German requests be met.[25] Although less outspoken, therefore, the new government remained quite critical of the treaty and slowed down remarkably the conclusion of the negotiations by asking the USA to adjust the draft to its requests – some of which the USA suspected of being just a mask for more substantial hostility.[26] As late as November 1967, according to a report by a US diplomat, not one among the 50 or 60 top West German politicians and officials supported the NPT.[27]

The reasons for this hostility were never completely spelled out, but in spite of the number of explanations offered at the time it is quite clear that the paramount issue was the political and symbolic importance of the treaty. Bange stresses the creation of 'a volatile and dangerous situation – both in a domestic and an international setting – through the combination of secret national goals and the personal futures of the protagonists. Both Strauss and Barzel seem to have aspired to topple Kiesinger by raising national emotions over issues of nuclear defense and national status'.[28] It was not nuclear armament *per se*, however, that West Germany was seeking, although parity with the other powers was an important issue, and there were echoes of the *Gleichberechtigung* debate of the 1930s throughout this period. Rather, the achievement of a nuclear status through NATO was seen as an instrument which might allow the Federal Republic to continue its previous policy based on the Hallstein doctrine and the search for a reunification of Germany from a position of strength. A nuclear Germany within NATO might exchange its potential rearmament for a more flexible Soviet attitude towards reunification, or use the threat of its nuclear rearmament as a bargaining chip. The formal renunciation to even a theoretical parity, on the contrary, could be swallowed by the Bonn government only with the greatest difficulty. Thus it is somewhat symbolic of the passing of an era that Adenauer's last speech advocated the creation of a federated Europe armed with nuclear weapons.[29] A non-nuclear West Germany, on the other hand, was finally bound to come to terms with the status quo and modify its previous revisionist policies. At the very least, it would have to adopt a much more conciliatory tone towards East Germany and the other East European countries. In short, the NTP made clear that there would not be a nuclear West Germany contesting the partition of the country.

For Italy the NTP was not a matter of vital interests as it was for West Germany, but it still retained a crucial importance. The Italian government had staked all its chances to be placed on an equal footing with the other European powers on achieving a nuclear status through NATO and the USA. Now it had to come to grips with the sudden realization that its policies had been based on a wrong assumption and that the USA had a different set of priorities. Italian uneasiness had already surfaced, even during the first phase of the 18 power negotiations,[30] and the Gilpatric report had elicited some concern lest any new US initiative in the field of arms control might have any negative implications for Italian nuclear aspirations.[31] While supporting détente and non-proliferation in principle, the Italian government led by Aldo Moro believed that there would not be much progress in the Geneva talks and that the ENDC was useful mostly for scoring propaganda points.[32] All the Italian steps inside the committee must be seen against this background, including Foreign Minister Fanfani's suggestion of a temporary moratorium as an alternative to a non-proliferation treaty in July 1965 and the subsequent tabling of a unilateral declaration of non-acquisition in September.[33]

In the following sessions of the ENDC the Italian predisposition to support a treaty went hand in hand with the request of the safeguard of a nuclear option for the European allies, including the possible creation of a European Union fully equipped with nuclear weapons.[34] As the chances of setting up a MLF faded away, and the creation of NATO's NPG was seen at best as a face-saving palliative, a possible European nuclear force acquired a growing relevance as the only course of action for non-nuclear states such as Italy and West Germany.[35] An internal Foreign Ministry memo clearly summed it up: '[...] we have an interest not only to eventually participate to a limited nuclear sharing, but also not to jeopardize the chance of a future European nuclear force'.[36] In March 1966 Prime Minister Moro plainly stated that Italy was favourable to any measure bound to stop the dissemination of nuclear weapons, but that it had also committed itself to the principle of nuclear sharing inside the alliance.[37]

All these attempts to square the circle came to an end by late 1966, when the Italian Foreign Ministry was shown the early Soviet–American NPT draft. It was immediately perceived in Italy as a 'radical step away from the original draft of August 1965', as it abandoned all attempts to reconcile non-proliferation with the principle of nuclear sharing. After defining its position in a number of very restricted meetings,[38] the Italian government concluded that that 'the new draft had a number of potentially dangerous implications for the principles on which Italy had based its Atlantic and European policies for many years'[39] and that Italy could accept a treaty only if its security was clearly protected by an American nuclear guarantee and if it was not discriminated against. Besides, noted an internal memo, the treaty would also end up giving France 'a net political-military hegemony within any continental European political association, which would be a further incentive for the Gaullist policy of excluding Great Britain from the European community'.[40]

As the conclusion of a treaty was still uncertain, some diplomats seemed to believe that Italy may be better off by keeping open the option of reaching a threshold status, which would enhance the country's freedom of manoeuvre.[41] When the Italian Supreme Defence Council met on 20 February, this possibility was actually raised and the president of the republic, the Social Democrat Giuseppe Saragat, seemed willing to consider a national nuclear option. Eventually this drastic choice was discarded, however, and the Council approved a policy of pressures on the USA, hoping to make the treaty more favourable to Italian national interests.[42]

The following months saw Italian diplomacy hard at work in raising a large number of criticisms against the treaty, from its unlimited duration to the nature of the controls. The State Department noted how among the European allies West Germany and Italy had expressed the strongest reservations,[43] and the CIA added that surprisingly Italy seemed the most opposed to the treaty:[44] 'the extent and seriousness of the opposition is disquieting. It tends further to separate Europe from the United States, in ways which may prove to be cumulative'.[45] Yet the early reactions of the USA seemed to display a limited interest in listening to what the Italians had to say, and State Secretary Rusk did not hide his disappointment towards the Italian attitude.[46]

As Italian diplomacy stepped up its efforts to obtain a number of substantial modifications in the text from the USA,[47] it also started a series of close discussions with German politicians and diplomats which clearly show the extent of both countries' resentment. Contacts between the two diplomacies on the issue of non-proliferation had begun very early on, but they were accelerated by the disclosure of the new draft. In September 1966 the German Foreign Minister Gerhard Schröder wrote to Fanfani suggesting a close cooperation between the two governments on this issue. The Italian reply was interested but cautious, as the government was careful not to commit itself too early against a possible entente between the superpowers.[48]

Then in January 1967 the Italian ambassador in Bonn, Luciolli, told the director of the Auswärtiges Amt, Frank, that the new draft was regarded in Rome with the utmost concern, and that accepting it without any changes would amount to a veritable 'final capitulation'.[49] The German embassy in Rome also sought the reaction of the Italian Foreign Ministry with a memo which raised a number of objections very similar to the Italian ones – meeting the full approval of Italian diplomacy.[50] Nevertheless, when the German ambassador to the Atlantic Council, Grewe, tried to shape a common strategy between the two governments, his approaches met with a crucial dilemma, namely which country should go first in leading an open battle against the treaty.[51] The Head of the NATO Office of the Italian Foreign Ministry, ambassador Simonetti, then suggested to the German embassy in Rome that the two countries should keep their cooperation at a very informal level and that they act in parallel in order not to give the impression of a conspiracy. From a tactical point of view, he argued, it would be better to present separately the points of view of their respective governments, possibly changing the motivations of their criticisms.[52] A similar proposal was repeated a few weeks later by a diplomat of the Italian embassy in Bonn who insisted that there should not be any common actions but a very close consultation – a suggestion which met the full approval of his German counterpart, who declared to prefer 'a de facto parallelism to an organized bilateralism'.[53]

These close consultations reached their climax during the crucial months of April and May 1967, when the Italian Prime Minister Aldo Moro met twice with the German Chancellor Kurt Georg Kiesinger on 24 April and 30 May. During their first meeting both expressed their concerns about the treaty. Moro stated that Italy was favourable to a more limited solution, such as a temporary moratorium of the same time span as NATO. Such a solution, Moro said, would avoid the discrepancy between the limited duration of the Alliance and the unlimited obligations of the NPT. Besides, Moro criticized the Soviet–American inclination to impose their *de facto* nuclear monopoly upon the non-nuclear countries, a trend which could have unforeseen consequences. The American attempt to crystallize the situation seemed to him 'unwise', all the more so as the USA, in order not to antagonize the Soviet Union, was unwilling to take into consideration all the Italian suggestions, even if Moscow had already achieved a considerable advantage once the West had decided to abandon the MLF project. Finally, Moro seemed concerned about the possible consequences of this treaty on the future of European integration, as it seemed to give the Soviet Union the right to interfere with the evolution of Europe, should the latter ever evolve into a Federal State which might inherit the nuclear weapons of its member states. Kiesinger shared all of Moro's concerns, voicing his reservation in an even harsher tone than that of his Italian counterpart. Both agreed that a close cooperation and consultation between their governments was of the utmost importance.[54] Such cooperation, they repeated during their second meeting in May, was crucial for protecting NATO – which both regarded as indispensable – from any possible negative consequences. The basic problem, Moro concluded, was for Italy a psychological one – of its rank and status among the nations.[55]

It is hard to assess whether the German–Italian objections to the draft were entirely sincere or if they were merely instrumental, a barely disguised attempt – as the US strongly suspected – to postpone or even halt the conclusion of the NPT negotiations. In the following months some of the tension began to melt down as the USA partly acquiesced to their allies' criticism. Step by step, the initial draft treaty was altered in order to accommodate some of the Italian and German requests, modifying article X (about the duration) and introducing article VI (about the commitment of the nuclear powers to negotiate in good faith their own nuclear disarmament). This reasonable compliance to at least some of the objections partially defanged the German–Italian hostility, as it forced both countries to adopt a less antagonistic attitude. Yet the overall principle of the treaty remained a hard pill to swallow, and each country tried to postpone signing as far as possible – both took advantage of the Czech crisis to postpone signing until early 1969. Italy did not actually ratify until 1975, and it did so only after a heated domestic debate. In the end, however, both countries had no alternative but to accommodate to the choices of their major ally, as neither of them was willing to risk a straightforward confrontation over such a difficult and delicate issue.

Conclusions

The extent of the Italian and German criticism of the NPT must be fully gauged against the background of the creeping crisis in US–West European relations of the second half of the 1960s. The juxtaposition between the NPT negotiations and the Vietnam War created a mental short circuit in the minds of a number of diplomats and politicians in both countries which linked the two events in an unexpected way. By 1965, expressions of concern for a possible Soviet–American deal over the heads of the Europeans were already commonplace, particularly in those countries such as West Germany and Italy which had the strongest interest in the development of a nuclear sharing formula inside NATO. As early as May 1965, Fanfani had asked Rusk whether the 'Soviets might be trying to link the problem in Vietnam with talks on European problems, such as the MLF'.[56] Such concerns were by no means limited to the private discussions of the foreign ministers: in December of the same year, for instance, a similar fear of a possible linkage was explicitly mentioned by the Austrian *Salzburger Volksblatt*, in which an editorial on the war remarked that for the USA the only possible solution in Vietnam was 'a honourable retreat with the diplomatic help of the Soviet Union. This would have a high price. This price was Germany'.[57] By early 1966, when the Soviets displayed an increasing reluctance to lend a helping hand in solving the crisis in Vietnam during the visit of Harold Wilson to Moscow, NATO Secretary General Manlio Brosio interpreted this stiffening of their attitude as a way to pressure the USA into making more concessions in the negotiations about disarmament. In the gloomy, pessimistic interpretation of the NATO crisis that he entrusted to the pages of his journal, Brosio made no mystery of his fear that the USA would end up paying a high price to extricate themselves from Vietnam and that the NPT would turn out to be the ideal ground for a Soviet–American compromise – at the expense of Western Europe and NATO. His view was shared by the Italian ambassador to the USA, Sergio Fenoaltea, who did not fear 'that the Soviets would force the Americans to a bad peace in Asia, but that they might offer a honourable peace in Asia extracting a heavy price in Europe'.[58] Shortly afterwards, in July 1966, the British Minister for Disarmament, Lord Chalfont, made a similar point – although from a completely different perspective, since he actually favoured progress in the arms control field – when he noted that the situation on the ground in Vietnam had deteriorated enough to soften the US position on disarmament, making Washington more amenable to the British suggestions that a future NPT bar all possible forms of German access to nuclear weapons.[59]

According to a number of US documents, Chancellor Kiesinger expressed similar concerns lest 'US global responsibilities in Vietnam would not force the US to some degree to sell out German interests'.[60] Johnson, therefore, was urged by his aides to meet the German's preoccupations by persuading him that the USA was not counting on Moscow to bail itself out of the Vietnamese predicament.[61] Undersecretary of State Nicholas Katzenbach also repeated the concept at the May 1967 meeting of the 'American Council on Germany' – at the height of the uproar about the NPT – that the USA was not pursuing détente at the expense and behind the backs of its friends, and its engagement in Vietnam testified its commitment to the European allies – and not the contrary.[62] One wonders, however, what the effect of these reassurances might have been. Schooled in the tradition of *realpolitik*, most Western European diplomats could not help noticing that at the same time of the escalation in Indochina there were indeed some other steps which reinforced their fears that the dialogue between the USA and the USSR might turn out to contain some dangerous implications for their countries. While the American military commitment in Vietnam grew, the whole structure of the transatlantic association was in fact undergoing a serious redefinition that affected in depth the nature of the relationship between Washington and its allies, reinforcing their fears of a downsizing of their importance for US foreign policy.

The Italian Foreign Ministry, moreover, was adamant in its belief that the central element of the NPT was the denuclearization of the Federal Republic of Germany, which it regarded as a fundamental goal of Soviet foreign policy. Once the Federal Republic had been deprived of a nuclear option, noted a gloomy Foreign Ministry memo of May 1967, it would be deprived of any possible bargaining chip to negotiate its reunification, and it would be forced to accept the European status quo. This would contribute to the consolidation which Moscow had been seeking since the end of the Second World War, and in turn such a consolidation might imply the progressive denuclearization of all of Western Europe, gradually eroding and perhaps totally eliminating the American presence in Europe.[63] A few years later the doyen of the Italian diplomatic corps, Roberto Ducci, would sum up this depressing perspective with one of his typically caustic remarks:

Lyndon Johnson sold out the European Union to the Soviet Union in order to have peace in Vietnam: this is the main reason behind the harsh pressure exerted on Germany and Italy so that they would gracefully castrate themselves renouncing to have a nuclear defence of their own. The result of Johnson's policy was that Gerald Ford was forced to take upon himself the shame to take down the Stars and Stripes in Saigon, while at the same time a mortal blow was dealt to the project of an European Union.[64]

This episode offers a number of important insights into the dynamics of the Cold War and of the transatlantic security system. The first and foremost is the centrality of the nuclear question for the foreign policy making elite of all the parties involved. Throughout the negotiations, nuclear weapons combined a deep symbolic meaning with a crucial strategic significance: for the Soviets, denying their acquisition to West Germany seems to have been the key to the stabilization of Europe, the indispensable precondition for going any further in the implementation of detente; for the USA, they were the key bargaining chip either to strike a deal with the main adversary or to strengthen the cohesion of the alliance; whereas for the Germans and the Italians they retained all along the aura of the crucial instrument with which to achieve their most ambitious foreign policy goals. From the US and the Soviet point of view, therefore, there is no doubt that the NPT was a cornerstone in their approach to détente, as it cemented their dialogue in the field of arms control much beyond the early bond created by the partial test ban treaty of 1963.

A second consideration regards the perception of détente as a much more complex phenomenon than the reduction of tensions between Washington and Moscow. Maybe the interconnection between the NPT negotiations and the Vietnam war should not be stretched too far, but it is clear that for many pro-American politicians in Italy and Germany the combination of these elements affected their perception of détente as not just an improvement of the US–Soviet relationship but as the possible ending of an entire phase of the international system, a dramatic realignment of forces which would require a serious rethinking of their countries' foreign policies. A third conclusion is related to the persistence of national goals and aspirations and of the traditional realist approach in the mindset of politicians and diplomats alike. For all the talk about the new dimensions of the international system, what comes out of this brief episode is the relevance of old-fashioned national interest, defended with equal vigour and stubbornness from all sides. A fourth and final point regards the amazing capacity of the USA to have its cake and it eat it too – to reach an NPT and to shape the orientation of the Western bloc. In spite of all the protests, the USA retained huge leverage with which to corral Italy and Germany where it wanted: eventually both had no alternative than to adjust to the rearrangement of NATO and to the international realignment that the USA orchestrated between 1966 and 1968. In short, the episode sums up quite clearly the complexities, ambiguities and, ultimately, the fundamental asymmetry of the transatlantic security structure – as well as the crucial role of the USA in shaping it.

Notes

1 John Wilson Lewis and Xue Litai, *China Builds the Bomb*, (Stanford: Stanford University Press, 1988), in particular pp. 186–89 for the description of the first test.

2 Report to the President by the Committee on Nuclear Proliferation, January 21, 1965. Personal Papers of Roswell Gilpatric (PPRG), Box 10, John F. Kennedy Library, Boston, MA (JFKL). See also Francis J. Gavin, 'Blasts from the Past: Proliferation Lessons from the 1960s', *International Security*, volume 29, number 3, (Winter 2004/05), pp. 100–135; Hal Brands, 'Rethinking Nonproliferation: LBJ, the Gilpatric Committee, and U.S. National Security Policy', *Journal of Cold War Studies*, volume 8, number 2, Spring 2006, pp. 83–113
3 Anna Locher and Christian Nunlist, 'What Role for NATO? Conflicting Western Perceptions of Detente, 1964–66', paper presented at *NATO, the Warsaw Pact and the Rise of Détente, 1965–1972*, Dobbiaco, 26–28 September 2002, p. 22. Tel. from the Dept. of State to the Embassy in the UK, July 22, 1965, Message from Foreign Secretary Stewart to Sec. of State Rusk, July 23, 1965, in *Foreign Relations of the United States* (FRUS), 1964–68, vol. XI, *Arms control and disarmament*, pp. 229–32. David Tal, 'The Burden of Alliance: The NPT Negotiations and the NATO Factor, 1950–68', in Christian Nuenlist and Anna Locher (eds) *Transatlantic Relations at Stake. Aspects of NATO, 1956–1972*, (Zurich: ETH, 2006), p. 111.
4 Glenn Seaborg, *Stemming the Tide. Arms Control in the Johnson Years*, (Lexington: Lexington Books, 1987), p. 164.
5 'Lettera di informazione dell'Istituto Affari Internazionali', n. 2, 10 novembre 1966 'La conferenza sul disarmo dal 14 giugno al 25 agosto 1966', Archivio Istituto Affari Internazionali (IAI).
6 Vol. XI of the *Foreign Relations of the United States*, 1964–68, contains many examples: see for instance Message from Chairman Kosygin to President Johnson, undated (but January 1966), in FRUS, 1964–68, vol. XI, *Arms control and disarmament*, pp. 277–81.
7 *Memorandum of conversation*, February 27 1964, in FRUS, 1964–68, vol. XI, *Arms control and disarmament*, pp. 24–25.
8 Thomas Alan Schwartz, *Lyndon Johnson and Europe. In the Shadow of Vietnam*, (Cambridge, MA: Harvard University Press, 2003), Massimiliano Guderzo, *Interesse nazionale e responsabilità globale. Gli Stati Uniti, l'Alleanza atlantica e l'integrazione europea negli anni di Johnson, 1963–1969*, (Firenze: Il Maestrale, 2000); Helga Haftendorn, *NATO and the nuclear revolution: a crisis of credibility, 1966–1967*, (Oxford, New York: Clarendon Press, Oxford University Press, 1996); Andreas Wenger, Christian Nuenlist and Anna Locher (eds). *Transforming NATO in the Cold War. Challenges beyond Deterrence in the 1960s*, (London: Routledge, 2006).
9 J. Nathan, 'The Heyday of the New Strategy: the Cuban Missile Crisis and the Confirmation of Coercive Diplomacy', *Diplomacy and Statecraft*, vol. 3, no. 2, 1992. Lloyd C. Gardner, 'Fighting Vietnam. The Russian American Conundrum', in Lloyd C. Gardner and Ted Gittinger (eds), *International Perspectives on Vietnam*, (College Station: Texas A & M University Press, 2000), pp. 23–57. Gardner also makes this point several times in *Pay Any Price. Lyndon Johnson and the Wars for Vietnam*, (Chicago: Ivan R. Dee, 1995).
10 Memorandum of Conversation Between Vice President Humphrey and the Soviet Ambassador (Dobrynin), March 12 1965, in FRUS, 1964–68, vol. XIV, doc. 103.
11 Memorandum of Conversation, March 26, 1965, in FRUS, 1964–68, vol. XIV, doc. 104.
12 Telegram From the Embassy in the Soviet Union to the Department of State, 21 July 1965; Information Memorandum From the Assistant Secretary of State for European Affairs (Leddy) to the Under Secretary of State (Ball), November 25 1965, both in FRUS, 1964–68, vol. XIV, docs 119 and 140.
13 Telegram From the Embassy in the Soviet Union to the Department of State, 17 April 1965, in FRUS, 1964–68, vol. XIV, doc. 107. On George Ball and the war, see David Di Leo, *George Ball, Vietnam, and the Rethinking of Containment*, (Chapel Hill, NC: The University of North Carolina, 1991); on McCloy, Gardner, 'Fighting Vietnam', p. 34.
14 Paper Prepared in the Policy Planning Council, March 23 1966, in FRUS, 1964–68, vol. XIV, doc. 157.
15 Memorandum from the Ambassador at Large (Harriman) to President Johnson and Secretary of State Rusk, October 3 1966, in FRUS, 1964–68, vol. IV, p. 691.
16 Memorandum of Conversation, October 14; Memorandum From the Ambassador at Large (Thompson) to Secretary of State Rusk, October 14 1966, both in FRUS, 1964–68, vol. XIV, docs 180–81. See also Gespräch des Bundesministers Schröder mit dem britischen Außenminister Brown, 4 November 1966, in *Akten zur auswärtigen Politik der Bundesrepublik Deutschland* (AAPD) *1966*, (Munich: Oldenbourg, 1997), b.2, doc. 360.
17 Anatoly Dobrynin, *In Confidence. Moscow's Ambassador to America's Six Cold War Presidents*, (New York: Random House, 1995), pp. 162–63.

18 Memorandum of Conversation, 22 September 1966, in FRUS, 1964–68, vol. XI, doc. 152, pp. 371–72.
19 Memorandum of Conversation, 10 October 1966, in FRUS, 1964–68, vol. XI, doc. 158, p. 390. Lyndon B. Johnson, *The Vantage Point: Perspectives of the Presidency, 1963–1969*, (New York: Holt, Rinehart and Wilson), 1971, p. 478.
20 Seaborg, *Stemming the Tide*, pp. 194–98.
21 Paul Buteux, *The Politics of Nuclear Consultation in NATO, 1965–1980*, (Cambridge: Cambridge University Press, 1984).
22 Oliver Bange, 'NATO and the Non-Proliferation Treaty. Triangulations between Bonn, Washington and Moscow', in Wenger, Nuenlist and Locher, *Transforming NATO*, pp. 166–68.
23 Haftendorn, *NATO and the Nuclear Revolution*, p. 157.
24 Ibid., pp. 160–68.
25 Memo of conversation, 8 February 1967, in FRUS, 1964–68, vol. XI, doc. 435
26 Intelligence Memorandum, 'Status of the Non-Proliferation Treaty Negotiations', 28 February 1967, in *Declassified Documents Research System*, DDRS, 1995, f. 252, doc. 3034.
27 Memo from Edward Fried of the NSC staff to the President's Special Assistant (Rostow), 3 November 1967, in FRUS, 1964–68, vol. XV, doc. 235.
28 Bange, 'NATO and the Non-proliferation treaty', p. 164.
29 George C. McGhee, *At the Creation of a New Germany: From Adenauer to Brandt: An Ambassador's Account*, (New Haven, CT: Yale University Press, 1989), p. 220.
30 Ambassador Cavalletti on 2 July and 23 July 1964, in Archivio Storico del Ministero degli Affari Esteri (ASMAE), Fondo Bettini, b. 10, 'Partecipazione italiana ai negoziati per il disarmo', doc. no. 186, vol. 4, and doc. 192, vol. 5.
31 Ministero degli Affari Esteri, Gruppo di Lavoro sulle questioni del disarmo, Appunto (Visto dal Presidente del Consiglio), 'Progetto Britannico di accordo sulla non disseminazione delle armi nucleari', June 3 1965, in Archivio Centrale dello Stato (ACS), Archivio Moro, Serie 3.
32 Memorandum of Conversation, 20 April 1965, in Lyndon B. Johnson Presidential Library (LBJ Library), NSF, Country file-Italy, b. 196, f. Italy Memos, Vol. III 1/65–10/65.
33 *International Negotiations on the Treaty on the Non-Proliferation of Nuclear Weapons*, (Washington, DC: US Arms Control and Disarmament Agency, 1969), p. 19; Diario Fanfani, 29 and 30 luglio 1965, in Archivio Storico Senato, Carte Fanfani; See also 'L'Italia e i negoziati per il trattato di non diffusione', 29 agosto 1967, typewritten book by Amb. Emilio Bettini, ASMAE, Fondo Bettini, b. 7, pp. 33–39.
34 'L'Italia e i negoziati per il trattato di non diffusione', pp. 51–55. See also Conferenza del Comitato delle 18 potenze sul disarmo, sintesi delle sedute dal 14 giugno al 25 agosto 1966, in IAI, Gruppo di studio sulla politica del disarmo, lettera di informazione n. 2, 10 novembre 1966.
35 On the German Gaullists see Christoph Bluth, *Britain, Germany and Western Nuclear Strategy*, (Oxford: Clarendon Press, 1995) pp. 160–68;
36 Appunto riservato del Ministero degli Esteri, 'Visita in Gran Bretagna dell'On. Nenni', 16 luglio 1966, in ACS, Archivio Nenni, serie governo, b. 114, f. 2382.
37 'L'Italia e i negoziati per il trattato di non diffusione', pp. 59–60.
38 Diario Fanfani, 4 febbraio 1967, in Archivio Storico Senato, Carte Fanfani.
39 'L'Italia e i negoziati per il trattato di non diffusione', pp. 75–79.
40 Appunto. Accordo di non-disseminazione nucleare, 5 febbraio 1967, in ASMAE, Fondo Bettini, b. 1.
41 Il Direttore Generale degli Affari Politici al Consigliere Diplomatico del Presidente del Consiglio, 'Politica nucleare degli Stati Uniti', 22 febbraio 1967, in ACS, Archivio Moro, Serie 3.
42 Diario Fanfani, 20 febbraio 1967, in Archivio Storico Senato, Carte Fanfani. 'L'Italia e i negoziati per il trattato di non diffusione', pp. 125–26.
43 Memorandum from J. Leddy to the Acting Secretary, Italian and other country views on NPT, February 14, 1967, in LBJ PL, Personal Papers of F. Bator, b. 31.
44 Intelligence Memorandum, 'Status of Negotiations on the Non-Proliferation Treaty', May 8, 1967, in DDRS, 1995, fiche 252, doc. n. 3035.
45 Draft Memorandum for the President, 2 February 1967, in DDRS, 1996, f. 260. n. 3073.
46 Tel. 133734 from Dept of State to American embassy Rome, February 8, 1967, in National Archives and Records Administration (NARA), RG 59, Central Foreign Policy Files 1967–69, Box 1729, Folder DEF 18–6 2/1/67.
47 Conversazione Nenni-Foster, 13 marzo 1967, e conversazione Nenni-Humphrey, 31 marzo 1967, both in ACS, Archivio Nenni, serie governo, b. 114, f. 2383, Foster e b. 2383, Humphrey. Tel.

5095, 5097 e 5101, from American embassy Rome to State, 1 April 1967, in NARA, RG 59, Conference Files, b. 438, f. VP's trip to Europe, vol. III, memcons; 'L'Italia e i negoziati per il trattato di non diffusione', cit., pp. 132–36; Appunto. Considerazioni preliminari sulle risposte americane al questionario tecnico da noi consegnato al signor Foster, 8 aprile 1967, in ASMAE, Fondo Bettini, b.1.
48 Carlo Masala, *Italia und Germania. Die deutsch-italienischen Beziehungen 1963–1969*, (Cologne: SH Verlag, 1997).
49 Anlage zu Abschluss eines Non-Proliferations-Vertrages, 12 Januar 1967, in Politisches Archiv des Auswärtigen Amtes, (PAAA), Bestand 150.
50 Appunto, 'Memorandum tedesco sul Trattato di Non proliferazione', 13 aprile 1967, in ASMAE, Fondo Bettini, b.1.
51 Wilhelm G. Grewe, *Rückblenden 1976–1951,* (Frankfurt: Propyläen, 1979), p. 699; Masala, *Italia und Germania*, p. 212.
52 Tel.117 aus Rom, 14 Februar 1967, in PAAA, Bestand 150.
53 Aufzeichnung: Italienische Haltung zu der Europa-Fragen, 23 März 1967, in PAAA, Bestand 150.
54 Aufzeichnung, 28 April 1967, in PAAA, Bestand 150.
55 Aufzeichnung, 5 Juni 1967, in PAAA, Bestand 150.
56 Memorandum of Conversation, 24 May 1965, in NARA, RG 59, Conference Files, b. 379, f. Visit of FM Fanfani.
57 Joachim Arenth, *Johnson, Vietnam und die Westen. Transtlantische Belastungen, 1963–1969,* (Munich: Olzog, 1994), p. 176.
58 *Diario di M. Brosio,* Fondazione Luigi Einaudi, entries of March 2 and November 18, 1966
59 Letter from Chalfont to Lord Hood, Burrows, Street, Barnes, Campbell, Smith, Beeley, Thomson, Zuckerman, July 4, 1966. Public Record Office, FO 371/187467 IAD 1052/155. I would like to thank Edoardo Sorvillo for providing me with a copy of this document
60 Gardner, 'Fighting Vietnam', p. 47. See also State Dept. report, 'Problems Ahead in Europe', undated (but 1967, in DDRS, 1984, f. 110, n. 1701). For a slightly different approach, 'Talking points – Force levels in Europe', February 27, 1967, in DDRS, 1993, f 131, doc 1537.
61 Guderzo, *Interesse Nazionale*, pp. 426–27.
62 Arenth, *Johnson, Vietnam.*
63 Appunto. Il Trattato contro la diffusione delle armi nucleari e la Conferenza sulla sicurezza europea, 22 maggio 1967, in ASMAE, Fondo Bettini, b. 2.
64 TE Ris. Dall'Ambasciata di Londra al Ministro degli Esteri, 'Il posto dell'Italia nel mondo degli anni ottanta', 27 dicembre 1979, in *Roberto Ducci,* (Rome: Ministero degli Affari Esteri), p. 221.

8

Power shifts and new security needs

NATO, European identity, and the reorganization of the West, 1967–75

Andreas Wenger and Daniel Möckli

Introduction

In 1975, Western statesmen convened under the auspices of four different institutions within a short period of time. These summit gatherings signaled a new diversification of the West's governance structures and a diffusion of political responsibility. First, there was a NATO summit in Brussels at the end of May. Its main purpose was to demonstrate that allied cohesion, having been absent during the turbulent transatlantic crisis of 1973/74, had been restored, now that the final phase of the Conference on Security and Cooperation in Europe (CSCE) had begun. Then, there was the European Council, in mid-July, which also met in Brussels. This was a new institution, set up to allow the nine member states of the European Community (EC) to provide strategic guidance on both EC matters and on European Political Cooperation (EPC), Europe's foreign policy structure that had been created in 1970. The third meeting was the CSCE summit in Helsinki at the end of July. This first multilateral East–West summit brought together 35 heads from Western and Eastern European states and from the USA and Canada to sign the CSCE Final Act, which reconceptualized security in Europe and provided a normative framework for peaceful change in Europe. The fourth and final summit took place at Rambouillet, France, in mid-November. On this occasion, the Group of Six (G6), which was soon to become the Group of Seven, was set up to enable the Western great powers to formulate joint responses to the pressing economic problems that were increasingly dominating the security agenda.[1]

By contrast, when the Harmel report was published in 1967, NATO was still the only relevant multilateral political structure that was able to coordinate and harmonize the West's Cold War policies. The Harmel exercise reformed NATO from within, strengthening its political functions and reshaping its institutional structures. NATO's then-new two-pillar security policy, together with its new force-planning and nuclear-consultation machinery, allowed it to shift the issues of a European settlement (including the German question) and of arms control (including the nuclear question) away from the bilateral Soviet–US "little détente" of 1963 and place these issues into the broader context of the multilateral European détente of the 1970s. Yet the political functions of NATO remained limited and closely linked to the Alliance's military strength: the allies were unable to agree on whether or not there was a need for a new political machinery; they were unable to reach a consensus on the development and long-term aim of their détente policies; they achieved a fragile, short-term compromise with regard to the balance between security and economy, but failed to define a sound financial basis for NATO and a functioning governance structure for regulating the West's monetary affairs; and they were unable to agree on out-of-area consultation, especially with regard to the Middle East.[2]

The transformation of transatlantic relations and Western political structures in the 1960s and early 1970s was triggered by a number of interlinked structural forces. First, the changing military balance—from US nuclear superiority to US–USSR nuclear parity—undermined the credibility of the US nuclear guarantee to its European allies. This in turn increased tension within NATO regarding military strategy and nuclear control. Second, the changing economic balance facilitated the evolution of the European Economic Community (EEC) and reshaped the distribution of economic power away from Washington and towards Europe. Third, a growing assertiveness in the global south meant that policy makers on both sides of the Atlantic had begun to think in terms of national, rather than Alliance, interests—which rendered it ever more difficult for the Alliance to agree on out-of-area policies for different regional settings. These three trends led to a fundamental restructuring of East–West relations at a time of emerging détente, on the one hand, and brought about the shift of political power from Washington to key US allies in Europe, on the other.

The power shifts that occurred in the late 1960s and early 1970s meant that security and defense could no longer be separated from the debate about the political and economic structures that governed the West. Western policy makers realized that there were forces at work within the transatlantic Alliance which reflected larger domestic and social changes and which made the status quo of transatlantic and European governance unsustainable. Foreign and security policies had to be anchored in domestic politics, which, throughout Western societies, were increasingly being undermined by protest movements aimed at what the protesters saw as an emptiness in, and a stagnation of, public institutions and governmental authority.[3] Given the growing interest in finding a common economic, social, and political exchange across the Cold War divide, policy makers in allied countries began to fear that NATO was being perceived by the Western public as a static and conservative institution that did no more than freeze the status quo. In domestic debates, questions of détente and nuclear control were being closely linked to the issue of sovereignty and political independence, and the question of burden sharing was being discussed in terms of wider financial and economic challenges. Thus, policy makers realized that their governance efforts would have to take public perception into consideration when dealing with issues of security and détente; balance the growing assertiveness of a distinct European identity with a more heterogeneous transatlantic identity; and achieve all this without endangering the interests and the unity of the West.

While the reorganization of the West during the 1960s and early 1970s did not follow any grand design, the role of human agency as a driver of institutional change should not be underestimated. Generational change and the arrival of a new set of leaders in key Western capitals resulted on several occasions in policy changes that facilitated institutional change. Thus, the multilateralization of the German question and the nuclear question in the context of NATO's transformation in the late 1960s cannot be understood without taking into account the dismissal of the old transatlantic elite (Dean Acheson, George Ball) in Washington and the growing influence of the SPD and Willy Brandt on foreign policy making in Bonn. The rise of Europe as a new political force in the early 1970s was tightly linked to the change of the French president in 1969 from Charles de Gaulle to Georges Pompidou and to the coming to power in 1970 of Edward Heath, the most pro-European prime minister Britain had ever had. And the restoration of US leadership and the reorganization of the West in 1974/75 was connected to the rise to power of Gerald Ford in Washington, Helmut Schmidt in Bonn, Valéry Giscard d'Estaing in Paris, and Harold Wilson in London.

By 1967, the Harmel exercise had signaled that the allies, accepting the risk of fragmentation within NATO, had grudgingly set out on the arduous task of trying to reach a new consensus on the political organization of the West. The key issue for the West's policy makers had already been outlined by Walt W. Rostow, from the Policy Planning Staff, in a memorandum to US Secretary of State Dean Rusk in late 1963:

> The atmosphere of *détente* and the assertion of more familiar nationalist impulses does not eliminate all the areas of common interest within the West, nor does it preclude continued movement forward in joint ventures which would, in effect, organize the world of diffusing power into a world of diffused responsibility.[4]

This, then, remained the key challenge for Western policy makers: how, in a world of diffusing power, could they best adapt the West's old governance structures—politically and functionally—to a new world of diffused responsibility?

Institutional diversification of the West's governance structures evolved in three distinct phases. In the first phase, from 1967 to 1970, the allies focused on the internal reform of NATO as a means of multilateralizing the German question and the nuclear question. A majority within NATO agreed that as long as these two questions remained unresolved, NATO would have to remain the bedrock of the West's governance structure. However, during the Harmel exercise, NATO member states, and in particular the USA, recognized that the political lead in the development of a European détente had to be left to the Europeans, especially the West Germans. In return, Bonn would have to accept its status as a permanently non-nuclear state in the Non-proliferation Treaty (NPT) and agree to coordinate its *Ostpolitik* in the multilateral structures of the Alliance. With regard to the evolution of East–West détente, the NATO member states made progress with their preparations for a security conference, linking the conference to progress of the Federal Republic of Germany's (FRG) *Ostpolitik*. The West's linkage strategy achieved its main purpose in 1970 with the signing of the Moscow and Warsaw treaties, which went a long way towards stabilizing Central Europe. For NATO, however, this meant that its political legitimacy would soon after come under renewed attack.

In the second phase, from 1970 to early 1974, diverging conceptions of détente, the beginning of European foreign policy cooperation, and growing economic and monetary differences prompted heated debates about how to further adapt transatlantic governance. Divergent European and US visions discounted the possibility of a consensus. While the USA focused on managing bilateral superpower relations, with little interest in the CSCE as the European multilateral variant of détente, the Europeans perceived the CSCE process as a unique opportunity to encourage the Soviet Union to subscribe to an expanded concept of security that included human rights. The CSCE became a catalyst for the rapid development of a European political identity, which raised the issue of the EPC's position vis-à-vis NATO. The breakdown of the Bretton Woods monetary system, and increasing trade bickering between the EC and the USA, underlined the governance deficits of the West.

Then the US "Year of Europe" initiative of April 1973—designed to expand and strengthen the Atlantic framework—prompted the Europeans to suggest a new bilateralism between the EC-Nine and the USA and to issue a declaration on their distinct European identity. The controversy over how to redesign the West peaked with the October War and the oil crisis in late 1973 and early 1974, as their conceptual differences translated into clashing policies in the Middle East and competing forms of energy governance.

Finally, the third phase of 1974/75 saw an agreement on how to reorganize the West into a pattern of diffused but hierarchically structured relationships. As the growing economic crisis undermined the cohesion of the EC and shifted power from Europe back to the USA, the limits of Europe's governance capability became exposed. The restoration of US leadership within NATO reflected the fact that Atlantic stability was now widely considered a higher priority than the establishment of a European identity, with the EPC losing much steam and in effect becoming subordinate to NATO. However, the scope of the Alliance remained limited, and the great powers created the G6/G7 to deal with those pressing economic and energy issues that had come to dominate the security agenda. This new political structure implicitly became the key steering tool of the new Western governance system, reflecting and at the same time reinforcing the weakness of existing multilateral institutions. Finally, the Helsinki Final Act became a symbol for the recovered cohesion of the West. As the USA threw its weight behind the European positions in the last phase of CSCE negotiations, the allies succeeded in transforming the conference into a long-term framework that enabled them to engage the Soviet Union in a continuing dialog on peaceful change in Europe.

It is along these three developmental stages that this chapter analyzes the reorganization of Western governance structures taking place between 1967 and 1975.

The Harmel script: the transformation of NATO, *Ostpolitik*, and détente in Europe, 1967–70

After the Berlin and the Cuban missile crises, the West's political elites realized that their people would increasingly demand a reduction of tensions between NATO and the Warsaw Pact. However, disagreement over the tricky question of who should take the lead in negotiating an opening between the two blocs soon increased the political tensions between the European states and the USA. The dynamic element in the post-Cuban environment was the bilateral relaxation in 1963 between Washington and Moscow—with the signing of the Limited Test Ban Treaty (LTBT) as its highlight—and what this limited bilateral cooperation meant for the internal organization of the Alliance. The US–Soviet negotiations clearly impinged on allied, and in particular on West German, sovereignty. After all, the German question—and the associated issue of post-World War II borders in Central Europe—and the nuclear question—and the associated issue of nuclear control and political independence—were at the centre of the emerging superpower *modus vivendi*. From a European perspective, it was simply unacceptable that the process of détente evolved top-down, formed by the global interests of the two superpowers. Together, the FRG and France were however strong enough to block the multilateralization of détente in 1963, because the next steps—including a nuclear non-proliferation treaty—would be multilateral and would need the consent of all allies.[5]

While most Western European states were in favor of increasing Europe's political clout, they disagreed both about the form and size of a future European polity, as well as about the relationship of such a polity to a NATO under US leadership. For French President Charles de Gaulle, US forces in Europe would have to leave before the historic process of détente could proceed. However, his vision of an independent European polity under French leadership was not popular with a majority of Europeans. Most Europeans felt that as long as the German question remained unresolved, a strong partnership with the USA would have to be the political bedrock of the West.[6]

In the wake of the Cuban missile crisis, de Gaulle had tried to increase French influence in Europe by forming a close partnership with the FRG. Forced to choose between Washington and Paris, a majority of West Germans favored a strong transatlantic security framework and rejected de Gaulle's vision of an intergovernmental grouping of continental European states (minus Britain) under French military and political leadership. Once it became clear that the Elysée Treaty of 1963 would not work, France decided to shift towards a bilateral détente policy, first forming a relationship with smaller East European states, then embarking on a rapprochement with the Soviet Union. These efforts culminated in de Gaulle's trip to Moscow in June 1966, a trip that came soon after the announcement by France that it would withdraw its remaining forces from NATO's integrated military command. These developments caused alarm among the rest of the Alliance: the ultimate danger of the Gaullist challenge to NATO was that it threatened to undermine the FRG's position in the post-war world which was that "Germany's politics and policy have to be conducted within the collective NATO framework and that a separate German policy is not feasible."[7]

NATO's 1966/67 crisis and reform

NATO's 1966/67 crisis had been in the making since 1963. Yet de Gaulle's actions of 1966 unlocked the Alliance and gave it a chance to define a new vision for NATO in a rapidly changing domestic and international environment. In the preceding three years, the allies had expressed the general consensus that NATO should be preserved beyond 1969, with or without France. At the same time, by 1966/67 it had become clear that NATO decision making was in need of reform and that its political functions had to be strengthened, should it continue to exist after its twentieth anniversary. The main aim of NATO reform should be greater European participation in a less hierarchical and a more political alliance. US President Lyndon B. Johnson realized that the USA had to abandon the hegemonic leadership style of the 1950s and exercise its leadership within NATO as *primus inter pares*. The Europeans had a legitimate role to play in international affairs, Dean Rusk told George Ball, and he felt it "important to draw a line between leadership and hegemony."[8]

NATO's institutional reform between 1966 and 1968 provided an effective solution to the Alliance's nuclear problems. Ambiguity on terminology relating to strategy—on the concepts of political warning, flexibility, and escalation—was a precondition for a political compromise between the remaining 14 allies on strategy and burden sharing. The agreement between the USA, Britain, and the FRG on strategy and burden sharing in their trilateral talks paved the way for the eventual adoption of flexible response, with the signing of MC 14/3 in December 1967.[9] As regards NATO's institutional reform, the establishment of the Nuclear Planning Group (NPG) was clearly the critical element. The NPG increased the role of the FRG in nuclear consultation and decision making. This in turn made it easier for the FRG to accept the NPT, on the one hand, and for the Soviet Union to accept a software solution for NATO's nuclear sharing problem, on the other. In effect, the NPT internationalized the touchy question of German nuclear control and paved the way for the breakthrough in superpower negotiation on strategic nuclear weapons and anti-ballistic missile systems in the early 1970s.[10]

At the same time, the Harmel exercise played a key role in restoring NATO's political purpose and its legitimacy as an instrument of détente. In essence, the exercise stabilized the consensus on NATO's new flexible response strategy and on its new force-planning and nuclear-consultation machinery in a multilateral political dialog on the future of East–West relations and on the German question. Two elements stand out in the Alliance's political deliberations: first, the report acknowledged the danger of a selective détente that would split the unity of the Alliance. While the Europeans acknowledged that the US presence in Europe would remain vital to a peaceful order, even after a European settlement, Washington agreed to give the lead in the development of political détente to its European partners. Second, the allies accepted that it was the primary responsibility of the FRG to define the development of political contacts between the two German states. In return, Bonn agreed in principle that NATO institutions would play a key role in harmonizing and coordinating the détente policies of the allies, in effect providing a forum for the monitoring of the FRG's internal debate and the progress of *Ostpolitik*.

With the Harmel report, NATO recognized that a European settlement would not be achieved top-down. Nor would it result from a policy that made the reunification of Germany a precondition for the improvement of East–West relations. On the contrary, the reconciliation of a divided Germany and a new political order in Europe would more likely result from a long and comprehensive historic process. In this process, NATO would have to both preserve the unity of the West and encourage the evolution of the East. It became apparent that both the USA and the FRG had reached a watershed in their post-war political development. In Washington, the rupture between President Johnson and key members of the old transatlantic elite such as Dean Acheson and George Ball in 1966 had signaled a new willingness to fundamentally reverse the post-war priorities of the USA in Europe and to focus on improving the political environment rather than on German unification. In Bonn, the 1966 election of the "grand coalition" government of Kurt Kiesinger, with Willy Brandt as foreign minister, fundamentally reoriented the FRG's East European policies, paving the way for the eventual breakthrough of *Ostpolitik* a few years later.[11]

NATO, the breakthrough of *Ostpolitik*, and the political limits of the Harmel compromise

Between 1968 and 1971, the Harmel script was followed by the West's preparations for a European security conference, which took place within the institutional structures of the Alliance. The initiative in the development of détente in Europe shifted from the East to the West. Eventually, in a remarkable exchange of communiqués, the two alliances defined the conditions for an all-European security forum. With its Reykjavik signal, NATO under US leadership linked progress on the security conference to progress on arms control. The Soviets would have to accept US and Canadian participation and negotiations on Mutual and Balanced Force Reductions (MBFR) in exchange for Western participation in the conference preparations and Western *de facto* acceptance of GDR participation.[12]

The German question was central to the political dynamic within NATO. Gradually, the FRG became the hub of multilateral preparations for a security conference between East and West, now referred to as the CSCE. With the formation of a new SPD–FDP

Government in October 1969, the linkage strategy of Brandt was put to the test. NATO decided to support the FRG's attempt to make progress on the CSCE conditional on progress on bilateral German-to-German *Ostpolitik*.[13] However, Western policy makers were nervous that Bonn's bilateral opening towards the East might lead to German neutralism. To hedge against the possibility of another Rapallo and to ensure *Ostpolitik*'s conformity with larger European interests, Paris lifted its veto on British entry into the Community, and launched the EPC and the project of European monetary union (see below). Washington, in turn, linked progress on the CSCE to progress on the four-power Berlin talks. This provided the USA with a monitoring device and a *de facto* veto on the progress of the FRG's new Eastern policies.

With the help of its allies, the FRG was eventually able to delay the CSCE long enough to conclude the key steps of its bilateral *Ostpolitik*. The breakthrough of the policy came during 1970. With the signing of the Treaty of Moscow in August, the FRG acknowledged the Soviet sphere of influence in Eastern Europe. Only four months later, Poland was able to secure Bonn's *de facto* recognition of its borders in the Treaty of Warsaw. West Germany had crossed its Rubicon, and thus the German question lost at least some of its political criticality. However, for NATO this meant that one of the key integrating factors of the Harmel consensus with regard to the political legitimacy of the Alliance had lost its importance.

Not surprisingly, by the beginning of the 1970s, NATO was in for a time of renewed discord. With the achievement of the Eastern treaties, the Western linkage strategy had served its main purpose. As a result, in late 1970, allied support for making the CSCE conditional on progress in intra-German relations started to slip, and disagreement between NATO members on the aim of Western détente policies soon intensified. Also, as economic and financial questions gained importance and were increasingly dealt with outside of the national security context, NATO proved unable to address these issues and lost some of its relevance as a Western governance instrument. This was also because it was incapable of harmonizing the allies' out-of-area policies and thus of functioning as a crisis management platform for global challenges. Prompted by the Middle East War in June 1967, the USA had proposed a new NATO body for the coordination of its members' Middle East policies during the Harmel exercise, a proposal which, however, had gone nowhere. More generally, US support for a corrupt and inept government in South Vietnam, held in power by seemingly unrestrained military escalation, damaged the USA's image throughout large parts of Europe, casting doubt on its leadership role in the Alliance, especially in terms of global affairs.[14]

The Harmel consensus had allowed NATO's successful transformation into a politically more balanced transatlantic relationship, while simultaneously engaging the Soviet Union and the Eastern European states in talks that would eventually lead to a wider European détente. With the successful multilateralization of the German question and of the nuclear question—no small feat, indeed—NATO had opened up the political space for an intensified debate about the reorganization of the West. Clearly, however, complementary political and economic structures would have to evolve before the West could position itself in a world of diffused responsibility.

European political identity, economic security needs, and transatlantic controversy over how to restructure the West, 1970–74

The fact that the transformation of NATO into a more political body could not satisfy Western governance needs became apparent in the early 1970s. European–US differences about the objectives and substance of détente widened to such an extent that the debates in NATO became increasingly unproductive. This ultimately prompted the Europeans to define their détente strategy in a forum of their own. The CSCE became the first major issue of European Political Cooperation that was set up by the EC member states in 1970 in order to develop a common European foreign policy. As the Europeans soon managed to take the lead in formulating Western CSCE policies, the broader issue of EPC–NATO relations, and consequently of Europe's role within the West and in the world, appeared on the transatlantic policy agenda. In a parallel development, with the shift of economic power from the USA to Europe, the issue of how to structure relations between the Community and the USA gained increasing attention. Furthermore, since the USA no longer exerted leadership in international monetary relations, the Bretton Woods system collapsed between 1971 and 1973, which had detrimental effects for the Europeans and brought to the forefront the issue of reform in Western monetary governance.

The US "Year of Europe" initiative of April 1973 was designed to forge a new transatlantic consensus on Western détente policies, European political identity, and economic governance, by further redefining the Alliance. However, the initiative resulted in some of the fiercest transatlantic clashes during the Cold War that lasted well into early 1974. In the early phase of the "Year of Europe", the main issue was Europe's insistence on being acknowledged by the USA as a second political decision-making forum in the West. But this debate gradually lost significance as the oil crisis, which erupted in the wake of the October War in 1973, caused energy and economic stability to become key security issues and put the search for effective economic governance structures at the top of the West's political agenda.

The détente disconnect and Europe's role in redefining pan-European security

The Europeans became increasingly unhappy with the US conception of détente in the early 1970s. The US tended to perceive détente as a static, stability-oriented project that would be shaped at the bilateral level between Washington and Moscow. In Washington, the emphasis was on military security, bilateral arms control, and the stability of the global status quo between the two blocs. Henry Kissinger, the chief architect of US foreign policy in the Nixon administration (1969–74), professed a particularly deep-seated skepticism towards any kind of multilateral diplomacy. Preferring great-power consultations and backchannel diplomacy, he was little interested in the role of the CSCE as the European multilateral variant of détente. This was also because he did not expect a fundamental change in the societal forces that were driving international affairs—human rights rhetoric would not change great-power relationships any time soon. Focusing on managing superpower relations instead, his efforts resulted in a series of bilateral agreements, signed at two superpower summits in 1972 and 1973, of which the SALT (Strategic Arms Limitation Talks) I treaty on nuclear armament control, the Basic Principles of Relations between the USA and the Soviet Union, and the Agreement on the Prevention of Nuclear War aroused the most public interest.[15]

While the Europeans appreciated the reduction of tension between the superpowers, they also resented the fact that they had little say in matters they felt went to the heart of European security. They were concerned about the possibility that the USA might subordinate their interests to stable relations with the Soviet Union. Fears about a superpower condominium peaked with the Agreement on the Prevention of Nuclear War in 1973.

From the perspective of many Europeans, this treaty would weaken the US commitment to the nuclear defense of Europe, and some even argued that the envisaged bilateral consultative machinery for times of crisis would undermine the UN Security Council and provide the basis for a US–Soviet "duopoly."[16]

With regard to specific European–US policy differences concerning détente, one bone of contention was the question of whether the West should prioritize MBFR or the CSCE. Washington made the case for focusing on arms control and for using the CSCE as a bargaining chip that could be traded for disarmament concessions. Realizing that they had only a limited say in arms control, the Europeans favored the CSCE, with its equal rights principle. They were generally much more positive about the CSCE than the USA was. This was partly because the CSCE was the only platform where they could actively and collectively engage in détente. Even more importantly, they perceived the CSCE to be a unique opportunity to engage the Soviet Union in negotiations about the parameters of European security.

Through the CSCE, the Europeans sought to demonstrate and expand to the East the norms and values that provided the basis for Europe's unification process. They were willing to meet the Soviet demand that Europe recognize the geopolitical status quo, on the condition that Moscow recognize human rights as part of an extended notion of European security. Accordingly, they argued for a complex three-stage conference model that would allow for long and thorough discussions. They aimed at achieving real, long-term changes and grass-roots improvements—just like the FRG did with *Ostpolitik* on the inter-German level. By contrast, Washington's main objective with regard to the CSCE seemed to be the wish to confront the East with exaggerated Western demands in order to highlight the closed nature of Communist regimes for propaganda purposes. Kissinger wanted a short "rubber stamp" conference, which he sought to push through as smoothly as possible so as to make sure that it would not have any negative repercussions on superpower détente.

The growing European–US disconnect regarding détente was the main reason why the Europeans started their own collective consultations on the CSCE in 1971. Another important factor was that the US and the Soviet Union decided, after secret talks in mid-1972, to separate MBFR and CSCE negotiations. This bilateral deal-making greatly irritated the Europeans. More importantly, without MBFR, the CSCE's focus shifted from military to political aspects of security, and more generally from issues of security to issues of cooperation. The effect was that NATO's difficulties in hammering out common Western positions for the CSCE increased further. Non-democratic allies such as Greece and Portugal found it difficult to go along with some proposals concerning human rights that were dear to the Europeans. With its southern flank, NATO found it very difficult in the early 1970s to act as a community of values. By 1972, it had lost its function as the key political forum for harmonizing East–West policies, with both the USA and Europe defining and pursuing their détente strategies outside NATO.[17]

Europe as a new political caucus in the West

The CSCE and the fear of a superpower condominium were not the only reasons why the Europeans began to assert their collective political identity in the early 1970s. As a result of nuclear parity between the superpowers, of the de-escalation of the German question, and of the growing strategic relevance of economic power, Europe's military dependence on the USA gradually shrunk, while its political room of maneuver increased.

Conversely, concerns about *Ostpolitik* helps to explain why European Political Cooperation (EPC) was launched precisely in 1970. Whereas West German Chancellor Willy Brandt was eager to set up the machinery needed for European foreign policy coordination in order to reassure his European partners that Bonn's foreign policy remained anchored in the West, the French, in particular, viewed EPC as an additional means to keep an eye on the FRG.

Also important, France and Britain were finally able to overcome their differences over Britain's membership of the EC, which had largely paralyzed the European integration process in the late 1960s and had prevented EPC from emerging earlier. French President Georges Pompidou lifted the French veto against Britain's accession to the EC and reversed de Gaulle's anti-British policy because he needed Britain to balance the FRG's ever-growing economic strength and its *Ostpolitik*, and also because he was eager to infuse new life into the Community. At their summit at The Hague in December 1969, the EC-Six eventually managed to agree on a package deal that allowed for Europe's first relaunch and for the first round of widening and deepening of the Community. This resulted in the accession of Britain, Ireland, and Denmark; the completion of the common agricultural policy; the beginning of monetary cooperation; and the establishment of EPC.[18] A particular boost to the notion of a European political identity was given by the fact that Edward Heath came to power in Britain in the spring of 1970. Unusual for a British prime minister, this leader of the Conservative Party pursued a distinctly pro-European and pro-French foreign policy and deliberately de-emphasized the special relationship with the USA. His "Europe first" doctrine provided the basis for trilateral Anglo-French-German leadership that came to mark EPC until 1974.[19]

Finally, there was a profound perception of US weakness and lack of leadership in Europe, which contributed to the collective political will of the EC countries to forge policies of their own. Vietnam and later Watergate conveyed the image of a superpower materially and morally in decline. As the US trade balance became increasingly negative and the dollar weakened, the Nixon administration appeared less and less willing and able to back the international economic system that it had itself created and began to lean towards unilateral policies geared towards US national interests (see below). In the field of diplomacy, Nixon and Kissinger showed very little interest in European and NATO affairs prior to 1973 and focused on getting out of Vietnam and changing US relations with the Soviet Union and China instead.

EPC became operational in November 1970, with the EC candidate countries participating from early 1972 on. It was based on a conspicuously minimalist conception. While membership was tied to the EC, EPC was set up as an intergovernmental forum outside Community structures. The roles of the European Commission and of the European Parliament remained very limited—which was a precondition for France's participation. Also, EPC had no permanent institutions and was based on a loose mechanism for political consultations only. Its performance was thus mainly dependent on the political will of, and the degree of political consensus among, member states. Displaying much self-confidence and ambition in this regard, the EC-Nine at their first summit in Paris in October 1972 announced the intention of converting, within eight years, their relationships into a European Union that included a foreign policy component and an Economic and Monetary Union (EMU).

And indeed, focusing on the CSCE, EPC had a successful start. Consultations on European détente led to quick and substantial results. By the time they went to Helsinki for the Multilateral Preparatory Talks (MPT) of the CSCE at the end of 1972, the EC-Nine had worked out a common position on the preparation, nature, and substance of the conference. They had definitely taken the lead from NATO in shaping Western strategy, the linchpin of which was the issue of freer movement. They were able to so simply because the USA considered the CSCE not important enough to impose their own policy preferences on their allies. Accordingly, in the context of the CSCE, NATO–EPC relations remained non-competitive, with US diplomats keeping a low profile at the conference and acting as loyal partners to their allies. This enabled the Europeans to pursue their agenda of change, even when transatlantic relations in 1973/74 deteriorated sharply. The MPT and the CSCE negotiations that followed in Geneva in mid-1973 became a catalyst for the rise of a European foreign policy in the early 1970s. What remained unaddressed before the "Year of Europe" was the larger issue of the significance of Europe's political identity for the Alliance.[20]

Trade rivalries and monetary turbulences, 1971–73

Parallel to the détente disconnect and the emergence of Europe as a political power, structural changes in the international economic system also brought important governance issues to the fore. US economic weakness contrasted with the new dynamism of the enlarging Community. The EC was bound to become an economic giant, representing 10 percent of the world's population, about 20 percent of global production, more than 25 percent of world trade, and nearly 40 percent of monetary reserves. Against the background of détente, many in Europe became critical of the US economic hegemony that had unfolded over the past decades. Conversely, with support for economic nationalism growing domestically, the USA became less and less willing to make economic sacrifices for the benefit of allies who had long overcome their post-war problems.[21]

One issue that gained significance was how to deal with the increasing trade rivalry between Europe and the USA. Confronted with a domestic mood of isolationism and Congressional pressure to reduce US overseas commitments, Nixon and Kissinger considered European trade concessions an important means to placate the US public. Although the Europeans would have none of this, Brandt proposed an institutionalized transatlantic link to deal with economic issues, in the form of a regularized EC–US dialog at a high political level. Pompidou, Heath, and several other European leaders rejected such a scheme, however, on the grounds that the enlarging Community was not yet ready to deal with the US as a single actor.

Also unresolved before the "Year of Europe" was the monetary crisis that had unfolded. In view of its economic weakness, the Nixon administration was eager to make the Bretton Woods system that had guided international monetary relations since the beginning of the Cold War more flexible. In August 1971, Washington went a step further and, in what came to be known as the "Nixon Shock," unilaterally suspended the convertibility of the dollar into gold. Nixon did lend a hand to the working out of a worldwide realignment of fixed parities among the major industrialized countries in the "Smithsonian Agreement" in December 1971. However, the Europeans had to realize that the USA was unwilling to stop the dollar from sliding, which rendered impossible any efforts to restore a system based on fixed exchange rates. In February 1973, the Bretton Woods system came to an end, and the currencies were subsequently floated.

Nixon's monetary policies irritated the Europeans, whose efforts towards European monetary cooperation was undermined by the currency crisis. Plans for European monetary union were both a response to the monetary turbulences and a means of taking

European integration to a higher level. However, overwhelmed by flows of unwanted dollars into their national reserves, some European countries, and particularly the FRG, were forced to float their currencies as early as 1971. As France rejected the idea of a collective European flotation against the dollar, the Europeans devised a European "currency snake" that would move within the "Smithsonian tunnel." This meant that the Europeans halved the margin within which their currencies were allowed to move against one another. Yet this system was disrupted when the pound sterling was forced to leave the snake and float, only weeks after the system was launched. In March 1973, the FRG again proposed a joint European floatation. The idea was that the Nine would maintain fixed exchange rates among each other but would cease to defend the fixed parity of the dollar. In other words, they would continue the snake but without the Smithsonian tunnel. However, as Britain, Ireland, and Italy felt unable to participate, the snake became rather short, which is why no significant monetary governance followed the collapse of the Bretton Woods system, either at the European or the transatlantic level.[22]

The "Year of Europe": competing models of Western governance

Having advanced superpower détente, restructured relations with China, and hammered out a Vietnam peace deal, Kissinger finally shifted attention to Western Europe in 1973. In a public speech on 23 April, he launched his "Year of Europe" initiative that proposed to adapt the transatlantic relationship to the conditions of the 1970s. Arguing that détente, the revival of Europe as a major power centre, and growing economic frictions had led to a "dramatic transformation of the psychological climate in the West," he made the case for a "fresh act of creation." Kissinger proposed that a "unifying framework" be set up to manage Atlantic diversity and asked the Europeans to recognize that their unification was "not an end in itself but a means to the strengthening of the West" and a "component of a larger Atlantic partnership." Europe, in Kissinger's view, had "regional interests" only, whereas the USA had global interests and responsibilities. Moreover, the Europeans should accept that the defense, diplomacy, and economic issues at stake were all "linked by reality" and needed to be addressed comprehensively. If the Europeans accepted these parameters and if there was a "spirit of reciprocity," the USA would commit itself not to withdraw any troops from Europe unilaterally. He concluded that the new transatlantic bargain ought to result in a "new Atlantic Charter," which would set the goals of the allies for the future.[23]

In effect, Kissinger proposed to strengthen Western governance by reopening the Harmel exercise and expanding the thematic scope of NATO. Yet, the Europeans disliked the initiative for several reasons. They felt they had not been adequately consulted for an initiative of such magnitude. Also, they were less pessimistic about the West's situation in general and saw little need for such a significant exercise. Moreover, Kissinger's approach of linking all issues in one governance framework was viewed with much skepticism by the Europeans, who feared that the USA might use military leverage to exert EC economic concessions. But what they resented most about the initiative was that it seemed to be an attack on European unity. Kissinger's point that Europeans had regional interests only, and no responsibility, did not go down well in Europe. Also, his idea to establish a confidential four-power group to steer the initiative was bound to inevitably undermine both EPC and the EC.

With the enlargement of the Community just accomplished, the priority of the Europeans was not the deepening of Atlantic unity, but the consolidation of the Europe of the Nine. Accordingly, against Kissinger's will, they devised a collective answer to the "Year of Europe." They dismissed both the idea of a new charter and the linkage approach. Instead, they argued for splitting the work and drafting two separate documents: one in NATO on transatlantic relations, and one between the Nine and the USA on their political and economic relations. In their draft declaration on European–US relations presented to Kissinger in September 1973, the Europeans proposed a new bilateralism between them and the USA regarding foreign policy and asked the USA to officially acknowledge them as a second political decision-making centre in the West. In order to underline their wish of being approached as a unitary actor, the Nine started to consult with the USA only through the Danish foreign minister, who was acting EPC president. In addition, the Nine also issued the "Declaration on European Identity," which defined the community of values that made the Nine distinct from other actors, and which argued that "the growing concentration of power and responsibility in the hands of a very small number of great powers mean that Europe must unite and speak increasingly with one voice if it wants to make itself heard and play its proper role in the world."[24]

Rather than revitalizing NATO, the "Year of Europe" gradually turned into a catalyst for European political unity. Although this provoked some sharp transatlantic exchanges in the summer of 1973, Kissinger eventually accepted the two-document approach. With the Watergate scandal escalating, Nixon was desperate to get something—anything—out of the "Year of Europe." More importantly, the French won US support for the European scheme when they complemented the draft of the Nine with a substantial draft on the Alliance. The idea initiated by Michel Jobert, Pompidou's foreign minister since March 1973 and key European figure in the "Year of Europe," was to make some symbolic concessions to the USA in the NATO declaration in order to win Washington's backing for a distinct political role for Europe. Thus, the French draft referred to the indivisibility of allied security, identified defense as a prerequisite of détente, pointed to the need to adapt NATO strategy, and committed the Europeans to maintaining sufficient defense force levels. This French scheme was the basis on which Kissinger, at the end of September 1973, accepted detailed negotiations on both draft declarations. On paper, at least, the Nine had come close to being recognized as an important political governance structure in their own right.[25]

The October War and the oil crisis: from European identity to economic governance

The Arab–Israeli War that started on 6 October 1973, and the ensuing oil crisis that was partly related to it, were both a low point and a turning point in the European–US conflict regarding the restructuring of transatlantic relations. All the controversies surrounding the "Year of Europe" that had been addressed at an abstract level now became practical political realities. This caused the deepest rift in the Alliance since the Suez Crisis. The October War revealed the stark differences in European and US threat perceptions and interests, the mutual lack of consultation and trust, and the desire of the Nine to make their own voice heard in international politics. Being much more dependent on Middle-Eastern oil than the USA, the Nine were heavily affected by the "oil weapon" (production cutbacks, embargo measures, and a quadrupling of the oil price) used by Arab oil producers to enforce a pro-Arab peace settlement. They partly blamed Nixon's previous refusal to deal with the Middle East for the crisis, and they strongly disagreed with Kissinger's view on crisis management during the October War, on the search for peace thereafter, and on what constituted an adequate response to the OPEC measures.

It was a classic case of an out-of-area disagreement in the Alliance. What was new was that the Nine finally succeeded in formulating a common Middle Eastern policy among themselves. After three years of difficult consultations in EPC, the Europeans issued their first "Declaration on Peace in the Middle East" on 6 November 1973, advocating a policy that Kissinger believed would undermine his shuttle diplomacy between Israel and the Arabs. Further policy differences emerged with regard to the issue of how to handle the unfolding oil crisis, i.e. of how to structure energy governance and the related aspect of North–South governance. The USA argued that the allies should jointly confront OPEC and build up an Atlantic consumer front to that end. Fearing ever more drastic OPEC measures, most Europeans did not have the stomach for such a policy, however. They preferred the French idea of a Euro-Arab dialog, which was about improving relations with the oil producers by establishing long-term cooperation and an increase in economic interdependence. The notion of Atlantic energy cooperation was also viewed with skepticism as the Community sought to formulate a European energy policy.[26]

In this context of transatlantic controversy, Europe's quest for US recognition of a distinct European political identity started to look increasingly surreal. From a US perspective, Europe was evolving too much in a Gaullist direction, with the political ambitions of the Nine weakening, rather than strengthening, the West. Having realized how divisive a common European foreign policy could be, Kissinger now sought to either "kill" EPC or at least to introduce measures to ensure that it would not attain a prominent role within the Western governance structures. Arguing that the USA needed an institutionalized and early say in European political decision-making, in December 1973, Kissinger suggested that EPC be linked to NATO. Conversely, the French, appalled that Europe had been "treated like a non-person" by the superpowers during the October War,[27] now sought to accelerate European political unification. Pompidou and Jobert proposed not only regular and informal summits of the Nine on foreign policy issues, but also urged their EC partners to move into European defense as a basis for greater European autonomy. Although Franco–US relations in the early 1970s had improved significantly compared to the de Gaulle era, they now became so strained that negotiations on a European–US declaration in late 1973 and early 1974 turned into a largely academic exercise.[28]

Towards the end of 1973, as the negative effects of the oil crisis were gradually felt in the West, the focus of the "Year of Europe" discussions shifted from Europe's role in Western diplomacy to the issue of economic governance. While the Europeans had managed to downsize the economic dimension of Kissinger's initiative as long as that initiative had been about trade, they could hardly do so now that the era of cheap and secure oil supplies seemed to have come to an end and that energy security had moved to the top of domestic policy agendas. Kissinger effectively relaunched the "Year of Europe" by putting forward a transatlantic energy initiative in an address to the Pilgrims Society of London on 12 December 1973. Warning the Nine that "Europe's unity must not be at the expense of Atlantic community" and that they had to choose between "creativity together or irrelevance apart," he invited them once more to join the USA in building a Western consumer bloc to break OPEC's power.[29]

At the Washington Energy Conference in February 1974, the USA succeeded in splitting the Europeans up. Facing a deepening economic crisis and US pressure, all of the Nine except France subscribed to the US scheme at the end of this highly confrontational conference. However, the scheme failed to translate into any effective Atlantic energy governance in subsequent months. Without the participation of France, no cohesive consumer bloc was feasible. Moreover, the USA soon realized that the other Europeans remained extremely reluctant to engage in Western energy cooperation. Worst of all, from a US perspective, the Nine decided to launch the Euro–Arab dialogue only weeks after the Washington Energy Conference, and despite Kissinger's objection. This provoked the last and most drastic negative US reaction of the entire "Year of Europe." On 15 March 1974, Nixon publicly announced that he would no longer tolerate the Nine "ganging up" against the USA and that he would withdraw US troops from Europe if Europeans continued to pursue foreign and economic policies contrary to US interests. Rarely has a US president confronted European allies with such harsh words. In early 1974, almost a year after the USA had initiated Western negotiations on reorganizing the West, consensus among the allies on both Europe's role in the world and on transatlantic economic governance seemed more remote than ever.[30]

Hierarchy back: great power consultations, NATO's reconsolidation, and the open question of Europe's role in the world, 1974/75

Three parallel developments explain why the West was able, in 1974/75, to overcome its political blockade and pragmatically restructure its relationships into what became a world of diffused but hierarchically structured responsibility. First, superpower détente was waning again. In Washington, the domestic support for détente was falling apart. Moscow, for its part, felt alienated by the way it was sidelined by Kissinger in his search for peace in the Middle East. Thus, as a result of the worsening of superpower relations, the USA became more willing to act as the leader of the West again. Conversely, as fears of a superpower condominium receded, an important element of European political cohesion no longer applied.[31]

Second, the remarkable dynamism that had characterized European integration in the early 1970s came to an end. This was partly because Heath, Brandt, and Pompidou all left the scene in the spring of 1974, which meant that trilateral leadership on European unification ended. With Harold Wilson in power in London, Euro-skepticism began to shape Britain's EC policies.[32] The European project also lost steam because of the serious economic crisis which unfolded in 1974/75, and which marked the third and most important development that affected the transatlantic search for new governance modes. The oil crisis brought an end to post-war economic stability and prosperity. With the high oil price intensifying the currency crisis of the early 1970s, most Western economies slid into recession. The hemorrhage of capital from industrial to oil-producing countries increased global monetary instability, and the net result of these developments on the global level was a power shift from the North to the South.[33]

However, power shifted in the West, too. On the one hand, within the Community, the power of the FRG grew at the expense of Britain and France. Growing economic disparities undermined solidarity within the Community and made collective crisis management in the EC framework increasingly difficult. Work towards an EC energy policy collapsed, not least because Britain found oil in the North Sea. Other key projects like the monetary union had to be put on the backburner, with the EC becoming almost as paralyzed as it had been during the late 1960s. On the other hand, power shifted from Europe back to the USA. The USA suffered much less from the economic crisis than

Europe. As Europe slid into recession, the USA managed to restore its economic power, thanks to a stronger dollar and a dramatic turnaround in the US balance of payments.

Washington managed to consolidate the centrality of the US dollar in the post-Bretton Woods era not least through bilateral deals with Saudi Arabia and Iran, according to which oil would continue to be priced in the US currency only and petrodollars would be recycled in US financial markets.[34] These deals must have looked ironic to those Europeans in particular who got blamed by Kissinger for attempting to handle the oil crisis by bilateral agreements with oil producers. Yet the fact was that much though Europe's military dependence on the US in the eyes of the Europeans had lost some significance during détente, its economic dependence on Washington was growing again in 1974/75, which reduced its freedom of maneuver once more. This in turn provided the material basis for the USA to restore its leadership in the West. As much as the new leaders in Bonn (Helmut Schmidt) and Paris (Valéry Giscard d'Estaing) disagreed with Britain's EC policy, they also agreed with Wilson and Kissinger that there was now a strong nexus between economic stability and national security and that the pressing problems of the time could be resolved only in a transatlantic framework.[35]

NATO reconfirmed: European identity subordinated to transatlantic unity

The notion of a distinct European political identity lost much of its impetus in this context. Work on the European–US draft declaration on the role of the Nine was discreetly discontinued. The "Year of Europe" ended with a NATO declaration signed at summit level in June 1974. This "Ottawa Declaration" failed to provide answers to all the problems that had troubled NATO in the early 1970s. Differences about issues such as burden-sharing, adequate levels of defense spending, and NATO's out-of-area role remained unresolved. Yet being based on the French draft submitted in the autumn of 1973, the declaration did symbolize a renewed Western commitment to NATO. It reconfirmed, in substance, the Harmel Report of 1967 in that it declared military security to be a precondition of a policy of détente. And by being the sole product of the "Year of Europe," it implicitly reflected a sense of predominance of NATO over EPC.

As it became clear that a European identity would not materialize anytime soon, the foreign policy governance mechanism of the Nine became a low-level entity. The Europeans went along with Kissinger's request to leave Middle Eastern diplomacy to the USA, issuing no further declaration for years. They pursued the Euro–Arab dialogue only very cautiously, so as not to irritate the USA. Talks on European defense led nowhere, which made it clear that the Nine would focus mainly on soft power issues. Moreover, discussions on how the European Union, which had been announced for 1980, should be structured were outsourced, for lack of agreement, to Belgian Prime Minister Leo Tindemans. As Europe reduced its political ambition and ceased its efforts to approach the USA as a single political actor, Kissinger no longer insisted on early US involvement in EPC decision-making. EPC continued to exist, but it was no longer perceived as a threat by Washington. The fact that the leaders of the Nine decided in December 1974 to meet three times a year as the European Council to deal with both EPC and EC issues at summit level could be interpreted as a renewed commitment to Europe's political structure; but it could also be seen as a reflection of the growing paralysis that had beset European institutions and weakened the governance capacities of the Nine. Given the danger of EC disintegration, the question of Europe's role in the world, which the Nine had addressed with so much verve in the early 1970s, receded into the background and remained wide open.[36]

The G6/G7: great power governance

The major issue still to be resolved about Western governance in 1974/75 was how to organize economic crisis management. At the NATO summit of May 1975, economic issues were addressed for the first time at the insistence of Schmidt. However, not all allies were in favor of NATO expanding to the economic field, and the Alliance framework was not really suited for economic decision-making. The International Energy Agency set up in November 1974 as part of the follow-up work of the Washington Energy Conference may have been originally conceived by Kissinger as the energy equivalent of NATO. However, with the European allies remaining lukewarm about US ideas of energy cooperation, the IEA never acquired the political dimension that would have made it a major Western governance tool.[37]

The concept of great power summits as a new structure for steering Western governance was the consequence of the obvious failure of existing Western multilateral institutions in dealing with the most pressing issues of the time. Leaders in Washington, Paris, Bonn, and London all came to believe that effective economic governance could best be achieved through informal great power consultations. While in the second half of 1974 France and the USA had continued to argue about whether to build Western energy policies on a consumer–producer dialog or on a Western energy bloc, they gradually came to realize that the only way forward that avoided mutual paralysis was through a pragmatic compromise. At the bilateral summit between Giscard and new US President Gerald Ford at Martinique in December 1974, Paris and Washington decided to no longer obstruct each other's policies but to work towards a joint energy strategy that included both Western cooperative measures and a dialog with producers. They further agreed that the USA, France, the FRG, Britain, and Japan, as the five major economies, should set up an informal group in which trusted representatives of the leaders could regularly consult on the oil crisis and on economic recovery.[38]

The idea of such a great-power caucus had several origins. For one thing, it went back to the so-called "Library Group," which had brought together the finance ministers of the Five (including Giscard and Schmidt) for secret discussions on how to deal with the monetary crisis in the early 1970s.[39] Furthermore, the idea strongly resembled the scheme which Kissinger had in mind to steer the "Year of Europe" initiative, and which Heath, Brandt, and Pompidou had rejected. Finally, it could even be argued that the caucus reflected the kind of great-power directorate de Gaulle had proposed in 1958—even though at the time the General would not have wanted the FRG and Japan at the table.

The decision to lift this new caucus to the summit level and to make it the implicit top of Western governance was taken by Giscard, Schmidt, Ford, and Wilson in the summer of 1975. Whereas Ford wanted to add Canada and Italy to the group, Giscard initially rejected enlarging it, so as to avoid demands by smaller EC countries for a seat at the table. The first summit in Rambouillet in November 1975 was eventually conducted as the G6, with Italy participating. When Ford invited Canada to the second summit, which was organized by the USA eight months later, the group became the G7. While this inner caucus of the West relapsed in later years into a formalized and bureaucratized institution, in the mid-1970s it was the key Western political structure, enabling leaders to pragmatically coordinate their policies. The G6/G7 signaled both a new spirit of allied cooperation and the reconstitution of US leadership, with the Europeans already at the first summit at Rambouillet accepting the dollar standard and the notion of floating exchange rates as two basic features of the emerging new international economic system.[40]

The Helsinki Final Act as a symbol for renewed Atlantic cohesion

The revitalization of the West in 1974/75 allowed the allies to bring CSCE negotiations to a successful close. When the superpower détente ended, Kissinger became a late convert to the CSCE. This was also because by doing so he hoped to silence those domestic critics who accused him of having pursued a status quo version of détente for too long, accommodating even the Soviet crackdown of dissidents. When in 1974 he began to pay more attention to the CSCE, Kissinger initially wanted to push the Europeans to a quick end of negotiations and suggested that they should define minimum goals, which he would then negotiate with the Soviet Union. However, he went along with the Nine's insistence on patience and open-ended goals and began to actively support their objective of wresting concessions from the Soviets with regard to freer movement and human rights.

During 1973 and 1974, the Europeans had swamped the conference with proposals in these fields and had achieved numerous tactical successes, committing the Soviets to specific measures and formulations. Yet while they were strong enough to resist Kissinger's call for an early end to the conference, they also lacked the power to achieve a large-scale final bargain with Moscow. Only once Kissinger had thrown his weight behind their positions did a final compromise become possible.

In the resulting Final Act, signed at the Helsinki summit on 1 August 1975, the West succeeded in making the Soviets subscribe to a widened conception of European security that added the security of individuals to the security of states. With the long-term CSCE process that was launched with the Final Act, the Western allies instituted a new political structure that allowed them to engage Moscow in discussions about the implementation of the agreement signed at Helsinki, and that would eventually provide a normative framework for peaceful change in Europe.[41] The fact that it was Kissinger who in the end made the Final Act possible reflected the restored leadership position of the USA. The fact that he defended essentially European positions was indicative of the Atlantic cohesion that had returned, once the painful process of diversifying the governance structures was overcome.

Notes

1 This chapter is an attempt at interpreting the many forces that were transforming the West during the late 1960s and early 1970s. As such, it builds on earlier archive-driven works by the authors and profits from other excellent works by a large group of scholars. We are especially indebted to a group of colleagues who, together with the authors, have organized and attended a series of multinational Cold War conferences in recent years, which have resulted in a number of edited volumes, including Daniel Möckli and Victor Mauer (eds), *European-American Relations and the Middle East: From Suez to Iraq*, (London: Routledge, 2010); Andreas Wenger, Vojtech Mastny, and Christian Nuenlist (eds), *Origins of the European Security System: The Helsinki Process Revisited, 1965–75*, (London: Routledge, 2008); Andreas Wenger, Christian Nuenlist, and Anna Locher (eds), *Transforming NATO in the Cold War: Challenges beyond Deterrence in the 1960s*, (London: Routledge, 2006); Vojtech Mastny, Sven G. Holtsmark, and Andreas Wenger (eds), *War Plans and Alliances in the Cold War: Threat Perceptions in the East and West*, (London: Routledge, 2006). See also Daniel Möckli,

European Foreign Policy during the Cold War: Heath, Brandt, Pompidou and the Dream of Political Unity, (London: I. B. Tauris, 2009).

2 On NATO's transformation, see Andreas Wenger, 'Crisis and Opportunity: NATO's Transformation and the Multilateralization of Détente, 1966–68,' *Journal of Cold War Studies*, vol. 6, no. 1, Winter 2004, pp. 22–74.
3 On the intersection between diplomatic history and social movements, see Jeremi Suri, *Power and Protest: Global Revolution and the Rise of Détente*, (Cambridge, MA: Harvard University Press, 2003); Andreas Wenger and Jeremi Suri, 'At the Crossroads of Diplomatic and Social History: The Nuclear Revolution, Dissent, and Détente,' *Cold War History*, vol. 1, no. 3, April 2001, pp. 1–42.
4 Rostow to Rusk, 'State of the World,' 17 September 1963, US National Archives, College Park MD (USNA), RG 59, Records of the Policy Planning Council, 1963–64, Entry 5041, Lot 70D199, Box 256, USSR.
5 On the limits of the little détente of 1963, see Anna Locher and Christian Nuenlist, 'What Role for NATO? Conflicting Western Perceptions of Détente, 1963–65,' *Journal of Transatlantic Studies*, vol. 2, no. 2, 2004, pp. 185–208; Andreas Wenger and Marcel Gerber, 'John F. Kennedy and the Limited Test Ban Treaty: A Case Study of Presidential Leadership,' *Presidential Studies Quarterly*, vol. 29, no. 2, 1999, pp. 460–87.
6 Anna Locher, *Crisis? What Crisis? NATO, de Gaulle and the Future of the Alliance, 1963–66*, (Baden-Baden: Nomos, 2010).
7 Memorandum, 'Possible Effects of the NATO Crisis on German Foreign and Domestic Politics', Undated, NSA, Non Proliferation Policy (NNP), Microfiche collection no. 713.
8 Rusk to Bundy, 26 January 1965, Lyndon B. Johnson Library, Austin, TX (LBJL), NSF, Country Files, Eastern Europe, Box 162, no. 24. On the 1966 NATO crisis see: Georges-Henri Soutou, 'La décision française de quitter le commandement intègre de l'OTAN,' in Hans-Joachim Harder (ed.), *Von Truman bis Harmel: Die Bundesrepublik Deutschland im Spannungsfeld von NATO und europäischer Integration*, (Munich: Oldenbourg, 2000), pp. 185–208; Frédéric Bozo, 'De Gaulle, l'amérique et l'alliance atlantique: une relecture de la crise de 1966,' *Vingtième Siècle*, vol. 43, July–September 1994, pp. 55–68.
9 See, for example, Helga Haftendorn, *NATO and the Nuclear Revolution: A Crisis of Credibility*, (Oxford: Clarendon Press, 1996); Wenger, 'Crisis and Opportunity,' pp. 48–59.
10 See, for example, Andrew Priest, 'From Hardware to Software: the End of the MLF and the Rise of the Nuclear Planning Group,' in Wenger, Nuenlist, and Locher (eds), *Transforming NATO in the Cold War*, pp. 148–61.
11 Final Harmel Report, East–West Relations Détente and a European Settlement, NATO Archives. www.nato.int/archives/harmel/harmel01.htm (accessed 3 December 2009).
12 See, for example, Michael Cotey Morgan, 'North America, Atlanticism, and the making of the Helsinki Final Act,' in Wenger, Mastny, and Nuenlist, (eds), *Origins of the European Security System*, pp. 25–45.
13 See, for example, Petri Hakkarainen, 'From Linkage to Freer Movement: the FRG and the Nexus between Western CSCE Preparations and *Deutschlandpolitik*, 1969–72,' in Wenger, Mastny, and Nuenlist (eds), *Origins of the European Security System*, pp. 164–82; Petri Hakkarainen, *Amplifying Ostpolitik: The Federal Republic of Germany and the Conference on Security and Cooperation in Europe, 1966–72*, (PhD thesis, University of Oxford, forthcoming).
14 Andreas Wenger, 'Crisis and Opportunity,' pp. 48–51.
15 Vojtech Mastny, 'Superpower Détente: US–Soviet Relations, 1969–72,' in David C. Geyer and Bernd Schaefer (eds), *American Détente and German Ostpolitik, 1969–1972*. (Washington, DC: Supplement No. 1 to the Bulletin of the German Historical Institute, 2004), pp. 19–25.
16 The term was coined by Ernst-Otto Czempiel, 'Entwicklungslinien der amerikanisch–europäischen Beziehungen,' *Europa–Archiv*, vol. 28, no. 22, 1973, pp. 781–90. On European fears of a superpower condominium, see also Georges-Henri Soutou, 'La problématique de la détente et le testament stratégique de Georges Pompidou,' *Cahiers du Centre d'Etudes d'Historie de la Défense*, no. 22, 2004, pp. 79–107.
17 Daniel Möckli, 'The EC-Nine, the CSCE, and the Changing Pattern of European Security,' in Wenger, Mastny, and Nuenlist (eds), *Origins of the European Security System*, pp. 145–63.
18 N. Piers Ludlow, *The European Community and the Crises of the 1960s: Negotiating the Gaullist Challenge*, (London: Routledge, 2006), chapter 7; Möckli, *European Foreign Policy*, chapter 1.
19 Möckli, *European Foreign Policy*, chapter 2.

20 Angela Romano, 'The Nine at the Conference of Helsinki: A Challenging Game with the Soviets,' in Jan van der Harst (ed.), *Beyond the Customs Union: The European Community's Quest for Deepening, Widening, and Completion, 1969–75,* (Brussels: Bruylant, 2007), pp. 83–106; Duccio Basosi, 'Helsinki and Rambouillet: US Attitudes Towards Trade and Security in the Early CSCE Process, 1972–75,' in Wenger, Mastny, and Nuenlist (eds), *Origins of the European Security System,* pp. 222–36.
21 Dieter Dettke, *Allianz im Wandel: Amerikanisch-europäische Sicherheitsbeziehungen im Zeichen des Bilateralismus der Supermächte,* (Frankfurt: Alfred Metzner Verlag, 1976).
22 Andreas Wilkens, 'Une tentative prématurée? L'Allemagne, la France et les balbutiements de l'Europe monétaire (1969–74),' in Elisabeth du Réau and Robert Frank (eds), *Dynamiques européennes: Nouvel espace, nouveaux acteurs, 1969–1981,* (Paris: Publications de la Sorbonne, 2002), pp. 77–103.
23 The speech is reproduced in Gerhard Mally (ed.), *The New Europe and the US: Partners or Rivals,* (Lexington, MA: Lexington Books, 1974), pp. 29–37.
24 'Declaration on European Identity by the Nine Foreign Ministers, Copenhagen, 14 December 1973,' in Christopher Hill and Karen E. Smith (eds), *European Foreign Policy: Key Documents,* (London: Routledge, 2000), pp. 93–97. On the Nine and the 'Year of Europe,' see Daniel Möckli, 'Asserting Europe's Distinct Identity: The EC-Nine and Kissinger's "Year of Europe",' in Matthias Schultz and Thomas A. Schwartz (eds), *The Strained Alliance: US-European Relations from Nixon to Carter,* (Cambridge: Cambridge University Press, 2009).
25 Michel Jobert, *L'autre regard,* (Paris: Grasset, 1976), p. 333.
26 Daniel Möckli, 'The EC-Nine and Transatlantic Conflict during the October War and the Oil Crisis, 1973/74,' in Möckli and Mauer (eds), *European-American Relations and the Middle East from Suez to Iraq.*
27 Jobert addressing the Assemblé Nationale on 12 November 1973, quoted in Jobert, *L'autre regard,* p. 344.
28 Möckli, *European Foreign Policy,* chapter 5.
29 The speech is reproduced in Mally, *The New Europe,* pp. 39–46.
30 Möckli, *Euroepan Foreign Policy,* chapter 6.
31 Ibid.
32 Uwe Kitzinger, 'Entry and Referendum Revisited,' in Roger Broad and Virginia Preston (eds), *Moored to the Continent? Britain and European Integration,* (London: University of London, 2001), pp. 79–94.
33 Fiona Venn, *The Oil Crisis,* (London: Longman, 2002).
34 Duccio Basosi, 'From Hierarchy to Hierarchy: The Transatlantic Relationship and the Global Economic Transition of the Long 1970s,' paper presented at the conference *Conflict and Community: Transatlantic Relations during the Cold War,* Tampere, Finland, 12 May 2008.
35 Möckli, *European Foreign Policy,* chapter 7.
36 Daniel Möckli, 'Speaking with One Voice? The Evolution of a European Foreign Policy,' in Anne Deighton and Gérard Bossuat (eds), *The EC/EU: A World Security Actor?* (Paris: Soleb, 2007), pp. 132–51.
37 Helmut Schmidt, *Die Deutschen und ihre Nachbarn,* (Berlin: Siedler, 1990), pp. 138 and 164; 'NATO-Gipfeltreffen in Brüssel vom 29. bis 30. Mai 1975,' *Akten zur Auswärtigen Politik der Bundesrepublik Deutschland 1975,* doc. no. 143.
38 Kissinger, *Years of Renewal,* pp. 624–26 and 686–97.
39 Helmut Schmidt, *Menschen und Mächte,* (Berlin: Siedler, 1987), pp. 193–97 and 213–15.
40 Basosi, 'From Hierarchy to Hierarchy;' Kissinger, *Years of Renewal,* pp. 692–97; Nicholas Bayne, 'Creating the Economic Summits,' in Nicholas Bayne and Stephen Woolcock (eds), *The New Economic Diplomacy: Decision-making and Negotiation in International Economic Relations,* (Aldershot: Ashgate, 2003), pp. 121–37.
41 Daniel C. Thomas, *The Helsinki Effect: International Norms, Human Rights, and the Demise of Communism,* (Princeton: Princeton University Press, 2001); Möckli, 'The EC-Nine, the CSCE.'

9

West Germany and the United States during the Middle East Crisis of 1973

'Nothing but a semi-colony'?

Bernhard Blumenau

'After all, we are nothing but a semi-colony!'[1]

Auswärtiges Amt official, October 1973

Introduction

This statement by a West German Auswärtiges Amt (Foreign Office) official is perhaps the best reflection of the mood and policies prevalent in Bonn in the autumn of 1973. In the course of the Middle East War of 1973, the Federal Republic of Germany (FRG) attempted to play a more independent role in international relations. It wanted to act as a sovereign state that could develop policies best fitted to reconcile its diverging interests, regarding its relations with the Arab world, its historic solidarity with Israel and its vital alliance with the United States. This policy, however, led to serious problems in Germany's relations with Washington. It was in that context that US Secretary of State Henry Kissinger criticized the Germans for having performed a 'blatant show of disunity'.[2] Shortly thereafter, the German government was reminded that, after all, Germany depended heavily on the United States – more than other European states – and could simply not afford to upset its most important ally.

This chapter argues that Bonn's decision to oppose Washington was caused by a multitude of reasons. They included Germany's new room for manoeuvre won by *Ostpolitik* that heavily relied on the maintenance of superpower détente. Moreover, its high dependence on Arab oil and its ambiguous relations with Israel and the Middle East also contributed to this decision. However, soon after Germany decided not to allow Washington to use its bases in the Federal Republic for resupply operations to Israel, it fell back on a more conciliatory policy towards the United States. This was due to the instrumental importance of the United States for Germany's security and with anything related to Germany's potential reunification.

The German–American relations will be assessed by focusing particularly on Bonn's diplomacy towards the United States. In 1973, relations between most Western European states and the United States were strained.[3] Focusing on the relations between the United

States and the Federal Republic of Germany is justified due to the special relationship between Washington and Bonn. Germany was at the front line of the Cold War and as a divided country it needed the cooperation of the occupying powers to overcome division. Moreover, because of its policy of *Ostpolitik*, Germany had a different position and interest in Europe and towards the United States than did its major European allies. Owing to limited space, this chapter will deal with the policies of other important European actors such as France and the United Kingdom only when they had a direct impact on Germany's policy. It will also leave out of consideration other important issues in transatlantic relations at the time such as the Declarations issue, the questions related to the Conference on Security and Co-operation in Europe (CSCE), relations with the East, arms limitations and the offset agreements.[4]

Literature on this particular aspect and period in German–American relations is practically non-existent. Major books on German foreign policy[5] and transatlantic relations[6] only mention it in passing. Recently, the British–American relationship during the Middle East War in 1973 has been the subject of an archival study.[7] This chapter, thus, fills a gap in literature and complements the historiography on the Yom Kippur War, as well as on transatlantic relations in the 1970s by adding the German dimension. Regarding the sources used, this text draws almost entirely from published and unpublished documents from the archives of the German Auswärtiges Amt and from memoirs of key actors in the period, such as the German Undersecretary of State Paul Frank, the US Ambassador to Germany Martin Hillenbrand and US Secretary of State Kissinger, to shed some light on this moment of dispute in transatlantic relations.

Factors for West Germany's policy towards the United States in autumn 1973

One of the most prominent factors is certainly the change that Germany's foreign policy underwent during the chancellorship of Willy Brandt. With *Ostpolitik* fully under way, West Germany had a broader margin for manoeuvre as it could now actively engage the East in general and East Germany in particular. It thus appeared in 1973 as if the formerly heavy dependence on the United States had weakened and that Bonn could focus more on genuinely German interests, even if that meant departing from the policy pursued by Washington. Brandt expressed this attitude in his memoirs, where he stated that he did not consider himself the chancellor of a defeated Germany but of a liberated one. He wanted to be treated as an equal and not as a pawn in Kissinger's great chess game.[8]

However, in order to maintain this new freedom, German foreign policy heavily depended on the general international environment. Détente was essential for *Ostpolitik*. Consequently, when there was the possibility that the United States might risk détente with the Soviet Union over the Middle East Conflict, the Auswärtiges Amt immediately suggested to 'concentrate their [i.e. European] activities on promoting a dialogue between both great powers'.[9] At the time, Bonn seemed to be more concerned about the United States' intentions than about the Soviet Union. As cables from the German embassy in Moscow imply, the Soviet leadership was very interested in keeping the tensions low, whereas Washington was perceived as being much more prone to risking détente because of the Middle East.[10] How much the Germans panicked about Washington's policy is shown in a comment that the German Undersecretary of State, Paul Frank, made to the Israeli ambassador in Bonn: 'Our policy on the conflict in the Middle East has, as a primary goal, preventing a

Third World War for which all causes exist'.[11] Consequently, it made sense for Bonn to avoid giving the United States excessive support in its possible endeavours to risk détente.

At the same time, there was a general mistrust of American motives. This was partially caused by Nixon's unilateral decision in 1971 to abandon the Bretton Woods system literally overnight.[12] Kissinger's badly received 'Year of Europe' speech in April 1973 added to the problems. Bonn was afraid that Washington might be tempted to cooperate more closely with Moscow at the expense of Europe, as this initiative granted Europe only a regional importance. Germany in particular did not feel treated like an equal by the United States.[13] This theme was of great importance again during the 1973 crisis.

Because of this perceived progressive marginalization of the Federal Republic, Bonn decided to enhance European cooperation, also and especially in political matters. The European Communities were supposed to become a more important international actor and according to Foreign Minister Walter Scheel, the Middle East Crisis was a great opportunity for this.[14] Nevertheless, Bonn's strategists were well aware that an increased importance of Europe could not be achieved against US opposition. They envisioned 'a long-lasting construction of European–American cooperation on an equal European–American basis'.[15]

Yet, when dealing with Germany's policy during the Middle East Conflict in 1973, the policies towards the Arab states and Israel cannot be neglected, especially in light of the special relationship between Germany and Israel as a consequence of the Holocaust. Moreover, Bonn's relations with the Arab world were strained. Diplomatic relations with most Arab states had been severed because of a *de facto* state visit of the East German Party Leader Walter Ulbricht to Egypt in 1965 and West Germany's subsequent diplomatic recognition of Israel. It took until 1974 until all relations with Arab states were restored. These relations should not be burdened again.[16] Since the late 1960s, Bonn's stance on Israel and especially on the Middle East Conflict had changed. Although Germany was hugely in favour of Israel's war against its Arab neighbours in 1967, public opinion and politics became more pro-Palestinian in the aftermath of the Six Days' War. On the one hand, the televised pictures of Palestinian refugee camps contributed to that.[17] On the other hand, Germany's increased dependence on Arab oil was also an important factor in that change. Frank pointed this out in a meeting with the Israeli ambassador: 'You will have to be aware that Western governments – not only the German one – will be more polite towards Arab oil producers in the future'.[18] Oil had become a weapon. That it was very influential in decision-making during the Middle East Crisis of 1973 is also obvious from a report issued by the Auswärtiges Amt:

> We have a big interest in an early end of the Middle East Conflict also since we import approximately 71% (about 503 million tons) of our oil from Arab producers including Libya and Algeria, which are parties to the conflict. We share this dependence with other Western European states and Japan while the US only imports 6% of its oil from Arab countries. Europe and Japan, thus, depend more on an arrangement with the Arabs than the US. This is another reason why we and our EC partners are trying to convince the Arabs that Europe takes a neutral stance in this conflict and expects not to be hit by oil reductions.[19]

Having a policy of neutrality in the Middle East Conflict was hence the best way to reconcile Germany's special responsibility to Israel while at the same time ensuring that the oil supply continued to be available.

The diplomatic crisis between Germany and the United States

For West Germany, the Middle East War started officially on 6 October 1973 at 15:30 local time, when the German ambassador to Israel was informed of the joint Syrian–Egyptian attack on Israel.[20] The Auswärtiges Amt created a crisis management group (*Krisenstab*) in Bonn and on the following day more information on the attack and on the position of other Arab states was available. Iraq was supportive of Syria and declared that it would nationalize US oil companies' assets because of Washington's pro-Israeli policy. Baghdad also called for an oil embargo against the states supporting Israel. The same applied to Kuwait, which also sided with Egypt and warned outside powers of taking sides in the conflict. Other states such as Tunisia and Jordan had a more hesitant stance on the conflict and decided not to get involved for the time being.[21]

In a meeting with the Israeli Ambassador Ben Horin on 8 October 1973, Foreign Minister Scheel explained Germany's policy of balanced neutrality in the conflict, which Ben Horin criticized as being 'too neutral'.[22] On the same day, Germany's embassy in Moscow cabled that the Soviet Union would tolerate the actions of Egypt and Syria but would probably not risk a confrontation with the United States over the Middle East Crisis.[23] The embassy in Paris also reported that France would take a pro-Arab stance on the crisis:

> Foreign Minister Jobert – after his talk with Pompidou – replied to a question on the issue of Arab aggression: 'est-ce-que [sic!] remettre les pieds chez soi represent [sic!] une aggression?' By this, Jobert gave a brief but important hint at the pro-Arab attitude of France.[24]

Meanwhile, the German ambassador in London was briefed that the British government feared the possibility of an oil embargo against the West, raising a concern which was at the core of European attitudes towards the conflict. Based on this information, the Auswärtiges Amt advised the federal government to maintain a neutral position in the conflict as this would reconcile best Germany's diverging interests.[25]

As for the United States, on 12 October, the embassy in Washington sent a cable stating that public pressure on the American government had risen in favour of supplying and supporting Israel in the conflict. It is possible that the United States had already started secretly resupplying Israel as of 9 October. Publicly, however, the United States was still pursuing a middle-of-the-road approach. This changed when Washington officially started its supply operations for Israel on 13 October.[26] At the same time, the German trade mission in Sofia informed the Auswärtiges Amt about Soviet flights to Syria and Egypt presumably providing those two belligerents with weapons.[27] The stakes were high. From Bonn's perspective, a possible superpower confrontation was not at all unlikely.

On 13 October 1973, in spite of its efforts to stay out of the conflict and to remain neutral, Germany was dragged into it. On this day, the Egyptians informed Bonn's ambassador in Cairo that the United States was showing a 'great level of activity' at its bases in West Germany. Egypt advised Germany to refrain from any action in favour of Israel, including support of resupply efforts. Cairo made this a matter of 'utmost seriousness'.[28] The Auswärtiges Amt immediately investigated this affair. It enquired the US embassy in Bonn and concluded that the Egyptian accusations were baseless. On the same occasion, the legal department of the Auswärtiges Amt circulated its legal assessment on the status of US war material in Germany:

There are no implications for the current situation from the Status of Forces Agreements of 1951 and 1959. If necessary, however, we could argue that the aim of these agreements was to grant the US the right to use its troops here to protect the Free World against the Eastern Bloc, but not to engage in military missions elsewhere. Moreover, the redeployment of US units, arms, jets etc is subject to agreements between NATO and the US. According to these agreements, the US would have to consult NATO, as this was done during the Vietnam War, for instance.[29]

With more states taking sides – such as Jordan on 15 October 1973 – Bonn also became increasingly concerned about the possibility of a fallout on superpower relations.[30] An internal document on the situation in the Middle East warned:

The repercussions of the Fourth Middle East War on the whole world are very serious. The biggest threat is the possibility of a confrontation of the great powers, which have so far tried to avoid this. […] US Secretary of State Kissinger hinted at a possible escalation of the situation and drew parallels with the situation on the Balkans in 1914.[31]

On 16 October, Minister Scheel had a discussion with US Ambassador Martin Hillenbrand during which he was informed that the United States had started resupplying Israel – also from bases in Germany – and that the United States considered support from its allies as crucial. As Hillenbrand warned: 'a lack of understanding on the part of some allies might do harm to the bilateral relations […]'.[32] Scheel expressed understanding and asked the ambassador to provide him with more information. He also pointed out that he did not want the Arabs to be informed about the shipments.[33] The next day, the US embassy gave details on the material that the United States intended to ship to Israel and which would leave Germany from Bremerhaven on an Israeli vessel.[34] The Auswärtiges Amt was consequently well aware of the resupply missions and of the involvement of Israeli ships.

Meanwhile, the German mission to NATO warned Bonn that US Ambassador Donald Rumsfeld had stressed that support from the European allies for the American resupply endeavours was a matter of crucial importance for the continuation of the alliance. Nevertheless, allied Great Britain and neutral Austria denied the United States the right to use their territories or airspace for resupply operations.[35]

Relations with the Arab states also became more strained. Egypt was upset about US flights from Germany to Israel and about alleged El Al flights from Frankfurt carrying war material to Israel. Emotions had been running high in the Arab world because of the perceived German support – albeit indirect – of US activities.[36] The political department (*Politische Abteilung*) in the Auswärtiges Amt, thus, advised Frank and Scheel to protest against American shipments from Germany to Israel by adverting to Germany's policy of neutrality and the risk of an oil embargo. They should also stress that those resupply operations were not covered by the treaties between Germany and the United States.[37] Consequently, on 23 October 1973, Frank met US Ambassador Hillenbrand and informed him that West Germany felt that US supply flights from or through Germany were no longer necessary. This was because the situation in the Middle East had changed with the ceasefire of 22 October.[38]

It was against this critical background that the Auswärtiges Amt was informed on 24 October 1973 by the Ministry of Defence that three Israeli vessels were waiting off

Bremerhaven port to be loaded with US material. The same news was also published in a local newspaper.[39]

The official Bonn was on high alert: if Israeli ships were stopping at German ports to be loaded with war material, the proclaimed German neutrality would be nothing but a shallow promise. Tensions with the Arabs would inevitably escalate.

Frank thus received US Chargé d'Affaires Frank Cash to protest strongly and to demand an immediate stop. He pointed out that having Israeli ships come to Germany lacked tact and sensitivity and that the ships would have to leave German territory at once. The third ship would not be loaded. Frank further complained that the German authorities had not been informed earlier. Cash protested – and as has been shown already, rightly so – that the Auswärtiges Amt had been notified of the ships on 17 October. He then inquired several times whether it would make a difference if US ships came to load the material but Frank strongly rejected that and wanted the whole action to be stopped immediately.[40] Moreover, an Auswärtiges Amt official leaked to the press a confidential internal note on the German decision to prohibit the use of its territory for American resupply efforts. Its wording and the fact that it was publicized displeased the Americans. Kissinger considered it a deliberate diplomatic manoeuvre to publicly disassociate Bonn from Washington in order to please the Arabs.[41] At the same time, Bonn instructed its ambassadors in Arab countries to immediately call on the foreign ministries of the host countries to explain the Bremerhaven incident and to point out that the German government had been unaware. The Egyptians became very upset and would not believe that German authorities were not informed about this major violation of German sovereignty. The Arab League also expressed its dissatisfaction with the recent developments and Gaddafi of Libya went so far as to threaten Europe with an oil embargo.[42]

On 26 October, Hillenbrand had another meeting with Frank and expressed Washington's disappointment about the German decision. He explained that the new German policy would lead to a weakening of the whole Western camp, as the Soviets kept on supplying the Arab states, thus creating an imbalance in the Middle East. Frank replied that Germany certainly did not want a major confrontation about this issue but wanted its sovereignty to be respected and needed to pay special attention to its dependence on Arab oil.[43]

Meanwhile, the German Ambassador in Washington, Berndt von Staden, met Kissinger to discuss the Middle East situation and the consequences for German–American relations. Kissinger was also utterly disappointed about the German decision, as it would affect vital aspects of the Alliance. He furthermore remarked that although the United States was acting in the interest of the West as a whole, the Europeans had disassociated themselves from the United States because of Arab oil blackmailing making NATO witness a 'blatant show of disunity'. The US would have to reassess its policy towards the Europeans once the crisis had been settled. The behaviour of the Europeans could have serious consequences. Von Staden pointed out that Bonn would not question NATO as such. He explained that Germany's policy was a consequence of the lack of consultation on the part of the United States and of the fact that resupply missions from Germany could no longer be justified once a truce was signed in the Middle East. Moreover, he stressed that Germany had been standing firm by the side of the United States – as one of the few American allies who did so – as long as the fighting was still going on, in spite of heavy Arab pressure. However, having ships from one of the belligerents – Israel – call at a German port to load war material was a major embarrassment for Germany's policy of neutrality and could not be tolerated.[44] The same reasoning was brought forward by

Minister Scheel in an interview some days later, and Chancellor Willy Brandt mirrored the same attitude in a letter to US President Richard Nixon of 28 October.[45]

In general, the memoirs of actors on both sides, Frank and Kissinger, show that it was not so much the German prohibition to use its territory for the US resupply actions that upset the bilateral relationship but rather the release of the harsh confidential note of the Auswärtiges Amt to the press. Bonn, however, argued that the publication was a mistake and not a deliberate act.[46]

The already grave situation was further exacerbated. On 25 October 1973 German time, the United States decided to have all troops go on DEFCON III, including the strategic nuclear forces and all the troops stationed in Europe. The allies had not been consulted beforehand and merely received information about it from the news.[47] It was only on 29 October that Ambassador Hillenbrand called on Frank to explain the urgency of the decision. According to him, the haste was necessary as the Soviet Union had intended to send troops to the Middle East. Thus, an immediate American reaction was needed, leaving no time for consultations. However, the United States would be willing to discuss how mechanisms for a timely exchange of information within NATO could be improved in the future. Hillenbrand then turned towards the Bremerhaven incident again and asked whether the United States could load the material on American ships. Frank finally agreed. In general, during this meeting, Frank used a conciliatory tone and tried not to add further tensions to the strained relationship. Moreover, he stressed Germany's ongoing commitment to the Alliance as such.[48]

Yet, in spite of Bonn's reassuring efforts, German–Arab relations remained strained. Although Egypt was placated a little by the – allegedly accidentally – published internal note, the fact that these resupply operations had taken place at all and that the federal government pretended not to have been informed about it increased tensions with the Arab world. Emotions were running high in Egypt and Libya.[49] The Netherlands had already become the victim of an Arab oil boycott because of – what was perceived in the Arab world – a pro-Israeli policy. Hence, it was clear to Bonn that these threats were not mere political manoeuvres but could actually be implemented. On 4 November, the Auswärtiges Amt warned again of the imminent risk of an oil embargo against the Federal Republic.[50]

Kissinger briefed the ambassadors of NATO countries about the reasoning behind the US decision to go on DEFCON III on 2 November. Von Staden reported that the atmosphere was serious but conciliatory. Kissinger stated his disappointment with the Europeans but also stressed that the United States would still consider the Alliance a centrepiece of American policy. He also underlined that he did not consider a lack of consultation as the major reason for the current tensions.[51] This, however, was Bonn's basic argument. One day earlier, Scheel had mentioned this in a talk with the French ambassador and Frank pointed out that 'only if full information and consultation is ensured, one can expect full solidarity'.[52]

On 6 November, the foreign ministers of the EC countries met to discuss the Middle East situation.[53] They adopted a declaration, which stressed their conviction that peace negotiations in the Middle East should be held within the framework of the UN under the auspices of the Security Council. Moreover, paragraph 3 of the declaration urged Israel to withdraw from the territories occupied after the 1967 War and demanded respect for the 'legitimate rights' of the Palestinian people.[54] The fact that this declaration had not been discussed with the United States prior to publication upset Kissinger. Moreover, the call for negotiations under the roof of the United Nations was obviously challenging the diplomatic strategy pursued by Kissinger, who was trying to broker a solution.[55] The declaration was clearly an attempt by the Europeans to appease the Arabs in order to prevent the use of the 'oil weapon'.

The Auswärtiges Amt was well aware of possible problems this could create. It, therefore, emphasized that the declaration merely expressed the preference of the EC member states and did not intend to interfere with other attempts to solve the crisis.[56] This policy paid off for Bonn with respect to the Arab states. During a meeting of Arab oil ministers, the majority of states were convinced that Germany was no longer pursuing an overly biased policy and put an end to pending threats of an oil embargo.[57]

Germany considered the tensions with the United States ended on 8 November 1973 as Chancellor Brandt pointed out during a meeting with the Italian Prime Minister Mariano Rumor. Nixon also shared this position.[58] However, for Kissinger, the tensions had not yet entirely disappeared.[59] Auswärtiges Amt officials were also still disgruntled about the recent events. Undersecretary Frank could not refrain from emphasizing his dissatisfaction with Washington's conduct of affairs: 'The FRG is an ally of the US. We see the importance of the great powers but we do also see the importance of Europe. We and Europe do not want to become a satellite of the great powers'. However, in retrospect he seemed to regret this candour as he then issued an order to keep this document confidential.[60] Possibly, the prior experience with the handling of internal documents caused him to be concerned.

Yet, officially Bonn was eager to show that tensions with the United States had ended. During the US Undersecretary of State Joseph Sisco's visit to Europe, Frank and Scheel were very reconciliatory. On the same day, the federal government, in a cabinet statement, once again emphasized the particular role the Atlantic Alliance played for Germany's security.[61] In addition, a solution was also found on the issue of future resupply missions. Federal Minster of Defence Georg Leber and his American counterpart James Schlesinger agreed that the United States could resupply Israel from the Federal Republic but only with US vessels. Consequently, Schlesinger renounced his threats of a withdrawal of American troops from Germany, which he had made earlier.[62] With the risk of an imminent oil embargo gone, the German statements once again showed the old pro-American rhetoric.

To French President Georges Pompidou, Brandt explained this policy like this: 'We have to find a strategy that accords an important role to the US as long as it remains crucial for maintaining a nuclear balance'.[63] This shows well the importance that Germany still accorded the United States in providing a nuclear shelter. Bonn simply could not afford to upset Washington to an extent that made its commitment to nuclear deterrence in Europe doubtful. West Germany's security stood or fell with the United States' credible commitment to it.

Finally, by mid-December 1973, friendly and cooperative relations between Bonn and Washington were fully restored. Even Kissinger used a conciliatory tone when he explained that the United States did not intend to limit Europe's responsibility but on the contrary wanted to strengthen it.[64] At another occasion, he said that he would 'not bear a grudge because of the European behaviour'.[65] The bilateral crisis had ended.

Diplomatic strategy

In autumn 1973, Germany pursued a strategy of calculated risk by disassociating itself to a visible extent from the policy of the United States in order not to upset its relations with the Arabs.

When dealing with the Arabs and the United States, Germany stressed its neutrality.[66] However, in the moment of crisis – when the Israeli ships were waiting off Bremerhaven Port to load the US material – Bonn had to make an *ad hoc* decision as its whole policy of neutrality was about to collapse. In that moment, it was decided to have the United States stop these actions immediately in order not to provoke the Arab states.[67] After all, it was noted that if the Dutch were boycotted solely due to some comments made by their foreign minister, Germany would face much more serious repercussions if it allowed Israeli ships to undertake resupply missions from its territory.[68] Under these circumstances, Bonn saw greater harm in provoking the Arab states than in challenging the United States.

Once the Nixon administration was upset and the damage was done, the question was how to deal with this. Therefore, Bonn wanted to embed German Middle East policy in the EC Political Cooperation (EPC) framework. Even before the Yom Kippur War, Bonn had intended to strengthen the European political integration process and now hoped to use the Middle East Crisis as an opportunity to do so. Bonn underlined the necessity of a common EC position on this issue.[69] Thus, West Germany refrained from formulating its own policy on the Middle East Conflict in order to avoid upsetting the Americans – and the Arabs for that matter – any further. As Frank points out in his memoirs, Bonn intended to use the EC to dispel criticism against Germany: 'European political cooperation and solidarity on that matter provided a certain shelter for Germany against verbal attacks from Israel'.[70]

Nevertheless, the longer the conflict lasted, the more difficult it became to unify all EC member states behind a unitary position. Yet, even during the EC summit of 17 and 18 December 1973, the Nine still managed to come to a common position on the Middle East, a position, however, that was already heavily contested by France.[71]

As Middle East policy was delegated to the EC, Bonn could shift primary attention again to the reparation of the damaged relations with the United States. During a meeting with Ambassador Hillenbrand on 25 October 1973 – one day after Germany had prohibited the use of its territory for resupply missions – Frank expressed the wish of the federal government not to let the tensions further escalate. He pointed out that it was important to relax the strained relationship. He even made a statement that had an air of desperation and that probably reflected the stress and problems he had been undergoing during the past few days: 'Now, Israel, the Arabs and even the US are upset with us. He is wondering whether that is the case because we did everything wrong or because we did everything right'.[72] Furthermore, the Federal Republic pointed out on several occasions – for instance in a letter from Brandt to Nixon – that the decision of 24 October did not question NATO as such, to show Germany's ongoing solidarity with the United States.[73] At another meeting between Frank and Hillenbrand, the former once again used a very conciliatory, almost submissive, tone: 'Moreover, he wanted to stress again that we have never prohibited anything to the US. We are in no position to do so. We merely voiced a demand'.[74] It is also worth noting that when Bonn decided to deny the US the right to resupply Israel from Germany, the situation in the Middle East War had already turned to Israel's favour. On 17 October, the Israelis had established a bridgehead over the Suez Canal and were besieging an Egyptian army. By 19 October, Israel was certain to have won the war and Bonn shared this perception.[75] Finally, on 22 October, the UN Security Council passed a resolution calling for a ceasefire in the Middle East that was co-sponsored by the United States and the Soviet Union.[76] Hence, when US resupply operations from Germany were stopped, Israel's survival was no longer at stake.

Two days later, on 31 October, Germany further relaxed tensions with Washington by allowing American ships to transport the material from Bremerhaven. Lastly, the Auswärtiges Amt decided to support the UN mission for the Middle East, mostly out of the belief that this would help to placate Washington. At the same time, the federal government took a very legalistic approach in justifying its decision to deny the United States the right to resupply missions. In the German point of view, the United States was under a legal obligation to consult its NATO allies before shipping material outside the NATO area.[77] Finally, Frank explained that the publishing of the internal Auswärtiges Amt note on the decision to have resupply missions stopped – the major source of American anger – was an accident and not at all a deliberate act.[78]

When analysing the German strategy vis-à-vis the US during the crisis, it is apparent that the conflict with Washington was not planned but rather an *ad hoc* decision. Confronted with increasing Arab pressure and an oil embargo that would harm West Germany's economy, Bonn decided to take the risk of brief tensions with the United States. Nevertheless, immediately afterwards Germany initiated a reconciliatory policy towards Washington in order to overcome these tensions.

Conclusion

Frictions between Bonn and Washington were caused by Germany's divergent interests. On the one hand, maintaining good relations with the protective superpower, the United States, had been a vital pillar of West German foreign policy ever since the foundation of the state. On the other hand, considerations – such as Germany's overwhelming dependence on Arab oil – as well as the need to maintain détente and, thus, *Ostpolitik* was another big motivation for Germany's policy in autumn 1973. Unfortunately, these interests were difficult to reconcile. In Bonn's perception, détente was more likely to be upheld – in that particular crisis – by departing from Washington's line. The same applied to Germany's desire to safeguard oil supplies. Therefore, on 24 October, Bonn decided to oppose Washington. This immediately led to tensions, which worsened when the United States unilaterally, and without prior consultation, set their forces in Germany to DEFCON III on 25 October. Consequently, to counter deteriorating German–American relations, Bonn enforced attempts to develop a more coherent EC policy on the conflict. Hence, while Middle East policies were delegated to the EC level, Germany could focus on repairing transatlantic relations again.

In the autumn of 1973, Germany tried to implement a more independent, more German foreign policy – and failed. The whole structure of the Cold War, with a divided Germany at its centre, did not allow Bonn to pursue a policy of brinkmanship for long. By Christmas 1973, the bilateral crisis had finally been – officially – overcome, although smaller tensions erupted again in 1974. However, only in the course of 1974, when most key politicians in the states concerned left office – Brandt, Scheel, Nixon – bilateral good relations were entirely restored. The new leaders of Germany and the United States, Helmut Schmidt and Gerald Ford, could then credibly re-enact the traditional show of German–American unity.

Although the German–American tensions in the autumn of 1973 reflect the generally strained transatlantic relations at the time, there are also some special factors that can be uniquely found in the relations between Bonn and Washington. *Ostpolitik* is one of those factors. The German variant of détente urgently required a general environment of relaxed tensions between the superpowers. Moreover, more so than France or the United Kingdom, West Germany needed the United States for its defence. Only the United States could provide the crucial nuclear deterrence so essential for Bonn's military concept. Therefore, any rupture in the relationship had to be overcome quickly. It is primarily for these reasons that the tensions between Germany and the United States were special and different from those between Washington and other European allies. The Federal Republic vitally needed the Western superpower. The United States reminded Germany of that as Brandt describes in his memoirs:

> At first, the reactions to our ideas were quite fierce in Washington. Our officials were even informed that from the US point of view, the Federal Republic had only limited sovereignty. The US reserves the right to implement measures as it deems necessary and appropriate to maintain international security.[79]

In 1973, West Germany was certainly no semi-colony. Nevertheless, it was not yet a fully sovereign state either.

Acknowledgements

I would like to thank Jussi Hanhimäki for very useful comments on earlier versions of this chapter.

Notes

1 A German Auswärtiges Amt official as quoted in 'Wir Standen Dicht an der Klippe,' *Der Spiegel* 29 October 1973, p. 25. My translation.
2 Botschafter von Staden, Washington, an Bundesminister Scheel: Unterredung mit dem amerikanischen Außenminister am 26.10., 26.10.1973, doc. 341, *Akten zur Auswärtigen Politik der Bundesrepublik Deutschland* (AAPD) 1973/III.
3 For the general argument see for instance Geir Lundestad, *The United States and Western Europe since 1945: From 'Empire' by Invitation to Transatlantic Drift*, (Oxford: Oxford University Press, 2003), p. 183.
4 Some other authors in this book also address issues that were very important in the German–American relations at the time but cannot be examined in this chapter, see the chapters by Benedikt Schoenborn, Leopoldo Nuti as well as Daniel Möckli and Andreas Wenger.
5 See for instance Helga Haftendorn, *Deutsche Außenpolitik zwischen Selbstbeschränkung und Selbstbehauptung. 1945–2000*, (Stuttgart, Munich: Deutsche-Verlagsanstalt, 2001), pp. 233–34; Gregor Schöllgen, *Die Außenpolitik der Bundesrepublik Deutschland: Von den Anfängen bis zur Gegenwart*, (Munich: Beck, 1999), p. 83; Christian Hacke, *Die Außenpolitik der Bundesrepublik Deutschland: Weltmacht Wider Willen?*, (Berlin: Ullstein, 1997), pp. 191, 193. Markus Weingardt assesses the crisis but predominantly only in so far as it touched upon German–Israeli or German–Arab relations, see Markus A. Weingardt, *Deutsche Israel- und Nahostpolitik: Die Geschichte einer Gratwanderung seit 1949*, (Frankfurt: Campus-Verlag, 2002).
6 In the comprehensive edition by Detlef Junker on German–US relations in the Cold War, the tensions during the autumn of 1973 are also only mentioned in passing, see Klaus Larres, 'West Germany and European Unity in U.S. Foreign Policy,' in Detlef Junker (ed), *The United States and Germany in the Era of the Cold War: 1968–1990*, (Cambridge: Cambridge University Press, 2004), p. 64. See also Helmut Hubel, 'Cooperation and Conflict in German and American Policies Towards Regions Outside Europe', p. 72 in the same volume. Geir Lundestad also does not address it in detail, see Lundestad, *The United States and Western Europe since*, p. 183.
7 Geraint Hughes, 'Britain, the Transatlantic Alliance, and the Arab-Israeli War of 1973,' *Journal of Cold War Studies*, vol. 10, no. 2, 2008.

8 Willy Brandt, *Erinnerungen,* (Frankfurt: Propyläen, 1990), pp. 186, 190.
9 Vortragender Legationsrat I. Klasse Redies an Minister Scheel: Aufzeichnungen über die Nahostlage und über die Möglichkeiten einer Beilegung der Krise, 17.10.1973, Zwischenarchiv (ZA) 104948, Politisches Archiv des Auswärtigen Amtes (PA), p. 5. All quotations from German sources are my translations.
10 Botschaft Moskau an das Auswärtige Amt: Nahost, 18.10.1973, ZA 104948, PA; Referat 310 an den Bundeskanzler: Sprachregelung des Auswärtigen Amtes zum Nahostkonflikt, 19.10.1973, ZA 104948, PA.
11 Gespräch Staatssekretär Dr Franks mit dem israelischen Botschafter Ben-Horin am 5. November 1973, 06.11.1973, ZA 104951, PA, p. 3. See also Vortragender Legationsrat I. Klasse Redies an Referat 013: Sprechzettel – Interview des Herrn Bundesministers für Rias Berlin (Hörfunk), 29.11.1973, ZA 104953, PA.
12 Willy Brandt, *Begegnungen und Einsichten: Die Jahre 1960–1975,* (Munich: Droemer Knaur, 1978), p. 387, Brandt, *Erinnerungen,* p. 277.
13 Andrew Pierre, 'Was Wird aus dem "Jahr Europas"?,' *Europa-Archiv,* no. 5, 1974, pp. 133–34, Paul Frank, *Entschlüsselte Botschaft: Ein Diplomat Macht Inventur,* (Munich: Dt. Taschenbuch Verlag, 1985), pp. 147–48. For more information on the 'Year of Europe' initiative, see Alastair Horne, *Kissinger: 1973, the Crucial Year,* (New York: Simon and Schuster, 2009), pp. 106–21, Jussi Hanhimäki, *The Flawed Architect: Henry Kissinger and American Foreign Policy,* (Oxford: Oxford Univ. Press, 2004), pp. 275–77, 348.
14 Vortragender Legationsrat I. Klasse Pfeffer an Minister Scheel: Ihr Fernseh-Interview über Allianz und Nahost am 28. Oktober 1973, 28.10.1973, ZA 104950, PA; Rundschreiben des Ministerialdirigenten Poensgen: Beziehungen Europa-USA, 16.10.1973, doc. 323, AAPD 1973/ III.
15 Botschafter von Hase, London, an das Auswärtige Amt: Gespräche BM Scheels in London, 23.11.1973, doc. 388, AAPD 1973/ III, p. 1880. Assistant Secretary of State van Well confirmed this: Günther van Well, 'Die Europäische Politische Zusammenarbeit in Der Außenpolitischen Sicht der Bundesrepublik Deutschland', *Europa-Archiv,* no. 17, 1973, p. 590.
16 Schöllgen, *Die Außenpolitik der Bundesrepublik Deutschland, p. 83.* Vortragender Legationsrat I. Klasse Pfeffer an Minister Scheel: Ihr Fernseh-Interview über Allianz und Nahost am 28.10.1973, 28.10.1973, ZA 104950, PA.
17 Weingardt, *Deutsche Israel- und Nahostpolitik,* pp. 192–94, 220.
18 Frank, *Entschlüsselte Botschaft,* p. 266.
19 Referat 310 an den Bundeskanzler: Sprachregelung des Auswärtigen Amtes zum Nahostkonflikt, 19.10.1973, ZA 104948, PA, p. 4.
20 Botschaft Tel Aviv an das Auswärtige Amt: Nahostkonflikt, 06.10.1973, ZA 104946, PA.
21 Errichtung eines Krisenstabes Nahost, 08.10.1973, ZA 104946, PA; Botschaft Bagdad an das Auswärtige Amt: Nahostkonflikt, 07.10.1973, ZA 104946, PA; Botschaft Amman an das Auswärtige Amt: Lage in Jordanien nach Ausbruch der Feindseligkeiten Ägypten–Syrien–Israel, 07.10.1973, ZA 104946, PA; and Die Lage im Nahen Osten, 15.10.1973, ZA 104946, PA as well as Botschaft Kuwait an das Auswärtige Amt: Kuwaitische Haltung im Nahostkrieg, 08.10.1973, ZA 104946, PA.
22 Gespräch des Bundesministers Scheel mit dem israelischen Botschafter Ben-Horin, 08.10.1973, doc. 314, AAPD 1973/ III.
23 Botschaft in Moskau an das Auswärtige Amt: Nahost-Konflikt, 08.10.1973, ZA 104946, PA.
24 Botschaft in Paris an das Auswärtige Amt: Lage im Nahen Osten, 08.10.1973, ZA 104946, PA, p. 1.
25 Botschaft London an das Auswärtige Amt: Britische Beurteilung des Nah-Ost-Konflikts, 08.10.1973, ZA104946, PA; Referat 310: Die Lage im Nahen Osten, 09.10.1973, ZA 104946, PA. For more information on the American Middle East policy in 1973, see for instance Patrick Tyler, *A World of Trouble. The White House and the Middle East – from the Cold War to the War on Terror,* (New York: Farrar, Straus, Giroux, 2009), pp. 137–75, and Alastair Horne, *Kissinger: 1973, the Crucial Year,* (New York: Simon and Schuster, 2009), chapters 6, 11, 12, 13, 15.
26 Botschaft Washington an das Auswärtige Amt: Nahost-Konflikt, 12.10.1973, ZA 194947, PA; and Botschaft Washington an das Auswärtige Amt: Nahost-Konflikt, 11.10.1973, ZA 194947, PA; Botschaft Washington an das Auswärtige Amt: Nahostkonflikt, 16.10.1973, ZA 104947, PA.
27 Handelsvertretung Sofia an das Auswärtige Amt: Nahostkrieg, 13.10.1973, ZA104947, PA.
28 Auswärtiges Amt an Botschaft Brüssel (NATO): Nahostkonflikt, 13.10.1973, ZA 104947, PA.
29 Sprechzettel, 14.10.1973, ZA 104947, PA, p. 1. For more information on the American troops in Germany see Richard Wiggers' article on 'From Supreme Authority to Reserved Rights and Responsibilities: The International Legal Basis of German-American Relations' and Bryan T. van

Sveringen's chapter on 'Variable Architectures for War and Peace: U.S. Force Structure and Basing in Germany, 1945–90', both in Detlef Junker (ed), *The United States and Germany in the Era of the Cold War, 1945–1990*, vol. I, (Washington: Cambridge University Press, 2004).
30 At the same time, the German Democratic Republic started a propaganda campaign against West Germany by alleging it of supporting Israel which led to démarches of the West German ambassadors in several Arab capitals strongly rejecting these accusations. See Referat 310: Im Anschluß an 176 vom 15.10., 16.10.1973, ZA 104947, PA; and Auswärtiges Amt an Botschaft Rabat und Beirut: Angebliche deutsche Waffenhilfe zugunsten Israels, 17.10.1973, ZA 104948, PA.
31 Referat 310: Die Lage im Nahen Osten – Sachstand, 15.10.1973, ZA 104947, PA, p. 3.
32 Gespräch des Bundesministers Scheel mit dem amerikanischen Botschafter Hillenbrand, 16.10.1973, doc. 322, AAPD 1973/III, p. 1559.
33 Gespräch des Bundesministers Scheel mit dem amerikanischen Botschafter Hillenbrand, 16.10.1973, doc. 322, AAPD 1973/III.
34 Gespräch des Bundesministers Scheel mit dem amerikanischen Botschafter Hillenbrand, 16.10.1973, doc. 322, AAPD 1973/III, footnote 12, p. 1562.
35 Botschafter Krapf, Brüssel (NATO) an das Auswärtige Amt: Nahost-Konflikt, 17.10.1973, doc. 324, AAPD 1973/III; Botschaft London an das Auswärtige Amt: Nahost-Konflikt, 17.10.1973, ZA 104948, PA; and Botschaft Wien an das Auswärtige Amt: Schutz des österreichischen Luftraumes, 18.10.1973, ZA 104948, PA.
36 Übersetzung: Brief der Botschaft Ägyptens an das Auswärtige Amt, 19.10.1973, ZA 104948, PA; and Ministerialdirektor Lahn an Staatssekretär Frank: Vorschlag den amerikanischen Botschafter zu einem Gespräch beim Herrn Minister oder bei Ihnen einzubestellen, 22.10.1973, ZA 104948, PA. As was pointed out by the Federal Ministry for Traffic later, there were, however, no proofs of war material being loaded on the El Al aircrafts. See Bundesministerium für Verkehr an das Auswärtige Amt: Nahostkrise, 05.11.1973, ZA 104951, PA. Ministerialdirigent Jesser: Entwicklung des Verhältnisses zwischen der Bundesrepublik Deutschland und der arabischen Welt seit Ausbruch des Nahost-Krieges am 6.10.1973, 23.10.1973, ZA 104949, PA.
37 Ministerialdirektor Lahn an Staatssekretär Frank: Vorschlag den amerikanischen Botschafter zu einem Gespräch beim Herrn Minister oder bei Ihnen einzubestellen, 22.10.1973, ZA 104948, PA.
38 Gespräch des Staatssekretärs Frank mit dem amerikanischen Gesandten Cash, 24.10.1973, doc. 335, AAPD 1973/III, footnote 4, p. 1639.
39 Gespräch des Staatssekretärs Frank mit dem amerikanischen Gesandten Cash, 24.10.1973, doc. 335, AAPD 1973/III, footnote 5, p. 1639. This news was first published by a Bremerhaven newspaper, see 'Bonn Is Singled Out,' *New York Times*, 27 October 1973.
40 Gespräch des Staatssekretärs Frank mit dem amerikanischen Gesandten Cash, 24.10.1973, doc. 335, AAPD 1973/III.
41 Henry Kissinger, *Years of Upheaval*, (Boston: Little, Brown & Co., 1982), p. 714.
42 Auswärtiges Amt an Botschaft Kairo, 25.10.1973, ZA104949, PA; Botschaft Kairo an das Auswärtige Amt: Beladung israelischer Schiffe in Bremerhaven, 26.10.1973, ZA104949, PA; Ministerialdirektor Lahn an Staatssekretär Frank: Besuch des Leiters des Büros der Arabischen Liga Herr Khatib, 25.10.1973, ZA 104949, PA; and Ministerialdirektor Lahn an Staatssekretär Frank: Interview des lybischen Staatspräsidenten Ghaddafi mit 'Le Monde' vom 23.10.1973, 25.10.1973, ZA 1049494, PA.
43 Gespräch des Staatssekretärs Frank mit dem amerikanischen Botschafter Hillenbrand, 25.10.1973, doc. 337, AAPD 1973/ III. Apparently, even Hillenbrand did not have much information on this issue either as he criticizes in his memoirs: 'Then all hell broke loose. [...] Frank called me in to find out what I knew. Frank [...] could scarcely believe me when I said I had no information. Little did he understand the dearth of information provided American ambassadors when the great men of the Nixon administration were personally involved.' in: Martin Joseph Hillenbrand, *Fragments of Our Time: Memoirs of a Diplomat*, (Athens, GA: University of Georgia Press, 1998), p. 328.
44 Botschafter von Staden, Washington, an Bundesminister Scheel: Unterredung mit dem amerikanischen Außenminister am 26.10., 26.10.1973, doc. 341, AAPD 1973/ III. The New York Times, also considered it the biggest NATO crisis since 1949, see 'Bonn Is Singled Out,' *New York Times* 27 October 1973, pp. 1, 11. Kissinger also bluntly expressed his disapproval by saying, 'I don't care what happens to NATO, I'm so disgusted', see Hillenbrand, *Fragments of Our Time*, p. 329.
45 Vortragender Legationsrat I. Klasse Pfeffer an Minister Scheel: Ihr Fernseh-Interview über Allianz und Nahost am 28. Oktober 1973, 28.10.1973, ZA 104950, PA, p. 5; Bundeskanzler Brandt an Präsident Nixon, 18.10.1973, doc. 342, AAPD 1973/III.

46 Kissinger, *Years of Upheaval*, pp. 714–16, Frank, *Entschlüsselte Botschaft*, p. 269.
47 Botschaft Washington an das Auswärtige Amt: US Alarmmaßnahmen im Rahmen des Nahostkonflikts, 25.10.1973, ZA 104949, PA. For more information on the DEFCON III crisis, see Horne, *Kissinger: 1973*, chapter 12.
48 Gespräch des Staatssekretärs Frank mit dem amerikanischen Botschafter Hillenbrand, 29.10.1973, doc. 343, AAPD 1973/ III. For more information on the decision-making process to go on DEFCON III and how this fitted into Kissinger's and Nixon's overall 'madman theory', see Jeremi Suri, *Henry Kissinger and the American Century*, (Cambridge, MA: The Belknap Press of Harvard University Press, 2007), p. 260.
49 Botschaft Tripolis an das Auswärtige Amt: Deutsche Haltung im Nahost-Konflikt, 30.10.1973, ZA 104950, PA; and Vortragender Legationsrat Fiedler: Vermerk über ein Gespräch mit dem ägyptischen Botschafter am 26. Oktober 1973, 29.10.1973, ZA 104950, PA.
50 Gesandtin Scheibe, Den Haag, an das Auswärtige Amt: Arabischer Ölboykott gegenüber den Niederlanden, 29.10.1973, doc. 345, AAPD 1973/ III; Referat 310: Sachstand – Die Lage im Nahen Osten, 04.11.1973, ZA 104951, PA.
51 Botschafter von Staden, Washington, an Bundesminister Scheel: Unterrichtung der NATO-Botschafter durch Außenminister Kissinger über Entwicklung und Stand des Nahost-Konflikts, 02.11.1973, doc. 356, AAPD 1973/ III.
52 Auswärtiges Amt an Botschaft London, Paris, Washington, Kopenhagen: EPZ; Nahost, 30.10.1973, ZA 104951, PA. For Scheel's meeting with the ambassador see Vermerk: Gespräch Bundesminister Scheel mit dem französischen Botschafter Sauvagnargues am 30. Oktober 1973, 30.10.1973, ZA 104951, PA.
53 For more information on how the EC dealt with the Middle East crisis see also the chapter by Andreas Wenger and Daniel Möckli in this book.
54 Übersetzung: Nahosterklärung der Neun Außenminister vom 6. November 1973, 06.11.1973, ZA104951, PA.
55 Kissinger, *Years of Upheaval*, p. 718. Botschaft Washington an das Auswärtige Amt: EPZ Nahost-Erklärung, 07.11.1973, ZA 104951, PA. For Kissinger's intention to exploit the Middle East conflict to increase US prestige see Suri, *Henry Kissinger and the American Century*, p. 258.
56 Runderlaß des Ministerialdirektors van Well: EPZ; Nahost, 07.11.1973, doc. 363, AAPD 1973/ III.
57 Botschaft Tripolis an das Auswärtige Amt: Lybisches Ultimatum, 07.11.1973, ZA 104951, PA.
58 Gespräch des Bundeskanzlers Brandt mit dem Ministerpräsidenten Rumor, 08.11.1973, doc. 365, AAPD 1973/ III; Frank, *Entschlüsselte Botschaft*, p. 269.
59 Ibid., p. 271.
60 Aufzeichnung: Besuch des lybischen Botschafters beim Herrn Staatssekretär Dr. Frank am 13. November 1973, 16.11.1973, ZA 104953, PA, p. 4. The last five words were manually underlined by Frank. See also his handwritten remarks on the cover page.
61 Referat 310 an Staatssekretär Frank: Gesprächsunterlage für Sisco-Besuch, 12.11.1973, ZA 104968, PA; and Referat 310 an Referat 240: Ortex zum Sisco-Besuch in Bonn, 14.11.1973, ZA 104968, PA; Leitlinien der Bündnispolitik, 12.11.1973, doc. 372, AAPD 1973/ III.
62 'US–Nato Dispute Still Unresolved,' *New York Times*, 11 November 1973, pp. 1, 26.
63 Gespräch des Bundeskanzlers Brandt mit Staatspräsident Pompidou in Paris, 26.11.1973, doc. 390, AAPD 1973/ III, p. 1899.
64 Kissinger, *Years of Upheaval*, pp. 724–26, Henry Kissinger, 'Rede des Amerikanischen Außenministers, Henry A. Kissinger, vor der Pilgrims Society in London am 12. Dezember 1973 über die Transatlantischen Beziehungen,' *Europa-Archiv*, no. 2, 1974, p. D45.
65 Ministerialdirektor van Well, z.Z. Brüssel (NATO) an Staatssekretär Frank: Vierertreffen am 9. Dezember 1973, 10.12.1973, doc. 410, AAPD 1973/ III.
66 Gespräch des Staatssekretärs Frank mit dem amerikanischen Gesandten Cash, 24.10.1973, doc. 335, AAPD 1973/ III and Gespräch des Staatssekretärs Frank mit dem amerikanischen Botschafter Hillenbrand, 15.10.1973, doc. 337, AAPD 1973/ III as well as Gespräch des Staatssekretärs Frank mit dem amerikanischen Botschafter Hillenbrand, 29.10.1973, doc. 343, AAPD 1973/ III.
67 To understand that this decision was really taken *ad hoc* see Frank, *Entschlüsselte Botschaft*, p. 268.
68 Gespräch des Staatssekretärs Frank mit dem amerikanischen Botschafter Hillenbrand, 25.10.1973, doc. 337, AAPD 1973/ III. For the embargo on the Netherlands, see for instance Desmond Dinan, *Europe Recast: A History of European Union*, (Basingstoke: Palgrave Macmillan, 2004), p. 145.
69 Runderlaß des Vortragenden Legationsrat I. Klasse Dohms, 19.10.1973, doc. 329, AAPD 1973/ III, p. 1609. See also for instance Runderlaß des Vortragenden Legationsrat I. Klasse Dohms: Zu

unserer Haltung im Nahost-Konflikt, 19.10.1973, doc. 329, AAPD 1973/ III, Botschafter Lebsanft, Brüssel (EG), an das Auswärtige Amt: 260. Tagung des Rates der Europäischen Gemeinschaften am 6.11., 06.11.1973, doc. 360, AAPD 1973/ III, p. 1759.
70 Frank, *Entschlüsselte Botschaft*, p. 255.
71 See for instance the talks between Brandt and Pompidou, Gespräch des Bundeskanzlers Brandt mit Staatspräsident Pompidou in Paris, 26.11.1973, doc. 390, AAPD 1973/ III. See also Runderlaß des Vortragenden Legationsrat I. Klasse Dohms, 18.12.1973, doc. 422, AAPD 1973/ III.
72 Gespräch des Staatssekretärs Frank mit dem amerikanischen Botschafter Hillenbrand, 25.10.1973, doc. 338, AAPD 1973/ III, p. 1653.
73 Bundeskanzler Brandt and Präsident Nixon, 28.10.1973, doc. 342, AAPD 1973/ III; Botschafter von Staden, Washington, an Bundesminister Scheel: Unterredung mit dem amerikanischen Außenminister am 26.10., 26.10.1973, doc. 341, AAPD 1973/ III; and Leitlinien der Bündnispolitik, 12.11.1973, doc. 372, AAPD 1973/ III.
74 Gespräch des Staatssekretärs Frank mit dem amerikanischen Botschafter Hillenbrand, 29.10.1973, doc. 343, AAPD 1973/ III, p. 1675.
75 Golda Meir, *My Life,* (London: Weidenfeld and Nicolson, 1975), pp. 364, 367–68. Gespräch Staatssekretär Dr. Franks mit dem israelischen Botschafter Ben Horin am 30. Oktober 1973 um 18.00 Uhr, 31.10.1973, ZA 104950, PA.
76 Tyler, *A World of Trouble*, pp. 162–63.
77 Gespräch des Staatssekretärs Frank mit dem amerikanischen Botschafter Hillenbrand, 29.10.1973, doc. 343, AAPD 1973/ III, footnote 22, pp. 1676–77; and for the original decision to refuse support see: Gespräch des Staatssekretärs Frank mit dem amerikanischen Gesandten Cash, 24.10.1973, doc. 335, AAPD 1973/ III. Vortragender Legationsrat I. Klasse Jirka an Ministerialdirektor Hermes: Nahostkrise, 26.10.1973, ZA 104949, PA; Botschafter Ruhfus: Sprechzettel für die Kabinettsitzung am 31.10., 30.10.1973, ZA 104950, PA; Botschaft New York (UNO) an das Auswärtige Amt: UN Emergency Forces, 26.11.1973, ZA 104953, PA; and Ministerialdirektor van Well an Staatssekretär Frank: Deutsche Beteiligung am Transport der VN-Friedenstruppe Nahost, 04.12.1973, ZA 104954, PA. Ministerialdirektor Lahn an Staatssekretär Frank: Vorschlag den amerikanischen Botschafter zu einem Gespräch beim Herrn Minister oder bei Ihnen einzubestellen, 22.10.1973, ZA 104948, PA; and Gespräch des Staatssekretärs Frank mit dem amerikanischen Botschafter Hillenbrand, 25.10.1973, doc. 337, AAPD 1973/ III.
78 Vortragender Legationsrat Niemöller an Staatssekretär Frank: Gespräch Staatssekretär Dr. Franks mit dem israelischen Botschafter Ben Horin am 30. Oktober 1973 um 18.00 Uhr, 31.10.1973, ZA 104950, PA.
79 Brandt, *Begegnungen und Einsichten*, p. 420.

10

The United States and the 'loss' of Iran

Repercussions on transatlantic security

Barbara Zanchetta

Introduction: NATO and the 'out-of-area' debate

In the aftermath of the 9/11 terrorist attacks against the United States, NATO invoked, for the first time in its history, Article V of the North Atlantic Treaty, therefore activating the collective defence mechanism of the Alliance. With the subsequent decision on the creation of a force to be deployed in Afghanistan, NATO embarked in its first ever truly 'out of area' mission. The test case of the Alliance's capacity for success is still ongoing, and it will take years, if not decades, to be able to assess the mission, its actual scope and impact on Afghanistan and on the region as a whole. Apart from the challenges and issues that remain to be addressed in terms of success or failure, this chapter focuses on the broad transformation of the Alliance. Today, the term 'out of area' reflects the widely acknowledged and accepted necessity of expanding NATO's 'mandate' to areas considered vital for the security of the member states, even if these areas are outside the legally defined boundaries of the Treaty. Yet, for decades this concept had remained a point of contention and division, without being either directly tackled or jointly discussed by the member states of the Alliance.

The history of the out of area debate and the controversy surrounding the legal boundaries and extension of the Treaty dates back to the signing of the North Atlantic Treaty itself. The geographical limitation – clearly defined in Article VI of the Treaty – reflected the necessities of the early Cold War. In 1949, the American and Western European utmost concern was to counter the emerging power of the Soviet Union. At the time, the immediate threat was posed by the presence of the Red Army in Eastern Europe, while Moscow's capacity to intervene in other areas – Iran, China, Korea, for example – appeared to be limited. At the same time, the United States, although committing to the defence of Western Europe, wanted to avoid potential involvement in European colonial conflicts, or in areas where it seemed unimaginable that US national security could be directly at stake.

Therefore, until the late 1970s, NATO's Article VI was repeatedly used to avoid or interrupt discussion of out of area issues, without even considering the possibility of common military action. A well-known episode is Secretary of State Henry Kissinger's outcry against the 'stampede of dissociation' by Washington's allies in the face of American requests for assistance in supplying Israeli forces during the Yom Kippur War. Kissinger was particularly critical of 'the legalistic argument' made by the allies that NATO's boundaries did not extend to the Middle East.[1] In fact, while throughout the decades there had been intensive inter-allied consultation at various occasions – Suez, Vietnam, Angola – the out of area issue was *not* formally addressed by NATO until 1980.

Between the 1950s and the mid-1970s the wars in Korea and Indochina, the growth in Soviet naval forces and Moscow's interventions in Africa (Congo, Angola, the Horn of Africa) had gradually unveiled a more geographically diffused nature of the threat.[2] For this reason, individual states undertaking operations in the 'periphery' might have expected political support from their allies. Yet, collective participation by NATO remained inconceivable. The security strategy of the Alliance simply did not extend to areas outside the north Atlantic territory.[3]

The events unfolding in the 'arc of crisis'[4] in the late 1970s revolutionized this basic concept, finally bringing the out of area debate to the forefront of NATO policies. The Carter Doctrine, announced in January 1980, and the subsequent creation of the Rapid Deployment Force (RDF) to support and sustain America's commitment to the region, forced the Europeans to consider the possible repercussions of the deployment of US forces to the Persian Gulf.[5] The need to define the Alliance's out of area posture gradually emerged and, from that moment onwards, remained at the centre of NATO's evolving and increasingly more global role.

The scope of this chapter is to trace the evolution of the Carter Doctrine and to assess the motivations behind the broad rethinking of American policy towards the Persian Gulf, which, in turn, impacted on the overall conception of transatlantic security. Focusing on events taking place *before* the Soviet invasion of Afghanistan, the analysis will point to the unfolding of events in Iran between 1978 and 1979 as the key element in determining the shift of US policy. The departure of the Shah and the creation of the Islamic Republic exposed the United States in a region of crucial strategic importance. The loss of America's closest and most important regional ally compelled Washington to foresee a direct military presence in the region. At the same time, the heightened sense of Western vulnerability unveiled in the aftermath of the Iranian revolution eventually led to the recognition that the traditional boundaries of the alliance between Europe and the United States were no longer sufficient to protect Western security.

Iran as the cornerstone of US policy in the Persian Gulf

America's troubled partnership with Mohammed Reza Shah Pahlavi started during the Second World War when US troops entered Iran for the first time, joining the British and Soviet occupation forces. After the end of the war, the crisis caused by Stalin's delay in withdrawing his troops signalled the importance that the emerging 'Western camp' assigned to maintaining a predominant influence over Iran.[6] In fact, as the Cold War gradually came to dominate the international scene, Britain and, increasingly, the United States tightened their relationship with the Shah in the context of the general drive to contain the expansion of the Soviet Union.

Despite some criticism from certain sectors of informed public opinion, until the 1953 CIA-sponsored coup, the image of the United States in Iran was generally positive. America represented the ideals of democracy and modernization in a country struggling to emerge from underdevelopment, dominant external influence and authoritarian rule. In the immediate post-war years, anger and resentment were commonly directed against the British colonial 'exploiters' who maintained their presence in Iran and, most importantly, administered the Anglo-Iranian Oil Company's rich revenues. In the early 1950s, Mohammed Mossadeq's nationalism emerged within this context and strengthened itself under the determination to promote the autonomous development of Iran. The decision to nationalize the Oil Company was the obvious first step in reducing foreign involvement in Iranian affairs while enabling the country to benefit from its own natural resources.[7]

However, from the perspective of London and Washington, the economic setback combined with the widespread perception of political instability, potentially open to communist infiltration, triggered plans on possible 'countermeasures'. Although initially the British and American leaders had been reluctant to intervene directly, with Churchill's return to power and the election of Eisenhower, the stage was set for 'Operation Ajax' – the CIA covert intervention that ultimately led to the removal of Mossadeq and the consolidation of the Shah's openly pro-Western regime.[8]

From that moment onwards, the United States was able to secure both the existence of a friendly government, geared towards the containment of Soviet expansionism, and the penetration of the Iranian oil fields. In concrete terms, and from the standpoint of a superpower engaged in an increasingly global Cold War, the 1953 coup (the first 'regime change' intervention of the US-CIA) was, therefore, a clear-cut success. At the same time, however, the coup inevitably, and irreparably, damaged the US–Iranian relationship. From the Iranian public's point of view, the United States had ruthlessly intervened in Iranian internal affairs to defend its own interests and to fulfil its global agenda. America came to be seen as just an 'ordinary' external power that was ready to exploit Iran's geostrategic significance while by no means assisting in the internal development of the country.

The events of 1953 also deepened the fissure between Iranian society and the Shah's autocratic rule, a rupture that would never be completely healed. However, without assessing the possible long-term consequences of its policies, Washington progressively strengthened its relationship with Tehran. Starting in the mid-1950s, and especially after the 1958 anti-Western coup in Iraq, the US aid programmes to Iran focused almost exclusively on reinforcing the country's military capabilities. After the proclamation of the Eisenhower Doctrine, the Middle East entered the Cold War 'chessboard' and the strategic importance of Iran became increasingly crucial for the United States.[9] Throughout the 1960s, Washington further developed its association with the Shah. For a combination of economic and geopolitical reasons, a positive relationship with Iran was in fact considered an essential asset in the formulation of security policies towards the Persian Gulf.

Despite the problems of the agricultural sector and its narrowly based political regime, Iran's economic progress 'under the leadership of an increasingly self-assured Shah' was deemed 'remarkable'. Between 1966 and 1969, the Iranian growth rate had proceeded at an annual rate of 10 per cent without incurring inflation or substantial increases in debt. This performance had been made possible by the rapidly increasing oil revenues, which enabled public development programmes and imports, with only minor strains on the country's foreign exchange position.[10] In short, Iran was a 'success story' among developing countries.[11] This conveyed general optimism in the United States for the future continuation of the Iranian development and modernization process.

In addition, close ties with the Shah for Washington were valuable from a military and strategic point of view. Iran allowed transit rights for American military aircrafts, thus providing the United States and the Western democracies with a secure air corridor between European NATO and Southeast Asia. Also, the Shah's regime offered hospitality for vital communication and intelligence facilities, advantageously located close to the border with the Soviet Union.[12]

Finally, during the 1960s oil had emerged as essential for the security of the West. The dependence of Japan and Europe on the largest proven reserves of petroleum in the world rendered access to the Persian Gulf absolutely vital for the 'free world'. If the flow of oil was interrupted, or if it went under control of unfriendly countries, the repercussions for the Western industrial economies would be incalculable. From this perspective, the pro-Western orientation of the Shah's regime was obviously crucial. Furthermore, the British decision to withdraw its presence from the Gulf by 1971 added strategic significance to the region entailing, from Washington's standpoint, a greater involvement in its defence.[13]

In the early 1970s, US President Richard Nixon therefore inherited a policy towards Iran that had been shaped by Washington's heavy reliance on the Shah's pro-Western and anti-communist credentials. Against this background, the Nixon administration formulated its own line of action, which eventually translated into a further and decisive strengthening of the links with the Iranian leader. Ultimately, Iran became the centrepiece of Washington's entire strategy for the Persian Gulf.

The basis of the US–Iranian relationship during the Nixon years was the administration's increased reliance on local powers for the defence of areas considered vital to American national security. Although this policy – labelled as the Nixon Doctrine – had been originally formulated in relation to Vietnam (providing the framework for the withdrawal of US troops), it rapidly evolved into the presidency's general posture. In its earliest formulation in relation to the Middle East (National Security Study Memorandum 66 of 1969), the policy recommended increased military and economic assistance to Iran and Saudi Arabia, the 'two pillars' responsible for maintaining regional stability. Although Saudi Arabia was mentioned and would remain an important US ally, Iran was clearly to become America's regional stronghold.[14]

The exchanges between the Iranian and American leadership confirm that the convergence of their policies was to a large extent motivated by the perception (either actual or crafted) of an external threat, i.e. coming from the Soviet Union directly or, most likely, by proxy. According to the Shah, Moscow was 'trying to dominate the Mediterranean by establishing control over a triangle with its points at Suez, Aden and Djibouti'. The broader objective was to access the Indian Ocean and, in due course, the Persian Gulf.[15] Moreover, the indication of rising radicalism in countries neighbouring Iran offered opportunities to the Soviets to extend their influence. In particular, the Shah was concerned about the situation in Iraq. According to his assessment, the Soviets were supplying Baghdad with offensive armaments, including aircrafts, missiles and hardware. These shipments were significantly strengthening the Iraqi military capabilities. In addition, Moscow was pressuring Baghdad to include Iraqi communists in the composition of its future government.[16]

Within this context, the Shah believed that Iran could play a crucial role in maintaining radical Arab or Soviet influence at an 'innocuous level'.[17] But this would require the further strengthening of his armed forces, with the additional acquisition of modern and sophisticated weapons. Despite the dangerous consequences that increased military investments could potentially entail – domestically, they would hinder the development of other sectors of the society, and internationally, they could alarm neighbouring countries – the Shah was determined to follow his course.[18] In concrete terms, this meant that the relations with the United States, Iran's chief provider of arms, would have to tighten more than ever before.

The American viewpoint is effectively summarized by Kissinger's definition of the Shah as a 'man of mission', determined to modernize his country. To this end, he was 'subtly pressing the idea of a "special relationship" with the US' which would give Iran a preferred treatment, both in economic terms[19] and on military credits. However, as underlined by the US National Security Adviser, the Shah was not 'entirely self-seeking'. His commitment to the West was, in fact, assessed as 'genuine'.[20] From this perspective, Kissinger referred to the Shah's definition of his country as an 'island of stability' – a phrase which would become ill-famed in the later part of the 1970s.

Interestingly, President Nixon's decisive strengthening of the US–Iranian relationship took place in late May 1972, on his one-and-a-half day stop in Tehran en route back to Washington from the first US–Soviet summit held in Moscow.[21] During the conversations in Tehran, Nixon told the Shah that in the future virtually no more limitations would be placed on his purchases of American military equipment. With this decision, the president overruled the conflicting recommendations of his advisers[22] and, in essence, enabled Iran to enter with full title the circle of America's closest allies.

The significance of Nixon's May decisions emerges in full only when the regional context is juxtaposed to the broader framework of US–Soviet relations. For Washington, the perception of a greater need to resist Soviet expansionism into the region – actual or even only potential – was the central motivation for strengthening the alliance with Iran. As Kissinger stated in his memoirs:

> The real issue in 1972 was that the required balance within an area essential for the security, and even more, prosperity, of all industrial democracies appeared in jeopardy. (...) Our friends – Saudi Arabia, Jordan, the Emirates – were being encircled.
>
> It was imperative for our interests and those of the Western world that the regional balance of power be maintained so that moderate forces would not be engulfed nor Europe's and Japan's (and as it later turned out, our) economic lifeline fall into hostile hands. (...) To have failed to match the influx of Soviet arms into neighbouring countries would have accelerated the demoralization of moderate forces in the Middle East and speeded up the radicalization of the area, including Iran's.[23]

For the US leadership, it was thus vital to reassure the Shah on America's continued commitment to the defence of the pro-Western orientation of the area. Within this framework, the May 1972 conversations provided tangible evidence of Nixon's intention to firmly sustain Iran's role as an anti-Soviet regional stronghold. In concrete terms, the President agreed to sell laser-guided bombs and F-14 and F-15 aircrafts,[24] then both considered among the most advanced and sophisticated US-produced weapons. The third concession was the agreement on the assignment to Iran of an increased number of uniformed technicians, the so-called 'blue suiters', to work with the Iranian military. In this way, Nixon gave weighty substance to the affirmation that he would not 'let down' his friends.[25]

Therefore, the ultimate strengthening of US–Iranian ties was inherently related to the developments taking place on the broader bipolar 'chessboard'. In other words, the competition with the Soviet Union was the central element shaping Washington's worldview and, in this context, Iran was a crucial asset – an asset which became all the more important during the era of détente. This basic outlook remained decisive in the formulation of America's policy throughout the 1970s. Consequently, between 1972 and 1976 Iran continued to be the largest recipient of US arms, purchasing almost one-third of total American sales.[26] The Ford administration maintained the basic guidelines of Nixon's policy and President Carter, in assuming office, displayed no intention of seeking a change of policy towards the Shah.[27]

Contrary to the promise of leading the country in a 'new direction' and the declared 'absolute commitment' to the promotion of human rights worldwide,[28] Carter's attitude towards Iran revealed, from the start, a remarkable continuity with the policies of his so-bitterly criticized predecessors.[29] The incoming administration in fact assigned more importance to American national security interests than to the values and principles posed at the centre of Carter's electoral platform: neither the declared objective of opposing human rights abuses nor the stated intention to focus on the local causes and dynamics of regional upheavals thwarted the development of US–Iranian ties. Despite the growing instability of the Shah's regime, which faced inflation, unemployment and increasing criticism from many sectors of civil society, during the first year of the Carter presidency, the close ties between Washington and the Iranian leader were repeatedly underscored. As a result, the Shah's preoccupations that Carter's human rights campaign would negatively impact on the development of the US–Iranian relationship rapidly subsided.[30]

In May 1977, Secretary of State Cyrus Vance visited Tehran and informed the Shah of the decision to proceed with the sale of F-16 aircrafts and of the President's intention to seek approval for the sale of sophisticated airborne warning and control systems (the AWACS). During the November 1977 meetings in Washington, the President and the Shah once again acknowledged their special relationship and outlined an understanding on the need to continue to satisfy Iranian defence needs. The timing of what would be the last visit to Iran by an American president dramatically revealed the flawed perceptions, within the United States, of the Iranian domestic turmoil and of the capacity of the Shah to maintain control over the internal opposition. Carter flew to Tehran and praised the Shah just when his leadership was confronted with increasing antagonism. On 31 December 1977, Carter declared:

> Iran under the great leadership of the Shah is an island of stability in one of the more troubled areas of the world. This is a great tribute to you, Your Majesty, and to your leadership, and to the respect, admiration and love which your people give to you.[31]

Only a few weeks later, riots broke out in Tehran and in other major cities, starting the anti-regime demonstrations, which would last, without interruption, until early 1979.

The 'loss' of Iran and the making of the Carter doctrine

The US administration did not foresee the collapse of the Shah's regime. Until late 1978, Carter received intelligence assessments indicating that there was no reason for immediate concern, Iran was 'not in a revolutionary or even a pre-revolutionary situation'.[32] On his part, the president had underscored the notion, developed by his predecessors, of Iran as a cornerstone of regional stability. According to National Security Council (NSC) staff member responsible for Iranian affairs, Gary Sick:

> The overriding consideration for US Iranian policy [...] was to ensure that the cooperative relationship that had been developed over nearly four decades would be preserved and that Iran would remain a strong, reliable and friendly ally in the vital region of the Persian Gulf. The importance of the security relationship was paramount.[33]

This well-established view, which Carter chose not to challenge, paralysed the administration's ability to conceive alternatives to the Shah's rule. Consequently, when it became impossible to defend what had been erroneously perceived as a solid anti-Soviet strategic ally, the United States was compelled to adjust its overall posture, initiating a process which led to the Carter Doctrine.

From Washington's standpoint, the implications of the Iranian revolution extended far beyond the borders of Iran and of the US–Iranian bilateral relationship. Carter's National Security Adviser Zbigniew Brzezinski summarized this position by underlining that the disintegration of Iran would be the 'most massive American defeat since the beginning of the Cold War, overshadowing in its real consequences the setback in Vietnam'.[34] As outlined above, the American strategy in the entire region, broadly defined as Southwest Asia, had been founded on the premise that Iran was and would continue to be a strong and stable regional power whose policies would, despite some divergences, essentially converge with those of the United States. This assumption affected decisions concerning US military deployments in Asia and in Europe, weapons procurements and long-term planning for force structure and readiness. Moreover, the relationship with Iran was inherently linked to the broad spectrum of US–Soviet relations and was, directly or indirectly, interconnected with other important American policies in the region.[35] The collapse of the Shah's regime also signified the impossibility of maintaining intelligence surveillance stations to monitor military developments in Soviet territory, sites which had been considered irreplaceable by the American intelligence community.[36] In addition, Iran was a crucial supplier of oil. Any disruption in the quantity of Iranian exports would inevitably impact on the price of oil defined by international markets, with severe repercussions particularly on Western Europe. In short, without relying on Iran it was difficult for the United States to envision alternative policies that would preserve American and Western interests.[37] As noted by Gary Sick, 'nothing less than a full-scale reconstruction of US global policies and assets would suffice'.[38]

In fact, the acknowledgement of the 'loss' of Iran initiated an extensive rethinking of the American role in the region. In the late 1970s, the United States had no military command strategically located close to the Persian Gulf, or specifically dedicated to coordinate operations in the area. The nearest US commands were either in Europe or in the Pacific.[39] Therefore, when the Nixon–Kissinger (and never abandoned) strategy of reliance on Iran collapsed, Washington had to enhance its own direct presence and military capabilities in the region, assuming directly the responsibility previously devolved to the Shah.

A few weeks after the departure of the Iranian leader, Secretary of Defense Harold Brown stated:

> We have made a policy decision about a more active role in the area. We told these countries things that they have not heard for a long time – namely, that the United States is deeply interested in the Middle East, we are very worried about what the Soviets are doing, we intend to be involved. That's a line no American administration has taken with them since Vietnam.[40]

Days later, he announced on television that the United States would be prepared to defend its vital interests in the Middle East with whatever means appropriate, including military force.[41] Interestingly, the focus was on the Soviet Union (and not on the internal dynamics of the Iranian turmoil). This, together with the reference to Vietnam, confirms the dominant Cold War mentality of the administration.

In March 1979, Brzezinski wrote a memorandum proposing a 'Consultative Security Framework for the Middle East'. Underlining that the fall of the Shah had added a new and dangerous dimension to the pre-existing problems in the region, and stressing the potential for Soviet penetration, Brzezinski drew a parallel with the late 1940s. 'Then too', he stated, 'a strategically vital region faced external threat, intra-regional conflicts, socio-economic privation, and local radicalism for which US power, wealth and leadership toward unity were the remedy'.[42] The Iranian revolution added unpredictability to an already unstable area. Hence, the need for a new security framework in which the United States would play a leading role. This meant that a greater US commitment to the defence of the region was needed, with more extensive security guarantees and an increased military presence. Furthermore, according to the US National Security Adviser, this shift in policy had to be unequivocal:

> To explain our new strategy toward the Middle East to friends in the region, allies, and to our own public will at some early point require a major Presidential pronouncement ... Such a statement should follow, not precede, tangible steps which demonstrate the viability of this approach.[43]

As early as March 1979, the basic elements of the future Carter Doctrine were, therefore, already present.[44] In the following months, 'tangible steps' in support of America's more assertive role were indeed taken: first, Washington started to transfer military aid to North Yemen in order to counter the Soviet-backed aggression of the South (the People's Democratic Republic of Yemen);[45] second, the policy of restraint towards the Horn of Africa, which had shaped Carter's attitude until late 1978, gradually shifted to more open support for Somalia in order to neutralize Soviet support for Ethiopia;[46] and, in July 1979, Carter authorized the CIA to supply assistance to the rebels fighting against the Soviet-backed government in Afghanistan.[47] These actions confirm that the entire Southwest Asian region had become linked to the Iranian crisis and to the perception of a looming Soviet threat.

In parallel with aid packages to various countries (or factions) to counter Moscow's supposed intention of advancing into the Gulf, Washington started to plan its own direct intervention capabilities and to consider the logistical means to sustain them. The discussion on a 'reaction force' able to respond to crises had been initiated already in 1977, but the actual planning for the force (which was to become the Rapid Deployment Force, or RDF) started only after the realization of US geostrategic vulnerability following the fall of the Shah.[48] In the summer of 1979, the Pentagon staff completed a document entitled 'Capabilities for Limited Contingencies in the Persian Gulf', which, pointing to the devastating consequences for the United States of Soviet advances in the region, exhorted the administration to place the Persian Gulf at the centre of US foreign policy interests.[49] Then, as the hostage crisis plummeted US–Iranian relations to a point of no return,[50] making it obvious that there was no possibility of resurrecting Nixon's 'twin pillar' strategy for the Persian Gulf, the implementation of the RDF became a concrete reality. At the NSC meeting on 4 December 1979 (i.e. *before* the Soviets entered Afghanistan), President Carter decided to seek access to military facilities in Kenya, Oman and Somalia in order to provide the necessary operational support for the effectiveness of the RDF.[51]

From Washington's standpoint, the Soviet invasion of Afghanistan in late December 1979 simply confirmed Moscow's aggressive and expansionist tendencies. This clearly added urgency to the redefinition of America's posture. However, the basic change of approach, which led to a firm commitment to the defence of the region, had already been initiated by the events unfolding in Iran. In January 1980 President Carter declared that 'any attempt by any outside force to gain control of the Persian Gulf region will be regarded as an assault on the vital interests of the United States of America, and such an assault will be repelled by any means necessary, including military force'.[52] This statement – the Carter Doctrine – thus resulted from a reassessment of American regional policy, which had been taking place for almost a year.

In sum, the Iranian revolution disclosed a crucial US vulnerability, a weakness and relative exposure to which the Carter Doctrine and the RDF sought to remedy. Inevitably, this fundamental shift in US policy reverberated on America's commitments to Europe – the operational theatre closest to the Persian Gulf – and on NATO – the forum potentially most affected by adjustments in American troop deployments.

Conclusion

The Carter Doctrine confirmed the continued centrality of containment for American foreign policy. Its formulation was similar to previous Cold War doctrines (Truman and Eisenhower, for example) and it formally expanded the perimeter of the areas under 'direct' US protection. Paradoxically, the administration that more than any other had criticized the excessive centrality of the Soviet Union in the formulation of American foreign policy in the end openly revealed a traditionally Soviet-centric worldview. The repercussions were, at least, twofold.

First, for decades Washington had neglected the Shah's problematic management of Iranian internal affairs in order not to jeopardize Iran's fundamental contribution to the broader strategy of containment of the Soviet Union. Although this attitude generally characterized the US–Iranian relationship during the Cold War, it is particularly during the 1970s that the overlooking of the complex local reality had far-reaching consequences. Despite the unequivocal signs of growing domestic unrest,[53] the Nixon administration proceeded with the strengthening of the partnership with the Shah. The increased reliance on Iran was, in fact, a crucial aspect of Nixon's innovative foreign policy. In an era of acknowledgement of limits, America delegated responsibilities while at the same time emphasizing the importance of resisting Soviet expansionism. This seemingly unavoidable Cold War outlook continued to shape America's policy towards Tehran throughout the 1970s. Consequently, once the turmoil in Iran reached its climax and the future of the Shah's regime became uncertain, the United States proved unable to effectively react with policies that could, at least partially, salvage American interests.[54] Instead, the US leadership almost immediately focused on the potential global setback caused by the loss of this crucially important alliance and, afterwards, on conceiving a comprehensive adjustment of policy. This ultimately led to the Carter Doctrine and to the definition of America's new and more active posture in the region.

Second, as a consequence of the Iranian revolution the Persian Gulf was placed at the centre of American interests and, more broadly, of Western security strategies. Although the decision to establish the RDF had been made unilaterally by the United States in late 1979, the Carter administration subsequently addressed the issue also within NATO. If American forces were sent to the Middle East to sustain the RDF there would be a 20–30 per cent decline in US troops available for deployment in Europe. The Europeans had to be aware of this potential drawback and, if need be, adjust their troop levels accordingly. Moreover, since Western Europe was more dependent on Middle Eastern oil than the United States, it seemed reasonable in Washington to demand that the Europeans consider the consequences of including the defence of the Gulf in the West's security strategy.[55] Despite resentment on the part of some European countries for the US decision on the RDF and a refusal to concede that this automatically translated into NATO's collective involvement in the Persian Gulf, a general willingness to compromise on the out of area issue did eventually emerge and was reflected in the Alliance's statements. In May 1980, the final communiqué of NATO's Defense Planning Committee for the first time formally recognized that 'the stability of regions outside NATO boundaries, particularly in the South West Asia, and the secure supply of essential commodities from this area are of crucial importance [...] the current situation has serious implications for the security of member countries'.[56]

The out of area issue remained at the centre of the debates within NATO until the Bonn summit of 1982, when the Alliance finally outlined a 'formula' to respond to conflicts in Southwest Asia based on 'consultation, facilitation, and compensation'. This meant that the allies would 'consult on out of area deployments' and that the Europeans would agree both 'to facilitate the transport of US troops and to compensate for the diversion of US assets'.[57] In the following years, the practical implementation of these decisions remained uncertain and the process reached a stalemate. This, however, does not diminish the importance of the change undertaken by the Alliance and the broad impact of the events in Southwest Asia on the conception of transatlantic security.

Generally, scholars have pointed to the Soviet invasion of Afghanistan as providing the real impetus to change. When assessing the unfolding of events in the region in late 1979, Iran and Afghanistan are coupled together as events with negative consequences for the United States. However, it is the Soviet move that is assessed as the turning point in triggering the fundamental shift in US policy.[58] Conversely, this chapter highlighted the importance of the loss of Iran in determining the potential exposure of the West in an area of crucial strategic importance and in producing the consequent adjustments of policy. In other words, Iran, more than Afghanistan, was the key.

In the immediate aftermath of the Soviet invasion, Brzezinski pointed to the absence of an effective barrier to Moscow's expansionism:

> If the Soviets succeed in Afghanistan, [...] the age-long dream of Moscow to have direct access to the Indian Ocean will have been fulfilled. Historically, the British provided the barrier to that drive and Afghanistan was their buffer state. We assumed that role in 1945, but the Iranian crisis has led to the collapse of the balance of power in Southwest Asia, and it could produce Soviet presence right down the edge of the Arabian and Oman Gulfs.[59]

In early January 1980, an NSC internal memorandum made references to an unconfirmed report that a Soviet division comprising at least 10,000 troops had taken up position along Afghanistan's border with Iran, within striking distance of Iran's oil fields. This raised questions on Moscow's 'real' intentions and on the possibility of Soviet advancement into Iran.[60] A few months later, NSC staffer Paul Henze went a step further, underlining that the possibility of a Soviet move into Iran was not inconceivable:

> I am concerned about the evidence we continue to get of steady, quiet build-up in the Transcaucasus for a Soviet military move into Iran. While I do not question current intelligence assessments that there is no indication that the Soviets are actually preparing to move, I am fearful that we are in danger of wishfully turning this rational assumption into a conviction that they will not move. I worry about the kind of mind-sets that afflict intelligence estimators and comfort policymakers and which led to conclusions, e.g. that the Soviets were not putting nuclear weaponry into Cuba in 1962 or that the dynasty was secure in Iran in 1978.[61]

While these assessments reflected the more extreme Soviet-centric views, by the end of the Carter administration these opinions (essentially expressed by the NSC) influenced policy-making more than any other.

From the US and Western European point of view, the two obvious reasons for concern in the late 1970s were the need to secure the continued flow of oil from the Gulf and the Soviet invasion of Afghanistan, which allegedly confirmed Moscow's aggressive and expansionist drive. It is not difficult to argue that both these factors would have had far less negative and far-reaching implications had the Iranian regime continued to function as a solid pro-Western asset.

It is striking to acknowledge that Iran, which for decades had been so central in the security strategy of the United States, in the brief time span of a few months passed from being one of America's closest allies to one of its most bitter enemies. Though tensions have repeatedly risen and abated between the 1980s and recent years, US–Iranian relations have yet to concretely improve. The legacy of hatred and mutual distrust that accompanied the birth of the Islamic Republic has not been overcome.

Today, while the West struggles to come to grips with the complexities of the mission in Afghanistan, it seems particularly timely to reflect on the potentially beneficial effects that improved relations with Tehran could represent. Iran is the country with the third largest population in the region; it is the world's fourth largest producer of oil and detains the world's second-largest reserves of natural gas.[62] And, it shares a 936-km-long border with Afghanistan. If the United States and its NATO allies still consider 'the stability of regions outside NATO boundaries, particularly in South West Asia' to be of crucial importance – and the continued priority assigned to Afghanistan points to the fact that they certainly do – then it would be valuable to assess the inherent linkages and multi-faceted interrelationships between the countries in the region once defined 'the arc of crisis'. In particular, it is difficult to imagine a stable and durable regional framework in Southwest Asia with the permanent isolation and exclusion of Iran.

Notes

1 Douglas Stuart, 'NATO's Future as a Pan-European Institution', *NATO Review*, Web Edition, vol. 41, no. 4, August 1993; Henry Kissinger, *Years of Upheaval*, (Boston, MA: Little, Brown and Co., 1982), p. 711.
2 Geoffrey Kemp, 'East-West Strategy and the Middle East-Persian Gulf' in Kenneth A. Myers (ed), *NATO – The Next Thirty Years. The Changing Political, Economic, and Military Setting*, (Boulder, CO: Westview Press, 1980), pp. 207–8.

3 For background on the out-of-area debate: Charles A. Kupchan, *The Persian Gulf and the West, The Dilemmas of Security,* (Boston, MA: Allen & Unwin, 1987), Chapters 7 and 8.
4 US National Security Adviser Zbigniew Brzezinski used this expression to define the area of concern of US foreign policy in the late 1970s: 'If you draw an arc on the globe, stretching from Chittagong (Bangladesh) through Islamabad to Aden, you will be pointing to the area of currently our greatest vulnerability', Memorandum for the President from Zbigniew Brzezinski, 'NSC Weekly Report, no. 81', December 2, 1978, Jimmy Carter Presidential Library (hereafter JCL), Donated Historical Material – Brzezinski Collection (hereafter DHM-BC), Subject file, box, 42.
5 Gianni Bonvicini, 'Out-of-Area Issues: A New Challenge to the Atlantic Alliance', in Joseph I. Coffey and Gianni Bonvicini (eds), *The Atlantic Alliance and the Middle East,* (London: Macmillan Press, 1989), pp. 2–3.
6 On the Soviet withdrawal crisis see, for example: Kenneth M. Pollak, *The Persian Puzzle. The Conflict between Iran and America,* (New York, NY: Random House, 2004), pp. 44–48.
7 For an account of the Iranian internal political forces in the early 1950s and the Mossadeq movement: James A. Bill, *The Eagle and the Lion. The Tragedy of American-Iranian Relations,* (New Haven, CT: Yale University Press, 1988), pp. 67–86; Ali M. Ansari, *Confronting Iran. The Failure of American Foreign Policy and the Next Great Crisis in the Middle East,* (New York, NY: Basic Books, 2006), pp. 19–53.
8 For a comprehensive account of the 1953 coup against Mossadeq: Stephen Kinzer, *All the Shah's Men: An American Coup and the Roots of Middle East Terror,* (Hoboken, NJ: Wiley, 2003). See also Pollack, *The Persian Puzzle,* pp. 63–71; Bill, *The Eagle and the Lion,* pp. 72–97 and the *New York Times.* www.nytimes.com/library/world/mideast/041600iran-cia-index.html (accessed 12 December 2009).
9 The Eisenhower Doctrine, proclaimed in a special message to Congress in January 1957, formally extended the US strategy of containment to the Middle East. To sustain America's role in the region, the United States supported the Baghdad Pact, signed in 1955, which included Turkey, Iran, Iraq, Pakistan, Great Britain and ended in 1958 following the coup in Iraq. The Baghdad Pact evolved into CENTO, signed in 1959, which included Turkey, Iran, Pakistan and the United States. These alliances signalled America's increased interest in the region.
10 National Intelligence Estimate 34–69, Washington, January 10, 1969, *FRUS, 1969–1972,* Volume E-4, Iran and Iraq, doc. no. 1.
11 There were, however, problems which still needed to be addressed. For example, the Intelligence Estimate pointed to the fact that the living conditions of the population in the countryside remained critical: 'The overall position of the peasant in the countryside has not yet changed very much, and efforts to alter attitudes, to raise living standards, and to increase production present a continuing challenge that seems destined to absorb the government's energies and attention for many years to come'. Another problem was that the Shah had concentrated the political power in his hands, thus the regime's political base remained narrow: 'Over the long term, economic development probably will not provide a satisfactory substitute for greater political participation. Hence, in a few years unrest may again begin to reach significant levels among politically aware elements. In time this could pose serious problems for the regime, particularly if dissent were to find support within the military,' ibid.
12 Record of National Security Council Interdepartmental Group for Near East and South Asia Meeting, Washington, April 3, 1969, *FRUS, 1969–1972,* Volume E-4, Iran and Iraq, doc. no. 10.
13 The intensified military presence of both superpowers in the Indian Ocean demonstrated the region's increased strategic significance. The United States had, in fact, acquired the capability to target Soviet territory with missiles launched from submarines (the Polaris A-3 missiles were deployed in 1968). On its part, the Soviet Union had steadily increased its naval presence and searched for ports to station or refuel its forces.
14 For the United States, Saudi Arabia was an important ally because reliance only on a Persian proxy would further complicate US relations with the Arab world. On the Nixon Doctrine: Robert S. Litwak, *Détente and the Nixon Doctrine. American Foreign Policy and the Pursuit of Stability, 1969–1976,* (New York, NY: Cambridge University Press, 1984).
15 Memorandum of Conversation, Washington, April 1, 1969, 10.00 a.m., *FRUS, 1969–1972,* Volume E-4, Iran and Iraq, doc. no. 8.
16 Telegram 4183 From the Embassy in Iran to the Department of State, October 13, 1969, 1300Z, *FRUS, 1969–1972,* Volume E-4, Iran and Iraq, doc. no. 23.
17 Intelligence Note, US Department of State to the Secretary from George C. Denney Jr., 'Shah's Views of Iranian Defense Needs on the Eve of US Visit', October 17, 1969, National Archives

(hereafter NA), Nixon Presidential Materials (hereafter NPM), NSC Files, Country files – Middle East, box 601, folder Iran Vol. I (1 of 3).
18 Ibid.
19 The Shah had, for example, proposed the so-called oil for arms deal. In essence, he asked the United States to buy more Iranian oil and, in turn, Iran would use the increased revenues to purchase US-produced armaments. For more details: Telegram 4185 From Embassy in Iran to the Department of State, October 13, 1969, *FRUS, 1969–1972*, Volume E-4, Iran and Iraq, doc. no. 24. It is important to note that this proposal could never be accepted by the US government, which could not grant special quotas to single countries, and neither directly control the import quotas of the American oil companies.
20 Memorandum From the President's Assistant for National Security Affairs (Kissinger) to President Nixon, Washington, October 21, 1969, *FRUS, 1969–1972*, Volume E-4, Iran and Iraq, doc. no. 29.
21 The 1972 Moscow summit between Nixon and Brezhnev is commonly considered the climax of US–Soviet détente. In Moscow, the two leaders signed the first agreement between the superpowers on the limitation of strategic nuclear weapons (the SALT I Treaty).
22 The Department of Defense opposed a commitment on the sale of F-14s and F-15s. Also Kissinger recommended not to make a commitment on these aircrafts; Memorandum From the Deputy Secretary of Defense (Rush) to the President's Assistant for National Security Affairs (Kissinger), Washington, May 18, 1972 and Memorandum From the President's Assistant for National Security Affairs (Kissinger) to President Nixon, Washington, May 18, 1972, *FRUS, 1969–1972*, Volume E-4, Iran and Iraq, doc. no. 195 and 196.
23 Henry Kissinger, *White House Years*, (London: Phoenix, 2000), pp. 1263–64.
24 The documents complied after the visit reveal that the only condition posed to the sale was that the aircrafts had to be operationally effective before being sold. Once the operational effectiveness of the new planes had been tested in the United States, the decisions on the purchases and their timing would be left to the Government of Iran.
25 Memorandum of Conversation, Tuesday, 30 May 1972 – 5:35 p.m. to 6:35 p.m., Saadabad Palace, Tehran, Iran, NA, NPM, NSC files, President's Trip files, box 487, folder: The President's Conversations (Part 2).
26 Memorandum to the President from Brzezinski, 'NSC Weekly Report # 32', 14 October 1977, JCL, DHM-BC, Subject file, box 41.
27 On the importance assigned by Carter to the two regional pillars: Memorandum for the President from Zbigniew Brzezinski, 'NSC Weekly Report # 8', 9 April 1977; for the importance of Iran, as the chief recipient of US arms: Memorandum for the President from Zbigniew Brzezinski, 'NSC Weekly Report # 32', 14 October 1977, JCL, DHM-BC, Subject file, box 41.
28 Gaddis Smith, *Morality, Reason and Power. American Diplomacy in the Carter Years*, (New York, NY: Hill and Wang, 1986), pp. 6–7.
29 On continuity and change during the Carter administration: Scott Kaufman, *Plans Unraveled. The Foreign Policy of the Carter Administration*, (DeKalb, IL: Northern Illinois University Press, 2008), pp. 5–27.
30 President Carter's human rights rhetoric had put the Shah on the defensive, inducing him to show some signs of reform. In mid-1976, during the US presidential campaign, the Shah took tentative steps to loosen his repressive regime, freeing some political prisoners. However, the pressure that the Iranian leader resented never came. After assuming office, the new US administration did not make human rights an issue in its policy towards Iran; Patrick Tyler, *A World of Trouble: The White House and the Middle East from the Cold War to the War on Terror*, (New York, NY: Farrar, Straus and Giroux, 2009), p. 219.
31 Cited in Bill, *The Eagle and the Lion*, p. 233.
32 Memorandum for the President from Zbigniew Brzezinski, 'NSC Weekly Report # 78', 3 November 1978, JCL, DHM-BC, Subject file, box, 42. Brzezinski referred to an assessment of the CIA published in November 1978.
33 Gary Sick, *All Fall Down. America's Tragic Encounter with Iran*, (New York, NY: Penguin Books, 1986), p. 28
34 Memorandum for the President from Zbigniew Brzezinski, 'NSC Weekly Report # 83', December 28, 1978, JCL, DHM-BC, Subject files, box 42.
35 For example, the US policies towards Israel, since Israel relied heavily on supplies of Iranian oil; Sick, *All Fall Down*, p. 47. Also, the US policies towards the Horn of Africa changed as a consequence of the loss of the alliance with the Shah. In particular, the importance of negotiating with

Somalia increased; Jeffrey A. Lefevbre, *Arms for the Horn. US Security Policy in Ethiopia and Somalia 1953–1991,* (Pittsburgh, PA: University of Pittsburgh Press, 1991), pp. 204–7.
36 For example, Director of CIA Richard Helms stated in the early 1970s: 'Ruling out Afghanistan as politically unfeasible, there is no place to which we could transfer these activities were Iran denied us. In time we hope that some of the important coverage now obtained from Iran can be picked up by overhead sensors, but for some years ahead the ground based facilities will remain absolutely essential if we are to keep our knowledge of the Soviet programs up to date;' Memorandum From Harold Saunders of the National Security Council Staff to the President's Assistant for National Security Affairs (Kissinger) Washington, April 16, 1970, *FRUS, 1969–1972,* Volume E-4, Iran and Iraq, doc. no. 63. Saunders forwarded Helms' memorandum to Kissinger.
37 No other country could replace Iran in guaranteeing Western influence in the region. The other regional 'pillar', Saudi Arabia, was not deemed capable of exercising the role played by Iran because it lacked the military infrastructure and technical expertise and had a ruling family fearful of building a strong military that could endanger the authority of the regime; Kupchan, *The Persian Gulf and the West,* pp. 70–71.
38 Sick, *All Fall Down,* p. 47.
39 James Mann, *Rise of the Vulcans. The History of Bush's War Cabinet,* (New York, NY: Viking Penguin, 2004), p. 83.
40 *International Herald Tribune,* 20 February 1979.
41 Secretary Brown on CBS News, *Face the Nation,* 25 February 1979, cited in Kupchan, *The Persian Gulf and the West,* p. 85.
42 Memorandum from Zbigniew Brzezinski, 'Consultative Security Framework for the Middle East', March 3, 1979, Cold War International History Project (hereafter CWIHP), 'The Carter Administration and the "Arc of Crisis" 1977–81', Declassified Documents prepared for A Critical Oral History Conference, The Woodrow Wilson Center, 25–26 July 2005.
43 Ibid.
44 This point is also made in Barbara Zanchetta, 'Human Rights versus Cold War. The Horn of Africa, Southwest Asia and the Emergence of the Carter Doctrine', in Max Guderzo and Bruna Bagnato (eds), *The Globalization of the Cold War. Diplomacy and Local Confrontation, 1975–1985,* (London: Routledge, 2010), pp. 78–80.
45 Lefebvre, *Arms for the Horn,* p. 199.
46 Lefebvre, *Arms for the Horn,* pp. 199–219; Zanchetta, 'Human Rights versus Cold War', pp. 78–82.
47 Steve Coll, *Ghost Wars. The Secret History of the CIA, Afghanistan, and Bin Laden, from the Soviet Invasion to September 10, 2001,* (New York, NY: Penguin, 2004), p. 46.
48 Zbigniew Brzezinski, *Power and Principle. Memoirs of the National Security Adviser, 1977–1981,* (New York, NY: Farrar Straus and Giroux, 1983), p. 456. On the perception of US vulnerability after the fall of the Shah: Raymond Garthoff, *Détente and Confrontation. US Soviet Relations from Nixon to Reagan,* (Washington, DC: The Brookings Institution, 1994), pp. 728–31.
49 Mann, *Rise of the Vulcans,* p. 79.
50 On the hostage crisis as marking the definite rupture in US–Iranian relations: Ansari, *Confronting Iran,* pp. 55–91.
51 Lefebvre, *Arms for the Horn,* p. 199–200; Brzezinski, *Power and Principle,* p. 446.
52 'The Carter Doctrine;' Jimmy Carter's State of the Union Address, January 23, 1980.
53 Already in the early 1970s, in fact, the US Embassy in Tehran reported on Iranian domestic unrest; Telegrams 668 and 5142 From Embassy in Tehran to the Department of State, February 24, 1970, *FRUS, 1969–1972,* Volume E-4, Iran and Iraq, doc. no. 49.
54 Scholars agree on the overall uncertainty of the policies of the Carter administration towards Iran in the critical months between late 1978 and early 1979; Bill, *The Eagle and the Lion,* pp. 216–60; Sick, *All Fall Down,* pp. 3–205; Ansari, *Confronting Iran,* pp. 55–91; Pollack, *The Persian Puzzle,* pp. 120–80.
55 Charles A. Kupchan, 'NATO and the Persian Gulf: examining intra-alliance behavior', *International Organization* 42, 2, Spring 1988, p. 320. In a weekly report to the President in May 1980, for example, Brzezinski underlined the necessity of building an effective security framework to protect US vital interests in the Persian Gulf and outlined the various military elements to consider. Among these, also NATO force implications; Memorandum to the President from Zbigniew Brzezinski, NSC Weekly Report 141, May 16, 1980, JCL, DHM-BC, Subject files, box 42.
56 Final Communiqué, NATO Defence Planning Committee, Brussels 13–14 May 1980. www.nato.int/docu/comm/49–95/c800513a.htm (accessed 10 December 2009).

57 Kupchan, 'NATO and the Persian Gulf', p. 322.
58 See, for example, Odd Arne Westad, 'The Fall of Détente and the Turning Tides of History' and Carol R. Saivetz, 'Superpower Confrontation in the Middle East and the Collapse of Détente' in Odd Arne Westad (ed), *The Fall of Détente. Soviet-American Relations during the Carter Years,* (Oslo: Scandinavian University Press, 1997), p. 23 and p. 90.
59 Memorandum for the President from Zbigniew Brzezinski, 'Reflections on the Soviet Intervention in Afghanistan', December 26, 1979, CWIHP, 'The Carter Administration and the "Arc of Crisis" 1977–81'.
60 Memorandum for Zbigniew Brzezinski from Jerry Schecter, 'SCC Working Group on Iran and Afghanistan: Public Posture', 14 January 1980, ibid.
61 Memorandum for Zbigniew Brzezinski from Paul B. Henze, 'Iran and the Soviets', 11 April 1980, ibid.
62 www.nationmaster.com/cat/ene-energy (accessed 10 December 2009).

Part II

Transatlantic security beyond the Cold War

Transatlantic security beyond the Cold War

11

The Warsaw Pact, NATO and the end of the Cold War

Jérôme Elie

Introduction

In the vast majority of studies, the end of the Cold War is synonymous with the collapse of the Soviet Union. The picture is one of a rapid and brutal structural change in the international system (from a bipolar to a unipolar configuration) that brought the old world order to an end. There is a strong sense of inevitability and determinism. Most books and articles devoted to this period are thus entrapped in a linear and almost teleological narrative mode that tries to explain why and how the USSR disappeared from the map or how and why Mikhail Gorbachev and his fellow reformers failed in their enterprise.

Indeed, an important controversy that emerged from this body of literature concerned the apparent failure of any specialist or commentator to anticipate one of the major turning points of twentieth-century international history. Noting that the Cold War was *the* historical phenomenon that, for almost half a century, had captured the "interest and attention of the Western intellectual community," Michael Cox has for example expressed his astonishment that its demise had not been forecast.[1] These criticisms were directed in particular at the realist school of international relations and Sovietologists as well as the intelligence services (especially the Central Intelligence Agency).[2]

This approach has implications for any analysis on how the Cold War alliances fit in the story of the end of the bipolar conflict. It describes a sudden and unavoidable disappearance of the Warsaw Treaty Organization (WTO) as well as the victory of the North Atlantic Treaty Organization (NATO). The rationale for the continuity of NATO is usually questioned and reflected upon only as regards the post-Cold War period.[3]

However, the end of the Cold War can be analyzed differently if it is considered as a "process" rather than an "event" or a "turning point." This major chapter of world history is more intelligible if we look at the years 1985–92 as a "transition period" between two world orders; a period when actors engaged in reflections on this transition. From the late 1980s, both the Soviets and the Americans viewed the possibility of ending the Cold War as implying a move beyond détente. Indeed, during these years, policy-makers and analysts on both sides of the Iron Curtain developed ideas on how to end the Cold

War, what the next world order should be, and how to manage the transition. This reflection was particularly important on a global scale, with a special focus on the United Nations Organization.[4] A logical and important question is therefore whether there were also regional elements of this thinking, especially as regards Europe. In other words, this chapter will investigate the thinking on the future of the Cold War alliances and the European military/strategic architecture during the late 1980s and early 1990s.

The Soviets were not necessarily pioneers in trying to overcome the bipolar conflict and proposing a new world and European order but their thinking did represent a more radical departure from their post-1945 practices and therefore had a greater impact on the evolution of the international system. The changes in their thinking and actual policies provided the key that would unlock the doors of the Cold War. Therefore, the analysis will first focus on Soviet thinking on the future of Europe and the WTO. Then, the American reactions and conceptions for NATO will be studied, especially with reference to the German unification process.

The WTO and Soviet plans for post-Cold War Europe

From the mid-1980s, building on a radical change in their world view, the Soviets developed a "New Thinking" about the international system that was gradually translated into policy directives and proposals for moving beyond the Cold War. "Gorbachevian diplomacy" was "a surprising mixture of pragmatism, voluntarism, and idealism—perhaps even of Utopia."[5] The "condition of mutual vulnerability engendered by nuclear weapons"[6] was the real original driving force behind New Thinking. It was thus based on a truly apocalyptic approach to the possible future of mankind and the overriding need to change course if global catastrophe was to be averted. Even though this New Thinking was largely idealistic and often inconsistent, it constituted a paradigm shift, comparable to a religious conversion or rather to a revolution in science in the Kuhnian sense.[7] Broadly speaking, it was an effort to "de-ideologize" interstate relations,[8] stressing the promotion of "common interests" and "universal human values" as well as the necessity to build a proactive, explicit system of cooperation for the promotion and maintenance of peace and stability. On the world scale, the new thinkers particularly campaigned for the "rebirth" of the United Nations Organization and "its restoration according to the blueprints of 1945."[9]

At the regional level, New Thinking also led to the development of ideas for Europe, under the label of the "Common European Home" (*nas obshchii dom*). This phrase was first used by Mikhail Gorbachev before his election as Secretary General in December 1984, when he visited London, but did not really constitute a novelty at the time. Indeed, similar expressions had already been used by Brezhnev and Gromyko in 1972, 1981, and 1983 with a very specific meaning. As explained by Hannes Adomeit, the purpose of the "Common European Home" rhetoric had always been to drive a wedge within the North Atlantic Alliance and "Gorbachev initially very much subscribed to such notions":

> Traditionally, the term was reserved almost exclusively for *Western European* audiences.
> It also had a decidedly anti-American connotation, its implication being that the United States, as a trans-Atlantic power, really had no business in that house.[10]

But as New Thinking developed and took root in the Soviet leadership, the terminology acquired a new content and meaning.[11] Building on the notion of balance of interests, disarmament and the idea of defensive military doctrines, Gorbachev retooled the Common European Home concept as a means to reduce military tensions and confrontation on the old continent.[12] He also believed that the division of Europe could be overcome on the basis of universal human values.[13] This new orientation had far reaching implications for the WTO's strategic posture and its future as a military alliance.

Given the weight of Mutually Assured Destruction in the development of New Thinking, the Soviet initiatives first focused on disarmament issues and particularly on nuclear weapons.[14] Nevertheless, the new thinkers eventually came to acknowledge Western fears and distrust over Soviet superiority in conventional weapons in Europe.[15] Soviet authorities thus showed an increasing willingness to work for disarmament in this field as well. Significantly, Gorbachev came to accept the notion of unilateral and even "disproportionately larger"[16] arms reductions in order to reduce the threatening image. This new stance was adopted in correlation with the concept of "reasonable sufficiency," which was first publicly mentioned in Gorbachev's address to the 27th Party Congress in February 1986.[17] The concept had an economic, cost-effective origin (the imperative to ensure the security of the state at a lower level of spending)[18] but the goal also became to maintain nothing more than parity with the West, which did not necessarily require "mirror" equality in stockpiles. It was thus a further incentive to reverse—through negotiations—the spiral of the arms race, and scale back the forces on the European continent. Designed to foster East–West trust and cooperation, this concept was also naturally expected to be reciprocated by the West.[19] It opened the way for a decisive progress in the Conference on Security and Cooperation in Europe (CSCE) follow-up meeting in Vienna (1986–89) and then led to the signature of the Treaty on Conventional Armed Forces in Europe (CFE) in Paris on 19 November 1990.

Interestingly, "reasonable sufficiency" was coupled with the adoption of a defensive military doctrine. This new approach was also formally adopted by the WTO in May 1987 and made public.[20] A communiqué read that the WTO members considered their military doctrine as strictly:

> defensive in nature and based on the need to keep the balance of military forces at the lowest possible level as well as the desirability of reducing the military potentials to sufficient levels as required for defense.[21]

It meant the adoption of a posture designed solely for territorial defense, i.e. to repel an aggression. Among other things, this entailed the elimination of offensive weapons and of capabilities necessary to conduct a surprise attack.

This evolution indicates that the Soviet proposals for improving European security went much further than simple disarmament or, rather, disarmament could not happen in isolation. This effort also implied important changes to military doctrines, as well as the adoption and institutionalization of confidence-building and risk-reduction measures.[22] The most obvious change in this respect concerned the setting up of a verification regime. Removing an earlier stumbling block and complying with an old Western request, the Soviets agreed to far-reaching procedures designed to ensure that agreements reached would be respected.[23]

It is important to understand that, even though they had come to accept asymmetrical arms reductions, the Soviets called for dialog and envisaged reciprocity in military reforms on both sides.[24] Most importantly, the Warsaw Pact members called for what could be termed a "joint *Glasnost*" on military doctrines as a major confidence-building measure:

> The States party to the Warsaw Treaty propose to the member States of the North Atlantic alliance to enter into consultations in order to compare the military doctrines of the two alliances, analyze their nature and jointly discuss the patterns of their future development so as to reduce the mutual suspicion and distrust that has accumulated over the years, to ensure a better perception of each other's intentions and to guarantee that the military concepts and doctrines of the two military blocs and their members are based on defensive principles.[25]

Or, as Gorbachev put it in 1987:

> [The Warsaw Treaty countries] have proposed to the NATO countries that everyone sits down together and compares the military doctrines of the two alliances in order to better understand each other's intentions.

According to his account, the "answer to that proposal was [then] silence."[26] However, it should be noted that, in October 1989, an agreement was reached between the two alliances to hold a seminar in Vienna in the early part of 1990 to discuss and compare military doctrines.[27] Much more progress would then be made on such confidence-building measures at the July 1990 NATO summit meeting in London and the November 1990 Paris summit of the CSCE. However, by this time the future of the WTO was already largely compromised.

According to Marie-Pierre Rey, from 1987 Mikhail Gorbachev also gradually described his vision for a new European architecture, "using the image of a four-level building":

> The Helsinki geopolitical order would serve as the foundations ... The first storey of the house would be built on collective security and based on the widest possible disarmament (nuclear, chemical and conventional) and, in the long-term, on the disappearance of military blocs and alliances. The second storey related to the peaceful resolution of conflicts. The upper two stories concerned a pan-European economic and trade cooperation and, finally, a real European cultural community, which would constitute the supreme achievement of this common home.[28]

In this context, the Soviets first advocated the gradual "simultaneous dissolution" of both the Warsaw Pact and the North Atlantic Treaty Organization as a means of "rejecting the division of Europe"[29] and creating a new "general European system of collective security."[30] From 1988, "the Soviet leaders no longer insisted on the dissolution of the alliances" but proposed instead "to progressively transform these alliances into political organizations that could actively contribute to the rapprochement."[31] The end result of this rapprochement was to be a merger of the alliances in the near future.

Importantly, the Americans were to participate in this new architecture. Indeed, at the Malta summit in December 1989, Mikhail Gorbachev confirmed to President Bush that the United States and Canada were no longer excluded from the "Common European Home" project and were expected to play a role in creating the new European structure.[32] This new architecture was to be built on the successes of the CSCE, which led the Soviets to call for a "Helsinki II" process. Thus, in Malta, Gorbachev called for a balanced and responsible approach to the question "What to do with institutions created in another age?" His opinion was that:

Existing instruments for supporting the balance must not be shattered but modified in accordance with the demands of the age. They must be utilized to strengthen security and stability and improve relations between states. Let NATO and the Warsaw Treaty Organization become to an even greater degree political, not just military, organizations; and let there be a change in their confrontational nature. It is good that our generals have already begun to grasp the spirit of the times, to visit each other, and to discuss the most complex questions.[33]

A year later, the Soviets also emphasized this new CSCE process and the transformation of the military alliances as a desirable framework for German unification.[34] Indeed, the prospect of German unification was intimately linked to the future of the Warsaw Pact and NATO, as one of the most important questions that quickly emerged in this context was: how would the unified Germany fit into the European military and security architecture? Would it be neutral, part of NATO, part of the WTO or of both alliances at the same time? Again, would the unified Germany become the cornerstone of a new architecture built on the basis of the CSCE? As will be explained in the next part, the Americans could not be persuaded to follow the path the Soviets suggested. The Bush administration decided that NATO should survive the end of the Cold War. On this basis, US officials rapidly decided to push for a full membership of the new Germany in NATO.

The liberation of Eastern Europe in 1989 put an end to the Soviet project and in the Spring of 1990, "Gorbachev's dream totally collapsed when Hungary started expressing its intention to leave the military structure of the Warsaw Pact," soon followed by Czechoslovakia and Poland. From this point, the Common European Home Project, "based on the parallel disappearance of the two military alliances, was obviously ruined by the sudden reinforcement of NATO and the quasi-death of the Warsaw Pact."[35] After German reunification, the German Democratic Republic's Warsaw Pact membership formally ended and the WTO disappeared in July 1991 after a final meeting of the Political Consultative Committee.

Western policies and reactions to the Soviet project certainly had an impact on the project's fate and will be analyzed in the following section. Nevertheless, it is also important to highlight Soviet responsibilities in the failure of this Common European Home idea. The weaknesses and inconsistencies in the Soviet New Thinking about Europe certainly played an important role.

First, at the conceptual level it is difficult to understand which type of governance the Common European Home would have followed. The main idea was to replace both military alliances by "integrationist international structures."[36] The new European system was thus to be built on the idea of joint management but it remains unclear how inclusive it was intended to be. Was it to be a new Concert of Europe, with only the great powers at the wheel or was it to allow for a wider participation? Which role would the West and East European partners have in such a framework and would the United States and the Soviet Union retain their *primus inter pares* status? Moreover, what was to be the pattern of the transition process? The vagueness could be explained by the fact that the Soviets might have considered that such issues were to be discussed and negotiated with interested partners, but the available documentation and literature is not clear on this point. As we shall see in the next section, this ambiguity also fuelled Western skepticism.

Second, despite the rhetoric and initiatives concerning the Common European Home, one should remember that, at least until late 1988, "Gorbachev concentrated on the reordering of relations with the United States" and Western Europe only "played a subsidiary role in Soviet policy towards the West."[37] For a long time, European issues were therefore not a real priority for the Soviet leadership but rather an instrument in their policy towards the United States.

The Common European Home concept also seems to have remained rather ill-defined and vague. For example, Vladislav Zubok has suggested that surprisingly the Soviets failed to fully take Eastern European countries into account in their thinking about the future of Europe:

> The Gorbachev leadership adhered to the illusory belief in "socialism with human face" as a possible third option for Eastern Europe, between old style communism and capitalism. And it was categorically against any direct interference, either by military or non-military means.[38]

This non-interventionist stance meant that "Gorbachev and his advisers had no new policy for Eastern Europe as they moved" and when the revolutions erupted in Eastern Europe, no contingency planning had been developed to deal with the situation.[39] The domestic problems that monopolized the Gorbachev leadership's attention from the first months of 1989, only reinforced this neglect. Geir Lundestad has talked about the American "non-policy towards Eastern Europe" in the early Cold War years.[40] As odd as this may appear, at the end of the bipolar struggle, this "non-policy" was a feature of Soviet diplomacy and it played an important role in the demise of the WTO:

> In the end, Eastern Europe, which had been the focus of the Soviet leadership from Stalin's and Khrushchev's times, was largely neglected by Gorbachev's foreign policy.[41]

Now that the Soviet intentions and their own responsibilities in the failure of their project have been established, it is necessary to turn to the analysis of the Americans and Western reactions to the Soviet proposals and their own visions for a post-Cold War Europe.

The United States, NATO and the future of Europe

With the end of the Cold War coming and the end of the division of Europe in sight, what was to be Western policy as regards the future of NATO? Moreover, how did the West and especially the United States react in the face of the Soviet initiatives and proposals outlined above? There are interesting parallels to be drawn with the American reception of the Soviet New Thinking about the United Nations. In the late 1980s and early 1990s, when the Soviets pushed for new ways of conducting international relations, the American approach to the transition remained very cautious and skeptical. The Americans actually showed very little in terms of new thinking and many analysts have noted their tendency towards the status quo during this period.[42] The aim was then to consolidate US gains and ensure the durability of Cold War practices and institutions. Nevertheless, this lack of intellectual innovation on the American side does not mean that there was total apathy at the policy level and should not be viewed cynically. First, the Americans had valid reasons to be suspicious about the Soviet new ideas and only started to shed this skepticism in the spring of 1989. Second, and more importantly, lessons from history were at play: the period seemed to vindicate the international policies followed by the United States since 1946–47 and the American administration acted vigorously to ensure continuity. Although the Soviet approach underwent a complete revolution, elements of continuity did prevail over elements of change in the American worldview and policies at the end of the Cold War.

It is noteworthy that some commentators and even policy-makers in the West did engage with Soviet ideas. For example, it is no secret that French President François Mitterrand[43] flirted with Gorbachev's idea and that the Soviets hoped that the Germans, in particular the social democrats, would support their project. As Marie-Pierre Rey put it, it is actually "only with the proposed confederation outlined by Mitterrand that Gorbachev's Common European Home finally found a real echo in Western Europe," although "the evolution of the European context, marked by the emancipation of the Central European Countries and by the German reunification ruined Gorbachev's project as well as Mitterrand's proposal."[44] At this time, some academics and commentators also began to believe that Europe could be turned into a multilateral arena for great power cooperation. According to some pundits, this would have meant a return to a system akin to the nineteenth century Concert of Europe.[45]

On the US side, 1989 was characterized by an "evolution of the Bush administration's policy from skeptical, watchful waiting to broad engagement with the Soviet Union."[46] It could be argued that a pattern of rapprochement really materialized and that the Americans gradually began to recognize the sincerity of New Thinking. Indeed, during the summer of 1990, the new atmosphere led to tangible results, with decisions taken at the NATO London summit in July and the CSCE meeting in Paris in November. The London Declaration invited the Soviet Union and other Warsaw Pact members to establish regular diplomatic liaisons with NATO and to develop a new cooperative relationship. In Paris, in addition to the "Charter for a New Europe," a Joint Non-Aggression Declaration was signed by the members of NATO and the WTO, thus formally ending the adversarial relationship.[47] However, the Reagan and Bush administrations never came close to accepting the Soviet proposals for a "Common European Home."

From 1987–88, the new Soviet attitude towards Eastern Europe was given particular attention by the US administration[48] and Congressional circles.[49] The Reagan administration did not go much beyond rhetoric as regards changes in Europe but with George Bush in the White House, the Americans began to be concerned about Gorbachev's "charm offensive" and the perceived need to regain the initiative. Despite a gradual US–Soviet rapprochement, this was to be done not by engaging with the new thinkers' concepts and proposals for the future of Europe and the military alliances but rather by countering Soviet rhetoric. In this way, the Bush administration did not show much sign of new thinking as it rather seemed to pursue an objective defined under the first Reagan administration, in National Security Decision Directive 75: "Prevent the Soviet propaganda machine from seizing the semantic high-ground in the battle of ideas through the appropriation of such terms as 'peace'."[50]

Thus, the Americans countered the Soviet concept of "universal human values" as a basis for the new European unity with the idea that the division of Europe could only end "through acceptance of common democratic values" or of "Western values." Indeed, the "concept of a 'commonwealth of free nations' was offered as an alternative to Gorbachev's call on Europeans to build a 'common European home'."[51]

The evolution of the German situation became a very important element in this respect. Indeed, fairly early on, considering US Cold War attitudes towards Germany, the Bush administration accepted the prospect of a rapid unification but insisted that it would not happen to the detriment of NATO and American leadership in Europe.[52]

There was therefore no chance of the Americans buying the Soviets' ideas for a disbanding or merging of NATO and the WTO or the establishment of relations between the unified Germany and both alliances. As George Bush bluntly explained to West German Chancellor Helmut Kohl at the February 1990 Camp David summit:

> [T]he Soviets are not in a position to dictate Germany's relationship with NATO. What worries me is talk that Germany must not stay in NATO. To hell with that! We prevailed, they didn't. We can't let the Soviets clutch victory from the jaws of defeat.[53]

Because of the American position, the CSCE never became the kind of regional organization envisaged by the Soviet new thinkers, even though the July 1990 NATO London Declaration, as well as the documents adopted at the November 1990 CSCE summit in Paris, did recognize and institutionalize the end of the bipolar confrontation in Europe. Indeed, the "Americans were worried about the possibility of discussing the German question into the most unwieldy European forum imaginable—the CSCE," because they feared they would not be able to control the agenda in such a context and that it "would be debated until the end of the century."[54]

In a sense, German unification followed or symbolized the pattern that led to the end of the Cold War on the world scene: the Western system swallowed the Eastern system. In the end, German unification came about through a "takeover" of the Eastern part by the Federal Republic of Germany rather than through a "merger." However, this process was not preordained since there were two paths to unification provided in West Germany's constitution.[55]

Similarly, the success of the American position on the German unification process and the durability of NATO was not a foregone conclusion. Maintaining the institutional status quo in Europe implied a skilful diplomatic activity, especially through the "2+4" mechanism.[56] As recognized by Philip Zelikow and Condoleezza Rice, the outcome dealt a blow to the Soviet Union and the new thinkers' projects for a new European order: "The harsh truth was that the American goal could be achieved only if the Soviet Union suffered a reversal of fortune not unlike a catastrophic defeat in war."[57]

How are we to interpret US policies and reactions as regards NATO and the post-war European order? The answer is simply that there was no major revision or modification of the US Cold War paradigm. It should be remembered that post-war American foreign policy was guided by a double paradigm: on the one hand, containment of and confrontation with the USSR, on the other, "leadership" within the Western camp. Whether they spoke of *Preponderance,*[58] *Empire,*[59] or *Hegemony,*[60] many authors have recognized that primacy over the West was part of the US Cold War axiom.[61] Wolfram F. Hanrieder has clearly explained this duality in relation to Europe:

> The restraint of the Federal Republic through international organization and treaties was at the core of Washington's post-war European policy of *double containment*: the containment of the Soviet Union at arm's length, and of West Germany with an embrace.[62]

It was also famously symbolized by Lord Ismay's formula concerning NATO's triple objective: "Keep the Russians out, the Germans down, and the Americans in."[63]

As a result of Soviet New Thinking and decline, the Americans agreed to drop the first part of their paradigm by engaging in close cooperation with the USSR. However, the type of cooperation that was established, as well as the process by which it was achieved, indicate that the second part of the paradigm remained unaltered. After the end of the Cold War, US foreign policy continued to be guided by a desire to lead and the best vehicle for this leadership remained NATO.

Indeed, as Brent Scowcroft once explained, the American position relied on a specific interpretation of Cold War history and international relations mechanisms that left very little room for Soviet New Thinking on Europe:

> Our first requirement was to prevent yet another repetition of the turmoil which had beset Europe in the twentieth century. American isolationism had played its part in those tragedies. The lesson we drew from this bloody history was that the United States had to continue to play a significant role in European security, whatever developed with respect to the Soviet Union. The vehicle for that role must be NATO. The Alliance was the only way the US could keep forces in Europe as a visible commitment to its security and stability. In addition, a united Germany as full member of the alliance was key to our presence. Germany held our bases: if it left the alliance, it would be difficult if not impossible to retain American troops in Europe. We needed Helmut Kohl's commitment to keep Germany in the alliance and American troops on its soil.[64]

Moreover, the Americans had always had mixed feelings about the European Community.[65] With the Cold War over, this approach did not change drastically. On the contrary, many US officials considered it even more vital to ensure that the United States would not be excluded from European politics after the creation of a European Union. Despite a longstanding rhetorical support for the European unification process, it was fundamental for the American administration to prevent the emergence of a potential rival superpower in Western Europe or a European regional hegemon. The leaked preliminary version of the Pentagon's Defense Planning Guidance (DPG) for the Fiscal Years 1994–99 was clear on the US objectives concerning the old continent:

> In Europe, the Pentagon paper asserts that "a substantial American presence in Europe and continued cohesion within the Western alliance remain vital," but to avoid a competitive relationship from developing, "we must seek to prevent the emergence of European-only security arrangements which would undermine NATO."[66]

Many US Congress hearings and publications from the early 1990s reflected these concerns. American politicians understood that the end of the Cold War could open up a "new era" in transatlantic relations and that this development was not necessarily positive.[67]

Conclusion

From the mid-1980s, policy-makers on both sides of the Iron Curtain came to perceive that the end of the Cold War was at hand. They realized that this context presented new opportunities and new challenges for the European continent. All the actors knew that they were living through a period of transition that had to be managed. They thus promoted their plans and ideas for the future. Eventually, the Americans accepted the reduction of tensions and even went quite far in establishing cooperation with Mikhail Gorbachev's Soviet Union. Nevertheless, they refused to disband the Cold War Western approaches and institutions, especially NATO. Continuity prevailed over elements of change in US foreign policy.

Some commentators have thus blamed the Bush administration since they believe it prevented the birth of a new European and world system and "missed opportunities to try to fashion an inclusive post-Cold War order based on a concert of powers—which were quite real." Indeed, for William C. Wohlforth, "the US response to German unification was at its heart a *denial* of any new world order."[68] This does not mean that the Americans did not develop any thinking or activity at the political level but rather that their plan for post-Cold War Europe was to ensure the continued presence of NATO.

Thus, while the Warsaw Pact vanished, NATO continued to exist despite the disappearance of its original *raison d'être*. To survive, NATO had to reinvent a role for itself. A remarkable aspect of this story is that, as far as currently available documents can show, while the American objective quickly became to maintain NATO in a post-confrontational European setting, very little thinking was developed before 1990 on NATO's future function in this context. Only after the end of the bipolar confrontation did the debate about NATO's post-Cold War role develop and stir some controversy in academic and political circles.[69] The political process really started with the July 1990 London summit and the adoption of a New Strategic Concept in November 1991.[70] The search for its new relevance notably involved discussions about its potential role in peace-keeping missions and "out-of-area" actions. Nevertheless, NATO's function and future remained vague, some still questioning whether this alliance made military sense years after the end of the Cold War.[71]

Despite a vague rationale for its continued existence, not only did NATO survive the demise of its enemy but it thereafter expanded to integrate former Warsaw Pact members. This expansion also provoked intense debates and recriminations especially in Russia. Indeed, many considered that by expanding NATO eastward the Americans violated a commitment made during the negotiations leading to the unification of Germany,[72] even though the archival record makes it clear that no such pledge was ever made by American officials. This question was not even discussed at the time since:

> Neither Gorbachev nor any of his advisers even thought to bring up the question of the expansion of NATO to other Warsaw Pact countries beyond East Germany. This was simply not an issue at the time. Gorbachev was still fully confident that the USSR would continue to "work with its allies" in the Warsaw Pact, and he therefore did not yet even conceive of the possibility that they might someday aspire to join NATO.[73]

Only later did Gorbachev and the new thinkers realize that the WTO was doomed and that their hopes for a new security architecture built on the CSCE framework would not materialize. As explained above, the Americans' willingness to preserve NATO and certain aspects of US Cold War policy played an important role in this respect. Nevertheless, in analyzing this failure, one should also remember the important weaknesses and inconsistencies in the Soviet project.

Notes

1. Michael Cox, 'The End of the Cold War and Why We Failed to Predict It', in Allen Hunter (ed), *Rethinking the Cold War*, (Philadelphia: Temple University Press, 1998), p. 157.
2. See, for example, Christopher I. Xenakis, *What Happened to the Soviet Union?: How and Why American Sovietologists Were Caught by Surprise*, (Westport, CT: Praeger Publishers, 2002) and Michael Cox, 'Memoirs of a Former Sovietologist—Getting the USSR Wrong: or Why we Failed to "Predict" the End of the Cold War', Paper Presented to the Nobel Institute Research Seminar, 4 April 2002.
3. See, for example, François Heisbourg, 'The Future of the Atlantic Alliance: Whither NATO, Whether NATO?', *The Washington Quarterly*, vol. 15, no. 2, spring 1992, pp. 127–39.
4. See Jérôme Elie, *The End of the Cold War as a 'Systemic Transition': Thinking about the New World Order in the Soviet Union and the United States, 1984–1992*, unpublished PhD Thesis, (Geneva: Graduate Institute of International Studies, 2007).
5. Marie-Pierre Rey, '"Europe is our Common Home": A Study of Gorbachev's Diplomatic Concept', *Cold War History* vol. 4, no. 2, p. 33. See also, Marie-Pierre Rey, 'Gorbachev's New Thinking and Europe, 1985–89', in Frédéric Bozzo, Marie-Pierre Rey, Nils Piers Ludlow and Leopoldo Nuti (eds), *Europe and the End of the Cold War: A Reappraisal*, (London: Routledge, 2008).
6. Steven Kull, *Burying Lenin: The Revolution in Soviet Ideology and Foreign Policy*, (Boulder, CO: Westview Press, 1992), p. 26.
7. Ibid., p. 6 and p. 17. See, Thomas S. Kuhn, *The Structure of Scientific Revolutions*, (Chicago: University of Chicago Press, 1970).
8. Mikhail Gorbachev, *Perestroika: New Thinking for our Country and the World*, (London: Collins, 1987), p. 143.
9. 'Shevardnadze – 45th General Assembly Session – Full Speech', *TASS Information Agency* (on LEXISNEXIS), 25 September 1990.
10. Hannes Adomeit, *Imperial Overstretch: Germany in Soviet Policy from Stalin to Gorbachev: an Analysis Based on New Archival Evidence, Memoirs, and Interviews*, (Baden-Baden: Nomos Verlag, 1998), pp. 246–47. (Emphasis in original).
11. For interesting Soviet developments on the 'Common European Home', see 'Common European Home Explained'. Source: Vitaly Zhurkin, 'A Common Home for Europe – Reflections on How to Build It', *Pravda*, 17 May 1989, p. 4, translated and reproduced in *The Current Digest of the Soviet Press* XLI/22, 28 June 1989, p. 15 and Vadim Zagladine, 'Notre Maison Commune', *Politique Internationale* 44, summer 1989, pp. 23–32.
12. See in particular, Mikhail Gorbachev, 'For a "Common European Home", For a New Way of Thinking', Speech at the CPSU Central Committee, Czechoslovak–Soviet Friendship Meeting, Prague, 10 April 1987, (Moscow: Novosti Press Agency Publishing House, 1987), pp. 27, 28 and 30.
13. Philip Zelikow and Condoleezza Rice, *Germany Unified and Europe Transformed: a Study in Statecraft*, (London: Harvard University Press, 1995), pp. 5–6.
14. Efforts on those issues began as early as 29 July 1985, when Mikhail Gorbachev announced a unilateral moratorium on nuclear testing, due to start on 6 August of that year, a very symbolic date: Hiroshima Remembrance Day.
15. On this theme, see Julie M. Newton, *Russia, France, and the idea of Europe*, (Basingstoke: Palgrave Macmillan, 2003), pp. 139–63.
16. Raymond Garthoff, *The Great Transition: American-Soviet Relations and the End of the Cold War*, (Washington, DC: Brookings Institution, 1994), pp. 407–8.
17. Raymond Garthoff, 'New Thinking in Soviet Military Doctrine', *The Washington Quarterly*, vol. 11, no. 3, summer 1988, p. 133 and p. 138.
18. See for example Alexei Arbatov's work on the subject: 'How Much Defense is Sufficient?', *International Affairs* (Moscow), April 1988, pp. 31–44; 'Parity and Reasonable Sufficiency', *International Affairs* (Moscow), October 1988, pp. 75–87. Alexei Arbatov (son of Georgi A. Arbatov) was then head of department at the Institute of World Economics and International Relations of the USSR Academy of Science.
19. See 'February 1986 plan for a Comprehensive System of International Security', point 1.iii and 1.v, in: Mikhail Gorbachev, *Political Report of the CPSU Central Committee to the 27th Congress of the Communist Party of the Soviet Union, February 25, 1986*, (Moscow: Novosti Press Agency Publishing House, 1986), pp. 94–95.

20 Vojtech Mastny, *Learning from the Enemy: NATO as a Model for the Warsaw Pact*, (Zurich: Center for Security Studies (CSS), ETH Zurich, 2001), p. 39.
21 '*Communiqué* issued by the Session of the Political Consultative Committee of the States Parties to the Warsaw Treaty', in: 'Letter Dated 29 Mai 1987 From the Permanent Representative of The German Democratic Republic to the United Nations Addressed to the General-Secretary', UN Doc. A/42/313 S/18888, p. 6. [Thereafter referred to as the 'WTO *Communiqué*']
22 These ideas were contained in embryo in the 'February 1986 plan for a Comprehensive System of International Security', (see point 2.iii).
23 See, for example, The declaration 'On the Military Doctrine of the States Parties to the Warsaw Treaty' and the 'WTO *Communiqué*' transmitted to the UN in: UN Doc. A/42/313 S/18888, p. 12.
24 See, for example, Andrei Kokochine, 'La meilleure défense: c'est la défense et uniquement la défense. Une invitation au débat', *Temps Nouveaux* (Moscow) 33, 1988, pp. 18–19.
25 'On the Military Doctrine', UN Doc. A/42/313 S/18888, p. 13.
26 Gorbachev, *Perestroika*, note no. 1, p. 143.
27 'The Foreign Policy and Diplomatic Activity of the USSR (April 1985-October 1989): A Survey Prepared by the USSR Ministry of Foreign Affairs', published in: *International Affairs* (Moscow), January 1990, p. 22.
28 Rey, 'Europe is our Common Home', p. 39.
29 'WTO *Communiqué*', UN Doc. A/42/313 S/18888, p. 7.
30 'Letter Dated 8 November 1989 from the Permanent Representative of Poland to the United Nations Addressed to the Secretary-General, transmitting a *Communiqué* on the Meeting of the Committee of Ministers for Foreign Affairs of the States Parties to the Warsaw Treaty', UN Doc. A/C.1/44/7, p. 6.
31 Rey, 'Europe is our Common Home', pp. 39–40.
32 See, 'At Historic Crossroads: Documents on the December 1989 Malta Summit', *Cold War International History Project Bulletin* vol. 12/13, fall/winter 2001, pp. 238–39, [Source: The notes of A. S. Chernyaev, Gorbachev Foundation Archive, Moscow, published in: Mikhail Gorbachev, *Gody trudnykh resheniy [Years of Difficult Decisions]*, (Moscow: Alfa-print, 1993), translated by Gary Goldberg.]
33 Document 10: 'Transcript of the Malta Meeting, December 2–3, 1989', Source: Gorbachev Foundation, Fond 1, Opis 1 available on the website of the National Security Archives. www.gwu.edu/~nsarchiv/ (accessed 5 December 2009).
34 Leon V. Sigal, *Hang Separately: Cooperative Security between the United States and Russia, 1985–1994*, (New York: The Century Foundation Press, 2000), p. 67–71.
35 Marie-Pierre Rey, 'The End of the Cold War: Soviet–American Relations and the Radical Changes in Europe' in: Pavel Palazhchenko and Olga Zdravomyslova (eds), *From Fulton to Malta: How the Cold War Began and Ended*, (Moscow: The Gorbachev Foundation/The World Political Forum, 2008), p. 65.
36 Vladislav M. Zubok, 'New Evidence on the "Soviet Factor" in the Peaceful Revolutions of 1989', *Cold War International History Project Bulletin* vol. 12/13, fall/winter 2001, p. 6.
37 Adomeit, *Imperial Overstretch*, p. 241. See also, pp. 251, 252.
38 Zubok, 'New Evidence on the "Soviet Factor"', p. 14.
39 Ibid., p. 7 and p. 11.
40 Geir Lundestad, *The American Non-Policy towards Eastern Europe, 1943–1947*, (Oslo: Universitetsforlaget, 1978).
41 Zubok, 'New Evidence on the "Soviet Factor"', p. 8 and p. 11.
42 See, for example, Alexander L. George, 'The Transition in US–Soviet Relations, 1985–90. An Interpretation from the Perspective of International Relations Theory and Political Psychology', in William C. Wohlforth (ed), *Witnesses to the End of the Cold War*, (Baltimore: The Johns Hopkins University Press, 1996), pp. 251–52; Kathleen Murray Shoon, *Anchors Against Change: American Opinion Leaders' Beliefs After the Cold War*, (Ann Arbor: The University of Michigan Press, 2002).
43 On François Mitterrand and the end of the Cold War, see in particular Hubert Védrine, *Les mondes de François Mitterrand: à l'Elysée, 1981–1995*, (Paris: Fayard, 1996); Samy Cohen (ed), *Mitterrand et la sortie de la Guerre froide*, (Paris: Presses Universitaires de France, 1998); Frédéric Bozo, *Mitterrand, la fin de la Guerre froide et l'unification allemande: de Yalta à Maastricht*, (Paris: Odile Jacob, 2005).
44 Rey, 'Europe is our Common Home', pp. 49–50.
45 See for example: John Mueller, 'A New Concert Of Europe', *Foreign Policy* no. 77, winter 1989/1990, pp. 3–16; James E. Goodby, 'A New European Concert: Settling Disputes in CSCE', *Arms*

Control Today, January/February 1991, pp. 3–6; Harald Mueller, 'A United Nations of Europe and North America', *Arms Control Today*, January/February 1991, p. 3 and pp. 6–8; James E. Goodby, 'Commonwealth and Concert: Organizing Principles of Post-Containment Order in Europe', *The Washington Quarterly* vol. 14, no. 3, summer 1991, pp. 71–90; See Neil Malcom, 'The "Common European Home" and Soviet European Policy', *International Affairs* vol. 65, no. 4, autumn 1989, pp. 659–76; Ole Waever, 'Three Competing Europes: German, French, Russian', *International Affairs* vol. 66, no. 3, July 1990, pp. 477–93; Ken Booth, 'Steps Towards Stable Peace in Europe: A Theory and Practice of Coexistence', *International Affairs* vol. 66, no. 1, January 1990, pp. 17–45; Clifford A. Kupchan and Charles A. Kupchan, 'After NATO: Concert of Europe', *The New York Times*, 6 July 1990, p. 25; Clifford A. Kupchan and Charles A. Kupchan, 'Concerts, Collective Security, and the Future of Europe', *International Security* vol. 16, no. 1, Summer 1991, pp. 114–61.

46 Arnold L. Horelick, 'US–Soviet Relations: Threshold of a New Era', *Foreign Affairs* vol. 69, no. 1, 1990, p. 54.
47 *NATO Handbook*, (Brussels: NATO Office of Information Press, 2001), p. 38.
48 See for example the following National Intelligence Estimates: NIE 11/12-9-88, May 1988, *Soviet Policy Towards Eastern Europe Under Gorbachev* and NIE 12–90, April 1990, *The Future of Eastern Europe* in: B. B. Fischer (ed), *At Cold War's End: United States Intelligence on the Soviet Union and Eastern Europe, 1989–1991*, (Washington, DC: Central Intelligence Agency, 2000).
49 See, for example, 'Implementation of the Helsinki Accords: Gorbachev, "Glasnost" and Eastern Europe, Hearing before the Commission on Security and Cooperation in Europe', 100th Congress, 1st Session, 18 June 1987, (Washington, DC: US Government Printing Office, 1987); 'Implementation of the Helsinki Accords: Gorbachev, Changing United States Attitudes on Eastern Europe and the Soviet Union, Hearing before the Commission on Security and Cooperation in Europe', 100th Congress, 1st Session, 28 October 1987, (Washington DC: US Government Printing Office, 1988); 'Implementation of the Helsinki Accords: East European Perestroika: United States and Soviet Foreign Policy Options, Hearing before the Commission on Security and Cooperation in Europe', 100th Congress, 1st Session, 15 March 1988, (Washington, DC: US Government Printing Office, 1988); 'Eastern Europe in the Gorbachev Era: Implications for US Policy', Report prepared for the Subcommittee on Europe and the Middle East of the Committee on Foreign Affairs, US House of Representatives, 101st Congress, 1st Session, December 1989, (Washington, DC: US Government Printing Office, 1990).
50 National Security Decision Directive 75: 'US Relations with the USSR', Washington, DC: The White House, 17 January 1983, p. 3.
51 Zelikow and Rice, *Germany Unified*, p. 28.
52 For an interesting US Congress Hearing on this issue, see: 'Implementation of the Helsinki Accords: German Unification and the CSCE Process, Hearing before the Commission on Security and Cooperation in Europe', 101st Congress, 2nd Session, 3 April 1990, (Washington, DC: US Government Printing Office, 1990).
53 George H. Bush and Brent Scowcroft, *A World Transformed*, (New York: Alfred A. Knopf, 1998), p. 253.
54 Zelikow and Rice, *Germany Unified*, p. 127.
55 On this, see ibid., pp. 201–5.
56 On this, see, in particular, ibid. and Frank Costigliola, 'An "Arm around the Shoulder": The United States, NATO and German Reunification, 1989–90', *Contemporary European History* vol. 3, no. 1, 1994, pp. 87–110.
57 Zelikow and Rice, *Germany Unified*, p. 197.
58 Melvyn P. Leffler, *A Preponderance of Power: National Security, the Truman Administration and the Cold War*, (Stanford: Stanford University Press, 1992).
59 Geir Lundestad, *'Empire' by Integration: the United States and European Integration, 1945–1997*, (Oxford and New York: Oxford University Press, 1998) and *The American 'Empire' and Other Studies of US Foreign Policy in a Comparative Perspective*, (Oxford and Oslo: Oxford University Press and Norwegian University Press, 1990).
60 David P. Calleo, *Beyond American Hegemony: the Future of the Western Alliance*, (New York: Basic Books, 1987).
61 For Melvyn P. Leffler the willingness to dominate the Western Hemisphere was not necessarily a result of US–Soviet relations. It could be traced back to an amalgam between the ideas of MacKinder (and Mahan), technological developments, the natural evolution of the Monroe Doctrine and the war against the Axis powers. See, Melvyn P. Leffler, 'The American Conception of National Security

and the Beginnings of the Cold War, 1945–48', *A.H.R. Forum*, *American Historical Review* np. 89, April 1984, pp. 346–81.
62 Wolfram F. Hanrieder, *Germany, America, Europe: Forty Years of German Foreign Policy*, (New Haven: Yale University Press, 1989), p. 6. (Emphasis added).
63 As quoted in: Geir Lundestad, 'American-European Cooperation and Conflict: Past, Present, and Future', in: Geir Lundestad (ed): *No End to Alliance: the United States and Western Europe: Past, Present and Future*, (Basingstoke: Macmillan, 1998), p. 245. Lord Ismay, a British General, was the first NATO Secretary General from 1952 to 1957.
64 Bush and Scowcroft, *A World Transformed*, pp. 230–31. See also pp. 196–97.
65 See: Lundestad, *'Empire' by Integration*, and Geir Lundestad, *The United States and Western Europe since 1945: from 'Empire' by Invitation to Transatlantic Drift*, (Oxford: Oxford University Press, 2003).
66 Patrick E. Tyler, 'US Strategy Plan Calls for Insuring no Rivals Develop', *The New York Times*, 8 March 1992, p. A1.
67 See especially: 'United States–European Community Relations: Entering a New Era, Report of the 34th Meeting of Members of Congress and of the European Parliament, 6–9 January 1990', (Washington, DC: US Government Printing Office, 1990) and 'Europe and the United States: Competition and Cooperation in the 1990s', Study Papers submitted to the Subcommittee on International Economic Policy and Trade and the Subcommittee on Europe and the Middle East of the Committee on Foreign Affairs, US House of Representatives, (Washington, DC: US Government Printing Office, June 1992).
68 William C. Wohlforth, 'German Unification: A Reassessment', in Arthur L. Rosenbaum and Lee Chae-Jin ed., *The Cold War – Reassessments* (The Keck Center for International and Strategic Studies, Monograph Series, 11/2000), p. 183 (Emphasis in original).
69 See, for example, Hugh De Santis, 'The Graying of NATO', *The Washington Quarterly* vol. 14, no. 4, autumn 1991, pp. 51–65; S. Victor Papacosma and Mary Ann Heiss (eds), *NATO in the Post-Cold War Era: Does It Have a Future?*, (London: Macmillan, 1995).
70 See, North Atlantic Treaty Organization, 'The Alliance's New Strategic Concept', *NATO Review* vol. 39, no. 6, 1991, pp. 25–32.
71 Jonathan Clarke, 'Replacing NATO', *Foreign Policy* no. 93, winter 1993–94, pp. 22–40.
72 See for example: Michael. MccGwire, 'NATO Expansion: "a Policy Error of Historic Importance"', *Review of International Studies* vol. 4, no. 1, pp. 23–42.
73 Mark Kramer, 'The Myth of a No-NATO-Enlargement Pledge to Russia', *The Washington Quarterly* vol. 32, no. 2, April 2009, p. 45.

12

The road to Saint-Malo

Germany and EU–NATO relations after the Cold War

Wolfgang Krieger

At their meeting in the French coastal city of Saint-Malo on 4 December 1998 President Jacques Chirac and Prime Minister Tony Blair issued a declaration in which they expressed their common position on the future of the European Union's (EU) Common Foreign and Security Policy (CFSP). They agreed that the EU needed '[…] the capacity for autonomous action, backed up by credible military forces, the means to decide to use them and a readiness to do so, in order to respond to international crises.'[1] At the same time they made clear that such a capacity and its uses should in no way diminish the contributions made to NATO by EU member states. Neither should it detract from the role of the Western European Union (WEU). Both NATO and the WEU would remain responsible for the 'collective defence of their members'. Concerning other military missions, the EU would only act where NATO decided not to become engaged.

While the Saint-Malo declaration did not spell out the parameters of a future EU military capacity in any detail, it did specify that the limited nature of potential EU crisis engagements were to be reflected in the organizational arrangements as well as the assigned military forces. The EU's military capacities would include intelligence and strategic planning only in so far as it did not duplicate WEU capacities. Its military forces would be drawn both from existing units assigned to the European pillar within NATO and from national and multilateral forces outside NATO. In more general terms, France and Britain agreed on the need for adapting their armed forces to new security risks and on the desirability of a strong and competitive European defence industry.

The overall intention of that declaration was clearly to impose tight limits on any future EU foreign and security policy. France and Britain agreed that the EU would develop a military capability only for international crises outside its own borders and only as an auxiliary to NATO, which would have the right of first refusal. They further stipulated that any related military capacities and all EU military missions would be dealt with in an intergovernmental fashion under the direction of the Council of the EU. This approach would effectively bypass the European Commission and the European Parliament. And it would give every EU member a veto right. In this way Paris and London sent out a clear message that defence matters, even when relating to peacekeeping or peace-enforcing missions, would primarily remain under national control and under NATO rather than under the EU umbrella.

The deeper significance of this Franco-British declaration only becomes intelligible if it is read against the wider background of how, after the end of the Cold War, both the EU and NATO tried to defend and to expand their respective political jurisdictions at a time when both had to adapt to a dramatically changed international environment.[2] As far as the institutional arrangements were concerned, the battle began way back in the 1950s and in many ways it still goes on today. All along the way it has reflected the highly divergent interests of the EU and NATO member states in matters of foreign and security policy. This drawn-out nature of the institutional conflict makes it impossible to reach a final conclusion on the historical significance of the Saint-Malo declaration. It may have been a historical watershed or it may have been a mere vignette to that Byzantine discourse called European integration.

By contrast it seems easier to assess the role played by Germany in that multilateral search for a new European security policy. But before we look at that issue we need to explore how France and Britain came to agree on the Saint-Malo declaration, under what circumstances Chirac and Blair held their meeting and what may have been on their minds at that time.

Back in December 1998 the public response to the Chirac–Blair meeting was one of surprise and uneasiness. What exactly were Paris and London up to? Did their joint declaration imply a ganging up vis-à-vis the rest of Europe? How might they play their cards as nuclear powers and as veto-powers on the United Nations (UN) Security Council in the arena of European security policy?[3]

There could be no doubt that Saint-Malo had brought the divergent French and British views of EU foreign and security policy closer together. 'One felt reminded of the days of the Entente Cordiale', as Maurice Vaïsse put it.[4] It happened at a time when France was in one of her cohabitation phases, with a conservative president forced to accept a socialist prime minister and cabinet. In Britain, Tony Blair had been in office for well over a year and had already won a remarkable reputation for resolving such difficult conflicts as the one in Northern Ireland. His prestige and boundless energy permitted him to steer a much more pro-European course at the same time as a much more interventionist one when it came to the international crises in the Balkans.

Then there was the institutional dimension with its long history of rivalry between on the one hand what has been called the 'integration of Europe', a complex set of policies initially pursued by only a few countries west of the Iron Curtain, and on the other hand the 'defence of Europe' to which some West European states contributed in NATO while others benefited as free riders outside NATO. Those two processes were in many ways pitted against each other from their very beginnings in the late 1940s. The essential difference between them concerned the role which the United States should or should not play in European affairs. The former process, which eventually led to today's EU, was essentially (but by no means exclusively) about limiting Washington's influence or even excluding it in certain policy areas. By contrast, the process related to NATO had very different objectives. From the European side it was mostly about getting the strongest possible American security guarantee while preserving as much as possible the different national options in foreign and defence matters.

However, the Americans did not see things in quite that way. Although Washington was willing to provide a strong yet limited security guarantee it expected to have a voice in European matters far beyond the realm of defence.[5] This difference in expectations is well expressed in a cartoon in the French satirical weekly *Le Canard enchaîné* featuring presidents Nicolas Sarkozy and Barack Obama at one of their first meetings. Says Sarkozy: 'Turkey's membership in the EU is a matter for the Europeans only.' To which Obama responds: 'I think I have to re-explain NATO to you.'

Although it is beyond the scope of this chapter to go over the 40 years of parallel and often tempestuous relationship between those two processes, it is important to point out that most integration steps on the side of 'Europe' were motivated by a more or less hidden desire to weaken American influence in Europe beyond the narrow sphere of defence issues and to keep tabs on the growing economic power of Germany, assuming that it would increase Germany's political and military weight to an undesirable degree unless harnessed by a further 'deepening' of European integration.

In this political game France and Britain played somewhat different parts, since Britain tried to limit such 'deepening' as much as possible and at the same time to emphasize the 'special relationship' with the Americans, while France was looking for ways to remain a great power with a global projection of influence and to maintain a fully independent foreign and defence policy. These tensions were habitually exploited by the Germans, who had far less sovereignty to lose given the constraints of the four-power regime between 1945 and 1990. Although pretending to work eagerly for more advances in 'Europe' they were in fact hoping that the French and the British could be relied on to keep a foot firmly placed on the brakes of the European integration vehicle.[6]

This political game was thoroughly upset by the sudden disappearance of the Iron Curtain. While NATO lost its central purpose of deterring a Soviet attack, the 'old Europe' (Donald Rumsfeld) was faced with a vast array of potential new members and an enormous agenda of economic transition. The result was a debate on the wisdom of a rapid 'widening' and its relationship with the publicly proclaimed need for 'deepening' in order to make the EU a more credible actor both on the European continent and in a newly globalized political and economic arena. Although defence matters did not at first seem overly pressing, they quickly became a major concern as the Gulf War to liberate Kuwait (1990–91) and the civil wars in Yugoslavia (from 1991) shattered the illusion of a new era of never-ending peace and prosperity.

Since the failure of the European Defence Community (EDC) in 1954 there had been no overall body for foreign and security policy-making within the framework of what in 1986 became the European Communities (and later on the EU). The European Political Cooperation (EPC), established in 1970, was merely an instrument of consultation among the membership as formalized in the Single European Act of 1986. While the larger member states did not wish to have their national foreign policies reduced by Brussels, some of the smaller members like the Netherlands rejected the idea of weakening the European Commission by allowing any new intergovernmental procedures. As a result, nothing was achieved in terms of a common (West) European security and defence policy.[7]

Then the Maastricht Treaty of 1992, which largely focused on establishing a common currency, created the CFSP as one of the three pillars of what was henceforth called the European Union. While broadening the area of external affairs in which the EU could operate, the actual process was a fairly weak one because it was governed by a need for unanimity in the EU Council. In other words, it depended entirely on reaching a consensus of all member governments on any given issue. The CFSP would not come under the domain of the EU Commission and would therefore be exempted from any further 'deepening' of the EU. In parallel, the agreement on monetary union acknowledged an opt-out clause for Britain and Denmark, which meant that international financial policy could not be an integrated part of EU policy-making either. If the CFSP was created in response to the EU's failure to play a meaningful role in ending the Yugoslav civil wars, it could at best be seen as a first step towards an institutional improvement. There was as yet no administrative unit to support this new policy area. Indeed there was not even a shadow of a military capability with which to make a meaningful contribution to international security.

Apart from the old rivalry with NATO it was the WEU that stood in the way of adding defence to the EU portfolio. Back in 1950 the WEU (or rather its predecessor, the Brussels Treaty Organization) had lost to NATO its mandate to plan and organize defensive forces. By the 1980s it had as much as suspended its supervisory role over the restrictions imposed on German weaponry when West Germany joined NATO in 1955. Then, in 1992, the WEU enjoyed a sudden revival. It was assigned the so-called Petersberg tasks. Among them were peacekeeping and peacemaking tasks and the use of military forces for humanitarian and rescue purposes. European states, whether EU members or not, were invited to join the revived WEU which in turn would make itself available to the CSCE, yet another international body which held the promise of providing an alternative to the older institutions such as the UN and NATO dominated by the old great powers of the Second World War era.

By putting the WEU in charge of an all-purpose European security policy, the leading powers would no doubt be France and Britain, given their experience and their capacity for military engagement in crises in developing countries, their nuclear deterrent forces and their permanent membership on the UN Security Council. At the same time Germany's influence would be weakened. By contrast, the two alternatives to a WEU-based structure would not have that effect in quite the same way. Any EU-based security structure might give Bonn/Berlin the leverage of being the number one net financial contributor in 'Europe' as well as certain numerical advantages in the European Parliament and in various EU decision-making processes because its population exceeded that of Britain, France and Italy by more than 20 million.[8] A NATO-based solution might bring back the traditional balancing game which Germany had played during the Cold War vis-à-vis France, Britain and the United States.[9] Vis-à-vis the smaller European states, particularly the new WEU members (and potential members) both in Eastern and in Western Europe, one could argue that the WEU solution held out the promise of a strong commitment to home defence since the WEU treaty obliges its members to territorial defence in more direct ways than does the North Atlantic Treaty.[10] Finally, by opting for the WEU, a European defence capability could be built independently of the 'sole remaining super power' (Samuel P. Huntington), the United States, who in turn would find it difficult to complain since the WEU and NATO had a long-standing mutually supportive relationship reaching back nearly five decades.

At the 1996 Berlin meeting of NATO foreign ministers, it was agreed that the WEU would manage the creation of a European Security and Defence Identity (ESDI) within NATO. That construct reached back to the old idea of a European 'pillar' that would need to be strengthened in order to match the already overbearingly strong American 'pillar' in NATO. It was now agreed that the Europeans could use NATO assets in missions that NATO did not wish to engage in. This would be done via WEU structures, based on a proposal made in 1993 that Combined Joint Task Forces (CJTFs) could be formed that used NATO assets and in which non-NATO-members could participate.

However, in the following year the Amsterdam treaty for yet another reform of the EU provided a sharp turnaround.[11] It established a set of organizational structures for dealing with the Petersberg tasks within the EU itself. Thus it made the WEU redundant because the EU would henceforth have its own military capability.

It was at this point in the EU reform process that the Saint-Malo meeting played an important role in getting the British to agree to a military role for the EU. As we have seen, they did so only under a very specific set of conditions, which asserted the principle of national sovereignty in the realm of defence policy. Nevertheless, it was due to the Saint-Malo agreement that the EU was able to make the next move along that twisted path. In June 1999 the office of a High Representative of the EU's Common Foreign and Security Policy pillar was created and Javier Solana, a former NATO General Secretary, was appointed to that post. At the same time the WEU was nearly shut down though Solana became Secretary General of WEU in the same year.[12]

This brings us to the role Germany played in this search for a new European security policy.[13] In fact, that role was much less prominent than one would have expected, given the additional economic and political weight Germany had allegedly gained from its unification in 1990. How is this weakness to be explained?

During the years immediately after German unification the German government was eager to make both the international public and its own citizens believe that united Germany would exercise the same kind of self-restraint to which people had become accustomed during the Cold War years.[14] But in reality most people, certainly most Europeans, found it difficult to believe that a considerable larger Germany, freed from the burden of the Soviet military threat, would refrain for very long from throwing around its weight in European and transatlantic affairs. There was much talk of a more assertive Germany, particularly as the government of Chancellor Helmut Kohl began to advertise its willingness to assume greater international responsibilities. Yet the first international crisis after unification, the war to liberate Kuwait, found the Germans in the humiliating position of having to watch their British and French partners at the side of the Americans while Germany (along with Japan) was forced by them to make an enormous financial contribution. (Some people would later calculate that the Americans may actually have made a handsome profit from those financial contributions.)

If self-restraint was a minor factor in Germany's weakness vis-à-vis the new security challenges the fear of Russia and the confusions created by Germany's internal military reforms were much more important. With hundreds of thousands of Russian (i.e. ex-Soviet) forces stationed in the eastern parts of Germany, the Bonn government was tied down by a most delicate relationship with Russia. (The last Russian units withdrew in August 1994.) It was making large loans and direct payments to Moscow. And the treaty which ended the four-power regime over Germany (the 'Two-plus-Four Treaty' of 1990) specified that the territories of former Communist East Germany were part of NATO but could not host any non-German NATO troops or any nuclear weapons. At the same time Germany had to reduce her military forces from nearly 600,000 to 370,000 and to provide the remaining forces with a completely new organizational structure. Given the new international security environment the bulk of the German tank forces had to be dismantled and a Rapid Reaction Force of 60,000 troops had to be established, trained and equipped.[15] For all these reasons Germany neither wished to take any steps which might upset Russia nor was it in a position to contribute significantly to the new types of international crisis intervention.

Matters were further complicated by domestic expectations with respect to military and security affairs. The German public was somehow under the impression that an entirely new European security architecture would emerge along the lines of the ideas promoted by German Foreign Minister Hans-Dietrich Genscher and by the political left. This new architecture would be based on a thorough reform of the UN (with a permanent seat for Germany on the UN Security Council) and on a withering away of the Cold War military alliances and forces. If the Warsaw Pact had been dissolved rapidly in 1991, what justification was there for the survival of NATO? Genscher's pet idea was to transfer European security matters to the CSCE (later called OSCE), which had evolved from the 1975 Helsinki conference that Genscher along with many others saw as a great triumph of West Germany's 'new *Ostpolitik*' (détente).[16]

However, the Genscherites, as we may call them, did not seem to notice that the spirit of that Helsinki meeting, and indeed the idea of endlessly creating mammoth international organizations, was totally incompatible with the spirit of the 1989 'springtime of nations' (Michael Howard). While Helsinki had cemented the Soviet-enforced borders, regimes and alliances in Eastern Europe, 1989 marked the revival of European nationalism and of the desire for ethnically defined borders and states.[17] As Henry Kissinger put it in a much-quoted article in March 1992: 'Ironically, the alphabet soup of institutions – EC, CSCE, WEU and the newest, as yet unlabeled candidate, the Europe from Vladivostok west to Vancouver – contribute to a rising nationalism. For they provide a menu to any country to choose whatever institution most favours its immediate national goals on any given issue – as happened on the issue of Yugoslavia.'[18] A month earlier, Czechoslovak President Vaclav Havel, formerly among the most prominent of anti-Soviet dissidents, had told the World Economic Forum in Davos: 'We have to abandon the arrogant belief that the world is merely a puzzle to be solved, a machine with instructions for use waiting to be discovered, a body of information to be fed into a computer.' The *International Herald Tribune* published excerpts under the headline: 'The Post-Modern World Is Sick of Systems.'[19]

All of this happened in direct contradiction to the dominant discourse of the German political left, and many people in other political camps, who insisted that the very concept of the nation state was to be scrapped as quickly as possible. No wonder they were left speechless when the revolutions of 1989 led to the formation of many new nation states. At the same time it became increasingly obvious that even the peoples of Western Europe had not given up on the idea of the nation state – despite decades of 'ever closer union' under the Brussels-led process of European integration.[20] Indeed, the drive towards German unification in 1989–90 held the same message, since the united Germany of 1990 was in essence a return to Bismarck's Germany of the 1870s, even if large chunks of territories were now lost and despite the more democratic constitution of 1949. Reconstituting the German nation had been a strong desire on the part of the German people, no matter how much the political left sought to deny that fact and even to prevent unification itself.[21]

Finally, there was the issue of constitutional limitations on the use of German armed forces. During the first years of the EU's failed policies in Yugoslavia, the Kohl–Genscher government had to operate under a political doctrine which held that the German constitution did not permit any military engagements other than for the immediate defence of German territory.[22] This view had become a convenient political myth during the 1980s, when any West German military engagement would have been impossible anyhow due to the limited sovereignty rights under the four-power regime. In 1991, after full sovereignty had been restored, the same reasoning was still used to justify Germany's non-engagement in the Gulf War. Psychologically, it was in large part based on the conviction that Germany should not engage in what was widely considered an aggressive and imperialist foreign policy on the part of the United States and its willing followers in Britain and France. When American protesters shouted 'no blood for oil' the majority of Germans were marching along in spirit. But how could this doctrine be upheld in the face of a European civil war (in Yugoslavia) in which Washington took no particular interest and which the EU had declared to be a matter for Europeans, i.e. primarily for the EU, to resolve? How could Germany be a mere bystander when thousands of people were being massacred in the Balkans and hundreds of thousands were driven from their homes?

In June 1994 the German constitutional court came up with a ruling which permitted such military engagements provided they took place under the authority of the UN and with the consent of a majority in the German federal parliament. In other words, the court confirmed the minority view that German military engagements would have been possible all along.[23] But now, by requiring a majority assent in parliament, it created yet another political myth. It prescribed that the German armed forces were under the immediate authority of parliament rather than under the executive. As a result, parliament would henceforth micro-manage military missions and operations, fixing not only the numbers of soldiers to be deployed but also their missions including the rules of engagement, while the government would have to scramble to find parliamentary majorities for each and every move. The result has been a tight limitation on what German forces can do during such missions. And since all of them are multinational missions, every commander of a peacekeeping or peacemaking operation in which the Germans participate has to conduct diplomatic negotiations with the German parliament. In a parliament of five political parties and given the volatile decision-making of German coalition governments, a commander may well ask whether it is worth the trouble having the Germans on the team. At the same time that new constitutional fiction made it possible to avoid any wider public debate on the realities of the emerging 'new world order' (George Bush, Sr.) and its manifold security challenges. In turn this left the field wide open to the preachers of pious illusions and self-serving ideologies.

Against this background it is easier to understand why the Bonn governments cut a less than admirable figure when it came to the pressing problems of European security institutions and new military capabilities inside the EU. Indeed, Germany changed its position several times during the NATO debate on a new command structure and on finding a way to reintegrate France into NATO's integrated military structures. At first it supported the French demand of a major command post in Southern Europe, thus going against the Americans, who insisted on keeping control of the Mediterranean and the Middle East. Then they suggested that the command might be rotated between the Americans and the French. Eventually, Bonn voted in favour of the American position, thus hurting the French, who then retreated to their former policy of staying away from NATO commands altogether.[24]

German policy on NATO expansion was somewhat more coherent. In December 1993, when it turned out to be impossible to transform the OSCE into an organization which could handle military forces and missions, German Defence Minister Volker Rühe proposed a straight course of NATO's eastward expansion. To the German public this was sold as a promise which Bonn had made to Poland in return for Warsaw's acquiescence in German unification and as an important step in improving Germany's security, because with the East Central European states in NATO Germany would be 'entirely surrounded by allies and friends'. The Americans hesitated at first, given the massive protests from Russia, but came around to Rühe's viewpoint in 1995/1996, when they began their own drive for NATO expansion.[25] The British were lukewarm, fearing for the coherence of the Alliance.[26] The French argued that EU expansion would have to come first, fearing that any such expansion, be it NATO or the EU, would primarily benefit their German rivals and was therefore less than desirable.

Eventually, the treaty between NATO and Russia and the Partnership for Peace Program provided an interim solution that made it possible in June 1997 to issue an invitation to Poland, the Czech Republic and Hungary to become NATO members. All three of them joined in 1999. France promoted the idea of issuing the same invitation to Slovenia and to Romania, the latter being Francophone but very backward in its transformation from Communism to democracy and to economic prosperity.

Although the Germans were happy to have those three new NATO members guarding their eastern borders, they were mortally afraid of the Russian response. This came to the surface during the Bosnian war of 1999, which Germany joined with a very small air force contingent based in Italy and to which the Kremlin was extremely hostile, staunchly backing Serbia to the hilt. The Kohl government, in its final year, was internally split on whether Germany could and should participate in a military mission if the UN Security Council, due to Russia's veto, failed to pass a resolution mandating such an operation. Foreign Minister Klaus Kinkel was opposed, whereas Defence Minister Rühe was in favour. Eventually, a UN Security Council resolution was passed which termed the Yugoslav situation 'a danger to international security'. This formula satisfied the incoming red–green coalition government under Gerhard Schröder. The decision was made to have the Bundeswehr participate in a NATO mission but in reality the new German government may well have believed that Serbia would pull back from the brink at the last minute.

As this was not the case, the NATO bombing campaign started in March 1999, making the German government extremely anxious to get Moscow to agree to yet another diplomatic peace initiative at almost any price (Ahtisaari/Chernomyrdin mission). Only the populist talent of Foreign Minister Josef Fischer and his brutal behind-the-scenes arm-twisting on his own Green party dissidents made it possible to keep German domestic support alive. The sheer luck of seeing all Bundeswehr bombers return safely to their bases was no doubt another crucial factor in keeping the domestic German situation under control.

Luckily for the Schröder–Fischer government there was much else going on besides the Yugoslav wars. Germany took the EU and WEU presidencies in the first half of 1999, faced with the shameful stepping down of the Jacques Santer EU Commission in the midst of financial scandals and widespread incompetency.[27] Germany's government offices and federal parliament moved from Bonn to Berlin. And former Chancellor Helmut Kohl, along with many of his political friends, became mired in a party finance scandal that dashed their hopes of replacing the red–green government any time soon. The great reforms of Europe's security institutions had been dropped quietly from the agenda, although Foreign Minister Fischer, in November 1998, had caused a small stir in NATO with his proposal that the alliance renounce officially any remnants of a nuclear first-use policy.[28]

Fischer's remarks were surely made to please his domestic audience. But they also served as a reminder that Germany, more than ever, was out of step on the entire issue of nuclear policies. While France and Britain were retaining and modernizing their nuclear arsenals and their posture of nuclear deterrence – to say nothing of the somewhat reduced but still vast American and Russian nuclear arsenals – the Germans quietly buried the consensus which chancellors Helmut Schmidt and Helmut Kohl had built during the heated days of the Intermediate Nuclear Forces debates less than two decades earlier. During all those years the Franco-German special friendship had never overcome those vital differences while the defence policies and views of Britain and the United States had remained a major source of German resentment against a more active German participation in international military missions.

If the foreign policies of Margaret Thatcher and Ronald Reagan had made the Germans more hostile to the idea of engaging in any external military operations, their attitude changed somewhat in the wake of 9/11. Now Germany began to participate in various international missions in Afghanistan, in Africa and the Persian Gulf. But this change was hardly reflected in German defence spending, which dropped to around 1 per cent of gross national product. Although Germans grudgingly accepted the need for certain military missions far away from home, they failed to understand the need for re-equipping the Bundeswehr with those weapons and logistics tools needed to participate effectively in such operations. Air- and sea-lifts were and still are the biggest gaps, along with armoured combat vehicles, attack (and other) helicopters, long-range bombers as well as drones and satellites for intelligence and command and control purposes. When German forces began to operate in the Balkans those weaknesses became painfully apparent. Intelligence was perhaps the weakest part since the Bundeswehr had no significant capability for gathering tactical intelligence on the ground and for protecting its military compounds. It had no battlefield human intelligence acquisition. German commanders had to beg their allies, particularly the Americans, for help.[29]

These weaknesses made it blatantly obvious that in the foreseeable future Germany had little to contribute to the ambitious project of making the EU an independent security actor. Much as it resented the Chirac–Blair initiative taken at Saint-Malo, Germany had no leverage to break the spirit of national sovereignty in defence matters which dominated the Saint-Malo meeting in December 1998.

In conclusion it seems as though the creation of the Euro may have weakened Germany's international position less than was intended by France and by others – though this is an issue on which the jury is still out – while the Saint-Malo declaration demonstrated that the German emperor had no clothes (or at least far less than expected) when it came to international security policy. Since 1998 Germany role in international security affairs has considerably changed. But will the 'Berlin republic' (that is united Germany) ever become a major actor in this field? It is too early to tell, as Zhou Enlai once said when asked what he thought of the effects of the French Revolution.

Notes

1 For the full text, see the home page of the British Foreign and Commonwealth Office www.fco.gov.uk/. On transatlantic and European security issues before and after Saint-Malo, see Paul Cornish, *Partnership in Crisis: the US, Europe, and the Fall and Rise of NATO*, (London: RIIA, 1997); Kori Schake, 'Building a European Defense Capability', *Survival* vol. 41, no. 1, 1999 pp. 20–40; Alyson Bailes, 'Europe's Defense Challenge', *Foreign Affairs* vol. 76, no. 1, 1997; Joachim Krause (ed.), *Unraveling the European security and defence policy conundrum*, (Bern: Peter Lang, 2003); Simon Serfaty, *Visions of the Atlantic Alliance: the United States, the European Union and NATO*, (Washington: CSIS, 2005); Lawrence Freedman, 'The Transatlantic Agenda: Vision and Counter-Vision', *Survival* vol. 47, no. 4, 2005/2006; Anand Menon, 'Empowering Paradise? The ESDP at ten', *International Affairs (London)* vol. 85, no. 2, 2009 pp. 227–46.

2 For the preceding rapprochement in Franco-British defence relations, see Jonathan Eyal, 'The Emerging Franco-British Security Alliance', *Wall Street Journal* (11 November 1994) p. 6; Jacques

Isnard, 'Paris et Londres renforcent leur cooperation militaire', in *Le Monde* (18 November 1994) pp. 1, 4; these steps are traced in Wolfgang Krieger, 'Grossbritannien setzt auf die WEU', in IP 2915, Stiftung Wissenschaft und Politik (Juni 1995); Andrew Shearer, 'Britain, France and the Saint-Malo Declaration – Tactical Rapprochement or Strategic Entente?', *Cambridge Review of International Affairs* vol. 13, no. 2, 2000 pp. 283–98. The wider historical background of Franco-British relations is deftly analysed in Robert and Isabelle Tombs, *That Sweet Enemy: The French and the British from the Sun King to the Present*, (London: Pimlico, 2007), Chapter 14.

3 Apart from the issues referred to here, the two parties also discussed defence issues unrelated to the European Union such as African security and their respective deployments of nuclear-armed submarines for strategic deterrence. For details, see Jolyon Howorth, *Defending Europe: The EU, NATO and the Quest for European Autonomy*, (New York, NY: Palgrave, 2003).

4 Maurice Vaïsse, *La Puissance ou l'influence: La France dans le monde depuis 1958*, (Paris: Fayard, 2009), p. 152.

5 For an excellent contemporary analysis, see Paul S. Gebhard, The United States and European Security, in *Adelphi Papers* 286, IISS London, 1994; a retrospective assessment is found in: Alyson Bailes, 'The EU and a "better world": what role for the European Security and Defence Policy?', *International Affairs (London)*, vol. 84, no. 1, 2008, pp. 115–30; for the wider historical context, see Anne Deighton and Gérard Bossuat (eds), *The EC/EU: A World Security Actor? 1957–2007*, (Paris: Soleb, 2007); Pierre Gerbet, *La Construction de l'Europe*, (Paris: Armand Collin, 2007), fourth edition.

6 Helga Haftendorn, *Deutsche Außenpolitik zwischen Selbstbeschränkung und Selbstbehauptung 1945–2000*, (Stuttgart: DVA, 2001); Eckart Conze, *Die Suche nach Sicherheit: Eine Geschichte der Bundesrepublik Deutschland von 1949 bis in die Gegenwart*, (Munich: Siedler, 2009); Georges-Henri Soutou, *L'Alliance incertaine les rapports politico-stratégiques franco-allemands, 1954–1996*, (Paris: Fayard, 1996); Marie-Thérèse Bitsch (ed.), *Le Couple France-Allemagne et les institutions européennes*, (Brussels: Bruylant, 2001); Amaya Bloch-Lainé, 'Franco-German Cooperation in Foreign Affairs: Security and Defense – A Case Study', in: Douglas Webber (ed.), *The Franco-German Relationship in the European Union*, (London: Routledge, 1999).

7 For a useful recent survey, see Jolyon Howorth, *Security and Defence Policy in the European Union*, (New York, NY: Palgrave, 2007); David P. Calleo, *Re-Thinking Europe's Future*, (Princeton University Press, 2003); an early analysis is found in Charles A. Kupchan and Clifford A. Kupchan, 'European Security, Past and Future', *International Security* vol. 16, no. 1, 1991, pp. 114–61.

8 The differences in defence expenditure between France (3 per cent of GDP), Britain (2.8 per cent), and Germany (1.6 per cent) are only vague indications of the exceptional position held by Paris and London. For the 1997 figures, see IISS (ed.), *The Military Balance 1998/99*, (London: OUP, 1998) p. 295.

9 Wolfram F. Hanrieder, *Germany, America, Europe: Forty Years of German Foreign Policy*, (New Haven, CT: Yale UP, 1989)

10 Article 5 of the Atlantic Treaty only requires each member '[...] individually and in concert with the other Parties, [to take] such action *as it deems necessary*, including the use of armed force [...]' By contrast, Article 5 of the WEU treaty (as modified in 1954) reads as follows: 'If any of the High Contracting Parties should be the object of an armed attack in Europe, the other High Contracting Parties will, in accordance with the provisions of Article 51 of the Charter of the United Nations, afford the Party so attacked all the military and other aid and assistance in their power.' In other words, member states must *automatically* use their entire military and other resources and are not at liberty to leave things up to their national decision-making process, a precondition laid down by the US Senate during the North Atlantic treaty negotiations in 1948–49.

11 Gisela Müller-Brandeck-Bocquet, 'Der Amsterdam-Vertrag zur Reform der Europäischen Union', in: *Aus Politik und Zeitgeschichte* no. 47, 1997, pp. 21–29; Lothar Rühl, *Conditions and Options for an Autonomous 'Common European Policy on Security and Defence' in and by the European Union in the post-Amsterdam Perspective*, (Bonn: ZEI, 1999).

12 Of course no international organization is ever shut down completely. The debate on what to do with the WEU still goes on. For the very modest list of remaining tasks, see its residual website www.weu.int/ (accessed 4 March 2010) and its 56-page brochure *WEU today* which dates from the year 2000.

13 Wolfgang Krieger, 'Die deutsche Integrationspolitik im postsowjetischen Europa', *Europa-Archiv* vol. 47, no. 18, 1992, pp. 515–26; Christoph Bluth, *Germany and the Future of European Security*, (London: Palgrave, 2000); Jens Hacker, *Integration und Verantwortung: Deutschland als europäischer Sicherheitspartner*, (Bonn: Bouvier, 1995).

14 On the illusions created during and after German unification, see Timothy Garton Ash, *In Europe's Name: Germany and the Divided Continent*, (New York, NY: Vintage, 1994); Andreas Rödder, *Deutschland einig Vaterland: die Geschichte der Wiedervereinigung*, (Munich: Beck, 2009).
15 Florence Gauzy, 'Soldats de métier, armées de conscription: les réformes militaires en Allemagne et en France dans les années 1990', in: CEHD, *L'image du militaire en Allemagne et en France aux XIXe et XXe siècles. Armées, soldats: regards croisés,* (Paris: Cahiers du CEHD, 2009); Detlev Bald, *Die Bundeswehr: eine kritische Geschichte 1955–2005,* (Munich: Beck, 2005); Wilfried von Bredow, *Militär und Demokratie in Deutschland,* (Wiesbaden: VS, 2007); Mary Elise Sarotte, *German Military Reform and European Security*, (London: IISS, 2001).
16 Genscher became foreign minister in 1974 and remained in that office until 1992.
17 For a contemporary analysis, see Samuel F. Wells (ed.), *The Helsinki Process and the Future of Europe,* (Washington, DC: 1990); Vojtech Mastny, *The Helsinki Process and the Reintegration of Europe: Analysis and Documentation, 1986–1990,* (New York, NY: NYU Press, 1992).
18 Henry Kissinger, 'The Atlantic Alliance Needs Renewal in a Changed World', in *International Herald Tribune* (2 March 1992) p. 5.
19 Ibid.
20 That phrase is quoted from the preamble of the Treaty of Rome of 1957 and has remained in force ever since.
21 A long and merciless list of such initiatives and statements (and of their authors) is found in: Jens Hacker, *Deutsche Irrtümer. Schönfärber und Helfershelfer der SED-Diktatur im Westen,* (Berlin: Verlag Ullstein, 1994); the influence of the '1968 activists' is portrayed in: Götz Aly, *Unser Kampf 1968: ein irritierter Blick zurück,* (Frankfurt: Fischer, 2008).
22 Karl-Heinz Kamp, 'The Bundeswehr in Out-of Area', *World Today* vol. 49, no. 9 (1993); Wolfgang Krieger, 'Toward a Gaullist Germany? Some Lessons from the Yugoslav Crisis', *World Policy Journal* vol. 11, no. 1, 1994.
23 Franz-Josef Meier, 'Germany's Defense Choices', *Survival* vol. 47, no. 1, 2005; Thomas U. Berger, *The Culture of Anti-Militarism in Germany and Japan,* (Baltimore, MD: JHUP, 1998).
24 Haftendorn, *Deutsche Außenpolitik,* p. 397; France eventually returned to NATO's military institutions in 2009. For an explanation from a former presidential security adviser, see Amiral Jacques Lanxade, 'Otan, la logique implacable de l'histoire', *Le Figaro,* 17 March 2009.
25 For contemporary views on NATO enlargement, see: Ronald Asmus et al., 'NATO Expansion – the Next Steps', *Survival* vol. 37, no. 1, 1995, pp. 7–33; Karl-Heinz Kamp, 'NATO Entrapped: Debating the Next Enlargement Round', in: *Survival* vol. 40, no. 3, 1998; Charles-Philippe David, *Future of NATO: Enlargement, Russia and European Security* (Montreal: MQUP, 1999).
26 In a speech on 23 February 1996 Prime Minister John Major had opposed NATO expansion, arguing that EU expansion should come first, press release of the British Embassy in Bonn D 10/96, 28 February 1996.
27 Bertrand Rochard, *L'Europe des Commissaires: Réflexions sur l'identité européenne des Traités de Rome au Traité d'Amsterdam,* (Brussels: Bruylant, 2003).
28 Paul Berman, *Power and the Idealists: Or, the Passion of Joschka Fischer and Its Aftermath,* (New York, NY: Norton, 2007).
29 Peter Goebel (ed.), *Von Kambodscha bis Kosovo: Auslandseinsätze der Bundeswehr seit Ende des Kalten Krieges,* (Bonn: Report, 2000).

13

EU–NATO relations after the Cold War

Hanna Ojanen[1]

NATO plays a special role as an institution of transatlantic relations. It is a defence alliance, and defence is a field in which the two sides, Europe and the USA, have interest in cooperating and where they are not competing against each other. This is how it has been for quite some time and how it still is. Defence still has a uniting function that few other policy fields would have. What has changed since the time of the Cold War, however, is that defence is no longer a monopoly of NATO, notably because of the development of the European Security and Defence Policy (ESDP). This chapter analyses the impact of this change on EU–NATO relations and, on a wider scale, on transatlantic relations.

Basically, the end of the Cold War put an end to a division of labour that had existed between NATO and the EU. The term 'division of labour' may not have been used then, but, factually, there was one in existence. In short, it stemmed from the different fields of the two organizations. One was a military alliance, the other an economic–political community, later becoming a political union. Thus, the difference between the two was clear, when it came to what tasks they would undertake.

What happens at the end of the Cold War is that both organizations change. NATO starts moving away from territorial defence as a main task. The EU, in turn, starts moving towards territorial defence. The two meet each other in the middle, in the field of crisis management that comes to be seen for both as an important part of their activities and international presence. For a while, the Western European Union (WEU) acted as a contact point of some sort between the two. Gradually, however, it faded away and a suitable form for direct relations between the EU and NATO had to be found.

This has not been easy: EU–NATO relations have been for the past 10 years a continued topic of political debate and controversy. This chapter delineates their relationship from where it started to how it was subsequently regulated, and proceeds to looking at what problems have been identified in this relationship. It is argued that understanding the true nature of these problems is a precondition for solving them. For this, it is helpful to try to bring up not only the explicit problems but also the implicit ones behind them, explaining both the evident and the veiled in debates on the EU and NATO and their common future.

While looking at the relations between the EU and NATO as relations between two organizations, or two collective actors in the field of security policy, this chapter also makes some assumptions and ontological claims. For an analysis of international relations where nation-states still are seen to be the main actors, organizations such as the two in focus here do not constitute real actors. Not being capable of independent action, they would then not be able of developing a relation between themselves, either. This chapter therefore assumes that they are independent actors and that their relations are a meaningful object of analysis. While doing so, the chapter also aims at contributing to the debate on multilateralism. It outlines a reading of the problems in EU–NATO relations as instances of the limits of effective multilateralism.

End of the Cold War, end of separation

During the Cold War, there clearly was a division of labour between the EU and NATO, even though it might not have occurred to anyone to call it such. The two simply operated in different fields and had different purposes. They essentially had different tasks, and so there was no need for them to cooperate or indeed be linked to each other in a particular way. On the contrary, it was seen that it would be better that they would not have any relations – in order to maintain the two organizations' nature and role.[2]

NATO was certainly a central part of the context in which the EC and later the EU grew. Knud Erik Jørgensen suggests that the absence of a European defence policy and a European army during the Cold War might have been the result of a very conscious political will to avoid such initiatives. In the Cold War bipolar environment, they might have risked a severe destabilization of international relations.[3]

The end of the Cold War meant also the end of traditional defence alliances – either the end of the organization as such, as for the Warsaw Pact, or the end of the most traditional *raison d'être*, as for NATO (and WEU). It also seemed to mean the end of specialization in the sense that both the EU and NATO started enlarging their fields of activity, starting to overlap more and more in what came to be called 'crisis management'.

From the point of view of NATO, it was a question of reassessing the threats. For the EU, the end of the Cold War meant a step towards security and defence cooperation, which coincided with the birth of the European Union. Why this direction was taken is an interesting question as such. Was there need for a new actor in this field? Or was there something inherent in the process of European integration that, in suitable external conditions, would simply lead to such a development? One way of explaining this is to see that disagreement with the USA leads to increased need to cooperate among the Europeans.[4] This might particularly apply to the period between 2003 and 2008. The formation of European defence policy within the EU has also been interpreted by scholars like Barry Posen as the EU balancing against the powerful position of the USA: military and defence unity would make the USA take the EU more seriously.[5] Further, the fact that US troops in Europe have been reduced, including in the Balkans, and installations closed (such as the Keflavík base in Iceland), whereas the new structures in Central and Eastern Europe are only skeleton structures with little permanent personnel,[6] might be a reason for developing European alternatives.

The chronological history of the ESDP is well known but not necessarily as logical as how it often is described. Even though the Maastricht Treaty of 1991 already defined the Common Foreign and Security Policy (CFSP) with the goal of a common defence, the actual start of the EU's transformation into a security and defence political actor can be located in the Amsterdam Treaty of 1997 (which entered into force in 1999). It brought new tasks for the Union in the form of the so-called Petersberg tasks, or tasks of crisis management, that is humanitarian tasks, rescue operations, peacekeeping and the tasks of combat forces in crisis management, including peacemaking. Such tasks were new to the organization, and demanding ones, too, as the EU did not have the capabilities required for them, such as combat forces. In December 1999, the decision was made to start putting together crisis management troops. There was also need for new decision-making and advisory organs: the Political and Security Committee (PSC), the EU Military Committee and the EU Military Staff. Many saw the physical presence of the military in the EU buildings as an important sign of change. Even more importantly, though, these new structures together with the new practice of EU Defence Ministers' meetings – even when informal – paved the way for the whole defence administrations and the defence forces of the Member States to enter the EU and its decision-making.

With the new means available, the EU started its first civilian and military crisis management operations in January 2003. At that point, it did not yet have a strategy or an idea of what it was to do with these capabilities. Again, in a sense, the development was not too logical: first came the tasks, then the means; first the operations, then the strategy. Indeed, the EU Security Strategy (ESS) was approved in December 2003[7] and is still the basic document describing the EU as a global security policy actor (cf. report on its implementation, December 2008[8]).

In 2004, the Constitutional Treaty was formally adopted with several new initiatives for what is now the European Security and Defence Policy (ESDP). Even though the treaty as such never entered into force, the contents were carried over to the Lisbon Treaty, and some of these were implemented long before its entrance into force,[9] notably the Battle Groups and the European Defence Agency (EDA). The tasks of the EDA are developing defence capabilities, promoting defence research and technology as well as armaments cooperation, and creating a competitive European Defence Equipment Market, and, finally, strengthening the European Defence, Technological and Industrial Base.[10] These functions relate to improving Europe's defence performance. More specifically, the agency works for 'a more comprehensive and systematic approach to defining and meeting the capability needs of the European Security and Defence Policy', to 'promote European defence-relevant research and technology', to promote European cooperation on defence equipment, both to contribute to defence capabilities and as a catalyst for further restructuring the European defence industry, and to work 'in close cooperation with the Commission' on steps towards an internationally competitive market for defence equipment in Europe. Finally, even joint strategic planning has been developing in the civil–military cell at the EU Military Staff and the Operations Centre. To what extent these developments have been paralleled in NATO is tackled below.

In all, the end of the Cold War thus brought the two organizations together. In theory, this is an excellent instance of an interesting new phenomenon of international relations: organizations that interact and that have to interact, even though they were not originally created with that task in mind. In such a situation, they face a need to develop rules for their interaction. In that very interaction, then, both emerge as something more than mere cooperation partners: they reveal themselves as autonomous actors jealous of their own decision-making rights and image. In practice, then, we have a situation that is in many ways problematic: the relations between the two do not seem to work too well. But just how problematic they are and what the problems really are is contested.

The role of the WEU

The story of the relations between the EU and NATO could not be told without taking into account the role of WEU. WEU can be seen as a repository of defence commitments, or a reserve actor; its history can be looked at as a rehearsal of relations with NATO, task expansion, enlargement and new structures – later repeated by the EU. It can also be an example of how difficult it can be to get rid of existing organizations and thus it tells something about the organizations' potential hidden functions.

WEU is based on the 'Brussels Treaty on Economic, Social and Cultural Collaboration and Collective Self-Defence', of 17 March 1948, by Belgium, France, Luxembourg, the Netherlands and the United Kingdom (the Federal Republic of Germany and Italy were invited to join later and the treaty was amended by the Protocol signed in Paris on 23 October 1954). It thus had general integrationist goals that then narrowed down to more purely defence-related issues. Such a specialization was problematic when, at the end of the Cold War, the very need for military alliances stemming from the old bloc divisions was questioned. Indeed, both NATO and WEU needed to broaden and renew their profiles, finding new tasks and identity. Moreover, WEU needed closer links to NATO in order to find the necessary capabilities for its new tasks, and thus to be credible in its new activism. For NATO, WEU served as its 'European pillar', a way of enhancing European commitment to common goals.

The Atlantic Alliance Summit gave in January 1994 its full support to developing the European Security and Defence Identity (ESDI) within NATO[11] and strengthening WEU; WEU-led operations using NATO assets were made possible, and the relations between the two organizations were developed by, for example, organizing joint Council sessions and signing a security agreement to facilitate the exchange of classified information and practical cooperation. The operational role of WEU was defined in the Petersberg declaration of 1992 where the tasks of the organization were extended from common defence to humanitarian and rescue tasks, peacekeeping tasks, tasks of combat forces in crisis management, including peacemaking. For these tasks, WEU did not dispose of forces or permanent command structures of its own, but military units (FAWEU's, Forces answerable to WEU) and headquarters were to be made available to WEU on a case-by-case basis, designated by the Member States and composed of national units as well as multinational formations. In addition, WEU could also use NATO assets and capabilities. The institutional structure of WEU was completed by a Planning Cell, a Situation Centre, a Satellite Centre and an Institute for Security Studies. WEU did undertake some operations,[12] but when the fiftieth anniversary of WEU was approaching in 1998, the topic of the day was already the fate of the organization and the possibility that it might be dismantled, as the treaty gives an opportunity for this after 50 years since its signing.

From the point of view of the EU, the deepening of the relations between WEU and the EU was one of the basic ways to develop the CFSP. WEU was the shortest way to military capabilities. At the same time, the EU was to be guaranteed the political decision-making right over WEU. Even though WEU itself voiced opposition to subordination,[13] the two organizations drew closer throughout the 1990s and, eventually, an agreement on WEU's gradual dismantling was achieved. WEU was first linked to the EU in the Maastricht Treaty. According to article J.4.2, the EU can request WEU 'to elaborate and implement decisions and actions of the Union which have defence implications'. At the same time, it had a double identity. From 1991, WEU was developed 'as the defence component of the EU and as the means to strengthen the European pillar of the Atlantic

Alliance. To this end, it will formulate common European defence policy and carry forward its concrete implementation through the further development of its own operational role'. The *rapprochement* also included the WEU Council and Secretariat-General moving from London to Brussels in January 1993.

The Amsterdam Treaty confirms WEU's role as an 'integral part of the development of the Union'. It provides the EU with access to an operational capability, complementing its own diplomatic and economic means for undertaking the Petersberg tasks now incorporated in the Treaty on European Union.[14] The Union will 'avail itself of' WEU to elaborate and implement decisions and actions of the Union which have defence implications. Yet, the Amsterdam Treaty also contains the goal of merging the EU and WEU: '[T]he Union shall accordingly foster closer institutional relations with the WEU with a view to the possibility of the integration of the WEU into the Union, should the European Council so decide'. The two declarations annexed to the treaty concerning WEU and the enhancing of cooperation between the two organizations contain indications of measures to be developed by the two to pull the EU and WEU closer, such as improving the compatibility of decision-making procedures, organizing joint meetings and harmonizing the presidency cycles.

Views on how to organize WEU–EU relations had ranged from the idea of political subordination[15] to complete merger. Belgium, France, Germany, Italy, Luxembourg and Spain presented in March 1997 a joint document on the gradual integration of WEU into the EU. It would take place in three phases. First, one would lay the foundations of a common European defence policy and harmonize the rules and procedures of both organizations. Second, the EU would assume the decision-making power to initiate military action, while WEU would be responsible for its implementation. The use of, for example, the WEU Situation Centre and the Satellite Centre by the EU should be furthered. In the final third phase, the competences of the institutions and bodies of WEU would be transferred to the relevant institutions of the EU.[16] This proposal was later supported by Austria, Greece, the Netherlands and Portugal, but 'strongly opposed' by Denmark, Finland, Ireland and Sweden, which were not prepared to go further than integrating the Petersberg tasks, and especially by the United Kingdom, afraid to jeopardize the transatlantic security guarantees.[17] In the end, a compromise presented by Finland and Sweden was instead adopted: the Petersberg tasks were transferred to the EU, but WEU's territorial defence mission was not.

In the Cologne European Council of June 1999, the issue was no longer WEU–EU merger but transferring some of the WEU structures to the EU, those that would be needed in the area of the Petersberg tasks. The Council also expressed the aim to take the 'necessary decisions' by the end of the year 2000; '[I]n that event, the WEU as an organization would have completed its purpose'.[18] The 'funerals' took place on 13 November 2000. Article V and the whole treaty stayed there, as well as the WEU's parliamentary assembly, the European Security and Defence Assembly.[19] Operational units such as the satellite centre in Spain were transferred to the EU.

Regulating the EU–NATO relationship

Once WEU was no longer there as a bridge between the EU and NATO, direct relations between the two had to be organized. After long negotiations, an agreement between the EU-15 was achieved at the Feira summit of June 2000 on the principles that

NATO–EU relations should follow: (a) consultation and cooperation between the two must take place in full respect of the autonomy of EU decision-making; (b) as the goal is to ensure efficient crisis management, the EU's objectives in military capabilities and NATO's defence capabilities improvement will be mutually reinforcing; (c) the two organizations are of different nature, and this will be taken into account; (d) the cooperation agreements shall reflect the fact that both organizations deal with each other on an equal footing; and (e) no member state of any of the organizations will be discriminated against.[20] Similarly, the EU–NATO declaration of 2002 talks about 'strategic partnership', acknowledges that the two are of a different nature, have their own interests and act with respect for one another based on their autonomy of decision-making. The declaration does not indicate whether these differences would lead to any possibility of a division of labour.[21]

The 'Berlin Plus' agreements, a set of cooperation agreements between the two organizations (the name refers to earlier NATO–WEU agreements) was finalized in 2003. One of the main ideas in these agreements was that the EU leans on NATO for the elements that clearly are of traditional NATO domain: the agreement includes the presumption of availability to the EU of NATO capabilities and common assets, access to NATO planning for EU crisis management operations, NATO command structures for EU-led operations, and procedures of release, monitoring, return and recall of NATO assets and capabilities, and consultations in case of EU-led operations making use of NATO assets. It also includes exchange of classified information between the two. The principle that the relations should respect the different natures of the two organizations was again repeated. The agreements have, however, led to a number of disagreements on their interpretation, including on what the assets in question are, or on which of the two would first take the decision to intervene (the 'first refusal' right).[22]

Why was there a need for a cooperation agreement? In addition to the simple reason that it would be better if the two cooperated than if they did not, there might be other reasons for having a cooperation agreement, too. Barry Posen argues that according to the Pentagon, the purpose of NATO cooperation with the EU through the 'Berlin Plus' procedure was to prevent the creation of an EU counterpart to SHAPE (the Supreme Headquarters Allied Powers Europe) and a separate EU army.[23] Thus, the challenge that NATO perceived to emanate from the EU could also serve as a basic reason for cooperation arrangements.

What does the relationship look like? When looking at how the EU perceives NATO, different images of the relationship emerge from different documents. The EU treaties, including the Lisbon Treaty, strongly reflect NATO's traditional position and role as Europe's main defence organization. NATO obligations have primacy over any EU arrangements. However, when we look at the ESS, even though NATO is praised there is an 'important expression' of the transatlantic relationship, the document mentions a mere 'strategic partnership between the two organizations in crisis management'.[24] NATO, then, would be calling for partnership, acknowledging the need for a stronger relationship with the EU.[25]

However described, the foremost practical problem perceived in the relations between the two has been unnecessary duplication.[26] Thus, the analysis of the EU–NATO relationship has accordingly concentrated quite a lot on how to avoid (too much) duplication and how to find, instead, a way of meaningfully dividing the tasks between the two organizations. For an optimist, there would be a good possibility here for efficient cooperation. The two organizations complement each other, work for the same goals and purposes, but bring different strengths. In short, the EU would bring in civilian capabilities, a broad spectrum of different tools to be used in external relations and elements of supranationality in keeping its Member States committed. NATO, then, would bring in military capacities, planning and command capacities, and US presence. Ideally, then, the two could divide the crises between themselves, either following a geographical division by regions or the phases of a crisis, whereby one of the two, the EU, would concentrate on preventing crisis and on post-conflict reconstruction needed after a crisis, and the other, NATO, would concentrate on the actual crisis management with military means. Many have indeed advocated such a specialization of roles and division of labour that would be based on the relative strengths of both organizations, and, thus, on the differences in their nature (which, after all, have been repeatedly referred to in all the documents). Thus, for instance, peacekeeping and stability tasks could be assigned to the EU, and high-intensity combat operations to NATO. Further, collective defence tasks and US participation, defence reform and the role of a 'reserve' presence in case the security situation in a given conflict area deteriorates would fall on NATO, whereas the EU's specialities would be a way of fusing civil and military components and making crisis management operations part of the Union's integrated approach (as in the Balkans) rather than seeing them as separate operations.[27]

Transatlanticism would thus be a defining contribution or task of NATO to European security policy. But even here, some changes might take place if a EU–US partnership were to develop. For instance, Sven Biscop argues that a broader EU–US partnership is needed than the one found in NATO, since the latter covers only the limited politico-military field. As such, it is not the most suitable forum to discuss EU–US cooperation in all other areas. Biscop goes on to argue that US willingness to accept the EU as the primary interlocutor, rather than 'attempting to steer EU policies by way of bilateral contacts with individual Member States',[28] could be increased by developing the state-like features of the EU in external relations, such as the EU 'Foreign Minister', empowered High Representative and its External Action Service now included in the Lisbon Treaty.

Yet, many also argue that such a division of labour is not only difficult to achieve but should not even be aimed at. Specializing too much may make organizations less responsive, less flexible and actually decrease their capacity for cooperation.[29] A division of labour between the EU and NATO would leave Europe dependent on the USA for global security, and reduce its ability to influence US policy and global events. It would also remove the incentive for Europe to develop deployable forces capable of conducting high-intensity combat operations beyond its own borders, thus perpetuating the current capability gap.[30] Even more, division of labour, responsibilities and risks would ultimately divide the allies politically.[31] Division of labour can be also be experienced politically as giving rise to subordination or the loss of joint decision-making power.[32]

Temptations of imitation: running into problems

In practice, the two organizations started becoming more and more similar to each other instead of cultivating the differences between them. There are several reasons for such a development. They imitate each other and are curious to learn from each other, or do not want the other to be perceived as more efficient. What has taken place in recent years is that the two have started going to the same places, following each other to the Balkans, to Sudan, to Afghanistan, to the Somali coast. They have also developed the same means, notably rapid reaction forces. They now have overlap in planning, and, with the Lisbon Treaty, also two partially overlapping mutual defence clauses. After all, they have more or less the same members and exist in the same world, so they would also tend to have a similar view as to what missions and what tools are legitimate or serve their own legitimacy.

What has taken place in practice between the two organizations is, first, certain devolution of tasks from NATO to the EU, or the EU taking over some of NATO's functions, notably as regards crisis management operations in Europe, but also in the defence-related planning of the Member States. The EU's military operation in Macedonia (2003) made use of NATO's assets and capabilities. The military operation EUFOR Althea in Bosnia-Herzegovina (2004) was originally also a NATO operation. In Somalia, the order was reversed as the EU went in first, followed by NATO.[33] The EU launched the military operation EU NAVFOR Somalia (operation 'Atalanta') to contribute to the protection of vessels delivering food aid of the UN World Food Programme (WFP) to displaced persons in Somalia as well as to the protection of vulnerable vessels cruising off the Somali coast, and to the deterrence, prevention and repression of acts of piracy and armed robbery off the Somali coast.[34]

Both also tend to develop the same means. The development of rapid reaction forces would be a case in point. The NATO Response Force (NRF), initiated by the US Secretary for Defense Donald Rumsfeld, was launched at the Prague Summit in November 2002. The idea was that of a highly ready and technologically advanced force that can be deployed wherever, and across the whole spectrum of NATO tasks, and as a demonstrative force also. It would also have an important internal function in being the driving engine of NATO's military transformation. In practice, the NRF has thus far contributed to vigilance and disaster assistance (for instance, protection of the 2004 Summer Olympics in Athens, support to the Afghan presidential elections in September 2004, assisting the USA in dealing with the aftermath of hurricane Katrina and the disaster relief effort in Pakistan[35]). Yet, the NRF has suffered from problems in getting the numbers right, and the goals are now already very much reduced. The very small number of American contingents became one of the obstacles. The decisions to deploy the NRF following hurricane Katrina or the Pakistani earthquake were difficult to reach; for instance, France objected, stating that NATO should concentrate on military tasks only.[36] In October 2007, NATO defence ministers acknowledged that the NRF has not delivered on its original intentions, leaving its future in doubt.[37] On the EU side, the same story unfolded just a couple of steps behind. In November 2003, Britain and France suggested the creation of EU Battle Groups (EUBGs) – a similar on-call arrangement albeit starting off smaller than the NRF. The full operational capability of the EUBGs was achieved on 1 January 2007, but they have not yet been used in operations. The reasons for this seem to be mainly financial.

There has also been some spreading of institutional innovations[38] from NATO to the EU: NATO was the inspiration behind the EU's new structures for military crisis management, notably the Military Committee, in addition to providing common standards aimed at enabling military cooperation.[39] Conversely, NATO also seems interested in some aspects of the EU. Ideas on how to reinvigorate the Alliance have often come from the EU model. For example, it has been argued that the agenda of the organization needed to be broadened à la EU, that it would need a new mandate, more capabilities, and a reform of its structures and governance.[40] There have been proposals of increasing the flexibility of NATO decision-making through mechanisms such as constructive abstention[41] or qualified majority voting to enhance the effectiveness of NATO decision-making with a larger number of members.[42]

In a sense, supranationality might thus be a comparative advantage of the EU. Some even argue that it is the EU's supranational character that could in the end save NATO.

Larrabee puts forth a concrete expression of this when arguing that the only way to increased European military capability is a greater degree of European defence integration: this is the only way to free up the investment funds needed for a transformation of European forces.[43] De Wijk argues that the very survival of NATO depends largely on the development of credible European military capabilities. As increases in national budgets are unlikely, funds can only be found by striving for a common defence, for example removing defence bureaucracies by developing a centralized defence bureaucracy in support of supranational decision-making.[44] Also role specialization and commonly owned capabilities are needed. Without supranational authority, a country not willing to deploy its capabilities could effectively block the entire operation. Such a supranational approach is by definition only possible through the EU.

Here, institutional innovations might also spread the other way. The influence of NATO might slow down the development towards supranational decision-making in EU defence. A difference between security and defence on the one hand and other policy fields on the other would be perpetuated also in that while a pronounced role of NATO and/or of the USA could be welcome in the former, it would not be possible for the latter. In the absence of such an influence, there would in all likelihood be increasingly strong links between the different policy domains.[45]

The EU's civilian crisis management capabilities have also inspired NATO. A widening of the scope of NATO activities towards the civilian side has led to suggestions of increasing cooperation with the EU. Helga Haftendorn sees NATO and the ESDP as each other's toolboxes, arguing that the 'Berlin Plus' could also be interpreted in the reverse sense of letting NATO use EU capabilities, and not only as letting the EU lean on NATO.[46]

In addition to crisis management tasks, the command and planning tasks would also seem to be overlapping more, even though the original agreements between the two organizations aimed at keeping these to NATO (and, at the same time, making these functions the real and effective link between the two). In December 2003, it was decided that the EU would establish a planning cell at SHAPE and that NATO would establish a liaison team at the EUMS (EU Military Staff).[47] Autonomous EU planning and command of operations was one of the critical elements that was seen to go against the role of NATO (see the responses to the 'Chocolate summit' of France, Belgium, Germany and Luxembourg in April 2003). Originally, there were two options for EU operations: in a so-called 'autonomous' operation, the EU makes use of facilities provided by any of the five Operation Headquarters (OHQs) currently available in the European Member States. The second option was through recourse to NATO capabilities and common assets (under the 'Berlin plus' arrangements). Since 1 January 2007, the EU has a third option for commanding, from Brussels, missions and operations of limited size, for the new EU Operations Centre within the EUMS is ready (using some EUMS core staff, as well as some extra 'double-hatted' EUMS officers and so-called 'augmentees' from the Member States).[48] The EU–NATO Capabilities Group started in May 2003 to coordinate the work of the two on capabilities, but became mere information exchange due to political difficulties between the North Atlantic Council (NAC) and the PSC.[49]

Instead of specialization, thus, the two would seem to have become more similar. In any case, the two organizations seem to shape each other to an unprecedented degree. They have an interest in how the other organization can further its own goals; they have an interest in maintaining their autonomy; and they have an interest in imitating whatever might emerge as a comparative advantage in institutional innovations, roles, tasks and power or authority. Both must demonstrate their added value and comparative advantages in crisis management, and even develop the same tools to meet the same needs.[50] Neither organization would like to give up its activities or functions, either, in order not to appear ill-prepared to confront different crisis situations.[51]

The two might have similar goals also because of legitimacy concerns: it is in their interest to have tasks that are generally perceived as legitimate, such as pursuing the goal of democratization (Sjursen, for instance, points out NATO's need to present its purposes and forge a basis of legitimacy for itself through democracy[52]). Other similar goals would be crisis management, spreading of stability through enlargement, and Security Sector Reform (SSR). While spurring each other, they, too, run into the same problems, notably in finding resources and in generating rationale for the rapid reaction forces. Finally, coordination (or lack of it) becomes a new problem on top of the existing ones, as in the case of Sudan. In April 2005, the African Union was calling for help; there was no formal discussion between the EU and NATO, some EU countries offering airlift through NATO, others through the EU. It took a month to discuss the options and then another month to agree on how to coordinate the actions, with, however, the end result being duplication. Later, however, joint EU–NATO headquarters were established in Addis-Ababa.[53]

Problems reconstructed

EU–NATO relations, thus, led to quite a number of problems, prompting the NATO Secretary General in 2006 to say that one of his main goals would be to 'to break the deadlock in the NATO–EU relationship and get away from replicating each others' initiatives'.[54] Replication and deadlock have frequently been pointed out as the main problems in EU–NATO relations.

Replication was referred to above as imitation. Overlapping profiles, tasks and memberships lead to synchronization problems and loyalty quandaries. Toje takes up the failures to synchronize the capability goals and points out the problem that countries would not be, for instance, ready to commit helicopters for the EU as they are afraid that NATO would ask why such resources are not already deployed in Afghanistan.[55]

Deadlock, then, refers to the problems on a high political level that effectively hamper efforts at remedying the situation. It was thought that the formal framework for dialogue would be meetings between the PSC and the North Atlantic Council (NAC), but that has not quite worked. Informal meetings do take place.[56] When the ambassadors meet, they are only authorized to discuss joint EU–NATO operations, of which there is only one, ALTHEA in Bosnia, and select capability initiatives. Issues like Afghanistan are not on the agenda. The explicit, stated reason for this are the relations between Cyprus and Turkey, blocking and counter-blocking each other.[57] In practice, the situation causes problems when, for instance, EU missions in Afghanistan and Kosovo are denied military protection from NATO.[58]

Various solutions have been proposed, too. Toje as well as Valasek[59] see that the reintegration of France in NATO's integrated military structure could further help EU–NATO meetings becoming a forum for the really important issues to be discussed. Toje also sees that the move could help overcome the differences in organizational cultures, and the EU would learn from NATO on issues such as pooling capabilities and joint funding.[60] New possibilities for bringing the two closer to each other culturally could include exchange programmes for officers and greater overlap between the new NATO Strategic Concept and the ESS.[61] Furthermore, it has been argued that improving Turkey's possibilities to participate in the ESDP could help EU–NATO relations, too.[62] After all, EU–NATO relations are in practice more ESDP–NATO relations, as Jolyon Howorth has pointed out.[63]

How the US view on how European defence evolves is, of course, another central variable in the equation. Toje argues that a paradigmatic shift is taking place in American policy towards Europe, visible in the willingness to rethink the 'three D's'. The current American view would be that a stronger EU defence policy is complementary rather than competing with NATO.[64] The value that a stronger and more capable European defence brings has been recognized.[65] But even here, complications might appear. It is interesting to note that a positive American view might be counterproductive. For instance Strömvik notes that the influence of the USA: the EU Member States feel more need to cooperate with each other when they disagree with the USA, and less when they are in agreement.[66]

Yet, the basic problem of EU–NATO relations might not be that they are too different from each other and should be brought closer; it can equally well be that they are too similar to each other. The situation is indeed paradoxical. There are convincing arguments for saying that they should actually be similar in order to cooperate: if they specialize too much, they become less flexible. Furthermore, if they concentrate on different tasks, the different threat and risk perception then comes to divide the allies. Different tasks may also induce subordination and loss of decision-making autonomy if one organization is able to decide for the other in a given situation. But if the two then increasingly resemble each other, we come to a situation where the overlap and similarity are such that they lead to redundancy: why would one need two of the same?[67]

In addition to redundancy, growing similarity seems also to imply less variation as to options in crisis management. It would not seem that crisis management is significantly improving in quality or quantity. The two organizations might even be replicating each other's mistakes, absorbed as they are in imitating each other. In the end, crisis management itself is perhaps the problem: we might see NATO and the EU less and less involved in crisis management in the future, and looking for other, less frustrating and less complicated tasks to prove their own usefulness.

If the goal instead was to distinguish the two from each other, one way would be the development of a global NATO. Ivo Daalder (now the US Ambassador to NATO) and James Goldgeier have argued for NATO to open up its membership to any democratic state in the world that is willing and able to contribute to the fulfilment of NATO's new responsibilities (stability in the world and addressing global challenges). Australia, Brazil, Japan, India, New Zealand, South Africa and South Korea are the countries that could in the future become formal members of the Alliance. This would require other structural changes[68] but eventually mean that the EU and NATO would clearly have different tasks and scopes, and serve different purposes.

Understanding the true nature of problems in EU–NATO relations is indeed a precondition for solving them. One way of approaching them is to divide the problems in explicit and implicit ones as, indeed, the stated concerns often seem to hide behind them other, more complicated issues. Thus, the explicit problem of which of the two organizations has the right to first decide whether they are going to do something on a specific crisis might hide the implicit problem of both organizations having problems in doing anything, due to the shared problems of lack of political will and lack of resources. Similarly, the explicit problem of one country hindering high level cooperation might hide the implicit problem that the countries can now play one organization against the other and have thus increased their possibilities to cause institutional problems of all kinds.

It is also possible to see, as Francis Fukuyama does, that we simply have here an instance of 'multi-multilateralism', a situation of overlapping and competing institutions that might actually be of value and worth promoting also as a way of permitting a certain forum-shopping for the Member States.[69]

An alternative way of reading the problems in EU–NATO relations is to see them as instances of the limits of effective multilateralism. On one level, the problem is the necessity to organize for cooperation between two organizations in a way that does not undermine the autonomy of either of them. On another level, the problem is the necessity to ensure the effective functioning of the organizations without undermining the autonomy of the Member States.

Notes

1 The author would like to thank Dr Basil Germond for excellent editing.
2 Information received from Alyson J. K. Bailes (referring to the period around 1997–99).
3 Jørgensen, Knud Erik, 'European Foreign Policy: Conceptualising the Domain', in Walter Carlsnaes, Helene Sjursen and Brian White (eds), *Contemporary European Foreign Policy*, (London: Sage Publishers, 2004), pp. 47–48.
4 Strömvik, Maria, *To Act as a Union. Explaining the development of the EU's collective foreign policy*. Lund Political Studies 142, (Lund: Lund University, Department of Political Science, 2005).
5 Posen, Barry R., 'European Union Security and Defence Policy: Response to Unipolarity?', *Security Studies*, vol. 15, no. 2, 2006, pp. 149–86.
6 Asle Toje, 'The EU, NATO and European Defence – A Slow train coming', *Occasional Paper* 74, December 2008, EUISS, European Union Institute for Security Studies, Paris, 2008, p. 15.
7 *A Secure Europe in a Better World. European Security Strategy*. Brussels, 12 December 2003, www.consilium.europa.eu/uedocs/cmsUpload/78367.pdf (accessed 8 November 2009).
8 *Report on the Implementation of the European Security Strategy – Providing Security in a Changing World*, Brussels, 11 December 2008, S407/08, www.consilium.europa.eu/ueDocs/cms_Data/docs/pressData/en/reports/104630.pdf (accessed 8 November 2009).
9 The Lisbon Treaty entered into force on 1 December 2009.
10 See the EDA website, www.eda.europa.eu/genericitem.aspx?area=Background& id = 122 (accessed 11 November 2009).
11 On the ESDI, see Guillaume de Rougé's chapter in this volume.
12 See, for instance, G. Wyn Rees, *The Western European Union at the Crossroads. Between Trans-Atlantic Solidarity and European Integration*, (Boulder, CO: WestviewPress, 1998) and André Dumoulin and Éric Remacle, *L'Union de l'Europe Occidentale. Phénix de la défense européenne*, (Brussels: Bruylant, 1998).
13 For instance, the President of WEU Assembly, Lluis Maria de Puig, in *Le Figaro* (17 March 1998), opposed a rigid subordination to the EU and emphasized WEU's own capacity to act. In his view, it would be regrettable if countries that are 'little involved' would be in the position to paralyse it.
14 See also the WEU ministers' declaration, Brussels July 1997: agenda for WEU's future development, in *WEU today*, March 1998.
15 Political subordination to the EU was an intermediate (French) solution before a merger, acceptable to the United Kingdom, which is against it, *Europolitique*, No. 2084, 15 November 1995.
16 Paper submitted by France, Germany, Italy, Spain, Belgium and Luxembourg on gradual integration of WEU into European Union. *Europe*, No. 6941, 24–25 March 1997.
17 See Sven Biscop, 'The UK's Change of Course: a New Challenge for the ESDI', *European Foreign Affairs Review* vol. 4, no. 2, 1999, pp. 253–68 (here p. 255) and Helene Sjursen, 'Missed Opportunity or Eternal Fantasy? The Idea of a European Security and Defence Policy', in J. Peterson and H. Sjursen (eds) *A Common Foreign Policy for Europe? Competing Visions of the CFSP*, (London: Routledge, 1998), pp. 106–7.
18 Declaration of the European Council on strengthening the common European policy on security and defence, 3 June 1999, and Presidency report on strengthening of the common European policy on security and defence, Cologne. In Maartje Rutten (compiled), *From St.Malo to Nice. European defence: core documents*, Chaillot Papers 47, (Paris: WEU Institute for Security Studies, 2001).

19 For details, see www.assembly-weu.org/en/ (accessed 8 November 2009).
20 Presidency Conclusions, European Council, Santa Maria da Feira, 19–20 June 2000. In Rutten, *From St Malo to Nice*.
21 Natalia Touzovskaja, 'EU-NATO Relations: How Close to "Strategic Partnership"?', *European Security*, vol. 15, no. 3, 2006, p. 240.
22 Ibid., pp. 241–42.
23 Posen, 'European Union Security and Defence Policy', p. 183.
24 *A Secure Europe in a Better World. European Security Strategy*.
25 'NATO: Safeguarding Transatlantic Security'. Speech by Jaap de Hoop Scheffer, Secretary General of NATO, at Columbia University, 20 September 2005; first press conference of the new Secretary General Anders Fogh Rasmussen 'Je souhaite vivement voir une amélioration de la coopération entre l'OTAN et l'UE' on 3 August 2009, www.nato.int/cps/en/natolive/opinions_56776.htm (accessed 8 November 2009).
26 Together with decoupling and discrimination, it makes the 'three Ds' that since 1998 were the US preconditions for EU–NATO relationship. In US Secretary of State Madeleine Albright's words, the key was to avoid 'what I would call the Three Ds: decoupling, duplication and discrimination'. Quoted in Martin Reichard, *The EU–NATO Relationship. A Legal and Political Perspective*, (Aldershot: Ashgate, 2006), p. 146.
27 Touzovskaia, 'EU–NATO Relations', pp. 249, 254.
28 Sven Biscop,*The European Security Strategy*, (Aldershot: Ashgate, 2005), pp. 124–26.
29 Jolyon Howorth, 'Why ESDP is Necessary and Beneficial for the Alliance', in Howorth, Jolyon and John T. S. Keeler (eds) *Defending Europe: the EU, NATO and the Quest for European Autonomy*, (New York, NY: Palgrave Macmillan, 2003), p. 234.
30 F. Stephen Larrabee, 'ESDP and NATO: Assuring Complementarity', *The International Spectator* (Rome) vol. XXXIX, no. 1, 2004, pp. 68–69.
31 Sten Rynning, *NATO Renewed. The Power and Purpose of Transatlantic Cooperation*, (New York, NY: Palgrave Macmillan, 2005), pp. 167, 174–75, 180–84.
32 Expert statement at the Defence Committee of the WEU Assembly, quoted in Touzovskaia, 'EU-NATO Relations', p. 248.
33 NATO had an operation from October to December 2008 (Allied Provider) that involved counter-piracy activities off the coast of Somalia. Responding to a request from UN Secretary-General Ban Ki-moon, NATO naval forces provided escorts to UN WFP vessels transiting through the Gulf of Aden, where growing piracy has threatened to undermine international humanitarian efforts in Africa. Concurrently, in response to an urgent request from the African Union, these same NATO naval forces escorted a vessel chartered by the AU carrying equipment for the Burundi contingent deployed to AMISOM. See Basil Germond and Michael E. Smith, 'Interest-Definition and Threat-Perception in the EU: Explaining the First ESDP Anti-Piracy Naval Operation', *Contemporary Security Policy*, vol. 30, no. 3, December 2009, pp. 573–93. See also 'Terminated operations and missions: Counter-piracy in the Gulf of Aden and off the Horn of Africa', www.nato.int/cps/en/natolive/topics_52060.htm#Terminated (accessed 8 November 2009).
34 See information on EU NAVFOR Somalia at the Council webpage, http://ue.eu.int/showPage.aspx?id=1518& lang = en (accessed 11 November 2009).
35 On the NATO Response Force, see NATO webpage www.nato.int/issues/nrf/index.html (accessed 11 November 2009).
36 Touzovskaia, 'EU–NATO Relations', p. 245.
37 Toje, 'The EU, NATO and European Defence', p. 16.
38 Alyson Bailes uses the terms parallelism, mutual borrowing and osmosis; see *Through European Eyes. An Anthology of Speeches by Alyson J.K. Bailes*, (University of Iceland Press, 2009), pp. 93–94.
39 Details also including WEU, Lars Wedin, 'Tre år I EU:s militära stab', *Kungliga Krigsvetenskapsakademiens Handlingar och Tidskrift*, vol. 208, no. 1, 2004, pp. 119–54.
40 Simon Serfaty, 'Thinking About and Beyond NATO', in Gardner and Hall (ed) *NATO and the European Union. New World, New Europe, New Threats*, (Aldershot: Ashgate, 2004), p. 86.
41 Şaban Kardaş, 'Inserting flexibility into NATO? Lessons for NATO from the EU', *Perceptions* (Ankara), vol. III, no. 3, 2004, pp. 197–245.
42 Celeste A. Wallander and Robert O. Keohane, 'Risk, threat, and security institutions', in Helga Haftendorn, Robert O. Keohane and Celeste A. Wallander (eds) *Imperfect Unions. Security Institutions over Time and Space*, (Oxford: Oxford University Press, 1999), pp. 45–46.

43 Larrabee, 'ESDP and NATO', p. 67.
44 Rob de Wijk, 'The Reform of ESDP and EU-NATO Cooperation', *The International Spectator*, vol. XXXIX, no. 1, 2004, pp. 71, 76.
45 See Hanna Ojanen, 'The EU and Nato: Two Competing Models for a Common Defence Policy', *Journal of Common Market Studies*, vol. 44, no. 1, 2006, pp. 57–75.
46 Helga Haftendorn, 'Koloss auf tönernen Füßen. Die NATO braucht eine realistische neue Zweckbestimmung', *Internationale Politik*, vol. 60, no. 4, 2005, p. 83.
47 de Wijk, 'The Reform of ESDP and EU–NATO Cooperation', p. 79.
48 On the EU Operations Centre, see the Council webpage www.consilium.europa.eu/showPage.aspx?id=1211& lang = (accessed 11 November 2009).
49 Touzovskaia, 'EU–NATO Relations', p. 247.
50 Thierry Tardy, 'The EU and NATO as peacekeepers: Open Cooperation *versus* Implicit Competition', in Hanna Ojanen (ed) *Peacekeeping – Peacebuilding: Preparing for the future*, FIIA Report 14, (Helsinki: The Finnish Institute of International Affairs, 2006), p. 31.
51 See Hanna Ojanen, 'Inter-Organisational Relations: the New Facet of European Security Policy', in Tuomas Forsberg, Timo Kivimäki and Liisa Laakso (eds) *Europe in Context. Insights to the Foreign Policy of the EU,* (Helsinki: Finnish International Studies Association, Publications N. 1, 2007), pp. 105–19.
52 Helene Sjursen, 'On the identity of NATO', *International Affairs,* vol. 80, no. 4, 2004, pp. 693, 696.
53 Touzovskaia, 'EU–NATO Relations', pp. 251–52.
54 Speech by NATO Secretary General, Jaap de Hoop Scheffer, at the SDA Conference, Brussels, 6 November 2006.
55 Toje, 'The EU, NATO and European Defence', p. 20.
56 Ibid, p. 21, see also Sinan Ülgen, 'The evolving EU, NATO and Turkey relationship: implications for transatlantic security', EDAM Discussion Paper Series, no. 2, 2008.
57 See, e.g., Heinz Kramer, 'Turkish Accession Process to the EU: the Agenda behind the Agenda', *SWP Comments,* no. 25, October 2009.
58 Ibid p. 19.
59 Tomas Valasek (2008), *France, NATO and European defence.* CER Policy Brief, www.cer.org.uk/pdf/policybrief_nato_12may2008.pdf (accessed 11 November 2009).
60 Toje, 'The EU, NATO and European Defence', p. 20.
61 Ibid., p. 21.
62 Ülgen, 'The evolving EU, NATO and Turkey relationship'.
63 Jolyon Howorth, *Security and Defence Policy in the European Union,* (London: Palgrave Macmillan, 2007).
64 Toje, 'The EU, NATO and European Defence', pp. 13–14.
65 Ibid, p. 17; see, for instance, the Summit Declaration issued by the Heads of State and Government participating in the meeting of the North Atlantic Council in Bucharest on 3 April 2008, www.nato.int/cps/en/natolive/official_texts_8443.htm (accessed 11 November 2009).
66 Maria Strömvik, *To Act as a Union. Explaining the development of the EU's collective foreign policy,* Lund Political Studies 142, (Lund: Lund University, Department of Political Science, 2005).
67 See Anne Deighton, 'The European Security and Defence Policy', *Journal of Common Market Studies*, vol. 40, no. 4, 2002, pp. 719–41.
68 Ivo Daalder and James Goldgeier, 'Global NATO', *Foreign Affairs,* vol. 85, no. 5, 2006, pp. 105–13.
69 Francis Fukuyama, *America at the Crossroads. Democracy, Power, and the Neoconservative Legacy,* (New Haven, CT: Yale University Press, 2006), pp. 158, 172.

14
Security of the EU borders in the post-Cold War era

Axel Marion

Introduction

'Border' is a term with special meaning for today's Europeans. In the past, borders have been at the core of national identities and they embodied the very nature of security in a continent composed of hostile countries. But since the late 1940s, their gradual disappearance in the process of European integration has symbolized collective progress towards peace and prosperity. Borders are now closely linked to the dynamics of integration.[1] Thus, looking at European borders, one can reasonably affirm that few political and geographical matters have undergone such a tremendous historical evolution over the last century.

However, this fact does not mean that security concerns over borders have abated in the context of the European Union (EU). The changing role of internal borders does not mean that the need to reassure the European community about external threats has disappeared, but rather that this task has been shifted to the 'external borders', which are still a work-in-progress. This change has consequences for the role and behaviour of Member States, as well as the strategies and programmes of the EU. The aim of this chapter is to present an overview of the different actions and measures taken over the past two decades in this field, as well as to analyse some of the paradoxes of the current situation.

Prior to this, it is useful to review some basic assumptions that apply to this topic. First, border security cannot be dissociated from global security and foreign policy concerns. As the border is nothing more than the spatial end of a definite community, all policies that concern other communities impact the border – and the opposite is also true. One cannot study border security issues without including them in a broader EU security and foreign policy approach.

Second, the internal and external aspects of security are closely linked. This is particularly the case when speaking about the role of the border: internal preoccupations such as terrorism, organized crime or illegal immigration have to be partially managed by measures oriented towards 'the outside' of the national (or communitarian) territory, and the border is the very point where concrete actions can be taken. Most authors agree on this point,[2] and the European Commission has also clearly recognized this: 'There is a general recognition that internal and external aspects of EU security are intrinsically linked'.[3]

Third, it is necessary to remember that the external borders of Europe are not one single entity. To put it simply, the Schengen borders are not equivalent to the EU external borders, which in turn are not equivalent to the 'broad' continental external borders – if it is even possible to define them. For practical purposes, one shall limit the analysis to the current EU and Schengen areas, but one has to keep in mind that European boundaries are an evolving concept.

Fourth, the diversity of threats that face contemporary Europe make it difficult to provide an overall definition of 'security' and simple measures to improve it. From weapons of mass destruction to climate change, through terrorism, illegal immigration, organized crime and pandemics, current threats need different – but coordinated – answers. If one adds the fact that every country or organization has its own legitimacy, priorities and tools, one can easily imagine the extreme complexity of security management issues.

Finally, one has to place this topic within the general transatlantic security relationship. Although its role has regularly been contested since the end of the Cold War, NATO still remains at the core of Europe's military defence. Up to today, the United States has maintained an important position in the security framework of the European continent, above all as a 'reassurance' partner – a role that has been more or less reactivated by the diffuse Russian threat, particularly since the Georgian conflict of August 2008. At the same time, assuming that 'the traditional form of defence is a thing of the past'[4] or at least far less relevant since the end of the Cold War, the EU has progressively shifted its security concerns towards 'soft' issues such as 'human security', 'comprehensive security', 'peacekeeping' and so on,[5] especially regarding its immediate neighbourhood. If the military dimension has been renewed through the Common Foreign and Security Policy (CFSP) and consecutive European Security and Defence Policy (ESDP), it is not conceived as a first-line tool for border management, but rather as a projection capacity for beyond European territory. Thus, it appears that to fulfil the objective of securing Europe's borders, the strategy of the EU mainly consists of 'police', 'development' and other 'soft security' policies. In this chapter these later aspects will be concentrated on.[6]

Security beyond the borders: the neighbourhood and general foreign policy

Priority of the 1990s: stabilization of the neighbourhood

The end of the Cold War engendered a major change in the perception of the security threat from Eastern countries. The feared 'Soviet Bloc' suddenly became a variety of economically and politically weak countries and, thus, the policies towards them had to evolve radically. Apart from the nuclear weapons problem (which was managed quite efficiently in the 1990s), the main preoccupation was the social and democratic development of the EU's Eastern neighbourhood. The war in the former Yugoslavia embodied all the fears that Western countries had at the time. As Sens states, 'after the Cold War, the emergence of intrastate conflicts (especially in the Balkans) made the stabilization of the volatile periphery of the continent a security priority'.[7]

The CFSP, implemented by the Treaty of Maastricht in 1992 and constituting the second pillar of the EU, responded to this challenge by taking a broad approach to the external relations of the EU. Numerous initiatives were taken during the 1990s to address the issue of Eastern Europe's development. The 'Pact on Stability in Europe' (1993) was initiated to resolve the border conflicts within countries: 100 agreements were concluded under the authority of the International Court of Justice.[8] This was followed notably by the 'Partnership and Cooperation Agreements' (1994) proposed by the EU and signed by almost all Eastern European states to ensure their progressive development towards Western European standards. Of course, the prospect of accession was the major motivation for Eastern countries throughout this process. 'Area issues' also appeared in the mid-1990s: the 'Euro-Mediterranean Partnership' (or 'Barcelona Process', initiated in 1995) was intended to enhance cooperation and mutual understanding on both sides of the Mediterranean. Shortly after, Scandinavian states asked for a strategy towards the Baltic region, which led to the 'Northern Dimension Initiative' (1997). In 1999, the ESDP complemented the EU security system by enhancing the military aspects.

The twenty-first century's new threats: the European Security Strategy, the European neighbourhood policy and the EU's regional policies

The terrorist attacks of 11 September 2001 generated a new paradigm in European security concerns. Linked with the fact that Eastern Europe was more or less stabilized and, for some countries at least, on the way to accession, the focus shifted towards the southern borders where cultural misunderstanding and immigration problems were becoming more worrisome. The need for a global strategy in security matters was also clearly expressed, and this led to the adoption of the European Security Strategy (ESS) by the EU.

This document[9] was prepared and presented by CFSP head Javier Solana and adopted by the Council in December 2003. It addresses three main issues: 'building security in our neighbourhood', 'address[ing] the threats (terrorism, crime, etc.)' and 'help[ing] create an international order based on effective multilateralism'. Without forgetting the Eastern issues, the document clearly focuses on the new threats to international and regional security linked to the post September 11 context and the so-called 'war on terror', which drew attention to the South. However, acknowledging that the European community was divided on how to react (the best example being, of course, the Iraq war), this document found the basic compromises and thus was neither revolutionary nor very ambitious. However, one can also argue that this is the main strength of this strategy.[10] Five years later, the EU was able to confirm its overall direction, nevertheless stressing the fact that a great deal still had to be achieved in terms of implementing the policy, in particular bringing together the internal and external dimensions.[11]

One of the three objectives of the ESS ('building security in our neighbourhood') soon took shape with the adoption of a European Neighbourhood Policy (ENP) between 2003 and 2004.[12] With this policy, the EU wanted neighbours (both Eastern and Southern) to adopt 'European values' and EU standards in economic, political and social domains.[13] It was complemented by a financial instrument[14] aiming to simplify the different measures still in place. The main objective was to ensure the stability of Europe's borderland by creating what Romano Prodi (then President of the Commission) called 'a ring of friends'[15] or, to put it more simply, 'good neighbours'.[16] However, it should also be seen as 'a testing ground for the European Union's strategic ambitions to be taken seriously as an autonomous and powerful actor in international politics'.[17] In this sense, the ENP can be considered as an EU tool for conflict prevention and crisis management in its neighbourhood.[18]

Following the adoption of these documents, the EU proceeded to implement its global and regional policies. Of course, the 2004 and 2007 enlargements changed the nature of regional security. The need to strengthen links with the new neighbours at the borders led to the adoption of renewed Eastern Partnerships,[19] which created bilateral tracks for discussion about free trade areas and visa liberalization. The Eastern issue was also completed by a 'Black Sea Synergy' created in 2007 as a regional cooperation initiative.[20] However, today's tensions between Russia and the EU (following the Georgian conflict and the 'gas war') as well as the recurrent instability of Ukraine do not create good conditions for progress in this field.

As the situation in the East was nonetheless on the way towards normalization, relations with the South remained a high priority as the problem of emigration was still increasing in this area. Thus, in 2006 the Commission announced a particular strategy for the management of the southern border, especially devoted to the reaction to and prevention of illegal immigration.[21] This 'security' approach was complemented by a more political one as illustrated by President Sarkozy's 'Union for the Mediterranean', finally integrated in 2008 by the other Member States in the Barcelona Process.[22]

One cannot finish this overview without a brief look at the Constitutional process that has preoccupied the EU for the past five years. Even if the first constitutional treaty had not changed the nature and fundamentals of the EU's security strategy, it would have represented an important step towards the better integration of actors and means (for example by the creation of a High Representative for Foreign Affairs), although it was not perfect.[23] With the adoption of the Treaty of Lisbon, the EU will at least have the possibility of moving forward on several points and could even codify some aspects of border security.[24]

Security at the borders: Schengen and the external dimension of internal security policies

One definition of 'border' is the point – or line – where the inside meets the outside (and vice versa). This 'meeting role' has never been as pertinent as today in the European context: about 300 million travellers cross the external border every year.[25] At the same time, more than 160,000 illegal immigrants are spotted by border guards, the great majority on the 'Mediterranean front'.[26] These figures underline the importance of efficient border management in today's EU. This preoccupation is reflected in European public opinion: 55 per cent of the EU population claimed to be concerned with the control of external borders[27] (although only 20 per cent believe that it should be one of the three highest priorities of the EU in the security field[28]). The rate is higher in Southern European countries (Portugal 69 per cent, Spain 66 per cent, France 64 per cent and Italy 63 per cent),[29] reflecting even greater concerns about the problem in this region.

This situation undoubtedly calls for action at the national and European levels. Completing the above-mentioned 'global' security and foreign policy strategies, some border-related measures have progressively been taken. They all underline the importance of considering internal and external security matters together, and of coordinated action between the national and European levels.

The Schengen system

The first real attempt at establishing common management of the external borders is the Schengen system, which was created by the homonym Agreement of 1985 and developed by a convention in 1990, which entered into force in 1995. This treaty was indeed a 'border agreement', since its main purpose was to suppress internal border checks between signatory states. Of course, in order to guarantee the success of this goal, the system implied a common strategy and common practices at the external boundaries of this community. Thus, article 6 of the convention states that border checks at the external borders must be systematic, equivalent in all parts of the Schengen borders, and take into account the interests of all Schengen countries.

A particularity of 'Schengen' is that it was designed by five EC Member States – France, Germany, Belgium, the Netherlands and Luxemburg – outside the framework of the Community. It was only in May 1999 that the Schengen *acquis* (formed by the treaty, the convention and the related legal texts and practises) was integrated into the EU legal order.[30] This means that the Schengen borders have never been equivalent to those of the EU. Apart from the fact that two new Member States (Romania and Bulgaria) have to wait until their full entry into the Schengen system, two Member States have deliberately remained outside (UK and Ireland), whereas three non-EU states are part of the system (Iceland, Norway and Switzerland).

One of the main purposes of the Schengen system is the management of immigration, in particular visa and asylum seekers. Different tools have been created to achieve this goal, such as the Schengen Information System (SIS – a database including all illegal and 'problematic' immigrants, operational since 1995), 'Eurodac' (a database concerning the asylum seekers and illegal immigrants seeking entry in one Member State, operational since 2003) or the Visa Information System (VIS – a database including all visa seekers, fully operational in 2012[31]). At the operational level, a 'Schengen catalogue of best practices on external borders' was issued in 2002 – a tool without legal power but designed for more integrated management by all national border guards. Finally, a 'Schengen Facility' programme of 960 million Euros for the period 2004–6 was created to provide new frontier states with infrastructure, training, etc.

It is difficult at present to evaluate the efficiency of the Schengen system.[32] However, it is clear that it has greatly contributed to changing the nature and management of the EU external borders. The following figures about land borders can be underlined: in 1995, Germany and France assumed 98 per cent of their surveillance; by 2003, the percentage was reduced to 42 per cent. With the accession of Eastern countries and Switzerland now being part of Schengen, the rate of control of land borders for these two countries now approaches zero per cent.[33]

The external dimension of the Area of Freedom, Security and Justice

In conjunction with the Schengen process, the EU has tried to clarify its strategy for better integration of the internal and external security challenges. This has been managed in accordance with the general programmes of action in the Area of Freedom, Security and Justice (AFSJ): the Tampere Programme (1999) and The Hague Programme (2005). Whereas the former identified the external border as a 'cornerstone' of EU security,[34] the latter was much more comprehensive about measures to be taken towards the management of security 'outside'. This comprised a dozen propositions, including the reinforcement of supervision of the level of control at the borders and the establishment of a data collection system between Member States.[35]

The Hague Programme was further complemented by a strategy on its external dimension,[36] which stressed the following measures: geographic prioritization (distinguishing between EU candidates and neighbouring countries); differentiation (no 'one-size-fits-all' strategy); flexibility; cross-pillar cooperation; partnership; relevance of external actions (coherence between internal and external measures); added value (efficiency); and benchmarking (evaluation). Finally, the Commission recommended better coherence and coordination between all 'external' actors of the EU, and the establishment of a 'rapid reaction' capacity.

Despite these recommendations, the implementation of the Hague Programme has not been fully successful. An evaluation made in 2007 concluded that the implementation is 'mitigated' to 'unsatisfactory', although the Border Management Policy is quoted 'satisfactory' to 'good'.[37] As for the ESS, one can then consider that if the vision of the AFSJ programme is still valid, progress needs to be made for its goal to be realized.

Integrated border management and the FRONTEX agency

The general lack of coordination regarding security issues, and particularly border issues, compelled EU authorities to act. The Laeken European Council of December 2001 initiated discussions on so-called 'integrated border management'. This concept should bring a 'comprehensive approach to border problems across administrative and national dividing lines under the management of dedicated professional skills', or, more simply, assure that 'border procedures [are] governed by modern economic strategies rather than slow bureaucratic structures'.[38] Following the decisions of the Council, the Commission delivered its main recommendations[39] in this field.

One of the main obstacles towards an integrated system concerned the border guards: should they be placed directly under the management of the EU, or stay under the control of national authorities? The Commission and some Western countries (including France and Spain) preferred the first option, but Eastern members strongly opposed placing their forces under a 'common' control, as they remain chiefly concerned with their external land borders. The European Council finally adopted a plan for the management of the external borders in June 2002, giving up the idea of a unique corps but calling for better cooperation and common standards.

This led to the creation, in 2005, of a 'European Agency for the Management of Operational Cooperation at the External Borders of the Member States of the EU' – better known as FRONTEX. As described in its regulation, the Agency 'shall [...] provide the Commission and the Member States with the necessary technical support and expertise in the management of the external borders and promote solidarity between Member States'.[40] Its tasks include coordinating operational cooperation between the Member States, training national border guards, risk analysis, research and development and special assistance when required. Following a decision made by the Council, FRONTEX is only meant as a support for Member States, who continue to be responsible for the surveillance of their external borders.

The Agency was apparently needed, as its importance grew quickly. The budget more than doubled between 2006 and 2007 (from 19.2 to 42.1 million Euros). FRONTEX was also reinforced by the Hague Programme, essentially by the creation of pools of national experts who can provide support to Member States, and by the establishment of a community border management fund. Finally, on 11 July 2007 the European Council approved the creation of 'Rapid Borders Intervention Teams', under the authority of FRONTEX 'for the purposes of providing rapid operational assistance for a limited period to a requesting member state facing a situation of urgent and exceptional pressure [...]'[41]

However, the implementation of FRONTEX has been rather slow and has generated some frustration. In 2007, Commissioner Frattini complained that only one-tenth of the boats, helicopters and planes promised to FRONTEX had been effectively delivered.[42] More recently, the French Minister of Immigration Eric Besson insisted that the Agency should be strengthened.[43]

Preparing the next steps

In February 2008, the Commission released two communications paving the way for further developments.[44] Aware that the Schengen visa policy had created negative reactions and could potentially hinder the openness of European territory and economic activity, it proposed facilitating the border crossing for bona fide travellers, as well as creating an electronic system of travel authorization for regular (and 'recommendable') visitors. Concerning illegal immigration, the Commission suggested two new tools – a global entry/exit registration and a European border surveillance system – intended to complement the Schengen tools. In order to finance the current and future tasks related to border issues, the EU established the 'External Borders Fund' for 2007–13, with about 1.82 billion Euros available. These measures and figures are a sign of continuing – and surely growing – concern about the control and management of external borders.

Looking for coherence

The different European policies towards the security of external borders present some strengths but also great weaknesses, and, perhaps more accurately, show deep paradoxes. In the long term, one can assume that these paradoxes will become the greatest obstacles towards the achievement of coordinated, efficient and ethical management of the EU's external borders.

Institutional coherence

The lack of institutional coherence is undoubtedly the most visible weakness of EU border policies. The interactions between Member States on the one hand and the Commission on the other, but also the variety of programmes, systems and agents inside the EU machinery all work against efficiency, clarity of decision-making and the legitimacy of the actors. It is also important to recall that the EU and the Schengen system (although fully part of the EU) do not share the same borders or the same tools. The intervention of other actors in the field of Europe's security – mainly NATO and the United States – as well as the different approaches of European countries regarding global security issues (i.e. the Iraq war) further complicates the picture.

There have however been reactions to this situation. The fact that co-decision – that is to say the involvement of the European Parliament and the qualified majority votes at the Council – has applied since 2005 in the context of border control[45] is a step in the right direction. The intended merging of all databases into one single instrument can also be seen as a positive development (although it may pose problems in terms of operational exploitation[46]). Public opinion is also calling for more decision-making at the European level for border control (70 per cent) and asylum policies (63 per cent)[47] – that is, calling for more coherence in these fields. Finally, concerning the EU–NATO relationship, the

'Berlin Plus' agreements (2003) allowed a better basis of cooperation through a negotiated division of labour.

Furthermore, separate actions by some Member States, such as Schengen in 1985, can actually be seen as an advantage, as ideas are tested separately and are not integrated into the EU corpus unless they have proved their efficiency and usefulness. Schengen is thus often seen as a 'laboratory' for European construction (although this is challenged by some authors[48]). In this context, the Treaty of Prüm signed in 2005 by seven Member States (France, Germany, Belgium, The Netherlands, Luxemburg, Spain and Austria), with the aim of improving cooperation against terrorism, cross-border crime and illegal migration, can be seen as an opportunity as well as a threat to the creation of a common framework for border security. But in the end, 'the building of common schemes to shape [the EU Member States] common Near Abroad requires a post-national definition of security, and hence the definition and adoption of common priorities, a common discourse and common positions, actions and strategies'.[49]

'East–West' coherence

Although the enlargement and Schengen processes embody the 'reunification' of Europe, border management presents the risk of creating new dividing lines between East and West. The new Eastern Member States thus have the impression that their Western counterparts have little confidence in their ability to manage the external border. The proposal of the 'old' Member States to create a unique corps of border guards was a sign in that direction. Therefore, the burden-sharing principle that lies behind this issue is not perceived in the same way from both sides of the former 'iron curtain': Western states seek more operational supervision in exchange for their financial support, while Eastern states are clearly opposed to any 'foreign' involvement.[50]

Another aspect of this issue concerns the new 'ruptures' between old neighbours created by Schengen and the external border control. Countries like Poland and Ukraine, which were close during the communist era and shared a free-visa regime and cooperation policies during the 1990s, are now separated by a 'hard' border. This, of course, has a negative, even counterproductive, impact on regional policies (as we will see below), and furthermore on public opinion: it consolidates the impression that Western countries do not feel concerned by Eastern issues.[51] Conscious of the need to improve this situation, over the past few years the EU has issued some proposals concerning 'local border traffic' (allowing special conditions of cross-border traffic for people living within 30 km of the border[52]) or visa facilitation policies with Eastern neighbours.

This relational problem between Eastern and Western Europe – linked to the more general distrust of Western public opinion towards newcomers as was seen in the 'Polish plumber' controversy – is clearly a threat to continental integration. To prevent this, one should recall that the views of East and West are similar regarding numerous security-related topics, such as recognition that Eastern countries are not a threat to European security but on the contrary need security as well.[53] Unless this issue is seriously taken into account, the risk of a 'new curtain'[54] remains.

Coherence towards neighbours

One of the main achievements of the EU since the end of the Cold War has been the stabilization of its Eastern neighbourhood. There is no doubt that the opportunity to be part of this vast area of prosperity – and finally accessing to the EU – motivated democratic, economic and social progress. With its neighbourhood policy, the EU maintains its objectives of stabilization and development of the 'far' European East and Mediterranean countries.

However, security strategies and external border management often work against these goals. It is indeed difficult to 'sell' partnerships and prosperity to neighbours if they are seen (and described) as threatening and if their citizens are not welcome in the EU territory. By challenging the free movement of people, which was one of the main revolutions for the post-Soviet countries, the Schengen system and all other border-crossing restrictions are casting a shadow on the development process, which requires the openness of European borders.[55]

We should wonder in particular whether the EU is pushing the security measures 'at the borders' too far rather than taking preventive actions 'beyond the borders', and if there really is coordination between the two aspects (although the ESS itself underlines the fact that the benefits of prosperity should be shared with the EU's neighbours[56]). In the case of immigration, for example, knowing that this issue will continue to grow, it appears to most researchers that prevention measures (such as improving economic development in the countries of origin) will be more efficient than maritime patrols or land border guards to reduce the phenomena. The EU and Member State authorities should face this paradox and find an appropriate equilibrium in order to avoid long-term European schizophrenia on this issue.[57]

Coherence towards values

Last but not least, there remains a deep paradox between current border management and European core values – i.e. the rights of the citizen, rule of law, etc. The different tools introduced in the Schengen context (SIS, Eurodac, VIS) are questionable in terms of their efficiency, proportionality and respecting the private sphere.[58] The introduction of biometrics data in the system reinforces this issue. According to some scholars,[59] the main problems lie in the lack of information given to the population – in particular, the right of people who have been refused entry to appeal the decision – and the democratic deficit in this process (or in the EU in general). Thus, it has been underlined that it was probably easier to have 'freedom-restrictive measures' at the European level rather than at the national one, as political and social opposition is less developed.[60]

Added to the remarks concerning the relative tightening of the external borders, the overall picture of this 'securitizing' Europe does not exactly correspond to the one it wishes to portray. The EU seems to have chosen to emphasize – at least for the moment – 'Security' rather than 'Freedom' or 'Justice',[61] despite claims that it does not.[62] In the long-term, the choice can prove dangerous.

Conclusion

The security of European borders is managed by two main tools: the global foreign and neighbourhood policy and border-focused policies. Since the end of the Cold War, numerous initiatives have been taken in both directions in order to improve border security. If Eastern frontiers were the main priority in the 1990s, there has been a shift to southern borders at the beginning of the twenty-first century, since the Mediterranean embodies the burden of illegal immigration as well as fears of terrorism.

If the stabilization and development of Central and Eastern Europe through enlargement is — as of today — the greatest success of the EU foreign and security strategy, there are still great weaknesses in European policies on these issues. In particular, we have shown the multiple paradoxes that face the EU when talking about border and/or neighbourhood policies, such as institutional relations between the EU and the Member States, the different perceptions between Eastern and Western countries, the opposition between securitization of the borders and open relations with neighbours, and the potentially damaging impact of securitizing measures on European values.

What are the future prospects? Future enlargements, which will certainly 'bring the EU closer to troubled areas'[63] (such as Iraq and Iran if Turkey joins the EU), will certainly demand the reinforcement of border controls. The United States is also waiting for greater involvement from the EU in regards to regional and global security — especially since the beginning of the Obama administration.[64] Finally, new issues such as energy or climate change (not discussed in this chapter) could also impact the management of European borders in the near future. These challenges will need clear and assertive answers from the EU. In any case, we can hope that cooperation between Member States and respect of the EU's core values will remain at the heart of the decision-making processes.

Notes

1 See Peter Hobbing, 'Integrated Border Management at the EU Level', in Thierry Balzacq and Sergio Carrera, *Security Versus Freedom? A Challenge for Europe's Future*, (Aldershot: Ashgate, 2006), p. 155.
2 See notably Malcolm Anderson, 'Internal and External Security in the EU: Is There Any Longer a Distinction?' in Stefan Gänzle and Allan G. Sens (eds), *The Changing Politics of European Security — Europe Alone?*, (Basingstoke: Palgrave Macmillan, 2007), pp. 31–46.
3 European Commission, *A Strategy on the External Dimension of the Area of Freedom, Security and Justice*, COM (2005) 491 (Brussels, 12 December 2005), p. 5. In the same document (p. 4), the Commission points out that 'the external dimension of justice and home affairs contributes to the establishment of the internal area of freedom, security and justice and at the same time supports the political objectives of the European Union's external relations.'
4 Sven Biscop and Jan J. Andersson (eds), *The EU and the European Security Strategy, Forging a Global Europe*, (London: Routledge, 2008), p. 169.
5 The Petersberg Declaration of the West European Union (1992) is a cornerstone in this process, leading to what will be known as the 'Petersberg Tasks.' See Helene Sjursen, 'Security and Defence', in Walter Carlsnaes, Helene Sjursen and Brian White (eds), *Contemporary European Foreign Policy*, (London: SAGE Publishers, 2004), p. 65.
6 For a discussion of the EU's projection policies in its frontier areas and their impact on NATO, see the contribution in this volume by Basil Germond.
7 Allan G. Sens, 'The Changing Politics of European Security', in Gänzle and Sens, *The Changing Politics of European Security*, p. 4.
8 Frédéric Charillon, 'Sovereignty and Intervention: EU's Interventionism in its "Near Abroad"', in Carlsnaes, Sjursen and White, *Contemporary European Foreign Policy*, p. 256.
9 European Union, *A Secure Europe in a Better World — European Security Strategy* (Brussels, 12 December 2003).
10 See Sven Biscop, 'The European Security Strategy in context: a comprehensive trend', in Biscop and Andersson, *The EU and the European Security Strategy*, pp. 5–20.
11 European Union, *Report on the Implementation of the European Security Strategy — Providing Security in a Changing World* (Brussels, 11 December 2008).
12 The Commission issued several papers in this field, including in particular: *Wider Europe — neighbourhood: a new framework for relations with our eastern and southern neighbours*, COM (2003) 104 (Brussels, 11 March 2003), *Paving the way for a new neighbourhood instrument*, COM (2003) 393

(Brussels, 1 July 2003), *European Neighbourhood Policy strategy paper*, COM (2004) 373 (Brussels, 12 May 2004).
13 The ENP was intended for the following countries: Russia (which has refused to be part of it), Ukraine, Belarus, Moldova, Algeria, Egypt, Israel, Jordan, Lebanon, Libya, Morocco, Syria, Tunisia and the Palestinian Authority. It was extended to Georgia, Armenia and Azerbaijan in 2004. Romania, Bulgaria, Turkey and the Western Balkans were not included (as candidate countries or 'special case').
14 European Commission, *Proposal for a Regulation of the European Parliament and of the Council Laying down General Provisions Establishing a European Neighbourhood and Partnership Instrument*, COM (2004) 628 (Brussels, 2004).
15 Romano Prodi, 'A Wider Europe – a Proximity Policy as the Key of Stability', 2002, quoted in Stefan Gänzle, 'The European Neighbourhood Policy: A Strategy for Security in Europe?' in Gänzle and Sens, *The Changing Politics of European Security*, p. 110.
16 Karen E. Smith, 'The Outsiders: The European Neighbourhood Policy', in Balzacq and Carrera, *Security Versus Freedom?*, p. 211.
17 Roland Dannreuther, 'The European Security Strategy's Regional Objective: The neighbourhood policy', in Biscop and Andersson, *The EU and the European Security Strategy*, p. 63.
18 Gänzle, 'The European Neighbourhood Policy: A Strategy for Security in Europe?', p. 113.
19 European Commission, *Eastern Partnership*, COM (2008) 823 (Brussels, 3 December 2008).
20 European Commission, *Black Sea Synergy*, COM (2007) 160 (Brussels, April 2007).
21 European Commission, *Reinforcing the Management of the EU's Southern Maritime Border*, COM (2006) 733, (Brussels, 30 November 2006).
22 European Commission, *Barcelona Process: Union for the Mediterranean*, COM (2008) 319, (Brussels, 20 May 2008).
23 See Milagros Alvarez, 'Common Security and Defence Policy in the Treaty Establishing a Constitution for Europe', in Gänzle and Sens, *The Changing Politics of European Security*, pp. 87–109.
24 Council of the European Union, *Consolidated versions of the Treaty on European Union and the Treaty on the functioning of the European Union* (Brussels, 30 April 2008): art. 77 (ex art. 62 TEC). '1. The Union shall develop a policy with a view to (c) the gradual introduction of an integrated management system for external borders'.
25 European Commission, *Preparing the next steps in border management in the European Union*, COM (2008) 69 (Brussels, 13 February 2008), p. 2.
26 In 2007, 163,903 illegal immigrants were detected. 80 per cent were detected in Spain, France, Greece and Italy. The figure increases slightly, especially at the southern border, according to FRONTEX (FRONTEX General Report 2007, pp. 14–15).
27 European Union, 'Awareness of key policies in the Area of Freedom, Security and Justice', *Flash Eurobarometer 252*, January 2009.
28 European Union, 'The role of the European Union in Freedom, Justice and Security polices areas', *Special Eurobarometer 290*, June 2008.
29 European Union, 'Awareness of key policies in the Area of Freedom, Security and Justice', *Flash Eurobarometer 252*, January 2009.
30 All the legislative corpus concerning the external border of Schengen is now compiled in the 'Schengen Border Code' (Regulation (EC) No 562/2006, 15 March 2006), which replaced part of the Schengen Convention and of the *acquis*.
31 European Commission, COM (2008) 69, p. 3.
32 Concerning SIS: Evelien Brouwer, 'Data Surveillance and Border Control in the EU: Balancing Efficiency and Legal Protection', in Balzacq and Carrera, *Security Versus Freedom?*, p. 140.
33 Hobbing, 'Integrated Border Management at the EU Level', p. 162.
34 One can also recall that for the period 1997–2003, 475.5 million Euros of the 888.5 million Euros available in the PHARE programme ('Justice and Home Affairs') were dedicated to border controls and customs. See Laura Corrado, 'Negotiating the EU External Border', in Balzacq and Carrera, *Security Versus Freedom?*, pp. 183–203.
35 See European Commission, *The Hague Programme*, COM (2005) 184 (Brussels: 10 June 2005).
36 European Commission, *A Strategy on the External Dimension of the Area of Freedom, Security and Justice*, COM (2005) 491, (Brussels: 12 October 2005).
37 European Commission, *Report on the Implementation of The Hague Programme for 2007*, COM (2008) 323 (Brussels: 2 July 2008).
38 Hobbing, 'Integrated Border Management at the EU Level', pp. 156–57.

39 European Commission, *Towards integrated management of the external borders of the Member States of the European Union* (Brussels: May 2002) and *A simple and paperless environment for Customs and Trade*, COM (2003) 452 (Brussels: 24 July 2003).
40 European Council, Regulation (EC) No 2007/2004 of 26 October 2004, art. 1, paragraph 3.
41 European Council, Regulation (EC) No 863/2007 of 11 July 2007, art. 1,1.
42 Stephan Keukeleire and Jennifer MacNaughtan, *The Foreign Policy of the European Union*, (Basingstoke: Palgrave Macmillan, 2008), p. 231.
43 *Communiqué: Eric Besson propose cinq mesures pour renforcer l'action de l'Union Européenne contre l'immigration irrégulière* (Paris: 18 September 2009)
44 European Commission, *Preparing the next steps in border management in the European Union*, COM (2008) 69 (Brussels: 13 February 2008) and *Examining the creation of a European Border Surveillance System* (EUROSUR), COM (2008) 68 (Brussels: 13 February 2008).
45 Council Decision 2004/927/EC.
46 Brouwer, 'Data Surveillance and Border Control in the EU', p. 150.
47 European Union, 'The role of the European Union in Freedom, Justice and Security polices areas', *Special Eurobarometer 290*, publication: June 2008.
48 Thierry Balzacq, Didier Bigo, Sergio Carrera and Elspeth Guild, 'The Treaty of Prüm and EC Treaty: Two Competing Models for EU Internal Security' in Balzacq and Carrera, *Security Versus Freedom?*, pp. 115–36.
49 Charillon, 'Sovereignty and Intervention', p. 261.
50 Hobbing, 'Integrated Border Management at the EU Level', p. 155–81.
51 'In Poland people entertain the fundamental suspicion that Western Europe is not interested in the region lying east of Germany' (Gesine Schwan, in 138th Bergedorf Round Table, 'Can the EU Ensure Europe's Security ?', 28–30 September 2007, Warsaw (Hambourg: ed. Körber-Stiftung, 2008), p. 39).
52 European Parliament and Council, Regulation (EC) No. 1931/2006 of 20 December 2006.
53 Jörg Monar, 'The external shield of internal security: the EU's emerging common external border management', in David Brown and Alistair J.K. Sheperd (eds), *The security dimensions of EU enlargement. Wider Europe, weaker Europe?* (Manchester: Manchester University Press, 2007), p. 67.
54 Gänzle, 'The European Neighbourhood Policy', p. 119.
55 Many authors stressed this paradox. See notably Keukeleire and MacNaughtan, *The Foreign Policy of the European Union*, p. 231–33; Dannreuther, 'The European Security Strategy's Regional Objective', p. 72–76; Charillon, 'Sovereignty and Intervention', p. 258.
56 'It is not in our interest that enlargement should create new dividing lines in Europe. We need to extend the benefits of economic and political cooperation to our neighbours in the East while tackling political problems there' (European Security Strategy, 2003), p. 8.
57 On the dichotomy between 'fortress Europe' and 'imperial Europe', see the contribution by Basil Germond in this volume.
58 See Juliet Lodge, 'Transparency, Justice and Territoriality: The EU Border Challenge', in Balzacq and Carrera, *Security Versus Freedom?*, pp. 257–77.
59 For example, Brouwer, 'Data Surveillance and Border Control in the EU', pp. 137–54.
60 Monar, 'The external shield of internal security', p. 54.
61 Keukeleire and MacNaughtan, *The Foreign Policy of the European Union*, pp. 233–34.
62 Corrado, 'Negotiating the EU External Border', in Balzacq and Carrera, *Security Versus Freedom?*, pp. 183–203. For this author, the choice of using the term 'management' rather than 'control' is a sign of openness.
63 European Security Strategy, 2003, p. 9.
64 'While the United States is changing its approach in a direction that is more compatible with European wishes, we are waiting for Europe to answer by sharing responsibilities', Philip Gordon, Deputy Secretary of State for Europe and Eurasia, in *Le Monde*, Paris, 13 October 2009 (author's translation).

15

Venus has learned geopolitics

The European Union's frontier and transatlantic relations

Basil Germond

'Even in an era of globalisation, geography is still important'.[1]

The 'power versus weakness' image has become a very common and popular way of depicting the divergences between the USA and the Europeans (or the European Union, EU) in the post-Cold War (and post-9/11) world.[2] Beyond the simplistic dichotomy between Mars and Venus, the recent literature on transatlantic relations has often discussed the reality and the myth of the so-called transatlantic gap.[3] Issues such as the representation of the world, the perception of threats, the security values, and the use of force have been highly debated. Now, it is generally recognized that the USA and the Europeans are facing similar risks and threats and are responding by projecting security outside in order to obtain security inside. However, the literature has emphasized that the strategies envisaged by the USA and the Europeans to cope with the current real or alleged risks and threats (and thus to project security outside) are rather divergent, if not opposite. Thus, while the USA seems to favour the use of force (hard power) and support unilateralism, the Europeans in general and the EU in particular emphasize soft power, favour a comprehensive approach to security and call for multilateralism. This has notably been illustrated by comparing the 2003 European Security Strategy (ESS) and the 2002 US National Security Strategy (USNSS).[4]

In this chapter, I show that this 'distinctive' European approach to security issues has not prevented the EU of developing a geopolitical vision that transcends the somewhat candid depiction of EU's strategic thought and security policies given by the literature. Indeed, a careful reading of the 2003 ESS and an analysis of the post-2003 EU practice in terms of projecting security (both at the Community and at the intergovernmental levels) reveal that the EU has assimilated the notion of the European frontier and consolidated its practice of intervention 'out-of-area' (to use a NATO concept), that is to say within its wider frontier zone. The EU's geopolitical ambitions and the exercise of its power beyond its external boundaries are, however, based on the EU's specificities; they thus encompass both civilian and military elements, as well as Community and intergovernmental components. In other words, Venus has learned geopolitics, but she has nonetheless kept her distinctiveness.

To illustrate this, I discuss the notion of the EU frontier, the EU geopolitical vision and the resulting practice of projecting security outside the EU's boundary. I conclude on the impacts of the EU's geopolitical vision on post-2003 transatlantic relations.

The concept of frontier and the projection of security

There was a time when the borders between kingdoms, empires or political entities were not fixed lines of demarcation but wide buffer zones. The words 'frontier' and *marches* were thus used instead of 'borders' or 'boundaries'. However, the emergence and the consolidation of nation-states, the worldwide diffusion of the Westphalian system, and the rule of public international law have reduced these frontier zones to linear segments, or in other words borders, whose peacetime function has mainly become a legal and an administrative one. In fact, the 'frontier era', characterized by a certain geopolitical anarchy has given way to the 'boundary era', characterized by order and stability. In 1959, while the Westphalian philosophy reached its peak with the *uti possidetis* principle shaping the decolonizing process, Ladis Kristof wrote that 'the international society in a frontier era is like the American West during open-range ranching: limits, if any, are ill defined and resented [...]. Under a boundary regime the international society resembles rather fenced ranching: each rancher holds a legal title to his land, knows and guards its limits'.[5]

Obviously, this is still the case today. However, the rise of the information age coupled with the end of the Cold War has begun to challenge the Westphalian system. Indeed, it has 'induced the globalization of the international system, the networking of the threats, and the broadening of the security agenda'.[6] Practically, borders are increasingly avoided and bypassed by the transnational networked forces (including criminal actors) as well as by the states, which are engaged in a globalized fight against the former, inducing the creation of deterritorialized networks of control, multilaterally defined responses and the projection of security outside the boundaries. Thus, the rigidity and the sealing of the boundary have a tendency to erode. The frontier is less conceived as a line of demarcation, but more likely as a zone extending as far away from the formal states' boundaries as it is necessary to exercise power.[7] The function of this frontier zone is to provide states (or groups of states – like the EU) with enough space to ensure their security, through the exercise of their power outside their polity, especially by projecting security outside, including peacekeeping, peace enforcement and peacebuilding, as well as combating incoming transnational threats such as illegal immigration, terrorism, and drug and arms smuggling.

The concept of 'projection' is not a new one. It did not emerge suddenly after the end of the Cold War, although the current concept of security places a particular emphasis on it, and although the current transnationalization of the threats requires acting outside one's own territory.[8] Indeed, as I have discussed elsewhere, the post-Cold War security system is characterized by a destatization and a deterritorialization of security, both at the level of the threatened object and at the level of the threatening subject.

> First, at the level of the threatened object, the notion of security is enlarged, inside states to societies and individuals, and outside states to regional institutions or even to the whole international system (destatization). Moreover, one does not care only

about the individuals within the state, but also about individuals within foreign states. Indeed, the security of the one depends on the security – or on the securing – of the other (deterritorialization). Second, at the level of the threatening subject, it is less a question of facing another state, but rather of responding to non-state threats, such as terrorism and organized criminality, or of responding to environmental threats such as climate change (destatization). Besides, these '(not) new threats' are essentially transnational and protean. They do not articulate within the state framework, but use the whole world as one sole network (the System of systems); they appear and proliferate 'elsewhere' but impact 'us' later, since they are not static and localized, but ubiquitous (deterritorialization).[9]

The new post-Cold War security policies put the emphasis on the projection of security 'upstream', that is to say pre-emptively rather than in response to an attack/nuisance (evolution from defence to security), and outside states' boundaries in order to respond to the destatization and the deterritorialization of security. In other words, one's own security depends on others' security and 'securing'. Thus, the assumption is that projecting security outside, abroad and 'upstream' allows obtaining security inside, home and 'downstream'. The evolution of the concept of security in general and of the concept of projecting security in particular is not only theoretical but translates into doctrinal change and operational practice.

The European states have modified their security policies and strategic concepts following the end of the Cold War. The current security policies in Europe did not appear *ex nihilo* but result from a gradual process that commenced in 1989 with the fall of the Berlin Wall and that have rapidly expanded after the 1991 Gulf War. From the beginning, the basic orientations of this process seemed clear, i.e. the need to project security outside, the importance of the non-military dimensions of security, and the necessity to cooperate within multilateral structures for the conduct of military operations as well as to face threatening non-state actors. However, this process underwent some phases of uncertainty, engendering debates on the strategic orientations to follow. Hence, the Europeans did not respond efficiently to the Bosnian crisis (1992–95), since at that time they had not yet achieved the transition that allowed them some years later to intervene in Kosovo (in the framework of NATO) or in 2003 in the Democratic Republic of Congo (in the framework of the EU). Moreover, the rhythm of assimilation of the new concept of security differs from state to state. Thus, before 1999 or even 2001, there was clearly no real concordance between the different security policies in Europe. Today, one can say that all the European states agree on the need to project security outside, although the means to employ and the intensity of the operations are still subject to many divergences. This does not necessarily mean that projecting security is the basis of the European strategic culture but it is certainly the principal element that is recurrent to *all* nationally defined security strategies in Europe. Indeed, the need to project security outside in order to obtain security inside is highlighted in the great majority of (if not in all) the main strategic documents released by the European states. Here are just a few examples taken from leading documents:

> The capacity to deliver effective military force in peace support and intervention operations, alongside our EU and NATO allies, is a vital component of our security policy. [The current threats] require a clear focus on projecting force, further afield and even more quickly than has previously been the case. This places a premium on the deployability and sustainability of our forces.[10]

Among their missions, armies created for national defence now have the principal task of projecting stability. [...] This potential for projection, which allows us to meet the enemy as quickly as possible and wherever necessary, characterises the present phase in which defence is seen and understood as an active, flexible and dynamic instrument.[11]

German security policy also has to take account of developments in geographically remote regions, insofar as they affect our interests. These are not static, but contingent on international constellations and developments. In the age of globalisation, interests can no longer be defined solely in geographical terms. [...] German security policy is forward-looking. The new risks and threats to Germany and Europe have their origin in regional and global developments, often far beyond the European area of stability.[12]

Projecting security has two components: a temporal one, i.e. the need to deal with crises and/or transnational threats at an early stage, and a spatial one, i.e. the need to act far away from home. Projecting security could imply to exercise the monopoly on the legitimate use of violence, the imposition of peace as well as the imposition of values. According to Heinemann-Grüder, 'the projection of security norms onto the outside world is seen as a function of self-image and the interests of particular interest groups'.[13] If this is true for the imposition of security norms, it is even truer for the very imposition of security. Indeed, the concept of projecting security is often linked with the one of intervention, and 'continues to be inextricable from the promotion of liberal democratic values'.[14]

Projecting security means that a state or a group of states (a coalition or a regional organization) aims at fighting transnational threats outside its boundary, at preventing or resolving conflicts abroad and 'out-of-area', as well as at imposing its own values/norms to others, with the aim of increasing its own security, by tackling the (alleged) source of threats, which can be located far outside the states' or European boundaries. Practically, the projection of security could consist in spreading development, good governance and security norms, in intervening for crisis prevention and management or even for enforcing peace (which require 'traditional' forces and power projection capabilities), and in combating transnational criminal actors.

EU's frontier and geopolitical vision

Since 2003, the EU has been increasingly involved in the dynamics consisting in projecting security outside its boundary, through diplomatic, economic, police and military activities. By doing so, the EU has been initiating a certain return to the 'frontier era'.[15]

Actually, two geostrategies currently coexist. The first one is known as the 'fortress Europe' strategy. It aims at making the EU impregnable by somehow hermetically sealing its external borders; this strategy is particularly put forward in the context of the fight against illegal immigration. The second strategy is that of 'imperial Europe'. It aims at obtaining security inside the EU by projecting security outside its external borders. The interpenetration of these two geostrategies has shaped four levels of borders and frontiers (Table 15.1). First, internally, the borders between member states are hardly more than administrative divisions; their interest in terms of security has a tendency to decline, in particular within the Schengen space. Second, the external outline of the EU is a legal and political boundary, or, in other words, the external limit of the sum of the member states. Since the end of the Cold War, its defence is guaranteed, and even if it symbolizes the ultimate wall against incoming transnational threats (such as illegal immigration[16]), its value in the framework of the new security policies is limited by the fact that security should now be searched outside the EU's boundary. Third, the 'neo-imperial' strategy has increased the relevance of the frontier zone between the EU and the very outer world, i.e. a wide space (mainly maritime, but also encompassing the EU's neighbouring states) separating the EU from the rest of the world. Its strategic depth should contribute to the security of the Union, but as the first frontline, this zone should also be secured itself. In other words, this frontier zone, or the EU *marches* has become the main theatre of the EU's external activities in the field of security. Fourth, the external limit of this buffer zone becomes the very far end of the EU's 'neo-imperial' zone of security, a *limes* in the Roman acceptation, i.e. the furthest edge of the empire.[17]

Balance between 'fortress Europe' (withdrawn attitude) and 'imperial Europe' (projecting security) has induced a multifaceted strategy. It consists in strengthening the external borders by consolidating the Schengen space,[18] collaborating with neighbouring countries to gain security (creation of transnational networks of control), and imposing EU norms and values as well as intervening and exercising power abroad (neo-imperialism). As a result, the EU's external borders (the wall of the fortress) are strengthened, and the Union's 'near-abroad' constitutes a buffer zone extending the 'EU-friendly' space up to the *limes* of the empire, that is to say 'pushing the threat of the outside away from EU's own borders'.[19]

The EU's land *marches* are in fact sovereign states' territories, which requires tact and diplomacy. To project security there, hegemonic tools (such as the European Security and Defence Policy – ESDP) should indeed be complemented with partnership tools (such as the European Neighbourhood Policy and the Union for the Mediterranean). In contrast, the EU's maritime frontier (i.e. the wider Mediterranean, the Black Sea, the Baltic Sea, and the Arctic Ocean) is a *mare 'quasi' nullius*. The EU can use this space to roll back its frontier, and thus to exercise its power and defend member states' interests far away from the EU's own territory.

The implementation of a broadened security agenda by the EU and its member states has engendered the broadening and the strengthening of the EU's geopolitical vision. The EU's own security now strongly depends on the security (or securing) of others, as

Table 15.1 The EU's borders and frontiers

Types of borders and frontiers	*Status and security function*	*Security value*	*Who is competent to provide security?*
Internal EU borders	Administrative divisions	None	Member states
External EU boundary	Legal external outline of the EU; Ultimate wall of the 'fortress'	Limited	Member states, the EU
Frontier zone (EU's 'near abroad' and maritime margins)	Buffer zone (*march*) between the EU and the outer world	High	Neighbours in cooperation with the EU and influenced by it
External borders of EU's neighbours	External limit of the 'EU-friendly' space (*limes*)	Limited (but subject to increase)	Mainly neighbours, somehow influenced by the EU

well as on the securing of areas where threats originate, and where the EU's interests are threatened. To combat transnational threats and to obtain security inside, the EU has to project security outside (to exercise its power) beyond its external border and even beyond its direct neighbours.

The EU's official documents, and notably the ESS, give striking examples of the EU's geopolitical ambition, although the term 'external borders' is still preferred to that of 'frontier', so as to obey the letter if not the spirit of public international law. Yet, this expression can be interpreted more extensively. Indeed, the geographically enlarged notion of European security has been clearly expressed in the ESS, the Neighbourhood Policy, as well as various other documents.[20] The ESS makes a clear reference to the growing strategic importance for the EU of regions such as the Balkans, the Mediterranean, the Black Sea, the Caucasus and even the Middle East; and the EU's *marches* are indeed considered as the essential theatre of the EU's projection of security. Thus, the EU's periphery/frontier zone is conceived as a space with a high security value: a space legally situated outside the EU's very territory, but *de facto* inside its zone of security interests and (in cooperation or concurrence with non-EU powers) of competences. Accordingly, 'with the new threats, the first line of defence will often be abroad [...]. It is in the European interest that countries on our borders are well-governed'.[21] This vision is not a purely EU construction, but it is also endorsed by the majority of the member states, including the United Kingdom, which considers that 'the EU has a vital role in securing a safer world both within and beyond the borders of Europe'.[22] Therefore, 'increasing the EU's visibility, spreading EU values, and increasing the EU's role on the world stage may become more representative of EU member states' national interests, and vice-versa'.[23]

This geopolitical vision, that is to say taking into account the security importance of the European frontiers and developing active strategies towards them, translates into a variety of policies. As shown in Table 15.2, the EU's means of action in its frontier zones are multiple and correspond to the EU comprehensive approach to security (crisis management, fighting transnational threats, and defence of the EU's interests),[24] as well as to

Table 15.2 Types of EU projection activities in its frontier zone

Types of activities	Community/intergovernmental	Example of operation/objectives
Promotion of good governance, the rule of law, and economic development	Community and Intergovernmental, but with a growing 'second pillarization'	EUPM BiH, Bosnia and Herzegovina: promotion of the rule of law in a neighbouring country
Peace enforcement, peacekeeping, and post-conflict stabilization and reconstruction	Mainly Intergovernmental, but with an important role played by the Commission	EUFOR BiH Althea, Bosnia and Herzegovina: post-conflict stabilization in a neighbouring country
Fight against transnational criminal actors and illegal immigration	Community, Third pillar, Specialized agencies	Operation HERA, off Senegal: Fighting illegal immigration outside EU's boundary
Protection of EU's core interests and those of the member states	Intergovernmental	EU NAVFOR Atalanta, Horn of Africa: protection of EU's maritime trade
External relations and common diplomacy	Community and Intergovernmental	European Neighbourhood Policy: Security through cooperation

its inter-pillar approach.[25] They encompass diplomatic, economic, police and military instruments.[26] More precisely, they concern the projection of good governance, the rule of law and economic development; peace enforcement, peacekeeping, and post-conflict stabilization and reconstruction; the fight against transnational criminal forces (human traffickers, terrorists, drug and arms smugglers, etc.); the protection of EU's core interests and those of the member states (for example energy security or maritime trade); and external relations and common diplomacy.

EU's geopolitical ambitions and transatlantic relations: friends or foes?

The EU's approach to security possesses three distinctive characteristics: first, security is understood comprehensively, i.e. in its broadened acceptation, including *intra*-state conflicts, international terrorism, proliferation of weapons of mass destruction, as well as various *infra*-military issues, such as transnational criminality, illegal immigration, energy security and even environmental degradations. Second, the EU intends to respond to the current risks and threats with a versatile strategy (or at least policies), using a variety of tools ranging from civilian to military assets. Third, the EU's institutional mechanism is dual, including the Community, or supranational level, and the intergovernmental level.

The EU has been an operational security actor only since about 2003; but, as discussed above, since then, it has rapidly developed its means of intervention abroad and its geopolitical vision, both at the intergovernmental level and at the Community level, although its ambitions have been rather limited until today. The EU is still prominently a civilian power, but it has understood the need to back its economic, diplomatic and normative power with a military and a police dimension.[27] Although the EU is rather a civilian power, it seems nonetheless that Venus has learned geopolitics, given that 'even in an era of globalisation, geography is still important',[28] and that the EU must defend its interests 'whose geographic scope often extends beyond the EU'.[29]

Having developed some geopolitical ambitions, not only does the EU play on the world stage, but it has also become a player on the Grand Chessboard (to use Zbigniew Brzezinski's expression[30]). There, 'the competitive nature of world politics means that one actor's geopolitical ambitions often enter in conflict with those of other actors'.[31] As for the EU, one can think of Russia's ambitions in the Ukraine, Georgia, and more generally speaking within the Black Sea region. The growing EU's geopolitical ambitions regarding the Eurasian Rimland has also been highlighted;[32] if ever the EU increases the exercise of its comprehensive power there, potential conflicts over spheres of influence may emerge with powers such as India, China or even Japan. Generally speaking, as the EU exercises its power outside its boundary, it may enter in conflict with other states' ambitions. When the exercise of power is not limited to economic might and civilian power but encompasses military and police interventions, and when it proceeds from a growing geopolitical ambition, thus resistance and opposition may well be expected. The Europeans are aware of this, and that is why they still favour 'effective multilateralism' over unilateralism and the use of force, be it in its 'near abroad' or anywhere in the world.

The question remains whether the development of some geopolitical ambitions by the EU could challenge NATO's *raison d'être* or hamper transatlantic relations. During the Cold War, Europeans and Americans agreed on the relevance of the Transatlantic Alliance to defend continental Europe and the Euro-Atlantic Sea Lines of Communication (SLOCs) against the Soviet Union. NATO's mission (defence against the USSR) and geographical zones of action (Continental Europe and the Atlantic Ocean) were agreed on both sides of the Atlantic, and NATO/transatlantic relations were the indisputable cornerstone of European defence.

However, after the end of the Cold War, the military (if not the political) relevance of NATO was questioned, and it became more difficult to agree on missions and geographical zones of action.[33] At the same time, the EU boosted its enlargement process (towards the North, the East and the South) and deepened its integration process (Maastricht, Amsterdam). When the ESDP was designed (1998–99), developed (1999–2003) and implemented (after 2003), many advocates of the transatlantic link (politicians and scholars) feared that it would constitute the deathblow for NATO.[34] Thus, the recent development of the EU's geopolitical vision, as well as its comprehensive and versatile practice of projecting security outside (including economic, diplomatic, political, administrative, police and military power) may be seen as a new challenge to NATO.

Actually, these dynamics within the EU rather tend to consolidate the transatlantic link. Indeed, the EU knows its priorities and its limits in terms of resources and capabilities. For the EU, projecting security is conceived as a comprehensive concept, encompassing both a civilian dimension (bringing development and good governance, including policing the EU's frontier) and a military one (peace operations). But it is clear that NATO is still essential as soon as it is a matter of high intensity interventions (as the Kosovo case highlighted). Since the end of the Cold War, NATO has indisputably been the main European tool to project forces and power outside, or, in other words, to intervene 'out-of-area' (although it has depended on US interest to proceed). NATO was in fact a pioneer in the field of projection, as its 1991 strategic concept made clear.[35] Although this rhetoric was certainly due in part to the battle for institutional survival, it however stated clearly what took years (in some cases a decade) for European states to stress in their own strategic and security documents. So, years before it was even imagined that the EC/EU may become an active security actor, NATO was engaged in the process of projecting security outside. The first post-Cold War decade culminated with the Kosovo air campaign (which showed that the Europeans could rely upon NATO to carry out military interventions) and the 1999 strategic concept, which clearly announced the future role of NATO (such as in Afghanistan) by placing a particular emphasis on crisis management and by specifying the notion of acting 'out-of-area':

> The security of the Alliance remains subject to a wide variety of military and non-military risks which are multi-directional and often difficult to predict. These risks include uncertainty and instability in and around the Euro-Atlantic area and the possibility of regional crises at the periphery of the Alliance, which could evolve rapidly. […] An important aim of the Alliance and its forces is to keep risks at a distance by dealing with potential crises at an early stage.[36]

The need to act far away from home in order to achieve security objectives was clearly explained by Secretary General Jaap de Hoop Scheffer in 2004:

> Our missions are changing. Projecting stability has become a precondition for our security. NATO's core function of defending its members can no longer be achieved by maintaining forces only to defend our borders. We simply can no longer protect

our security without addressing the potential risks and threats that arise far from our homes.[37]

For the Europeans *and* for the EU, NATO is still important, and they will certainly not liquidate it. But is the EU's comprehensive exercise of power outside its boundary a duplication of NATO in any regards? First, the EU has a comparative advantage in civilian power projection in general and in post-conflict stabilization and reconstruction in particular. Thus, NATO is naturally favoured for high-intensity warfare and the EU for peace-building (although both actors may be involved in these activities); 'the EU does not do war, but it does do police'.[38] This beneficial division of labour is not limited to the duality peace enforcement versus post-conflict stabilization and police mission. The EU is more versatile than NATO, which is limited to military actions or military-related activities (such as confidence-building measures, military cooperation, etc.). The EU, including the Commission and the specialized agencies, is thus best suited to deal with non-military actors, such as transnational criminals and illegal migrants. In brief, as reminded during the 2009 Strasbourg/Kehl NATO summit: 'efforts should be mutually reinforcing and complementary'.[39] However, the recent deployment of counter-piracy naval forces at the Horn of Africa by both the EU and NATO shows that the limit between complementarity and duplication is somewhat very narrow.

Second, NATO is a *transatlantic* organization; it means that NATO's involvement in such or such a conflict is subordinated to US willingness to act. In case Washington is reluctant, the military dimension of the EU offers a valuable alternative; with both NATO and the EU capable of acting outside (although in a limited way for the latter), the Europeans have not put all their eggs in the same basket.

Third, the deployment of EU forces could politically prove more acceptable than that of NATO in some cases. Indeed, the Alliance is often perceived as a puppet of the USA (by a part of Western public opinion, as well as by many developing countries).[40] Thus, it may sometimes be wiser to use the EU instead of NATO, as it could legitimize such or such an intervention, and 'other states may be more willing to respond to EU, rather than US, leadership'.[41]

The strengthening of the EU's geopolitical vision and the EU's exercise of power outside its boundary confirm that the EU is more than a burdening partner; it can efficiently complement NATO, and, thus, reinforce transatlantic relations. Now, its growing geopolitical ambitions confirm (in the eyes of the USA) that the Union can be reliable *and* that European NATO members are reliable. The EU has slowly operated a move back towards the 'frontier era', which, concretely, translates into policies and operations that tend to reinforce the EU's exercise of power beyond its external boundary. In learning geopolitics, Venus has developed her strategic vision and a practice of projecting security outside; it has also made the Europeans more credible vis-à-vis the USA. Consequently, this dynamic can reinforce, rather than hinder, transatlantic relations.

Notes

1 EU, *A secure Europe in a better world: European security strategy,* (Brussels: Council of the European Union, December, 2003), p. 7.
2 See notably Robert Kagan's seminal piece 'Power and Weakness', *Policy review*, June and July 2002, pp. 3–28; see also Robert Kagan, *Of Paradise and Power: America and Europe in the New World Order,*

(New York, NY: Knopf, 2003); for a critical analysis of Kagan's vision, see Michael Cox, 'Martians and Venutians in the new world order', *International Affairs*, vol. 79, no. 3, 2003, pp. 523–32.

3 See the 2009 special issues of the *British Journal of Politics & International Relations*, vol. 11, no. 1, 2009 and of *International Politics*, vol. 45, no. 3, 2008, both dedicated to transatlantic relations; for various points of view, see also Doug Bereuter and John Lis, 'Broadening the Transatlantic Relationship', *The Washington Quarterly*, vol. 27, no. 1, 2003/04, pp. 147–62; Erik Jones, 'Debating the transatlantic relationship: rhetoric and reality', *International Affairs*, vol. 80, no. 4, 2004, pp. 595–612; Kagan, 'Power and Weakness', Pierangelo Isernia and Philip P. Everts, 'Partners Apart? The Foreign Policy Attitudes of the American and European Publics', *Japanese Journal of Political Science*, vol. 5, no. 2, 2004, pp. 229–58; James P. Rubin, 'Building a new Atlantic alliance: restoring America's partnership with Europe', *Foreign Affairs*, vol. 87, no. 4, 2008, pp. 99–111.

4 Felix Sebastian Berenskoetter, 'Mapping the Mind Gap: A Comparison of US and European Security Strategies', *Security Dialogue*, vol. 36, no. 1, 2005, pp. 71–92; Sven Biscop, *The European security strategy. A global agenda for positive power* (Ashgate: Aldershot, 2005), pp. 109–11; Sven Biscop, 'The European Security Strategy: Implementing a Distinctive Approach to Security', *Sécurité & Stratégie*, the Royal Defence College (IRSD-KHID), Brussels, Paper No. 82, March 2004, pp. 29–31; Simon Duke, 'The European Security Strategy in a comparative framework: does it make for secure alliances in a better world?', *European Foreign Affairs Review*, vol. 9, no. 4, pp. 459–81; Gerrard Quille, 'The European Security Strategy: A Framework for EU Security Interests?', *International Peacekeeping*, vol. 11, no. 3, 2004, pp. 422–23.

5 Ladis K. D. Kristof, 'The Nature of Frontiers and Boundaries', *Annals of the Association of American Geographers*, vol. 49, no. 3, 1959, p. 281.

6 Basil Germond, 'From Frontier to Boundary and Back Again: The European Union's Maritime Margins', *European Foreign Affairs Review*, vol. 15, no. 1, 2010, p. 43. See also Bertrand Badie, *La fin des territoires: essai sur le désordre international et sur l'utilité sociale du respect* (Paris: Fayard, 1995).

7 In this sense, the frontier zone is broader than the 'fuzzy borders', i.e. these 'interfaces or intermediate spaces between the inside and the outside of the polity' as described by Thomas Christiansen, Fabio Petito and Ben Tonra, 'Fuzzy Politics Around Fuzzy Borders: The European Union's "Near Abroad"', *Cooperation and Conflict*, vol. 35, no. 4, 2000, p. 393.

8 Traditionally speaking, it was referred to as the 'projection of forces' or as 'the projection of power'. This concept was thus mainly linked to the notion of war: projecting forces and power was of strategic, operational or tactical value, with the aim of forcing the victory in war. It is still the case today in the event of military operations. However, in the post-Cold War era, projection is also a notion of peacetime. Actually, the notion of projection is not limited to forces and power and not restricted to military operations, but should be understood more comprehensively, as the projection of security.

9 Germond, 'From Frontier to Boundary and Back Again', p. 42.

10 Ministry of Defence, *Defence White Paper: Delivering Security in a Changing World*, presented to Parliament by The Secretary of State for Defence By Command of Her Majesty, (London: Crown, TSO, December 2003), pp. 4, 7.

11 Ministerio de Defensa, *Revisión Estrategica de la Defensa*, (Madrid: Secretaría General Técnica, May 2003), pp. 49–50 (English version: pp. 47–48).

12 Federal Ministry of Defence, *White Paper 2006 on German Security Policy and the Future of the Bundeswehr*, (Berlin, 2006), pp. 21–22.

13 Andreas Heinemann-Gruder, *Small States-Big Worries: Choice and Purposes in the Security Policy of the Baltic States*, (Bonn International Center for Conversion, Brief 21, February 2002), p.9.

14 Rebecca R. Moore, *NATO's New Missions: Projecting Stability in a Post-Cold War World* (Westport, CT: Praeger International Security, 2007), p. 5.

15 On the evolving nature of the EU's frontier, see Roberto Albioni, 'The Geopolitical Implications of the European Neighbourhood Policy', *European Foreign Affairs Review*, vol. 10, no. 1, 2005, pp. 1–16; Malcolm Anderson and Eberhard Bort (eds), *The frontiers of Europe*, (London: Pinter, 1998); Eiki Berg and Piret Ehin, 'What Kind of Border Regime is in the Making? Towards a Differentiated and Uneven Border Strategy', *Cooperation and Conflict*, vol. 41, no. 1, 2006, pp. 53–71; Christopher S. Browning and Pertti Joenniemi, 'Geostrategies of the European Neighbourhood Policy', *European Journal of International Relations*, vol. 14. no. 3, 2008, pp. 519–51; Christiansen, Petito and Tonra, 'Fuzzy Politics Around Fuzzy Borders'; Liam O'Dowd, 'The Changing Significance of European Borders', *Regional and Federal Studies*, vol. 12, no. 4, 2002, pp. 13–36; William Walters, 'The

Frontiers of the European Union: A Geostrategic Perspective', *Geopolitics*, vol. 9, no. 3, 2004, pp. 674–98; Jan Zielonka, *Europe Unbound: Enlarging and Reshaping the Boundaries of the European Union*, (London: Routledge, 2002); Jan Zielonka, 'How New Enlarged Borders will Reshape the European Union?', *Journal of Common Market Studies*, vol. 39, 2001, pp. 507–36.

16 Air transport induces that this external boundary is also present inside the EU territory, i.e. in the airports.
17 On the concept of *march* and *limes* and its relevance for the EU, see William Walters, 'The Frontiers of the European Union', pp. 674–98; on the four levels of borders/frontiers, see Germond, 'From Frontier to Boundary and Back Again'.
18 On Schengen, illegal immigration and the security of EU's borders, see the chapter by Axel Marion in this volume.
19 Browning and Joenniemi, 'Geostrategies of the European Neighbourhood Policy', pp. 531–32.
20 EU, *ESS*; Commission of the European Communities, *European Neighbourhood Policy: Strategy Paper* (Brussels, 2004), COM (2004) 373 final.
21 EU, *ESS*, p. 7.
22 Cabinet Office, *The National Security Strategy of the United Kingdom: Security in an interdependent world*, Presented to Parliament by the Prime Minister, by command of Her Majesty, (London: TSO, March 2008), Cm 7291, p.8.
23 Basil Germond and Michael E. Smith, 'Interest-Definition and Threat-Perception in the EU: Explaining the First ESDP Anti-Piracy Naval Operation', *Contemporary Security Policy*, vol. 30, no. 3, 2009, pp. 588.
24 On the comprehensive approach to security, see also Biscop, *The European security strategy*.
25 On the functioning of the inter-pillar structure regarding crisis management, see Catriona Gourlay, 'European Union Procedures and resources for Crisis Management', *International Peacekeeping*, vol. 11, no. 3, 2004, pp. 404–21.
26 For a recent study of these three instruments of EU's foreign policy, see Karen E. Smith, *European Union foreign policy in a changing world*, (Cambridge: Polity Press, 2008), pp. 54–75.
27 This has often been highlighted. See for example Christopher Coker, 'The ESDP: A Threat to the Transatlantic Alliance?', in Thomas L. Ilgen (ed), *Hard Power, Soft Power and the Future of Transatlantic Relations*, (Aldershot: Ashgate, 2006), pp. 59–70.
28 EU, *ESS*, p. 7.
29 Commission of the European Communities, *Energy Policy and Maritime Policy: Ensuring a Better Fit*, Commission Staff Working Document, Brussels, 10 October 2007, SEC (2007) 1283 provisional version, p. 4.
30 Zbigniew Brzezinski, *The Grand Chessboard: American Primacy and Its Geostrategic Imperatives*, (New York, NY: Basic Books, 1997).
31 Germond and Smith, 'Interest-Definition and Threat-Perception in the EU', p. 588.
32 James Rogers, 'From Suez to Shanghai: the European Union and Eurasian maritime security', *EU-ISS Occasional Paper*, no. 77, March 2009.
33 See for example Robert B. McCalla, 'NATO's Persistence after the Cold War', *International Organization*, vol. 50, no. 3, 1996, pp. 445–75; Celeste A. Wallander, 'Institutional Assets and Adaptability: NATO After the Cold War', *International Organization*, vol. 54, no. 4, 2000, pp. 705–35.
34 When two institutions that rely upon the same source of money and resources (the states) are engaged in similar missions, this obviously raises the question of inefficient and unsustainable duplication. As the EU comes second, it has naturally been widely criticized by many politicians and some academics. The literature discussing the impact of the ESDP on NATO is prolific; for different points of view, see for example Coker, 'The ESDP: A Threat to the Transatlantic Alliance?'; Jolyon Howorth, 'ESDP and NATO: Wedlock or Deadlock?', *Cooperation and Conflict*, vol. 38, no. 3, 2003, pp. 235–54; F. Stephen Larrabee, 'ESDP and NATO: Assuring Complementarity', *The International Spectator*, vol. XXXIX, no. 1, 2004, pp. 51–70; Christopher Layne, 'Death Knell for NATO? The Bush Administration Confronts the European Security and Defense Policy', *Policy Analysis*, 394, 2001, pp. 1–15.
35 NATO, 'The Alliance's Strategic Concept', agreed by the Heads of State and Government participating in the meeting of the North Atlantic Council (Rome, 8 November 1991).
36 NATO, 'The Alliance's Strategic Concept', approved by the Heads of State and Government participating in the meeting of the North Atlantic Council in Washington, DC, April 23–24 1999, *Press Release*, NAC-S(99)65, 24 April 1999, §20.

37 Jaap de Hoop Scheffer, 'NATO's Istanbul Summit: New mission, new means', Speech at the RUSI, London, 18 June 2004, www.nato.int/docu/speech/2004/s040618a.htm (accessed 15 January 2008).
38 Coker, 'The ESDP: A Threat to the Transatlantic Alliance?', p.63.
39 NATO, 'Declaration on Alliance Security', issued by the Heads of State and Government participating in the meeting of the North Atlantic Council in Strasbourg/Kehl on 4 April 2009, *Press Release*, 4 April 2009.
40 See Basil Germond, 'Multinational Military Cooperation and its Challenges: the Case of European Naval Operations in the Wider Mediterranean Area', *International Relations*, vol. 22, no. 2, 2008, pp. 173–91.
41 Germond and Smith, 'Interest–Definition and Threat–Perception in the EU', p. 589.

16

The rise and fall of criticism towards the United States in transatlantic relations

From anti-Americanism to Obamania

Tuomas Forsberg

"Anti-Americanism" became a catchword in transatlantic relations during the George W. Bush presidency (2001–8). Criticism towards the United States was already increasing during the Clinton administration in the late 1990s[1] but it became a truly palpable phenomenon in Europe at the beginning of the 2000s. Bush's early policy decisions that were seen as being unilateralist, most notably his refusal to sign the Kyoto protocol and rejection of the International Criminal Court, evoked a lot of criticism in Europe, but negative reactions became even more salient in 2003 as a counter-reaction to the war plans and to the actual launch of the war against Iraq. The German and French leaders, Gerhard Schröder and Jacques Chirac, openly resisted the war and did not support the UN Security Council resolution that would have mandated it. On 15 February 2003, millions of people marched for peace in the streets of the European capitals to the effect that the German and French philosophers Jürgen Habermas and Jacques Derrida argued that a truly trans-European civil society was born in opposition to the policies and dominance of the United States.[2] The image of the United States plummeted in public opinion polls.

What made these disagreements of the Bush era in the transatlantic relations different from the past was that they seemed to involve an emotional aspect and go across the various European nations independently of their historical background and actual political relationship with the United States. In the view of Marc Trachtenberg, "this crisis *was* very different from the NATO crises of the Cold War period, because [...] many in Europe were to jump to what were viewed as extreme anti-American conclusions."[3] Michael Cox argued that "one of the most important developments since 2001 is the degree to which trust has been eroded. [...] A Rubicon of sorts has thus been crossed and it is going to be extremely difficult to return back to the other bank."[4] Anti-Americanism, indeed, was seen as being here to stay. Ivan Krastsev argued that the twenty-first century could be labeled as an "anti-American century" in opposition to the twentieth that was an "American century."[5] In view of Andrei Markovits, anti-Americanism had been promoted to the status of West Europe's lingua franca.[6] Against this background many believed that the United States and Europe could not easily repair their mutual relations. In the view of Geir Lundestad, "most factors seem to indicate that the two have entered a new period compared to the Cold-War years."[7] Another prominent scholar, Robert Jervis, who started his scientific career by looking at the role of images in international relations, argued that "it will be hard for any future administration to regain the territory that was lost."[8]

Others regarded the criticism towards the United States in Europe before and during the Iraq war as a less serious thing for the future of the transatlantic relations. The negative attitudes were regarded as a more a less temporary phenomenon tightly tied to President Bush and his personal image as a "toxic Texan," trigger-happy cowboy. "It is abundantly clear," wrote Thomas Risse, "that negative feelings toward America stem from the Bush administration's policies rather than from some underlying resentments of the US in general."[9] Another optimist was Steven Kull, who argued that "there are numerous factors that can influence the future of the transatlantic relationship but it is likely that the force of public opinion is likely to be one pulling in a direction of reducing tensions."[10]

At present, it appears that those who believed that the negative attitudes towards the United States had more to do with President Bush and the policies of his administration were more correct than those who associated the criticism towards the United States to some more fundamental value difference or ways to assess what the United States is rather than what it does. Indeed, with Barack Obama being in power in the United States, the tensions of the Bush era in transatlantic relations seem to have been wiped out. The personal popularity of President Obama in Europe has greatly improved the image of the United States. Yet, it is perhaps too early to conclude that the opinion change towards the United States has everything to do with the president and nothing to do with any general trends in world views and attitudes towards the United States.

This chapter seeks to analyze the rise and fall of anti-Americanism in Europe from Bush to Obama. It first discusses the concept of anti-Americanism and theories of it in the light of the recent literature. Then, it presents the trends in opinion on the United States in Europe and discusses various explanations for them. Finally, on the basis of this analysis the chapter asks whether the change in image of the United States can be attributed to the existence and erosion of an anti-American bias. Essentially, this chapter is one of the first ones to test the various claims about European anti-Americanism in light of the changes in the US administration and its effects on the climate of attitude in transatlantic relations.[11] The chapter argues that the dramatic changes in the image of the United States prove that the anti-American bias during the Bush era was never very strong and therefore we should not believe that a correspondingly strong pro-American bias has emerged with Obama.

Anti-Americanism: conceptual starting points

The concept of anti-Americanism is very tricky. It is politically loaded and difficult to define. Its conveyed purpose is easily misunderstood, since it can be seen both as exaggerating the nature of criticism towards the United States and as belittling it by labeling the criticism deriving simply from an irrational and negative bias. For sure, it would be easier to talk simply about the image of the United States abroad, but for better and for worse, anti-Americanism is the term that has evoked heated debates and raised fundamental questions about the future of world politics and transatlantic relations.

The key question is whether anti-Americanism refers just to the surface of a pattern of negative opinions about the United States or to some deeper ideology, "*ism*," that explains the attitudes. For some, all criticism and negative statements about the United States represents anti-Americanism, for others anti-Americanism points to an emotional, unjustified, biased, or otherwise irrational and as such a systematic or repeated sentiment against the United States, or in the extreme, it is seen as a deep-seated strong hatred towards the United States that is also prone to violent behavior. Katzenstein and Keohane define anti-Americanism as "a psychological tendency to hold negative views of the United States and of American society in general" but they differentiate between opinion, distrust, and bias.[12] Opinion, even if mistaken, is still open to new information. Yet, opinion can harden into distrust and bias that systematically influence opinions despite new information that is available, because new information will be interpreted in accordance with the pre-existing negative scheme.[13]

By the same token, it is also partly a definitional question what the target of anti-Americanism is: in the narrow sense the target is only the current US administration and its policies, in the wider sense it is the American state, the American culture and society or even the American people or everything labeled as "American." Again, most studies adopt a middle-way: negative views of the current US administration, even if systematic, do not represent anti-Americanism unless backed by the negative views of the US society. People usually can differentiate their views about the leader, the people and the society: there is no strong correlation that if the leader of a country has a negative image that the society or the people could not be judged positively. Yet, as Robert Singh notes, "there exists a pronounced tendency among non-Americans to associate—and judge—the nation according to the incumbent in the Oval Office."[14]

We can also distinguish anti-Americanism according to the criteria of who is holding the negative views. The key distinction is between the leaders or the elite on the one hand and the masses on the other. The media can be seen as a third force or it can be seen either as a part of the elite or as a part of the masses. The distinction is important with regard to the question of who is driving the opinions about the United States in Europe. For example, Markovits has claimed that the European elites have been anti-American throughout centuries, whereas the masses have turned critical towards the United States only recently.[15] But in reality, the opposite claim can be seen as equally plausible: during the 1980s the masses formed the peace movement that demonstrated against the deployment of US missiles in Europe, whereas the political leaders endorsed it as a countermeasure to the deployment of Soviet missiles. During the Iraq war public opinion was widely critical towards the US-led war, even in those countries where governments supported the war and participated in it.

The view that anti-Americanism derives from a negative bias and does not just consist of a set of negative opinions underlines its psychological or emotional nature in opposition to its rational components. For example, Russell Berman argued that anti-Americanism is not a product of any genuine interests or values, but it is seen as an obsession or prejudice that "remains impervious to rational arguments or factual proof."[16] It is the "the hysterical surplus that goes beyond reason." The definition of anti-Americanism as obsession is also made famous by Jean-Francois Revel.[17] Yet, there is no need to assume that a negative bias, even if systematic, would be "hysteric" or "obsessive." People have several biases and sometimes they can be useful shortcuts to correct conclusions or be genuine reflections of their values rather than irrational prejudices. Moreover, if we explain negative attitudes through an anti-American bias, we should also explain positive attitudes through a pro-American bias. There is no objective baseline where anti-Americanism stops and pro-Americanism starts.

The operational question of how we define the bottom line that defines what sort of opinions are normal criticism and what is indicative of a bias is therefore often more important than the initial definition of anti-Americanism. For example, the former French Foreign Minister Hubert Védrine asserted that when he spoke of the United States as a "hyper power" it was a factual statement and not a criticism because the word "hyper" has no negative connotations.[18] The most obvious yardstick is when the negative language is out of proportion and reflects some sort of double standard. People can said to be anti-American if they would not be critical towards other states, countries, or people for the same reasons they are critical towards the United States, American society and culture, or Americans in general. The problem is that for some scholars, almost any criticism of the United States or refusal to follow its policies is interpreted as a sign of anti-Americanism. As Katzenstein and Keohane point out, "some authors distinguish correctly between opinion and bias but then make the error of accepting polling data as expressions of anti-Americanism."[19] Yet, it is a manifestation of anti-Americanism if people boycott American products because they do not like American capitalism but at the same time they can happily buy products of equally capitalist European companies. We can also try to compare the views among different nations or populations and think that variation in opinions about America or its policies that cannot be explained by any direct experience of it reflects some sort of a bias. Although there is no objective baseline for determining what is biased and what is unbiased, the variation in opinion cannot be explained by the same "rational" standards.

Most of the recent studies support the view that anti-Americanism was—at least during the Bush era—a significant, increased, but not a penetrating phenomenon. For example, Keohane and Katzenstein contend that with the exception of the Arab Middle East, bias is not deeply embedded in global public opinion.[20] In view of Giacomo Chiozza popular anti-Americanism is mostly benign and shallow and far from being a prejudice; the popular opinion of the United States takes a loose and multifaceted form in which negative and positive elements coexist with no apparent tensions.[21] Similarly, Davis Bobrow summarizes his review of international public opinion polls by contending that "there are significant numbers of America-skeptic publics but few clearly anti American ones."[22]

The big question is whether anti-Americanism is truly driven by policies—what the United States does—or by stereotypes motivated by ideologies—what the United States is. Richard Higgott and Ivona Malbasic argue that the principal source of anti-Americanism is policy driven.[23] Pierangelo Isernia concludes that "anti-Americanism is mostly driven by our assessment of what Americans do or what they think they do."[24] These assertions stand in direct contradiction with the view of Markovits, according to whom critical attitudes towards America have "little to do with the "real existing America" itself and everything with Europe."[25] Yet, the distinction cannot be absolute. Markovits, too, acknowledges that the policies of the Bush administration have had some additional effect in accelerating the trend.

There is thus no straightforward explanation neither of the causes nor the consequences of anti-Americanism. It is generally agreed that there was an increase in the negative opinions about the United States in Europe and elsewhere but not all want to explain this change by referring to an anti-American bias. The key message of much of the recent literature is that anti-Americanism as a bias is multi-causal and that the different causes, not just such a bias, interact in producing the negative image of the United States. Moreover, anti-Americanism needs to be contextualized, since the nature and many of the causes of negative attitudes are local. Indeed, the multi-causal nature of anti-Americanism is part of the explanation why anti-Americanism is so prevalent. Katzenstein and Keohane argue that the symbolism generated by America is so polyvalent that it continually creates a diversity of material on which to construct anti-Americanism.[26]

Views also differ with regard to the impact of anti-American opinions on transatlantic relations and other policy issues. In view of Keohane and Katzenstein it is surprising how little hard evidence, with the exception of the Middle East, can be found that anti-American opinion has had serious direct and immediate consequences for the United States on issues affecting broad US policy objectives.[27] Despite protests and negative opinions, European governments cooperated and were willing to cooperate with the United States in key issues, apart from a few well-known exceptions such as the German and French opposition to the Iraq war.

Starting from the fact that the climate of opinion in Europe changed when the Bush era ended and Obama's began, there are three possibilities of how to interpret the change. First, it can be assumed that there was a negative bias during the Bush era but that it has now developed into a positive one. The second option is to say that there has been a negative bias and it continues to exist despite the positive opinions now expressed of Barack Obama and the United States. The third possible interpretation is that there has never been a negative bias and anti-Americanism has only existed on the level of opinions. Let us first, however, have a look at how the change in the climate of opinion in Europe manifested itself when Obama became president of the United States.

The changes in the image of the United States from Bush to Obama

During the presidency of George W. Bush, transatlantic relations underwent a deep crisis. The crisis was visible at the level of both leadership and public opinion. In public opinion polls, desirability of US leadership had been historically on a rather high level but it dropped fast when Bush was elected president. The watershed year was 2002, when Bush coined the term of "axis of evil" and his administration started to plan the war in Iraq. The United States had received general sympathy because of terrorist attacks, but it started to fade away when the United States declared the "war on terror."[28] In the view of Europeans, the desirability of US leadership in world affairs went down from 64 percent in 2002 to 45 percent in 2003 and further to 36 percent in 2004. In Germany the number of those who rated the US favorably sunk from 78 percent in 2000 to 60 percent in 2002 and further to 45 percent in 2003 and 38 percent in 2004.[29] The decline of the US image was similarly clear but not as steep in France and Great Britain and several other European countries.

Transatlantic relations improved during Bush's second term as president from 2004 onwards. One reason for this improvement was that the French and the German leaders, Chirac and Schröder respectively, who had personified European rejection of US leadership during the Iraq War were replaced by Nicolas Sarkozy and Angela Merkel, who had a less strenuous relationship with Washington. Meanwhile in the UK, Gordon Brown was seen as moving some distance from President Bush compared with his predecessor, Tony Blair.[30] In public opinion polls, Europeans supported closer relations with the United States but overall perception of the relations remained cool, and the assessment of US influence on the word was negative.[31]

Towards the end of the Bush era there was a general feeling that almost any new US president would improve the image of the United States in Europe. Yet, in public opinion polls the Europeans did not believe that transatlantic relations would have improved had the Republican candidate John McCain been elected. Instead, half of Europeans thought that relations would change for the better if Obama was elected. This was also on Obama's agenda. During his campaign, Obama argued that the world will look at America differently when he becomes president.

Obama's popularity in Europe was striking. Europeans expressed more confidence in Obama than in their own political leaders. Obama's presidency was hailed very positively, especially in Germany and France. When Obama visited Berlin in summer 2008, more than 200,000 people gathered to listen to his speech at Siegessäule. In France and Germany, three-quarters of the population would have voted for Obama had they had the right to vote. In Eastern Europe and in the UK, the views were not as enthusiastic about Obama but more people were willing to support Obama over his rival candidate McCain. Obama's key message about multilateralism and willingness to listen to others was received positively in Europe. His early foreign policy initiatives demonstrated that he represented changes that had been on the European wish list. He announced that the Guantanamo prison would be closed down, troops would start to be pulled out from Iraq; he advocated nuclear disarmament and wanted to deal effectively with climate change. When visiting Europe in April 2009 Obama made a comment on anti-Americanism, saying that "there is an anti-Americanism that is at once casual but can also be insidious. Instead of recognizing the good that America so often does in the world, there have been times where Europeans choose to blame America for much of what's bad."[32]

After Obama was elected president, the changes in public opinion were, as expected, dramatic. According to the Pew Research Center's Global Attitudes Project, the favorability rating of the United States in France went up from 42 percent in 2008 to 75 percent in 2009. In Britain the rise was from 53 percent to 69 percent and in Germany from 31 percent to 64 percent (Table 16.1). Transatlantic Trends reported that the approval of the way the US president handled foreign policy issues increased from 19 percent in 2008 to 77 percent in 2009, when the respondents were assessing Obama instead of Bush.[33] For example, in Germany, only 12 percent approved Bush's policy in 2008 but 92 percent approved Obama in 2009 (Figure 16.1 and Table 16.2). Desirability of US leadership in Europe increased from 33 percent to 49 percent. A substantive number of people on both sides of the Atlantic, 41 percent of Europeans and 31 percent of Americans, believed that transatlantic relations had improved during the year when Obama

Table 16.1 US favorability rating

	1999/2000 (%)	2002 (%)	2003 (%)	2005 (%)	2006 (%)	2007 (%)	2008 (%)	2009 (%)
Britain	83	75	70	55	56	51	53	69
France	62	62	42	43	39	39	42	75
Germany	78	60	45	42	37	30	31	64
Spain	50	–	38	41	23	34	33	58
Poland	86	79	–	62	–	61	68	67
Russia	37	61	37	52	43	41	46	44
Turkey	52	30	15	23	12	9	12	14

Source: Pew Research Center 2009.

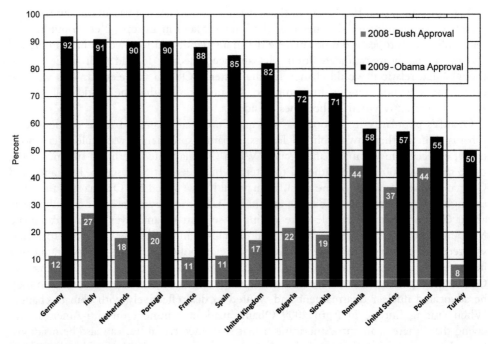

Figure 16.1 The Obama bounce.
Source: Transatlantic Trends 2009.

Table 16.2 Percent of population confident that the US president will do the right thing in world affairs

	Bush 2008 (%)	Obama 2009 (%)
Britain	37	7
France	13	91
Germany	14	93
Spain	8	72
Poland	41	6
Russia	22	3
Turkey	2	33

Source: Pew Research Center 2009.

had been elected President. In Germany, the perception of the role the United States plays in world politics changed from negative to positive.[34]

By contrast, the image of the United States did not improve much in Eastern Europe. In Poland and Romania, of the countries where opinions were polled, Obama was just slightly better approved than Bush was in 2008. In Russia, a majority of people (54 percent) believed that the United States is an unfriendly country and a quarter (27 percent) that it is a friendly country. The favorability rating remained the same as during the Bush administration (44 percent) and only 37 percent of Russians believed that Obama would do the right thing in world affairs.[35] Obama's personal popularity compared to Bush was visible in Turkey, but the Obama effect did not change the views about the United States, which continued to be broadly negative there.

Despite Obama's popularity, differences between the European and American views on policy choices remained almost the same as before. Although a majority of Europeans expected that Obama would be multilateral, a significantly lower number of people believed that the US is already behaving multilaterally. While both Europeans and Americans agreed on the importance of general values such as democracy and human rights, the biggest differences dealt with the acceptance of the use of military force. Although Europeans were more willing to support the US-led efforts to combat terrorism than before, only less than half of the people in Europe approved the US decision to deploy more troops in Afghanistan.[36] In Europe only 29 percent wanted to keep the military option against Iran, whereas in the United States the corresponding figure was 47 percent. Only one-quarter of Europeans believed that war is sometimes necessary, whereas almost three-quarters of Americans believed so.

The differences in views on policy issues were also visible in practice. The divergent attitudes culminated in the Afghanistan policy. In spite of Obama's new Afghan strategy, Europeans have not agreed to increase their military presence much in Afghanistan,[37] although some small changes in troop numbers and mandate took place. Indeed, the Europeans wanted to do something to please Obama and without Obama they would probably have done even less.[38]

Explanations: was there ever an anti-American bias or is it just latent now?

Most scholars writing on anti-Americanism did not expect that such a dramatic change in the image of the United States in Europe would have occurred, as happened when Obama was elected President. For example, Brendon O'Connor and Martin Griffiths posited that we are unlikely to see a decline in anti-Americanism as the United States rethinks its foreign policy in light of Iraq.[39] Markovits claimed that a change to a center-left administration in Washington, led by a Democratic president, would not bring about its abatement, let alone disappearance.[40] Even if anti-Americanism had been caused by the mistaken policies of the Bush administration and was not a centuries old factor, if it has hardened into a bias, then it would have taken time to remove the bias again.

Katzenstein and Keohane discerned three potential factors that could have explained the rise of anti-Americanism.[41] First there is the tendency to react against the global hegemon, whoever it is. It is common not to like those who are wealthier or more powerful and, in international relations, there is the additional need to be wary of those who possess superior power because of international anarchy. Second, there is the backlash globalization that finds its target not only in multinational companies but also in the United States. Third, there is the view that conflicting identities or conflicting values, for example religiosity, best explain the rise of anti-Americanism. Although these explanatory sketches are popular in mainstream thinking and literature, Katzenstein and Keohane argue that anti-Americanism is not well explained by any of them. The United States is still a hegemon, although perhaps slightly weakened, and if the standing in US power were the decisive factor, one would have expected a significant change in Russian attitudes rather than in Germany. Globalization continues and with a worldwide economic decline its effects are felt even more clearly than before and would be just another reason to blame the United States. Neither have identities and values changed overnight, although it can be argued that the social democratic parties have been in decline in Europe and that Obama represents values that are closer to the European mindset than those represented by Bush.

Indeed, when explaining anti-Americanism, it is often important to distinguish between two questions: first what causes anti-Americanism in general and second what causes the fluctuations and change in the image of the United States? If anti-Americanism is explained by some constant deep structural cultural or ideological elements in European societies, then it is not likely that we are able to explain changes in the climate of opinion by the same factors. By the same token, if we explain the criticism towards the Bush administration by referring to anti-Americanism, do we need to explain the popularity of Obama by referring to pro-Americanism?

The first possibility to consider is that the negative views of the United States during the Bush era stemmed from an anti-American bias and that with Obama the negative bias was now eroded and a new pro-American bias was formed instead. Such a change in bias could have occurred because the election of Obama was more than simply a change in personnel. When Obama changed policies, Europeans have been willing to adopt a more positive view of not just the administration but the whole country and its leadership in world affairs. For example, Dominique Moïsi explained that the election of Obama showed that the identity of America was not as fixed as it had seemed.[42] In particular, the Germans seem to have changed their view of the United States after Obama was elected President. "Germans seem to clearly like Obama and are beginning to renew some of their warmth toward the US," commented Steven Kull on the results of an opinion poll in summer of 2009.[43]

It is also possible to argue that the anti-American bias that existed during the Bush era, and even before, continues to exist during the Obama era. Many commentators suspect that this is the case. "Anti-Americanism didn't begin with George Bush and it won't end with an Obama" wrote David Aaronovitch.[44] "Obamania" is thus just a passing phenomenon on the political surface: Obama's popularity in Europe will inevitably decrease with time.[45] Skeptics claim that enthusiasm for Obama will cool down at the first real test and anti-American sentiment will see an upsurge again, perhaps even stronger than before because of the disappointment caused by Obama. During 2009, according to some observers, there was already a general trend toward a return to more negative reporting about America, its people and its president.[46] The Europeans expected Obama to visit Europe sooner than he did and there were a number of similar minor disappointments. For example, the allies were not consulted beforehand of the appointment of James Stavridis as the new Supreme Allied Commander, although it was accepted that traditionally the post belongs to an American. Some were critical of Obama's refusal to release more photos related to the Abu Ghraib prison scandal and others were concerned of protectionist measures in US trade policy. Yet, so far none of these criticisms have lessened the positive image of the United States.

What, however, may have changed on a more permanent basis are the discursive structures of what is possible and acceptable to say about the role of the United States and transatlantic relations. For example, in Germany expressing critical views of the United States is no longer a taboo in the election campaigns of the major parties. Public opinion polls may be insufficient to capture the change that has taken place in the way it is legitimate to speak publicly about the United States in Europe.

Finally, there is the view that neither critical views of Bush nor positive views of Obama reflect any particular anti- or pro-American bias. The sheer volatility in the image of the United States makes this interpretation look most plausible. In other words, there has never been a particularly strong anti-American bias in Europe and therefore Obama did not bring about any major changes in it. Europeans criticized the United States for what it did and not for what it was. The bias that existed was not so much anti-American but more tied to George W. Bush and his administration.[47] As Philip Gordon, now the Assistant Secretary of State for Europe and Eurasian affairs in the Obama administration, together with Jeremy Shapiro noted in 2004, "the European public is not as "anti-American", as is often assumed, but anti-Bush."[48] McCain would not have been enough to remove the bias, but Obama's election to president was. If and when Obama's policies start to contradict European interests and values, the European governments and public opinion are likely to become more critical again but not anti-American in any deeper sense. Normally, negative and positive images of the United States coexist and only a small majority of Europeans can be said to have a strong anti-American bias. Although criticism towards the United States was already growing during the Clinton era, in particular among the foreign policy elites of the "old Europe," it was only Bush and his administration that really made the criticism fly off and turn down pro-American sentiments. The negative attitudes of the larger public did not settle into a bias during the Bush era but were able to change quickly when the United States offered a new fresh face in the form of Obama.

Anti-Americanism during the Bush era manifested itself more in the form of opinions and attitudes than in the form of behavior. Keohane and Katzenstein have argued that "even high levels of expressed anti-Americanism do not translate readily into government and individual action."[49] The European opposition to the war in Iraq that led to government decisions not to support it was more an exception than proof of a fundamental breakdown of cooperation in transatlantic relations. The more relevant aspect of anti-Americanism was probably what governments and people did not do than what they did because of their negative attitudes towards the United States. Disagreements during the war in Iraq and other incidents suggest that anti-American opinions can matter at specific circumstances. Moreover, over the long-term anti-Americanism can erode the institutional basis upon which transatlantic relations are based.

If the impact of anti-American attitudes on policies could be deemed as rather marginal, so seems to be the impact of "Obamania." This implies that key policy decisions are based on interests and commitments rather than represent emotional statements related to the negative image of the United States. The fact that European governments have been slow in increasing their troops in Afghanistan in spite of the wishes of Obama simply proves that they did not do it during the Bush era simply because they did not like Bush or the United States. As one observer cynically concluded, "no amount of charm and flattery, no degree of self-abasement and apology for American 'arrogance' is going to get any meaningful reciprocity from the Old Europeans."[50]

Conclusions: the future of anti-Americanism in Europe and its impact on transatlantic relations

The starting point of this chapter was the dramatic change in the US image in Europe during the first year of Barack Obama's presidency. Whereas the Bush era was characterized by negative attitudes and distrust towards the United States and a related discourse of European anti-Americanism, Obama's term as President of the United States started with positive attitudes towards the United States and expectations of improving transatlantic relations and a related discourse of "Obamania."[51]

Three options about the relationship of anti-Americanism and "Obamania" have been outlined in this chapter. First, there may have been a big change in bias due to Obama, and the European climate of opinion has moved from anti-Americanism to pro-Americanism. Although there has been a change in opinions, it is, however, unlikely that the bias would have changed so quickly. It is possible that there is no sudden swing from one bias to another but that those who used to be negatively biased towards the United States have now become more neutral, and those who were neutral against the United States during the Bush era have now become more positively biased. There is some indication that Obama has affected the way the United States and its society is perceived in Europe. Yet, it would be an exaggeration to talk about a pro-American bias forming in due to Obama.

Second, it is possible to argue that there was a negative bias towards the United States in Europe and it continues to exist despite the personal popularity of Obama. In other words, according to this argument, "Obamania" is only a temporary surface phenomenon and it is unlikely to last for long. Soon Europeans will return to criticizing the United States whatever it does. Although it is likely that Obama's popularity will diminish and criticism towards the United States grow, the problem is that the evidence that once proved the existence of an anti-American bias of the masses has almost entirely disappeared. Indeed, given the nature of the change, it is now easy to conclude that those stressing the deep and constant nature of a significant anti-American bias in Europe were wrong, although structural elements and features of anti-Americanism that have been detected in many studies have most certainly remained intact and may be mobilized despite Obama.

It is, however, most natural to accept the third view of how the change in the climate of opinion was possible according to which there was never a strong anti-American bias in Europe despite the existence of critical opinions during the Bush era. Consequently, there is not a strong bias in favor of the United States either due to Obama. The election of Obama did not mean that the differences in values and interests between the United States and Europe were eradicated. In continuation, therefore, if the United States is criticized it will be more because the values and interests differ, not because there is an anti-American bias.

The image of the United States in Europe will be important for the future of transatlantic relations, but not in the most direct and obvious way. In the short run, neither negative nor positive views are likely to lead to any fundamental policy changes. If the image of the United States influences government policies, it affects more what Europeans refrain from doing rather than what they do. Moreover, in times of crisis, images can be crucially important for some key decisions reflecting the degree of trust since it cannot be rationally assessed due to surrounding uncertainties. Finally, over the long term, negative or positive views may develop into more long-lasting biases that shape the institutional basis and frames of transatlantic relations—the Bush era demonstrated that if there was a positive bias during the Cold War, it had eroded during the 1990s, but the Obamania phenomenon instead demonstrated that no strong negative bias had emerged in Europe during the Bush era.

Notes

1 See for example the article by the now Vice President Joseph Biden, 'Unholy Symbiosis: Isolationism and Anti-Americanism', *The Washington Quarterly*, vol. 23, no. 4, 2000, pp. 7–14.
2 Jürgen Habermas and Jacques Derrida, 'February 15, or, What Binds Europeans Together: Plea for a Common Foreign Policy, Beginning in Core Europe', in Daniel Levy, Max Pensky and John

Torpey (eds) *Old Europe, New Europe, Core Europe. Transatlantic Relations After the Iraq War*, (London: Verso, 2005), pp. 3–13, [originally published in *Frankfurter Allgemeine Zeitung* in 2003].
3 Marc Trachtenberg, 'The Iraq Crisis and the Future of Western Alliance', in David Andrews, *The Atlantic Alliance under Stress. US-European Relations after Iraq*, (Cambridge: Cambridge University Press, 2005), p. 225.
4 Michael Cox, 'Beyond the West: Terrors in Transatlantia', *European Journal of International Relations*, vol. 11, no. 2, 2005, p. 208.
5 Ivan Krastev, 'The Anti-American Century', *Journal of Democracy*, vol. 15, no. 2, 2004, pp. 5–16.
6 Andrei Markovits, *The Uncouth Nation. Why Europe Dislikes America* (Princeton: Princeton University Press, 2007).
7 Geir Lundestad, 'Introduction'. In Lundestad (ed), *Just Another Major Crisis? The United States and Europe Since 2000* (Oxford: Oxford University Press, 2008), p. 14.
8 Robert Jervis, *American Foreign Policy in a New Era* (New York: Routledge, 2005), p. 137.
9 Thomas Risse, 'Beyond Iraq: The Crisis of the Transatlantic Security Community', *Friedenswarte*, vol. 78, no. 2–3, 2003, p. 180.
10 Steven Kull, 'Can the Circle Be Unbroken? Public Opinion and the Transatlantic Rupture' in Lundestad (ed), *Just Another Major Crisis?*, p. 248.
11 Sophie Meunier 'Anti-Americanism and the Financial Crisis', Paper Presented at the Meeting of the American Political Science Association, Toronto, September 2009.
12 Peter Katzenstein and Robert Keohane, 'Varieties of Anti-Americanism: A Framework for Analysis', in Katzenstein and Keohane (eds), *Anti-Americanisms in World Politics*, (Ithaca: Cornell University Press 2007), p. 19.
13 On cognitive and motivational biases, see Janice Gross Stein, 'Building Politics in Psychology', *Political Psychology*, vol. 9, no. 2, 1988, pp. 245–72.
14 Robert Singh 'Are We All Americans Now? Explaining Anti-Americanisms', in O'Connor and Griffiths (eds), *The Rise of Anti-Americanism*, p. 43.
15 Markovits, *The Uncouth Nation*, p. xx.
16 Russell Berman, *Anti-Americanism in Europe: A Cultural Problem* (Standorf: Hoover Institution, 2004).
17 Jean-François Revel, *L'obsession anti-américaine. Son fonctionnement, ses causes, ses inconséquences* (Paris: Plon 2002).
18 Hubert Védrine, 'On Anti-Americanism', *Brown Journal of World Affairs*, vol. 10, no. 2, 2004, p. 117.
19 Peter Katzenstein and Robert Keohane, 'Varieties of Anti-Americanism: A Framework for Analysis', in Katzenstein and Keohane (eds), *Anti-Americanisms in World Politics*, p. 23.
20 Keohane and Katzenstein,'The Political Consequences of Anti-Americanism', in Katzenstein and Keohane (eds), *Anti-Americanisms in World Politics*, p. 276.
21 Giacomo Chiozza, *Anti-Americanism and the American World Order* (Baltimore: The Johns Hopkins University Press, 2009), p. 4.
22 Davis Bobrow 'Anti-Americanism and International Security: Indications in International Public Opinion', in Richard Higgott and Ivona Malbasic (eds), *The Political Consequences of Anti-Americanism* (Abingdon: Routledge, 2008), p. 121.
23 Richard Higgott and Ivona Malbasic, 'Introduction: The Theory and Practice of Anti-Americanism – A Brief Introduction', in Higgott and Malbasic (eds), *The Political Consequences of Anti-Americanism*, pp. 1–12.
24 Pierangelo Isernia 'Anti-Americanism in Europe During the Cold War', in Katzenstein and Keohane (eds), *Anti-Americanisms in World Politics*, pp. 57–92.
25 Markovits, *The Uncouth Nation*, p. 201.
26 Peter Katzenstein and Robert Keohane, 'Conclusion: Anti-Americanisms and the Polyvalence of America', in Katzenstein and Keohane (eds), *Anti-Americanisms in World Politics*, pp. 311–16.
27 Keohane and Katzenstein, 'The Political Consequences of Anti-Americanism', in Katzenstein and Keohane (eds), *Anti-Americanisms in World Politics*, p. 275.
28 Cox, 'Beyond the West: Terrors in Transatlantia'.
29 Pew Research Center Global Attitudes Project, 'Global Unease with Major World Powers,' 27 June 2007.
30 David Hastings Dunn, 'The Double Interregnum: UK-US Relations beyond Blair and Bush', *International Affairs*, vol. 84, no. 6, 2008, pp. 1131–43.
31 *Transatlantic Trends, Key Findings 2008*, (Brussels: The German Marshall Fund of the United States and Torino: Compagnia di San Paolo, 2008) and Transatlantic Network 2020, 'Talking Transatlantic', British Council 2008.

32 Jon Ward, 'Obama Speaks Forcefully to Europeans', *The Washington Times*, 4 April 2009.
33 *Transatlantic Trends, Key Findings 2009* (Brussels: The German Marshall Fund of the United States, 2009). www.transatlantictrends.org.
34 World Public Opinion, 'Obama Changing the Way Germans See US', 3 June 2009, www.worldpublicopinion.org/pipa/articles/breuropera/614.php?lb=breu& pnt=614&nid=&id= (accessed 30 October 2009).
35 Pew Research Center Global Attitudes Project, 'Confidence in Obama Lifts U.S. Image Around the World, 23 July 2009 and Ellen Barry, "U.S.'s Critics, Now Muted, Are Eager to Growl Again; A Wait-And-See Attitude on Obama, But Russians Are Widely Anti-American"', *The International Herald Tribune*, 6 July 2009.
36 Pew Research Center Global Attitudes Project, 'Confidence in Obama Lifts U.S. Image Around the World'.
37 Reuters, 'Europe Wary of Sending More Troops to Afghanistan', *Euraractiv.com*, 29 September 2009.
38 Edward Cody, 'Europeans Reluctant to Follow Obama on Afghan Initiative', *The Washington Post*, 3 April 2009.
39 Brendon O'Connor and Martin Griffiths 'Introduction: Making Sense of Anti-Americanism', in O'Connor and Griffiths (eds), *The Rise of Anti-Americanism* (London: Routledge, 2006), p. 5.
40 Markovits, *The Uncouth Nation*, p.5.
41 Peter Katzenstein and Robert Keohane, 'Conclusion: Anti-Americanisms and the Polyvalence of America', in Katzenstein and Keohane (eds), *Anti-Americanisms in World Politics*, pp. 307–9.
42 Robert Marquand, 'For Europe, Obama Revives Positive Image of America's Unique Identity', *Christian Science Monitor*, 17 November 2008.
43 World Public Opinion, 'Obama Changing the Way Germans See US'.
44 Jeff Jakoby, 'Obama Lovefest Won't Last', *The Boston Globe*, 9 November 2008.
45 David Aaronovitch, 'Eventually, We Will All Hate Obama, Too', *The Times*, 22 July 2008.
46 See e.g. Leo Cendrowicz, 'Is Europe Falling Out of Love with Obama', *Time*, 5 March 2009; Soeren Kern, 'European Anti-Americanism in the Age of Obama', *The Brussels Journal*, 7 July 2009 and Werner Weidenfeld, 'In Spite of Europe's Obamania, Transatlantic Relations Remain Tricky', *Europe's World*, no. 13, Autumn 2009.
47 Chiozza, *Anti-Americanism*, p. 197.
48 Philip Gordon and Jeremy Shapiro, *Allies at War. America, Europe and the Crisis over Iraq* (New York: McGraw-Hill, 2004).
49 Keohane, Robert and Peter Katzenstein 'The Political Consequences of Anti-Americanism', in Katzenstein and Keohane (eds), *Anti-Americanisms in World Politics*, p. 303.
50 Janet Daley, 'Europe's Passion for the States is Unlikely to be Reciprocated', *The Daily Telegraph*, 13 April 2009.
51 See e.g. Alvaro de Vasconcelos and Marcin Zaborowski (eds), *The Obama Moment. European and American Perspectives* (Paris: European Union Institute of Security Studies, 2009).

17

Strategic culture and security

American antiterrorist policy and the use of soft power after 9/11

Jérôme Gygax

Through the National Security Act (1947) to the Homeland Security Act (2002), the United States has fundamentally redefined its security paradigm. Antiterrorist laws, passed between 2002 and 2008 in the framework of the "Global War on Terrorism" serve varying objectives, ranging from the apprehension of criminals to the control over the flow of commercial and private data. Although the idea and concept of terrorism embracing both tactic and ideology is difficult to define, any definition embraces the expression of a Western system of values and implicitly serves to reaffirm them.[1] In 1952, Arnold Wolfers defined national security as a system directed to creating an absence of a threat to a society's essential values. This definition establishes a link between security concepts and culture.[2]

In this chapter we are interested in the evaluation of the concepts of "threats" and "security" by the United States discussed as reflections on a redefinition of their security doctrine.[3] What were the effects of the 11 September 2001 attacks on American and transatlantic strategic and security cultures?[4] Can we affirm, as the historian W.L. Hixson claims, that these attacks led to a renewal of a warlike culture, seen as a response to a crisis in American society through a reaffirmation of its national identity and its cultural hegemony?[5] We will focus on three stages: the first is the period of the conceptualization of the antiterrorist doctrines (1970s to 1980s); the second is the transition after the fall of the USSR (1990s), followed by the third which is a systematic application of these doctrines after the attacks of September 2001.

The range of institutional and legal transformations accompanying this process is debated today. The debate raises the question if there is an "American way of war" that is exportable to other actors in the international system? As David A. Baldwin writes, "Just as teams compete to be champions, so states compete for security." We could also add: "to define what security is."[6] In fact, experts are divided over the importance of cultural determinants of security. Some postulate the continuity of security doctrines from before and after 9/11,[7] whereas for others the break has been radical and revolutionary, accompanied by a change in the collective American identity which has become "militant."[8] The phenomenon of the militarization of society is a consequence of this transformation, and it is wedded to a global security market in full development.[9]

Is the concept of *soft power*, defined by Joseph S. Nye in the 1990s, anything more than the expression of new forms of influence derived from new technological tools in the service of globalized security?[10] Nye does not forget to remind us that no modern state has been able to develop a military power capable of exercising hegemony over the long term.[11] In this chapter, we will highlight how the means used in the fight against terrorism has cleared the path for the use of asymmetric measures in the form of pre-emptive action replacing the deterrence practice of the Cold War period. The European Union, the United Nations (UN), and NATO, as well as regional organizations (such as the Organization of American States (OAS) and Association of South-East Asian Nations (ASEAN)) seem to have accepted this new strategic configuration, a veritable "strategic culture" initiated by the United States, responding to their new security agenda.[12]

The conceptualization of asymmetric antiterrorist doctrines

The signing of the National Strategy for Combating Terrorism (NSCT) in February 2003, gave the United States the right to use its geostrategic and economic advantages to defeat its enemies, now defined as terrorists. In fact, this law originated 30 years earlier in an effort to renew American security strategy following two major "shocks:" the massacre at the Olympic Games in Munich in September 1972 and the traumatic retreat of US troops from Vietnam.[13]

Following the attack at the Olympic Games, Palestinian terrorism, described as fanatical, irrational, and amoral was, for the first time, uncoupled from its territorial claims, of ending the "illegal occupation" of territories held by Israel since the June 1967 war.[14] Israel, which had become the indispensable ally of the United States in the Middle East, found support for its antiterrorist laws and a framework to legitimize the maintenance of its occupation for years to come.[15] In July 1979, during a meeting of the Jonathan Institute in Jerusalem, Israeli Prime Minister Menachem Begin, in the presence of a number of journalists and Western statesmen, including G. Will, R. Moss, C. Sterling, and George Bush, insisted on the necessity of promoting the theme of terrorism in relation to the USSR.[16] At the end of the 1970s, a CIA report advocated structural reforms in the fight against terrorism:

> It is a problem of enormous complexity, made all the more so by the diverse and sometimes ambiguous sources of the threat, and one which places great demands on our intelligence capabilities. [...] So is the whole phenomenon of the use of security assistance as a means of projecting power, which means we need to detect and understand the implications of the military and economic assistance programs, grants and sales, training and advisory agreements, base rights and exchange programs which can be used to extend the reach and influence of adversary nations.[17]

This report highlighted some of the key elements in American security strategy which were to come: the extension of the capacity to reach out and influence its adversaries; the sharing of intelligence between departments; and the use of information technologies and communication directed to these ends.[18] Two years later, the State Department established the first list of terrorist states before President Reagan called for the establishment of "perfect security" against those he considered responsible for the ultimate violation of human rights.[19] Reagan was then supported by military–industrial milieus, neoconservatives, powerful think tanks such as the Committee on the Present Danger (CPD), the Heritage Foundation, and RAND (which maintained close links with the military–industrial complex). These "modern monasteries" assured doctrinal continuity up to the presidency of George W. Bush (2001–9).[20]

President Reagan signed the first security directive, National Security Directive (NSDD 30), in April 1982, which was titled "Managing Terrorist Incidents." The purpose of this document was the improvement of response mechanisms as well as the reorganization of jurisdictions and responsibilities in the counterterrorist struggle (FBI, CIA, National Security Agency, Department of Defense (DoD), Department of Justice).[21] Two years later, and six months after the explosion of the Korean Airlines flight, NSDD 138, "Combating Terrorism" (3 April 1984) established the modalities of operations conducted against groups or states, implicated in terrorism. This directive extended various types of sanctions against their supporters.[22] It was thus specified that all means of communications available would be employed in this struggle. The Denton Act, introduced by Republican Senator Jeremiah Denton in March 1984, aimed at preserving the balance between liberty and security. In this law, security was recognized as a liberty placed above all others. A terrorist act was defined as a federal crime, constituting:

> The knowing use of force or violence against any person or property in violation of the criminal laws of the United States or any State, territory, possession, or district, with the intent to intimidate, coerce, or influence a government or person in furtherance of any political or ideological objective.[23]

The following month, four separate bills on "international terrorism" were proposed in Congress, adding a warning against those "threatening democratic states." Each of the following security directives (NSDD 179, NSDD 180, NSDD 205, and NSDD 207), between 1985 and 1986, extended the security sphere while trampling upon state sovereignty. NSDD 207, the National Program for Combating Terrorism specified that "terrorism" in itself, without defining the place or the target, committed by anyone, constituted a threat to national security. This gave the United States the right to unilaterally and pre-emptively respond to any threat of attack. In the same vein, the Strategic Defense Initiative (SDI), launched in March 1983, anticipated the deployment of a "security" umbrella and supported the financing of technologies geared at winning future conflicts. The USSR was thus presented as a sponsor of "state terrorism".

A series of presidential Executive Orders (EOs) were signed during the following decade. They applied systematic economic sanctions against organizations and individuals suspected of terrorism aiming to "threaten or disrupt the Middle East Peace Process."[24] The names of Al-Qaeda and Bin Laden appear in an amendment to this law for the first time in 1998.[25] That same year, the Americans revised their special operations doctrine against terrorist threats.[26] Two kinds of special operations, *information* and *psychological*, became legitimate in order to influence information and public opinion: "to influence their emotions, motives, objective reasoning, and ultimately the behavior of foreign governments, organizations, groups and individuals."[27]

Thus, the psychological nature of terrorist operations authorized a response which implemented such exceptional means. At the end of the 1980s, Ronald Reagan had established the necessary legal framework for the conduct of pre-emptive counterterrorist operations on a global scale. The reorganization of the Defense Department in 1986 reinforced its prerogatives by bringing in new legal instruments allowing for the projection of power outside of the United States in the context of deterritorialized wars.[28] Public opinion and individuals, no longer states, became the protagonists in a new kind of conflict whose heart was information and mediatization before an international audience.[29]

The 1990s: a window of opportunity for the reaffirmation of the new American leadership

The absence of a threat since the end of the Cold War called into question the capacity of the United States to maintain its status as a superpower.[30] Developing nations aspired to redefine the terms of their relations with the West while pressuring the United States to withdraw its forces stationed in certain regions of Asia and the Far East.[31] The fall of the USSR, in addition to having made nuclear deterrence obsolete, confirmed the idea that future wars would be frontless, asymmetric, and would advantage the side possessing the most doctrinal coherence.[32]

The two presidential terms of William J. Clinton (1993–2001) saw intense debates over the proper means to insure a change in American "strategic culture" to guarantee the maintenance of its leadership.[33] The Pentagon and the CIA took care to define the new threats according to an interprative frame which was culturally acceptable to the majority.[34] The "window of opportunity" created by the absence of a direct rival encouraged visions of material technological advances, especially in communications, which would be called the "Revolution in Military Affairs" (RMA).[35]

The Defense Department and the neoconservatives shared a common approach towards the role of the United States as the sole guarantor of international order. They aspired to pursue the projects of the Reagan era by following unconventional strategies by integrating the domestic security sector and national defense.[36] This desire partly reflected the experience in Vietnam and the defeat on the home front of domestic opinion. By 1992, the Defense Planning Guidance document (DPG-1992) called for maintaining American primacy by completing Reagan's SDI.[37] A report by the Center for Strategic and International Studies (CSIS) entitled *Foreign Policy into the 21st Century: The US Leadership Challenge* co-authored by Z. Brzezinski, L. Hamilton, and R. Lugar, asked that no one heed the sirens of isolationism: "As much as we as a country might feel tempted to turn inward, we simply have too much at stake in other parts of the world to do so."[38]

To return to the conditions surrounding the larger transformation of security policy, one must underline the publication of several studies written for the military at the beginning of the 1980s, such as that of Kupperman and Associates. These aimed at demonstrating the foreseeable difficulties in the event of a reorganization of the existing security structures, particularly jurisdictional conflicts within the bureaucracy.[39] Gorbachev also experienced the obstacles of the bureaucratic apparatus in the face of his desire for reform between 1984 and 1989. The American and Russian situations were certainly not comparable, but nevertheless, Reagan was able to exploit the climate of insecurity and fear in order to conduct his political "revolution." Just before the 1984 Los Angeles Olympic Games, he passed a series of antiterrorist legislations defined as "emergency measures". A few years later, a change in the "security culture" at the national level was still the order of the day. A RAND study estimated that a minimum of five years would be necessary for a transformation of the "security culture" of the United States provided that there was an unconditional adherence of the elites which was an imperative condition for a wider national acceptance.[40]

It was without a doubt not entirely fortuitous that at the beginning of the 1990s Joseph Nye, former Assistant Undersecretary of State in the Carter Administration, proposed his concept of *soft power*, reflecting the capacity of the United States to get other powers to accept its "agenda" without resorting to force.[41] In the same vein, Samuel Huntington, who was a member of RAND, defended a new cultural conceptualization of international power relations with his "Clash of Civilizations" thesis.[42] These two theses, without any obvious linkages, exposed in complementary terms certain fundamental aspects of the debate on the possible transition towards new strategic concepts.

The threat to American security took shape at the end of the 1990s following the first attack against the World Trade Center in 1993. This was followed three years later by attacks against American targets on Saudi Arabia (1996), then in Kenya and Tanzania (1998) and finally the September 11 attacks in New York and Washington (2001), which culminated in the idea of a resurgence of a "new terrorism" in American consciousness, according to the sociologist Albert J. Bergeson.[43] This terrorism has the following characteristics:

- It takes the form of networks and it is more global.
- It is more difficult to identify.
- Its objectives are more vague and diffuse, or even non-existent.
- It is more religious.
- Its violence is more indiscriminate.

The forecast of "superterrorism" was already present in campaigns waged by experts at the Pentagon and in the Reagan Administration between 1983 and 1984 where countless predictions of imminent attacks on American soil were made and publicised in the national and local press.[44] However, by "crying wolf," no one believes you anymore. Bin Laden and his Al Qaeda network made a lie of this assertion. Bin Laden had nonetheless been described in the media as the potential sponsor of cyber-attacks against "critical infrastructures" well before September 2001.[45] Al Qaeda was depicted as an invisible enemy capable of profiting from new technologies and networks, all the while acting in secret. In 1998, the former assistant to the Secretary of Defense, John Hamre, declared on CNN that "We are facing the possibility of an electronic Pearl Harbor [...] There is going to be an electronic attack on this country some time in the future."[46] These warnings were reiterated by Allan B. Caroll from the National Infrastructure Protection Center, in December 1999, and again in February 2001 by its new director, Ronald Dick.[47]

The fact that these attacks finally happened against "critical" infrastructure allowed the implementation of a technological and asymmetric defense strategy. Al Qaeda is defined in official documents as a non-state actor whose aim is to overthrow societies, cultures, and values on a global scale.[48] It is interesting to highlight the "conspiracy-like" nature of their action, hiding their subversive operations at the intersections of crime and war. We thus create a new category of "ideological criminals."[49] In December 2001, the FBI created a *cyber division*.[50] This strategic renewal, elaborated over two decades has been validated, along with its technological options with civilian and military implications.[51] These technologies have additionally resulted in erasing the traditional demarcation between domestic and foreign spheres.[52]

The new concept of "threat" (as described above), has abolished the distinction between domestic and international policies by linking police surveillance and political or economic intelligence in the case of terrorist finance networks.[53] The September 11 attacks have thus transposed the ideological conflicts of the Cold War into the realm of culture.[54] For the neoconservative Robert Kagan, the September 11 attacks have given America its veritable identity.[55] For other observers this event marks the beginning of a process of "total globalization" in which the United States has demonstrated its desire to remain the nucleus of the world system.[56]

The nature of the institutional revolution in the service of *soft power*?

Neither the CIA nor the FBI officially bears responsibility for the security failure of 11 September 2001, attributed to the lack of the centralization of information. This rough explanation permitted the continuation of previous programmes, comprising measures recommended by the National Commission on Terrorism, including the report which was published a few months before the attacks containing the following main ideas:[57]

- fusion of criminal and intelligence activities;
- suppression of safeguards and legal restrictions in the carrying out of those activities which fall outside of the system of mandates that establish legislative control over those operations reinforced under the Clinton administration;[58]
- extension of the recruitment of staff, including among former terrorists;
- surveillance of foreign nationals on American soil.[59]

Although the centralization of intelligence programs have been a continuous task for all presidencies since Richard Nixon,[60] the fusion of intelligence services after 2001 substantially increased control over all sensitive data in all the areas of society (economic, political, military, cultural, or scientific), conforming to the hopes expressed by the DCI two decades before, in 1977.[61]

The Patriot Act and the Homeland Security Act established the department of the same name (DHS) in 2002. With the Intelligence Reform and Terrorism Prevention Act in 2004, the new institutional architecture was put in place, including one of the essential components, the capacity to fight against cyber-terrorism. A Computer Emergency Readiness Team was created within the DHS.[62] Domestic terrorism was from then on defined according to intentions rather than actions—"appears to be intended"—applying the doctrine of pre-emption to Homeland defense.[63] According to the Patriot Act, computer hacking, carried out from distant computers, is a terrorist act: the enemy is someone with the intention of attacking critical infrastructures—information, communications, financial services, energy resources, transport, and distribution—irrespective of their geographical or physical location.[64]

Thus the figure of the enemy of the state becomes diffuse and difficult to discern. In his work entitled *Enemies of Intelligence*, published in 2007, the historian Richard K. Betts, a former member of the National Commission on Terrorism, classifies these enemies in three categories: "exterior," "inherent," and "innocent."[65] The first are "rogue states" and other opponents of the policy of the United States; the second represents the blockages inherent in the system as well as the limits of the cognitive process; finally, this consists of the individuals who unintentionally obstruct the conduct of antiterrorist operations. In his view these persons should be removed from positions of influence. A culture of secrecy becomes the norm in this fight against the "conspirators", the blacklisting of political opponents is condoned and to this is added the criminalization of certain formerly legal activities. Effective prevention of danger and an acceptance of the compromise of freedoms is central to the Denton Act passed some 20 years earlier. The search for security justifies the sacrifice of other liberties or values deemed as secondary.[66] The integration and centralization of the intelligence services was accepted by the majority of citizens in the context of a crisis without demur. Everyone assumes that these transformations only affect the "enemies" of the state and does not directly concern them.[67]

The definition of spheres of power as informational and no longer territorial is fundamental to this institutional restructuring. In 1960, the American sociologist Daniel Bell conceptualized a post-industrial society based on power residing in "intelligence technology." Some years later, Z. Brzezinski returned to the mechanisms of a technological and electronic revolution, implementing a strategy of global domination by and for information based on a "diplomacy network."[68] The American DoD played a considerable role in calling for an "information dominance" in all types of conflicts. Its research organ, the Defense Advanced Research Projects Agency (DARPA) has also conducted research to "map" the internet recording everything from traffic to topology creating databases. This is put into the service of the long term objectives of the infowar or informational war. This effort is called the Cooperative Association for Internet Data Analysis (CAIDA).[69] The Network Centric Warfare (NCW) elaborated during the previous decade responds to the priorities of the fight against transnational threats after 9/11.[70] Military and political intelligence, divided into 15 agencies with their own bureaucracies, contravenes democratic transparency. This is illustrated by the new importance given to "illegal" operations that, as opposed to "covert" activities, escape Congressional supervision.[71]

American law now does not consider the control of digital data as a constitutional violation. Indeed, for the Supreme Court these data are "means" or "technological support" towards other ends. The term espionage thus does not apply to the content of data that are not protected from external interference.[72] Amongst the first to be aimed at are financial networks. Banking institutions have the duty to exchange information under the threat of being excluded from the American market and liable to penalties. The principles of "due diligence" and "compliance" thus force every actor on the international scene, state or non-state, to comply with American laws.[73]

One also wonders after 11 September about the significance of *soft power* as the ability to manipulate the level of threat by sharing a certain representation of it with others. Did the USSR not collapse from an intractable perception of its "world vision," ideology, and value system.[74] Did the Communist ideology not experience difficulty in resisting the expansion of an information society, while denying the competitive market of ideas? Generally, there was a marked improvement in America's ability to exploit the sub-state wars coupled with the use of infowar.[75] Security also became a more diffuse concept applicable to all sectors of society, including individuals in their daily lives.[76] According to A.B. Zegart, intelligence has become the ultimate weapon of postmodern conflicts as long as the United States is the sole superpower of cyberspace capable of controlling virtual space.[77] Beyond traditional boundaries is drawn a *noopolitique* that delimits cognitive spaces (*noosphere*) that are no longer territorial.[78] We have passed from a national definition of security in 1947 to an ideologically diffuse one in 2002. The Homeland is no longer definable in terms of territory to defend but a system of values to protect.

Homeland security and civil defense, fear as a tool of social change

The Homeland Security Act (2002) and its department, DHS, legalised spying in the United States itself, a practice formerly prohibited by the National Security Act (1947).

The same notion of "Homeland" reflects the acceptance of the dematerialization of the war front, shifting from security of the state to that of the individual and radically putting into question the principle of sovereignty. The Federal Emergency Management Agency (FEMA) edited a brochure about mobilization entitled "Are you ready?" in August 2004, which was reminiscent of the "Civil Defense" programs in the 1950s. These were elaborated by the Psychological Strategy Board (PSB). The PSB upheld the principle that future conflicts would only be won on the domestic front, with the morale of the nation becoming an essential component of power.[79] The reinforcement of the resilience of the American people would prepare them for the sacrifices necessary to safeguard their values.[80] Information campaigns, relayed by private institutions, affected the emotions of the public while artificially modifying the perception of danger.[81] As Oakes underlines:

> If emotions are cultural artefacts, they can be intentionally, even self consciously formed, molded, manipulated, worked out, and worked upon. [...] Civil defence specialists developed a plan to bring the public psychology into conformity with the requirements of national security.[82]

Paul Nitze, the author of directive NSC-68, father of the National Security State, was partisan to a policy of psychological mobilization. He was joined a few years later by the Committee on the Present Danger (CPD) followed by Ronald Reagan and numerous other neoconservatives who considered any "appeasement" as a compromise of American ideals and injurious to national security.[83] After 9/11, Secretary of Defense Donald Rumsfeld resuscitated the spirit of the Nitze doctrine by demonstrating how geopolitical ambitions could be concealed behind ideals. He privately declared, "Keep elevating the threat. [...] Make the American people realize they are surrounded in the world by violent extremists."[84]

One of the vehicles of mobilization after the attacks of September 2001 was popular culture and film. It is no coincidence that a large number of metaphorical Hollywood films from the 1950s, with the theme of external threats such as Martian invasions and the end of the world, have been readapted in new big budget productions.[85] These give the threat a polymorphous character, espousing and reflecting the doctrinal renewal.[86] These "strategic fictions" make the threat seem real and credible. They train people to be favorably disposed to the ideas of the Executive and the Pentagon through entertainment.[87] Never has propaganda appeared so dematerialized and easy to sell and export outside American borders.[88]

During the second term of George W. Bush (2005–9), dissenting opinions were censured and the opposition marginalized, while those lacking patriotism were seen as conspirators. The media relayed sensational content and the more liberal among them were forced to resort to self-censorship from fear of being subjected to boycotts and financial sanctions.[89] Numerous political organizations, public events, and meetings have been criminalized, linked to terrorists or terrorist organizations by the FBI.[90] The return of the unofficial practice of "black lists," recalling the darkest days of McCarthyism, caused individuals to fear being subjected to public defamation.[91] In recent years there has been a proliferation of lists of individuals or legal persons wanted for their alleged involvement in criminal organizations. This is a practice that is widespread beyond American borders. Hunting the ideological enemy can even be observed on university campuses where think tanks such as "Campus Watch" have asserted the duty of denouncing political disloyalty on campus and encouraging the denunciation of such courses and the persons who give them. This recalls the initiatives of neoconservative organizations, close to the CPD, Accuracy in Media (AIM) and Accuracy in Academia (AIA), which pursued the same goals of controlling the ideological orthodoxy during the presidency of Ronald Reagan.[92]

Emotions, particularly fear, are vectors capable of guaranteeing social change, while assuring public adhesion to a normative and discursive apparatus.[93] The Copenhagen School of Political Science has analyzed this process of "securitization" through which an existential threat generates the acceptance of measures seen as securing values that are endangered.[94] Security is becoming almost "virtual" because it reflects the system of values of a particular elite. The "Homeland" becomes a new sacred entity that needs to be defended against virtually all forms of subversion and conspiracy, wherever it is found.[95]

The United States is by far the most well-placed to exploit borderless conflicts. The information market is much more homogeneous than it appears, both concentrated and closed to outside influences, which represents an advantage in the service of defining and disseminating ideas to the outside, made possible after 11 September 2001.[96] NATO is progressively integrating the American concept of Homeland into the Transatlantic Homeland.

Exportation of the strategic culture and the birth of the Transatlantic Homeland

NATO, fruit of the security representations of the Cold War, seemed to be deprived of a mission after 1991 and lost its legitimacy not only in the eyes of the allies but also the international community. At the end of the 1990s, the review "Security Dialogue" reported an inevitable fracture within the organization:

> Only if European and US threat perceptions and policies match will NATO be the preferred framework for action. […] It is difficult to see how the idea of a transatlantic community of values can be sustained. […] In the end, this means that NATO won't last.[97]

Europe made progress with the adoption of a policy of dialog in the face of terrorism, and its diplomacy saw encouraging results in the Middle East. Only the United States and Israel remained skeptical towards this policy which they described as "soft on terrorism."[98] Israel continues to deny that the EU dialogue with the Palestinian authorities in defining the boundaries of a state.[99] Following the terrorist attacks against American interests in Nairobi, Kenya (1998), NATO was asked to mobilize against these new transnational threats. Bruce Hoffman explains the different attitudes towards terrorism among the transatlantic partners by the fact that the United States has an international approach while that of the European states is above all national and thus more limited.[100]

Since October 2001, the American "war against terror" has put other actors on the defensive.[101] The Europeans face an evident coordination problem with the enlargement of the concept of security, separate from territory and transposed to a global level.[102] Before the Council of the European Union adopted guidelines for a common security policy, each European state sought to communicate its policy intentions in a scattered manner, trying to limit the use of warlike discourse while preserving their credibility in the eyes of international opinion.[103] The attacks in Madrid (2004) and London (2005), with no proven links to Al-Qaeda, increased tensions within the EU. Spain and Great Britain were among the more Atlanticist powers.[104] Since March 2004, with the election of the new Prime Minster José Luis Rodriguez Zapatero, Spain has indicated its intention to rejoin the European family without breaking its commitments to the United States. The first years thus translated into an undeniable crisis of transatlantic consensus.

NATO will be given missions that it did not have during the previous decade. It will perpetuate its role as a vehicle for American engagement in European security affairs while pursuing its enlargement incorporating Moscow's former satellites and relaying the security doctrines to the new members.[105]

Within a few months, NATO became the primary framework for the fight against terrorism, acting as the disseminator of the new security standards vis-à-vis its members and partners.[106] At the Prague Summit (November 2002), directives concerning the anti-terrorist fight were developed, making the "Military Concept for Defence against Terrorism" its official policy. Operation Active Endeavour (OAE) became, under NATO auspices, a mission to securitize the entire Mediterranean up to the gates of the Black Sea by 2009. Since August 2003, NATO controlled the military forces in Afghanistan, the International Security Assistance Force (ISAAF). The following year it demonstrated to the entire world its capacities to prevent terrorism and bioterrorism by establishing a task force and its deployment to secure the Olympic Games in Athens (2004). It was at the Riga summit (November 2006) that the notion of Transatlantic Homeland was finally adopted.[107] The Homeland embodies a community of not only American but also transatlantic and Western values with NATO as the new guarantor.

One must take a nuanced approach, however, to avoid making the allied powers seem subservient. If the European states have accepted a redefinition of the tasks of the Alliance, this did not mean that they have abandoned their ambitions for common defense or that NATO has become the sole framework, as demonstrated by the development of the European Security and Defence Policy (ESDP).[108] However, it is difficult to deny that a common security policy has become inconceivable outside of the Alliance as it has become the central military and civilian co-ordination organ.[109] On their side, the United States demonstrated that it still prefers to have freedom of manouvre by using bilateral frameworks when it suits it. This has led some experts to say that NATO is only playing a subsidiary role in the fight against terrorism.[110]

The effect of American pressure to transform the "security culture" engendered notable resistance that weakened rather than reinforced the Alliance. Some were tempted to practice what Robert A. Pope has called "soft balancing," that is, the use of non-military means, such as economic might, to counter American dominance.[111] This temptation will without doubt be attenuated by the new presidency of Barack H. Obama, who has tried to soften the doctrine of his predecessor in the sense of a renewed dialog that does not, however, put into question the fundamentals of the antiterrorist fight. NATO's sixtieth anniversary in April 2009 gave rise to celebrations that were meant to show the unity of its members and the health of the organization. Similarly, France, traditionally reluctant to conform to the Atlantic framework, an expression of its Gaullist legacy, rejoined the ranks under the presidency of Nicolas Sarkozy (2007–), which matched Sarkozy's aspiration to return France to the status of a Great Power.[112]

The UN at its General Assembly on 8 September 2006 adopted a "global counterterrorism strategy."[113] Regional organizations, including the OAS and the ASEAN, took note of the effects of the new strategy, which challenged institutional regimes, violating their spheres of sovereignty.[114] According to the figures, there are no fewer than 23 countries that have agreed to act as intermediaries in American military operations, sheltering their armed forces; 89 countries have authorized the Americans to use their airspace; 76 approved landing rights; and 142 have issued orders to freeze the bank accounts of organizations suspected of being affiliated with terrorists.[115]

No state can pretend to ignore that a refusal to collaborate could lead to reprisals or stigmatization as a terrorist support network. The new security policies have led to many abuses and violations of human rights. As Renée de Nevers said, terrorism is fought above all through non-military means, with law enforcement and intelligence gathering.[116] In February 2009, an international commission composed of eminent jurists (ICJ) specifically denounced the abuses caused by the adoption of emergency laws and the regular practice of spying and secrecy of the current policy. The danger lies in legalizing what appears to be legitimate.[117] Indeed, intelligence activities conducted in secret have been at the heart of many violations in third countries which were reinforced by their repressive policies, paving the way for the persecution and torture of political opponents.[118] UNESCO has played a role, although heavily criticized, in the defense of cultural spheres against systematic penetration and application of information technologies for security.[119]

The United States is at present the only state to practice pre-emption. NATO itself has not as yet engaged in offensive operations outside of Afghanistan. Its members risk more interventions though under the pretext of the solidarity of its members (article 5 of its charter) to defend the transatlantic Homeland. The adoption of preventive measures and principles of asymmetric war by the European members may become more blatant as they increase their engagement in Afghanistan or an enlarged theatre of operation.[120] The risk of an indefinite extension of the conflict is undermining the credibility of the United States and its allies in the eyes of world opinion and particularly in Arab countries. Rapidly becoming the largest civil–military organization in peacetime, NATO defies anyone to try and question its existence. An instrument of peace that is above all a weapon of war that, like all bureaucracies, responds to its own rules. The warning applies to powers outside this "community of values" and those who call into question the merits of its missions or even its very existence.[121] The United States is carrying on its shoulders, like the mythic figure of Atlas, the burden that it has taken upon itself, as the last, only and sole superpower, "provider" of security at the global level.[122]

Conclusion

Security doctrines are not radically modified overnight, but are the result of a long-term process allowing the legitimation and of the use of asymmetric force by the technological superiority acquired during the Reagan era and entrenched through security legislations. As the source of power is not static, the "strategic culture" remains flexible and modular, influenced by "external pressures." This American strategic culture and view of security, while asserting the universality of its defense model, based on its experience and values, imposed a de facto hegemony of norms and values on others. As stipulated in the National Security Strategy (NSS 2002):

> There is a single sustainable model for national success—ours—that is right and true for every person in every society [...] The United States must defend liberty and justice because these principles are right and true for all people everywhere.[123]

The process of merging domestic and international security is imposed on the allies of the United States who are then faced with the necessity of adapting their "security culture" and accepting the American approach to terrorism as part of a larger scheme.[124] NATO managed to perpetuate its existence, despite the temporary absence of a mission. It remains the preferred channel through which the Americans retain influence over European affairs by making them accept a common defense of the Transatlantic Homeland.

The revolution in communications technologies has supported the realization of *soft power* as a new power, following the construction and distribution of networks; these networks are not governed by democratic principles of distribution but by "power laws."[125] Like a road map, the communication channels are divided into a web more or less dense and complex depending on the size of the arteries, the challenge is to design the maps, to determine the rules and signals, designing the paths to take according to circumstances. One can predict that in terms of "zones" (or regions) some will be isolated, made to disappear, while others will become important hubs.[126]

Thus, one cannot deny the reinforcement of the capacity of the United States, in less than a decade, to set the agenda for other actors.[127] In fact, the concept of *soft power* should include (beyond mere influence by attraction) the ability to "dictate the agenda" by imposing concepts through the use of intermediaries and specific technologies, which J. Nye never explained.[128] As Armand Mattelart said, "The concept of soft power reflects the hidden side of globalization doctrines, namely the thinking of the military establishment."[129] Tom Ridge, the director of the DHS was, in turn, very clear when he addressed the Electronic Industries Alliance in 2002: "Computer networks have become incorporated in the development of hard military power, but they have also become the mainstay of soft power."[130]

Understanding terrorism as the hatred of Western values by a radical Islam is without any real foundation. Yet this thesis in conjunction with the idea of a clash of civilisation. has been growing acceptance with the general public. The fight against terrorism is, as noted in this chapter, a pretext for the deployment of the new option of asymmetric warfare. The rapidity of technological change and the capacity to adapt to it are important facets of power and the cultural approach to security is key to understanding this phenomenon.[131] Europe has had another bitter experience as it struggles to coordinate its imposing bureaucratic structure. On the other hand, the speed with which the United States took action after 2001 by adopting a range of security laws (the Patriot Act, the Homeland Security Act, NSS) demonstrates its capacity to retain its power, by reformulating its "grand strategy" over half a century and revolutionizing its pre-existing institutional and structural frameworks.[132] Henceforth, the information war may take the form of a "war of identity" in which all borders, including cognitive ones, can be challenged.[133] The boundaries between hard and soft power are likely to disappear as they are merged in the new security framework thus defined.

Notes

1 Adrian Guelke, *The Age of Terrorism and the International Political system*, (New York, I. B. Tauris, 1995), p. 14.
2 Johan Eriksson and Giampiero Giacomello, 'Closing the gap between international relations theory and studies of digital-age security', *International Relations and Security in the Digital Age*, (New York, Routledge, 2007), p. 2; Arnold Wolfers, 'National Security as an Ambiguous Symbol', *Political Science Quarterly*, no. 67, 1952, p. 485–88. The author states that security is also measured by the absence of fear that these values will be attacked. Wolfers states that when a state aspires to increase its security, it creates suspicion that this nation is concealing aggressive goals.

3 K.M. Fierke, *Critical approaches to international security*, (Cambridge: Polity, 2007), p. 14. It needs to be established how, in an information society, the dissemination of information can become a means of production like any other service provided by security institutions.
4 For a definition of strategic culture and culture of security, see Keith Krause, 'Conclusions: Security Culture and the Non-proliferation, Arms Control and Disarmament Agenda', *Contemporary Security Policy*, no. 19, 1998, pp. 221–22. This explains the difficulty of showing the role of cultural factors outside of the language process.
5 Walter L. Hixson, *The myth of American diplomacy, national identity and U.S. foreign policy*, (London: Yale University Press, 2008), p. 304.
6 David A. Baldwin, 'The concept of security', in Michael Sheehan (ed.), *National and International Security*, (Burlington: Ashgate, 2000), p. 46.
7 Andrew J. Bacevich, *The limits of power, the end of American exceptionalism*, (New York: Metropolitan Books, 2008), p. 118; John Prados, 'Intelligence for Empire', in Andrew J. Bacevich (ed.), *The Long War, a new history of U.S. national security policy since World War II*, (New York: Columbia University Press, 2007), pp. 302–34; Paul Rogers, *Global Security and the War on terror, elite power and the illusion of control*, (New York: Routledge, 2008).
8 Chalmers Johnson, *The Sorrow of Empire, militarism, secrecy, and the End of the Republic*, (New York: Metropolitan Books, 2004), p. 22.
9 Hixson, *The myth of American diplomacy*, p. 294; Fierke, *Critical approaches*, p. 39; see also R.A. Hinde and H.E. Watson, *War: a cruel necessity? The bases of institutionalized violence*, (New York: Tauris, 1995), pp. 145–49.
10 Joseph Nye invented this concept in 1990 in his work *Bound to Lead* (New York: Basic Books, 1990), and developed 'smart power' in his work *The Powers to Lead*, (Oxford: Oxford University Press, 2008). According to him, soft and hard power reinforce one another. This concept overlaps with intangible resources such as the influence of culture, values, communication capacity, scientific, and technological influence.
11 Joseph S. Nye, 'The Changing Nature of World Power', *Political Science Quarterly*, no. 105, 1990, p. 192.
12 Christoph O. Meyer, *The Quest for a European Strategic Culture*, (New York: MacMillan, 2006), p. 11; Jürgen Haacke, *ASEAN's diplomatic and security culture*, (New York: Routledge, 2003).
13 After the hostages were taken in Munich, a 'Cabinet Committee to Combat Terrorism' was established by an executive order of President R. Nixon.
14 Guelke, *The Age of Terrorism*, pp. 149–59.
15 D. Allin and S. Simon, Comprendre le soutien des Etats-Unis envers Israël, www.diplomatie.gouv.fr/fr/IMG/pdf/AFRI%2025.pdf (accessed 10 January 2010).
16 Noam Chomsky and Edward Herman, *La Fabrication du consentement*, (Marseille: Agone, 2008), p. 297, Claire Sterling, published in 1981, 'Les Réseaux de la terreur', qui servirait de référence à l'administration Reagan.
17 1977 Director of Central Intelligence Report on The Intelligence Community, Secret, March 1977, in archives of the CIA, Washington.
18 In 1974, Brian Jenkins of the RAND Corporation published a work entitled: *International Terrorism: A New Kind of Warfare*, viewing terrorism as a conspiracy. See also John B. Wolf, 'Controlling Political Terrorism in a Free Society', *Orbis*, no. 19, Winter 1976, pp. 1289–1308.
19 Bacevich, *The Limits of Power*, p. 27; Guelke, *The Age of Terrorism*, p. 148.
20 Tony Smith, *America's Mission, The United States and the Worldwide struggle for democracy in the Twentieth Century*, (Princeton, 1994), p. 323. Reagan called for the pursuit of a "democratic revolution."
21 During Reagan's first term, experts relayed the position of the administration, such as Dr. Kupperman, announcing a technological "superterrorism" on the horizon. They wanted to "take the initiative in declaring war" stated in John W. Amos and Russel H.S. Stolfi, 'Controlling International Terrorism: Alternatives Palatable and Unpalatable', *Annals of the American Academy of Political and Social Science*, vol. 463, sept 1982, pp. 80, 81, 83.
22 The directive was never declassified, but an extract was prepared by the NSC outlining some of its provisions. National Security Archives, www.gwu.edu/~nsarchiv/NSAEBB/NSAEBB55/index1.html (accessed 10 January 2010). The bombing of flight KL007 remains disputed. It should be recalled that in 1955, the CIA planned to blow up a Chinese airliner en route to a conference of non-aligned countries, while in March 1962 Operation Northwoods planned to blow up a US airliner to justify intervention in Cuba.

23 Cited in *Review of the News*, 9 May 1984, p. 53, in CIA archives. Law S.2469 made terrorism a federal crime and gave the FBI the necessary competences.
24 Executive Order (EO) 12947 of 23 janvier 1995, and EO 13099 of 20 août 1998.
25 Article by Bernard Lewis, 'Licence to Kill, Usama bin Ladin's Declaration of Jihad' in *Foreign Affairs*, November-December 1998, pp. 14–19; see also Hixson, *The myth of American diplomacy*, p. 288.
26 Joint Pub 1–02 of 17 April 1998, cited in Joint Pub 3–05, Doctrine for Joint Special Operations, 17 December 2003, www.dtic.mil/doctrine/jel/new_pubs/jp3_05.pdf (last accessed 10 January 2010), p. GL-11. This definition matched that contained in US law: Title 50, sec 1801. It stated that such acts can take place on or off of American soil.
27 Joint Pub 3–05, section II, 8. The information war is defined by Daniel Ventre as "all means to achieve and secure the dominance of information to support the political and military strategies, through the manipulation of information systems and the information of the enemy, and at the same time providing security and protection of one's own information and information systems in order to increase their effectiveness." In Daniel Ventre, *La guerre de l'information*, (Paris: Lavoisier, 2007), pp. 21–22.
28 The Goldwater-Nichols *Department of Defense Reorganization Act of 1986* (Washington, DC: GPO, 1986), Public Law 99–433.
29 Susan D. Moeller, *Packaging terrorism, co-opting the news for politics and profit*, (Chichester: Wiley Blackwell, 2009), pp. 18, 22, 27.
30 Daniel Ventre, *La guerre de l'information*, (Paris: Lavoisier, 2007) pp. 53–54; Stephen Burman, *The State of the American Empire, how the USA shapes the world*, (Brighton: Earthscan, 2007), p. 13.
31 Christopher Layne, 'From Preponderance to Offshore Balancing, America's Future Grand Strategy', *International Security*, no. 22, 1997, p. 104; Aaron L. Friedberg, 'The future of American power', *Political Science Quarterly*, no. 109, 1994, pp. 10–11.
32 Andrew Martin, 'Popular culture and narratives of insecurity', in Andrew Martin and Partice Petro (ed.), (London: Rutgers, 2006), p. 106; Bernard Wicht, *L'OTAN attaque, la nouvelle donne stratégique*, (Geneva, 1999), p. 97; Martin Van Creveld, *La Transformation de la guerre*, (Paris: Editions du Rocher, 1998), p. 258.
33 Armand Mattelart, 'An Archeology of the global era: constructing a belief', *Media, Culture & Society*, no. 24, 2002, p. 609; Richard K. Betts, *Enemies of Intelligence, Knowledge and Power in American National Security*, (New York: Columbia University Press, 2007), p. 2. According to the author, before 9/11 experts thought that it would take a revolution to finally adapt the framework of the *National Security Act*, 1947.
34 Bacevich, *The limits of power*, pp. 33–36; Manuel De Landa, *The War in the Age of Intelligent Machines*, (New York: Zone Books, 1991).
35 Robert J. Pauly Jr. Tom Lansford, Jack Covarrubias, *To Protect and Defend US Homeland Security Policy*, (Burlington: Ashgate, 2006), p. 18.
36 The *National Security Strategy* NSS 1990 called for the projection of power through the creation of a truly global police force. See Johnson, *The Sorrow of Empire*, pp. 18–20.
37 Andrew J. Bacevich (ed.), *The Long war, a new history of U.S. National Security Policy*, (New York: Columbia University Press, 2007), p. 33.
38 Report of the Center for Strategic & International Studies, 'Foreign Policy into the 21st Century: The U.S. Leadership Challenge', (CSIS, Washington, DC: September 1996), p. 37.
39 Robert H. Kupperman and Ass. Inc., 'Low Intensity conflict', vol. 1, Main Report, Ad-A 137260, Fort Monroe, VA, US Army Tradoc, 1983, pp. iv, vi–vii.
40 Dewar James, et al., *Army culture and planning in a time of great change*, Santa Monica, CA, RAND corp., 1996, pp. 2–3, 8, 42; the studies of some specialists affirm the possibility of a change in beliefs, contrary to realist and neorealist doctrine, Keith Krause, 'Conclusions: Security Culture and the Non-proliferation, Arms Control and Disarmament Agenda', *Contemporary Security Policy*, no. 19, 1998, pp. 219–39; the review *Relations Internationales* dedicated its second issue in 1974 to the question of collective mentalities and to the national character and indicated that they were not stable over time; J.-B. Duroselle, 'Opinion, attitude, mentalité, mythe, idéologie: essai de clarification', *Relations Internationales*, no. 2, 1974, pp. 4–24.
41 Joseph Nye, *Bound to Lead: The changing nature of American Power*, (New York: Basic Books, 1990).
42 Huntington established a new intellectual and moral hierarchy in his book.
43 Robert M. Cassidy, *Counterinsurgency and the global war on terror, military culture and irregular war*, (Westport, 2006), p. 12 and Albert J. Bergesen and Omar Lizardo, 'International Terrorism and the World System', *Sociological Theory*, vol. 22, no. 1, 2004, p. 42.

44 On 8 May 1984, Dr. Robert Kupperman of CSIS announced: "My guess is you're going to see a bomb against the State Department," on 21 May 1984, the *Washington Times* headline on page 2: "U.S. found ill prepared for terrorism," on 24 June *The Washingtonian* dedicated a special edition on terrorism with the headline: "Where will Terrorists Strike Next?"
45 In December 1998, the DCI George Tenet issued a directive in which he intensified the efforts of the CIA to declare that the United States was at war, see Betts, *Enemies of intelligence*, pp. 110, 127.
46 Eriksson and Giacomello, 'Closing the gap', p. 8.
47 Ibid. p. 68–69.
48 Cassidy, *Counterinsurgency*, p. 14.
49 Betts, *Enemies of intelligence*, p. 6; see the declaration of Brian Sheridan, Assistant Secretary of Defense for Special Operations and Low-intensity Conflict, before the subcommittee on emerging threats and capabilities of the Committee on Armed Services, United States 106th Congress, Department of Defense and Combating Terrorism, March 24 2000.
50 See le projet *Infragard*, a public-private partnership directed by the FBI and the private sector, www.infragard.net.
51 Elinor C. Sloan, *The Revolution in Military Affairs*, (Montreal: McGill University Press, 2002), p. 148.
52 Heinz Vetschera, 'Civil-military relations and democratic control: A European security policy perspective', in NATO defense college (ed.), *Military Assistance to the civil authorities in democracies: case studies and perspectives*, (Frankfurt: Peter Lang, 1997), pp. 15–16.
53 Jessica T. Mathews, 'The Information Revolution', *Foreign Policy*, no. 119, 2000, p. 64.
54 Michael C. Williams, *Culture and Security, symbolic power and the politics of international security*, (New York: Routledge, 2007), p. 41; Jim Garrison, 'America as Empire: Global Leader or Rogue Power?', in Earthscan (ed.), *Human and Environmental security, an agenda for change*, (London, 2005), p. 203; Luis Fernando Ayerbe, 'Amérique latine et Etats-Unis: néoconservatisme et guerre culturelle', *Cultures et mondialisation, résistance et alternatives*, (Paris, 2000), pp. 102–3.
55 R. Kagan, cited by Scott Lucas, *The Betrayal of dissent*, (London: Pluto Press, 2004), p. 184.
56 Mohammed Dahbi, 'English and Arabic after 9/11', *The Modern Language Journal*, no. 88, 2004, p. 628; Leon T. Hadar discusses the adoption of a strategy of global revolution from the Bush administration, serving a pro-Israeli policy. Leon T. Hadar, 'The New American Imperialism vs. the Old Europe', *Journal of Palestine Studies*, no. 32, 2003, p. 74.
57 Amy B. Zegart, *Spying Blind, The CIA, the FBI and the Origins of 9/11*, (Princeton: Princeton University Press, 2007).
58 According to the *Foreign Intelligence Surveillance Act 1978* which institutionalized the process of supervision.
59 Betts, *Enemies of intelligence*, p. 173.
60 John Prados, 'Intelligence for Empire', in Andrew J. Bacevich (ed.), *The Long War, a new history of U.S. national security policy since World War II*, (New York: Columbia University Press, 2007), p. 304.
61 Klaus Günther, 'World Citizens between freedom and security', in David Dyzenhaus (ed.), *Civil Rights and Security*, (Toronto: Ashgate, 2009), p. 382.
62 Signed on 26 October 2001, the Patriot Act is an abbreviation for: Uniting and strengthening America by providing tools required to intercept and obstruct terrorism act. In 2002 and 2003 the 'National Strategy to secure cyberspace' was introduced. Among the most important laws under the Patriot II H.R. 3037 The Antiterrorism Tools Enhancement Act of 2003; H.R. 3040 and S. 1606 The Pretrial Detention and Lifetime Supervision of Terrorists Act 2003; H.R. 2934 and S. 1604, The Terrorist Penalties Enhancement Act of 2003.
63 Mary N. Layoun, 'Visions of Security, impermeable borders, impassable walls, impossible Home/Lands?', in Andrew Martin and Patrice Petro (eds.), *Rethinking Global security, Media popular culture and the War on terror*, (London: Rutgers University Press, 2006), pp. 48–49.
64 Myriam A. Dunn, 'Securing the digital age, the challenge of complexity for critical infrastructure protection and IR theory', *International Relations and Security in the Digital Age*, (New York: Routedge, 2007), p. 93.
65 Richard K. Betts, 'The soft underbelly of American Primacy: Tactical advantages of Terror', *Political Science Quarterly*, no. 117, 2002, pp. 19–36. Betts also claims that Al-Qaeda rebels against American soft power. Richard K. Betts, *Enemies of intelligence, Knowledge and Power in American National Security*, pp. 9–12.

66 K. M. Fierke, *Critical approaches to international security*, (Cambridge: Polity, 2007), pp. 39–42; David A. Baldwin, 'The concept of security', in Michael Sheehan (ed.), *National and International Security*, (Burlington: Ashgate, 2000), p. 46.
67 Jeremy Waldron, 'Security and Liberty: the image of Balance', in David Dyzenhaus (ed.), *Civil Rights and Security* (Toronto: Ashgate, 2009), pp. 192–94.
68 Armand Mattelart, 'An Archeology of the global era: constructing a belief', *Media, Culture & Society*, no. 24, 2002, p. 599–600; Z. Brzezinski, *La Révolution technétronique*, (Paris: Calmann-Lévy, 1971), translated from English by Jean Viennet, 1971, 387 p. [original title: *Between two Ages, America's role in the Technetronic era*]. At the time Brzezinski believed that 65 per cent of global communications came from the United States.
69 Ibid. p. 148.
70 Ken Dark, 'The changing form of post-Cold War security', in Dartmouth (ed.), *New Studies in Post-Cold War Security* (Brookfield: Dartmouth, 1996), pp. 12–16; Mattelart describes how in the 1990s a project to reorder the world through networks crystallized. Armand Mattelart, 'Société de la connaissance, société de l'information, société de contrôle', *Cultures et conflits*, no. 64, 2006, p. 168.
71 The ' plausible deniability ' clause is in the law, U.S.C. title 50, sect 413b, the 'covert action' is defined as a government activity in contrast to the illegal operations, conducted by the Pentagon, which do not require Congressional approval. In 2006, the new name given to the Director of Operations of the CIA became the National Clandestine Service.
72 James B. Ferguson, 'Information Warfare and National Security: Some First Amendment Issues', in Stuart J.D. Schwartzstein (ed.), *The Information Revolution and National Security Dimensions and Directions*, (Washington, DC: The Center for Strategic & International Studies, 1996), pp. 38–40.
73 The first principle allows the acquisition of information on third entities, the second calls for submission to the rules laid down. However, as noted by Xavier Raufer these two principles do not account for cultural differences that may influence the security culture. X. Raufer, "La guerre contre la terreur," *La Nouvelle Revue d'histoire*, no. 40, janv-fevr. 2009, pp. 53–54.
74 In 1996, Katzenstein explained how national security interests depend on the construction of a "self identity," Peter J. Katzenstein and Social Science Research Council (U.S.). Committee on International Peace & Security, *The culture of national security: norms and identity in world politics*, (New York, Columbia University Press, 1996), p. 59–60; see J.F. Metzl who explains the exploitation of existing prejudices. Jamie Frederic Metzl, 'Popular diplomacy', *Deadalus*, no. 128, 1999, p. 178.
75 Bernard Wicht, *L'OTAN attaque, la nouvelle donne stratégique*, (Geneva, Georg ed., 1999), p. 97; Daniel Gourré, 'The Impact of the Information revolution on strategy and doctrine', in Stuart J.D. Schwartzenstein (ed.), *The Information revolution and National security dimensions and directions*, (Washington: The Center for Strategic and international Studies, 1996), pp. 218–19.
76 Johan Eriksson and Giampiero Giacomello, 'Closing the gap between international relations theory and studies of digital-age security', *International Relations and Security in the Digital Age*, (New York: Routledge, 2007), p. 2; Elinor C. Sloan, *The Revolution in Military Affairs*, (Montreal: McGill University Press, 2002), p. 147; Jessica T. Mathews, 'The Information Revolution', *Foreign Policy*, no. 119, 2000, pp. 64–65.
77 Amy B. Zegart, *Spying Blind, The CIA, the FBI and the Origins of 9/11*, (Princeton: Princeton University Press, 2007), pp. 166–67; in February 2009 the ICJ denounced the use of technology and intelligence to penetrate the private sphere. International Commission of Jurists, 'Assessing Damage, urging action,' (Geneva, 2009), p. 13.
78 Until now, Russia has found it difficult to resist the cultural influence relayed by the networks of private foundations funding the new "independent" media. See Boris Pétric, "Dossier, les élites russes à l'épreuve de la culture d'influence", in *La Croix*, 6 May 2005. Most of the "freedom fighters" of the revolutions of Eastern Europe were aided in one way or another by organizations such as Freedom House, National Endowment for Democracy, Open Society, etc.
79 Susan D. Moeller, *Packaging terrorism, co-opting the news for politics and profit*, (Chichester, West Sussex: Wiley Blackwell, 2009), p. 4; The PSB was created 4 April 1951 by a secret presidential directive that legally reduced psychological activities outside of the United States. See G. Oakes, who describes how a program of 'emotion management' was developed, Guy Oakes, *The Imaginary war, civil defense and American Cold war culture*, (Oxford: Oxford University Press, 1994), p. 47.
80 Ibid., p. 33, p. 47; war itself can be seen as a tool of psychological warfare. The battle is organized so as to destroy the morale of the enemy in order to destroy the opposing system.

81 Patricia Mellencamp, 'U.S. television since 9/11 and the war in Iraq', in Andrew Martin and Partice Petro (ed.), *Rethinking Global security, media popular culture and the War on Terror*, (London: 2006), pp. 117, 128; studies on the psychology of the media have shown that emotions paralyze our ability to question information we are given.
82 Oakes, *The Imaginary war*, p. 33, p. 47.
83 Lucas, *The Betrayal of dissent*, p. 92
84 Andrew J. Bacevich, *The limits of power, the end of American exceptionalism*, (New York: Metropolitan Books, 2008), p. 112.
85 Some examples: "War of the Worlds" (S. Spielberg, 2005); "When Worlds Collide" (S. Sommers, 2008); "The Day the Earth Stood Still" (S. Derrickson, 2008).
86 Jean-Michel Valentin, *Hollywood, le Pentagone et Washington, les trois acteurs d'une stratégie globale*, (Paris: Autrement, 2003).
87 Doug Davis, 'Future-War Storytelling, national security and popular film', in Andrew Martin and Patrice Petro (ed.), *Rethinking Global Security, media popular culture and the war on terror*, (London: Rudgers, 2006), p. 15, James Castonguay, 'Intermedia and the war on terror' in ibid. recounts the ties between American intelligence and film directors, the Institute for Creative Technology at the University of Southern California has among others inspired film scripts about terrorism. *Die Hard* by John McTiernan (1988) was a product of this collaboration. See also R.A. Hinde and H.E. Watson, *War: a cruel necessity? The bases of institutionalized violence*, (New York: Tauris, 1995), p. 146.
88 See the notion of *Military-Industrial-Entertainment Network* (MIME-NET) used by James DerDerian. Propaganda is elaborated to educate people about a complex body of doctrine.
89 Scott Lucas, *The Betrayal of dissent*, p. 137, p. 174; Hixson, *The myth of American diplomacy*, p. 288.
90 Lisa Rein, 'Federal Agency Aided Md. Spying, Homeland Security Dept. gave information to State police', in *Washington Post*, 17 February 2009, B01.
91 Moeller, *Packaging terrorism*, p. 27; James Castonguay, 'Intermedia and the war on terror', in Andrew Martin and Patrice Petro (ed.), *Rethinking Global Security, media popular culture and the war on terror*, (London, 2006), pp. 151–53; see the report *International Commission of Jurists*, Communiqué de Presse, Geneva, 16 February 2009, p. 13.
92 'Campus Watch' by Daniel Pipes, reply by Michael Massing, The New York Review of Books, vol. 53, no. 12, July 13, 2006; for the AIA see James D. Hunter, *Culture Wars, the struggle to define America*, (New York: Basic Books, 1991), p. 214.
93 Christoph O. Meyer, *The Quest for a European Strategic Culture*, (New York, 2006), p. 32.
94 Barry Buzan, 'Rethinking Security after the Cold War', in Michael Sheehan (ed.), *National and International Security*, (Burlington: Ashgate, 2000), pp. 329–52.
95 The invention of the concept of noosphere is attributed to Theilard de Chardin in 1947, it means half of the performance of our brains, and by extension it came to mean the cognitive spheres of influence. See also Jamie Frederic Metzl, 'Popular diplomacy', *Deadalus*, no. 128, 1999, pp. 187–90.
96 Charles William Maynes proclaimed in 1998 the supremacy of ' American soft power ', explaining that for neoconservatives, interventions in the internal affairs of other states never seemed so important. For Maynes it was a unique moment that transformed relations between states. Charles William Maynes, 'The Perils of (and for) an Imperial America', *Foreign Policy*, no. 111, 1998, p. 41.
97 Peter Van Ham, 'Security and Culture, or, why NATO won't last', *Security Dialogue*, vol. 32, no. 4, 2001, pp. 393–407.
98 Bruce Hoffman, 'Is Europe soft on Terrorism ?', *Foreign Policy*, no. 115, 1999, p. 73.
99 Renée de Nevers, 'NATO's international security role in the terrorist era', *International Security*, vol. 31, 2007, p. 37.
100 Hoffman, 'Is Europe soft on Terrorism?', p. 65
101 Klaus Günther, 'World Citizens between freedom and security', in David Dyzenhaus (ed.), *Civil Rights and Security*, (Toronto: Ashgate, 2009), p. 385.
102 Christoph O. Meyer, *The Quest for a European Strategic Culture*, (New York, 2006), p. 37; Stephanie B. Anderson, *Crafting EU Security policy, in pursuit of a European identity*, (London, 2008), pp. 93–96; the threat promotes economic interdependence, see Christopher Layne, 'From Preponderance to Offshore Balancing, America's Future Grand Strategy', *International Security*, no. 22, 1997, p. 102.
103 Christoph O. Meyer, *The Quest for a European Strategic Culture*, (New York: MacMillan, 2006), p. 3; in the directive of 28 January 2003, this needed to be done according to 'democratic values'; Klaus Günther described the creation of transnational security architecture, in Klaus Günther,

'World Citizens between freedom and security', in David Dyzenhaus (ed.), *Civil Rights and Security*, (Toronto, 2009), pp. 380–82.
104 Armand Mattelart, 'Société de la connaissance, société de l'information, société de contrôle', *Cultures et conflits*, no. 64, 2006, p. 176. According to the author, soft power is nothing more than strategic doctrine to preserve cultural hegemony.
105 Katzenstein, *The culture of national security*, p. 520; Stephanie B. Anderson, *Crafting EU Security policy, in pursuit of a European identity*, (London: Lynne Rienner, 2008), p. 104.
106 Michael C. Williams, *Culture and Security, symbolic power and the politics of international security*, (New York: Routledge, 2007), p. 41; for a discussion of the 'new threats' to NATO, see Didier Bigo, 'L'idéologie de la menace du Sud', *Cultures et conflits*, (Paris, 1991), p. 10.
107 'Transatlantic Homeland Defense', CTNSP/INSS Special Report (Washington, D.C.: Center for Technology and National Security Policy, Institute for National Strategic Studies, National Defense University, May 2006), www.NDU.edu/ctnsp/pubs/324–005_PO6–210016.pdf (accessed 10 January 2010].
108 On the ESDP, see the contribution by Hanna Ojanen in this volume.
109 David S. Yost, 'Transatlantic Relations and Peace in Europe', *International Affairs*, vol. 78, no. 2, 2002, pp. 277–300
110 de Nevers, 'NATO's international security role', pp. 34–35
111 Robert A. Pape, 'Soft balancing against the United States', *International Security*, vol. 30, no. 1, 2005, pp. 7–45
112 Ibid. p. 64
113 This took the form of a resolution and a plan of action. See www.un.org/french/terrorism/strategy-highlights.shtml (accessed 10 January 2010).
114 Jürgen Haacke, *ASEAN's diplomatic and security culture*, (New York: Routledge, 2003), pp. 231–32.
115 M. Shamsul Haque, 'Government Responses to Terrorism: Critical Views of Their Impacts on People and Public Administration', *Public Administration Review*, vol. 62, September, 2002, p. 172
116 de Nevers, 'NATO's international security role', p. 65
117 International Commission of Jurists, 'A culture of secrecy is becoming pervasive', Communiqué de Presse, Geneva, 16 February 2009, p. 5.
118 Robert Ricigliano and Mike Allen, 'Cold War Redux', in Andrew Martin and Patrice Petro (ed.), *Rethinking Global Security, media, popular culture and the war on terror*, (London: Rutgers, 2006), pp. 89–90.
119 The UN and especially UNESCO have attempted to regulate the impact of communication technologies, slowing the commercialization of cultural property. In its agenda for the 1990s, UNESCO called for the protection of cultural identity, see also UNESCO, 'Les principaux jalons de l'action entreprise pour promouvoir une nouvelle approche de la sécurité', 1994–99, www.unesco.org/cpp/fr/paix/jalons.htm (accessed 10 January 2010). On 20 October 2005 UNESCO adopted a convention on cultural diversity against the advice of the United States and Israel. It warns against the dangerous concentration of means of expression and distribution channels. Syed Husin Ali, 'Impact des médias nord-américains dans le Tiers Monde', *Cultures et mondialisation, résistances et alternatives*, (Paris, 2000), p. 92.
120 The new American Secretary of Defense Robert M. Gates states in his speech before the National Defense University, on 29 September 2008, the guidelines for the future. The Global maneuver would generally be well regarded as a communication operation which would be a battle of arguments. See Vincent Desportes, 'Relire le discours du nouveau secrétaire à la défense américain', *DSI*, no. 44, pp. 32–33.
121 Anatol Lieven, 'The Secret Policemen's Ball: The United States, Russia and the International Order after 11 September', *International Affairs*, no. 78, 2002, p. 249. The author compares the anti-revolutionary character of American actions after 9/11 to the Holy Alliance of 1815.
122 In 2003, the United States still represented 45 per cent of all global defense spending. See Niall Ferguson, 'Power', *Foreign Policy*, no. 134, 2003, this author also denies the influence of American soft power, the security market is estimated at 100 billion US dollars annually.
123 Citation pulled from NSS 2002, cited by Chalmers Johnson, *The Sorrow of Empire, militarism, secrecy, and the End of the Republic*, (New York, Metropolitan Books, 2004), pp. 286–87; see also John Prados, 'Intelligence for Empire', in Andrew J. Bacevich (ed.), *The Long War, a new history of U.S. national security policy since World War II*, (New York: Columbia University Press, 2007), p. 304, 315.
124 Hoffman, 'Is Europe soft on Terrorism?', p. 65

125 Joseph Nye was a former Assistant Secretary of Defense; with William A. Owens they reveal their vision of the future potential of new communication capacities, see Daniel Gourré, 'The Impact of the Information revolution on strategy and doctrine', p. 219.
126 Albert-László Barabási, *Linked,* (London, 2003), p. 72, p. 162.
127 Keith Krause, 'Conclusions: Security Culture and the Non-proliferation, Arms Control and Disarmament Agenda', pp. 219–39.
128 Some authors such as Katzenstein have criticized Nye for failing to demonstrate the relational implication so soft power, Peter J. Katzenstein and Social Science Research Council (U.S.). Committee on International Peace & Security, *The culture of national security: norms and identity in world politics,* (New York, 1996), p. 504; others prefer to talk about 'sticky power' holding the others prisoner in an American institutional fabric, Walter Russell Mead, 'America's Sticky Power', *Foreign Policy*, no. 141, 2004, p. 46–53.
129 Armand Mattelart, 'An Archeology of the global era: constructing a belief', *Media, Culture & Society*, no. 24, 2002, p. 600.
130 Cited by Johan Eriksson and Giampiero Giacomello, 'Closing the gap between international relations theory and studies of digital-age security', *International Relations and Security in the Digital Age,* (New York, 2007), p. 16; directive JCS-2006 defines the operations influences and determines that it is in the cognitive sphere that battles can be lost or won. Cited by Ventre, *La guerre de l'information,* p. 54.
131 Mathews, 'The Information Revolution', p. 65.
132 See John Lewis Gaddis, 'A Grand Strategy of Transformation', *Foreign Policy*, no. 133, 2002, p. 56.
133 John Arquilla and David Ronfeldt, 'Cyberwar is coming', *Comparative strategy*, no. 12, 1993, pp. 141–65; The information war will be a form of conflict that attacks the 'central nervous system' of states; Daniel Gourré, 'The Impact of the Information revolution on strategy and doctrine', in Stuart J.D. Schwartzenstein, ed., *The Information revolution and National security dimensions and directions,* (Washington: The Center for Strategic and International Studies, 1996), p. 225; Ventre, *La guerre de l'information,* p. 21; Nye finally rebutted the point in 2003 in 'The Velvet hegemon'. He asserts that soft power has the ability to manipulate the agenda of other powers. Joseph S. Nye, 'The Velvet Hegemon', *Foreign Policy*, no. 136, 2003, p. 74.

18
European security identity since the end of the Cold War

Guillaume de Rougé

Identity is a complex notion, particularly when applied to international politics.[1] As any pocket dictionary would suggest, its definition is all the more ambivalent: identity is the fact of being the same, i.e. the fact of being what you are – hence, its main synonyms are unity and singularity – as well as the fact of being the same as something else – hence the notion of resemblance and symmetry. As far as the European Union (EU) is concerned, this identity's dialectic deals on the one hand with what divides and gathers European multiple identities and, on the other hand, with what could make the EU a global actor among others on the world stage. How not to quote here the Jacques Delors' famous 'OPNI' (Objet Politique Non Identifié – Unknown Political Object), as well as his oxymoron 'Nation-States Federation' that coined the *sui generis*, but also undetermined nature of the EU? This dialectic is particularly important in relation to security and defence policies, which take a lion's share in Member States constitutive identities. Divided and torn between the two superpowers during the Cold War, Europe had no security identity and was simply not able to prove that it was European; hence, de Gaulle's calls for a 'European Europe', a fully assumed tautology, and Kissinger's teasing: 'Europe? Which phone number?'

The debate over the European security identity dates back to the end of the Second World War and the beginning of the construction of Europe, with the 1947 Dunkirk Treaty, the 1948 Brussels Treaty and the rise and fall of the European Defence Community in the early 1950s. But the phrase 'European security identity' itself dates back to John F. Kennedy's plan for a 'European pillar in the Alliance' in 1962. Since its inception, the concept of a 'European pillar in the Alliance' – notwithstanding the more implicit concept of an American pillar – has been at the heart of transatlantic misunderstandings. However, despite many transatlantic crises – including France's withdrawal from NATO's integrated military structure in 1966 – it was widely accepted as a pillar of NATO itself, through which the USA could provide an existential guarantee to Western Europe during the Cold War. Nevertheless, a proper European security identity gradually emerged during the period of détente, to which the 'Common Declaration on European Identity' adopted by the European Community's (EC) Nine a few weeks after the Helsinki Opening Conference can testify.[2] In contrast, Kissinger's 'Year of Europe' (also in 1973) was largely perceived by EC Member States as an American attempt to impede the crystallization of a European identity. Whereas Kissinger stated that European unity was not an end in itself but only a way to reinforce the West as a whole, French Foreign minister Michel Jobert reproached the USA for treating Europe as a 'non-person', i.e. disregarding its identity.[3]

Although the two superpowers gradually relinquished their duopoly on European strategic affairs, the idea that a European identity would create a European *subject*, and no longer just an *object* of international affairs, gained credibility.[4] Important initiatives emerged during the 1980s, mostly through the European Political Cooperation, but also through Franco-German initiatives and in the Western European Union's (WEU) awakening, gradually (re)introducing a defence component to Europe's strategic horizon. Quasi-mechanically, at the end of the Cold War, the European security identity re-emerged as the European Security and Defence Identity (ESDI), i.e. a European pillar of the Alliance. However intransigence eventually prevailed on both sides of the Atlantic, and renewed Franco-American disagreements overturned attempts to rebalance an outdated transatlantic trade-off. True, Bosnia's challenges gradually raised hope for a settlement, but the ESDI concept never managed to live up to Europeans' or Americans' expectations. As transatlantic dilemmas worsened on the eve of the Kosovo conflict, an autonomous European Security and Defence Policy (ESDP) gradually replaced the untested ESDI concept, but is still looking forward to getting the better of a renewed transatlantic relationship.

From 1990 to 1991: the birth of ESDI

ESDI: 'D' for defence?

Immediately after the end of the Cold War, the very notion of ESDI crystallized transatlantic misunderstandings and the Franco-American *kriegspiel* in particular. From the French point of view, the emergence of the EU as a source of stability and defence in Europe would allow the USA to fine-tune its European strategic equation, optimizing its military footprint through a progressive withdrawal without hindering its room for manoeuvre on the global stage. According to this vision, the Alliance would be rebalanced to make room for Europe. NATO's integration system would be loosened, and eventually replaced by a European crisis management response whose organization still had to be defined, but would be partly restructured without the USA, on the basis of a Franco-German agreement and within the framework of the WEU. Despite its long-term approach, this vision instantaneously worried the US administration and most EC members. A European defence component would vindicate the isolationist trends in the US Congress and provoke the massive US military withdrawal that it was supposed to forestall. As early as February 1990, US National Security advisor Brent Scowcroft told the French that 'if the EEC is politically integrated, we will resent being kept out of decision-making, which will have consequences for us (i.e. the US)'.[5] Admittedly, the Bush administration was prone to play on Congress's fears of being dragged into a conflict by the Europeans. But more importantly – and G.H. Bush followed in Kennedy's and Kissinger's steps here – potential transatlantic strategic parity could not question American leadership in the Alliance. An even more radical vision gradually emerged, mostly from the Pentagon, led at that time by Richard Cheney, according to which the EC should never have jurisdiction in defence matters nor even seek to obtain an identity in the field. Transatlantic strategic parity must thus be prevented. In the highly uncertain post-Cold War context, a new transatlantic trade-off took place: NATO offered comfortable strategic reassurance to Western Europe which, in return, supplied the US 'grand strategy' with legitimacy and authority through political support and 'willing and capable' forces.

Admittedly, the Alliance Declaration from the London summit in July 1990 recognized 'the move within the European Community towards political union, including the development of a European identity in the domain of security'.[6] As Mitterrand stated at the Press Conference these were 'a few words that have demanded a lot of time and talks'.[7] Nevertheless, as German reunification in the Alliance was almost secured at that time, the US seized the opportunity to enhance its primacy by strengthening NATO's political role through cooperation with the Eastern countries and, more importantly, by reaffirming NATO's military integration system and extending it toward a new security role through the creation of multinational forces.

Such a rapid reaffirmation of NATO, officially aimed at limiting the decline of Western European defence budgets and avoiding the 're-nationalisation' of Western European – read German – defence policies, clearly ran against the French vision. Despite some Franco-German hesitancy during the summer of 1990 – Mitterrand put some pressure on Kohl by threatening to withdraw French Forces stationed in Germany (FFA), whereas Kohl was focusing on the last steps toward reunification, sealed in Moscow on 12 September – the two countries confirmed their first call for a Common Foreign and Security Policy (CFSP) in April.[8] Furthermore, an agreement was reached on the improvement of the Franco-German Brigade, as a prelude to the Eurocorps – which would be very controversial one year later (see below) – and made new proposals in a 6 December common letter to the Italian presidency of the European Council. European defence was eventually introduced via the WEU at the Political Union Intergovernmental Conference (IGC) opening on 15 December. The Franco-German proposals to implement ESDI already incorporated the two sides of the compromise eventually agreed to in Maastricht one year later, the WEU being as much conceived as the defence component of the EU, with 'organic link' between the both, as the European pillar of the Alliance. Once this fundamental Franco-German agreement was secured at the end of 1990, French policy was able to show more pragmatism, albeit in a very national way. Foreign Minister Roland Dumas' speech on 10 October at the National Assembly testifies to this:

> A common defence policy will not be implemented from scratch [...] But it is a necessary direction if we want Europe to reach its full maturity. The WEU can become the pillar of a common defence policy [...] This is not about substituting a collective approach to current national responsibilities. Security is the business of all; defence is the business of each one. The political Union will make the junction between security and defence.[9]

As a corollary, discrete and open-minded 'Quad' talks (comprising the USA, France, the UK and Germany) took place during the winter of 1990–91. Agreeing with the WEU-NATO institutional double-hat arrangements promoted by London and officially aimed at fostering the European pillar, the French Permanent Representative to the Alliance pleaded for WEU robust planning and operating capabilities, and his interlocutors eventually acknowledged that reform of NATO's integrated system was required.[10] According to the new trade-off in the making, reforming the Alliance, building a European pillar in it and reintegrating France were the three faces of a same problem.[11] However, intransigence would eventually prevail in Paris, and in Washington too.

Intransigence prevails

Mitterrand refused to involve France in what he deemed an uncertain NATO journey and rather confirmed the European choice. To him, nothing guaranteed that a French first step would give birth to a reformed Alliance and a real transatlantic partnership. True, the WEU appeared more and more as a roundabout strategy. It maintained the long-term but nonetheless platonic horizon of European defence, as it did not meet the capabilities and operational needs of the new, albeit uncertain, strategic context. As one of Mitterrand's main counsellors at the time, Hubert Vedrine, wrote in December 1990, that the WEU 'bears more problems than solutions'.[12] Moreover, French diplomats already acknowledged in May 1990 that strategic priority would consist in force projection, Command, Control, Communication and Information (C3I), demanding new types of cooperation with US forces, hence with NATO, in non-article 5 crisis management.[13] The Gulf War largely confirmed the weakness of French Armed Forces compared to the USA and, albeit to a lesser extent, to the British forces. Both French Foreign Affairs and Defence Ministries now saw the strengthening of the European pillar in the Alliance as the only viable option, and French reintegration as its logical consequence. The time had come 'to choose influence against independence at any cost'.[14] The following briefing for the president reflects this new state of mind:

> One can imagine that those of the Allies which are the weakest supporters of a European Defence Identity's emergence would accept the creation of a symbolic force, a European equivalent of the Franco-German Brigade, which would give us a political satisfaction without weighting on military realities, as the dependence on NATO 'C3I' would still be total. Hoping to get rid of this dependence by developing a complete autonomous European C3I capability in a purely WEU framework appears without doubt as wishful thinking.[15]

But Mitterrand stood firm. Disproving the accusations against France as a conservative if not reactionary player, he opposed a static vision of the Cold War collective defence institutions – almost placing NATO's and the Warsaw Pact's futures on the same track – in favour of a dynamic vision of the European security architecture built on the EU, the WEU, the CSCE and possibly Mitterrand's own pan-European Confederation project.[16]

Therefore, France refused to cast the WEU aside, as it was the only way to preserve – and avoid any *a priori* limits to – the embryo of European defence. A pillar in the Alliance was required but the European pillar outside the Alliance was still the ultimate aim. Gradually recognizing its narrowing room for manoeuvre, France pleaded for national forces' coordination in the WEU to create a European Rapid Action Force aimed at operating in non-article 5 missions. But the French project would soon be pre-empted by US–UK efforts to implement a NATO Rapid Reaction Force in the post-Gulf War context that shed a new light on the European capabilities deficit.

On the other side, the USA and UK resented that ESDI, understood as an embryonic autonomous European defence pillar, might jeopardize NATO's integration system and hamper American influence in Europe. Already mentioned during the informal Quad talks in December, the USA's bottom line was firmly reaffirmed, with British support, in the

253

Bartholomew–Dobbins Telegram, sent to the Nine WEU members on 22 February 1991, on the eve of a WEU summit, and a few days before the launch of ground operations in Iraq:

> We understand the political problems of developing a 'European Defense Identity' which has no apparent European role, but we believe the solution must not come at the expense of NATO. The further one goes in this direction (even if only in words, let alone actions), the more one accentuates the separateness of Europe and America in security and defense. [...]
>
> The objective of a European pillar should not be to relieve NATO of its responsibilities in this area, nor carve out new defence missions in Europe.[17]

Furthermore, both the American and the British governments pushed for rapid NATO reform, including the implementation of the Allied Rapid Reaction Corps' (ARRC). The Franco-German response, consisting of the Eurocorps proposal, elaborated between June and October, was perceived as a provocation in Washington, despite Paris and Berlin's efforts to appease the controversy surrounding this nascent 'European army'. Hence, from June 1991 onwards, the ESDI lay at the heart of a new *kriegspiel* in the run up to NATO's Rome summit in November and EU's Maastricht summit one month later. Admittedly, in the Maastricht's WEU Annex Declaration, 'WEU Member States agree on the need to develop a genuine ESDI and a greater European responsibility on defence matters [which] will be pursued through a gradual process'.[18] However, the compromise was clear between the WEU as 'the defence component of the EU' and as 'a means to strengthen the European pillar of the Atlantic Alliance'. European common defence must be '*compatible* with the Atlantic Alliance', whereas the emerging ESDI and the Alliance must interact 'on the basis of transparency and *complementarity*'.[19] A compromise that was all the more obvious as stated in the Maastricht Treaty itself:

> the eventual framing of a common defence policy, which might in time lead to a common defence [but] shall not prejudice the specific character of the security and defence policy of certain Member States and shall respect the obligations of certain Member States under the North Atlantic Treaty and be compatible with the common security and defence policy established within that framework.[20]

More than the Gulf War, the implosion of Yugoslavia in June 1991 acted as a catalyst for the ESDI debate. Although the crisis initially put Maastricht at risk, France tried to seize the opportunity to prove the relevance of the WEU. Bush and Clinton's hesitation regarding Bosnia, especially in deploying troops on the ground, confirmed the necessity of filling in the gap created by what the French perceived as the first evidence of US strategic withdrawal. But Bosnia's consequences would partly upset French expectations. Far from being managed by the EC and WEU, the crisis testified to the renationalization of foreign policies and *de facto* European weakness. After Germany's unilateral 'recognition policy' and British refusal to deploy troops under the WEU flag, the UN took the lead, but US engagement through NATO became a priority from 1993 onwards, eventually regaining a leading role in European security.

Nevertheless, the Balkans War set in motion an important dialectic. First, although NATO still guaranteed US engagement, its limits became apparent in Bosnia, and the Europeans, notably the British, began to acknowledge that US engagement and assistance would no longer be automatic. Second, in return, France now acknowledged that US support must be guaranteed, as a crisis management operation could upset Alliance solidarity. But third, Bosnia showed (and Kosovo would forcefully show in 1999) that once engaged, the USA was prone to unilateralism and resisted any political control or operational subordination, as the major Lift and Strike transatlantic crisis illustrated. Reopened in 1994, the whole ESDI debate would muddle through these three contradictory poles until the Franco-British compromise sealed in Saint-Malo in December 1998.

From 1992 to 1997: ESDI'S rise and limits

ESDI's rise ...

The main lesson from Bosnia was that Europe's room for manoeuvre was extremely narrow. Without US engagement, Europe was militarily impotent, and thus also politically insignificant; but in cases of US engagement, Europe was dependent on the Pentagon, hence, once more, politically impotent. Nevertheless, from the summer of 1993 onwards, the *de facto* rapprochement between France and NATO created an opportunity for the new right-wing coalition in power to plead 'from the inside' for a reformed integrated system that had proven outdated in Bosnia, albeit in the 'cohabitation' governmental context French reintegration was not on the agenda, at least not yet.[21] On the one hand, France henceforth explicitly acknowledged, notably in the Defence White Book published in April 1994,[22] that the WEU's role was designed for non-article 5 operations only. On the other hand, France promoted the idea of having two coexisting planning and command structures: the traditional integrated one for collective defence (article 5) and a more flexible one for crisis management. As the European pillar, ESDI must take place within the Alliance, but not within NATO.

In the Bosnia war context, this new thinking will largely meet UK's voluntarism, but also give new impetus to the new Clinton's administration approach, whose diplomatic offensive took place at the Alliance Brussels Summit on 10–11 January 1994. In order to reaffirm the leadership of NATO – and the US – in Europe, the US proposals consisted of the Partnership for Peace – a tacit prelude to the eastern enlargement of the Alliance – and, more importantly, as far as ESDI was concerned, the Combined Joint Task Force (CJTF) concept. From the US point of view, CJTF was initially aimed at improving the interoperability and flexibility of NATO structures and forces,[23] gradually inserting PfP member States forces, and developing – but also better controlling – ESDI by establishing European capabilities 'separable but not separate' from the command structure. From the USA's point of view, CJTF had to maintain the integrated structure's centrality and avoid any duplication of the chain of command. Therefore, the new thinking embodied its own limits in 1994 already. For Mitterrand, officially, the summit marked the end of the suspicion previously raised by the European identity embodied in the WEU. The European defence identity's recognition that 'had been, let's face it, torn to US consent in Rome [in November 1991], seemed all the more natural in Brussels'.[24] But the Elysée Palace was in fact very sceptical, and the Government would eventually recognize the limits of the CJTF in 1994 and 1995.[25]

... And limits

True, a North Atlantic Council (NAC, the highest Alliance institution) 'consultation' and not 'decision', as previously requested by the USA, was obtained by France in the summit declaration, and ESDI appeared in the first paragraph of the Declaration. But whereas France had initially tried to seize the opportunity to reform the military structure through the CJTF concept, its ambitions now had to be downsized. As Gabriel Robin asserted, the CJTF approach was a 'low cost' compromise for the French: 'rather no European Army than a European Army at the expense of NATO's dismantling'.[26]

In theory, planning and command structures had to reflect the nature and level of national contributions, so that the Europeans could reach their objectives, i.e. conduct operations autonomously, without the USA but with NATO assets or with limited US support, and contribute substantially to a US-led operation, should it occur.

But the WEU could not conduct an operation autonomously, as 1996 exercises and Bosnia post-war IFOR–SFOR (implementation force–stabilization force) operations still demonstrated.[27] European national or multinational structures were too weak, and there was still no palliative except NATO collective assets … Or, more precisely, assets belonging to the US but assigned to NATO, as strategic airlift, air refuelling and C4ISR. As Philip Gordon pointed out in 1996:

> Since automatic access to US national means is out of question – no country will make its national assets automatically available to an alliance without a veto over their use – Europe must accept the dilemma that the French have (intentionally or not) underlined: it must either put the resources behind developing independent capabilities or accept dependence on the US. This is a reality that CJTF cannot be expected to resolve.[28]

Moreover, an 'informational umbrella' could replace the Cold War's nuclear umbrella, and US progress in the so-called Revolution in Military Affairs (RMA) could widen the transatlantic gap.[29] Hence, as hinted in Bosnia and confirmed in Kosovo, the Europeans' role would be reduced to political endorsement and part-time force multiplier in US-led coalitions.[30] Strengthening transatlantic interoperability became a priority, but required preliminary European market consolidation – a first step was made with the OCCAR in November 1996[31] – but the 'fortress America' could try to impede it, prone as it was to pre-emptively denounce the hypothetical 'fortress Europe'.[32] Furthermore, the USA did not hesitate to stress that it had less interest in cooperating with the EU than vice versa. As a transatlantic working group reported in 1996:

> In the US, economic and technological considerations may never prove strong enough to create sufficient momentum behind transatlantic cooperation. US incentives for cooperation must stem in the first instance from the likelihood of coalition military operations and from the fact that cooperative armaments programs will be a major force multiplier when the US is fighting alongside allies.[33]

Nevertheless, as they could neither take on complete duplications nor put the Alliance at risk, the Europeans had to cooperate with their US counterparts in armaments procurements, although this involvement would neither automatically prevent European forces from being treated as auxiliaries nor *per se* give new impetus to NATO's Europeanization prospect.

Quite logically, the USA would take advantage of these capabilities imbalances to promote its interests in NATO and preserve the integrated military structure. Washington refused to create new command structures dedicated to non-article 5 crisis management, arguing that such operations could put Alliance solidarity at stake. Any CJTF staff, even the non-integrated ones (national or multinational staffs like the Eurocorps) should ultimately be subordinated to SACEUR (Supreme Allied Command Europe). As a corollary, although the chain of command should reflect the countries that deploy forces, states that would not provide troops could keep assigned positions in headquarters staff, according to the tacit assumption that, considering European weaknesses, US presence in the command structure would still be required for the time being.[34]

Consequently, as the CJTF concept alone hardly met European and American expectations because of technical and political hurdles, diverse options have been suggested at the official or observer's level, aimed at achieving further Europeanization of the Alliance at the major NATO command levels: the strengthening of the Deputy SACEUR's powers;[35] SHAPE's (Supreme Headquarters Allied Powers Europe) full Europeanization, pending SACLANT's (Supreme Allied Commander Atlantic) Americanization, comprising the USA and Canada, with Brussels headquarters staying as the Alliance's politico-military centre;[36] regional command decentralisation through CJTF headquarters staff nucleus, as SACLANT (General Sheehan) suggested; and last but not least, a reform of SACEUR as a *supporting commander* in case of national, *ad hoc* (Eurocorps for instance) or WEU-led CJTF operations.[37]

Yet the Europeans had no choice but to take ESDI seriously in order to solve the new transatlantic conundrum. France would follow two complementary paths under Jacques Chirac's Presidency. First, major national defence reforms – mainly 'professionalization', but also the pursuit and acceleration of the reforms launched since 1991 – aimed at upgrading national armed forces.[38] And second, with British and, to a lesser extent, German support, the pursuit of France's rapprochement with NATO aimed at obtaining a Europeanization of its command structure in exchange for a French full return. By confirming CJTF implementation process and the Deputy SACEUR's enhanced responsibilities, the Alliance summit in Brussels (13 June 1996) consecrated ESDI, and the word 'integration' disappeared from the Communiqué, although it mentions 'a single, multinational command structure, respecting the principle of unity of command [and] the continued involvement of the North American Allies across the command and force structure'.[39]

The Berlin Summit has raised expectations too high on both sides, to which the escalation surrounding the Allied Forces Southern Europe (AFSouth) Command's quarrel can testify. The negotiations on French reintegration – maybe, in the end, precisely because they were perceived as zero-sum game negotiations – eventually failed in the autumn of 1996.[40] 'Intentionally or not', to paraphrase Philip Gordon, France demonstrated that a European pillar or 'caucus' in the current NATO system was nothing more than an illusory, albeit necessary roundabout, as the WEU had been a few years earlier.

As a consequence, France was sidelined for a while, but the most important victim of this failure was the ESDI itself, as no *modus vivendi* or *modus operandi* between NATO, the EU and the WEU had emerged. The merger of the WEU and EU, promoted by Germany and France, seemed like the best institutional path. True, Paris had temporarily put up with London's predictable refusal in the run up to the 1996 IGC, giving priority to NATO reform, including its own reintegration, judging as a corollary that, in case of difficult transatlantic negotiations, and despite its weaknesses, WEU would still prove useful to avoid EU's institutional blockades and preserve the European solidarity clause (article V of the Brussels treaty).[41] The failure of French reintegration and the Amsterdam Treaty nevertheless opened an era of gradual absorption of the WEU by the EU.

Eventually, the schizophrenia surrounding the ESDI debates since 1990 had to be addressed, and the UK would be one of the most important players. Tony Blair understood on the eve of the Kosovo War that he had to 'cross the Rubicon'[42] of European defence, implementing the European Security and Defence Policy (ESDP) ... in order to save NATO.

From 1998 onwards: from ESDI to ESDP

ESDP versus ESDI

From the December 1998 Franco-British summit in Saint-Malo onwards, ESDI has progressively been overtaken by the ESDP. There has been a lot of valuable research done on this agreement and its enduring consequences.[43] To put it in a nutshell, Saint-Malo was a compromise between means and ends, capabilities and autonomy, i.e. between British will to save NATO's political framework through transatlantic interoperability, and French will to pursue European autonomy through credible military forces.

The Kosovo crisis demonstrated that the Europeans still lacked the capacity to manage a crisis in their own backyards, but also confirmed that if the USA was ready to get involved in a European crisis in the future – and it could refuse next time – it would be, as was already hinted at in Bosnia, on its own terms, and at a rather high political, military and financial cost for Europe. Furthermore, Kosovo confirmed that NATO did not shape the US military anymore, and the 'coalition of the willing', not yet an official principle of US foreign policy, was nonetheless hinted at in Kosovo.

As a corollary, whereas Saint-Malo was initially perceived in Europe as a journey from 'burden sharing to autonomy', it was still perceived in the USA as a departure from the single 'burden sharing' motto toward a renewed European 'balancing' – and deeply French-rooted – project. Therefore, the USA initially responded to the ESDP process as they had reacted to French policy almost a decade earlier. Madeleine Albright's '3D' – no delinking (or decoupling) of the transatlantic link, no discrimination against non-EU NATO members, and no duplication of NATO assets[44] – even when positively reformulated as '3I' by NATO General Secretary Lord Robertson (indivisibility, inclusiveness, improvement) were exact copies of the political red lines defined in 1990. True, some Americans began to support the ESDP process.[45] But most of them were disappointed, as European investments in capabilities did not follow the course. NATO's new procurement mechanisms (DCI – Defence Capabilities Initiative – and New DCI) quickly proved to be a dead end, whereas European ones (the Helsinki Headline goal, in particular the objective of 60,000 troops deployable in 60 days) were only launched as an embryonic European planning system. As a result, London began to 'back pedal', on ESDP's operational aspects as soon as the end of 2000, whereas Paris, and Berlin to a lesser extent, tried to implement the unprecedented progress made at the institutional level.

Then came the 9/11 attacks and the intervention in Afghanistan, which opened a new era but nonetheless confirmed three dynamics: first, the new global dimension of threats and risks in the world; second, the unilateralist drift of the US Administration and its focus on Asia and an arc of crises from Morocco to Indonesia at the expense of Europe; thirdly, at the European level, the renewed importance of Atlanticism in British foreign policy and the return to a 'counterweight' stance in France ... all trends that would be catalysed by the Iraqi crisis one year later.

Toward a new EU–US partnership?

Since the end of the Cold War, as Scowcroft warned in early 1990, the USA has resented being deprived of a voice in European defence and security matters. But such warnings have been largely theoretical, as America's soft power – and hard power as well, notably via its armaments industry – preserved its influence in Europe, although it was unable to prevent the emergence of the ESDP. Deeper evolutions explain the recent shift in opinion in Washington, in particular the gradual recognition of the ESDP during G. W. Bush's second term. The last 20 years have eventually convinced the Americans that the EU was not trying to 'balance' the USA, as it had previously thought. 'Euro-Gaullism', according to Ronald Asmus, has died out.[46] Admittedly, these last decades have also shown that the EU neither could nor, to a certain extent, wanted to support US foreign policy *per se*, as Washington had previously expected it too. As the EU has not taken on the burden that it is supposed to – which Afghanistan confirms – neither ESDI in NATO nor ESDP in the EU meets US interests, at least not yet. However, European reservations vis-à-vis Bush's foreign policy were not only motivated by a lack of will, means or even common strategic culture, but also by the fear of being dragged into a conflict – or crusade – by the USA – a reversal of the traditional transatlantic conundrum.

Nowadays, notably since Barack Obama's election, both sides of the Atlantic seem more inclined to pragmatism and still see the Alliance as necessary. But beyond insistence on better EU–NATO cooperation and so-called 'complementarity', proposals for a renewed EU–US partnership have emerged at last in Washington. The USA henceforth wishes as much as the EU to be able to act jointly and widely acknowledges that NATO is neither the only nor the best place for EU–US strategic dialogue.[47] As James Dobbins stresses – and slightly exaggerates on purpose – NATO cannot act without the EU anymore, whereas the EU can act alone.[48] True, maintaining ESDP in civil and civil–military affairs will make the EU everything but a real strategic partner for the US, and a EU–US partnership beyond NATO will not give ESDP *ex nihilo* the impetus it needs to be an autonomous and responsible partner. Therefore, EU–US military cooperation will still demand pragmatic cooperation in NATO for the time being, without falling into old ESDI traps. The answer henceforth lies in Europe, not in the USA, to which the French full return to NATO's command (except the Nuclear Planning Group) testifies. Even if it is obviously too early to draw conclusions from this French evolution, it is eventually confirmed when most of its allies, notably the USA, wish to reform NATO and to implement a new transatlantic cooperation beyond NATO. Whether or not the EU and the USA will still see themselves as irreplaceable mutual partners, one can hope that, considering the demanding global challenges ahead, both will at least leave the transatlantic misunderstandings of the post-Cold-War era behind them, to History.

Notes

1 For a good overview of the theoretical debate, see Jean-Yves Haine, L'Eurocorps et les Identités européennes de Défense, (Les Documents du C2SD, SGA – Ministère de la Défense, 2001), pp. 45–92; for a stimulating theoretical analysis on the triptych made of Europe, Identity and Defence, see Paul A. Chilton, 'La défense européenne, condition nécessaire à la formation d'une identité européenne?', in Bastien Nivet (ed.), La défense Européenne, quel objet pour quels outils d'analyse? Repenser la Défense européenne, Revue Internationale et Stratégique, no. 48, hiver 2002/2003, pp. 75–147.

2 Declaration on European Identity (Copenhagen, 14 December 1973). www.ena.lu/declaration-european-identity-copenhagen-14-december-1973-020002278.html (accessed 10 January 2010).
3 More specifically, Jobert also reproached the USA for marginalizing the Europeans in the Kippur War settlement. For a synthesis, see Maurice Vaisse, La puissance ou l'influence, La France dans le Monde depuis 1958, (Paris: Fayard, 2009), pp. 190–94.
4 As Samuel Wells has stated in this volume, the US 'divide and rule' traditional policy vis-à-vis Europe began to decline at the end of the 1970s (see his chapter in this book).
5 To what François de Rose answered: 'Do not look for an institutional solution, do not frame the problem this way. The solution only lies in the future good political relationship between the EC and the US.' French Nationals Archives (FNA), 5AG4, CD92, note du 5 February 1990 (Hubert Vedrine), 'compte-rendu des discussions de l'ancien Ambassadeur de Rose avec le général Scowcroft, Kissinger et Brzezinski'. All translations are by the author.
6 Declaration on a transformed North Atlantic Alliance issued by the Heads of State and Government participating in the meeting of the North Atlantic Council ('The London Declaration'), London, 6 July 1990; §3, www.ena.lu/ (accessed 10 January 2010).
7 Président François Mitterrand, Press Conference, Brussels, 11 January 1994. Cited in FNA, 5AG4 CD 92.
8 CFSP is one of the common proposals for the Intergovernmental Conference contained in the Franco-German letter to the Irish Presidency of the European Council on 19 April 1990.
9 Foreign Minister Roland Dumas' Address at the Assemblée nationale, 10 October 1990, Cit. in Claire Tréan, Politique Etrangère, vol. 1, no. 1, IFRI, 1991.
10 For a detailed analysis of these informal negotiations, see Frédéric Bozo, *De Yalta à Maastricht. Mitterrand, la fin de la guerre froide et la réunification allemande*, (Odile Jacob, 2005), especially pp. 328–36.
11 Ibid., p. 333.
12 FNA, 5AG4 CD 92. 19 December 1990, note d'Hubert Vedrine: 'Or, si nous n'avons aucun attachement particulier pour l'UEO qui a de nombreux défauts, c'est la seule base à partir de laquelle on peut bâtir quelque chose, du moins tant que l'Union politique à 12 ne sera pas clairement dotée de compétences en matière de politique étrangère et de sécurité.'
13 FNA, 5AG4 CD 92: Gabriel Robin (Atlantic Alliance French Permanent Representative), Réflexions sur la réforme de l'Alliance, Prospective 1995–2000, June 1990; Philippe Guelluy, A/S: Rénovation de l'Alliance Atlantique, 2 May 1990, 28 May 1990.
14 FNA, 5AG4, CD 92, MAE, A. S. Débat franco-américain sur l'avenir de l'OTAN, Jean-Marie Guéhenno (Director of a marginalized Policy Planning Staff, Centre d'Analyse et de Prévision, at that time), 26 March 1991.
15 FNA, 5AG4, CD 92, Note (confidentiel) A. S. La France, l'OTAN et l'UEO: vrais et faux problèmes de l'intégration, [anonymous], 2 February 1991.
16 Few of Mitterrand's speeches better express his views than the one he gave at the Ecole Supérieure de Guerre on 11 April 1991, where he reaffirmed France's Gaullist legacy and refused a full return to the NATO military integrated structure, www.doc.diplomatie.fr/basis (last accessed 10 January 2010).
17 FNA, 5AG4 CD 96, Non papier, 'Conception globale des Etats-Unis concernant le développement d'une identité européenne de sécurité'.
18 Declaration of the members of the WEU and of the EU on The Role of the WEU and its Relations with the EU and with NATO, Maastricht, 10 December 1991.
19 Ibid. Italic added by the author.
20 Maastricht Treaty, Title V article J4.
21 See Jacques Chirac's address, 8 February 1993, Paris. Cit. in Robert Grant, *France's new relationship with NATO, Survival*, vol. 38, no. 1, Spring 1996; Pierre Lellouche, 'France in search of Security', *Foreign Affairs*, vol. 72, no. 2, Spring 1993.
22 *Livre Blanc sur la Défense*, la Documentation Française, April 1994, pp. 32–33: 'Henceforth, clearly recognized as the EU defence component, [WEU] must aim to make a Europeans' autonomous military action possible, except in case of aggression putting at stake the main guarantee of the North Atlantic Treaty.' ['Désormais clairement reconnue comme composante de défense de l'Union Européenne, [l'UEO] doit se fixer pour objectif de rendre possible une action militaire autonome des Européens, en dehors des cas d'agression mettant en jeu la garantie principale du Traité de l'Atlantique Nord.']
23 See Charles Barry, '*NATO's CJTF in theory and practice*', *Survival*, vol. 38, no. 1 Spring 1996, pp. 81–97, and Terry Terriff, *US Ideas and Military Change in NATO, 1989–1994*, in Theo Farrell and

Terry Terriff (eds), *the Sources of Military Change: Culture, Politics, Technology*, (Boulder, Co: Lynne Rienner Publishers, 2002).
24 Interview given to AFP, 9 January 1994. In FNA, 5AG4 CD 92.
25 FNA, 5AG4, CD 92, 22/04/94, Note de Jean Vidal et du Général Quesnot à l'attention du Président. Alliance Atlantique – GFIM [CJTF]; 29/04/94, diffusé le 6 juin. Secrétariat Général du Gouvernement (SGDN). Confidentiel. Compte-rendu de la réunion interministérielle tenue le lundi 18 avril 94 à 16h sous la présidence de Bernard de Montferrand (Prime Minister Edouard Balladur's diplomatic advisor).
26 Gabriel Robin, 'Un concept en quête de substance', *Revue de Défense nationale*, Paris, mars 1995, p. 92: 'Plutôt pas d'armée européenne qu'une armée européenne qu'il faudra payer du démantèlement de l'OTAN.'
27 Robert Grant, 'The Military Challenges of Transatlantic Coalitions', *Chaillot occasional Paper*, no. 15, 2000; Pauline Neville-Jones, 'Dayton, IFOR and the Alliance relations in Bosnia', *Survival*, vol. 38, no. 4, Winter 1996, pp. 45–65.
28 Philip Gordon, 'Recasting the Atlantic Alliance', *Survival*, vol. 38, no. 1, Spring 1996, pp. 32–57.
29 Robert Grant, 'The Military Challenges of Transatlantic Coalitions', *Chaillot Occasional Paper*, no. 15, 2000; James P. Thomas, Adelphi Paper, No. 333, May 2000, Institute for Strategic Studies. On the use of information superiority by the USA, see Jérome Gygax's contribution in this volume.
30 The Europeans 'could be confronted with an unpleasant alternative: either excluded for good from the US system, incapable of participating in coalitions except as political endorsers, or merged as functional bit-parts incapable of autonomous action, [with] equally unpleasant consequences [...]: duplication and decoupling.' Etienne de Durand, *The United States and the Alliance*, Transatlantic Serie, Ifri Note no. 23, Paris, 2000.
31 European armament cooperation started in November 1996 with the creation of the OCCAR Convention (Organisme Conjoint de Coopération en matière d'Armement) by Germany and France, then joined by Italy and the UK, then Belgium.
32 *Transatlantic armament cooperation: into the XXIst century*. 17–19 April 1996, Paris. A US-CREST Conference Report, US-Crest, Arlington, Virginia, 1996.
33 Ibid.
34 Barry, *'NATO's CJTF in theory and practice'*, pp. 81–97.
35 Which could only be British or French. See Stanley R. Sloan, *NATO's Future: beyond collective defense*, (Washington, DC, Congressional Research Service, September 1995), pp. 30–32; Robert Grant, 'France's new relationship with NATO', *Survival*, 1996, endnote 80.
36 Admiral Paul David Miller (SACLANT until October 1994), *Retaining Alliance relevance, NATO and the combined joint task force concept*, (National security paper no. 15, 1994, Institute for Foreign Policy Analysis, in association with the Fletcher School of Law and Diplomacy, Tufts University, Cambridge, MA). His successor General James Sheehan, pleads for the creation of a *Resource command*, deemed too radical for the time being, but a prelude to ACT created in 2002.
37 Cf. Barry, *'NATO's CJTF in theory and practice'*.
38 In 1996 French force projection capabilities were still under 20 per cent. For a good overview of Chirac's 'strategic revolution', see Shawn Gregory, *French Defence Policy into the Twenty-first Century*, (New York: Palgrave Macmillan, 2000). Chapter 3: The Reform of Defence, pp. 67–103.
39 Final Communiqué, Meeting of the North Atlantic Council in Defence Ministers Session, Brussels, 13 June 1996. The wording of the NAC Ministerial Meeting's Final Communiqué (Berlin, 3 June 1996, §7.4) is slightly different and a bit confusing: it calls for 'the ability to mount NATO non-Article 5 operations, guided by the concept of one system capable of performing multiple functions.[...] The CJTF concept is central to our approach for assembling forces for contingency operations and organising their command within the Alliance. Consistent with the goal of building the European Security and Defence Identity *within NATO* [whereas the Brussels Communiqué speaks of "ESDI within the Alliance"] these arrangements should permit all European Allies to play a larger role in NATO's military and command *structures* [whereas the Brussels Communiqué speaks of one single structure] and, as appropriate, in contingency operations undertaken by the Alliance.' (emphasis by the author).
40 For a balanced and detailed account of Franco-American negotiations, see Charles Cogan, *French Negotiating behavior: Dealing with la grande nation*, (Washington: USIP Press, 2003), pp. 191–217 (French version, Jacob-Duvernet, 2008).
41 And to a lesser extent, the Parliamentary Assembly could be useful. Interview, French Diplomat, February 2008.

42 Jolyon Howorth, 'The European integration and Defence: the ultimate challenge?', Chaillot Papers, no. 43, November 2000, p. 25.
43 See Jolyon Howorh, 'Britain, France and the European Defence Initiative', *Survival*, vol. 42, no. 2, 2000.
44 See Madeline Albright, 'The Right Balance Will Secure NATO's Future', *The Financial Times*, 7 December 1998.
45 Charles Kupchan, 'In Defense of European Defense: An American Perspective', *Survival*, vol. 42, no. 2, Summer 2000.
46 Ronald Asmus, 'New purposes, new plumbing, refunding the Atlantic Alliance', *The American Interest*, November–December 2008.
47 Alliance Reborn: An Atlantic Compact for the 21st Century, January 2009, written by The Washington NATO Project; Lead Author: Daniel Hamilton; Co-Authors Charles Barry, Hans Binnendijk, Stephen Flanagan, Julianne Smith, James Townsend. Ronald Asmus, 'New purposes, new plumbing, refunding the Atlantic Alliance', *The American Interest*, November–December 2008; Coll., *Re-wiring the US-EU relationship*, December 2008, European Council on Foreign Relations.
48 Alliance Reborn: An Atlantic Compact for the 21st Century, January 2009.

19

A realistic reset with Russia

Practical expectations for US–Russian relations

James M. Goldgeier

Meeting for the first time in London on 1 April 2009, Russian President Dmitry Medvedev and US President Barack Obama declared in their joint statement they were 'ready to move beyond Cold War mentalities and chart a fresh start in relations between [the] two countries'.[1] It was rather startling that nearly 20 years after the fall of the Berlin Wall, the leaders of the two nations believed they needed to stress their readiness to overcome Cold War mentalities. But is it really Cold War mentalities that have been the problem? The dashing of expectations that has occurred often in the past two decades should lead us to be somewhat sober about the prospects going forward, despite the Obama administration's worthy goal of pushing the 'reset button' and its early achievements. Looking back through the history of the intervening years can help us understand why we have made such little progress in forging a strong US–Russian relationship since the hopeful days after the collapse of Communism. Doing so reveals that the problems in the relationship have been caused not by lingering Cold War mentalities, but rather by two very different visions of the *post*-Cold War world, as well as by the sharp asymmetries in power that emerged when the Soviet Union imploded. Although Medvedev and Obama followed their April meeting with a productive summit in Moscow in July as well as a follow-on meeting in September on the margins of the UN General Assembly meetings, we should be realistic about what we can expect given the underlying differences in both worldview and power that will continue to exist.

A false start

The rush of events that occurred as the Soviet Union unravelled seems rather surreal in retrospect: Boris Yeltsin standing on a tank in August 1991, staring down a drunken band of coup plotters; the Baltic countries and then Ukraine declaring their independence; Yeltsin meeting with the leaders of Ukraine and Belarus in the Beloveschaya forest in early December 1991 to effectively declare the end of the Soviet Union, followed by Mikhail Gorbachev's formal admission a few weeks later that the state built by Lenin and Stalin was no more.

In early 1992, a triumphant Yeltsin visited Camp David to meet with George H.W. Bush. Yeltsin was enthusiastic about the prospects for US–Russian friendship. Gorbachev had been the darling of the West for his programmes of *perestroika* and *glasnost*, opening up the Soviet system, and creating opportunities for both democracy and the stirrings of a market economy. To outmanoeuvre his Soviet rival in 1991, Yeltsin had decided to be more pro-democracy, more pro-market and more pro-Western than Gorbachev, hoping to garner American support to ensure his defeat of the Communists.

Meeting at Camp David in February 1992, Yeltsin pressed Bush to declare that America and Russia were now allies rather than using the more ambiguous phrase 'friendship and partnership'. Bush demurred, saying 'We are using this transitional language because we don't want to act like all our problems are solved'.[2] Although Bush missed an opportunity to draw closer to Yeltsin (towards whom the American president never had the warm feelings he displayed towards Gorbachev), 'Cold War' mentalities did not linger too long into the 1990s (outside of certain Republican circles on Capitol Hill or old-school Communists in Russia), and certainly not in the relationship between Bill Clinton and Yeltsin. A new American Cold War policy would have focused on containment, which was not a policy that Clinton or his top Russia adviser, Strobe Talbott, were going to pursue. Meanwhile, for the Russians, a truly Cold War mentality would have emphasized undermining the American-led order by trying to rebuild a network of proxy states to balance the West; Yeltsin instead was a prime cause of the independence achieved by the *post*-Soviet States, and he did not stand in their way as they (and he) pursued closer ties with America and the West.

The American policy in those years had conceptual flaws, but not due to a desire to continue the Cold War. Rather, the policy reflected a misguided belief that the Russian elite would accommodate itself to the dramatic geopolitical changes that were occurring in Europe and come to see the value of creating a large zone of stability and security in a part of the globe that gave rise to two world wars and the Cold War.

The American approach

As America began to develop a policy toward the former Communist world, it worked within a framework first enunciated by Bush in May 1989, when the president called for an effort to foster a 'Europe Whole and Free'. At the time, there was no detailed strategy for accomplishing this task, but over the course of the 1990s, the policy consisted of three main components: integrating Central and Eastern Europe into Western institutions, stopping genocide in the Balkans, and reaching out to Russia.

NATO's first *post*-Cold War enlargement occurred in 1990, when the territory of the German Democratic Republic became part of the West German state. Although negotiations had been tense at times, and many misunderstandings would result later from those conversations, the unified Germany remained a full member of NATO.

Little more was done on NATO's outreach to the East until the Clinton administration entered office in 1993, but the alliance soon stepped up its efforts to build ties to the Central and Eastern Europeans. At his first NATO summit in Brussels in January 1994, Clinton and his fellow heads of State and government announced the Partnership for Peace programme, which would be open to all East European and former Soviet nations, including Russia. PfP, as it became known, was designed to build strong military-to-military ties in the belief that the military was the institution most capable of blocking reform in these societies in transition. When Yeltsin was first told about this programme, at a meeting he held at his dacha with US Secretary of State Warren Christopher in October 1993, the Russian leader asked for reassurance that partnership did not mean NATO membership for the former Soviet satellites. Christopher replied, 'Yes, that is the case, there would not be even an associate status'. Yeltsin excitedly told his American guest, 'This is a brilliant idea, it is a stroke of genius'. He presumably did not worry too much when Christopher added that 'we will in due course be looking at the question of membership as a longer term eventuality ... Those who wish to can pursue the idea over time, but that will come later'.[3]

It was therefore a shock to Yeltsin that, by autumn 1994, the United States began to move ahead on an enlargement strategy, although Clinton was clear that he would not do anything that would harm his Russian counterpart before the latter's re-election in July 1996. Once Yeltsin was safely re-elected, the policy sped up. In 1997, NATO issued invitations to Poland, Hungary and the Czech Republic; those three nations joined the alliance at its fiftieth anniversary summit two years later. In 2004, seven more countries joined NATO, to be followed at the sixtieth anniversary summit in 2009 by the formal welcome to the newest members, Albania and Croatia. As it developed these ties across Europe, NATO had assisted former Communist countries with their reform programmes, made respect for human rights an essential condition of membership and paved the way for the European Union to expand across the continent by providing the necessary security and stability.

Bush's 'Europe whole and free' mantra gave way to Clinton's similar refrain of a peaceful, undivided and democratic Europe, which finally in 1995 led to the second part of the overall strategy: the effort to bring peace to the Balkans. The Bush administration tried to leave the war in Bosnia for the Europeans to solve, but to no avail. Clinton promised in the 1992 campaign to do more, but in his first couple of years in office did little in the face of the horrific violence that continued to unfold. Finally, in November 1995, thanks to a combination of NATO air strikes, a resurgent Croat military offensive, and tenacious negotiating by American envoy Richard Holbrooke, the Dayton Accords brought an end to the war. Three years later, the Clinton administration began preparing for another conflict with Slobodan Milosevic, this time to deter genocide in Kosovo. After negotiations failed to produce agreement, NATO in March 1999 went to war for the first time in its history, and 78 days later, succeeded in coercing the Serb leader to surrender. A year later, Milosevic was toppled from power.

NATO has continued its outreach into south-eastern Europe in the decade since the Kosovo war. Macedonia will join Croatia and Albania as new NATO members as soon as it can resolve a dispute with Greece over the name of the country. And Bosnia, Serbia and Montenegro all joined the PfP in 2006.

The twin efforts of NATO enlargement and the effort to pacify the Balkans have been remarkably effective. Although tensions remain in Bosnia and the peace in Kosovo is tenuous (even the members of the Alliance are divided over recognizing the independence of that tiny nation), the United States and its European partners have used NATO quite effectively as part of the strategy to achieve the vision of a continent whole and free. But that effort has had tremendous repercussions on the third component of the strategy – the effort to reach out to Russia and include it in the West.

Reaching out to Russia

Whereas George H.W. Bush did seem rather ambivalent about his relationship with Yeltsin even after Russian independence, Clinton was not. In his initial months as president,

Clinton devoted little time to foreign policy, but what time he did devote was largely towards Russia. He announced a large American assistance package at his first meeting with Yeltsin in April 1993 in Vancouver. When Yeltsin carried out a military assault against extremist forces in the Russian parliament later that year, Clinton supported him wholeheartedly. For Clinton, Russian reform was not just a national security priority; it was a means of ensuring a decline of the American Cold War defence budget to enable the president to fund cherished domestic programmes (the so-called 'peace dividend'). For Clinton, Boris Yeltsin was the embodiment of a new democratic Russia that would work closely with the West, as occurred, for example, with the withdrawal of the Red Army from the Baltic States.

When Clinton spoke of a Europe peaceful, undivided and democratic, he meant one that included Russia. In January 1994, after his visit to Brussels for the NATO summit and a stop in Prague to show support for the leaders of Central Europe (where disappointment was rampant that NATO membership was not going to be fast-tracked for the leading aspirants), he went to Moscow to demonstrate that his policies were designed not to leave Russia out. In a televised 'town hall' meeting geared to reach the younger generation, the president urged the Russian people to find a 'new definition of Russian greatness' (i.e. one that did not involve intimidating and dominating neighbouring countries) and said that as Russians did so, 'I hope that my nation and I can make a positive contribution, in the spirit of genuine and equal partnership'.[4]

Unfortunately, as time went on, it became clear that the different elements of the American policy towards Europe worked at cross purposes. Clinton knew that NATO enlargement was a bitter pill for Yeltsin; that's not only why the process was slowed down until after the Russian presidential election in July 1996 but also why the United States invited Russia to become a member of what became the G8. (Clinton thought giving Yeltsin a platform alongside other major world leaders could help soften the blow of enlargement.) Clinton also understood that the Russians were angry about American policy in the Balkans, and thus supported US Secretary of Defense William Perry's dogged effort to find a way for Russia to participate in the NATO-led Implementation Force (IFOR) that was set up to keep the peace after the Dayton Accords were signed in November 1995.

Clinton tried to convince Yeltsin that neither his NATO enlargement policy nor his Balkans policy was directed against Russia. He even told Yeltsin that NATO might be open some day to a democratic Russia. Yeltsin once said to Al Gore after the vice president made a similar statement, 'Nyet, nyet, that doesn't make sense. Russia is very, very big, and NATO is quite small'.[5] Clinton and his team created the Permanent Joint Council (the precursor to the NATO–Russia Council), announced with great fanfare in Paris in May 1997 – before NATO formally invited Poland, Hungary and the Czech Republic to join the alliance – to show that Russia's sensitivities were being taken into account.

Regardless of whether Yeltsin himself accepted that NATO was not a threat to Russia, and no matter what Clinton said about the policy, enlargement had a corrosive impact on the relationship. The Russians argued it was because they had been betrayed. After all, in February 1990, US Secretary of State James Baker had told Gorbachev that 'there would be no extension of NATO's jurisdiction for forces of NATO one inch to the east'.[6] But that conversation was a preliminary discussion about Germany, not the rest of Europe, and Gorbachev was not ready to make a deal at that time. Although the final agreement on German unification did limit NATO deployments in the former East

German territory until Soviet troops had departed, the sides had not discussed NATO's future in places such as Poland and Hungary.[7]

Harder for Yeltsin to take, in fact, was probably the memory of his discussion with Warren Christopher in October 1993, when the Secretary of State had led Yeltsin to believe that Russia had truly been able to kill the idea of NATO enlargement. But whether the Russians felt betrayed or not was less important than the most obvious fact of the enlargement process: the United States was too powerful vis-à-vis Russia not to proceed with an enlargement strategy. For the Americans, it would have been politically and morally damaging not to include Central Europe into an alliance that is the symbol of transatlantic unity, and since they could do so, they did.

For the United States, the policies were designed to create greater stability, and American officials argued to their Russian counterparts that this stability was good for Russia. But it did not look that way from Moscow's vantage point. The areas that were becoming part of the West had formerly been within Moscow's sphere of influence. The break up of the Soviet Union moved Russia's borders farther from the centre of Europe than they had been in centuries. Now these lands were becoming integrated into Western institutions. And the bombing of the Serbs in March 1999 was the last straw. It may not have raised the spectre of 'World War III', as Yeltsin declared, but the air campaign largely wiped away whatever pro-American sentiment still existed in Russia. As former Russian Deputy Prime Minister Yegor Gaidar told Strobe Talbott at the time, 'Oh Strobe, if only you knew what a disaster this war is for those of us in Russia who want for our country what you want'.[8] From a traditional geostrategic perspective, Russia had suffered enormous blows in the first *post*-Cold War decade, leading Yeltsin's successor, Vladimir Putin, to conclude that the collapse of the Soviet Union 'was the greatest geopolitical catastrophe of the century'.[9]

Cooperation elsewhere stalls

During the 1990s, hope for cooperation on two major strategic issues – arms control and the Iranian nuclear programme – foundered. It is impossible to know whether progress on either issue would have been possible had the United States forgone the opportunity to expand NATO, but there is little doubt that NATO enlargement made efforts to cooperate in these other strategic areas more difficult. At precisely the moment that the enlargement process began to move forward in 1995, so did the Russian effort to assist Iran in building a nuclear reactor in Bushehr.

Bill Clinton himself feared that enlargement might hinder his effort to scale back the Russian–Iranian relationship. Conservatives were urging the president not to attend a ceremony in Moscow in May 1995 to commemorate the fiftieth anniversary of the defeat of Nazi Germany. Clinton colourfully told his staff, 'I'm going to Russia because of the dogs we have in this hunt, but we've got to do something on Iran. Joe Lunchbucket out there in Ames, Iowa, doesn't care about NATO enlargement. He cares about whether this ol' boy is going over there to Russia and let those people give the new ayatollah an a-bomb'.[10]

NATO enlargement also appeared to have an impact on arms control. In January 1996, the US Senate ratified START (Strategic Arms Reduction Treaty) II (signed by George H.W. Bush and Yeltsin in 1992), but Congress prohibited the administration from unilaterally reducing the US arsenal below START I levels until the Russian Duma ratified START II. Alexei Arbatov, deputy chairman of the Duma's Defence Committee, explained why that wasn't going to happen: 'First there is no money for it. Secondly, the treaty is considered to be unfair on technical grounds. And thirdly, the general background – the determination of NATO to expand to the East – is very unfavourable to the treaty'.[11] Duma ratification finally occurred four years later, but in 2002, Russia reacted angrily to the American abrogation of the Anti-Ballistic Missile Treaty by announcing it was not bound by START II any longer.

Looking back, looking forward

Rather than merely seeing the US–Russian relationship in the George W. Bush years as one that failed to live up to the promise of the Bush–Putin friendship of 2001 that emerged even before the attacks of 11 September, it is important, when thinking about the prospects for a 'reset', to understand the trajectory we have been on since the end of the Cold War. The emergence of the United States as the global hegemon in 1991, accompanied by the swift descent of Russia from Cold War superpower to failed state, created an imbalance of power that made a true partnership (much less the 'alliance' Yeltsin called for in 1992) extremely difficult. The United States defined its interests in a peaceful and prosperous Europe in ways that Russia found objectionable, and there was not much that Moscow could do to change the evolving dynamic.

Putin understood this trend when he assumed the presidency in 2000, and he vowed to rebuild Russia economically and thus politically. He also came into office with a different worldview from that of Yeltsin. Yeltsin, particularly in the early years, showed genuine interest in Russia being seen as part of the West. Putin showed no such desire. What the latter has demonstrated is a fixation on control over the foreign policies of the countries in his neighbourhood, an attitude that reflects a nineteenth-century spheres of influence approach (and one that President Obama sought to counter in his public address in July in Moscow when he argued that zero-sum thinking belonged to the past).

With the benefit of high energy prices, Russia built huge foreign currency reserves, no longer needing to come hat in hand to the G7 and IMF for support. And as the United States became bogged down in Iraq, and then suffered its worst financial crisis since the 1930s, the world's leading power no longer seemed so dominant. For Russia, the rise of Moscow's power and what seemed to be a decline of Washington's was what made the notion of a reset so appealing, since perhaps it could lead to a relationship built on a more equal basis, and one that accepted Russian domination of the former Soviet space.

When the Obama administration entered office in 2009 promising to reset relations, the Russians jumped at the chance to recreate an aura of 1972–73, when the United States, weakened by war and recession, recognized Moscow's emergence as a major power and pursued détente, with arms control as the defining issue on the agenda. Strategic arms control is the one global issue on which America and Russia are on a relatively equal footing, and the Russians are delighted that the Americans want to go back to the era of big, formal treaties, which George W. Bush had refused to go along with in his first term. (The Strategic Offensive Reductions Treaty agreed to by Bush and Putin was three pages, and was only called a treaty as a sop to the Russians for not making more of a fuss about the American abrogation of the Anti-Ballistic Missile Treaty.) The United States hoped that an agreement in late 2009 on arms control before the expiration of START could help form the foundation of a relationship in which other cooperative endeavours – on counterterrorism, counterproliferation, Afghanistan, Iran and North Korea, for example – might be built.

It does seem that despite all of the dashed hopes of the past two decades, there was a window of opportunity in 2009 to move forward in a relationship that hit its nadir at the end of the Bush presidency. The two American foreign policy issues that antagonized the Russians so intensely in 2008 – defence against long-range Iranian missiles and the prospect of NATO Membership Action Plans for Ukraine and Georgia – are off the table, and the United States and its West European allies seem determined not to let continued Russian unwillingness to abide by the terms of the cease-fire in Georgia (as well as Moscow's decision to end the OSCE and UN missions in that country) derail possible cooperation in other areas. The Obama administration is not trying to create the kind of 'linkage' strategy that has at times characterized American policy in the past.

President Obama decided not to deploy the Bush administration's proposed missile defence system in Poland and the Czech Republic. Instead the president decided to shift to a forward, sea-based system (built around Aegis-equipped warships armed with the SM-3 missile) to counter the short-range and medium-range missile threat from Iran. The new sea-based system would be based in the eastern Mediterranean (and possibly the Black Sea and Persian Gulf) to protect American allies. Over time, the system may incorporate forward-based radar systems in Turkey, the Gulf region and possibly the Caucasus, as well as land-based mobile interceptors (including in Poland). The Obama administration believes that this system is more attuned with the actual Iranian threat and provides a defence for all NATO allies. The Russians may come to rue the day they applauded the decision not to deploy a mere 10 interceptors in Poland given the robustness of the Obama plan, but for the moment, Russia is quite pleased that the new administration shelved the Bush plan.

The other irritant for Russia, NATO Membership Action Plans for Ukraine and Georgia, was removed as a pressing problem even before Obama became president. At the NATO foreign ministers meeting in December 2008, the alliance approved annual national review programmes for both nations. These efforts will serve the same purpose as the Membership Action Plans, but without use of the word 'membership'. Since neither Georgia nor Ukraine has a prospect of membership within the next decade, the review programmes have allowed for the NATO relationships with both countries to continue without causing any immediate heartburn in Moscow. At their 60th anniversary celebrations, Alliance members declared, 'NATO's door will remain open to all European democracies which share the values of our Alliance, which are willing and able to assume the responsibilities and obligations of membership, and whose inclusion can contribute to common security and stability'.[12] The first two have been standard criteria throughout the post-Cold War enlargement process; enunciating the third has ensured that the hurdle is higher for Ukraine and Georgia given their disputes with Russia. President Obama added an additional threshold when he was in Moscow in July 2009, stating that a majority of the population of an aspirant must support membership, a line clearly directed at Ukraine.[13]

President Obama has taken advantage of the breathing room created by shifts on missile defence and enlargement to deftly change the atmosphere of the relationship. His call for a 'reset' was met with great approval from President Dmitry Medvedev, Foreign Minister Sergei Lavrov, and others, and his meeting with Prime Minister Putin in July was judged quite favourably. The joint statement issued by the two presidents in London in April listed numerous areas of potential cooperation, not only in the arms control sphere but on Afghanistan, North Korea, trade and elsewhere. Obama and Medvedev followed that effort in July with a framework agreement on strategic arms control. Significantly, Russia agreed to allow American supplies to cross its territory into Afghanistan. Refreshingly, the April statement did not shy away from noting that differences between the two countries remain, not only on missile defence (on which they continued to express disagreement in July) but also on the implementation of the cease-fire in Georgia. In the London meeting with Medvedev, Obama even raised his concern about the beating of human rights activist Lev Ponomarev that occurred just prior to the summit, just as in an interview with a Russian newspaper prior to his July visit to Moscow he questioned the treatment of jailed businessman Mikhail Khodorkovsky.

Getting concrete results

As the July summit demonstrated, arms control was the centrepiece of cooperation on the US–Russian agenda in 2009 not only because the sides perceived a common interest in a new treaty but because the stakes involved are relatively low compared to other big-ticket issues. Obama has linked US and Russian nuclear reductions to his larger effort on non-proliferation; decreasing American and Russian arsenals is part of his comprehensive strategy in the nuclear sphere to promote the idea of a world ultimately free of nuclear weapons. For the Russians, not only does a new arms control agreement with the United States put Moscow alone on the stage with the world's leading power, but it forces the United States to go to the lower levels the Russians would be forced to go to for financial reasons anyway.

As NATO and Russia continue to rebuild a relationship that was shattered by the Russia–Georgia war, they have shown an ability to begin pursuing concrete cooperation (for example on Afghanistan) even while continuing to disagree about Georgia. When a NATO–Russia Charter was first discussed in the mid-1990s, US Secretary of Defence William Perry saw the conversation as 'an academic discussion with no practical nature'.[14] In many respects, through its iterations as the Permanent Joint Council and now the NATO–Russia Council, there has been little progress in producing practical results. Given the common challenge of combating terrorism and piracy, there are real opportunities for joint training and exercises. NATO and Russia should work to build on the limited steps that have been taken to date, for example, in the few Russian deployments as part of NATO's Operation Active Endeavour in the Mediterranean.

Still, we should be cautious about how much we can expect overall in the US–Russian (and by extension, the NATO–Russian) relationship. While the United States, for example, is determined to prevent Iran from developing nuclear weapons, Russia seems more concerned that Iran might one day achieve a rapprochement with the United States, thereby delivering yet another blow to Russia's traditional geopolitical approach. And while Medvedev has appeared to signal a willingness to consider tougher sanctions on Iran, Putin has not. Even on Afghanistan, where the two countries have a clear interest in preventing a resurgence of the Taliban, the Russians are ambivalent at best about an American victory.

The Russians have approached the reset believing that the United States is operating from a position of weakness given the two wars and the financial crisis, and certainly the mood in Washington is not as triumphant as it was in the 1990s. But while President Obama has been clear that there are limits to American capabilities and that the United States needs other countries to solve common problems, the huge disparities in power between these two nations remain. The United States, despite all the problems of recent years, is still the world's most powerful country. It possesses an unrivalled military, the globe's leading economy, and a dominant diplomatic and cultural position. Europe is an economic heavyweight, and China is moving into the front ranks, but the United States maintains its leading position.

Russia, on the other hand, remains quite weak. It has rebounded dramatically from the 1998 economic crisis, but the hard currency reserves Putin built up during his presidency have been sorely tested in defence of the rouble. Investments in the energy sector are insufficient for Russia's future economic development, and the demographic trends are devastating. Russia's military inflicted damage on Georgia, but it is a shadow of its Soviet self. This Russian weakness, the lack of global reach, is in fact the main reason that a new Cold War was never going to re-emerge after 1991. The Cold War was a worldwide military, economic, diplomatic and ideological competition. That is no longer possible. The more traditional Russian spheres of influence approach is far more troubling to American policymakers than any 'Cold War' mentality, and it is particularly dangerous in Moscow's continued efforts to intimidate Georgia. The Russian belief that it is only secure if it dominates its neighbours undermines the continued American push for a Europe whole and free.

As we ponder the prospects for a reset, we should recall that Bill Clinton came into office in 1993 talking about the importance of multilateralism, the UN and partnership with Russia. But as the United States pursued its interests, its actions inevitably caused frictions with Moscow. As Clinton did, Obama, too, will grow frustrated with the limits of multilateralism in general and the UN in particular, and like all American presidents (and Russian ones, for that matter), he will pursue what he believes are the country's interests, as he did with his missile defence proposal. When it comes to European security, the United States and Russia still define their interests quite differently. Russia will continue to push back against the American approach as it defines its own view of its security needs in Europe, but for all its renewal in the Putin years, its leverage remains quite limited.

For the reset to be successful over the long run, the United States and Russia, as well as NATO and Russia, will need to do what has already been signalled in the interactions in the first year of Obama's presidency: acknowledge the differences but seek areas of cooperation where possible. Perhaps most important is to keep expectations in check so that we are not disappointed once again as we have been so often since the end of the Cold War. Achievements are possible, but the two nations will continue to define their interests differently on many of the major issues in the relationship.

Notes

1 An earlier version of this chapter has been published in Policy Review, www.hoover.org/publications/policyreview/51403357.html (accessed 9 December 2009).
2 James A. Baker III and Thomas M. DeFrank, *The Politics of Diplomacy: Revolution, War and Peace 1989–1992*, (New York: G.P. Putnam's Sons, 1995), p. 625; 'Statement issued by Presidents Bush and Yeltsin, February 1, 1992', US Department of State Dispatch 3, 3 February 1992, pp. 78–79.
3 From Secretary Warren Christopher's meeting with President Boris Yeltsin, 22 October 1993, Moscow. Declassified in response to a Freedom of Information Act request, 8 May 2000.
4 Serge Schmemann, 'Clinton in Europe; on Russian TV, Clinton Backs Reforms', *New York Times* 15 January 1994.
5 James M. Goldgeier and Michael McFaul, *Power and Purpose: U.S. Policy toward Russia after the Cold War*, (Washington: Brookings, 2003), p. 194.
6 Philip Zelikow and Condoleezza Rice, *Germany Unified and Europe Transformed: A Study in Statecraft*, (Harvard: Harvard University Press, 1995), pp. 180–83.

7 Mark Kramer, 'The Myth of a No-NATO-Enlargement Pledge to Russia', *Washington Quarterly*, April 2009.
8 Goldgeier and McFaul, *Power and Purpose*, pp. 251–52.
9 See Putin's 2005 state of the nation speech, quoted at www.msnbc.msn.com/id/7632057/ (accessed 9 July 2009).
10 Strobe Talbott, *The Russia Hand: A Memoir of Presidential Diplomacy*, (New York: Random House, 2002), pp. 159–60.
11 Goldgeier and McFaul, *Power and Purpose*, p. 292.
12 The 2009 NATO summit declaration on alliance security, www.nato.int/cps/en/natolive/news_52838.htm?mode=pressrelease (accessed 10 December 2009).
13 'Remarks by the President at the New Economic School Graduation,' Gostinny Dvor, Moscow, Russia, the White House, Office of the Press Secretary, July 7, 2009, www.whitehouse.gov/the_press_office/remarks-by-the-president-at-the-new-economic-school-graduation/ (accessed 9 December 2009).
14 James M. Goldgeier, *Not Whether But When: The U.S. Decision to Enlarge NATO*, (Washington: Brookings, 1999), p. 97.

20

The Obama administration and transatlantic security

Problems and prospects

Jussi M. Hanhimäki

Proposals for a new American foreign policy were many during the 2008 presidential race. The Obama campaign promised to end the war in Iraq, embark on a diplomatic initiative with Iran without preconditions, pursue a new, comprehensive strategy vis-à-vis Russia, strengthen the transatlantic alliance, combat environmental change, stop genocide in Darfur and fight poverty throughout Africa. Obama promised to do all these things while pursuing a policy that 'advances American national interests without compromising our enduring principles'.[1]

This sounded impressive. If you only elect Obama, the Bush doctrine would be dead and buried. America would have a new leader that would not be driven by simple-minded ideological excesses. The forty-fourth president would reverse course, bring back thousands of Americans from a mishandled war and dazzle the world with his winning diplomacy. He would make America respected again, not (just) because of its military prowess but by using the irresistible appeal of the American dream of which he was such a shining example. Soft power was 'in', hard power was 'out'.

The message and the messenger were greeted with much enthusiasm around the world, particularly in Europe. When he visited Berlin in the summer of 2008, crowds went wild. In many people's minds the election of the first African-American president showed how far the United States had progressed in its multiculturalism while Europe – old and new – was still stuck in the ancient regime of white rule. Obama's inauguration was one of the highest rated media events throughout Europe in early 2009, with commentators around the continent heralding the historic moment upon us all. It was as if the US president 'had been "elected" on both sides of the Atlantic'. Mathias Müller von Blumencron, the editor of *Spiegel*, even referred to Obama as the 'world's president'.[2]

As of this writing, Barack Obama has been in office for less than a year. He is a very different leader than his predecessor, preferring engagement and consultation to uncompromising leadership. This became evident during his first trip to Europe in April 2009, as Obama used all his persuasive powers to try and forge an international consensus behind his major foreign policy goals. The three key issues that he focused upon – the economic and financial crisis; Afghanistan; nuclear proliferation (and nuclear strategy more broadly) – set the stage for transatlantic relations for the remainder of the year.

Indeed, it was clear that throughout this whirlwind tour of Europe (with additional stops in Istanbul, Ankara and Iraq), Obama managed to earn, not unexpectedly, the adulation of crowds and public praise from European leaders. According to *Transatlantic Trends*, Obama enjoyed 77 per cent approval ratings within the EU and Turkey for his handling of international affairs.[3] And he earned the trust of the Norwegian Nobel Committee which, in October 2009, awarded the American president the much-coveted Nobel Peace Prize. In the words of Assistant Secretary of State Philip Gordon: 'there is more trans-Atlantic unity than at almost anytime in the post-World War II period'.[4]

But hold on. By the fall of 2009 doubts about Obama's commitment to a renewal of transatlantic relations had seeped in. In early October 2009, the UK-based *Economist* declared that a new 'Atlantic Gap' had emerged, that 'the honeymoon between Europe and Barack Obama's America is over'. According to 'Charlemagne' EU leaders were disappointed with the lack of progress on emission targets and what many considered meagre results of the September G20 meeting in Pittsburgh. Meanwhile the Americans were becoming increasingly exasperated with the Europeans ability – as seen from Washington – to refrain making a true commitment to the conflict in Afghanistan. Not all was going wrong. Yet, tensions that have always characterized transatlantic relations appeared to be back. In fact, while Obama remained popular, even *Transatlantic Trends* noted that significant differences of opinion remained over climate change, Afghanistan and Iran.[5]

Indeed, the initial European euphoria about a new era in transatlantic relations has been replaced by confusion and disappointment. As James Joyner of the Atlantic Council wrote, while Obama is 'saying all the right things in public about transatlantic relations and NATO [he is] adopting a high-handed policy and paying little attention to Europe'.[6] Other countries – from China and Russia to the many trouble spots in the Middle East – and global questions – from the environment to the economy – command the agenda. There was little nostalgia for the Bush years. But the inconvenient truth that Obama's election may have meant a change in rhetoric and style but not necessarily in substance was starting to sink in. The United States was going to pursue its interests – be they related to economic prosperity or national security – in ways that were not always aligned with or identical to those of European nations. For those in Brussels, London, Paris and Berlin it was looking much less than 'change they could believe in'.

Economic engagement over protectionism

'[Barak Obama] had always planned for the economy to be his priority. Just not this economy'. The financial crisis was in large part responsible for Obama's victory in November 2008 over John McCain. But the banking failures and foreclosures that spiralled into what is called the worst economic crisis since the Great Depression dominated not only the last stages of the presidential campaign. By the time he reached office, it was clear that Obama's approach to dealing with the crisis was bound to have a major impact on the first years of his presidency. Along with the – perhaps ill-advised – attempt to revamp the mess that is otherwise known as the American health care system, it was certainly a top priority of his first year in office.[7]

The crisis may have been heavily (although by no means only) American in its origins. But it quickly became clearly global in its consequences. Few countries were spared. In the spring of 2009 the OECD predicted that the world economy would shrink by 2.75 per cent in 2009 and output by four per cent. The predictions for 2010 were no brighter: despite creeping optimism that the bottom of the economic cycle may have passed, unemployment figures were approaching double digits in many rich countries in the autumn of 2009.[8]

The challenge facing the Obama administration – as well as European, Asian, Latin American and almost all governments around the globe – was how to beat this crisis without reverting to policies that the electorates in most of these countries seem to instinctively prefer. In particular, how to counter the seductive idea of promoting purely national solutions to a global set of problems? More to the point: how to avoid a slide to 'murky' protectionism that, while potentially popular at home, would in all likelihood further deepen and most certainly prolong the crisis?[9]

Initially, the prospects were troubling for any committed free trader. During the campaign, Obama had said he would renegotiate the NAFTA and bring about an era of 'fair trade'. Democrats in the Congress had managed to put on a hold on a number of trade deals – with Panama, Colombia and South Korea – negotiated by the Bush administration. Concerned over the direction of the president-elect, British Prime Minister Gordon Brown warned Obama against the dangers of protectionism within a week of the November 2008 election.

The real international outcry, however, started with 'buy American'. In early 2009 the House of Representatives passed an $819 billion stimulus package which required that infrastructure projects carried out under the programme use US-made iron and steel. The Senate version of the bill went even further, specifying that all manufactured goods used in the projects be homemade. Europeans, Japanese, Australians and others were soon crying wolf, complaining about such protectionist measures. By the time the American Recovery and Reinvestment Act (ARRA) was eventually signed by Obama on 17 February 2009, concerns about an American slide towards protectionism had not been abated, despite the president's public assurances that he would not allow any sidestepping of current trade agreements.

To his credit, Obama soon showed that his approach would be nothing like the one that had so manifestly failed in the 1930s. There was reassuring rhetoric and action to try and bring a new measure of responsibility to the battered US financial system. Some of this may have been mere scoring of points from the electorate – such as the righteous anger directed at all those executives who still take their fat bonuses even as their investors had lost much of their money. Perhaps there is even reason to hope that the crisis has given rise to what Obama, in his inaugural address, called a 'new era of responsibility'.

In the international arena, the G20 meeting in London in early April was, by most yardsticks, a key moment. It marked the new president's international debut, a moment he could truly set down the priorities of the new administration's economic foreign policy. Here he was, with a group of other leaders that between them accounted for roughly 90 per cent of the world economy, ready to rewrite the rules of global finance and financial institutions.

In practice, the major results of the G20 meeting included increased regulation of international financial markets, a commitment to closing down tax havens, regulating hedge funds and capping bank executives' pay. In addition to such commitments, G20 agreed to pump over a trillion dollars to the IMF and the World Bank. Not quite the new economic order but an impressive signal of collective action nonetheless. Beyond these measures, one of the most significant signals came in the form of a frank rejection of protectionism. Obama and China's leader, Hu Jintao, for example, released a joint statement affirming that the two countries – sometimes tipped as the G2 – were 'committed to resist protectionism'.[10]

The follow up to the London summit – the G20 meeting in Pittsburgh in late September 2009 – was equally ebullient in its rhetoric. Obama billed it as the opening of a 'new era of engagement' while Britain's Prime Minister Gordon Brown applauded the way in which 'the world is coming together to do what it should have done many years ago, and we recommended many years ago to create a system that can prevent crises as well as deal with them when they occur'.[11] What Brown was referring to was not entirely clear to most observers who, justifiably, suspected the beleaguered Labour leader for trying to use the international setting to rescue his falling popularity at home.

Most remarkably, however, the September G20 summit took place in what seemed like a very different world economy. The global gloom of the spring was giving way to signs of recovery. 'World emerging from recession', was the OECD's perspective in early September. The fact that job losses had been less severe than anticipated were interpreted as a sign that the worst was already over. In Europe, only Britain was still struggling – allowing some continental sceptics to claim that the Anglo-Saxon economic model was clearly 'inferior' to the continental one. In the United States, after hitting a 26-year high (10.2 per cent) in October 2009, US unemployment rates declined for the first time, according to figures released on 4 December. To be sure, at 10 per cent the numbers remained high, more than double the situation in late 2007 (when the US unemployment rate was 4.9 per cent).[12]

The key element in the Obama administration's approach to the economic crisis was the sheer acknowledgement that American economic interests were best served by global cooperation and by revitalizing some of the key international institutions that, although mainly of America's own creation in the aftermath of the Second World War, had fallen into disrepute over the past decades.[13] It should be stressed, though, that this does not in itself mean a paradigm shift: ever since the United States emerged as a global player – and particularly since the end of the Second World War – its economic security has been tied to the rest of the globe. At the same time, none of the reassuring rhetoric should be taken to mean that the Obama administration is immune to political pressures from American trade unions and popular sentiment. With 69 per cent of Americans 'strongly agreeing' that the Obama administration should focus primarily on domestic economic issues – with similar, if somewhat lower, figures in Europe – it is evident that such notions as 'buy American' were easily viewed as the best recipe for saving American jobs. Faced with economic hardship people do tend to turn inwards. The crisis that began in 2007 has been no exception.[14]

Yet, on the economic front Obama's mantra about engagement was in fact put into practice. The G20 meetings did confirm the message of the president's inaugural address. Obama's America showed that it was 'ready to lead again'. In the context of transatlantic economic relations – still one of the cornerstones of the global economy – this was good news. The same is not necessarily true of a set of interrelated crises in a region that has played an increasingly important role in US foreign and national security policy since the 1970s.

A two-front war in the Arc of Crisis

In the late 1970s Zbigniew Brzezinski – with the help of eager journalists and academics – coined the term the Arc of Crisis, defined by George Lenczowski as 'an area stretching from the Indian subcontinent in the east to the Horn of Africa in the west'.[15] Thirty years later, it appears that the arc remains fuelled by constant conflicts which remain as – if not even more – central to American foreign and security policy as the 1979 Islamic Revolution in Iran and the Soviet invasion of Afghanistan. The main trouble spots that the Bush administration grappled with are here: Iraq, Iran, Afghanistan, Pakistan, the Palestinian–Israeli conflict. It was in this region that the now sidelined neo-conservatives had a brief but disastrous influence on the Bush administration's foreign policy. They may have referred to it as the Greater Middle East but the area was the same as the one that has preoccupied every administration since the days of the Carter presidency.[16]

Within the arc of crisis the president has inherited a set of almost intractable problems that may not be of the administration's making but have preoccupied the president ever since he took office in January 2009. Ironically, the legacy of Obama's foreign policy hinges on the content and success of the policies towards the same region that defined the presidency of George W. Bush. Or, as Brzezinski puts it in 2009: 'the first order of business for NATO members is to define together, and then to pursue together, a politically acceptable outcome to its out-of-region military engagement in Afghanistan'.[17]

America is at war on two fronts. In early October 2009 there were over 120,000 US troops in Iraq and roughly 68,000 in Afghanistan. Although the prospect of a full blown civil war in Iraq – despite repeated and often large-scale acts of violence – appears to have abated in the last year, the opposite is the case in Afghanistan. The Taliban has made a strong return and the war has spread to the tribal regions of neighbouring Pakistan. While Obama himself repeatedly labelled Iraq the wrong war during his campaign, he pinpointed Afghanistan as the central front of the so-called war on terror (a term that seems to stick), 'a war of necessity' from the perspective of US and global security. Whether this is true hardly matters. Obama's rhetoric has confirmed that the country that fought back the Soviets for a decade only to see the rise of the Taliban and the invasion of the United States and its allies remains plagued by increasingly bloody military activity. As Obama put it at West Point on 1 December 2009: 'Afghanistan is not lost but for several years it has moved backwards'.[18]

There are other problems in the region. Iran, inconveniently located between Iraq and Afghanistan, presents another potential for crisis or, perhaps worse, humiliation. Moreover, Iran is implicated in the ongoing conflicts in Iraq and Afghanistan and continues to pursue its nuclear programme despite international pressure. The perpetual Arab–Israeli conflict may momentarily command fewer headlines than one is accustomed to. But here, also, the situation appears to be moving – once again – from extremely bad to something worse. With a new hawkish prime minister in Israel in the form of Benjamin Netanyahu and a strengthened Hamas refusing to budge down, the Palestinian question appears insoluble. Better, or so the forty-fourth president appears to signal, to leave the issue to his erstwhile secretary of state. At the south-west corner of the arc, Somalia remains the prototype failed state and pirates terrorize the Gulf of Aden.[19]

In fact, if one looks for continuity from the Bush administration it is found in the realm of the ill-defined yet ever-present war on terrorism. Already in his inaugural address Obama came uncomfortably close to that Bushism 'You're with us or you are against us' as he reminded his audience that the memory of 11 September 2001 was not forgotten. Americans, he exhorted, 'will not apologize for our way of life, nor will we waver in its defence, and for those who seek to advance their aims by inducing terror and slaughtering innocents, we say to you now that our spirit is stronger and cannot be broken; you cannot outlast us, and *we will defeat you*'.[20]

The trouble is that the Obama administration has no magic wand by which such a victory might be achieved.

Is there any cause for optimism? Can the Obama magic transform the arc of crisis into something less volatile? Perhaps. At the moment, however, it seems that his policy amounts to winding down one war and escalating another. To many Europeans this is not a particularly convincing or reassuring strategy.

In Iraq Obama has set in motion a gradual withdrawal of all American troops by the end of 2011. Before that – by August 2010 – the US combat mission should be over. If nothing else, a process of Iraqization is now under way. The administration has promised to end the war 'responsibly'; in addition to the phased withdrawal of American troops, the United States will engage in diplomatic efforts, combat a humanitarian crisis that is visible throughout the region due to the 5.2 million Iraqis (19 per cent of the population) who have been rendered either refugees or Internally Displaced People (IDPs). For this effort the administration has promised 2 billion US dollars. Obama has also pledged to 'make sure we engage representatives from all levels of Iraqi society – in and out of government – to forge compromises on oil revenue sharing, the equitable provision of services, federalism, the status of disputed territories, new elections, aid to displaced Iraqis, and the reform of Iraqi security forces'. What if things deteriorate and sectarian violence surges? The answer is simple. The United States 'reserve[s] the right to intervene militarily, with our international partners, to suppress potential genocidal violence within Iraq'.[21]

Will this work? Time can only tell. What seems evident, though, is that there is no major change from the previous administration's strategy. Indeed, the irony of Obama's Iraq policy is that Congressional Republicans are more supportive of the president's approach than Democrats. It would be a great historical irony if, a decade after the American-led intervention, a re-elected President Obama would herald the building of a stable, perhaps even democratic, Iraq as a major foreign policy achievement of his first term. Perhaps in the future the American president can even announce his visit to Iraq beforehand, rather than keeping it secret for security reasons as Obama did in early April 2009.

If Iraq is possibly on the mend, Afghanistan is another story. Throughout 2009 the basic idea seemed to be that another surge – partly civilian, partly military – would reverse the deteriorating security situation in this country (and parts of neighbouring Pakistan). Indeed, the January 2009 Obama–Biden agenda called for withdrawal from Iraq 'so that we can renew our military strength, dedicate more resources to the fight against the Taliban and al Qaeda in Afghanistan'.[22] This is the 'right war' (or the 'war of necessity') Obama had preached throughout the presidential campaign. But is it? Few others – while offering no real options to the current strategy – seem to believe so.

Warnings have been issued from everywhere. From Russia, veterans of the Afghan war – including Boris Gromov, the general who oversaw the final Soviet withdrawal – have been particularly outspoken. 'One can increase the forces or not [but] it won't lead to anything but a negative result', Gromov said in February 2009.[23] In the United States, Boston University Professor Andrew Bacevich made the point about the limits of military power in his widely discussed book that was published in 2008. He summed it all up rather neatly: 'we can't remake Afghanistan and don't need to'.[24] On a broad level, it is difficult to disagree: nation-building – and that is essentially what we are talking about – has rarely worked; the history of US foreign policy is filled with failures in this area (from Haiti in the first half of the twentieth century to Vietnam during the Cold War).

For all his considerable charm and persuasive skills, Barack Obama is finding it very hard to convince his transatlantic allies that they need to increase their contribution to the Afghan cause. Certainly, in the spring of 2009 European leaders praised the new strategy in Afghanistan. 'When it comes to Afghanistan, this summit and this alliance has delivered', NATO's outgoing Secretary General Jaap De Hoop Scheffer declared in Strasbourg in early April. Others agreed, taking turns to praise Obama's new approach. But they did so with a caveat that was neatly summed up by the French president. 'We completely support the new *American* strategy in Afghanistan', exhorted Nikolas Sarkozy on 3 April.[25]

As far as the Europeans are concerned the new strategy is America's. It is not truly transatlantic. While Obama referred to Europe's 'strong down payment' in Afghanistan, his words could not mask a more sobering reality. At the Strasbourg summit European leaders agreed to provide only token practical support. In subsequent months this imbalance has become increasingly clear. In 2009 America's NATO allies sent roughly 5,000 more trainers and police – on short-term assignments – to help monitor the Afghan elections and train the country's military. In contrast, Americans have increased their troop levels by more than 50 per cent: from 38,000 to roughly 60,000. In the spring of 2009 Americans totalled less than half of the 58,000 members of the International Security Assistance Force (ISAF). By December they accounted for roughly two-thirds.[26]

In 2010 the Afghan campaign will clearly become Obama's war. Once the 30,000 US troops and an additional 5,000 soldiers from other NATO countries are in place, there will be a total of 140,000 foreigners in Afghanistan. Will they be able to stabilize the country and allow the United States to begin troop withdrawals in 2011 as Obama has promised? As of this writing signs are not particularly encouraging. Not only is Obama drawing criticism from all quarters at home and abroad, but the Taliban is publicly welcoming the additional targets of its unconventional military campaign. As a Taliban commander told BBC news: 'Obama is sending more troops to Afghanistan and that means more Americans will die. With just a handful of resources we can cause them even more casualties and deaths'.[27]

Such threats – realistic or not – are helpful in understanding why the Europeans, so eager to be photographed next to Barack Obama, have been reluctant to commit more resources to the Afghan campaign. Most European leaders see such support as a political nightmare. In Europe, De Hoop Scheffer opined in April 2009, 'fighting is not very popular'.[28] What he really meant was that war casualties, likely to increase with more troops in a conflict area, are the surest way to political catastrophe. This was particularly the case in 2009 when most voters – in the United States and Europe – clearly preferred using economic resources to support recovery at home than an uncertain and ill-defined military mission abroad. Indeed, many Europeans have difficulty seeing the light at the end of this particular tunnel. If the Soviets could not stabilize Afghanistan with 130,000 troops is there any point in increasing the numbers of the ISAF to similar levels? Will the presence of more foreign troops simply boost the Taliban cause and further hurt the credibility of the Kharzai government (already badly damaged by corruption charges and the election fiasco of 2009)?

When it comes down to Afghanistan, Europeans also have an institutional problem not fully appreciated by the Americans. In simple terms: where does EU policy end and NATO policy begin? Would a firmer European commitment within the context of the alliance simply further complicate the much-awaited European Common Foreign and Security Policy?

In the end, the basic danger for the United States is clear. Instead of 'Afghanistanizing' the conflict with European support, the Obama administration is well on its way towards Americanizing it. Burden-sharing – always a tricky issue in transatlantic security relations – still has its limits. Nor can Obama expect that the American public will treat kindly a president who may well be able to end one war only to replace it with another. Even the most silver-tongued orator will eventually reach the limits of his persuasive skills.

Such considerations can lead to two problematic outcomes: (1) forget about a nation-building effort in Afghanistan and accept an increasingly important role for the Taliban as a provider of future stability; or (2) further increase the direct US role. As General David Petraeus, head of the US Central Command (and the architect of the famed 'surge' in Iraq), put it in an interview in early 2009, the war in Afghanistan was going to be the 'longest campaign in a long war'. When asked how long, his response was ominous: 'There are predictions one doesn't hazard'.[29] In early December, the sentiment was echoed by General Stanley McChrystal, the commander of US troops in Afghanistan. McChrystal chose to cite Winston Churchill's statement after the defeat of Rommel's Army in El Alamein during the Second World War: 'it was not the end, nor even the beginning of the end, but it might be the end of the beginning'.[30]

It is difficult to describe the situation in Afghanistan as anything but a no-win situation in which the ultimate casualty – almost without fail – will be the Afghan people. They are unlikely to experience even a semblance of stability any time soon. Instead, most of them will struggle for survival as a resurgent Taliban, an incompetent local government and a somewhat larger foreign force exchange control over various parts of territory. Whatever may happen to Barack Obama's political fortunes as a result is surely insignificant by comparison.[31]

Much like the economic crisis, dealing with the arc of crisis – and its current focal point, Afghanistan – has the potential for either bringing America and its allies together or tearing them further apart. But while questions of economic security tend to have the ability to focus politicians' minds and increase the tendency towards cooperation, the state and future of a mountainous country in Central Asia that controls few natural resources seems to have the opposite effect. As so many times in the history of transatlantic relations, an out-of-area crisis – and Afghanistan is most definitely 'out-of-area' – is exposing the limits of transatlantic unity.

Nuclear stakes

On 5 April 2009 Barack Obama stopped in Prague. In the Czech capital, the president was keen on addressing one of the most worrisome legacies of the Cold War. 'No nuclear war was fought between the United States and the Soviet Union, but generations lived with the knowledge that their world could be erased in a single flash of light. Cities like Prague that had existed for centuries would have ceased to exist', Obama declared. He then added: 'Today, the Cold War has disappeared but thousands of those weapons have not'. This, though, was not the crux of the problem. As Obama explained:

> In a strange turn of history, the threat of global nuclear war has gone down, but the risk of a nuclear attack has gone up. More nations have acquired these weapons. Testing has continued. Black market trade in nuclear secrets and nuclear materials abound. The technology to build a bomb has spread. Terrorists are determined to buy, build or steal one. Our efforts to contain these dangers are centred on a global non-proliferation regime, but as more people and nations break the rules, we could reach the point where the centre cannot hold.

To much applause, Obama outlined his plans. He would start reducing US nuclear stockpile, negotiate a new Strategic Arms Reduction Treaty (START) with Russia, press the US Congress to ratify the Comprehensive Test Ban Treaty (CTBT), strengthen the Non-Proliferation Treaty (NPT). Obama announced new initiatives to make sure nuclear secrets would not be passed on to terrorists and rogue states. Throwing in the trademark slogan 'yes we can', he earned the adulation of a large crowd in the Czech capital.[32]

It was and remains a bold vision. But it is not as complete a volte-face as some might have hoped. In fact, Obama injected a degree of realism by, first, acknowledging that he may not live long enough to see a nuclear weapons free world and, second, by making it clear that the controversial missile defence programme was a bargaining chip of sorts. The United States would continue developing a 'cost-effective' system as long as Iran's nuclear ambitions were not checked. However, '[i]f the Iranian threat is eliminated, we will have a stronger basis for security, and the driving force for missile defence construction in Europe will be removed'. How the 'elimination' would arrive he did not specify. But one assumes that Obama was thinking in terms of engagement and diplomacy, direct or via those – like Russia and China – who may have some influence on Iran's policies.[33]

Obama's vision received a mixed reaction. In the United States it gave rise to partisan bickering, with a number of Republicans arguing that the president is an irresponsible fool. Former Speaker of the House Newt Gingrich (Republican, Georgia) told Fox News that 'it's very dangerous to have a fantasy foreign policy'.[34] To be sure, such critics – notable for finding in Obama's speech something he did not say – were in the minority. Even Obama's former rival John McCain was complementary. 'Concerning President Obama's commitment to the removal of nuclear weapons from the Earth, I certainly support that ambitious goal', McCain said at a press conference in Tokyo.[35]

In Europe, there has been support for the idea but scepticism about the reality. The *Economist* noted that North Korea's missile tests and the subsequent Chinese and Russian action at the UN Security Council – that virtually coincided with Obama's Prague speech – was a clear demonstration of the difficulties in working towards a nuclear free world. 'Nuclear weapons cannot simply be wished away or uninvented', the British-based journal noted. Yet, in what amounts to a relatively strong endorsement, the *Economist* added: 'Mr. Obama is right. This and more are the work of decades. The world may never get to zero. But it would help make things a lot safer along the way if others act in concert'.[36] The key 'others' include two European nuclear powers of which only one – Britain – has expressed an interest in cutting down its nuclear forces in the future.

Nuclear weapons are indeed a minefield of international diplomacy. At the moment the key questions have to do with proliferation rather than force reduction. What is 'right' about having an NPT that essentially grants the right for nuclear weaponry to the five countries that – hardly by accident – are also the five permanent members of the UN Security Council? Even if one accepts the treaty's inherent inequalities as a fact of life, what to do about countries like Iran (which is in the treaty but continues to defy UN calls to end its suspect nuclear programme), those who made no secret of their nuclear ambitions but left the treaty (North Korea), or even those who simply did not join but are in possession of a nuclear arsenal (India, Pakistan and Israel)?

From the perspective of transatlantic security, however, nuclear weapons policy has always offered a unifying theme. As early as November 1949 NATO defence plans called for insuring 'the ability to carry out strategic bombing including the prompt delivery of the atomic bomb. This is primarily a US responsibility assisted as practicable by other nations'.[37] In subsequent decades nuclear sharing became part of NATO's strategic doctrine, with the understanding that the United States was in a special position to decide how much 'sharing' actually were to take place at the level of decision-making (not all that much). But deterrence – in the form of an American nuclear umbrella – was accepted as the ultimate guarantee of security.

Since the end of the Cold War there has been much debate about the role that nuclear weapons should play in NATO's overall strategy. Deterrence has not disappeared. In the early twenty-first century Belgium, the Netherlands, Germany, Italy, the UK and Turkey all host NATO (US) nuclear weapons. Britain and France also have their own arsenals.[38] Nevertheless, as the likelihood of an attack against NATO countries dissipated after the Cold War, NATO nuclear policy changed. By 1999, when NATO's last Strategic Concept was approved, non-proliferation had become a key ingredient of Alliance policy. As a result of the Heads of State meeting held in Washington in April 1999 stated: 'The goal of the Alliance and its members is to prevent proliferation from occurring or, should it occur, to reverse it through diplomatic means'.[39]

A decade later it seems clear that NATO needs something more. Proliferation has occurred and may well be occurring as we speak. Diplomatic measures have so far done little to convince states into putting the genie back in the bottle. If nuclear proliferation truly is a key issue affecting transatlantic security, the Alliance needs to be far more effective. This will undoubtedly be one of the key questions addressed when NATO prepares its new Strategic Concept in 2010.

There are, though, two important caveats. The first one is the simple practical implementation of any non-proliferation strategy. If diplomatic means are not enough to stop proliferation, then what is one to do? As of this writing, Iran continues its nuclear programme, even threatening to build 10 new nuclear plants in its territory. The Obama administration is faced with an uncomfortable situation in which its efforts to reach out with a diplomatic olive branch have been consistently thwarted and the choice appears to be, as the *Economist* puts it, between an 'Iranian nuclear bomb, or the bombing of Iran'.[40] Before that choice comes to a head, Americans and their European allies will undoubtedly try to strengthen the sanctions regime. But given less than full cooperation from Russia and China such efforts are unlikely to yield a volte-face from the fervently defiant government of President Mahmoud Ahmadinejad. It is likely that at some point in 2010–11, the Obama administration – struggling with the consequences of its deepening commitment in Afghanistan – will thus have little choice but to accept the existence of a nuclear armed Iran. For given America's recent record on preventive (or pre-emptive) military action, the bar for engaging in any kind of first strike is very high.

On the whole this may not be entirely bad news. But when viewed from Pyongyang and taken together with Chinese and Russian reluctance to condemn North Korean missile tests, it means that the Obama administration's already battered diplomatic credibility is in danger of evaporating entirely when it comes down to dealing with nuclear non-proliferation. In the early months of 2009 Susan Rice's efforts at the UN Security Council were fruitless and the North Koreans have felt no need to worry about the series of verbal condemnations from the United States and its allies. 'There is no need for the six-party talks any more', read a statement from Pyongyang's foreign ministry on 14 April 2009, further affirming that North Korea 'will strengthen its nuclear deterrent for its defence by all means'.[41] To make the point clear, less than a month later North Korea conducted its second underground nuclear test in three years. There seems to be scant hope that diplomacy alone will make Kim Jong Il relent. One thing is clear. As long as one small country can play this kind of game with impunity, non-proliferation will remain a noble dream.

Second, while there is broad agreement on both sides of the Atlantic about the value of non-proliferation, there is less of a consensus about the lowering of NATO's missile defences. Will European concerns about their security be heightened as America's nuclear umbrella diminishes? From today's perspective it may seem like a far-fetched scenario to imagine European leaders – let alone the general public – demanding that Americans keep their nuclear weapons on their respective territories. However improbable their actual use remains, nuclear weapons have, throughout NATO's history, been a symbolic guarantee of the permanence of the transatlantic security project. Their continued presence may be required for that project to remain viable.

This is something that became clear in September 2009 when Obama scrapped the missile defence agreement negotiated by the Bush administration with Poland and the Czech Republic. What particularly annoyed decision-makers in Prague and Warsaw was the manner and sudden nature of Obama's decision. On 1 September 2009, National Security Advisor James Johnson had affirmed Radoslaw Sikorski. Poland's foreign minister, of America's 'unwavering commitment to Poland's security and defence'. He further stressed that Washington would 'engage in a strategic dialogue with Poland' as part of an ongoing review of ballistic missile defence. About two weeks later, on 17 September, the administration announced that it was changing the Bush administration's missile defence plans; there would not be land-based systems in Poland and the Czech Republic. The Polish defence ministry's spokeswoman's commentary was laconic: 'catastrophic'.[42]

The irritated comments that this public turnaround – which had in fact been the subject of consultations between the respective governments – provoked were in part related to Polish sensitivities of the timing: 1 September was the seventieth anniversary of the German attack on Poland; 17 September the same for the Soviet attack. But more importantly, the announcements confirmed in the minds of many East Europeans that the days of 'New Europe' were firmly in the past and that – hoping to seal a new START and support for his policies vis-à-vis Iran – Obama's foreign policy had become far too accommodating towards Russia.[43] As a strong critic of the administration's policies, James Joyner of the Atlantic Council, puts it: 'President Obama promised he would win America friends where, under George W. Bush, it had antagonists. The reality is that the US is working hard to create antagonists where it previously had friends'.[44]

Unfair though such a critique may be, the reality is that in the first year of its tenure, the Obama administration has not managed to live up to the – unrealistically high – expectations that greeted it in early 2009. It is too early to talk about a transatlantic crisis. But what stockbrokers refer to as a 'correction of the market' has surely taken place as Europeans have come to accept the uncomfortable truth that Obama pursues his nation's interests before any other concerns. And these interests are likely to clash, on occasion, with the goals of all, or some, NATO countries. The Bush Doctrine may be history. Yet, a year after the election of the first African-American president, it is evident that the Obama Doctrine is unlikely to please all Europeans, all of the time.

Continuity and renewal

Plus, ca change. Although the Obama administration came into office with an outpouring of goodwill and enthusiasm for change, it could hardly bring about a complete transformation in US foreign policy. American *interests* and the global leadership role that the United States plays have not changed. Any American president will have as his (or in the future her) foremost task to safeguard those interests and that leadership position. One need not look further than Barack Obama's inaugural address to see that the new president was not about to accept for his country anything other than the pre-eminent position among the family of nations. 'We are ready to lead once more', Obama promised the cheering crowds in Washington on 20 January. The major front of the war on terror may have shifted to Afghanistan. But it goes on. In other fields as well, there is plenty of continuity from the previous administration. As Peter Barker of the *New York Times* put it: 'Obama is carefully choosing his battles, and otherwise keeping intact much of the foreign policy architecture that he inherited, while cloaking it in new language. The new emphasis on diplomacy still advances many of the same goals and national interests'.[45]

In terms of transatlantic relations change was always likely to be a relative concept. In general, European publics from Lisbon to Helsinki and from Dublin to Bucharest still love Obama, because he *is* so different – in every conceivable way – from George W. Bush. In less than a year, the Obama administration has engaged in some path-breaking diplomacy. In large part due to the president's personal charisma, the United States appears very much 'ready to lead again'. Many allies in Europe welcome this. The trouble is that the United States still demands something in return for its shows of goodwill. Multilateralism is a fine buzzword. But national and regional interests are still realities that continue to limit the extent of co-operation, be it in the field of international economics, ongoing military conflicts or long-term strategic goals.

NATO and transatlantic relations are changing. Most importantly, diplomacy has made a serious comeback as a method of pursuing US foreign policy. But one central fact remains: a proclaimed unity of purpose does not automatically translate into an agreement over policy when it comes down to questions of security. This is particularly true when it comes down to issues considered 'out-of-area' (as Afghanistan so manifestly is). Nor is there anything surprising about it. The United States is a superpower with global interests; Europe remains an ill-coordinated grouping of states with mainly regional interests. Or, to put it in narrower terms: NATO is still fundamentally a regional security alliance not a global peacemaker. Not even eight years of Obama is likely to change that.

Notes

1 From the Obama campaign's website, http://origin.barackobama.com/issues/foreign_policy/ (accessed 1 April 2009).
2 Interview with von Blumencron, 11 December 2008, www.democracynow.org/2008/12/11/president_of_the_world_editor_of (accessed 8 December 2009) 'US Relations at the Outset of the Obama Presidency,' *European Foreign Affairs Review*, vol. 14, no.1, 2009, pp. 1–6.
3 *Transatlantic Trends,* 9 September 2009, www.gmfus.org/trends/pressinfo.html (accessed 3 March 2010)
4 'Obama-Vertrauter Gordon,' *Spiegel,* 6 November 2009, www.spiegel.de/politik/deutschland/0,1518,659658,00.html (last accessed 5 December 2009).
5 Ibid. 'The Atlantic Gap,' *Economist,* 1 October 2009, www.economist.com/world/europe/displaystory.cfm?story_id=14539983 (accessed 5 October 2009); Barry Eichengreen, 'The Dollar Dilemma', *Foreign Affairs* vol. 88, no. 5, 2009, pp. 53–69.
6 James Joyner, 'Europe's Obama Fatigue', *Foreign Policy*, 29 October 2009, www.foreignpolicy.com/articles/2009/10/29/europes_obama_fatigue (accessed 5 December 2009).
7 'Wolves at the Door', *Economist*, 6 November 2008, p. 7.

8. The OECD Economic Outlook Interim Report, March 2009, www.oecd.org/document/51/0,3343,en_2649_34487_42464883_1_1_1_1,00.html (accessed 3 March 2010).
9. For an elaborated set of recommendations by a group of distinguished economists see an e-book edited by Richard Baldwin and Simon Evenett, *The collapse of global trade, murky protectionism, and the crisis: Recommendations for the G20*, 2009, http://graduateinstitute.ch/corporate/page5892_fr.html (accessed 6 April 2009).
10. 'How President Obama managed to unlock the G20 Summit', *Telegraph*, 5 April 2009, www.telegraph.co.uk/finance/financetopics/g20-summit/5105508/How-President-Obama-managed-to-unlock-the-G20-Summit.html (accessed 10 December 2009).
11. Cited in 'G20 leaders map out a new economic order at Pittsburgh summit', *Guardian*, 26 September 2009, www.guardian.co.uk/world/2009/sep/25/g20-summit-economy-bonuses-deficits (accessed 4 October 2009).
12. 'World emerging from recession says OECD', *Business & Leadership*, 3 September 2009, www.businessandleadership.com/news/article/15518/leadership/world-emerging-from-recession-says-oecd (accessed 24 October 2009). 'Employment Situation November 2009', Department of Labor Statistics, U.S. Department of Labor, 4 December 2009, www.bls.gov/news.release/pdf/empsit.pdf (accessed 5 December 2009).
13. On this see Stephen Brooks and William Wohlforth, 'Reshaping the World Order: How Washington Should Reform International Institutions', *Foreign Affairs*, March/April 2009, pp. 49–63.
14. Transatlantic Trends, September 2009, www.gmfus.org/trends/2009/docs/2009_English_Key.pdf (accessed 4 October 2009).
15. George Lenczowski, 'The Arc of Crisis: Its Central Sector', *Foreign Affairs* vol. 57, no. 4, Spring 1979, pp. 796–820.
16. For a recent overview see Patrick Tyler, *A World of Trouble: The White House and the Middle East – from the Cold War to the War on Terror*, (New York: Farrar, Straus & Giroux, 2009).
17. Zbigniew Brzezinski, 'An Agenda for NATO: Toward a Global Security Web', *Foreign Affairs* vol. 88, no. 5, September–October 2009, p. 7.
18. 'Obama Address on the New Strategy in Afghanistan and Pakistan', 2 December 2009. For a full text and video, www.nytimes.com/interactive/2009/12/02/world/middleeast/20091202-obama-policy.html (accessed 5 December 2009).
19. See Jeffrey Guttleman, 'The Most Dangerous Place in the World', *Foreign Policy*, March/April 2009, pp. 60–69.
20. Inaugural address can be found on www.cnn.com/2009/POLITICS/01/20/obama.politics/ (accessed 6 April 2009).
21. Obama-Biden Iraq Agenda, 21 January 2009, www.cfr.org/publication/18311/obamabiden_iraq_agenda_january_2009.html (accessed 6 April 2009).
22. Ibid.
23. Cited in the *Guardian*, 13 February 2009, http://blog.luciolepress.com/2009/02/13/gen-boris-gromov-last-russian-commander-of-troops-in-afghanistan-warns-us-afghanistan-taught-us-an-invaluable-lesson-it-has-been-and-always-will-be-impossible-to-solve-political.aspx?ref=rss (accessed 3 March 2010).
24. Andrew J. Bacevich, *The Limits of Power*, (New York: Metropolitan Books, 2008), p. 62.
25. Sarkozy cited in 'Obama asks NATO for help in Afghan war', MSNBC News, 3 April 2009, www.msnbc.msn.com/id/30025192/ (accessed 9 April 2009).
26. 'Down payment' cited in 'NATO leaders pledge police for Afghanistan,' MSNBC News, 4 April 2009, www.msnbc.msn.com/id/30042575/ (accessed 5 December 2009).
27. 'Taliban vow to fight US troop surge in Afghanistan', BBC News, 2 December 2009, http://news.bbc.co.uk/2/hi/south_asia/8390466.stm (accessed 5 December 2009).
28. Vivienne Walt, 'As NATO Gathers, Its Future is Looking Cloudy', *Time*, 2 April 2009.
29. 'Interview with General David Petraeus', *Foreign Policy*, January–February 2009, p. 50.
30. 'The beginning or the end? The urge in Afghanistan', *Economist*, 5 December 2009, p. 55.
31. For a pessimistic take see Ahmed Rashid, *Descent into Chaos: The United States and the Failure of Nation Building in Pakistan, Afghanistan, and Central Asia*, (New York: Viking, 2008).
32. Full text of Obama's speech can be found in www.whitehouse.gov/the_press_office/Remarks-By-President-Barack-Obama-In-Prague-As-Delivered/ (accessed 5 December 2009).
33. Ibid.
34. 'Gingrich decries Obama's nuclear policy', UPI, 5 April 2009, www.upi.com/Top_News/2009/04/05/Gingrich-decries-Obamas-nuclear-policy/UPI-73731238964117/ (accessed 6 December 2009).

35 'McCain backs Obama's call to end nuclear weapons', *Geo World*, 10 April 2009, www.geo.tv/4-10-2009/39492.htm (accessed 6 December 2009).
36 'Safe without the bomb?', *Economist*, 11 April 2009, p. 15.
37 'The Strategic Concept for the Defense of the North Atlantic Area', 29 November 1949, p. 5, www.nato.int/docu/stratdoc/eng/a491129a.pdf (accessed 6 December 2009).
38 Ian Anthony, *The Future of Nuclear Weapons in NATO*, (Stockholm: SIPRI, 2009), www.sipri.org/research/disarmament/nuclear/researchissues/carnegie/nato/view (accessed 3 March 2010). For an estimate of US nuclear weapons in Europe see p. 27.
39 'The Alliance's Strategic Concept', 24 April 1999, www.nato.int/docu/pr/1999/p99-065e.htm (accessed 6 December 2009).
40 'An Iranian nuclear bomb, or the bombing of Iran?' *The Economist*, 3 December 2009, www.economist.com/displayStory.cfm?story_id=15016192& source = most_commented (accessed 14 December 2009).
41 'US Condemns North Korea over Talks Exit', 14 April 2009, www.google.com/hostednews/afp/article/ALeqM5jbD8UuE6MUNwYGz1jilXVwDE8wXw (accessed 16 April 2009).
42 'White House Press Release', 1 September 2009; *Foreign Policy Bulletin*, December 2009, p. 140; 'Remarks by Secretary of Defense Gates and Vice Chairman of the Joint Chiefs of Staff General Cartwright', 17 September 2009, *Foreign Policy Bulletin*, December 2009, p. 141–46. 'U.S. scraps missile defense shield plans', CNN, 17 September 2009, http://edition.cnn.com/2009/WORLD/americas/09/17/united.states.missile.shield/index.html (accessed 6 December 2009).
43 For more analysis on US–Russian relations, see James Goldgeier's chapter in this volume.
44 James Joyner, 'Europe's Obama Fatigue', *Foreign Policy*, 29 October 2009, www.foreignpolicy.com/articles/2009/10/29/europes_obama_fatigue (accessed 5 December 2009).
45 Peter Barker, 'On Foreign Policy, Obama Shifts, but Only a Bit', *New York Times*, 16 April 2009, www.nytimes.com/2009/04/17/us/politics/16web-baker.html?hp (accessed, 18 May 2009).

21

Is the present future of NATO already history?

Jean-Jacques de Dardel

NATO–OTAN: the letters are exactly reversed in English and French, the two official languages of the organization. This is a symbol perhaps of the fact that the Alliance, as so many things in life, can be seen from two opposite angles. For those who have only nice things to say about it, NATO is described as 'the most successful alliance in history'. A catchy phrase which is far from being intrinsically wrong – although as a Swiss onlooker, I would add with a smile that as an alliance of states bent on developing their core values and defending militarily against outer foes, the old Swiss Confederation can also apply for the main prize in that martial beauty pageant.

Another, somewhat disrespectful description of the North Atlantic Alliance would underscore the fact that NATO basically never did was it was preparing to do, and was brought to do what it had not expected to. Indeed, it long prepared for the Third World War, but never fired a shot at the enemy it kept in check. When it did fire shots, it did so in a state of legal un-preparedness, against a foe it had until then not considered an enemy. Every time it acted, it did so outside the territorial scope it had first assigned itself. When it grew, it was mostly by ingesting former enemies it had never dreamt of welcoming in its midst. When it developed interoperability on a larger scale, it had to do so by including in its forces Soviet materiel, such as MIGs and BTR-70s and TR-85 tanks. And whereas it prepared for battle against a mighty enemy, it is now toiling against an elusive Taliban and sending warships against pirates assailing tankers with ladders as was done to castles in the Middle Ages. Whereas it should rejoice at the thought of making up the lion's share of the world's military might and having grown to almost three times its initial membership, it is struggling to find a new impetus and to assert its *raison d'être*.

Does the truth lie in between those two views? Or is it not that, just as both NATO and OTAN refer to the exact same reality, both sides of the coin are true? Symbolically, I would say that just as a coin stands little chance of staying on its edge if it is not spun, what links both visions of NATO is the dynamics of political and security evolutions. It is, I believe, through a better understanding of those dynamics, of the flow of events and matching decisions, that a solution to the quandary of a good and useful, versus an obsolete and cumbersome Alliance can be solved.

NATO's sixtieth

On 4 April 2009, NATO celebrated its 60th birthday in a highly symbolic setting across the Franco-German border. The symbolism referred to the origins of the Organization, created as a bulwark against menacing Soviet forces.[1] No symbolic reference was made to the present openness and outreach of the Alliance, however, since no guests were invited at the ceremonies. The summit was, somewhat surprisingly, held as a members-only event, excluding all partner countries. That marked an apparent low point in the evolution of the Partnership for Peace, that worthy post-cold war complement to the North Atlantic security construct. (The views expressed here are, hence, not only personal, but truly that of an outside observer, not privy to the inner workings of the North Atlantic Council.)

Undoubtedly, an anniversary is always a time of remembrance and of assessment of the past, leading to a review of the accomplishments that have led to the present. But when it brings together heads of state and government under the helm of an organization strained by ongoing adversities, the pause and thinking afforded by an anniversary is also a convenient time to lay out a vision for the future, based on a general stocktaking as well as the latest updates on perceived trends and challenges.

We know that these updates are precisely what the Alliance has been focusing on. Not only did it prepare for a jubilee summit at a time of financial and economic turmoil and crisis flare ups, it also set forth to adopt a declaration calling for a new strategic concept, to be drafted within a year and a half so as to be tabled at the next NATO summit in Lisbon in late 2010. The new strategic concept is to replace the one previously adopted in 1999 at the Washington summit commemorating NATO's fiftieth anniversary, a conference attended by all member and partner states, two years before the dawning of a new age of terrorist threats, at the height of the latest Balkan wars. Is it outdated today, and if yes, by how much? To assess the probabilities of the Alliance's ability to come up with a viable and lasting new strategy, we can retrace some main elements of its recent history, compare its visions for the future 10 years ago and subsequent reality as it has unfolded. We should thus try to come up with an estimate of the ability of the Alliance, its partners and of the International Security Community to meaningfully predict the future as it tries to make the appropriate choices in the face of rapidly evolving circumstances.

1989–2009: milestones and the acceleration of change

Should we retrace the full 60 years of the Alliance? Suffice it to say that its first 40 years were referenced by the Cold War, whereas the next 20 years have unfolded in a totally different – and definitely warmer, if not hotter – setting. The enemy NATO had been created to keep in check was no more after the implosion of the Warsaw Pact in 1991. Europe experienced momentous changes as the Soviet empire collapsed remarkably peacefully. Soon thereafter Yugoslavia went from cement white to the reddish brown stains of wars and strife. Central Asia and the Caucasus reappeared on the world map, the market economy triumphed and the major tugs of war of conflicting ideologies seemed to have disappeared for good.[2]

The 20 years that separate us today from the fall of the Berlin Wall have undeniably seen immeasurably greater changes than the former 40. In fact, they have been so dynamic as to warrant an analytical division in two separate decades, each one more eventful than the whole of the Cold War period. Viewed from a NATO standpoint:

- NATO first developed a new Strategic concept and extended its circle of affiliates in 1991 as it created the North Atlantic Cooperation Council (NACC), soon to be complemented by the Partnership for Peace (PfP) in 1994, and replaced altogether by the Euro Atlantic Partnership Council (EAPC) in 1997. Moreover, the Alliance went from enlargement to enlargement to further enlargement, as it ingested three former Warsaw Pact countries in 1999,[3] then seven others in 2004[4] and two new members, Albania and Croatia, most recently at Strasbourg–Kehl–Baden Baden.
- NATO commenced out-of-area operations in the Adriatic Sea[5] in 1992, a sea change indeed! then in Bosnia,[6] before launching a first concerted war campaign in 1999 when it attacked Milosevic's rump Yugoslavia to rescue the Kosovars and establish peacekeeping forces on the ground.[7]
- The core article 5 of the North Atlantic Treaty, whereby allies agree to use force to fend off an attack perpetrated on the North American or European territory of one of its members, was applied for the first time after the 2001 9/11 attacks on the USA. Even though it was done in a clearly defensive manner – NATO AWACS patrolling the American sky and NATO ships patrolling the Mediterranean Sea – invoking article 5 was in itself a major milestone.
- Soon thereafter, not only did the Alliance resort to force with the blessing of a UN mandate, it was also aided for the first time in its newly launched military campaign against the Taliban in Afghanistan by a good number of partner countries. Even Switzerland, which had entered the PfP in 1996 and the Euro Atlantic Partnership Council (EAPC) at its inception in 1997, first joined ISAF – however modestly – when it was launched in 2002. It is worth noting that NATO's main operation today falls outside of article 5 and is also accompanied by an unexpectedly high number of caveats, a series of limitations that the Alliance was not originally prepared to contend with.
- The Afghan campaign marked the beginning of *far* out-of-area operations,[8] which brought the Alliance to substantially widen its scope of action, both geographically and in the nature of operations. It thus proceeded to deterritorialize security, as it tried to safeguard security within the borders of its members by lashing out at far away sources of terror and insecurity.
- NATO went on to further extend its partnerships as it established an institutionalized Mediterranean dialogue, and novel ties with the Arabian Gulf countries as well as with far Asian partners such as South Korea, Japan and Australia. Today, at 28 members, 22 EAPC partner states and 18 countries otherwise brought into an extended dialogue, NATO is a far cry from the 12 original member states defending on their own against ill deeds from Moscow.
- Importantly, NATO has also embarked on a policy of careful cooperation with some other international organizations, foremost the UN and the EU.

But the Alliance was not the only one to change substantially. Its evolutions have also been matched by parallel changes in other major organizations and in the international environment:

- The EU has also evolved considerably: from 1989 to 2008, its member countries have also expanded from 12 to 27.[9] It introduced a common currency in 1999.[10] In the field of security, it laid the grounds for a common European Security and

Defence Policy in 1992 at its Petersberg summit, and acknowledged its necessary military kinship with NATO through the 1994 Berlin+ agreement.
- Russia, the former main foe, has ebbed and flowed since 1989. It first opened its borders, its economy and its foreign policy towards the West. It went on to recreate collaborative ties with its former domestic republics through the creation of the Commonwealth of Independent States in 1991. It pursued its new geopolitical goals through the creation of the Shanghai Cooperation Council as of 1996 and more formally in 2001 and then through the Collective Security Treaty Organisation in 2002. All the while both regenerating and endangering its own economy, waging two wars in Chechnya, averting a further conflict in Dagestan[11] and developing its huge energy resources.
- Beyond Russia, the other BRIC (Brazil, Russia, India, China) countries have emerged as major players, whereas Pakistan's stability was repeatedly tried, as was the Middle East's.

Most of these changes and evolutions were already in place 10 years ago when NATO celebrated its fiftieth anniversary. The strategic concept it crafted for itself at the turn of the century took these overall changes in account. The Alliance had first outlined a strategic concept in 1991, immediately after the end of the Cold War, when it suddenly had to reassess its purpose, decide on a future and prove its relevance. So that first concept was strongly marked by the decision the Alliance took to turn to its former foes and extend a hand of partnership and cooperation. That first new era document was revised eight years later, 'committing the Allies not only to common defence but to the peace and stability of the wider Euro-Atlantic area'.[12] Thus, within a decade, NATO had analysed and adapted to the new openness of international relations, which had also seen new dangers and crises flare up and drag the Alliance for the first time into open warfare.

What of today?

Today, many aspects of the 1999 strategic concept seem to remain viable and useful. As NATO's Secretary General Jaap de Hoop Scheffer is keen to say:

> Il n'est pas non plus question de dire que le concept stratégique de 1999 est dépassé: à bien des égards, si vous le relisez aujourd'hui, vous verrez qu'il n'a pas si mal résisté aux outrages du temps.
>
> (It would also be way out of line to say that the 1999 strategic concept is outdated: in many respects, if you read it over today, you will see that it has withstood the test of time rather well.)

But he then also adds:

> Mais il faut aussi reconnaître que le concept stratégique était très marqué par les opérations de soutien à la paix (l'Alliance était massivement présente en Bosnie, et en pleine opération du Kosovo); il est naturellement antérieur au 11 septembre et à la résurgence de la menace terroriste internationale; et il a été élaboré et adopté à 16.[13]
>
> (But it should also be acknowledged that the strategic concept was heavily influenced by ongoing peace support operations (the Alliance was massively committed

in Bosnia and operations were in full swing in Kosovo); it of course predates September 11 and the resurgence of the international terrorist threat; and it was drafted and adopted among 16.)

So that strategic concept, although still largely valid, was overly marked by the operations and challenges of the day. Why, may we ask, would it turn out to be otherwise for the new strategic concept now in the workings? How will the thinkers and decision-makers tasked to devise and adopt a new concept avoid being overly influenced by present day worries, so as to steer a truly forward leaning course?

Today's challenges and menaces

Indeed, in this respect, what are, in fact, the parameters that we know to be in place today, the long-term trends in the field of menaces and the search for security? What are on the one hand the long-term challenges that NATO, its partners and all international security strategies must face in the age of globalization, of information technologies revolution, of climatic and environmental change – and, on the other hand, which ones may appear to be more circumstantial than long lasting?

Lasting threats

If the prevalence of terrorism in different parts of the world ever since the nineteenth century is any measure to go by, the age of hyper-terrorism[14] as it began before the dazed eyes of hundreds of millions of TV viewers on 11 September is not about to fade away. The mere widening effect of media coverage of any attack ensures that terrorism will long remain a very easy underdog's way of asserting a certain form of asymmetric power. For its part, organized crime will also remain a dark side of human systems. It may be locally defeated from above; it may be made to lose its grip on communities exasperated enough to revolt. However, let us not be too candid about the complexities of human nature. Both of these threats are well recognized and taken into account. But now, on top of this, new fears arise in the face of climate change, renewed nuclear proliferation,[15] cyber attacks, open seas piracy, fragile states,[16] to name only the most frequently mentioned. The hierarchy of these ills varies according to one observer or the other. Yet, all of them are seen as lasting elements of the brave new world we must cope with.

In more general terms, we must recognize that the fastening pace of globalization is an absolutely unavoidable civilizational trend, which carries priceless advantages in the fight against poverty, disease, alienation and even natural disasters as prevention and relief are accelerated. But it is also fraught with new security risks, as breakdowns in the distribution of natural resources, most prominently energy, can affect ever-widening circles of consumers.

Circumstantial threats

We may risk a forecast: these parameters and security risks will long have to be addressed by any security strategy. On the other hand, the 2008–10 triad will probably go down in history as being marked by specific crises, which need not be considered particularly perennial. That seems to be the case of the distinct Georgian crisis unleashed in August

2008. This is not to say that this crisis is nearing a satisfactory solution, and that it can easily be set aside as short-term epiphenomena. Much to the contrary, it remains at the core of one of the main objectives of the Atlantic Alliance, and that is to better relations with Russia and enter in a longer lasting phase of substantial cooperation with Moscow. Yet, if the NATO Secretary General feels that he can refer today to the Bosnian and Kosovo crisis of yore as having too heavily impacted on the strategic concept of 1999, then surely Georgia does not outweigh those two hot spots and can thus be seen as circumstantial.

This also seems to be the case for the current financial and economic crisis. It definitely is a shame and a dread for most, as it caused a recession seldom seen, the worst in our present lifetimes. As it impacts on all economies, states, systems and individuals, it is bound to affect the means at the disposal of those seeking to provide security, and it is sure to weigh on the capabilities side of any strategic equation. But there again, economic cycles being what they are, the world will recover within a few years as it re-enters a phase of growth, however muted and hopefully better balanced.

Specificities of the day

Much more specifically and circumstantially, other novelties are bound to influence any present rethinking of concepts. The new US administration has already proven that it really is geared towards change and *aggiornamento*. The prerequisites for a renewed international dialogue among allies but also with rivals and possible foes, a better balancing of interests and different viewpoints, seems to be convincingly in place. The next NATO strategic concept will owe a lot to this new window of opportunity. Other important steps forward will rightly weigh on contemporary minds: the French reintegration into the military structures of the Alliance; the new surge in Afghanistan, both military and civil; a reappraisal of the meaning and aims of a policy of enlargement; and other such orders of the day are bound to find their way in a restyled overall strategy, ensuring years of fruitful cooperation[17] – and unabashed speech-making.

In view of what we have just outlined, we should not find the wording of the Declaration on Alliance Security, adopted at the recent summit, surprising. Moreover, some aspects of the new strategic concept, which will be drafted in the coming months, although they are still to be delineated and decided on, are already hinted at in that Declaration. Surely, the new Concept will include orientations on at least four main matters.[18]

The first will be the definition itself of the kind of world and of security that Allies are ready and willing to protect, one relying on dialogue and cooperation rather than confrontation and overpowering, where the USA will develop its 'smart power' potential, whereas most Europeans and other partners may enhance the means of their 'soft power'. That will warrant a renewal of the political, philosophical and sociological ties that bind the USA as well as Canada and the Europeans, and the EU in particular, so that a more trusting relationship may flourish, devoid of the negative emotions and endless rivalries[19] which, I understand, have even been echoed on Mars and Venus.

The second will thus have to deal with a renewal and a qualitative improvement of the relationship with Russia, as that major other pole of security in the Euro-Atlantic zone, still influential the world over, and a possible vehicle for stability through a strategic partnership with the democracies of the West or, if it feels cornered into isolation and irrelevance, a cause of concern and of crisis flare ups.

The third will have to deal with the use of force – and the appropriate means of power. It has become increasingly apparent that whereas outright wars can be waged massively by the superior means at the disposal of NATO and its main members, such short and mighty wars never lead by themselves to a lasting solution of a crisis. Bombing Serbia took slightly over two months. Toppling the Taliban took five weeks. Defeating Saddam's Iraq took a mere three weeks, and defeating the Georgian army took Russia a few days. But in no case has that use of force cleared the way for a stable peace. Much to the contrary, initial military advantages have been followed by immensely more costly quagmires, much higher casualties, endless peacekeeping and peace enforcing. NATO will thus have to move beyond exclusively military responses and the political body of the Alliance will have to come up with novel ideas to secure the peace.

The fourth question that will have to be resolved will hence be that of the juncture between military means and civilian efforts, security and human security, peace enforcing and nation building. This should lead to the development of a doctrine of cooperation and separation of responsibilities among different regional and world organizations, in NATO lingo, the development of the 'comprehensive approach'. In this context, a clarification of the working relations between NATO and the European Union will probably be given top priority during the discussions.

Revolutionary times

That is the 'present future' of NATO.

Yet, as has been repeatedly suggested, we may well question any supposed linearity of the foreseen evolution, and guess that the pace of change today is so fast that what holds true and plausible in the present setting has an ever-shortening use-by date. Indeed, we seem to live through more revolutionary than evolutionary times. It may not be enough to notice that we continue to address the challenges of the twenty-first century with a mentality and means pertaining to the twentieth.[20] Beyond the obvious general slowness of response one experiences in the absence of imperious necessity to adapt, there needs to be a reappraisal of the parameters of the present days' circumstances. As one of the former NATO Special Advisors for Central & Eastern European Affairs, Chris Donnelly, put it recently at a conference exploring NATO's past,[21] compared to Cold War times, the world has been undergoing a revolution for the past 20 years. Indeed, we may add, an ongoing revolution, akin to a landslide or like the controlled turmoil of a nuclear reactor. And such overwhelming motion should call for a radical change of posture and an athletic balance control to keep on top of things. Yet, international organizations still rely on peacetime procedures and mentalities – and so does NATO, even if it is engaged in war-like operations in Afghanistan.

Change keeps surprising us

In this hot geyser of our times, many events, however foreseeable they may have at first seemed, happened and unravelled in such a way as to cause changes and consequences that were not that readily predictable. Through the multiplier effects of globalization, the different local energy crises initiated by Russia against its neighbours, Belarus, the Ukraine and Georgia, impacted more or less heavily on other countries – and certainly on risk assessments in broader terms. The one cyber attack on Estonia, unleashed in 2007, although limited to one small country, led to a flurry of activities in a field until then focused on the sole effects of electromagnetic impulsions. This is what may well happen now that an extensive system of network spying masterminded by China seems to have been uncovered. Kosovo, first its riots and unsteadiness, then its independence, did not cause a major crisis, as had long been feared. Yet, Georgia did, on its own terms,[22] and caused actions and reactions in the field and at political and military headquarters that had not been predicted. This did change the course of international relations. And, of course, the economic crisis we are now facing is of far greater proportions than any former contingency planning had ever suspected.

What is predictable is that unpredictable change will happen

In view of these notable past events, we can only guess what new happenings might soon reroute the path of evolution: some dangers and trouble spots are known. That is certainly the case of Pakistan, today one of the most volatile countries, a most complex and worrisome pole of attention. It may once again be the case of the Ukraine, profoundly split as it is between pro-Russians and pro-Westerners, even though Ukrainians have until now been remarkably and commendably restrained in their internal differences, as they have shown a certain realism in their foreign policy that was lacking in some parts of the Caucasus. The Caucasus, in particular, that will long remain a possible trouble spot, as any ethnic and historical map of this most ancient cradle of civilization will tell. Well beyond Georgia and its separatist provinces, the frozen conflict between Azerbaijan and Armenia over Nagorno–Karabakh is far from over, Armenia and Turkey have yet to solve their profound differences, and the Russian autonomous republics of the South West are far from stable and prosperous. I am not sure Moldova and Transnistria will remain off the radar screen forever after the domestic situation is stabilized in Chisinau and relations with Romania restored. But even if these possible hot spots are widely acknowledged as such, it remains quite arbitrary to predict the course that events will take there.

The coming surge in Afghanistan, both in military and civil terms, may well enable an eventual withdrawal of foreign forces from the country. But no one is certain at this juncture that the situation will not derail there, in ways whose only predictable aspects are that they will affect the whole of NATO, its member countries and the security system as a whole. Iran is being engaged and wooed back into the international arena. But its regime was able to thrive for too long on being both an outcast and a beacon to a certain world that it may now readily normalize its relations with the West. Given the dangers of nuclear proliferation, and the ties that Iran nurtures with numerous extremist groups, Teheran will remain an unpredictable factor for some time to come. The Middle East, and specifically Israel and some of its immediate neighbours, will also remain a hearth of unpredictable flare-ups. Central Asia, although less volatile, has not solved a number of tensions and is experiencing a resurgence of Russian versus American influence.[23] Not to mention the major unrest that remains possible in such giants as India and China, and whose consequences, if they come to a head, are bound to profoundly affect our overall sense of security. Fragile and failed states on the African continent will also continue to be sources of instability, with wide-ranging effects as massive migration and refugee flows have already shown over time.

We need not be doomsayers, and there is no intention on my part to thwart any emerging optimism that may be derived, for instance, from observing the new US administration become more pragmatic, open to international cooperation and intent on lowering threat levels in various parts of the world, particularly those which I have just mentioned at length. And given a possible new level of cooperation among emerging or established major powers, local crises could well be defused. But not everything will be solved at once. The new world order has not yet found its point of balance and stability, if ever one is to be found, given the rising multipolarity which will warrant constant balancing acts. New dangers are also lurking in traditional crisis areas and possible new ones, such as the far north, as the struggle for resources widens. In other words, the only thing that is predictable is that NATO – like other organizations and governments – will have to face rapidly changing contradictory forces and events for which it will not have fully prepared.

Adapting step by step or continuously

And so, we may now come to the crux of the matter: is NATO going to limit itself to developing a new strategic concept valid for the next 10 years, or is it going to lower its sights and strive for a shorter time frame for its new doctrine? Will it altogether devise ways to develop its adaptability, so that it may continually keep in pace with shifting circumstances? Given the certainty of uncertainty, given the fact also that NATO cannot merely work on its deterrence role against set and known enemies, but will have to face unpredictable and shifting challenges, what is needed is not only a new strategy, a new positioning and a new credo. What is called for above all is a new flexibility of structures and decision-making processes. Of course, as the Secretary General well put it, 'NATO's missions have changed; it has also reformed its structures accordingly. This is what we call 'transformation' in our jargon: 'simplification of the chain of command, encouragement of new capability initiatives focusing on the deployability of forces, creation of the NATO Reaction Force, the NRF.'[24] But transformation, that is the capacity to adapt structures to changing needs on a step-by-step path, may soon not be enough. What NATO is most probably going to experience is a need for a more radical systemic and organic change. It will sense the necessity to radically adapt its structures, methods and procedures to overcome its inherent inertia and adapt to the velocity of evolution of challenges and threats.

'Transformation' is under way

Indeed, NATO may well try to reduce the number of its special committees, which number 430 today. It may go on streamlining some decision-making procedures and rationalize the work of its different secretariats in order 'to create a leaner and more cost-effective organization'.[25] But it will not readily change the complexity of decision-making, with 28 or perhaps soon 29 members, if it does not overhaul its basic working procedures. NATO has of course already tried to tackle this problem and intense negotiations are going on under the label 'Headquarters reform'. As a step forward NATO decided some time ago to cut back on the number of meetings it holds in the EAPC format: as often as possible, 'troop contributors only' meetings replace EAPC reunions, focusing on the matters at hand, without undue loss of stamina. But those alterations in procedures do not yet represent a full systemic change. Knowledge management, lines of communication and the fusing of different components – military and political, military and civil, core NATO and partners, as well as NATO and other international organizations – is not optimal yet. Whereas the revolutionary clock of events, crises and geopolitical mishaps keeps on ticking.

This is of course not specific to NATO: no organization can go from a few members to a full arena of dozens of members without experiencing dire difficulties in decision-shaping and -making. The EU certainly has had to face the same dilemma and is far from having found the solution. For those who are committed to democracy – the prevalence of parliaments, the exercise of sovereign rights – there can't be anything wrong with the principles that translate into this often-laborious decision shaping. But the necessary search for consensus may also be seen as a liability when an organization must act rapidly to rise to an outer challenge. Specially when faced with an inextricable situation, when the cohesive effect of sudden shock does not apply, no top-heavy organization can consistently keep the decisional pace that is warranted to act effectively. Paraphrasing Fukuyama's observations in his book *After the Neocons* published before the Obama phenomenon, NATO could get a second wind as a security organization in a context of Washington's renewed appetite for multilateralism but on the condition that the NATO decision-making machinery be streamlined so as to avoid the type of difficulties that occurred during the Kosovo war when all Allies had to agree on lists of bombing targets.[26]

One solution to this general problem would be to preposition caucuses, subgroups and thematic coalitions of the willing at the political level and set up standing task forces ready to act decisively. The NRF created as of 2003 is a major step in that direction. More could be done along those lines, where countries would commit in advance to certain tasks or sets of responses and then act on the principle of consensus among the subgroup. Article V operations would not be hollowed, since the obligations derived from that article would remain untouched. But we know that, in effect, most NATO operations are conducted outside the framework of Article V.

Another solution could be that basic or critical and strategic decisions be taken by consensus but the implementing measures would then be decided on by a simple or qualified majority. For example, do all 28 members really need to agree on each word of a press statement condemning the testing of a ballistic missile prohibited by the UNSCR, or would it not be sufficient that consensus be reached on the principle of a condemnation?

Such pre-established task forces and subgroups need not mean that NATO or parts thereof would automatically contribute to a global gendarme role for the Alliance. The debate about the full extent of NATO's reach will have to come to fruition within the new strategic concept itself, and not be left to creeping globalization and overextension. The USA will no doubt continue to see things through the eyes of a fully global power, intrinsically connected to all crisis situations. Whereas many a European NATO member will want the Alliance to remain focused on the transatlantic segment of the planisphere, a proposition that will necessitate a thorough discussion of the limits and contingencies of NATO's scope of action.

The global approach: a change of paradigm

One option would be to define areas and situations where NATO would automatically be seen as the core organization bearing the brunt of crisis management and operations, as opposed to offering subsidiary support to other organizations or *ad hoc* coalitions – provided a UN mandate is given. Indeed, better coordination with other international organizations and non-member countries will also inevitably come to be considered a priority. There is nothing new in such an ambition. But what must be striven for is far more than mere daily cooperation on the ground, enabled once headquarters negotiated their terms. The goal should rather be to develop an ability to convene rapid cooperative structures, according to pressing new needs. What is called for is modernizing multilateralism. As the World Bank Director Robert Zoellick put it: 'We need to help overhaul the institutions and regimes of multilateralism, some established over 60 years ago, to meet the necessities of a very different era'.[27]

Options and question marks

This poses a particular question as to the viability of a core NATO versus an extended partnership. Can NATO with 28 members, perhaps more, remain flexible and geared towards both quick responses and extended partnerships? How should it fit into the widening global structure? As the main military arm of the UN? Or as a *primus inter pares* alongside the EU, the fledgling Russian sponsored Collective Security Treaty Organization (CSTO), perhaps Asian and, most particularly, Chinese forces? Moscow has repeatedly expressed the wish to bring about a new security architecture, and it will no doubt come forward with its own ideas on the subject. Will its thinking be marred by a fixation on containment of NATO expansion, or will it be willing to engage the Alliance on terms that could expand the possibilities of partnership for non-NATO members? And how is this debate, also favoured by President Sarkozy's France, going to avoid the new formation of spheres of influence according to twenty-first century criteria, which would certainly run counter to the better logic of globalization?

When these pitfalls are recognized and sidestepped through intensive debate and collaboration, there well may come a time when NATO will become an accepted and sought after service provider to other regional groupings, be they as overlapping as the EU or as distinct as any Asian organization. Could it be that NATO airlift support to the African Union's missions and capacity building for the African Standby Force (for peacekeeping) are just the first examples of such a development?

In conclusion: wither the partnership?

Which brings us both to the conclusion and back to the main proposition of this address: whatever the findings of the group of eminent persons called in to draft the new strategic concept, whatever the outcome of the arbitration between different standpoints and interests, NATO is bound to have to go on adapting to changing circumstances in ways that will often remain beyond the grasp of planners and analysts. Thus, the need for increasing flexibility and shorter response times will impose itself on the Alliance.

In this context and from our own vantage point, we do foresee a quandary that the Alliance is going to have to face head on, and not dismiss, as it has tended to do in these last months. What role will NATO attribute to its non-member partners, the first circle belonging to the PfP EAPC structures, and then the outer circle of non-institutional member countries, which may yet expand to much greater numbers than is the case today?

As NATO moves towards a more comprehensive approach to problem solving, including police, civil and developmental elements, as it tries to develop working links and procedures with other international organizations, it is bound to want to rely on those partnerships it has already established. And over 15 years on, the Euro Atlantic Partnership community has proven itself a net provider of added value. The Partnership has thrived on its inner wisdom, that which has enabled it to help reform the security sector and harness the resources of friends but not allies. It has also thrived on the wisdom of countries with no wish to join it, but ready to engage in fruitful cooperation.[28] Thus, the Partnership remains a solid asset for the extension of security.

But the lead up to the Strasbourg–Kehl–Baden Baden summit and the focus the Alliance has set on its disturbed relationship with Russia has distanced it from the partnerships it has already established. If these are to remain meaningful and fruitful for all, NATO will have to include in its adjustment to the pace of change mechanisms that enable the motley crew of established institutional partners to feel they are taken seriously. We could then witness a process of 'concentrification', if you allow me the word, whereby NATO proper would be complemented by EAPC Council members, recognized and upgraded as such full members, the outer circle comprising partner states, the 'World Partners' as opposed to the Council Members. Because strengthening the Council is another solution to the problems of fast paced enlargement.

But then again: whatever I say today, the future is bound to be different ...

Notes

1 The North Atlantic Treaty was signed in Washington DC on 4 April 1949 by 12 Western nations. The subsequent admission in 1955 of the newly created Federal Republic of Germany – which only joined the UN 18 years later – was met with the creation of the Warsaw Pact in May 1955.
2 Since China had already adopted a new economic course, and communist proselytism has subsided everywhere, this led to Francis Fukuyama's much decried but seldom read insightful essay on the 'End of History', *The National Interest*, Summer 1989.
3 Czech Republic, Hungary, Poland.
4 Bulgaria, Estonia, Lettland, Lithuania, Romania, Slovakia, Slovenia.
5 Operation Sharp Guard, 1992–96.
6 Operation Deny Flight, 1993–95; then IFOR, 1995–96 and SFOR, 1996–2004.
7 KFOR, 1999–ongoing.
8 Even though the Balkan campaigns in Bosnia and against Serbia to protect Kosovo were strictly speaking out-of-area operations, i.e. out of the mainland territories of NATO member states, and even though NATO involved itself rather indirectly in some aspects of the war in Iraq, it is the campaign in Afghanistan which heralded the beginning of a marked geographical extension of logistics and operations, whereby NATO projected forces very far from its usual bases.
9 Since the end of the Cold War, the EU has taken in Austria, Finland, Sweden in 1994; Cyprus, the Czech Republic, Estonia, Hungary, Latvia, Lithuania, Malta, Poland, Slovakia, Slovenia, all in 2004; Bulgaria and Romania in 2007.
10 As an accounting currency; coins and notes entered circulation in 2002.
11 'Dagestan is not a second Chechnya' but Dagestan 'is now suffering from escalating street warfare.' in *Russia's Dagestan: Conflict Causes*, International Crisis Group, Europe Report No. 192, (ICG – 3 June 2008).
12 *NATO Handbook*, 2006, p. 18. The Handbook lists eight political elements of the Strategic Concept: a broad approach to security, encompassing political, economic, social and environmental factors, as well as the Alliance's defence dimension; a strong commitment to transatlantic institutions; maintenance of the Allies military capabilities to ensure the effectiveness of military operations; development of European capabilities within the Alliance; maintenance of adequate conflict prevention and crisis management structures and procedures; effective partnerships with non-NATO countries based on cooperation and dialogue; the enlargement of the Alliance and an open door policy towards potential new members; continuing efforts towards far-reaching arms control, disarmament and non-proliferation agreements.
13 Discours du Secrétaire général de l'OTAN M. Jaap de Hoop Scheffer à la Fondation pour la Recherche stratégique, Paris, 11 mars 2009.
14 That term referring to large-scale terror, of the 9/11 sort, including bacteriological, chemical and radiological menaces, was coined by François Heisbourg in *Hyperterrorisme: la nouvelle guerre*, (Editions Odile Jacob, 2001).

15 Whereas a few years ago, terrorism and organized crime seemed interlinked as the most prominent threat, while nuclear issues had subsided, the latter and climate change are now generally seen as topping the list, as the Swedish Foreign Minister Carl Bildt puts it: 'But if I had to identify the two most difficult strategic challenges that the international community will have to handle in the years ahead – apart from the obvious one of global terrorism – I would cite global climate change and nuclear proliferation', Carl Bildt, in *Perspectives on International Security*, Adelphi Paper 400–401, December 2008.

16 As the World Bank President Robert Zoellick puts it, 'One billion people, including about 340m of the world's extreme poor, are estimated to live in fragile states. […] Fragile states' neighbours are also at risk, often suffering from the hardships caused by refugee flows, warring groups, contagious diseases and transnational criminal networks that traffic in drugs, arms and people' in *Fragile States: Securing Development*, Survival, vol. 50, no. 6, December 2008 to January 2009, pp. 67–84.

17 Negotiating a new Strategic Concept may well give the Allies an opportunity to iron out some of the differences that have appeared among them as of late.

18 As was well outlined by Bernard Adam, Director of the Groupe de recherche et d'information sur la paix et la sécurité (GRIP), in *La Libre Belgique*, 27 March 2009.

19 Indeed, as recently as on February 19, 2009, the European Parliament barely accepted a resolution on a rapprochement between the EU and NATO, by 293 versus 283 votes – even though 21 EU member states are part of the Alliance, and all are members of the EAPC.

20 A point repeatedly made by the NATO Secretary General, as in his 11 March 2009 speech in Paris.

21 NATO at 60 – A Conference Exploring NATO's Past Through its Archives, 13 March 2009.

22 The Georgian crisis and the subsequent recognition of Abkhazia and South Ossetia by Moscow is certainly not a consequence of the evolution of the Kosovo situation, even if Kosovo is referred to by Russia in an awkward bid to justify its uncomfortable posture.

23 The Kirghiz government decision to close a US military base is one latest example of this trend.

24 Speech by the Secretary General of NATO, Jaap de Hoop Scheffer, to the National Assembly, Paris, 12 February 2009.

25 Declaration on Alliance Security issued at the Strasbourg/Kehl Summit on 4 April 2009.

26 Francis Fukuyama, *After the Neocons; America at the Crossroads*, (Yale University Press, 2006), pp. 172–74.

27 Robert Zoellick, *Fragile States: Securing Development*, p. 83.

28 See Jean-Jacques de Dardel, *PfP, EAPC, and the PfP Consortium: Key Elements of the Euro-Atlantic Security Community*, Connections, The Quarterly Journal, Summer Supplement, 2008, pp. 1–14.

Index

Aaronovitch, David 226
Acheson, Dean 17, 19, 20, 25, 51, 104, 108; North Atlantic Treaty negotiations 3, 5, 8, 9, 10, 11–12
adaptation: French-US relations, aim of independence and 58–59; to nuclear warfare 39–40; unpredictable challenge and 295
Adenauer, Konrad 52, 62, 77, 94–95
Adomeit, Hannes 156
Afghanistan 13, 138–39, 145–46, 177, 186, 225, 227, 241, 268, 273; EU-NATO relations and problem of 189, 213–14; European Union (EU) in 259, 274; International Security Assistance Force (ISAF) 240, 279, 289; major front in "war on terror" 284; nation-building effort in 280; out-of-region engagement in 277, 278–79, 298n8; Soviet invasion of 139, 146, 147, 148, 277; Taliban in 270, 277, 278, 279–80, 287, 289, 293; US deepening commitment in 282, 292, 294; US-Russian cooperation on, potential for 268–69, 270
After the Neocons (Fukuyama, F.) 296
Ahmadinejad, Mahmoud 282
Ahtisaari, Martti 176
Ailleret, Charles 63; Ailleret-Lemnitzer exchange 63
Air Defense Ground Environment (NADGE) 64
Al-Qaeda 233, 239
Albright, Madeleine 258
Algeria 7, 45, 48, 125, 204n13; conflict in 54, 60
Allied Rapid Reaction Corps (ARRC) 254
Angola 139
Arab-Israeli War (October, 1973) 115–17
Arab League 128

Arbatov, Alexei 267–68
Arc of Crisis, wars in 139, 148, 276–80; *see also* Afghanistan; Iran; Iraq; Pakistan; Palestine; Somalia
Area of Freedom, Security and Justice (AFSJ) 198–99; external dimension of 198–99
Armenia 204n13, 294
Arndt, Adolf 84
Aron, Raymond 35–36
Articles of North Atlantic Treaty: Article 2 7, 8, 11, 12; Article 5 4, 6, 7, 8, 10, 11, 14n14, 138 178n10, 184, 296; Article 6 138; Article 9 48–49
Asia 98, 141, 144, 275, 289, 297; Arc of Crisis in 258; Association of South-East Asian Nations (ASEAN) 232; Central Asia 280, 288, 294; CIA activity in 23; Communism in 25, 28; East Asia 17, 19, 79, 90, 91; mutual defense aid in 53; Northeast Asia 23–24; nuclear weapons in 24; Southeast, military operations in 54, 91–92; Southwest Asia 145, 147, 148; US force withdrawals from 234; US strategy for 17
Asmus, Ronald 259
asymmetric antiterrorist doctrines 232–34, 235
asymmetric arms reduction 157
asymmetric warfare 241, 242, 291
Atlantic Alliance: Bahr's *Planungsstab* and 80, 82, 83; Brandt's loyalty to 75, 81–82; "Common European Home" rhetoric and 156; European institutions within framework of 50; European uncertainties caused by withdrawal of France from NATO 79; France, Fourth Republic and 45–55; France, Gaullist position on 58–59, 60, 63, 66, 68, 70–72, 83; France, withdrawal from

301

INDEX

NATO 79; France and initiatives at origin of 47–48; geographic area of, France-US differences on 48; Georgian crisis and core objectives of 291–92; integration of, Korean War and 50; integration within, French initiatives 48–51; MC Directive 70, technocratic and strategic bankruptcy of 41–42; military aid, Franco-American difficulties over 52–53; New Look US policy and 32, 34, 36, 37, 40; Non-Proliferation Treaty (NPT), effect on 89–99; North Atlantic Alliance 58, 156, 260n6, 287; nuclear defense of, impossibility of 32–42; politico-military interpretation 49; Prague Spring (1968) and future of 81–82; SHAPE and strategic weight of France in 50–51; Standing (Permanent) Group in Washington 34, 42, 43, 49, 50, 53, 55, 60, 61, 72n11; Summit (January, 1994) 183; West Germany, security and importance of 130; Western European Union (WEU) and 254; *see also* NATO

Atlantic Council 20, 34, 41, 44n39, 55, 66, 68, 96, 274, 283; goals of, redefinition of 79; High Atlantic Council, proposal for 49–50, 55; policy directive (December, 1956) 38–39; *see also* North Atlantic Council

Atlantic Pact 7, 9, 45–46, 48, 50, 53, 56n8, 56n14; German question and French distrust of 51–52

Atomic Energy Commission (AEC) 22, 30n2, 31n19, 33

Attlee, Clement 6

Auriol, Vincent 47, 50

Auswärtiges Amt (German Foreign Office) 83, 89, 96, 123–24, 125, 126–27, 127–28, 128–29, 130, 132

Azerbaijan 204n13, 294

Bacevich, Andrew 278

Bahr, Egon 76, 78–79, 80, 81–82, 83–85; *Planungsstab* and Atlantic Alliance 80, 82, 83

Baker, James 266

Baldwin, David A. 231

Ball, George 91, 104, 107, 108

Balladur, Edouard 67

Bange, Oliver 94

Barker, Peter 284

Barman, Russell 220

Bartholomew-Dobbins Telegram (February, 1991) 254

Barzel, Rainer 94

Begin, Menachem 232

Belarus 204n13, 263, 293

Bell, Daniel 237

Bergeson, Albert J. 235

Berlin: Atlantic Council in 68; Bahr and security for 81; Barack Obama, speech at Siegessäule 223; 'Berlin Plus' agreements 185, 188, 201; blockade of 4, 8, 11, 48; Brandt's return to 75; crisis in 58, 60, 76; fall of Wall in 84–85, 208, 263; Federal Parliament, move from Bonn to 176; four-power talks in 109; NATO Summit (June, 1996) 172, 257; occupation zones in West of 18; Soviet threat to access to West of 76–77; Wall construction, effect on Brandt 77–78; *see also* Brandt, Willy; West Germany

Bermuda Summit (December, 1953) 60

Bernardini, Giovanni 76

Besson, Eric 200

Betts, Richard K. 236

Beuve-Méry, Hubert 51

Bevin, Ernest 3, 4, 5–6, 7, 8, 9, 10, 11, 12

Bidault, Georges 36, 46–47, 48, 49–50, 55

bilateralism 8–9, 96, 106, 115

Billotte, Gaston-Henri-Gustave 46, 47

Bin Laden, Osama 233, 235

Biscop, Sven 186

Blair, Tony 69, 169, 170, 177, 222, 258; Blair-Chirac initiative at Saint-Malo (December, 1998) 169–70, 177

Blumenau, Bernhard 123–37, viii

Bluth, Christoph 76

Bobrow, Davis 221

Bonn (Hotel Petersburg) WEU Summit (June, 1992) 289–90

Bonn NATO Summit (June, 1982) 147

Bonnet, Georges 7

"border," special meaning of term for Europeans 194

Bosnia, NATO engagement in 66, 69, 176, 187, 189, 198n8, 208, 211, 254–55, 255–56, 258, 265, 289

Bozo, Frédéric 49

Brandt, Willy 74–75, 94; alternatives to NATO, exploration of 79–82; Atlantic Alliance, loyalty to 75, 81–82; Berlin Wall, effect on 77–78; East-West conflict, development of new concepts in 76–79; Egon Bahr and 76, 78–79, 80, 81–82, 83–85; Franco-German "Study Group," on European security 80; German-American friendship, staunch supporter of 77; Harvard University lectures 78; Middle East crisis (1973) 124, 129, 130, 131, 132; mutual and balanced force reductions (MBFR), ambition for 76; peaceful coexistence, promotion of idea of 77; political rise 75; power shifts and new security needs 104–5, 108, 109, 112, 117, 119; reunification post 1989, support for 84–85; Tutzing speeches 78; West Berlin, Soviet threat to access to 76–77

Brazil 190, 290

Brezhnev, Leonid 76, 84, 156

Brosio, Manlio 98

Brown, Gordon 222, 275, 276
Brown, Harold 144–45
Brussels 'Chocolate' Summit (April, 2003) 69, 188
Brussels NATO Summit (January, 1994) 183, 255, 264, 266
Brussels NATO Summit (June, 1996) 257
Brussels NATO Summit (May, 1975) 103
Brussels Pact (1948) 4–5, 8, 17, 47, 48, 55, 183, 250; automaticity, model in 7; collective defense arrangements under 6; continental leadership of France and 55; drawing up of 4; military dimension 11
Brzezinski, Zbigniew 144, 145, 147, 212, 234, 237, 276, 277
Bush, George H.W.: Bush-Kohl Summit, Camp David (February, 1990) 162
Bush, George H.W. (and administration of) 158, 161–62, 164, 175, 232, 251, 264, 265–66, 267
Bush, George W. (and administration of) 251, 273, 275, 277, 283, 284; antiterrorist policy and use of soft power 233, 238; Bush Doctrine 273, 283; Bush-Putin friendship, potential for US-Russian relations 268; criticism of US, rise of 218, 219, 221, 222, 223, 224, 225–27, 228; US-Russian relationship 268–69

Le Canard enchaîné 171
Caroll, Allan B. 235
Carter, Jimmy (and administration of) 70, 143, 144, 146–47; Carter Doctrine 139, 143–44, 145, 146
Cash, Frank 128
Central Intelligence Agency (CIA): Church Committee and 22; covert operations 22–23; creation of 22; Korean emergency and build-up in 23; Office of Policy Coordination (OPC) and 22–23; paramilitary operations 23
Chalfont, Alun Gwynne Jones 98
change: challenges in transatlantic security in global world 291–93; in current strategic concept, need for 290–91; milestones and acceleration of (1989–2009) 288–90; options for change in transatlantic security 297; prediction of unpredictability in 294–95; in US attitude to NPT, first signs of 91–93
Chen Jian 28
Cheney, Richard 251–52
Chernomyrdin, Viktor 176
China, People's Republic of 138, 212, 271, 274; emergence as major player 290, 294, 298n2; establishment of 17; intervention in Korean War 23, 24, 25, 28–29; Mutual Friendship with Soviet Union, Treaty of (February, 1950) 17–18; nuclear stakes 281, 282; nuclear testing by 89–90; Politburo, views on Korean War 28–29; protectionism, declaration of resistance to 275; spy network masterminded by, uncovering of 293–94; US relations with, post-Vietnam restructuring 112, 114
China's Road to the Korean War (Chen, J.) 28
Chiozza, Giacomo 221
Chirac, Jacques 64, 67, 68, 69, 70, 169, 170, 177, 218, 257; Blair-Chirac initiative at Saint-Malo (December, 1998) 169–70, 177
Christopher, Warren 265, 267
Churchill, Winston S. 6, 46, 60, 280
circumstantial threat 291–92
civil defense in US 237–39, 246n79
Clinton, William J. (and administration of) 218, 227, 234, 264, 265–66, 267, 271
Cold War: bipolar system of world of 1; Middle East, Eisenhower Doctrine and 140; process of transition from 155–64; traditional defense alliances 181; United States, NATO and future of Europe after 160–63, 164; Warsaw Pact and Soviet plans for post-Cold War Europe 156–60, 163–64
command integration: and French independence, problem of 59–64; under US, UK and French leadership, need for 107
'Common Declaration of European Identity' 250–51
'Common European Home' rhetoric o' 156
Common Foreign and Security Policy (CFSP): EU border security 196; EU-NATO relations 181–82, 183, 191
Comprehensive Test Ban Treaty (CTBT) 281
Conference on Security and Cooperation in Europe (CSCE) 84, 103, 124, 157, 164, 172, 174, 253; European political identity, catalyst for development of 105–6; European unification and 111; focus shift from military to political 111–13; Helsinki Summit (July, 1975) 103, 120; Malta Summit (December, 1989) 158–59, 166n32; Multilateral Preparatory Talks (MPT) 112–13; Paris Summit (November 1990) 158, 161, 162; Rambouillet Summit (November, 1975) 103, 119–20
Copenhagen EC Summit (December, 1973) 131
Council of Europe 12, 14n6
Couve de Murville, Maurice 61
Cox, Michael 155, 218
Cuba, missile crisis in 58, 91, 106, 107, 148, 243n22
Cuillaumat, Pierre 61
Czech Republic 174, 265, 266, 269, 280, 281, 283; NATO membership for 176
Czechoslovakia 78, 81, 97, 159

Daalder, Ivo 190
de Dardel, Jean-Jacques 287–99, viii
David, François 32–44, viii

INDEX

de Gaulle, Charles 45, 50, 55, 79, 83, 105, 107, 119, 250; Fifth Republic, NATO and 58, 60–61, 62–63, 65, 67, 70, 71; September 1958 memorandum 61–62
de Hautecloque, Jean 47
de Rose, François 66
de Tassigny, Jean de Lattre 50
De Wijk, Rob 188
Debré, Michel 61
Défense nationale 65–66
Deighton, Anne 3–16, viii
Delors, Jacques 250
Denton, Jeremiah 233
Derrida, Jacques 218
détente: pan-European security and 110–11; waning of 117
Deutschland-Plan (SPD) 78
Dick, Ronald 235
Dobbins, James 259
Dobrynin, Anatoly 91
Donnelly, Chris 293
Ducci, Roberto 98–99
Duckwitz, Georg Ferdinand 84
Dulles, John Foster 32, 33–34, 36, 52; Atlantic Council speech (April, 1954) 34
Dumas, Roland 252
Dunkirk Treaty (1947) 250

East Germany (Democratic Republic) 75, 76–77, 78, 81, 86, 95, 164, 173, 108124
East-West conflict: Brandt and development of new concepts in 76–79; Eastern Partnerships, renewal of 197; Europe as lightning rod for 42 economic engagement 274–76
The Economist 274, 281, 282
Eden, Anthony 37, 52
Egypt: 72, 125, 126, 127, 128, 129, 131, 204n13
Eighteen Nations Disarmament Committee (ENDC) 90, 92, 95
Eisenhower, Dwight D. (and administration of) 20, 24, 32, 33, 36, 38, 41, 42, 60, 61, 77; Eisenhower Doctrine 140
Elie, Jérôme 155–68, ix
Ely, Paul 61
Emmel, Egon 84
Enemies of Intelligence (Betts, R.K.) 236
Entspannungszone (zone of détente in West Germany) 78
Erhard, Ludwig 93–94
EU border security: Area of Freedom, Security and Justice (AFSJ) 198–99; coherence, search for 200–202; Common Foreign and Security Policy (CFSP) 196; East-West coherence 201; Eastern Partnerships, renewal of 197; European Neighbourhood Policy (ENP) 196–97; European Security Strategy (ESS) 196–97; External Borders Fund 200; external dimension of AFSJ 198–99; FRONTEX agency 199–200; future developments 200, 203; Hague Programme (2005) 198–99; institutional coherence 200–201; integrated border management 199–200, 202–3; neighbourhood stabilization, priority of 1990s 195–96; neighbours, search for coherence towards 201–2; regional policies of EU 196–97; Schengen system 197–98, 198–99, 200; special meaning of term "border" for Europeans 194; Tampere Programme (1999) 198–99; transatlantic relations and EU frontier 206–14; values coherence towards 202
EU-NATO relations: Arab-Israeli War (October, 1973) 115–17; Blair-Chirac initiative at Saint-Malo (December, 1998) 169–70, 177; Bosnian War (1999) 176; Common Foreign and Security Policy (CFSP) 181–82, 183, 191; Czech Republic, NATO membership for 176; deadlock in, problems of 189–91; *détente,* pan-European security and 110–11; *détente,* waning of 117; economic disparities within EU, growth of 117–18; Euro-skepticism in UK 117; European defence, NATO membership and 170–71; European integration, process of 170–71; European Political Cooperation (EPC) 103, 111–13, 116; European political identity 109–17, 118–19; European Security and Defence Policy (ESDP) 180, 181–82, 188, 190; G6/G7, great power governance 119–20; Germany and, limitations on use of armed forces 174–75; Germany and, post 9/11 177; Germany and, post-Cold War 169–77; Germany and, search for new security policy 173–74, 175–76; Harmel Report (1967) 103–4, 105, 106, 108–9, 114, 118; Helsinki CSCE Summit (July, 1975) 103, 120; Hungary, NATO membership for 176; imitation, temptations of 186–89; institutional diversification in Western governance structures 105–6; Maastricht Treaty (1992) 171–72; monetary turbulences 113–14; mutual and balanced force reductions (MBFR) 111; NATO institutional reform (1967/8) 107–8; NATO reconsolidation (1974/5) 117–20; nuclear first-use policy, Fischer's call for renunciation of 176–77; oil crisis, economic governance and 115–17; *Ostpolitik* 75, 83, 105, 106–7, 108, 109, 111, 112, 123–24, 132–33, 174; Partnership for Peace Program 176, 255, 264, 265, 289, 297; Poland, NATO membership for 176; post-Cold War situation 180–91; regulation of, post-Cold War 184–86; Saint-Malo declaration (December, 1998) 169–70, 177; security policy-making, lack of overall control

in Europe 171; Strategic Arms Limitation Talks (SALT) 110, 150n21; trade rivalries 113–14; traditional defence alliances, end post-Cold War of 181; transatlantic cohesion, Helsinki CSCE Summit (July, 1975) and 120; transatlantic elites, change in 104–5; transatlantic unity, European identity and 118–19; US dollar, consolidation of centrality of 118; US role in European affairs 170–71; US-USSR nuclear parity 104; Western European Union (WEU) 169, 172–73, 174, 176; Western European Union (WEU), role post-Cold War of 183–84; Western governance, competing models of 114–15; "Year of Europe," US initiative 106, 110, 113, 114–15, 116–17, 118, 119, 125, 250–51

Euro Atlantic Partnership Council (EAPC) 289, 295, 297, 298

Eurocorps 66, 252, 254, 257, 259n1

Europe: "border," special meaning of term for Europeans 194; Brussels Pact (1948) 4–5, 6–7, 8, 17, 47, 48, 55, 250; 'Common Declaration of European Identity' 250–51; continental leadership of France, Brussels Pact (1948) and 55; Dunkirk Treaty (1947) 250; EU-US partnership, potential for 259; European Defence Community (EDC) 12, 21, 50, 51, 52, 54, 55, 171, 250; 'European pillar in Alliance' 250; European Security and Defence Identity (ESDI) 251–55, 255–58, 258–59; European Security and Defence Policy (ESDP) 251, 258–59; European Security and Defence Policy (ESDP), ESDI and 258–59; European Security Strategy (ESS) 182, 185, 190, 196–97, 199, 202, 206, 211; France, withdrawal from NATO 79, 250–51; institutions within framework of Atlantic Alliance 50; integration of, process of 170–71; as lightning rod for East-West conflict 42; political identity, catalyst for development of CSCE 105–6; politics in, NAT and US effect on 11; reaction to NATO MC Directive 70 41; security identity post-Cold War 250–59; unification of, CSCE and 111; US focus on prior to Korean War 19–20; Western European Union (WEU) 251; *see also* EU border security; EU-NATO relations; France and NATO

Europe-puissance, programme of 71

European Community (EC) 103; EC-Nine Summit (Paris, 1972) 112; EC-Six Summit (Hague, 1969) 112

European Council 9, 69, 103, 118–19, 184, 191n18, 252; Laeken Council (December, 2001) 199

European Defence Community (EDC) 12, 21, 50, 51, 52, 54, 55, 171, 250

European Economic Community (EEC) 104
European Monetary Union (EMU) 112
European Neighbourhood Policy (ENP) 196–97, 204n 13
European Political Cooperation (EPC) 103, 111–13, 116
European Reconstruction Programme (ERP) 10, 53
European Security and Defence Identity (ESDI) 251–55, 255–58, 258–59; ESDP and 258–59; Europe, effect on 251–55, 255–58, 258–59; intransigence over 253–55; limits of 255–58; origins of 251–55; rise of 255
European Security and Defence Policy (ESDP) 13, 180, 181–82, 188, 190, 195–96, 210, 213, 240; ESDI and 258–59; EU-NATO relations 180, 181–82, 188, 190; Europe, effect on 251, 258–59
European Security Strategy (ESS) 182, 185, 190, 196–97, 199, 202, 206, 211
European uncertainties caused by withdrawal of France from NATO: Atlantic Alliance 79
European Union (EU) 13; Copenhagen EC Summit (December, 1973) 131; EC-Nine Summit (Paris, 1972) 112; EC-Six Summit (Hague, 1969) 112; economic disparities within, growth of 117–18; Fiera Summit (June, 2000) 184–85; geopolitical ambitions, transatlantic relations and 212–14; Maastricht Summit (December, 1991) 254; regional policies 196–97; Summit (December, 2008) 71
External Borders Fund 200

Fanfani, Amintore 95, 96, 97
Fiera EU Summit (June, 2000) 184–85
Fifth Republic in France 58–72
Fischer, Josef 176
Ford, Gerald (and administration of) 105, 119, 132, 143
Foreign Policy into the 21st Century: The US Leadership Challenge (CSIS) 234
Forrestal, James 9
Forsberg, Tuomas 218–30, ix
Fourth Republic in France 45–55
France: Ailleret-Lemnitzer exchange 63; colonial policy, NATO and 53–54; continental leadership under Brussels Pact (1948) 55; doubts about NATO 51–54; Eurocorps 66, 252, 254, 257, 259n1; foreign policy, evolution during Fourth Republic 46–47; Franco-British Summit (Saint-Malo, 1998) 69, 258; Franco-German "Study Group," on European security 80; Franco-German troubles, French leadership on 11–12; Gaullist position on Atlantic Alliance 58–59, 60, 63, 66, 68, 70–72, 83; Indochina, problems in 45, 52–53, 54, 98, 139; initiatives at origin of Atlantic Alliance 47–48; leadership in Europe,

305

INDEX

difficulties for 5; legal objection of US participation in Alliance 47–48; and NATO, back together 70–72; Tactical Air Control Command (CATAC) 61; transatlantic policies of Fourth Republic 45; Velentin-Ferber agreements 65; withdrawal from NATO 79, 250–51

France and NATO: acceptance of French views about NATO 71; Atlantic integration, French initiatives at 48–51; back together 70–72; colonial policy 53–54; command integration and French independence, problem of 59–64; continental leadership of France, Brussels Pact (1948) and 55; de Gaulle and September 1958 memorandum 61–62; demands of Fourth Republic, lasting nature of 54–55; doubts 51–54; expectations of NATO, French disappointment with 60; Fifth Republic 58–72; Fourth Republic 45–55; genesis of NATO, Fourth Republic and 44–51; hardening of de Gaulle stance 63–64; initiatives of France at origin of Alliance 47–48; inside of beside NATO, problem for France 67–69; military aid, difficult Franco-American relations on 52–53; nuclear issue 64–65; original organization of NATO, Fourth Republic and 44–51; outsider status, French initial desire for 46–47; overall Atlantic environment 69–70; progressive divorce between 51–54; rearmament of Germany, initial French doubts towards Alliance 51–52; relationship between, adjustments to 65–66; September 1958, memorandum of 60–61, 61–62; strategic division of labour among allies, de Gaulle's conception of 62–63; tripartite leadership, French demand for 55; warming of Fifth Republic to NATO 66–67

La France et la dédense de l'Europe (de Rose, F.) 66

La France et l'Alliance atlantique: le faux problème de l'intégration (Renouveau Défense) 67

Franco-British Summit (Saint-Malo, 1998) 69, 258

Frank, Paul 124–25, 128, 129, 130, 131, 132

Frattini, Franco 200

FRONTEX agency 199–200

frontier, concept of 207–9

Fuchs, Klaus 17

Fukuyama, Francis 191, 296

G6/G7: G6 becomes G7 103; great power governance 106, 119–20

Gaddafi, Muammar 128

Gaidar, Yegor 267

Gardner, Lloyd 90–91

G20 274, 275, 285n9, 285n11; London Summit (April, 2009) 71; Pittsburgh Summit (September, 2009) 276

Genscher, Hans-Dietrich 174

Georgia 195, 197, 204, 212, 269–70, 271, 281, 292, 293, 294; crisis in, core objectives of Atlantic Alliance and 291–92

Germond, Basil 206–17, ix

Gilpatric, Roswell 89–90, 95

Gingrich, Newt 281

Giscard d'Estaing, Valéry 58, 64, 65–66, 70, 105, 118, 119

Goldgeier, James M. 190, 263–72, ix

Gorbachev, Mikhail 84–85, 155, 156–57, 158–59, 159–60, 161, 164, 234, 263, 264, 266

Gordon, Philip 227, 256, 257, 274

Gore, Al 266

Gouin, Félix 46

Griffiths, Martin 225

Gromov, Boris 278

Gromyko, Andrei 92–93, 156

Gruenther, Alfred 37–38

Gygax, Jérôme A. 231–49, ix

Habermas, Jürgen 218

Haftendorn, Helga 75, 94, 188

Hague Programme (2005) 198–99

Hahn, Walter 82

Haig, Alexander M. 66

Haiti 278

Hallstein, Walter (and doctrine of) 94

Hamilton, L. 234

Hamre, John 235

Hanhimäki, Jussi M. 133, 273–86, ix

Hanrieder, Wolfram F. 162

Harmel, Pierre (and doctrine of) 81; Harmel Report (1967) 103–4, 105, 106, 108–9, 114, 118

Harriman, Averell 91–92

Harvard University, Brandt lectures 78

Havel, Vaclav 174

Heath, Edward 105, 113, 117

Heinemann-Grüder, Andreas 209

Helsinki CSCE Summit (July, 1975) 103; transatlantic cohesion, importance of 120

Henze, Paul 148

Higgott, Richard 221

Hillenbrand, Martin 124, 127, 128, 129, 131

Hixson, W.L. 231

Hoffman, Bruce 239

Hofmann, Arne 77

Holbrooke, Richard 265

homeland security in US 231, 236, 237–39, 242

Horin, Ben 126

Howard, Michael 174

Howorth, Jolyon 190

Hu Jintao 275

Humphrey, Hubert 91

Hungary 78, 159, 265, 266, 267; NATO membership for 176

Huntington, Samuel P. 172, 235

Hussein, Saddam 293

306

imitation, temptations of 186–89
Inchon landing in Korea 27–28, 29
India 190, 212, 276, 281, 290, 294
Indochina, French problems in 45, 52–53, 54, 98, 139
integrated border management 199–200, 202–3
International Herald Tribune 174
International Monetary Fund (IMF) 268, 275
Iran 7, 15, 118, 138–39; Anglo-Iranian Oil Company 140; autocratic rule of Shah in 140; bilateral relationship with US, collapse of 143–46, 146–47; Carter Doctrine in 143–46; cornerstone of US policy in Persian Gulf 139–43, 146; economic development and US relations with 140–41; Kissinger on alliance with 142; Nixon Doctrine in 141; Obama promise of diplomatic initiative with 273; Revolution in (1979) 139, 148; US arms provision for 141–42, 143
Iraq 13, 69, 126, 140, 141, 203; European opposition to war in 227; Obama pledge to end war in 273, 278; pull-out of forces from 223; US foreign policy in light of 225; War in 196, 200, 218, 219, 220, 222, 227, 254
Isernia, Pierangelo 221
Ismay, Hastings Lionel 74, 162
Italy: hostile reaction to Non-Proliferation Treaty (NPT) 93–94, 95–97, 98–99; membership of Western European Union (WEU) 52

Japan 4, 17, 29, 119, 125, 141, 142, 190, 212, 275, 289; economic recovery in 25–26; need for rehabilitation of 10
Jervis, Robert 219
Jobert, Michel 115, 116, 126, 251
Johnson, James 283
Johnson, Lyndon B. (and administration of) 77, 79, 89–90, 92, 98, 99, 107, 108
Jordan 126, 127, 142, 204n13
Jørgensen, Knud Erik 181
Joyner, James 274, 283

Kagan, Robert 235–36
Katzenbach, Nicholas 98
Katzenstein, Peter 220, 221, 222, 225, 227
Kennan, George 17
Kennedy, John F. (and administration of) 77, 250, 251
Keohane, Robert 220, 221, 222, 225, 227
Kharzai, Hamid 279
Khodorkovsky, Mikhail 270
Khrushchev, Nikita S. 60, 76–77
Kiesinger, Kurt G. 79, 80, 81, 94, 96, 97, 98, 108
Kim Il Sung 24–26, 28–29
Kim Jong Il 282–83
Kinkel, Klaus 176

Kissinger, Henry 65, 74, 83, 138–39, 142, 144, 174, 250–51; power shifts and new security needs 110, 111, 112, 114–15, 115–17, 118, 119, 120; West Germany and US in Middle East Crisis (1973) 123, 124, 125, 127, 128, 129–30
Kohl, Helmut 68, 85, 162, 163, 173, 174, 176–77, 252; Bush-Kohl Summit, Camp David (February, 1990) 162
Korean War 27–28; alternative history 29; atomic strategy 21–22; Chinese intervention, objectives of 28–29; Chinese Politburo, views of 28–29; defense expansion, debate on 18; Europe, US focus on prior to 19–20; impact of 23–24; Inchon landing 27–28, 29; intelligence operations, growth of 22–23; invasion by North of South (June, 1950) 17; lessons from history 29; military build-up 19; NATO restructuring 20–21; North Korean initiative 25, 29; policy of US, evaluation of 24–29; SAC, expansion of 21–22, 29; Soviet assistance for North Korea, agreement on 25; Soviet leadership, role in North Korean invasion 24–26; Soviet Union, policy on 25–26; Soviet Union, surprise at US response to Northern attack 25–26; strategic priorities of US 17; strategic programs, impact on 24; strategy of US, evaluation of 24–29; United States, defence perimeter in Asia, Acheson's view 25; United States, immediate response to invasion by North 26; United States, unpreparedness for 26–27; Yalu River, US agreement on advance to 26–28
Kosovo, engagement in: NATO 69–70, 189, 208, 213, 251, 255, 256, 258, 265, 290–91, 292, 294, 296, 298n8
Kosygin, Alexey N. 92
Krastsev, Ivan 218
Krieger, Wolfgang 169–79, ix–x
Kristof, Ladis 207
Kull, Steven 219, 226
Kupperman and Associates 234

Lange, Halvord 54
Larrabee, F. Stephen 188
Lavrov, Sergei 269
Lebanon 61, 204n13
Leber, Georg 130
LeMay, Curtis E. 21
Lemnitzer, Lyman L. 63
Lemonnier, Emile-René 51
Lenczowski, George 276
Lenin, Vladimir I. 263
Lisbon Conference (February, 1952) 32
London Summit (July, 1990) 158, 161, 162, 164, 252
Loth, Wilfried 76

307

INDEX

Lovett, Robert A. 23–24
Luciolli, Mario 96
Lugar, Richard 234
Lundestad, Geir 160, 218–19
Luns, Joseph 74

Maastricht Summit (December, 1991) 254
Maastricht Treaty (1992) 67, 68, 171–72, 181, 183, 254
MacArthur, Douglas 23, 26–28, 29
McCain, John 223, 227, 274, 281
McCarthy, Joseph R. 18; McCarthyism 238
McChrystal, Stanley 280
McCloy, John 91
McGhee, George 80
Macmillan, Harold 37, 61
McNamara, Robert 93
Macovescu, George 82
Major, John 68
Malbasic, Ivona 221
Malta CSCE Summit (December, 1989) 158–59, 166n32
Mao Zedong 25–27, 28, 29
Marion, Axel 194–205, x
maritime communications 40–41
Markovits, Andrei 218, 220, 225
Marshall, George C. 17, 20, 47; Marshall Plan 4, 17, 53
Martino, Gaetano 54
massive retaliation, doctrine of: Dulles' Atlantic Council speech (April, 1954) 34; NATO MC Directive 48 34–38; NATO MC Directive 70 37–42; nuclear deterrence 32; planning for, MC Directive 48 and 34–36; US NSC Directive 162 33–34; Western nuclear defense, origins of 33–34
Mattelart, Armand 242
MC Directive 48 34–38, 40; Atlanticization of nuclear war 34–36; boldness of 35; conventional and nuclear war, boundary between 35–36; defense of Europe, UK doubts on US plans for 37; deterrence, strength through possibility of victory 35; innovative subtlety of 35; massive retaliation, planning for 34–36; moral determination 35; paving way for Directive 70 37–38; Soviet Union, possibility of victory over 35; subtle nature of 35; tactical nuclear weapons 36
MC Directive 70 37–42; cost of 41; essence of 39–40; European reaction to 41; fantastic accounts of 41; logistics 40–41; maritime communications, importance of 40–41; Minimum Essential Force Requirements (1958–63) 39; objectives of 39–41; paradox of fate of 39; preparatory studies for 38–39; radical views of Pentagon, imposition of 39; SACEUR command 39–40; short-range tactical nuclear weapons, deployment of 40; strategic bankruptcy of 41–42; survival and retaliation 40–41; technocratic bankruptcy of 41–42; UK position on 41
Medium Term Defense Plan, NATO and 20
Medvedev, Dimitry 263, 269–70
Mendès-France, Pierre 55
Merkel, Angela 222
Méry, Guy 65–66
Michelet, Edmond 46
Middle East 175, 211, 274, 290; anti-American bias in 221, 222; Arab-Israeli conflicts 109, 115, 277; Crisis in (1973) 123–33; Eisenhower Doctrine and 140; energy governance and policy clashes 106; European "Declaration of Peace in the Middle East" 116; European dialogue on terrorism in 239; Greater Middle East 277; Israel, indispensable US ally in 232; Kissinger and search for peace in" 117, 118; moderate forces in, demoralization of 142; NATO boundaries and 139; out-of-area consultation 104; Peace Process 233; Rapid Deployment Force (RDF) in 139, 145, 146, 147; Suez Crisis (1956) 54, 55, 60, 115, 131, 139; unpredictability of 294; US National Security Study Memo 66 (1969) 141; US-Soviet confrontation in 144–45
Middle East Crisis (1973): DEFCON III, US forces on 129; diplomatic crisis between West Germany and US 126–30, 132; European Declaration on 129–30; oil as weapon in 125, 128; *Ostpolitik* and German reaction to 124, 132–33; policy of Germany towards Arab states and Israel 125, 127–28; West German policy towards US, factors influencing 123–24, 124–25, 132; West German strategy during 130–32, 132–33
Military Committee (MC) of NATO 34, 38–39, 39–40, 107; *see also* MC Directive 48; MC Directive 70
Milosevic, Slobodan 265
Minimum Essential Force Requirements (1958–63) 39
Mitterand, François 58, 64, 65, 66, 67, 68, 161, 252, 253
Moch, Jules 53
Möckli, Daniel 103–22, x
Moisi, Dominique 226
Mondale, Walter 58
Le Monde 51
monetary turbulences 113–14
Monnet, Jean 12
Morgenthau, Hans J. 94
Moro, Aldo 95, 96–97
Morocco 22, 204n13, 258; Franco-American relations over 53

308

Moscow Medvedev-Obama Summit (July, 2009) 263, 270
Moss, Robert 232
Mossadeq, Mohammed 140
Müller von Blumencron, Mathias 273
Multilateral Force (MLF) 90, 93, 94, 95, 97
Multilateral Preparatory Talks (MPT) 112–13
multilateralism 8–9, 181, 191, 196, 206, 212, 223, 271, 284, 296, 297
mutual and balanced force reductions (MBFR) 76, 86, 108, 111
Mutual Defence Assistance Act (MDAA, 1949) 52–53
Mutual Defense Act (1949) 10–11
Mutual Friendship Treaty China-Soviet Union (February, 1950) 17–18

Nagorno-Karabakh 294
Nasser, Gamal Abdel 60
National Security Act (1947) 22, 231, 237–38, 244n33
National Security Agency (NSA), creation of 23
National Security Council (NSC) 17, 18; NSC-10/2 (June, 1949), approval of 22–23; NSC-162 Executive Directive 33–34; NSC-68 Report, cost implications 18, 19, 24; Psychological Strategy Board 23
neighbourhood stabilization 195–96, 201–2
de Nerval, Gérard 32
Netanyahu, Benjamin 277
de Nevers, Renèe 241
New Look on nuclear deterrence 24, 32, 34, 36, 37, 40
New York Times 284
Niedhart, Gottfried 75
Nitze, Paul H. 17, 18, 238
Nixon, Richard M. (and administration of) 70, 83, 142, 144, 145, 146, 236; Nixon Doctrine 141; power shifts and new security needs 110, 112, 113–14, 115, 117; West Germany and US during Middle East Crisis (1973) 125, 129, 130, 131, 132
Non-Proliferation Treaty (NPT): blunt talk between US and USSR on 91–93; change in US attitude to, first signs 92–93; change in US attitude towards, first signs 91–93; effect on Atlantic Alliance 89–99; Eighteen Nations Disarmament Committee (ENDC) 90, 92, 95; Italy, hostile reaction to 93–94, 95–97, 98–99; Multilateral Force (MLF) 90, 93, 94, 95, 97; negotiations for, early phase 89–93; transatlantic relations, impact on 89–99; US-West European relations, crisis in 93–94, 97–98; West Germany, hostile reaction to 93–97, 98–99
Norstad, Lauris 37
North Atlantic Alliance 58, 156, 260n6, 287

North Atlantic Cooperation Council (NACC) 289
North Atlantic Council 20, 33, 34, 41, 50, 51, 53, 54
North Atlantic Treaty (NAT, 1949) 3–13, 17; American lectures for Europeans 9–10; Article 2 of 7, 8, 11, 12; Article 5 of 4, 6, 7, 8, 10, 11, 14n14, 138 178n10, 184, 296; Article 6 of 138; Article 9 of 48–49; bilateralism 8–9; bipolar system of Cold War world 1; combined command under US, UK and French leadership, need for 10; community-building clause, difficulties with 8; Dean Acheson and negotiations for 3, 5, 8, 9, 10, 11–12; duration of, issue of 7; economic objectives, need for sacrifices in 9–10; effects of 12, 13; Ernest Bevin and negotiations for 3, 4, 5–6, 7, 8, 9, 10, 11, 12; European Defence Community (EDC) and 12, 21, 50, 51, 52, 54, 55, 171; European politics, US effect on 11; European Reconstruction Programme (ERP) 10; Franco-German troubles, French leadership on 11–12; Germany, military protection for West of 12; Germany, need for rehabilitation of 10; ideological contours of Cold War world 1; issues involved 6–8; January-April, climactic months 5–6; Japan, need for rehabilitation of 10; membership issues, difficulties over 7; multilateralism 8–9; negotiation process, climax of 8–10; public diplomacy towards 2–3; ratification in US, UK and France 11; Robert Schuman and negotiations for 3, 5, 8–9, 10, 11; secret diplomacy towards 2–3; short-term outcomes 10–12; Soviet Union, ideological warfare against 9, 10; strategic revolution of 12; traditional security, need for sacrifices in 9–10; UK Foreign Office, aim for Atlantic rather than European community 12; UN and NATO, relationship between 7–8
North Atlantic Treaty Organization (NATO) 12–13; acceptance of French views about 71; Air Defense Ground Environment (NADGE) 64; alternatives to, Brandt's exploration of 79–82; Berlin Summit (June, 1996) 257; Bermuda Summit (December, 1953) 60; Bonn Summit (June, 1982) 147; Bosnia, engagement in 66, 69, 176, 187, 189, 198n8, 208, 211, 254–55, 255–56, 258, 265, 289; Brussels Summit (January, 1994) 183, 255, 264, 266; Brussels Summit (June, 1996) 257; Brussels Summit (May, 1975) 103; existential external threat and success of 4; institutional reform (1967/8) 107–8; Kosovo, engagement in 69–70, 189, 208, 213, 251, 255, 256, 258, 265, 290–91, 292, 294, 296, 298n8; London Summit (July, 1990) 158, 161, 162, 164, 252; MC Directive 48 34–38; MC Directive 70

309

37–42; Medium Term Defense Plan and 20; military build-up for 19–20; Military Committee (MC) 34, 38–39, 39–40, 107; NATO-OTAN, opposite perspectives on transatlantic security 287; Nuclear Planning Group (NPG) 71, 93, 94, 95, 107–8, 121n10, 259; Ottawa Declaration (June, 1974) 65, 118; and 'out of area' debate 138–39, 146–48; partnership in, future for security in 297–98; post-Cold War world of 12–13; Prague Summit (November, 2002) 187, 240; rapid reaction force 38; reconsolidation (1974/5) 117–20; restructuring after Korean War 20–21; Riga Summit (November, 2006) 240; Rome Summit (November, 1991) 254; Strasbourg/Kehl Summit (April, 2009) 214, 279, 288, 298; Supreme Allied Commander, Europe (SACEUR), establishment of 20; transformation due to Korean War 24, 29; Washington Summit (April, 1999) 265, 288; West Germany, role within, disputes over 21; withdrawal of France from 79, 250–51; *see also* MC Directive 48; MC Directive 70

nuclear deterrence 21, 22, 24, 32, 64–65, 70–71, 133; defense of Atlantic Alliance, impossibility of 32–42; first-use policy, Fischer's call for renunciation of 176–77; French and British forces of 172, 176–77; issue for France and NATO 64–65; massive retaliation, doctrine of 32; North Korean moves towards 282–83; nuclear testing by China 89–90; obsolescence of 234; transatlantic security nuclear stakes and 280–83; West Germany, US and 130

Nuclear Planning Group (NPG) 71, 93, 94, 95, 107–8, 121n10, 259

nuclear war: Atlanticization of 34–36; atomic strategy, Korean War and 21–22; conventional and, boundary between 35–36; deterrence, strength through possibility of victory 35; MC Directive 48 and tactical nuclear weapons 34, 35, 36, 37, 38; tactical nuclear weapons 22, 24, 31, 39, 40, 63, 64, 65, 88; Western nuclear defense, origins of 33–34

Nuti, Leopoldo 89–102, x
Nye, Joseph S. 232, 234–35, 242

Oakes, Guy 238
Obama, Barack H. (and administration of) 71, 171, 226, 240, 259, 296; criticism towards US in transatlantic relations 219, 222, 223–24, 225, 226, 227–28; transatlantic security and 273–74, 274–75, 275–76, 277–80, 280–81, 282, 283–84; US-Russian relations 263, 268, 269–70, 271
O'Connor, Brendon 225
Office of Policy Coordination (OPC) 22–23
oil crisis, economic governance and 115–17

Ojanen, Hanna 180–93, x
Organisation of Petroleum Exporting Countries (OPEC) 116
Ostpolitik 75, 83, 105, 106–7, 108, 109, 111, 112, 123–24, 132–33, 174
Ottawa Declaration (June, 1974) 65, 118

Pahlavi, Mohammed Reza Shah 139, 140–42, 143, 144, 145, 146
Pakistan 149, 187, 277, 278, 281, 290, 294
Palais Rose Council (May, 1950) 11
Palestine 125, 129, 232, 239, 277
Paris CSCE Summit (November 1990) 158, 161, 162
Partnership for Peace (PfP) 176, 255, 264, 265, 289, 297
Pearson, Lester B. 54
Perry, William 270
Petraeus, David 280
Planungsstab (planning group) 80, 82, 83
Pleven Plan (October, 1950) 12, 51, 56n26
Poland 75, 78, 81, 109, 159, 166, 175, 201, 224, 265, 266, 267, 269, 283; NATO membership for 176
Politique étrangère 67
Pompidou, Georges 64, 65, 70, 105, 112, 113, 116, 117, 119, 130
Ponomarev, Lev 270
Pope, Robert A. 240
Posen, Barry R. 185
Prague NATO Summit (November, 2002) 187, 240
Prague Spring (1968) and future of Atlantic Alliance 81–82
Prodi, Romano 196
Putin, Vladimir 267, 268, 269, 271

Raflik, Jenny 45–57, x
Ramadier, Paul 47
Rambouillet CSCE Summit (November, 1975) 103, 119–20
Rapacki, Adam 78, 84
Rapid Reaction Forces 38, 173, 186, 187, 189, 253
Reagan, Ronald (and administration of) 161, 177, 232–33, 234, 235, 238, 239, 241
Revel, Jean-Francois 220
Rey, Marie-Pierre 158, 161
Rice, Condoleezza 162
Rice, Susan 282
Ridge, Tom 242
Riga NATO Summit (November, 2006) 240
Risse, Thomas 219
Robertson, George I.M. 258
Robin, Gabriel 256
Rome NATO Summit (November, 1991) 254
Roshchin, Alexei 90

Rostow, Walt W. 105
de Rougé, Guillaume 250–62, viii
Rühe, Volker 175, 176
Rumor, Mariano 130
Rumsfeld, Donald 127, 171, 187, 238
Rusk, Dean 92–93, 96, 97, 105, 107
Russia: Bush-Putin friendship, unrealized potential of 268; Commonwealth of Independent States (CIS), creation of 290; Moscow Medvedev-Obama Summit (July, 2009) 263, 270; nuclear stakes 281, 282; *see also* US-Russian relations

Saint-Malo declaration (December, 1998) 169–70, 177
Salzburger Volksblatt 97–98
Sandys, Duncan 41
Santer, Jacques 176
Saragat, Guiseppe 96
Sarkozy, Nicolas 59, 66, 69, 70, 71, 171, 197, 222, 240, 297
Saudi Arabia 22, 118, 141, 142, 235
Scheel, Walter 76, 125, 126, 127, 129, 132
Scheffer, Jaap de Hoop 213–14, 279, 290–91
Schengen system 197–98, 198–99, 200
Schlesinger, James 130
Schmidt, Helmut 105, 118, 119, 132, 176–77
Schmidt, Wolfgang 77
Schoenborn, Benedikt 74–88, x
Schröder, Gerhard 96, 176, 218
Schuman, Robert 3, 5, 8–9, 10, 11, 50, 53
Schumann, Maurice 83
Scowcroft, Brent 163, 251, 259
security: identity in Europe, post-Cold War 250–59; policy-making, lack of overall control in Europe 171; projection of, concept of 207–9; *see also* transatlantic security
Sens, Allan G. 195
September 1958, memorandum of 60–61, 61–62
Shapiro, Jeremy 227
Sheehan, John J. 257
Sick, Gary 143–44
Sikorski, Radoslaw 283
Singh, Robert 220
Sisco, Joseph 130
Sjursen, Helene 189
Smith, Walter Bedell 23
social change, fear as tool of 237–39
soft power 236–37
Solana, Javier 173, 196
Somalia 145, 146, 187, 192n33, 192n34, 277
Soutou, George-Henri 58–73, 76, x
Soviet Union: assistance for North Korea, agreement on 25; blunt talk with US on NPT 91–93; GDR, occupation of 17; leadership of, role in North Korean invasion of South 24–26; Moscow US-Soviet Summit (May, 1972) 142, 150n21; Mutual Friendship with China, Treaty of (February, 1950) 17–18; NAT and ideological warfare against 9, 10; New Thinking about United Nations 160; policy on Korean War 25–26; possibility of victory over, MC Directive 48 and 35; power of, respect for 6; Prague coup (1948) 4, 33, 47, 55n4, 81–82; problem for US of 18; surprise at US response to Northern attack in Korea 25–26; US-Soviet confrontation in Middle East 144–45; US-USSR nuclear parity 104
Spaak, Paul-Henri 9, 41
Speicher, Peter 77
Der Spiegel 273
Stalin, Josef 25–26, 27, 28–29, 263
Standing (Permanent) Group in Washington 34, 42, 43, 49, 50, 53, 55, 60, 61, 72n11
Stavridis, James 226
Stehlin, Paul 51
Sterling, Claire 232
Stikker, Dirk 9
Strasbourg/Kehl NATO Summit (April, 2009) 214, 279, 288, 298
Strategic Air Command (SAC): expansion of 21–22, 29; nuclear weapons, build up of 22; overseas bases, construction of 22; Soviet Union, defence against 22
Strategic Arms Limitation Talks (SALT) 110, 150n21
Strategic Arms Reduction Treaty (START) 267–68, 281, 283
strategic bankruptcy of MC Directive 70 41–42
strategic culture, US exportation of 239–41
strategic reserve, importance for US of 36
Strauss, Franz-Josef 41, 94
Strömvik, Maria 190
Sudan 186, 189
Suez Crisis (1956) 54, 55, 60, 115, 131, 139
Supreme Allied Commander, Europe (SACEUR) 50, 52; Ailleret-Lemnitzer exchange 63; establishment of 20; Eurocorps and 257; German forces and authority of 52; MC Directive 70 and 39–40; NATO MC and Atlanticization of nuclear war 34, 35, 37, 38, 39–40, 41; tactical coordination and 66
Supreme Allied Commander Atlantic (SACLANT) 41, 43n33, 257, 261n36
Supreme HQ, Allied Powers Europe (SHAPE) 39, 42n8, 49, 50, 185, 188, 257; and strategic weight of France in Atlantic Alliance 50–51
Syria 126, 204n13

Tactical Air Control Command (CATAC) 61
tactical nuclear weapons 22, 24, 31, 39, 40, 63, 64, 65, 88; MC Directive 48 34, 35, 36, 37, 38; short-range weapons, deployment of 40
Taft, Robart A. 20

311

INDEX

Taiwan 17, 25, 26, 28
Talbott, Strobe 264, 267
Taliban 270, 277, 278, 279–80, 287, 289, 293
Tampere Programme (1999) 198–99
Taylor, Maxwell D. 36
technocratic bankruptcy, MC Directive 70 41–42
Thatcher, Margaret 177
Thompson, Llewellyn 92
Tindemans, Leo 118
Toje, Asle 189
Trachtenberg, Marc 218
trade rivalries 113–14
transatlantic elites, change in 104–5
Transatlantic Homeland, birth of 239–41
transatlantic relations: anti-Americanism and 219–22; bias against US, reality of? 225–27; criticism towards US and 218–28; EU frontier and 206–14; and EU geopolitical ambitions 212–14; frontier, concept of 207–9; future of anti-Americanism in Europe, impact on 227–28; geopolitical vision, EU frontier and 209–12; image of US, changes from Bush to Obama 222–27; NPT impact on 89–99; policies of French Fourth Republic 45; security, concept of projection of 207–9; *see also* EU-NATO relations; France and NATO
transatlantic security: adaptation in face of unpredictable challenge 295; Arc of Crisis, wars in 276–80; challenges for today 291–93; change, milestones and acceleration of (1989–2009) 288–90; change, need for in current strategic concept 290–91; change, prediction of unpredictability in 294–95; circumstantial threats 291–92; continuity, renewal and 283–84; economic engagement 274–76; global approach, paradigm change and 296–97; international relations, surprise at change in 293–94; lasting threats 291; NATO-OTAN, opposite perspectives on 287; nuclear stakes 280–83; Obama administration and 273–84; options for change 297; partnership in NATO, future for security 297–98; protectionism, rejection of 275; revolutionary times 293–96; sixtieth birthday of NATO 288; specificities of new strategic concept 292–93; strategic concept, durability of 290–91; transformation, progress in 295–96
Transatlantic Trends 274
transatlantic unity, European identity and 118–19
Truman, Harry S. (and administration of) 4, 9–10, 13, 17, 18, 20, 23, 26, 27, 28, 36, 46, 47
Tunisia 126, 204n3; Franco-American relations over 53
Turkey 7, 15, 17, 22, 46, 71, 171, 189–90, 193, 203, 204n13, 224, 269, 274, 282, 294

Ukraine 197, 201, 204n13, 212, 263, 269, 293, 294
Ulbricht, Walter 125
United Kingdom: defense of Europe, doubts on US plans for 37; Euro-skepticism in 117; Foreign Office, aim for Atlantic rather than European community 12; Franco-British Summit (Saint-Malo, 1998) 69, 258; position on MC Directive 70 41
United Nations (UN) 156, 232; Article 51 of Charter 4, 15n22, 178n10; General Assembly 92; General Staff Committee 46; Kissinger's diplomatic strategy, challenge to 129–30; NATO and, relationship between 7–8; Security Council 26, 46, 170; Soviet New Thinking about 160
United States: Afghanistan, deepening commitment in 282; anti-Americanism and transatlantic relations 219–22; anti-terrorist policy post-9/11 231–42; approach to US-Russian relations 264–65; Asia, mutual defence aid in 53; asymmetric antiterrorist doctrines, conceptualization of 232–34; Atomic Energy Commission (AEC) 33; bias against, reality of? 225–27; bilateral relationship with Iran, collapse of 143–46, 146–47; blunt talk with USSR on NPT 91–93; Bush-Kohl Summit, Camp David (February, 1990) 162; Carter Doctrine, development of 143–46; civil defense 237–39; criticism towards, transatlantic relations and 218–28; defence perimeter in Asia, Acheson's view 25; dollar value, consolidation of centrality of 118; Homeland Security Act (2002), security and 231, 236, 237–39, 242; image of, changes from Bush to Obama 222–27; immediate response to invasion by North Korea 26; Iran, cornerstone of policy in Persian Gulf 139–43, 146; Korean War, unpreparedness for 26–27; leadership, 1990s and potential for reaffirmation of 234–36; lectures for Europeans from 9–10; Medium Term Defense Plan, NATO and 20; moral commitment to defence of Europe 20; Moscow Medvedev-Obama Summit (July, 2009) 263, 270; Mutual Defence Assistance Act (MDAA, 1949) 52–53; Mutual Defense Act (1949) 10–11; National Security Act (1947) 22, 231, 237–38, 244n33; National Security Agency (NSA), creation of 23; National Security Council (NSC) 17, 18; NATO and 'out of area' debate 138–39, 146–48; New Look on nuclear deterrence 24, 32, 34, 36, 37, 40; NSC-162 Executive Directive 33–34; NSC-68 Report, cost implications 18, 19, 24; NSC Executive Directive 162 33–34; Office of Policy Coordination (OPC), CIA and 22–23; Patriot

Act (2002) 236, 242, 245n62; relations with China, post-Vietnam restructuring of 112, 114; role in European affairs 170–71; social change, fear as tool of 237–39; soft power, institutional revolution in service of 236–37; strategic culture, exportation of 239–41; strategic reserve, importance of 36; Transatlantic Homeland, birth of 239–41; US-Soviet confrontation in Middle East 144–45; US-USSR nuclear parity 104; Vandenberg resolution (1948) 4; "war on terror" 196, 222, 231, 277, 284; West European relations, NPT and crisis in 93–94, 97–98; West German relations with during Middle East Crisis (1973) 123–33; 'Year of Europe,' Kissinger's initiative of 106, 110, 113, 114–15, 116–17, 118, 119, 125, 250–51

US-Russian relations: American approach to 264–65; atmosphere change, post Obama 269–70; Bush-Putin friendship, unrealised potential of 268; concrete results, aim of 270–71; cooperation in other spheres, difficulties on 267–68; false start 263–64; Obama and promise of resetting 268–69; power, imbalance of 268; reaching out to Russia 265–67

Vaïsse, Maurice 170
Valasek, Tomas 189
Valentin-Ferber agreements (July, 1974) 65
Valluy, Jean Étienne 36
Vance, Cyrus 143
Vandenberg resolution (US, 1948) 4
Védrine, Hubert 221, 253
Versailles Treaty (1919) 3, 9
Vietnam 53, 63, 79, 90, 91–92, 109, 112, 114, 139, 141, 144–45, 232, 234, 278; War in 70, 92, 97, 98, 99, 127
Vogtmeier, Andreas 76
Von Staden, Berndt 128, 129

"war on terror" 196, 222, 231, 277, 284
Warsaw Pact 64, 78, 79–80, 81, 82, 83, 84, 106, 174, 181, 253, 288, 289, 298n1
Washington Energy Conference (February, 1974) 116–17
Washington NATO Summit (April, 1999) 265, 288
Wells, Jr., Samuel F. 17–31, x
Wenger, Andreas 103–22, x–xi
West Germany (Federal Republic) 33, 36, 40, 41, 42, 52, 55, 77, 78–79, 109, 114, 117, 119; Atlantic Alliance, importance for security of 130; Auswärtiges Amt (Foreign Office) 83, 89, 96, 123–24, 125, 126–27, 127–28, 128–29, 130, 132; Berlin, blockade of 4, 8, 11, 48;
Bush-Kohl Summit, Camp David (February, 1990) 162; *Deutschland-Plan* (SPD) 78; diplomatic crisis with US over Middle East 126–30, 132; *Entspannungszone* (zone of détente) 78; Eurocorps 66, 252, 254, 257, 259n1; European community, reintroduction to 5; Franco-German "Study Group," on European security 80; hostile reaction to NPT 93–97, 98–99; limitations on use of armed forces 174–75; NAT and military protection for 12; NAT and policy regarding 3–4; need for rehabilitation of 10; *Ostpolitik* (détente) 75, 83, 105, 106–7, 108, 109, 111, 112, 123–24, 132–33, 174; *Planungsstab* (planning group) 80, 82, 83; policy towards US, factors influencing Middle East Crisis (1973) 123–24, 124–25, 132; post 9/11 and EU-NATO relations 177; post-Cold War and EU-NATO relations 169–77; rearmament of Germany, initial French doubts on 51–52; recovery of, threat to French European leadership 52; relations with US during Middle East Crisis (1973) 123–33; role within NATO, disputes over 21; search for new security policy 173–74, 175–76; strategy during Middle East Crisis (1973) 130–32, 132–33; zonal solution for Germany, discussions on 9

Western European Union (WEU) 48; Atlantic Alliance and 254; Bartholomew-Dobbins Telegram (February, 1991) 254; Bonn (Hotel Petersburg) Summit (June, 1992) 289–90; EU-NATO relations 169, 172–73, 174, 176; Europe 251; German membership 52; Italian membership 52; role post-Cold War of 183–84
Western governance, competing models of 114–15
Western nuclear defense, origins of 33–34
Will, George 232
Wilson, Harold 98, 105, 117, 118, 119
Wischnewski, Hans-Jürgen 84
Wohlforth, William C. 164
Wolfers, Arnold 231

Yalu River, US agreement on advance to 26–28
'Year of Europe,' Kissinger's initiative of 106, 110, 113, 114–15, 116–17, 118, 119, 125, 250–51
Yeltsin, Boris 263, 264–65, 265–66, 267, 268

Zanchetta, Barbara 138–52, xi
Zapatero, José Rodrigues 240
Zegart, Amy B. 237
Zelikow, Philip 162
Zhou Enlai 29
Zoellick, Robert 297
Zubok, Vladislav 160

eBooks – at www.eBookstore.tandf.co.uk

A library at your fingertips!

eBooks are electronic versions of printed books. You can store them on your PC/laptop or browse them online.

They have advantages for anyone needing rapid access to a wide variety of published, copyright information.

eBooks can help your research by enabling you to bookmark chapters, annotate text and use instant searches to find specific words or phrases. Several eBook files would fit on even a small laptop or PDA.

NEW: Save money by eSubscribing: cheap, online access to any eBook for as long as you need it.

Annual subscription packages

We now offer special low-cost bulk subscriptions to packages of eBooks in certain subject areas. These are available to libraries or to individuals.

For more information please contact webmaster.ebooks@tandf.co.uk

We're continually developing the eBook concept, so keep up to date by visiting the website.

www.eBookstore.tandf.co.uk